A NEW ECONOMIC HISTORY OF AMERICA

GERALD GUNDERSON

North Carolina State University, Raleigh

McGraw-Hill Book Company

New York   St. Louis   San Francisco   Auckland   Düsseldorf
Johannesburg   Kuala Lumpur   London   Mexico   Montreal   New Delhi
Panama   Paris   São Paulo   Singapore   Sydney   Tokyo   Toronto

Library of Congress Cataloging in Publication Data

Gunderson, Gerald.

A new economic history of America

Includes index.
1. United States—Economic conditions.   I.   Title.
HC103.G86   330.9'73   75-33366
ISBN 0-07-025180-0

A NEW ECONOMIC HISTORY OF AMERICA

1 2 3 4 5 6 7 8 9 0   D O D O   7 8 3 2 1 0 9 8 7 6

This book was set in Times Roman by National ShareGraphics, Inc.
The editors were J. S. Dietrich and Claudia A. Hepburn;
the cover was designed by Scott Chelius; the production supervisor was Judi Allen.
The drawings were done by Fine Line Illustrations, Inc.
R. R. Donnelley & Sons Company was printer and binder.

Contents

Preface

During its initial preparation, this volume was tentatively titled *Solutions: A New Economic History of America.* Since then, however, *solutions* has been dropped because of its rather presumptuous sound and to avoid possible confusion with other texts that are so titled because they are an instructor's key to end-of-chapter questions. Nevertheless, the term still captures a number of the basic themes in the work. At the first, and most direct level, it expresses the continuous tension in economic affairs between desires, on the one hand, and the comparatively limited ability to meet them, on the other hand, which results in the need for accommodations, or difficult choices, at each point in time. This phenomenon of opportunity cost will be readily apparent throughout the work and *solutions* seems to express it well. Second, it also expresses an important corollary of this ongoing fact of scarcity—that innovative, or problem-solving, activity which attempts to override this omnipresent problem. This attempt has never completely succeeded, of course, but in the American experience it has produced a fairly continuous outpouring of improvements which have expanded the economic capabilities of the economy. This is much less noticeable at any given moment, but in retrospect it becomes one of the prime concerns of historical explanations. Innovative activity never quite succeeded in creating Utopia, but in falling short it systematically altered the course of economic affairs. Last, *solutions* also has a third meaning. In the past decade there has been considerable innovation in economic history itself. There are substantial reasons for believing that these efforts represent more than simply an adding to the already extensive backlog of hypotheses in history. They have produced explanations that are more inclusive than ever, and that can with-stand a wider range of potential contradiction. Economic history has become more useful. Many of these advances have been incorporated in this volume, and some make their initial appearance here in order to round out topics which the "new economic history" has not yet had an opportunity to reformulate. In the sense of presenting better explanations of past economic affairs, therefore, the volume could rightfully be titled *Solutions*.

This book really began about the third time a student in my classes suggest-ed that the class lectures were far more useful than the available reading materi-als and that it would be much better to assign a transcript of the lectures. Subsequently the book has been helped along by the explicit comments of stu-dents who read the resulting class handouts and by the implicit message of puz-zled looks when particular points were not clear. The work took major steps forward when a member of the publishing field, Leroy Craig, Jr., took an enthusi-astic personal interest in it and when economic historians of such reputation as Jeffery Williamson, Gary Walton, and Gavin Wright gave it a good professional judgment. The staff at McGraw-Hill has been very patient while all the final pieces were being put together. But it was my family who sacrificed the most, and indirectly contributed the most to the book. So it is only appropriate that this book be dedicated to them—to Margaret, David, and Laura—who gave up all those Saturdays and evenings so that the next generation might have a more usable past.

GERALD GUNDERSON

A NEW
ECONOMIC
HISTORY
OF AMERICA

Economics and History

A copy of the daily *New York Times* usually contains more than fifty pages and if you were to read all of it conscientiously—from the front page through all the fine print of the stock, bond, and commodity quotations to the weather forecast in the back—the next day's edition would be out before you turned the last page. Of course, only proofreaders and fanatics read every word of a newspaper. Most of us turn to the items that interest us: the price of our mutual fund, the major league ball scores, or the weather expected over the weekend. Then we skim through the rest of the paper and set it aside. It is time to leave for dinner, a movie, or a meeting.

Just as reading the daily paper is only one of the possible activities that compete for our attention each day, so is it also only one part of the record of our behavior which we leave behind us. Each day adds also to the accumulation of books, videotapes, government documents, business forms, building excavations, tombstones, and trash landfills—more or less permanent evidence for future scholars to catalog and interpret. Nor is modern man unique for his outpouring of tattletale residue. There are enough bones, ruins, pottery shards, pictographs, and ancient manuscripts available to keep anthropologists and classicists busy for some time. Frequently historians bemoan the lack of some specific information which would help them reconstruct a particular aspect of the past, but more basically the problem with historical material is that there is far more of it than existing scholarship can completely assimilate. Historians frequently produce excellent portrayals of some specific event or situation in the past, but when they broaden their horizons to describe larger and more complex phenomena the quantity of available evidence becomes overwhelming.

Suppose, using the techniques of a historian, you were to investigate a specific event in the past, perhaps the invention of a particular metal-stamping machine. You would certainly read the patents covering the innovation and interview any individuals associated with it who were still alive. You would probably also check contemporary trade journals and local newspapers as well as any commentaries other historians had made concerning the invention. By this point the facts and impressions you had accumulated would probably have begun to coalesce into tentative explanations. Yet it is likely that there would be a few inconsistencies and some missing segments to the hypothesis, so you would resume searching, modifying, and reconciling to develop a better account. Finally, if you were fortunate—a large portion of such efforts end in failure—you would produce an explanation which would appear plausible and would survive contradiction by available evidence. The results might be good, but they would have required considerable trial and error and numerous man-hours. Consider, then, what would be entailed if you were to write a comprehensive history of the entire American metal-stamping industry. Obviously there would be many individual events to incorporate, each requiring an effort comparable to the herculean one outlined above. But now the scope of the study would be expanded so much that it would no longer be possible to consider it in isolation from the rest of the economy. It is difficult to discuss the development of metal-stamping machines without reference to what metals were available and at what prices and locations. Prevailing incomes and the existing substitutes for metal products shaped the demand for equipment to form metal. Tariffs, taxes, zoning laws, and immigration regulations also shaped the industry's behavior.

Pity the poor historians, then, with far more information than they can reasonably expect to tabulate, digest, and report in a lifetime (and their research funds perhaps due to run out in four months). What can they do? Somehow they must devise some shortcuts—some way of developing the major portions of the topic without assembling it ad nauseam from every available bit of evidence. They must be selective, much as we are in reading the newspaper. They must select those facts they believe important, glance over the remainder for any obvious supplements, and then proceed to assemble the story. In essence, to practice their craft historians must structure their accounts by a framework, or ordering, or—to use the term often uttered with mistaken distaste by "practical" people—*theory*. Theory is simply a collection of the operating rules one uses, explicit or otherwise, to explain why events occur as they do and to separate the important from the unimportant forces. Theory is the historians' shortcut, their combination filter and pipewrench which allows them to build a coherent explanation out of what is otherwise an overwhelming avalanche of information.

THEORY IN HISTORY

Any account of consequence of the past must utilize some theory, or theories, but there are almost unlimited numbers of theoretical orderings which could be used. For example, the American Civil War—that recurrent topic of American historiography—might be explained by political, economic, class, legal, or climatic forces, or combinations thereof. Each individual category, in turn, could use one of numerous possible alternative explanations of how that respective force affected and interacted with the two regions and their institutions. And when historians begin with one of those theories as a tentative explanation of that period, it influences the evidence they gather and the order in which they assemble it. Not surprisingly, histories of the United States contain nearly as many explanations of what brought about the Civil War as there are historians writing about it.

Theory is the all-important skeleton of history but historians cannot agree on how its bone structure is assembled, or even generally shaped. Some historians doggedly tell their students that the Civil War was caused by certain specific forces. Many, however, have turned to a more candid presentation, assigning an anthology of alternate explanations to their classes. It may make history more colorful, varied, and possibly more exciting for a historical interpretation to be deemed final, but it comes at a high cost. The most interesting and productive questions in history are the "hows" and the "whys." Those answers require some touchstone, or standard, by which preferred explanations can be judged and, if necessary, rejected; some basis by which hypotheses can be credited as probable or improbable. The great opportunities to illuminate the workings of human society intrinsic in history's vast domain depend on measures which allow judgments and discrimination. A "usable past" can be built only out of some proven guidelines as to how human societies operate—in short, out of accepted theory.

The theory used to organize an account of the past is crucial. The emphasis, causation, conclusions, and quality of those conclusions depend primarily on the framework on which the narrative is assembled. What follows may seem a long digression before we turn to America's economic history, but it is necessary. Without this explicit structure there could be literally thousands of possible presentations of the material. The best economic theory presently available is an immensely productive resource with which to construct economic history. It diverts us from appealing but unlikely explanations—which form the great majority of cases—to those usually indicated by human behavior. It also leads to some novel and rather striking observations on our past, often in direct contradiction to traditional views of history. But that is part of the story yet to come.

ECONOMIC HISTORY

Mention economic history and many people immediately think of Karl Marx and Charles Beard. The association is unfortunate because in two crucial dimensions it is incorrect. Marx and Beard believed that all important human activity, and thus the portrayal of its history, was explained by economic forces. Most contemporary economic historians do not believe that economics is the sole driving force of the world. In fact, the nature of economic activity as they understand it allows them to distinguish what is, from what is not, economic activity. Reading an economic history might give one the impression that economics is assumed to be all-important, but that merely reflects the specialization of the writer's energies. Similarly, medical textbooks which discuss blood, bones, or nerves do not imply that doctors believe that each specifically is the entire account of life.

Marx would have been considered an economist, albeit an unorthodox one, in his day, while Beard was a historian preoccupied with economic forces. That difference in credentials is far less important today than a common obsolescence of their works when measured by the standards of contemporary economic theory. Their scholarship is very old when compared with more recent developments in economic science. Since their time economic theory has been logically extended and tested repeatedly against observed behavior. Its usefulness as a discriminating, explanatory device has grown accordingly until today we can say that many of the supposed economic relationships on which Marx and Beard constructed their narratives are incorrect.

Fortunately, the counterpart of this increased ability to discredit some proffered economic relationships is the positive attribute of providing a better explanation of what did happen. With the possible exception of demography, economic theory provides the best developed and most powerful framework available today for constructing history. Obviously it has shortcomings, just as do the most developed areas of man's knowledge. Some of those gaps will undoubtedly be filled in the future as economists continue to refine their theory. Those developments will continue to be applied to economic history so that it, too, will evolve. Even so, the advances achieved within it recently are almost revolutionary and the narrative of the past it now provides is well worth the effort to pursue.

Inside Economic Society: Desires versus Capabilities

Our checkbook is usually exhausted before the month is, and if it is not, it often means that we have curtailed expenses by not replacing the tires on the car, by not moving to an apartment with carpeting and a patio at $20 more per month, or by postponing that winter vacation in Jamaica until next year. These personal decisions reflect the individual choices an economic system forces upon almost all human beings. Such choices also express the major, underlying problem confronting all economic societies.

Human beings themselves are the root of the economic problem; they have always wanted more goods and services than their capabilities allow them to provide. Most people would like more material goods and will make sacrifices to obtain them. Economists euphemistically title such behavior "self-interest"—humans prefer more items and more of each item. The name of the behavior is not important, but recognizing that the acquisitive trait is basic to humans is crucial to understanding economic societies. Such observable, repetitive behavior, coupled with people's capacity to gratify that behavior, is the foundation of economic activities.

Nature is neither harsh nor lenient toward people's efforts to satisfy their economic desires; it is indifferent. By far the most important constraint in human beings' efforts to wrest goods from the earth is humans themselves—their knowledge in converting the natural environment into economic output. We are often told that there is a limit to the earth's resources. That observation is correct, but it is incorrect to conclude that humans must some day dissipate their environment and existence on this planet. People cannot destroy matter; rather, they convert resources from one state to another in the production of goods. The correct statement would be that when people use their environment to satisfy their desires they alter it through states of decreasing usefulness, given any prevailing level of knowledge. In a static world with no additions of technology, human society would be inexorably ground under by diminishing returns. Western history demonstrates that our economic experience has not been static, however. Human beings' incentives and abilities have expanded the technology available to us and, therefore, our capacity to wrest output from nature. Today New York, Chicago, and Los Angeles stand on land which 1,000 years ago was the site of a few Indian huts. Australians raise wheat and wool where only 300 years ago aborigines struggled to obtain a livelihood from the arid land. From Chile, New Guinea, and the Congo comes copper, a metal now useful to us but which most natives of those countries still would not recognize. The contest is knowledge versus diminishing returns. In retrospect, knowledge is the winner by a large margin.

Thus, the product of human beings' minds struggles to cope with the desires of their hearts. Knowledge, and new increments to it, works to satisfy our desires. It might be presumed that some day knowledge will catch up. One recurrent group of social optimists assert that we have, in fact, solved the production problem and now all we need is some minor tinkering with the distribution process. Both that assumption and the optimists have neglected to consider a crucial factor, however; human desires are not constant. In fact, they are remarkably elastic. Desires expand so readily that they always outdistance the capacity of our knowledge to satisfy them. When our stomachs are filled with hamburger we want sirloin. When we have had enough sirloin we want to add candlelight, champagne, and soft background music. We could replace the backyard swimming pool with an Olympic-sized model and add a cabana, a sauna, and a larger terrace complete with lawn furniture, landscaping, and gas lanterns. So far our imagination has barely been scratched.

Each time you drive downtown you wish the state highway department would widen and straighten that road. Those slums you pass on the way to the office should be replaced by new apartments and their tenants given enough help to have decent food, clothing, education, medical care, and a playground for the kids. The car you drive is three years old with its share of rust and dents and it is starting to burn oil and. . . . It is possible but not likely that some day in the future our abilities will catch up to our expansive desires. In any case, our concern here is with the past and that record is clear. Human desires have increased so easily that output has never had the slightest chance of catching up.

Scarcity = Hard Choices

Human desires have always exceeded the resources available to them and, therefore, some desires have always gone begging. Which are satisfied and which, because they are of lower priority to us, are not is the nitty-gritty of any economic society. We are compelled to make choices. Resources committed to producing color television sets or corn flakes or polio vaccine cannot be used to make classrooms or evaporated milk or interstate highways. A decision to produce one good or service simultaneously denies the possiblility of making other goods or services by wearing out some of that finite stock of inputs from which all economic output must draw. Every resource or input which people's ingenuity has mustered contains an alternate price. The true cost of any product is the opportunities to produce other products forgone by its production. Every economic good could contain the following label: "Caution: Scarcity prevails. Using this good will reduce your ability to obtain other goods."

All economic organizations must face up to scarcity. Each must find some way to ration its available resources among the larger set of conflicting desires. Economic groups can grapple with scarcity in different ways, but either explicitly or implicitly the choices must be made. Harsh and inflexible as it may seem, scarcity and the ensuing choices and unsatisfied desires are a normal part of life. Our intuition often argues that it is not normal and that examples of neglected desires which keep popping up either in current affairs or in historical accounts must indicate a malfunctioning of the economic system. Oddly enough, however, poverty, airport delays, and poor repair service on your car in the 1970s, and accounts of child labor, crowded tenements, and nonexistent sewage systems in the 1800s are examples of normalcy rather than defects in economic affairs. We could eliminate poverty, build more airports, and train more mechanics, but it could be done only by diverting resources from other activities. In the nineteenth century children could have stayed in school longer; housing could have been improved; and citywide sewer systems could have been installed; but only at the cost of having fewer family doctors; more bread to substitute for less meat, milk, and vegetables; and no overcoats for winter. We can always find examples where human desires which we think are important are neglected. They are not necessarily ignored because people do not want to satisfy them or because no one knows of their existence. They usually remain unattended to because individuals place more value on other goods.

Our conceptions and standards of what is "adequate" or "necessary" or "subsistence" living standards are shaped by prevailing conditions around us. Families who have incomes substantially below the current average are considered poor while families with relatively large incomes or holdings of wealth are considered rich. Such standards and definitions are very elastic, however; the meanings of rich and poor, minimum and substandard, and comfort and subsistence change subtly but certainly as income levels rise and fall. In the colonial period families whose real incomes were less than $50 per year would have been considered poor. At the time of the Civil War, $250 per year was required to avoid poverty. In the 1920s a family had to have at least a $1,000 yearly income, and in 1970 a household of four needed $3,700 to escape the official government onus of having insufficient purchasing power for a minimum standard of living.

Each generation of Americans has enjoyed a higher income and has, therefore, raised its expectations and standards above those of its predecessors. This condition has, in the past, not been appreciated and subjected the economy's performance to double jeopardy. Not only is it difficult to suppress the premise that unsatisfied desires in the past are a sign of trouble, but we also tend to judge the past by our present standards. Handle the economic past with care! The performance of an economy in any period should be judged by the capabilities and objectives of the era, not by how well past generations anticipated what our judgments of them would be and, therefore, what they could do to best satisfy that future scrutiny.

People can choose to make their struggle with scarcity an individual battle or they can join with others in a common cause. In practice there are gains from cooperation, gains so large that only a few hermits have adopted the individual approach. Cooperation allows us to specialize in particular activities in which we can become more proficient and productive. Cooperation allows human beings to accumulate and use a much larger body of knowledge than one individual could. Cooperation allows us to share the special talents of many individuals—Walter Cronkite, Billie Jean King, Marian Anderson, Jonas Salk, and R. Buchminster Fuller. Robinson Crusoe may find comfort in the solitude and self-sufficiency of his desert island for a while, but he will soon tire of no electricity, no frozen foods, and no *Time* magazine. Most of us have revealed our preferences for the amenities of civilization. We have shown by our behavior that we prefer productive cooperation to sparse independence. We cannot avoid making choices, however, because choosing is meshed into the social framework of cooperation from which we generate our output. Economics, then, is a process of social choice.

The Province of Economic History

Economic history is the record and explanation of how societies have made their economic choices. It reports the endowments an economy used to perform its tasks, such as the institutions, the knowledge currently available to facilitate production to meet human desires, the preferences of the population, and the resources available for production. Economic history also records how well an economy has done with its opportunities. It records this by such means as per capita incomes, how these incomes have been divided among individuals, how consistent the economy's performance has been, and, finally, how well the economy has grown and adapted to change over time—which is a central issue of economic history.

Economic history is all these things—and more. The economic component of history is specified very precisely by the domain of economic choice. Economic history is that subsector of history which relates how societies employed those resources which had alternate, conflicting uses. That component of human activity is broader than commonly assumed. Much economic activity concerns what many people believe to be the mundane things of life, namely, food, clothing, and shelter, although Julia Childs, Christian Dior, and Eero Saarinen, respectively, would quarrel with that characterization. Economics is also indigenous with the more esthetic components of life. Schools, churches, rock concerts, underground newspapers, and neighborhood parks also consume resources, and all these activities must necessarily disappear when they cannot compete successfully for those resources.

Our parents may have told us that "money can't buy happiness." However, that did not stop them, or ourselves for that matter, from trying to prove otherwise. Of course, money cannot buy happiness—it is not sold in quart containers over the counter; neither are beauty or health or love. But money can buy things which we believe will *contribute* to happiness and beauty and health and love. Money buys the car and the gas to take us out of the noise and congestion of the city for the weekend. Money buys cosmetics and pays the barber. Money buys medical care and vitamins and Contac capsules. Money pays for dinner and Winter Carnival tickets for that brown-eyed brunette in Psych 10. Money cannot buy a sunset—a sunset is not an economic good in that it uses resources which could be turned to other applications (except possibly in Los Angeles)—but money does buy a home on a hill where that sunset can be better seen or a trip to Lake Champlain where it is at its best. Money cannot buy immortality but it can extend life and ameliorate or eliminate illness. Money cannot eliminate all the dirt and ugliness in the world, but it can pay for the architect's fee to design more pleasing buildings, roads, and business signs. In short, economic choices impinge on most of our activities. They are the exclusive criteria in only a few activities, but there are very few in which they do not play some part. The world is not composed of white noneconomic sectors and black economic sectors; rather, almost all the world is varying shades of gray. To borrow part of the analysis which economists use to describe decisions in an economic framework, economic goods are only one of a number of resources that people have with which they seek satisfaction in the broadest meaning of the word. They assemble them in various combinations, mixing and substituting economic and noneconomic elements as the circumstances warrant. There are diminishing returns to using economic resources exclusively, as there are to relying only on noneconomic inputs. A little economic resource mixed with a lot that is noneconomic adds a great deal to satisfaction and vice versa. Understandably we use both for most activities.

ECONOMICS FOR HISTORY

People have a choice as to the system they use to make their social choices. Three distinctively different ways of organizing an economy, and mixtures of those three, have survived the test of time. The *traditional* society has existed ever since people joined together in hunting and living bands and began to share their economic tasks. It still exists today in the villages of lesser developed economies, often coexisting with more developed sectors nearby. The logic of the organization is repetition—a rigid recycling of assigned tasks. The society applies strong pressures of tradition and custom on individuals and groups to continue in their designated roles. Sons continue in their father's occupation, daughters in their mother's, the village's rice output is divided in set proportions, and seniority clearly places a person in his or her slot in the social hierarchy. Such a society is strong in one function—reproducing what has been done before. Inversely, it is poor in preparing to accommodate growth and change. Growth tears a traditional society apart because growth implies reorganizing production techniques, moving laborers, and abandoning obsolete enterprises. When substantial growth occurs, a traditional system of economic organization must fade away in practice even if its forms linger on. At that point either of the other two systems of organizing an economy must develop.

One of those systems is a *planned* economy in which all the necessary choices among alternates are made by a planning authority. That authority could be one person, a group of people, or a legislative body whose function consists of issuing directives which are implemented by a working staff. The authority would plan production from existing factories and construct new ones; supply the necessary raw materials and labor to the factories; provide railroads, warehouses, and grocery stores to move the goods to their consumers; and ensure that the apartments, barbershops, parks, and veterinarians required by the populace were available. In short, the planners would have to anticipate everything, coordinate everything, and, when something unexpected developed, adjust everything. An adequate planner need be only superhuman. Lacking such personnel, most economic bodies that use centralized decision making have adopted an expedient. They plan only a portion of the choices, the ones they believe important. The lesser choices, such as the output of matches, the assortment of shoe sizes, and sometimes the content of novels, are delegated to minor officials. At times the planners use part of another type of system of economic organization to make these lesser choices. Within constraints set by the planners the third system, the *market* mechanism, goes about its autonomous task of easing the planners' burdens. Let us look a little more closely at this system.

The Market System

The market system is of particular interest to us because most American economic history has developed under its guidance. Of the three systems for organizing an economy, its functioning is the most puzzling and elusive. Although in relatively sophisticated economies such as our own it is shaped by a long precedent of law and institutions, its essential ingredient is the natural, spontaneous, and repetitive responses of individuals. It requires only people doing what they want to do. The market system coordinates and shapes into a consistent aggregate the economic actions individuals exhibit in their self-interest. It is actually an immense collection of individual markets, one for each effectively different good or service. Individual markets are interlocked in varying degrees so that consistent overall choices are achieved. A market is simply a process by which the desires of the consumers (demand) are reconciled with the capacities of the producers (supply) for a particular item. This is where we reconcile what we choose with the realities of what we can provide.

A market is neither a gathering nor a location but rather the process of buying and selling an individual good or service. Perhaps it is best conceived of as a special type of auction where, responding to price changes, buyers and sellers alter the quantity of goods they offer to buy or sell. The price is the central gear in the market's "machinery." On the one hand it efficiently summarizes all relevant information about the market, incorporating and approximately weighing all the factors affecting the availability of the good. It sums up the effect of potential buyers' incomes, the price of possible substitute products, the cost of inputs used in the product, and the best technology available for that production. The price says it all, but it also enforces the collective valuation it expresses. When transactions occur in a market they are not between buyers with vague, wistful desires and sellers with well-intentioned largess. All buyers must pay (eventually if not immediately) for the goods they acquire. That, in turn, reduces correspondingly the claims they can make on the remainder of society's output. All sellers must receive enough to acquire the resources necessary to produce the product, otherwise their account books condemn them to limbo and the resources go to those who can pay for them.

When individuals consider how much of a particular good they will purchase, they usually weigh its price against the prices of available substitutes. Colonial farmers, for example, used wool material in clothing and bedding, but they could also use varying amounts of linen, cotton, silk, or deerskin. The higher they found the price of wool, the less of it they would be inclined to buy and the more they would use other types of cloth as substitutes. Generally individuals, or the collection of individuals which comprise the buyers in a market, purchase more of a good (during any given time period) as its price decreases. This behavior is formally expressed by a demand curve, or schedule, drawn on a graph, as in Figure 1-1.

Sellers in a market are also pulled between alternative choices, but because they view the market from the opposite side their response to prices is the reverse of that of buyers. Higher prices for their product make it easier for them to command resources for production and encourages them to offer larger quantities for sale. At 5 cents per yard colonial weavers would have found it worthwhile to produce some wool cloth, but at 10 cents per yard many would have abandoned linen or hybrid materials entirely for wool. Imports of wool cloth would undoubtedly have increased and farmers would have taken land away from cattle and pumpkins to pasture sheep. The seller's behavior can also be expressed formally as a supply curve, or schedule, on a graph, as in Figure 1-1.

Figure 1-1 depicts buyers and sellers adapting to the current price of wool. Unable to affect current prices by their own individual actions, they are assumed to react by varying the quantity of wool they buy or sell. Collectively, however, the behavior of buyers and sellers must affect the price of a good. If, for example, the price of wool was initially 8 cents per yard, colonial buyers would purchase ($q1$), less than suppliers would offer for sale ($q2$). This difference is formally

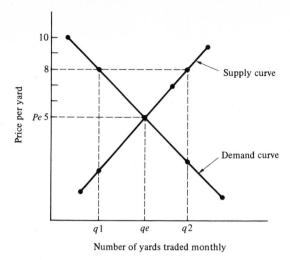

Figure 1-1   The wool market.

called excess supply, but in common experience it is simply unsold stocks which we know would cause price reductions. Excess supply self-destructs—as the price falls buyers increase their purchases while sellers reduce the quantity they find profitable to offer. The adjustment continues until all excess supply is eliminated—that is, until the price has fallen to the level where the supply and demand curves intersect. That price occurs at the equilibrium level in the market, the one combination of price and quantity (*Pe, qe*) which accommodates both buyers and sellers simultaneously. Had the price started below the equilibrium level, buyers would have asked for more goods than sellers would have been willing to supply (excess supply) and the price would have been bid up until it reached the value at *Pe*.

Obviously buyers and sellers in a market are concerned with quality, credit terms, warranties, and so forth, as well as price and quantity. These dimensions are included in market solutions, although it is difficult to incorporate them into a standard representation such as Figure 1-1. Such considerations have had important effects in American economic history. For example, changes in the information available about the conditions in distant markets or the certainty with which goods could be expected to arrive caused colonial port merchants to alter the quantity of goods they held in inventory, their pricing practices with newly arrived goods, and their participation in local manufacturing enterprises.

A market incorporates all these factors and arrives at a solution, striking a balance between society's desires for the one product as opposed to its desires for other products that could be gained by using its resources in other ways. This solution is illustrated in Figure 1-1 where that part of possible market activity which is actually carried out is depicted as the area to the left of the equilibrium quantity *(qe)*. Those portions of the supply and demand curves to the right of the equilibrium quantity, however, are inactive (except possibly when the market is adjusting toward an equilibrium). The inactive portion of the demand curve represents demands of less priority which are overruled by purchases of other products and, analogously, the unused upper section of the supply schedule which cannot justify coercing resources from their other employments.

The Market as Shock Absorber

One market, responding in conjunction with all others, reaches the basic economic decisions in an economy. It makes those choices not just once, but continuously. Even in a seemingly timeless traditional society, where technology and efficiency improve slowly, random changes are constantly intruding on the economy. Rainfall varies and thus so do the crops and the fishing in the rivers, clay deposits are depleted or discovered, and governments change, altering tax laws and trading rules along with officials. A system of markets incorporates such changes into the collective schedules of behavior of the buyers and sellers. The demand and/or supply curve, in turn, shifts, causing adjustment toward a new equilibrium price and quantity.

Notice the effect of the discovery of a more productive variety of cotton on the colonial wool market, initially comfortably settled at equilibrium. This new element appears in the demand curve, as buyers incorporate the lower price of cotton material into their patterns of behavior. In Figure 1-2 the demand curve has shifted from its original position, D_1, downward (or to the left) to D_2. This reflects the logical response of cloth consumers who buy less wool at any given price once cotton cloth becomes more competitive.

This shift of the demand curve throws the market out of equilibrium and sets up an excess supply which forces price and quantity to the new equilibrium at the intersection of the supply curve *(S)* and the new demand curve (D_2). The demand curve would also have moved in the same direction if colonial incomes had fallen or if wool dresses had become unfashionable. If cotton had experienced a blight or incomes had increased, or if wool carpeting had become "essential" in every "self-respecting" colonial home, the demand curve would have shifted upward. That also would have started market adjustments leading to a new equilibrium combination of price and quantity.

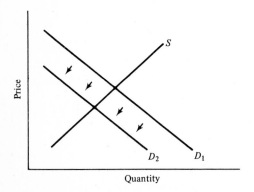

Figure 1-2   Colonial wool market—a decrease in demand.

Analogously, changes which affect the behavior of sellers appear in the supply curve. If sheep in colonial America had been depleted by an outbreak of anthrax, the price of raw wool would have increased. The original supply curve S_1, depicted in Figure 1-3, would have shifted upward (or to the left) to S_2 as the impact of the disease took effect. This shift also begins an adjustment to a new equilibrium. The price, originally at P_1, causes an excess demand $Q_2 - Q_1$, when the supply curve shifts to the left. This forces the price to rise to P_3 where both the quantity demanded by consumers and the amount offered by sellers are pulled into equality at Q_3.

Resources for Production

Wool fibers are just one of a number of inputs, such as weaver's services, looms, and buildings, used to produce wool cloth. Economists label these resources *factors of production* and divide them into three broad categories of labor, land—all natural resources, not just tillable acreage—and capital—man-made production facilities. Some authorities use four classifications by dividing labor services, even from an individual, into two groups: routine labor services and entrepreneurial (innovative or managerial) skills. Either method of classification can be misleading, however. The categories are relatively old descriptions which originated at a time when society was viewed as being composed of mutually exclusive, antagonistic groups. In practice, it is very difficult to find resources which are pure examples of any one of these groups. Farmers, for example, might own land but it would yield very little unless it was plowed (labor) and fenced (capital). Even range land requires cattle (capital) and some minimal supervision (labor) to be productive. Farmers require some education and/or experience (human capital) themselves to rise above routine corn shucking so that they can manage a farm.

Few resources are composed entirely of one factor, but in some, one factor predominates. When an economy puts such resources to work, their relative abundance can dictate the patterns in which they are used. The first few immi-

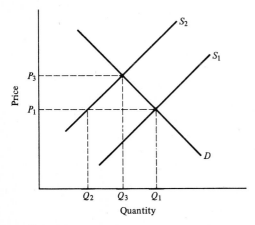

Figure 1-3 The wool market—a decrease in supply.

grants to America arrived with only a few capital resources and found themselves facing a vast supply of natural resources. Naturally they used their capital and labor resources carefully in contrast to the nonchalant manner with which they approached land. Any potential labor service was too valuable to be neglected. Convicts were not allowed to languish in jail but were farmed out to employers to work out their sentences. In contrast, the colonists treated trees and soil as if they were unlimited. They leveled forests and depleted soil and then abandoned them for virgin tracts.

Inputs may decrease in price also. A new breed of sheep or lower prices of hay or even just unusually good weather can lower the price of wool fibers. That will make the task of supplying wool cloth at any given price easier for suppliers and will be reflected by a rightward (or downward) shift of the supply schedule. With given demand (such as D in Figure 1-3) the market will move toward a lower equilibrium price and a larger equilibrium quantity. An identical adjustment in the market for wool cloth could have been caused by another change, an improvement in technology. When the minimum quantity of inputs required by existing knowledge to produce a given output decreases, producers offer more output at any given price (expressed as a rightward shift of the supply curve). Technology, however, is too central a force in economic history to be included merely as an adjustment in a market. We shall give it coverage more deserving of its consequence in a separate section later in this chapter.

Elasticity

Most graphs drawn to illustrate the functioning of a market tend to express graceful symmetry in the drafting rather than the behavior of the participants. Supply and demand curves are not necessarily straight lines which intersect each other at exact 45-degree angles. In fact, examining the forces which determine their shape, it appears unlikely that most would have that configuration.

When suppliers increase the quantity of a good they offer and consumers decrease the amount they purchase in response to an increase in its price they do so in the context of the alternatives open to them. Producers can increase their output of wool cloth, but to do so they must bid the necessary land away from pasture for cattle, weavers away from linen manufacture, and loom makers away from carriage construction. Consumers can be induced to buy more wool cloth but only to the extent that they are convinced that the money would not be better spent on other things. These options determine how much producers and consumers will alter their response in terms of quantity to a change in price, or, in the more formal term of the economist, the *elasticity* of the respective schedule. If pasture land for sheep is readily available and there are numerous potential weavers and crafts workers in the labor force, then the output of wool cloth can be substantially expanded by a small increase in its price. If, however, there are only a few such resources, or they are not readily adaptable to employment in wool production, a relatively large increase in price will coax out only a modest increase in the quantity supplied. These contrasting possibilities can be seen in Figure 1-4 where S_1 portrays the elastic supply curve whose output can be increased readily by small price increases. S_2 represents the inelastic supply where the scarcity of potential inputs compels a big increase in price to obtain expanded output.[1] Analogously, demand curves can be elastic (tending toward horizontal on a graph), reflecting ready substitutes for the good, or inelastic (appearing more vertical), expressing a paucity of substitutes.

The concept of elasticity may seem to be a dull, elusive abstraction in a textbook but it explodes into action when a market adjusts to new conditions. Elasticities are the economic trade-offs potentially available in a market, and when a market adjusts, some of these options must be exercised. If an increase in demand, as from D_1 to D_2 in Figure 1-4, occurs in a market where supply is elastic, most of the adjustment will be made by an increase in the equilibrium quantity. A slight increase in price from P_0 to P_1 can mobilize enough additional resources to increase output from q_0 to q_1. If supply is inelastic, however, as in S_2 in Figure 1-4, most of the burden would be borne by price rather than quantity. With only a few additional inputs available which could increase output, most of the adjustment is made by the big jump in price from P_0 to P_2. It "rations out" the new demand by substantially increasing the cost to any consumer who persists in using the product.

Elasticity—an economy's contingency plan—explains why some villages become ghost towns while others switch to electronics or plastics or antique shops and continue to grow when the local textile mill closes. Elasticity explains why Americans have taken up do-it-yourself projects as home-repair costs have risen but not home remedies as doctor bills have increased. And elasticity explains why cotton continues to be used extensively in clothing while the ice man has all but disappeared from American neighborhoods.

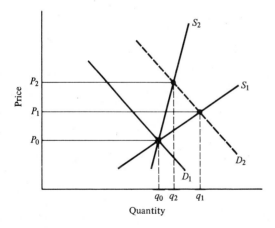

Figure 1-4 The wool market—differing elasticities.

---

[1] Notice that the two curves are drawn on the same graph, which automatically constructs them relative to the same measurement units of price and quantity. It is possible, as every introductory economics textbook stresses, to make almost any schedule appear elastic or inelastic on a graph by varying those units of measurement. The only foolproof method of indicating elasticity is by gauging the percentage change in quantity relative to the change in price.

RESOURCE COSTS AND SPENDING

One person's monthly payments are another person's income. The payments businesspeople must make to the owners of resources for their services become purchasing power, ready to be returned into the economy's circular flow of expenditures as the next cycle of demand. Paychecks received by millwrights, interest credited on savings accounts, and the weekly check from the roomer upstairs reappear in another pocket. When a market economy arrives at a price and quantity for a particular good, it simultaneously decides the inputs necessary for its production and their respective prices. Those payments to factors reflect and enforce (tempered somewhat by random factors) the valuation which society places on their efforts. They explain, in turn, who has the votes which decide the goods provided in the next round.

With the income from the resources they own in hand, individuals may choose either to spend or to save their money. Every once in a while the newspapers carry the story of the discovery of tens of thousands of dollars buried in coffee cans under the floor of a shack of a miser who died in poverty. In contrast, there is your kid brother or sister who was always borrowing ahead three months on his or her allowance and, even now, is forced to sell real estate on the side in the evenings and on weekends to keep up with the bills. Misers and kid brothers and sisters average out, however. Most Americans at most times have chosen to spend most (but not all) of their income. From the evidence now available it appears unlikely that any sizeable sector of the economy ever saved more than 15 percent (therefore consumed less than 85 percent) of their income. Similarly, it also appears unlikely that in normal conditions any large group of consumers spent more than 95 percent (thus saved less than 5 percent) of their current income.

Thus, year after year, Americans have chosen to withhold some of the resources available to them from consumption's extinguishing end. The labor, capital, and land services thus released have been channeled into increasing the economy's stock of capital. Savings were converted into improving farmland and public schools and into additional milling machines, warehouses, canals, and street lighting. As has been obvious to so many scholars writing American history, this in turn increased the capacity of the economy and contributed to higher levels of output in subsequent years. But this has not been the major source of American growth as so many have assumed. In explaining the past in our economy, the process of productivity increase is much more important than that of capital accumulation. It is so important, and so central to historical explanation, that we must examine that process before we can begin to recount the history.

THE LONG VIEW

There is an understandable myopia about human activities. Most of each day is taken up with that day's events. History, on the other hand, is farsighted. It sweeps over much of our daily activities looking for those forces which produce major changes through time. Economic history adopts a similar long view. All decision making on economic questions necessarily concerns conflicting uses of resources. Most economic choices allocate present capabilities among the larger number of possibilities for their use. The existing stock of resources is organized and employed according to the best of the existing technology. The hard choices are made. Some desires are satisfied—many more are not. But the solution of the present economic problem contains the seeds of its own destruction.

The human response to present scarcities overflows the confines of the present, continuously modifying the economic parameters of the future. Economic man and woman, whether driven by profits, personal pride, or laziness, use as few inputs as possible to accomplish their tasks. They use the most efficient techniques at their disposal and are naturally sympathetic to any better innovations that either they or others develop. Mr. Suds was making profits running the local laundry but found he could make more if he kept his equipment busy in the evening washing bedding for nearby rest homes. Ms. Letterhead discovered she had five more minutes for drinking coffee if she numbered and cross-referenced the incoming accounts payable. And Professor Chalk has substantially revised her lectures in microbiology because of the appearance of a new textbook and several pioneering journal articles. Normal self-seeking human behavior not only adapts itself to scarcity, but it constantly assaults it. Scarcity has never been defeated; in fact, it is self-rejuvenating and as full of life as ever. However, human behavior forces a process of continuous change and adaptation. That process is the most important part of the past which we attempt to narrate as economic history.

Productivity

Human behavior keeps attempting to expand the limits of society's economic capability. These changes also evidence themselves in a more basic form as improvements in the productivity of resources. Every economic good or service can be conceived as resulting from the collection, organization, and employment of a bundle of inputs of factor services. Steel, for instance, is the end product of labor, coal, iron ore, and blast furnaces. Haircuts require a barbershop, electric clippers, and a barber's time. A steel-mill manager or a barber uses as few of these inputs to provide a given output as knowledge permits. The amount of input(s) required to provide a certain output—minutes of barber's time per haircut or tons of coal per ton of steel produced—is the current level of productivity.

Through time people learn to perform tasks more efficiently and productivity increases. Blast furnaces are redesigned so that a ton of steel requires 1.3 tons of coal rather than the earlier 1.6 tons. Barbers using faster clippers can give five instead of four haircuts in an hour. Such improvements in productivity are the primary source of that growth in production which makes more output available to a representative consumer. When it requires less coal to produce a ton of steel our available supplies of coal can be used to produce more steel. On the other hand, the "extra" coal freed by greater productivity in steel making may be used to produce more electricity, chemicals, or foreign exchange earnings from exports. This is economic progress—raising the productivity of our inputs so that some of them become unnecessary. The redundant resources can then be turned to satisfying other human desires by producing goods which were previously unattainable.

Increasing Productivity, It Is Not

There are some processes which masquerade as economic improvements and which large numbers of individuals believe contribute to growth. They are hollow expectations, however, because they do not generate productivity increases—the major source of rising per capita incomes. Employment is one such supposition. Maintaining full employment is a major goal of public policies today, and with good reason. The experience of the 1930s demonstrated that unemployment can inflict sizeable losses of economic welfare on our society. When people, machines, and land are idle, the economy is not producing what its full capability allows. Programs which move an economy toward full employment are certainly proper and productive. But they do not *cause* growth! Full employment is making the most of our present capabilities. Growth is the process of expanding those capabilities. The goal of full employment is to put all our resources to work. The objective of growth is to use as few resources as possible so that some can be freed for additional tasks. Employment for the sake of employment often contradicts the objective of increasing productivity. Jobs created merely to keep people busy do not usually result in gains in efficiency.

Another strategy often advocated to promote growth is to increase the rate of investment in the economy. This would be done by consuming less of current output (that is, saving more) and channeling those released resources into expanding the productive capability of future years. This strategy does not cause growth in any basic sense of improving the efficiency with which resources are employed, but it can raise output per capita by giving each worker more resources with which to work. In recent years the prescription of increasing the flow of capital into an economy to raise incomes has been especially popular for lesser-developed nations. The disappointments which have resulted from such policies provide additional (negative) illumination as to what constitutes growth. Development planners constructed impressive dams, roads, port facilities, and steel mills, only to have them operate at a fraction of capacity because technicians or repair personnel or raw materials of sufficient quality were not available. Additional capital can increase output, but only if conjunctional inputs of complementary composition are available with it. It is very difficult to leapfrog an economy ahead in development by pushing on a few supposedly "key sectors." At any given time even the simplest economy contains large numbers of established relationships between economic units. These have reached their existing balance by a process, often prolonged, of adaptation, learning, and investment. One new resource, even a relatively large one such as many foreign-aid projects have been, cannot be expected to shock all these subtle, nurtured associations overnight into a complete new network resembling a modern economy.

Historically the American economy has been able to productively incorporate any additional capital resources made available to it. Americans have chosen, however, in the face of conflicting objectives, to curtail capital accumulation well short of the amount which would be possible as well as productive. Resource services plowed back for future use cannot be enjoyed today. You cannot have your cake and eat it too, and Americans have shown a hearty appetite for eating now. That has probably been a wise decision. Higher levels of capital accumulations reduce consumption in favor of future, albeit augmented, consumption. But with productivity rising in the economy, incomes increase through time without any additional investment whatsoever. Saving for the future then appears to be a transfer from the poor to the rich.

In the American experience, new capital has aided growth mostly by serving as a vehicle for better technology rather than improving the productivity of conjunctional inputs. Some improvements in knowledge can be put into use without any additional investment. Sometimes a production manager can put down a trade magazine after reading of a new method, march out into the assembly area, push the machines into a new pattern, and increase output. Such improvements are called unembodied progress. More frequently, though, advances must be "embodied" in new capital. Some improvements in machinery require a different gear arrangement or larger bearings or stronger steel in stress points and they can be effected only by building a new machine. Embodied technological improvements require new capital but they do not necessarily require more capital. As an economy produces goods and services it wears out some of the factors it employs, including the capital stock. Some placements of capital would be required each year merely to replace that quantity which depreciates in use. Any net additions to society's inventory of capital would come in addition to replacement investment. But investments made either to replace worn-out capital or to increase the total stock can raise the level of productivity if they embody better technology. In practice, replacing old with more efficient equipment has increased productivity much more than simply increasing the amount of equipment.

Improvements in productivity do not imply a specific path of economic development. Gains in productivity come where you can find them. It is tempting to assume that if one nation follows the pattern that other successful nations have followed, it, too, will be successful. However, this follow-the-leader guideline is usually misleading. Opportunities vary from place to place and from time to time. The more developed economies pioneered the path they followed, raising their productivity by the difficult route of hammering out improvements in technology and organization as they went. Why duplicate all their work when their current technology might be simply copied? Besides, it is not at all clear what path the most developed economies did follow. A variety of patterns have proven successful. The usual stereotype of growth includes such symbols as industrialization and urbanization. England's and Germany's records seem to conform to that image. But in other economies, manufacturing and cities appeared to develop later in response to growth in other sectors. Before the Civil War the majority of Americans lived and worked on farms; their level of per capita incomes was higher than, and the improvement in their productivity was at least as fast as, any other nation at that time. Growth does not come from building steel mills or skyscrapers. Growth comes from increasing the productivity of production processes, whether that lies in growing cocoa, weaving textiles, making toothbrushes, or—producing steel.

Inside Productivity Change

In recent years the doctors who specialize in productivity have been watching, exercising, measuring, poking at, and generally diagnosing their patient. There have not been many of them at work and their tools have often been crude, but a hazy picture of the creature's metabolism has begun to emerge. The findings are tentative but for the first time we have an approximation of the why, when, where, and how of productivity increases. Our interpretation of the economic past is obviously in for some substantial changes.

Sudden, dramatic increases in productivity are unusual for an innovation. Most improvements occur as small but frequently made alterations. Their development seldom rouses the interest of a casual observer: it is about as exciting as watching the grass grow. If you consult an almanac you can find the year in which a particular device was introduced—the steamboat in 1807, the telegraph in 1844, and the Bessemer process in 1864. Those dates can be misleading, however. One might assume that the particular innovation appeared full-blown that year and immediately played a major role in the sector which employed it. In practice most inventions go through a period of experimentation and adaptation even after they are officially presented to the public. Not only that, but after they have been generally adopted they continue to undergo refinements, improvements, and often specialization to particular uses. Innovations should be looked upon as evolving, not occurring.

There are undoubtedly numerous reasons for the gradualness of productivity improvements, but learning by doing is certainly an important one. Individuals can theorize, speculate, simulate, and hypothesize, but only when ideas are actually implemented is much of the process perfected. To borrow an old cliché, there is no substitute for experience. The "learning curve" has appeared in so many studies that it must be considered a general phenomenon. Productivity improves as the cumulative output increases. These gains do not require any improvement in technology, any increases in the basic stock of knowledge. They result from experience on the job such as streamlining the flow of materials, consigning certain processes to a subassembly sequence, and learning to tighten bolts in a specific pattern to facilitate final adjustments. Out of these trial-and-error efforts, shortcuts, and minor experiments come a sizeable part of the total gains from improved efficiency.

Innovations usually improve gradually and they seldom improve in isolation. Techniques interact, industries interact, and techniques and industries interact. They rise together, pulling and pushing each other along. Improvements in one industry usually feed into others. The development of plastic wrap improved the packaging of foods (and leftovers), reduced the drudgery of trash removal, and lengthened the construction season (by enclosing building activity in all-weather cocoons). Electricity obviously lengthened the working day but it also improved mine safety by providing a spark-free source of lighting and power, and increased the flexibility of factory layouts by replacing the cumbersome steam engine with electric motors for individual pieces of equipment.

Productivity gains tend to be ubiquitous rather than localized for several other reasons. New developments in knowledge complement and encourage other improvements. Technology is not a series of chunks of information that can be modulized—one section pulled out and used independently of the others. Individual "bits" of information are intertwined, each is usually supported by others, and in turn supports other bits. A new or improved bit compels reshuffling all along the chain, setting off a search to close newly created gaps and weak links. Discoveries in the technology of petroleum refining may provide information and clues which lead to new findings in storage batteries or cattle feed.

Progress does not arrive suddenly in a big crate. It comes slowly but steadily in numerous little packages.

Differing Growth Rates

Human inventiveness may be universal but that does not imply that productivity will increase uniformly. In fact, the evidence asserts just the opposite. Growth rates (the percentage increase in productivity) differ among industries, among nations, and through time. These differences are not merely random. On the contrary, there are compelling reasons for growth rates to differ.

Innovative effort by individuals is itself an economic good. It competes with other possible uses for resources. Lab technicians, test tubes, and microscopes can be pressed into the search for the cause of cancer but they might also be used to produce more smallpox and polio vaccines. Similarly, the expected fruits of inventive efforts promise certain returns. Individuals who—or firms that—build a better washing machine or light bulb or mousetrap will be rewarded for it. It could result in more profits, a raise, royalties, a promotion, or a banquet in their honor by the chamber of commerce. Individuals and decision units are constantly being pressured by these costs of, and returns to, innovative activity. They are frequently not even aware of the forces which push them sometimes to expand, sometimes to contract their creative efforts.

Industries usually experience their greatest productivity gains during their earliest year. Those gains decline as the industry grows older. In the first years of an industry there are likely to be more profitable opportunities which have not yet been used. The typical pattern of the growth of output of a product also encourages more innovative activity in the early years. Output usually grows in the form of an "S-shaped" or a Gomperz curve, as illustrated in Figure 1-5. In the first years not only does output increase, but the rate at which it rises increases as well. During this stage, profits in the new industry attract large increases in capacity and output begins to pour out of all the resulting new plants. Later the surge of investment is completed, the initial demand satisfied, and the rate of growth of output begins to decline. (This turn is indicated in Figure 1-5 as point A.) Thereafter the growth rate continues to slacken. Total output continues to grow because rising incomes and population continue to increase demand, but new products and technology begin to challenge the product's traditional markets. Finally this competition more than offsets the expansive forces, output

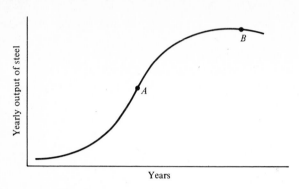

Figure 1-5 Gomperz curve for steel.

reaches a maximum (point *B* in Figure 1-5), and thereafter declines. The future for the industry obviously looks much brighter during its earlier development than it does toward the end. When profit rather than output is the focus, the contrast is even sharper. The reversal from above-average profits during the early expansion to below-average profits in the later stages produces a tremendous percentage change. A decline from a 15 percent return on capital to a 5 percent return, for instance, is a change by a factor of 3. It also produces a sharp differ-ence in the expected returns from possible innovations. There is much more incentive to innovate for an industry with high profit margins, growing output, and new investment than there is for one with lower margins, a small (and/or decreasing) profit rate, and little new investment.

For the last two centuries there also appears to have been a systematic pattern in the growth rates of the most developed nations. The estimates are subject to some doubt—the earlier the year the less direct statistical evidence exists. Nevertheless, the estimates suggest that growth rates have been increasing. That should not be surprising. There are several reasons that the successful rate of innovative activity should be increasing. There has been a continuous increase in the population and, of course, in the number of people working at economic tasks. Consequently, more individuals are positioned where they can devise inno-vations. More house painters have the opportunity to experiment with different brushes, more corporate managers can reshuffle their businesses' structures, and more kernels of seed corn might be mutated and larger ears grown. The opportu-nities are larger and so are the rewards. More people and rising per capita in-comes increase the quantity sold of most products. The larger the market for the improved product, the larger the gain from an improvement. Directly or indirect-ly, expanding economic activity encourages a relatively larger effort to raise pro-ductivity. A larger economy encourages a faster rate of improvement in society's productivity and economic welfare.

Growth and Not-So-Growing Industries Wall Street has recently spent much of its time searching for companies in emerging "growth industries." The label is new but the phenomenon is not. In the 1600s tobacco was a growth industry, in the 1830s textiles were, in the 1870s steel and railroads were, and in the 1920s automobiles, radios, and farm equipment were considered exciting. A growing economy—which is the only reasonable framework in which to consider the American economy—always has some growth industries. Some sectors inevitably experience a faster-than-average rate of expansion as the structure of productivity and demand changes. There are also, inevitably, some declining industries. While some products start up the Gomperz curve, others reach the top and then contract. In the 1960s, computers, electronics, and fast-food franchises were given sizeable markups, but most of the above-mentioned previous favorites were selling at sizeable discounts. Railroads were cutting down schedules and tearing up track. Steel and textile firms were pressuring Congress to enact quotas against younger, more energetic competition.

Declining industries use resources just as all other industries do, and in this world of scarcity they must compete against those alternate uses for them. The growth process keeps adding to, and shifting, the possible alternate uses. In the market system, prices wrench some of them away from the declining sectors and shove them into other uses to which society is assigning higher priority. Often the transfer is effected so gradually that individuals involved barely notice, but if the resources resist the proddings the clout can become brutal. Decreasing sales erode profits and lead to either efforts at retrenchment or inevitable bankruptcy. In either case the result is idle factories, jobs which disappear, and stocks and mortgages worth only a fraction of their previous value.

A retrogressive industry is not pleasant and some individuals (especially politicians) cannot admit that any industry could undergo such a setback. They blame the decreasing numbers of farms on government policy (or the lack thereof) and the railroad's trouble on poor management. These sectors, like the stagnant shoe, steel, and ocean shipping industries, are alleged to be "essential." They cannot be allowed to wither away. But neither first-rate management nor major government intervention is able to slow the retreat much. The forces leading to contraction are much too powerful to constrain. Some potato farmers may think themselves "essential," but right now there are too many potatoes and the market is telling some growers that they would be much more useful assembling refrigerators or operating a motel. Some rail lines may feel "essential," but right now the patronage on most indicates they are not. Most people seem quite content not to use them. There are runs operating because of government mandate where the conductors eagerly await a passenger to break the monotony. Such service would be much more productive if the right-of-way were converted to a strip park and the conductor set to work caring for its grass, trees, and flowers.

Misleading Analogies   The market economy is not easy to understand. It works unobtrusively and quietly in reaching a massive number of decisions, each a finely balanced compromise between conflicting goals. It absorbs and reconciles the effects of hurricanes, droughts, improvements in productivity, shifts in tastes, and increases in income. All this is very difficult to fit on a score card, even a large one. Understandably, observers try to find shortcuts in describing and characterizing economic activity—shortcuts such as analogies.

Biological analogies are the favorite. Economies are said to be "reaching maturity," "sick," "healthy," "coming of age," or "drawing to the end of an age." But economies do not photosynthesize, or grow and die like rhododendrons. An economy, basically, is ongoing human behavior—a collection of social transactions which involves scarce resources. Human behavior in the setting of an economy does not appear to age, at least not in any way similar to that in which individuals and plants do. Social responses to similar economic conditions appear remarkably consistent over long periods of time. Economic behavior has a newness, an aura of discovery about it. This despite the fact that it is usually repeating once again what has been done over and over before. A historical perspective is one of those luxuries most people can forgo. Chronologically the American economy is well into its fourth century. But economically it has no age. Designating it a "young economy," "old economy," or "middle-aged economy with a few gray hairs" is meaningless. It is a collection of people doing what they consider best with existing opportunities. That is timeless.

Analogies from physical science are also common. Economies are described as "taking off," "gathering momentum," "breaking down" (presumably like airplanes, rolling rocks, and old rusty machinery, respectively). Such illustrations are misleading. An economy may grow continuously and it may grow at an increasing rate but that does not imply that growth is self-sustaining. Growth results from increasing productivity and that, in turn, results from an environment which encourages and disseminates improvements in efficiency. One increase in productivity, however, does not create another. Unless the underlying growth generation process continues, the improvements in productivity cease and growth slows to a stop.

An economy is a pattern of social relations, not mechanical connections. Neither does it function (or malfunction) as a single unit. Unlike a machine which may stop completely when a gear or shaft breaks, economies can continue even after the loss of one of their components. Self-seeking behavior substitutes, rearranges, and builds new connections around a gap resulting from such major happenings as wars, crop failures, or government edicts. Among economic systems a market economy is most proficient at compensating for any major rifts which appear suddenly in the economic structure. But most of the dislocations in economic life do not arrive suddenly and full-blown. They build gradually by an accumulation of modest pressures before they appear large and dramatic. This is where the resiliency of the market completely outclasses other economic systems. It begins to incorporate and adjust to these small changes as soon as they occur. Well before the public's interest begins to designate some economic adjustment as a problem, the market has been at work incorporating the change. Thus, the characterization of a "crisis" or "turning point" or "revolution" is usually inappropriate to a market system. The process of economic change moves gradually, absorbing changes as it goes. Other types of history may recount sharp breaks in the patterns described, but in economic history most of the sudden turns occur in the eye of the beholder, not in the processes themselves.

Two additional forces are important to recognize when we recount America's economic past. While neither is a cause of growth in itself, both are so entwined with the growth process and the expansion of the American economy that they must also be considered among the sources of growth. The first of these is *economies of scale.*

Economies of Scale

In their quest to minimize the cost per unit, producers usually encounter a general relation in economic costs called *economies of scale.* Costs depend not only on how inputs are combined but also on the size of the production effort—the quantity of inputs employed. Certain inputs are relatively large in themselves. To produce at their most efficient level they must work in conjunction with large quantities of other inputs. An automobile assembly plant requires an extensive division of labor to achieve the lowest cost per car. When each assembler is responsible only for installing five screws, and a welding robot is constructed to make only one L-shaped bead on a fender, it takes at least 200,000 cars annually to justify that form of organization. It also takes a very large amount of petroleum to fill the most efficient-sized oil tankers. Those now coming off the skids of shipyards in Japan, Sweden, and Britain are built to carry 300,000 tons of oil products. If that cargo were gasoline, for instance, it would be enough to supply 800,000 American-built cars for a full month. Actually, even larger oil tankers could carry their cargoes at even less cost per ton but there are not enough markets in the world with several times 800,000 cars to keep such a ship busy.

Automobile plants produce cars cheaper at larger volumes than at lower volumes, and the cost per ton of hauling oil decreases as tankers get larger. These are economies of scale, as illustrated in Figure 1-6. When a firm begins to produce almost any given item, it often discovers it can reduce its cost per unit as it expands output. More inputs—labor, materials, transportation services, and correspondence—are flowing through the plant and this increases the opportunities to rechannel and save on some of them. As a company becomes larger it may find it can save by providing its own fleet of delivery trucks, or receive a discount on a larger volume of steel bars, or spread the cost of newspaper advertising over more sales, or introduce more specialized equipment on the assembly line.

Economies of scale are important in the economic affairs of a society, but they are not all-important; that is, they are not universal and where they do exist there are limits to the savings through size. Businesses can become inefficient from being too large as well as too small. This is illustrated in Figure 1-6 where, to a point, average unit costs decrease as output expands, but with further increases in output costs stabilize and then begin to increase. (Economists often refer to the output level at minimum cost as the "optimum size" of the firm, since either the incentive to maximize its net returns or the competition from other producers pressures the firm to organize its production facilities at this level.) Firms which produce some types of goods must be relatively large in order to reach their optimum size. Plate glass, gasoline, and Dream Whip are feasible only when they are produced in a large manufacturing unit. On the other hand, dry cleaners, lettuce farms, and home builders need not be large to provide their services efficiently. But "large" and "small" are relative terms. The corner gro-

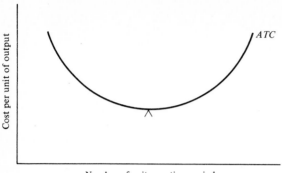

Figure 1-6 Economies of scale.

cery store is large relative to the market it serves, whose customers would otherwise be forced to drive 2 miles to buy a pound of coffee or a quart of milk. A steel mill comprising 800 acres of buildings, railroad sidings, and ore docks may be relatively small. It is now a cliché to say that American business has grown bigger. Like most clichés it has some truth, but standing alone it is a misleading statement. The size of a business is important only when related to its market. While many business operations have grown larger, so have most markets for their services. The outcome of this contest between size and purchasing power is not at all obvious, and is an issue we will encounter several times in the course of spanning American economic history.

The size of the firm relative to its market is only one of several ways economies of scale have affected economic organization and performance in the past. No business person, past or present, can ignore its implications with impunity. One obvious implication is that entrepreneurs, either from the pull of profits or the push of competition, organize their production efforts at the optimum size. Through time that size will probably change. Business units will adjust their size in response. They will also be adjusting in more subtle ways, such as location. Given the choices embodied in economies of scale of unit costs to size, the placement of factories, workshops, and warehouses on the landscape becomes important. Costs of doing business are influenced by location. Business people will tend to minimize the total cost per unit of output delivered to their customers rather than just that portion of costs resulting from production. Gains from a large, efficient plant may be offset by higher transport costs, higher property taxes, a higher burglary rate, problems in recruiting a labor force, or inaccessibility to marketing or service specialists. Sometimes substantial economies of scale overrule other cost components and that dictates the location decision. Other businesses—such as produce dealers, law firms, and golf courses—must be near their customers. Business people weigh these respective costs, organizing and locating their operations as their particular mix dictates. The various cost components change with time and in relation to one another. Consequently, both the organization and location of business operations undergo modifications as they are adapted to the changing conditions. In the first half of the nineteenth century, mills clustered around sharp drops on rivers which could be used for water power. In the late nineteenth century, manufacturing was located near its work force and the railroad station in the center of town. In the midtwentieth century, factories followed cars and trucks out to the suburbs.

A given economy of scale merely expresses a range of production efficiencies which varies with the amount of output. It is not a new addition to knowledge which can be applied to increase productivity. Yet, ironically, it can be a source of higher incomes and productivity in an expanding economy. American history, particularly the earliest periods, illustrates how important that force can be. Per capita incomes of Americans during that era grew because knowledge about economic processes was improving. But they also increased because the rapid growth of population, capital, and natural resources created larger markets which could use more efficient production methods, that is, economies of scale. More customers allow a general store to be split into a grocery store, a hardware store, and a pharmacy. A larger flow of farm products enables middlemen to specialize and provide grain elevators and loading docks. And banks, insurance companies, and wholesalers take over the functions previously handled by the jack-of-all-trades port merchants. We do not have any overall quantitative measure of how important this force was in relation to other gains, such as improving technology. But in the judgment of some scholars who have examined the period closely, it is very important. In the one available study of the period which has examined productivity change, that of ocean shipping, it was found to be the most important factor.

SUGGESTED READINGS

Carr, Edward Hallett: *What Is History?* Vintage Books, Random House, New York, 1961.

Davis, Lance E.: " 'And It Will Never Be Literature': The New Economic History, A Critique," *Explorations in Economic History,* Fall 1968.

Fishlow, Albert and Robert W. Fogel: "Quantitative Economic History: An Interim Evaluation, Past Trends and Present Tendencies," *The Journal of Economic History,* March 1971.

Heyne, Paul T.: *The Economic Way of Thinking,* Science Research Associates, Inc., Chicago, 1973.

Kuznets, Simon: *Toward a Theory of Economic Growth,* Norton, New York, 1968.

Lee, Dwight R. and Robert F. McNown: *Economics in Our Time: Concepts and Issues,* Science Research Associates, Inc., Chicago, 1975.

Lipsey, Richard G. and Peter O. Steiner: *Economics,* 4th ed., Harper & Row, New York, 1975.

Mansfield, Edwin: *Technological Change,* Norton, New York, 1971.

North, Douglass C.: "Economic History," in *International Encyclopedia of the Social Sciences,* Crowell Collier & Macmillan, New York, 1968.

Samuelson, Paul A.: *Economics,* 9th ed., McGraw-Hill, New York, 1973.

Wright, Gavin: "Econometric Studies of History," in Michael D. Intriligator (ed.), *Frontiers of Quantitative Economics,* North Holland, Amsterdam, 1971.

European Initiatives and American Reactions

The American economic experience began by accident. In 1492, Columbus was searching for Asia when North America blocked both his path and his hopes. Initially there was some prospect that the Caribbean might be merely an outpost of Asia or could be skirted to reach Asia's treasures, but those possibilities were destroyed when Magellan circled the world two decades later. His voyage proved that the Western Hemisphere was not Cathay or its environs; it was an entire continent system in its own right, far from the previously known world. Hereafter the development of America could proceed only on its own merits.

In the 1500s, however, there was not much promise in the economic development of America. Europeans could find only a few products on the two new continents for which the rewards justified the efforts to bring them back home. These dismal prospects existed despite the sophisticated Indian civilizations in Central and South America in 1492 and despite the great economic development of this hemisphere since 1492. The limited prospects were not a result of European ignorance of the opportunities in the new land, either. Shortly after the journey of Columbus, numerous explorers had disclosed many of the details of geography and resources of the new lands. Cabot and Cartier had explored the Atlantic shore of what is now the United States, while Ponce de Leon and De

Soto had traversed Florida and the Gulf Coast. Cortez had conquered Mexico. Balboa had crossed Panama and discovered the Pacific Ocean. Pizarro had pushed down the western coast of South America, overcoming the Incas. Only fifty years after Columbus, Coronado had explored what is now the southwestern part of the United States, including Kansas. In short, substantial exploration of America had been completed quickly and the basic parameters of the continents were known. Now what could be done with it?

In the 1500s, most of the great resource base of the Western Hemisphere was prohibitively expensive for European use. Had America's great stock of soil, minerals, water, and timber been located conveniently next to Europe, it would have been immediately pressed into production. But it was not. The long, expensive ocean voyage that separated America and Europe in the sixteenth century made America's natural wealth only slightly more useful to Europe than if it had been 3 miles deep in the Atlantic Ocean.

Thus the constraint which explained the slow initial development of North America was the very high transportation costs between America and Europe. These rates were a direct reflection of the relative inefficiency of ocean shipping of those days and the resulting consumption of large quantities of shipping resources to transport cargo. Most of America was not an economic resource in 1500 because it was effectively removed from participation in the economies operating at that time.

Most of the possible products of the Western Hemisphere were excluded from trade with Europe by these high freight costs. The only feasible way by which much development of North America could take place in the sixteenth century was by a reduction of those costs. Pending that development, only high-valued products whose final sale price could absorb those high freight rates could participate in European-American trade.

EARLY DEVELOPMENT IN SPANISH AMERICA

Much of Columbus's experience in the New World paralleled this major quandary which he had himself initiated—what to do with this new world. Flush with the instant and enormous success of discovery, his second trip to America attracted 1,200 men and 17 ships. His plans of establishing a central outpost at Hispaniola, however, were repeatedly frustrated. Its inhabitants were more interested in searching for gold or plundering the nearby Arwark Indians. Many settlers preferred to return to Spain rather than farm the islands. Columbus' third and fourth voyages attracted diminishing enthusiasm, and Queen Isabella ordered him to search for a passage to Asia rather than attempt to develop the Caribbean area.

Spain's notable success in the New World came not in the Caribbean region per se, but rather as a consequence of its conquest of the relatively sophisticated Indian civilizations bordering the region. The Aztecs, the Incas, and the Chibchas (who lived in the area now encompassed by Colombia) had accumulated far more gold than the poorer Arwarks and Caribs of the Caribbean Islands. The Spanish seized it and then went on to acquire much larger quantities via a new resource they had brought with them—European mining technology. The Spanish also reaped substantial gains by deposing the top leadership of the Indian societies while retaining and controlling the remainder of the organization of the economies to produce cattle, tobacco, and cotton.

Meanwhile the islands of the Caribbean languished in the sun, and there was even less activity there than there had been immediately before Columbus. The European population, never very large, diminished as the settlers drifted back to Spain or migrated to the mainland. The original Indian population had been decimated by the first attempts at colonization, and one major group, the Arwarks—probably initially numbering about 300,000—disappeared entirely. This somnolence lasted until the 1620s when new developments in sugar culture brought explosive growth to the islands. Colonists representing all the major European powers poured into the area, bringing substantial numbers of Negro slaves with them. By the mid-1600s many of the smaller islands of the southeast Caribbean (the Lesser Antilles) were almost completely settled. Barbados, for example, had more than 40,000 inhabitants, more than the entire population of the American colonies that year. Sugar was profitable and it was produced almost exclusively, to the neglect of foodstuffs and other supplies. Americans soon discovered this ready market for their flour, meat, horses, and lumber products to the south of them. Thus, this development, coinciding with the early period of the American colonies, had an important effect on the latter's development.

TWO SEPARATE ECONOMIES MEET AND MERGE

The impressment of the Indians by the Spanish was only one instance of a much more general interaction between those two civilizations. The sixteenth century witnessed extensive borrowing and adapting of technology and tastes between the two hemispheres, an exchange through which both the European and Indian civilizations reaped some gains. Although both economies were primarily agricultural, there was a striking difference in the crops each raised. Most of the Indian crops were unknown in Europe before Columbus, crops such as tobacco, potatoes, corn, beans, squash, pumpkins, tomatoes, peanuts, avocados, chocolate, vanilla, or chilies. Today it is hard to conceive of the Eastern Hemisphere without some of these products. Imagine Ireland without potatoes, Italy without tomatoes, and India without the curry made from chilies.

Europe introduced a long list of products to the Americans, including grains (such as wheat, barley, and rye), sugar, onions, cabbage, peas, and fruits (such as apples and peaches). By introducing domesticated animals the Europeans also filled an especially noticeable gap in the farming opportunities of the natives. The indigenous livestock included only dogs, turkeys, and, in the South American mountains, the llama. As a result, the pre-Columbus Indians had to carry all overland cargo on their backs, they had no power strong enough for heavy plowing, and their meat supply was limited to wild game. The Europeans introduced horses, cows, oxen, hogs, chickens, and sheep to the economies of the New World. They also added other notable improvements to native technology. The Indians were unable to use any metal other than copper, which was soft enough to be hammered into usable forms. This meant that before 1492 any noncopper implements were necessarily made from stone, bone, and wood. Firearms and gun powder from the white man greatly expanded the Indian's hunting capacity.

From the vantage of the present, the American economy of a few hundred years ago appears very underdeveloped, even primitive. On the other hand, viewed from the perspective of the total length of economic history, that economy is very comparable to ours both in time and in economic development. Columbus and his European contemporaries thought of the Indians as aborigines but, given the earlier history of the New World, it is surprising how similar the two societies were. For an unbelievably long period of about 25,000 years, the economies of each hemisphere developed independently. There is no evidence that any products or technology crossed between the two worlds before Columbus, except for that which the first few natives brought with them across the Bering Strait. It was a remarkable arrangement, one of those rare cases which offers a social scientist a test-tube-like isolation of a social process which in this case was the entire development of a civilization! It is clear that the same forces which brought productivity increases and higher living standards in the Old World were at work in the Americas. Even more surprising was the timing of those advances. As in Europe, they accumulated very slowly during the long first period of development and then increased much more rapidly in that relatively short period just before Columbus. There were some obvious differences, of course, but many of these were a reflection of adaptations to different conditions. The Indians did not develop the technology Europeans did with metals and that, more than anything else, accounted for the subjection of the New World to the Old. But the Indians did develop substantial improvements in agriculture, architecture, textiles, handcrafts, and food processing. Some of their inventions (such as canoes, snowshoes, and hammocks) would have been useful in Europe if the Europeans had developed them before discovering America. The irony is that the Indian and European stages of development were so comparable, but that the small margin of difference the Europeans held was enough to overwhelm the Indians when they met. Had the Indians been just a few hundred years earlier on their 25,000 year course, the age of exploration and colonization might well have been reversed. The scenario could have read: A fleet of boats directed by Emperor Montezuma reached the coast of Portugal. Three decades later the Aztecs conquered Spain and North Africa, the Incas destroyed Paris, and the Iroquois claimed all the British Isles.

Most of the economic history which has been written about early America tells of Europeans in America, an understandable perspective. Nevertheless, Europeans accounted for only a small proportion of America's economic activity in its early years. Though seldom mentioned (and then only poorly recorded), the Indians generated most of the economic activity in those years. The major development of that period was the introduction and adaptation of European technology into the native economy.

European technology and products preceded European settlers in restructuring the economy of the New World. All the way across the continent frontier blazers found the Indians had already been substantially "Europeanized": they had adopted European animals, borrowed European skills, and were eager to trade for European goods. These changes make it difficult to visualize the economy of the Indians before 1492. Most of the reports about Indian civilization were made after the transformation had taken place. There were some (often substantial) costs of the initial contacts between the two civilizations. Large numbers of Indians succumbed to measles and smallpox brought by the somewhat less-susceptible white man. Then many of the survivors were pushed out or exterminated by the incoming colonists. Farther inland, however, large populations of the natives were not troubled by the newcomers for centuries to come, and in those societies two consequences almost certainly occurred: The introduction of new products and skills both raised the per capita income of the Indians and concurrently caused them to reorganize their economic activities.

Such reorganization occurred in the early seventeenth century when horses were brought to the Great Plains from Mexico. Only then did the Indians have the necessary mobility to effectively overcome the buffalo. The vulnerable animal added large quantities of meat and hides to the Indians' incomes. With this improvement came the economic organization of the Plains Indians and their distinctive teepees. The economy would have appeared as strange and exotic to an Indian living along the Missouri River in the fifteenth century as it does to us today. Before 1600, settlements in the Plains were confined to a few wooded areas along the rivers. Some agriculture was possible there but in the broad stretches of prairie between the rivers the sod was too tough to work.

Another example of the reorganized economic activities of the Indians as a result of contact with Europeans can be seen in a Sierra Club art book of the Southwest canyon country. Typically you will find a picture illustrating the "eternal serenity" of Navaho life. In the foreground a woman is weaving elaborate patterns in a wool blanket while in the distance sheep are grazing at the foot of a tall, red cliff. Life goes on the way it always has—except there were no wool blankets and no sheep until after 1500. The "timeless life" of the Navaho is relatively new and so are the famous Indian blankets they sell at roadside stands.

NORTH OF THE RIO GRANDE

Before 1600 Europeans were engaged in two profitable types of economic enterprise in North America, although neither of these activities resulted in permanent settlements there. Shortly after—or perhaps even before—1504 when Cabot explored the northern coast of North America, European fishermen duplicated his path across the North Atlantic. They were attracted by the rich source of fish along the coastal banks but found it difficult to transport the fish back to Europe. Initially the catch was salted on board the fishing boats to preserve it through the long trip home, but that proved cumbersome. Soon "shore fisheries" were established because processing could be done more easily on land. Nevertheless, these shore fisheries were not permanent settlements; each year when the fishing was completed they were abandoned until the next season.

The fishermen also developed the profitable sideline of trading with the Indians for furs. Manufactured goods such as iron kettles, nails, mirrors, beads, and wool blankets were brought from Europe to trade for pelts of muskrat, otter, mink, and, the most valued of all, beaver. The Indians in turn collected furs at the coastal fishing locations, drawing them from the interior of North America. This was one reason the French did not explore the interior of North America until after 1600; the entrepreneurship of the natives, which brought the furs to the coast, made such ventures unnecessary.

Major portions of both the coast and the interior of North America had yet to be explored in detail in 1600. Florida, the Gulf Coast, and the southwest of what is now the United States had become well known and their geography was a challenge only to map makers. This geographical knowledge was a result of Spanish efforts which had paralleled their settlement to the south. Extensive exploration of these areas had seemed worthwhile to the Spanish because of the possibility of their productive use. Areas north of the Spanish regions had not seemed as promising and therefore had received very little subsequent exploration. But around 1600, interest in the more northern regions of North America resumed as a result of decreasing ocean freight rates which were converting this area of the world into an economic attraction. Champlain paddled his canoe into the Great Lakes, Henry Hudson discovered his bay and his river, and settlement began on the Atlantic Coast.

Several locations had previously been attempted as colonies but had been abandoned as failures. Early settlers gave up their bases in Newfoundland and Roanoke Island to return to Europe. A second group of colonists on Roanoke mysteriously vanished; where they went is unknown but why they left is understandable. In the early seventeenth century no permanent settlement on the Atlantic Coast had good economic prospects; one on the sand dunes of Cape Hatteras was even less promising. The Spanish town of St. Augustine was successful only because of its location, not because of any products it produced. It was established as a naval base to help defend the Spanish galleons, carrying gold and silver, against British and French privateers.

What proved to be the first successful colony began with prospects fully as dismal as those of all its predecessors. In 1607, the Virginia Company began two settlements, one at Jamestown, and one at Kennebec, Maine. Kennebec was quickly abandoned as unproductive. Jamestown also proved disappointing; in fact, the colonists had decided to leave and were in the process of closing down the outpost when another ship arriving from Europe persuaded them to stay in order to try some other possibilities. The advice eventually proved to be good. During the first few years, however, the colonists experimented with all the products that were expected to be profitable—profitable as predicted from the distant perspective of Europe—with little success. They searched for the Northwest Passage. They hunted for gold and silver. They tried raising grapes to make wine. Then finally, in 1613, they planted a few tobacco plants. With that event Jamestown became the first settlement to be economically productive above the Rio Grande River—more than 120 years after Columbus.

Most of the remainder of the Atlantic Coast remained unprofitable, however. In 1619 a ship of dissidents bound for Jamestown strayed north of their course and landed at a place they named Plimoth. The small colony suffered through years of isolation and hardship in the 1620s. Their struggles have been lauded ever since in history books as dedication to their beliefs, but any such small, isolated colony on the New England coast in the early 1600s was certain to encounter those hardships, whatever its doctrines. Conditions were improved in 1629 when the Puritans founded the Massachusetts Bay Colony at Boston. They had also come for noneconomic reasons, but they came in such numbers—about 20,000—and with such wealth that their aggregate presence made the regional economy more productive. This same influx of immigrants also settled Rhode Island, New Haven, and the rich farmland of the Connecticut River Valley running through western New England. The Dutch followed in Hudson's footsteps to establish settlements at Manhattan and along the Hudson River.

The Maryland Colony, just north of Jamestown, was established. in the 1630s. It, too, was conceived as a sanctuary for religious dissenters, but tobacco quickly became the prime concern of its citizens. Just as in Virginia, the profitability of the crop attracted a large number of immigrants. Maryland grew much faster than the other "dissident" settlements in New England. Profits, not ethics, appear to have been the more powerful incentive.

The extensive histories on record of these first settlements run in direct contradiction to their economic importance. In the first few years the colonies were not only small, isolated, and underdeveloped, but were also of marginal economic importance. The early years consisted of hardship, risk, trial and error. Many crops and methods of raising them were tried, most of which were either abandoned or modified. Commerce depended on the long, unpredictable, and expensive voyage to and from Europe. There was little domestic market within which products could be exchanged. No doubt the knowledge and experience gained during this first period were useful to later colonists but that consolation did not change the hardship of the first settlers.

America's first settlers made less than full returns on their resources. Soon, however, the rewards equaled and then surpassed the income from comparable European employments. While the first colonists came to a location which had dismal economic prospects and, therefore, their immigration suggested strong noneconomic objectives, later settlers were considering an attractive environment in their decision to immigrate. This latter group may also have been attracted by some of the noneconomic facets of America, but the economic influence was sufficient in itself to explain their migration. Furthermore, many of the latter came under arrangements which were prima facie evidence that their motivation was primarily economic. Clearly the Pilgrims came for noneconomic reasons, but they and other widely publicized groups like them were only an early and tiny minority of American immigrants. Most American immigrants arrived at a time when their expected economic returns in the New World compensated for the cost of their relocation.

Colonial America, 1670–1720

In 1670 there were slightly more than 100,000 residents of the American Colonies. More than half of these lived in Massachusetts and Virginia; the remainder were scattered along the coast from southern Maine to North Carolina. Even at tidewater there were substantial stretches of unsettled country. The city of Philadelphia, for example, had yet to be established and there were almost no colonists in Pennsylvania. Boston, the largest city in the Colonies, had only about 4,000 inhabitants; New York fewer than 3,000; and Newport, Rhode Island, less than 2,000. With this precarious a foothold in North America it is understandable that much of the American's economic activity was tied back to the established economies of Europe. Domestic demand was so small and scattered that almost no local products could be expected to be profitable if they were sold exclusively in the Colonies. Thus, the colonists were constantly searching for local products which could be bartered for imports from Europe. In 1670 that list was very limited: tobacco, fish, furs, deerskins, and lumber products. These were almost the only products which could absorb the relatively high transport costs of crossing the Atlantic and still yield any net returns to American producers.

Even while American opportunities appeared limited in 1670, the constraints were beginning to fall away. During the subsequent century freight rates fell and the domestic market grew. Combined with other gains, such as improvements in technology, these forces yielded a century-long expansion in the colonial economy. Using population as an indicator, there were about twenty times as many Americans in 1770 as there had been in 1670. (See Figure 2-1.)

In the fifty years after 1670 this expansion was obviously well under way. Population quadrupled, existing towns and settled areas expanded, and new ones were formed, so that by 1720 few of the regions along the Atlantic Coast from Charleston, South Carolina, to Portland, Maine, were still completely uninhabited. Such expansion seldom simply expands in multiples of existing patterns, of course, and the experience of this half-century is no exception. Some regions grew faster than others and all altered their economic functions somewhat in response to changes in demand brought about by the expansion. The "growth sectors" of the Colonies of this period were South Carolina and Pennsylvania, two areas which began the period almost completely unpopulated. The expansion of each was propelled by the robust demand for their exports, rice in the case of South Carolina, and flour, bread, and meat in the case of Pennsylvania. Many of the other relatively unsettled colonies of 1670 also expanded rapidly in this period. Connecticut, Rhode Island, New York, and New Jersey expanded their economies of mixed farming, generally characteristic of Northern agriculture. Delaware, Maryland, and North Carolina thrived on the tobacco culture established in nearby Virginia. In contrast, the larger established colonies of Massachusetts and Virginia grew less rapidly—although the tripling of population which each recorded in the period is small only in relation to the very high rates of the nearby colonies.

New England   New England's economy received a major blow at the beginning of this period. As the frontier edged out of the lowlands and river valleys into the hills, it increasingly infringed on the preserves of the local Indians. In 1675, the majority of the tribes in southern New England struck back. Their numbers were large compared to the militia the colonists were able to field, and using the guerrilla tactics of surprise they terrorized much of New England until

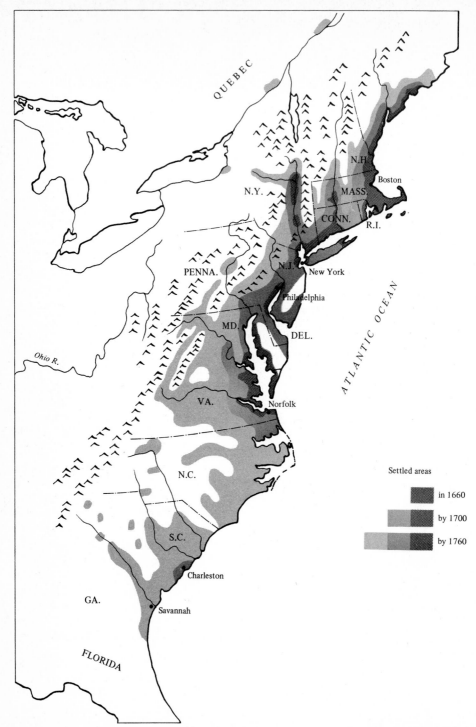

Figure 2-1 *(Source: Ross Robertson,* History of the American Economy, *3d ed., Harcourt Brace Jovanovich, New York, 1973, p. 52.Copyright 1955, © 1964, 1973 by Harcourt Brace Jovanovich, Inc. and reprinted with their permission.)*

1678. During King Phillip's War—as the conflict became known—the Indians destroyed or forced the abandonment of settlements in the Connecticut River Valley, in southern Maine, and in eastern Massachusetts. Even venerable Plymouth was attacked. Boston was swollen with refugees from the receding frontier. Eventually the Indians were killed or driven from the region but not without heavy costs. The colonial militia suffered large losses in numerous battles, including 300 killed in two major defeats in western Massachusetts. Some of the abandoned towns were not resettled for some twenty years, and, particularly in the north, it was not until the 1700s that the frontier resumed its advance into the interior.

In contrast to the problems of the interior during the period, Boston thrived in its role of leading seaport and entrepôt for the American Colonies. With an excellent harbor, established ship-building and supply facilities, and a head start in size and experience, Boston became the marine shipping center of the Colonies. Its merchants dominated the coastal trade and, partly for that reason, held a commanding position in the importation and distribution of goods from Europe also. In addition, Boston shippers were leaders in opening and developing the West Indian and Southern European trades during the era. By 1720 Boston had developed into a busy, crowded, complex, world port city, as we shall see when we return to it shortly to examine a cross section of colonial life in 1720.

The Middle Colonies From 1664 to 1691 the colony of New Amsterdam underwent an identity crisis. Its governance switched back and forth between the Dutch and the English until 1674 when the latter finally gained permanent control and gave the settlement the now familiar name of New York. Even then, however, the dispute over who would control the colony continued between rival English groups. Part of the question was an extension of the struggle for power then occurring back in the mother country. England's governance was settled in 1688 by the "Glorious Revolution" when the forces of representative government triumphed over the crown. This denouncement soon influenced the colonial governments in America where, in many of the colonies, an analogous conflict between the perquisites of the Empire officials and the local colonists had been raging. New York, for example, finally regained a representative assembly and a permanent charter in 1691.

The uncertainty caused by the turmoil in the colony's government did not appear to disrupt day-to-day economic activity much, however. In the thirty years from 1670 to 1700 the area's population tripled from 6,000 to 19,000 and settlement developed along most of the lower Hudson River. Whatever the influence that the machinery of a colonial government could bring to bear—and these governments tended to be relatively small operations—it was overwhelmed by the improving prospects in colonial agriculture resulting from abundant productive land and growing markets.

Nearby New Jersey had a similar experience. It also underwent a period of strife until its charter was finalized, but agriculture in the colony kept expanding, seemingly oblivious to any such goings-on. Starting from a mere handful of resi-

dents in 1670, the colony had 14,000 by 1700. By 1720, a total of 37,000 inhabitants lived in a belt running across central New Jersey from Philadelphia on the
southwest to New York City on the northeast. Jersey folk exported not only such
standard colonial products as cattle and grain, but also more exotic fare such as
melons and peaches. It was during this era that the state acquired its nickname of
the "Garden State," seemingly so incongruous to the urbanized, industrialized
area today.

Southwest from New Jersey across the Delaware River lay the American
colony which made the most dramatic advance during this fifty-year period.
William Penn acquired a proprietory grant to the area in 1681 and immediately
set to work filling it with European immigrants. Being a sometime persecuted
Quaker himself he naturally attracted various ostracized religious groups—of
which there were quite a few in Europe at this time—to the colony. Along with
the Quakers came Huguenots, Episcopalians, Baptists, Presbyterians, Mennon-
ites, and Amish, the latter still providing local color and a large source of tourist
revenue to the Pennsylvania Dutch region today.

While the displeasure of the European establishment encouraged many of
the immigrants to Pennsylvania, it was fortunate local natural endowments which
made the colony so successful. Southeastern Pennsylvania is laced with navigable
rivers such as the Delaware, the Schuylkill, and the Susquehanna, which provided
direct, inexpensive connections with existing world markets. Beginning right at
the edge of these river terminals was fertile land capable of producing large yields
of corn, wheat, and cattle fodder. With markets for such products developing in
the Caribbean and Southern Europe, it was a fortuitous combination of land,
location, and time.

The influx began in 1682 and continued strong into the eighteenth century.
By 1690, the region which had, just ten years before, held only a few hundred
Dutch and Swedish settlers, claimed 11,000 inhabitants. Philadelphia, with several thousand residents at that time, was already becoming a major colonial city.
Thirty years later the population of the colony had tripled to more than 30,000
and the settled area had advanced 40 miles west of the Delaware River. From this
region, as well as from west New Jersey and upper Maryland, came increasing
quantities of grain, lumber, and livestock destined for export markets. It was
necessary to mill the grain into flour at a location—usually in the countryside—
where water power was available. Eventually, however, almost all exports from
the region, whatever their required preparation, were funneled out through Philadelphia. By 1720 that city had become so active in baking, preserving, grading,
packing, loading, selling, insuring, and shipping these exports that within a forty-
year period it had grown to become America's second largest city.

The Southern Colonies   The tobacco colonies of Maryland, Virginia, and
North Carolina were not growing quite as rapidly as their northern neighbor,
Pennsylvania, during this fifty-year period, but they had a head start of more
than fifty years of growth. Thus, even while the other regions gained on it during
the period, the upper South remained the major center of colonial population

English Tobacco Imports from America (including reexports)

Year	Millions of Pounds	Year	Millions of Pounds
1620	0.1	1722	35.0
1630	0.5	1730	41.0
1672	17.6	1740	41.0
1682	21.4	1745	55.0
1688	28.4	1755	64.0
1708	30.0	1760	85.0
1717	32.0	1775	102.0

Source: Adapted from U.S. Bureau of the Census, *Historical Statistics of the United States, Colonial Times to 1957,* U.S. Government Printing Office, Washington, D.C., 1960.

through these fifty years. In 1670 almost half of all Americans lived in this area. Even by 1720 more than 37 percent of the colonial population was still living there.

The prime attraction, of course, was tobacco. Encouraged by a growing demand in Europe and abundant, productive land bordering Chesapeake Bay, production increased secularly throughout the colonial period. This pattern of output is sufficient to explain the area's population experience. Tobacco culture was—and it still is—very labor-intensive. Two or three acres of the crop kept a worker busy for an entire year. The plants had to be started in seedbeds early in the year in order to complete the long cycle. The ground was prepared by burning brush over it to kill off tobacco fungus and weeds. Each plant was transplanted and then hilled, weeded, and pruned through the summer. Another particularly unpleasant task was worming the plants, removing and killing each bug by hand—an unavoidable task in the era before insecticides. Finally each harvestable leaf had to be removed, stored, dried, graded, and packed in large barrels for sale. These tasks frequently overlapped with the beginning of work on the next crop.

The lower South grew very rapidly from 1670 to 1720 but because settlement had only begun in 1670 it retained a frontier aura for much of the period. Exports of rice and indigo, which became so characteristic of the region in the later colonial period, were not yet evident, nor were the aristocratic and plantation forms of social organization they encouraged. South Carolina's major exports were naval stores (pitch, tar, ship spars, and so forth), lumber products, and meat, and the primary market for them was the West Indies. In that regard it more closely resembled the colonies of Connecticut and Rhode Island than the nearer Southern economies. Most of the colony's agricultural efforts were centered in the higher (interior) piedmont area. There were occasional cleared sections in this naturally wooded area but most of the region was given over to cattle which roamed range-style through the forest. Almost all the colony's commerce was channeled through Charleston, a natural entry point to the interior on the otherwise sparsely settled coastline.

Like New England on the other flank of the settled area in this period, South

Carolina suffered through a major Indian war. In 1715 the Yamassee war forced many of the colony's residents from the interior to take refuge in Charleston, leaving their homesteads to be razed by the Indians. The Yamassee and the Lower Creeks were pushed west and south in the following year and held back by a series of new fortified settlements. It was not until the 1730s, however, that the thirteenth colony, Georgia, was founded, and settlement developed along the then southern frontier, the Savannah River.

Colonial Economic Life in 1720

History is a hopeless muddle without some understanding of the order and inter-action of events, so that is the general pattern we have followed in considering the colonial economy up to the present demarcation of 1720. Simply recounting previous occurrences, however, can also hinder our comprehension of the past if we are not familiar with the general forces and conditions which propel such events. For this reason we shall pause at 1720, as an approximate midpoint where we can examine in more detail a cross section of colonial economic life. After this digression we shall complete our trek across the colonial period.

Colonial Occupations   In retrospect, our knowledge of the resource endow-ment of the Colonies indicates where the colonists would most likely have found profitable activities—as in fact they actually did. In colonial America the number of settlers and the capital resources at their disposal were very limited compared with the quantity of natural resources they could use in production. All workers had a relatively large amount of land, trees, water, rocks, and minerals at their disposal. Factor prices in the Colonies reflected this endowment: capital and especially labor were expensive while land and lumber were cheap. These prices were not merely a peculiar feature of a market economy. They reflected condi-tions so fundamental in America that any form of economic organization would have been forced to acknowledge them and adapt to them.

Europeans arriving in the Colonies were forced to adjust to relative factor scarcities different from those existing in the Old World pattern. Adjustment, or adaptation, was not a superficial or a simple process; it required substantial resources and time. In practice, a nation's knowledge is embodied in economic "packages" such as machines, factories, and its structure of economic organiza-tion. These packages incorporate the effect of relative factor prices into their design in that, either implicitly or explicitly, their technology is developed for a particular set of input prices. Once a package has been developed, however, the prices are frozen into its structure and it is usually difficult to adapt the package to new prices without reworking much of its technology. American colonists carried with them much of the current knowledge of Europe, but it took work, experimentation, and time before they could employ that knowledge to use the resource endowment of America.

A high price tag on an item encourages people to use it carefully. Labor and capital in colonial America carried such price tags because their use in any of a number of ways would have yielded high returns. Conversely, the soil, trees, and wildlife had low price tags. The colonists used them extensively in production. So much—or so many—of them were available that their expenditure in one use detracted very little from their availability for another. In some cases, trees were more a nuisance than a resource. Farmers, road builders, and real estate developers destroyed them at a rate which would horrify a modern conservationist. Farmers used the land with the same intensity they applied to trees. Soil was tilled for a few years with little effort given to maintaining its fertility. If the soil's productivity declined substantially, the farmers simply moved to another area.

Prodded by this abundance of nature, most colonists took occupations in the natural resource, or extractive, industries. Agriculture was the predominant colonial advocation. In the early eighteenth century about 90 percent of the labor force was primarily employed in agriculture but the typical farm family had several other ways in which it supplemented its income. Tending crops occupied much time, from planting to harvest. Other days were spent hunting, fishing, clearing land, making potash and pearlash (which were shipped to England to make glass), building fences and roads, grinding grain, making tools and furniture, and locating cattle in the woods. In New England farmers collected maple syrup, and in the South they gathered pitch for calking ships.

The Maritime Sector　Other important colonial industries also made extensive use of natural resources. Fishing, especially for cod and mackerel, was important along the northern coast. In those days, before refrigeration, fish could be eaten fresh or preserved by salting and drying. The coastal port cities, such as Boston, Salem, Gloucester, Newport, Philadelphia, and New York, constituted the market for colonial catches, but that market was small because the cities were small. Even in 1790, only four American cities had a population greater than 10,000. The best of the preserved fish was sent to markets in southern Europe while the lowest grades were sold in the Caribbean area for the slaves on the sugar plantations.

Whaling was another important maritime industry. Initally whaling was a local industry in that small boats operated from numerous ports off New England and eastern Long Island. As the supply of whales in the local water was exhausted, whaling was undertaken with larger, well-equipped ships which operated in all the oceans. The bases for these operations were concentrated in a few ports, such as New Bedford and Nantucket. The most important product from these efforts was whale oil, which at that time (prekerosene as well as pre-Edison) was the best available fuel for lamps. Whale oil was also used as a lubricant for machinery, as were animal and vegtable fats. Spermaceti, a type of wax taken from the whales, was used to make candles. Whalebone was used for tools, jewelry, and other small miscellaneous items.

Shipping and ship building were two other important maritime activities of New England. The rocky landscape that hindered agriculture formed excellent harbors and inlets along its coast. Here ships were built, moored, outfitted, and repaired. Nearby forests provided the necessary strong timbers; numerous crafts workers and suppliers congregated to provide ropes, sails, chains, and metal fittings. Other merchants provided rations for the crews, insurance and financing for cargoes, and barrels and ballast. Ships built in New England were the least expensive to buy and the most efficient to operate of their day. Furthermore, the colonists, as citizens of the British Empire, were allowed to carry commerce between all ports within the Empire—which was the world's largest trade network at that time. The income acquired in this commerce as well as that made from selling ships to other mariners in the British Empire earned foreign exchange just as surely as if goods had been exported abroad. Colonial shipping services helped provide that necessary export component which allowed the Colonists to reap the gains from participating in international trade.

Industry and Crafts   No one would mistake early America for an industrialized economy. Both its comparative advantage and its directed energies were in extractive production. Nevertheless, some factories, mills, and workshops were inevitable. Of course, they were nowhere near the size and organization of their counterparts today, but they were "industry" by the standards of the eighteenth century.

Few agricultural products could be used without some processing. Grain had to be ground and the resulting flour packaged. Meat was preserved. Vegetables and fruits were dried or sometimes kept in cool cellars. Some of these processes were done on the farm where the crop was grown, but some could be more efficiently processed elsewhere. Almost every village or town had its own grist mill. Most were small, much smaller than the most efficient-sized mill would have been, but they served their function satisfactorily; that is, they processed locally grown grain, most of which was consumed locally. A few mills were large and operated at optimum size. In port cities such as Philadelphia, where a sizeable volume of grain was ground into flour for export, flour mills were quite large by standards of colonial enterprise.

In many ways the mills were typical American undertakings of that day. They were designed to economize on expensive American labor by using pulleys, gears, and inclined planes where a mill hand would otherwise have been necessary. They used water to power the mill and even continued to use it for some time after English mills had converted to steam power. The mills used wood extensively in their mechanical system rather than the iron of which gears, nails, and braces were usually made.

Wood Products   The entire Eastern seaboard was covered with trees when the colonists arrived. Development of the area implied that many of those trees had to be removed. Much of the lumbering—if that term is used very broadly— was done by farmer-frontier folk whose primary intention was to clear land for agriculture rather than to obtain lumber. Their operations were slow and sporadic, seldom totaling more than 2 acres per farm in a year. They did use some of the trees for heavy timbers for their first homes and barns, and others were split for fence rails. The best grades of wood were used for making furniture, tool handles, and other household implements. Some wood was burned for its ashes, which were used to make potash and pearlash, and was barreled and sold to colonial merchants who in turn exported it to glassmakers in Europe. Some was also used to make soap and to bleach cloth in the Colonies.

In addition to the sizeable amount of timber used for household operations, lumber products from sawmills were an important colonial industry. During the early part of the colonial period, lumber mills were located at almost every sharp drop along a stream which was near a few trees. The falling water provided the power for the mill and the stream was a convenient channel to transport both the logs and the finished lumber. As the colonial period progressed and more of the Atlantic seaboard was cleared and settled, lumbering specialized into areas where the best areas of timber remained. Northern New England and the piedmont region of the Carolinas became large producers of lumber and wood products.

Exports of lumber from the Colonies, though important, never achieved a magnitude comparable to its natural abundance. Lumber occupies considerable shipping space relative to both its weight and value. As a consequence, the delivered price is substantially increased because the high freight cost must be included in that final price. Baltic lumber was cheaper in London than American lumber was, even though American lumber was less expensive in America than Baltic lumber was in Scandinavia. The major destination for colonial lumber exports was the West Indies. A similar phenomenon was at work in the domestic trade of firewood. Being as abundant and cheap as it was, wood was the natural fuel for home heating. As the frontier moved inland, however, locally obtainable supplies became exhausted, and overland transportation was so expensive that, even while potential firewood was destroyed in order to clear land along the frontier, by 1700 the price of firewood delivered to port cities reached $5 to $10 per cord. At such prices enough fuel for two weeks would cost a laborer a month's wages. By 1715 Boston was already importing coal from Nova Scotia and England. Another adaptation in the face of rising fuel prices was the development of the Franklin stove, which used only about one-third the fuel to heat a given area as did the huge, inefficient colonial fireplaces.

Wood was, nevertheless, such an abundant raw material that when it came to a choice of construction materials it captured most of the market—even though the threat of major fires constantly concerned citizens in the colonial cities and one of the steps they took to reduce that danger was to require that buildings be constructed of brick, stone, or some other noncombustible material. Lumber was so much cheaper, however, that the regulations were widely ignored and frequent exhortations about the public safety failed to override the stark differences in costs.

The low price of lumber encouraged its extensive use but the growth of the economy almost guaranteed it. The colonial population was increasing rapidly. At constant per capita income levels, that increase ensured a demand for lumber to build the homes, barns, stores, warehouses, and wharves the additional population would require. But those incomes were rising, which provided an additional component for demand. The typical frontier person, who in the first year constructed a crude house out of hewn timbers and shakes, increased both income and wealth through hard work. A few years later that person was often able to build a second house. This one was larger and more expensive, and it required a great deal of mill-cut lumber. The farmer often also added new barns and sheds. Colonial towns, though small, were also growing. In response to such demands, sawmills produced large quantities of planks, boards, clapboards, and shingles. Another major product was barrel staves and headings. In an age when glass was relatively expensive (and tin cans, plastic bags, cardboard boxes, and polyethylene wrapping were unknown), barrels were ubiquitous containers.

Even all these uses of wood failed to consume the great quantities accumulated in clearing land, and timber was necessarily destroyed so that farming could be expanded. Understandably, frontier people treated the forest very casually as they carved their homesteads out of it. Pioneers first cleared underbrush, lower tree branches, and small trees from the areas they expected to develop. This initial clearing allowed sufficient sunshine to grow corn, pumpkins, and squash the first year. Somewhat larger trees were felled and burned later, as time permitted. Large trees were seldom felled by cutting unless they were destined for a sawmill. Usually they were unceremoniously stripped of their bark and they were allowed to die. Later they were burned around the trunk until they toppled, then they were burned more until their ashes could be scattered over the ground as fertilizer.

The Iron Industry   The capital scarcity of the American Colonies should have prevented the colonists from undertaking any major effort in the iron industry. Then, as now, the different phases of iron processing used relatively large amounts of capital equipment. However, the American colonial period coincided with an era of special problems in the world's supply of iron. Until about 1750, pig iron was smelted with charcoal rather than coke. In the 1500s England had assumed leadership in iron production, but from 1600 to 1750 her scarcity of timber stifled growth in the smelting of ore into pig iron.

The colonists literally had wood to burn and by the requirements of that day they also had ample supplies of iron ores. In the 1600s they extracted "bog iron" from swamps or ponds near the Atlantic coast. These sources were limited, however, so that in the 1700s mining shifted westward to the richer rock ores found in an arc running from Vermont through western Massachusetts, New York, and Pennsylvania to Maryland. During much of the period the colonists exported pig iron across the Atlantic, but after 1750 when improvements in technology allowed England to use her own abundant coal to smelt it, these exports ceased.

The colonial iron industry was actually a composite of three phases of iron processing: mining the ore, smelting the ore into pig iron, and forging the pig iron into metal articles. Occasionally each of these phases was performed at a separate location, but often two or even three were undertaken at the same site. Mining was obviously restricted to the location of the ore, but the smelting and manufacturing were free to be done wherever economic considerations dictated. The very expensive cost of transporting ore during this period tended to keep the smelting process near the mine, but another consideration, the availability of charcoal and water power, sometimes removed it from the source of ore. The locations of smelting and manufacturing were decided by analogous considerations. Sometimes the two processes were performed together to reduce the cost involved in reheating the metal, but more often they were separated by the high costs required to service a diverse, uncertain market for iron manufactures from a few centralized sources. A large part of the colonial market for iron products originated in agriculture and much of that market was for "custom" products. Many metal articles were hammered out by the local blacksmith, possibly under his spreading chestnut tree, in response to the orders of local farmers. At roughly the same time he might be making metal braces for barn construction and fashioning shoes for a particularly wide-footed horse, neither of which could be expected to be standard products of a foundry. The "village smitty" was a logical substitute for the extremely large inventory of metal articles a local shopkeeper would otherwise have been required to maintain to supply the requirements of the local population. The blacksmith bought crude iron in bars and hammered it into the spikes, hammerheads, bits, stirrups, ax blades, skillets, and wagon wheels which the colonists used. Only the most common items such as nails, shovel heads, and kettles were produced by anything resembling factory organization. The highest-quality metal products or those requiring special craftsmanship were usually imported.

The village blacksmith was only one of many crafts workers who served the local markets. Cobblers, coopers, clockmakers, wheelwrights, saddlers, chandlers, and tinsmiths, among others, turned out an extensive array of items. While the variety of products may seem large, the total quantity was limited. Only coastal cities were large enough to continuously support a major portion of this wide spectrum of workers. Most small towns or villages claimed only a few. Often a mason or a wheelwright was shared between villages; that is, a wheelwright maintained a shop in one village but delivered wares to neighboring towns. Or a mason traveled from one construction site to another within an area of several towns. The paths of traveling crafts workers were often duplicated by other purveyors to human desires, such as salespersons and ministers. Peddlers supplemented the infrequent trips that rural residents made to town. Traveling ministers conducted regular worship services, weddings, and funerals in locations where the populace was too scattered to justify a full-time preacher. This manner of providing services has largely disappeared from America today, but the conditions which encouraged and justified it have also disappeared. The proliferation of local crafts workers and "direct-to-the-customer" services in the colonial period was a necessary accommodation to the small, fragmented colonial marketplaces. Local markets were too small to support specialized production of most products and high transportation costs prevented the importation of most items from distant sources. The colonists developed this system as the best accommodation to an economic environment which had certain handicaps. Nostalgia for this age of independence and handcrafting often obscures some of its costs. Handcrafted items were usually more expensive than mass-produced ones. Furthermore, despite our association of "handcrafted" with quality, many such items were not carefully made. Many artisans were only part-time crafts workers. They made barrels in the winter before lumbering in the spring and farming in the summer and fall, or they made saddles in the front of the barn while they kept cattle and corn in the rear. Much of the crafts worker's skills were acquired in an ad hoc manner. Apprentices were common in cities, but in rural areas people often learned skills by trial and error.

Colonial Merchants   Merchants performed a very large role in the colonial economy, acting not only as retailers and wholesalers but also intermittently as bankers, commodity dealers, insurance agents, real estate brokers, landlords, postal workers, manufacturers, and agents for other merchants. They were not superhuman, they were only doing the tasks necessarily given to them by the small, nonspecialized colonial economy. They were the commercial sector's counterpart to the roles performed in other sectors by blacksmiths, peddlers, and traveling masons.

Colonial merchants were forced to be jacks-of-all-trades in order to complete their primary function as salespeople. Many customers could (or would) purchase goods only if they were advanced credit for the sale; hence, the merchants became part-time bankers. Some farmers could buy the merchants' wares only if they would in turn market the farmers' crops; therefore, the merchants became commodity dealers, buying and reselling farm products. Merchants could not depend on regular delivery of high-quality goods from their suppliers and, as a consequence, were forced to employ agents in other parts to obtain such goods, to finance and organize ships which initiated trade with other ports, and even to underwrite manufacture of some products themselves.

Household Production   The colonial household accommodated itself to the same small markets which shaped the activities of crafts workers and merchants. Most items consumed at home were produced at home, especially in rural areas. This self-sufficiency, however, should not be confused with subsistence. The colonial farm family had a higher standard of living than most of its contemporaries in the rest of the world. While the colonists made most of the products they used, the colonial landscape made their efforts highly productive. America's characteristic abundance of natural resources intensified the incentives for self-sufficient activities produced by high transportation costs. The returns the colonists could make in certain lines of self-sufficient activities kept those activities out of the marketplace.

Families on the frontier were most self-sufficient, often limiting their purchases off the farm to salt, flour, gunpowder, and nails. Such extreme self-reliance, however, declined through time for both individual farms and for agriculture on the whole. As farming in an area developed, incomes rose and barriers to transportation were reduced. Farmers sold more produce and bought more of the items they consumed. Few frontier folk ventured into the wilderness merely to measure themselves against the challenge; most expected their efforts would result in commercial farms and higher incomes in the future.

A frontier family began farming with the same methods the Indians had used for centuries before. Using only a hoe, they planted corn into hills scattered across the floor of the forest. Three months after it was planted it supplied a fresh vegetable; in four months the kernels could be used to make cornmeal, corn mush, and corn pudding. Horses ate the unground dried kernels. The cornstalks were fed to the livestock and corncobs made good fireplace fuel. Most farms made a little corn whiskey.

In the first years of farming in a frontier area, corn kernels were pulverized into meal by means of a "sweep mill," a large mortar and pestle arrangement made from a hollowed-out log to hold the kernels, and from a grinding weight which was suspended overhead on the end of a flexible tree trunk which could be raised and lowered so the weight could pound the corn. This was slow work. The sweep mill produced only a few handfuls of meal at one time. Whenever a grist mill was established in a local area, it replaced most sweep-mill grinding. The larger size of the grist mill made it much more efficient—in fact, indispensable— if the farmers wished to grind more corn than was used by one household alone. The grist mill's size also explained why it was not established immediately when a farming area began to develop; a certain volume of grain was necessary to make it profitable. (Wheat cannot be ground into flour in a sweep mill; its culti- vation in any area was necessarily postponed until a grist mill was established.)

Many contemporary observers remarked how casually colonial frontier fam- ilies cared for their livestock. Horses, oxen, cows, and hogs were turned loose to support themselves in nearby wooded areas. The cattle foraged on patches of grass, plants, and leaves in the woods; hogs lived on acorns, chestnuts, and roots. Farmers usually provided supplements to such diets only during the winter months. Animals were given varying amounts of hay, corn, turnips, cabbage, pumpkins, apples, and household scraps. Not surprisingly, frontier livestock of- ten appeared an emaciated lot which yielded only limited quantities of milk, meat, or plowing power. Many died from exposure or attacks by wolves. Despite this seeming callousness of the pioneers toward their animals, there was an evi- dent logic to their practices. The returns from such animal husbandry were small, but so were the costs. The woods were free, the animals interfered with few other economic activities there. In the absence of these unusual practices of animal care, no milk, no meat, and no hides could have been obtained from those wood- land areas.

As frontier areas became more densely settled, "forest farming" was re- duced. There was less uncleared, unclaimed woodland and livestock was more likely to invade nearby fields of corn or cabbage. Farmers installed more fencing and certain land was specialized into pasture. Animals were given more shelter and supplementary feed during that part of the year outside the growing season. As developments altered the costs of livestock raising in an area, farmers adopted husbandry practices which appear much more conventional.

Pork was a natural product to raise in the colonial economy and large amounts were consumed. Most colonists preferred to raise the woodhog, a large, rangy animal capable of obtaining most of its own sustenance by foraging in the forest. Given a little supplementary corn in the winter, it often grew to weigh 200 pounds within eighteen months. Furthermore, the woodhog behaved just like all other pigs: it compulsively uprooted rocks and stumps—a very productive habit for an economy which was constantly engaged in clearing and improving new land.

The colonists ate a fairly large amount of their pork fresh; preserving it either by smoking or salting were time-consuming tasks. Processing pork for distant markets was further discouraged by high transportation costs over land. On the other hand, because of its size and its conditioning in the woods, the woodhog was able to travel long distances. Farmers drove them to coastal markets from the interior, distances which were upward of 200 miles toward the end of the colonial period. There they were slaughtered, either for local consumption or for export.

The colonists also had fairly large amounts of mutton, an inevitable by-product of raising sheep for wool. They ate some beef, but less than Americans have since the Great Plains and refrigerator cars were incorporated into the economy. There were, however, large numbers of cows in the Colonies which provided plentiful supplies of milk, cream, butter, and cheese. Most farms also kept poultry from which came meat, eggs, and feathers. Most farmers supplemented their own production of food by fishing in nearby rivers and ponds and by hunting deer, ducks, and turkeys.

Farming was so common and towns were so small in colonial America that every household was near a source of fresh vegetables. Onions, peas, carrots, turnips, cabbages, and melons had been introduced from Europe and were raised in large quantities, but the most successful crops were native ones which the Indians had improved through selective breeding for thousands of years. Corn was the most important but pumpkins, squash, and beans were also sizeable crops. Potatoes, which originated in the Western Hemisphere, were grown more successfully in Europe than in the Colonies; despite all the evidence to the contrary, some colonists insisted that potatoes were poisonous. They became more important after the Revolution when areas more hospitable to their cultivation were settled, such as northern New England and upstate New York.

Like the Indians before them, the colonists gathered wild plums, berries, grapes, and nuts from the forest. But they also planted large numbers of apple, peach, and cherry trees which had been brought from Europe. Fruit was not the most important product of these trees, however: cider was the most common drink in the Colonies. Some families estimated a year's supply at twenty barrels. At today's prices that would have been expensive drinking, but at that time 50 cents per barrel was a common rate. Even with such copious consumption, some localities produced more fruit than they used. Often it was left to fall from the trees for the cows and the hogs.

The colonists made most of their own clothing, including the cloth as well as the final articles. Wool was probably the most common material at this time; sheep were raised everywhere in the Northern Colonies where wolves had been eradicated. Linen was used extensively in women's and children's clothing. It was the most common "soft" fabric of the day—cotton was scarce because of the large amount of time it took to separate the seeds from the fiber. Each of these fibers had particular disadvantages, however, and much of the cloth the colonists made was of mixtures of them. Jeans, a combination of wool and cotton, made tough fabric for outdoor work clothes. Fustian, a lighter fabric composed of flax and cotton, was used extensively in the South. Linsey-woolsey, more serviceable than its name might sound, was also used for work clothes.

These fabrics required a great deal of labor when made on a home loom. Understandably, the colonists knitted large numbers of socks, caps, sweaters, mittens, and shawls to supplement their output from weaving. Another substitute for cloth, especially on the frontier, was the soft and durable deerskin used for hunting shirts, breeches, leggings, and moccasins. Most of these items of home-made clothing were rough but functional. For the heavy, outdoor work that comprised much of colonial life, they served admirably. For the wealthy, or many residents of port cities, or a farm family's Sunday trip to church, however, the colonists demanded better tailoring. The materials from which quality clothing was made, and sometimes even the clothes themselves, were imported from Europe.

Many farm families tanned animal hides and shaped the resulting leather into articles such as boots and shoes, coats, breeches, belts, gloves, and harnesses. Good leather required more skillful tanning than most families were capable of, however, and thus numerous tanneries—with full-time artisans—were established. These produced the best quality leather, used in binding books, upholstering furniture, and making saddles. Scraps of leather were made into leather thongs which were used to wrap, tie, or secure various items. Rope and twine were expensive and rubber bands, paper clips, and masking tape unknown.

Colonial households were also self-sufficient in other areas. The families tried their hand at amateur carpentry, making chairs, tables, bedsteads, boxes, brooms, and tool handles. They also made rugs, blankets, soap, and candles. Most children received a short formal education in "readin', writin', and 'rithmetic" from the town school, but most of the knowledge colonists used in making a living was acquired through experience. The household even provided most of its own medical care; many home remedies were made from plants, either wild or from the herb garden.

Colonial Cities—Circa 1720

Colonial America was clearly not an urbanized society. Indeed, colonial cities would be small towns by contemporary standards. Boston, the largest American city of that period, had about 12,000 residents in 1720. Our current perceptions can be very misleading, however, colored as they are by what is familiar to us. Colonial Boston was actually one of the largest cities in the British Empire, comparable in size to the larger English provincial centers, such as Bristol and Falmouth, although much smaller than the predominant center of England and the Empire, London. Also, the proportion of Americans living in urban centers made the Colonies among the most urbanized societies at that time—which might seem surprising in that one would suppose that a society with such an obvious comparative advantage in natural resource and agricultural-intensive activities would be predominantly rural. That tendency, however, seems to have been more than offset by the commercial concentration associated with the relatively high levels of American market specialization and trade.

Around 1720 Boston was America's most developed example of that commercial agglomeration and trading activity. As well as serving the regional market of southeastern New England—one of the largest in the Colonies at that time—it was also an entrepôt for all of colonial America. Ships owned and outfitted in Boston serviced much of the coastal trade among the Colonies and were also the major carriers between the Colonies and Europe or the West Indies. Boston's waterfront saw literally thousands of arrivals and departures of boats of all sizes each year so that on any given day, unless the weather was prohibitive, the harbor was busy with ships casting off and tying up, loading and unloading. By 1720 the harbor was lined with more than fifty piers, some of them several hundred feet long and boasting—by the standards of that day—huge warehouses.

Much like the other larger colonial cities, Boston's raison d'être was trade. Small manufacturers and crafts workers were operating but they primarily served the local commercial sector rather than producing for an export market. The layout of the town then understandably focused on the waterfront with the most expensive and intensively utilized real estate immediately beside the wharves. The offices of the major merchants were located in this busy, crowded zone of economic agglomeration. Here the (usually) small shipments of products collected from the interior and along the coast were consolidated into outgoing shiploads, and incoming cargoes were broken into lots for distribution throughout the Colonies. By 1720, these merchants had already achieved a rudimentary specialization with certain firms emphasizing their trade in fish, rope, leather, flour, or sugar.

Mixed among the offices of the major traders were the smaller, but more numerous shops serving the general public with basic items such as dry goods, groceries, and clothing. These enterprises had also developed a fair degree of differentiation by 1720 so that there were shops whose primary trade was stationery, musical instruments, lanterns, mirrors, hats, shoes, or medicinal drugs. The shops where the artisans sold their own products were also concentrated along the waterfront. There were the usual collection of tailors, carpenters, cordwainers, bricklayers, and blacksmiths, but more personalized services were also available from wigmakers, glovers, watchmakers, painters, barbers, and goldsmiths. If this diverse pattern of distribution failed to meet some demands of potential buyers, they could frequently supplement it by "vendues," or auctions, of consignments of imported goods, or by occasional entrepreneurs, such as visiting sailors, who rented space in a tavern to display their goods. Even traveling peddlers who usually kept to the back country occasionally risked the ire of the city merchants to hawk their wares along the city streets.

Farther down the waterfront, beyond the commercial piers, were the shipyards—fourteen of them in 1720. From here came more than 200 new vessels a year, enough to equip the Boston traders and, combined with the efforts of other New England shipwrights, a good portion of the entire British Empire as well. A couple of blocks back from the waterfront, intermingled with the artisans' shops, the first residential area of Boston appeared. These were the slums of the 1700s, crowded wooden tenements which were gradually displaced by the substantial brick and stone buildings of the expanding business district. Better-quality housing, both country mansions and more moderate dwellings, stretched off to the west. Beyond the narrow neck of land connecting Boston to the interior—since expanded to a wide peninsula by extensive land fill—were the "suburbs," such as Roxbury and the beginning of the agricultural countryside.

Within Boston one was never very far from the favorite institution of the town—or, for that matter, almost any colonial crossroads—the tavern. This was not the same kind of establishment we associate with the name today, but rather the multipurpose gathering spot more closely resembling the English pub. One could go to the The Blue Anchor, The Rose and Crown, Hall's, Bull's Tavern, The Three Mariners, or The Sign of ye Turkie Cock in Fish Street for a drink of rum. But at various such establishments one could also pick up mail, eat lunch, rent a room, conduct business deals, attend an auction of imported goods, or see a performance of a traveling road show.

The tavern served as the locale for a number of activities which now take place separately in commodity exchanges, real estate and insurance offices, hotels, restaurants, and theaters. In each town of any magnitude there was usually a recognized establishment where merchants congregated at a particular hour to arrange business deals. In the larger towns, such as Boston, there were usually several taverns where traders conventionally gathered each day. Each tavern tended to attract individuals with a particular type of business interest. At one inn, for example, ownership shares in ocean-going vessels might be bought and sold. (This was the colonial equivalent of maritime insurance, and was achieved by spreading one's assets among a variety of shipping ventures rather than risking all in a single vessel.) Other taverns might be forums for trading local commodities or various categories of imported goods.

Such regular gatherings in taverns, as well as the various other interchanges which occurred there, were one of the earliest examples of agglomeration appearing in colonial America. In any society at any stage of development some economic activity is best accomplished by face-to-face exchange. Quantities and types of goods either available or desired fluctuate widely from day to day, terms must be ironed out in contracts, and financing must be arranged on new sales. Many American markets are now large enough that such activities can be carried out in locations and institutions especially adapted to them. In colonial America, however, the volume of transactions was much too small to support such specialized firms as insurance companies or stock exchanges. Most such functions were delegated to the local tavern, that convenient crossroads of colonial life.

Not everything in Boston went as smoothly and prosperously as might be inferred from the above description. Like other societies at other times inhabitants of the city found themselves troubled by a variety of irritants, all associated

with specific conditions of the period but ultimately growing out of that ubiquitous and timeless reality of human affairs—scarce resources. One of the most
feared occurrences of the era was a fire, which could sweep through the closely
ordered wooden buildings destroying a good portion of the town. Boston's fire-
fighting capabilities were among the best available in the world at that time, but
low-volume hand pumps and pulling down buildings in the path of a blaze could
not stop a major conflagration. It would have been possible to substantially
reduce the probability of a major fire but the costs would have been prohibitive.
Buildings could have been built of stone or brick rather than wood, but that
would have doubled or tripled the cost of most dwellings. Buildings could also
have been separated by lawns or wider streets or parkways rather than being built
with one outside wall abutting the next. In terms of the cost of land in central
Boston where marked agglomeration of activity occurred, however, that would
also have been quite expensive. Fire was simply one of those problems Bostonians had to learn to live with—and worry about each night.

One consolation resulting from its recurrent major fires was that Boston was
periodically able to restructure its road network to better accommodate its expanding operations. After each of the great fires of 1690, 1691, and 1711, the
right-of-way for city streets was widened and straightened before buildings could
be reconstructed along the outdated prefire boundaries. One can appreciate such
ill-gotten gains when driving in Boston today. Many of the older city streets have
again become obsolete after a long period in which modern building codes and
fire-fighting techniques have suppressed such major fires.

Some of colonial Boston's afflictions rode into it on the channel of its economic lifeline, maritime commerce. Yellow fever arrived in 1693 and measles in
1713, but the most feared were smallpox epidemics which took the lives of large
numbers of residents in 1702 and 1710. Later in the 1700s immunization against
smallpox became understood and accepted and thereafter reduced the severity of
each outbreak. In 1720, however, such outbreaks could be prevented only by
complete isolation and quarantine from the rest of the world, and for Boston,
whose raison d'être was trade with and for those hazardous localities, that was
simply impossible.

Boston's other proclaimed ailments read like a list compiled by modern big
city mayors. The concentration of commercial activity not only benefited merchants but also shoplifters and burglars. In the relative anonymity of the cosmo-
politan city they were able to slip away and dispose of their purloined wares.
Some parts of the town were sufficiently dangerous that the night watch refused
to patrol alone or even in pairs. Possibly that caution resulted from the type of
person who was attracted to the job. One embarrassing night thieves stole the
door off the night guards' office while they slept inside.

Complaints of traffic congestion in the city streets were continually directed
at the selectmen (town councilmen). Laws were enacted against "galloping or
speeding" horses and wagons. Load and size limits were imposed on wagons.
Conversely, selectmen frequently had to warn those who were impeding traffic by
piling firewood or construction in the roadway, or were extending a building onto

the public way. Another group of complaints concerning the high cost of land were frequently heard.

One complaint that Bostonians had made frequently in the earlier colonial period was becoming less frequent by 1720. Reports of loose horses and yelping dogs continued to reach the selectmen frequently (ownership of dogs was restricted by prohibiting anyone with an annual income of less than £20, or about $100, from owning one) but complaints of stray hogs rummaging in garbage or backyard gardens became infrequent. It indicated that Boston was becoming a conscious metropolitan center and had now shed many of its countryside characteristics.

The Supply of Labor in the Colonies

Americans have always been a do-it-yourself people. In recent years the high cost of labor services compelled us to that recourse. Rather than pay someone else $8 per hour, we paint the house ourselves, add another bedroom in the basement, and serve the canapes at our parties. Real wages in the colonial period were much lower than they are today; nevertheless, labor was expensive relative to capital and natural resource inputs. Wages may have been only 30 cents per day, but with land at $1 an acre and with the substantial services one could purchase from machinery for $1, labor was a costly input.

Several examples of adaptation by the colonists to expensive labor have already been reviewed—the organization of flour milling, the dominance of extractive industries, and certain farming practices. These responses were obvious examples of the ubiquitous accommodation which the colonists were compelled to make to expensive labor. One part of that accommodation was the immediate rationing of, and substitution for, labor—the short-run response to labor scarcity. The other part was the incentives which functioned to increase the quantity and productivity of labor over a longer period.

One obvious source of new labor, and a very important one throughout the colonial period, was immigration. In their formative years, colonial governments encouraged immigration. Given the very small populations of the Colonies, each new citizen helped raise the economic returns to established citizens. The colonists recognized that a larger local economy allowed more rudimentary economies of scale. Colonial governments awarded acreage to each new free citizen or to each citizen who imported servants.

As the Colonies grew, the efforts of colonial governments to encourage immigration subsided. Some immigrants, attracted by the higher labor incomes in the Colonies, came at their own expense. On the other hand, many potential new residents were excluded by the cost of passage to America; for average wage earners it constituted their entire income for several years. This high price in itself did not make the voyage unprofitable because the additional incomes an immigrant could earn in the Colonies would easily pay for the voyage, but most persons did not have access to that much money at one time. The problem was not profitability but liquidity. Understandably, an institution was devised to overcome this bottleneck of ready cash—the contracts of indenture.

An indentured servant was required to serve a certain number of years in the Colonies in return for his passage to America. This arrangement was very popular; in some colonies nearly one-third of the population had come as indentured servants. A body of colonial law was developed to safeguard the rights of both servants and masters. Servants were entitled to their own property and to food, clothing, shelter, and medical care if sick. When their specified servitude was completed they were usually given about 50 acres of land. Once signed, the contract of an indentured servant could be resold or even rented to someone else. Ship captains, who often accepted people's indentures in payment for their passage, usually resold them to someone in the Colonies. Farmers, crafts workers, and merchants bought or sold the contracts as their demands for such labor changed.

The length of indenture was the "price" in the market for indentured servants. It varied according to the supply and demand for servants. Since the indenture was payment for ship passage, the length of service would be expected to be that number of years in which the earnings of a servant, above his or her expenses (discounted by the interest cost imposed by waiting for this repayment), equaled the passage cost. If the specified number of years being contracted for were low, individuals were attracted into servitude because they could quickly complete their obligation and have the opportunity for an unencumbered, higher income in America. On the other hand, if the length of the contracts were long, colonists had good reason to buy them because the years of service received from such servants more than repaid their cost. In the early colonial period servitude of seven years was common, but the length of the obligation decreased until just before the Revolution, at which time three years was typical. This reduction reflected falling passage costs and rising incomes in the Colonies during this time. It was becoming easier for a man to buy his way into America.

Some indentured servants came to America voluntarily, others did not. England sent many of her convicts and debtors to the American Colonies; it was cheaper than supporting them in prison. The Colonies were not pleased to have these new arrivals and an entrance tax was often placed on them. Their indenture usually involved ten years since they then had to work off the amount of the tax as well as their passage. Another group of indentured servants was considered voluntary but the conditions of their indenture suggest otherwise. Drunk or befuddled English citizens often realized they had become indentured servants only after the ship was at sea on the way to America. Britain passed laws against such deception, but it was a difficult practice to stop. There were profits to be made in delivering indentured servants, and there was a hazy distinction between persuasion and coercion.

Efforts by the Americans to reduce the labor scarcity went well beyond importing workers. All through the colonial period, birth rates were exceptionally high by historical standards, in some cases reaching a level of fifty-five births per 1,000 inhabitants per year. Planners in underdeveloped economies today believe that birth rates of thirty to forty per 1,000 are too high in that such increases in population threaten to dissipate hard-earned increases in production. But colonial America was not an underdeveloped economy by the standards of that day. A rapid increase in population was not considered a problem—it was an asset. For the society in general, more inhabitants allowed the economy to become more specialized and more efficient. To many individuals in particular, larger families offered economic advantages. Colonial America was predominantly an agricultural economy, and, as numerous observers have remarked, farms have certain advantages over urban areas as places to raise children. Costs in the country— particularly food but also housing and clothing—are lower. In addition, rural children can contribute more to a family's livelihood. City children can sell newspapers or do simple household chores, but farm children at an early age can be shelling corn, gathering eggs, or watching the sheep. In fact, the traditional American school year with its long summer vacation was designed to ensure that the children were home during the busiest season of farm activity.

Most couples like children and often would like to have more of them than they do. The constraint is economic; like houses, cars, and stereotape systems, children cost money. One might expect, therefore, that as incomes rise, birth rates would also rise. However, the cost of raising children has risen with incomes; in fact, in Western societies it appears to have risen even more and thus has reduced the average number of children per family. Colonial America was a rare exception to this tendency. Incomes there were among the highest in the world during the 1700s and yet, because America was an agrarian economy, the cost of having and raising children was relatively low. Americans responded with the outstanding performance characteristic of them when they decide something is worth undertaking. The domestic growth rate of population in the colonial period is among the highest known in world history.

The other method of augmenting the labor supply, besides increasing the number in the work force, is to increase the productivity of each worker. In practice this requires some form of investment in individuals to improve their skills, namely, education. There was nothing in the Colonies which could be called a conventional system of primary education. Some towns, especially in New England, supplied public schooling for all the children of their inhabitants. But most education was provided through a variety of arrangements, such as private schools, cooperative programs, tutors, itinerant teachers, and instruction from older family members. The school year was usually shorter than it is today and subject to many more variations and interruptions. Few students went beyond the fourth year. Despite this seemingly haphazard arrangement, Americans appeared to receive the education they required. The average colonist certainly received more education than his Western European counterpart. Travelers through the Colonies, even in frontier areas, noted an almost universal literacy among the populace. The colonists' speech often betrayed their rural environment and much of their writing was less than graceful, but their skills in rhetoric did serve the purpose.

Capital in the Colonies

The same forces which caused labor to be scarce in colonial America also caused capital to be scarce. During the seventeenth and eighteenth centuries, improvements in technology and transportation converted large quantities of natural resources in America into economic resources. Labor and capital, attracted by higher earnings, moved across the Atlantic to use the New World's natural wealth. Resources would be expected to continue to move until earnings (wages to labor, and profits and interest to capital) were equalized between America and Europe. Such a transference did occur; in fact, it continued throughout the entire colonial period. Nevertheless, earnings continued to be higher in America than in Europe. While this labor and capital migration tended to reduce the difference in rewards, falling transportation costs increased the difference by increasing the resource base with which labor and capital worked in America.

The transfer of capital from Europe to America was a common, recurring process throughout the colonial period. Understandably, institutions and channels developed to carry out the process. Most of the transfer was effected by Europeans making loans to colonial citizens who in turn imported goods with the proceeds. Loans to individuals were frequently renewed as part of a pattern in which the total indebtedness of the colonists to Europe increased over time. In the mutually acceptable quid pro quo, Europeans received larger earnings for their capital than they could earn in Europe and Americans made more from using these borrowed resources than it cost them in interest.

The colonists did not borrow money from the English by going to a bank or selling bonds or offering a mortgage on their real estate. Europe was too far removed and credit markets there too small to support such arrangements. Rather, the colonists obtained credit through commercial relations with English exporters. Colonial merchants purchased most of their imports on credit and usually extended credit to their customers when they resold the goods. These loans were subsequently paid, but were then renewed when additional imports were purchased. The effect of this arrangement was a continuous volume of outstanding loans from Britain to the Colonies, tied to the trade between them.

This arrangement of providing credit may seem bizarre and awkward today but it was a logical adaptation to conditions at that time. A primary concern of British investors was the security of their capital. Liens or mortgages on property in the Colonies were a doubtful asset. British courts and sheriffs found it very difficult to enforce claims against the strong-willed colonists across the Atlantic. For this reason, they tied their credit to assets over which they did have control— the products they shipped to the Americans.

The colonists always used some foreign capital. It was particularly important during the first years of settlement, but with time the percentage of foreign capital declined. The Colonies generated a large amount of their own capital. Most of their economic activity was in agriculture, and most of their increase in capital occurred as investments in farming. This happened because the development of colonial agriculture necessitated creation of capital. Trees had to be removed, fences erected, barns and sheds built, and additions made to the herds of livestock. For the most part these improvements were done by the family's labor. While they expected to increase their future income through such efforts, they also added to the stock of capital in the Colonies.

Although it was much less important than agriculture, commerce was also a

major economic activity in the Colonies and was another source of capital creation. Profits from marketing and trade were reinvested in buildings, wharves,
warehouses, and inventories. Manufacturing—as we understand it today—was
not important in the colonial economy, but handicrafts and household manufactures were common. They, as well as ocean shipping and the processing of agricultural and natural-resource products, were sources of additional capital. In
fact, almost every type of colonial economic activity was probably a source of
capital. Capital was such a productive resource that its return (interest) was very
attractive. No colonist could avoid saving (the act which creates capital) without
paying a correspondingly high penalty for not augmenting the sparse capital
stock in the Colonies.

The American Colonies, 1720–1776

Momentum is a misleading word by which to describe the process of economic
development. An economy does not grow merely because it has been growing,
but rather because the conditions which caused that previous growth have persisted. If, however, it were possible for some historical periods to be characterized
as possessing momentum—the obvious continuation of the basic conditions
yielding growth—then the late colonial period in America would certainly be so
designated. Starting with a population of around 470,000 in 1720, the number of
people had increased by nearly six times by the beginning of the American Revolution. (See Table 2-1.) In the span of less than sixty years, the settled area moved
out from a relatively narrow strip paralleling the Atlantic Coast to reach—and
even to begin to overflow—the Appalachian Mountain Range to the west. In
addition, behind that advancing frontier the established areas of the economy
were undergoing reorganization. Some of the coastal towns, located at a conflu-
ence of expanding domestic and international commerce, were becoming substantial cities. The nearby countryside was changing also. The farms altered their
products to serve the expanding markets of both the cities and their foreign
commercial contacts. Products such as vegetables, small grains, and hay replaced
the likes of beef, wool, and whiskey. The casual use of land characteristic of the
early colonial period also receded. Farmland next to coastal centers—as a result
of the combination of expanding demand and falling transportation costs—was
becoming much more expensive and thus was used progressively more intensively. It was, in other words, a dynamic, expansionary period, indicating that well
before such conventionally perceived benchmarks of economic development as
independence or industrialization occurred, expansion and innovation were commonplace in the economy.

New England By any common measure, New England grew very well in
the late colonial period. Population more than quadrupled, Newport joined Boston as a major American port, and a sizeable portion of southern New England
was settled, cleared, and brought into productive agriculture. This performance,
however, was overshadowed by even more robust expansion of colonies farther
south so that, measured by standards of this particular era, New England ap-

Table 2-1   Population of the American Colonies, 1630–1780

	1780	1750	1720	1690	1660	1630
Maine[1]	49,000					
New Hampshire	88,000	28,000	9,000	4,000	2,000	*
Vermont	48,000					
Massachusetts[2]	269,000	188,000	91,000	57,000	35,000	1,000
Rhode Island	53,000	33,000	12,000	4,000	2,000	
Connecticut	207,000	111,000	59,000	22,000	8,000	
Subtotal	714,000	360,000	171,000	87,000	47,000	
New York	211,000	77,000	37,000	14,000	5,000	*
New Jersey	140,000	71,000	30,000	8,000		
Pennsylvania	327,000	120,000	31,000	11,000		
Subtotal	678,000	268,000	98,000	33,000	5,000	
Delaware	45,000	29,000	5,000	1,000	*	
Maryland	245,000	141,000	66,000	24,000	8,000	
Virginia	538,000	231,000	88,000	53,000	27,000	3,000
North Carolina	270,000	73,000	21,000	7,000	1,000	
South Carolina	180,000	64,000	17,000	4,000		
Georgia	56,000	5,000				
Subtotal	1,334,000	543,000	197,000	89,000	36,000	
Grand Total	2,726,000	1,171,000	466,000	209,000	89,000	5,000

[1] Until 1760 Maine was included in Massachusetts.
[2] Includes the population of Plymouth, officially independent until 1691.
*Less than 1,000.
Source: Adapted from U.S. Bureau of the Census, *Historical Statistics of the United States, Colonial Times to 1957,* U.S. Government Printing Office, Washington, D.C., 1960.

peared to be a laggard. From having about 37 percent of the total population of the Colonies in 1720, the region's share slipped to 26 percent by 1780. Boston's once dominant position in American maritime shipping was eroded and was surpassed by ports to the south, such as New York, Philadelphia, and Charleston.

New England's basic disadvantage was that it was not successful in developing any thriving staple export, such as wheat, tobacco, naval stores, or rice, as were some of the other colonies. The region did, however, increase its exports of such products as lumber, fish, whale oil, potash, meat, butter, and cheese. But no particular product appeared which was an obvious successful combination of local capabilities and robust international demand. New England's experience in this period is a common one in economic development. Sometimes a region is fortunately located as technology and consumer preferences evolve—and sometimes it is not.

Boston's relative decline as a shipping entrepôt was linked to this failure to develop a major export from the home port. In the early part of the colonial period the volume of commerce through any given port was usually too small to support direct ocean voyages to other distant commercial ports, and Boston had moved into this void, consolidating the imports and exports of the Colonies for international shipments by (respectively) distributing and collecting them along the American coast. As other port cities grew, however, their trade became sufficiently large to be reorganized into direct shipments. As the exports of wheat, tobacco, and rice increased from (respectively) Philadelphia, Norfolk, and Charleston, each city developed its own direct trade with major correspondent ports and then, naturally, built the ships to carry it. The efficiency of trade gained, but Boston was the loser. In 1776 the port was barely larger than it had been in 1720. Meanwhile the other major colonial ports had continued to grow—right past Boston.

New England was not entirely on the losing side of the decentralization of maritime trade, however. One of the colonial ports which prospered by initiating direct international commerce in the later colonial period was Newport, Rhode Island. That port continued to receive many of the articles it imported from Europe via Boston, but it developed and supplied the markets for its exports in the West Indies directly. Horses, meat, cheese, and other products collected from the region of Narragansett Bay and eastern Long Island Sound were shipped south to Barbados and nearby islands.

Those products aboard ships outward bound from Newport reflected the state of New England agriculture in the late colonial period. In the early years of colonization local agriculture could produce any product it found worthwhile; there was almost no competition from distant sources. High transportation and handling costs shielded New England producers from the competition of other regions, even in those crops in which the area was markedly inefficient. Such barriers receded—that is, freight and handling costs were reduced—as the period progressed. Farmers in New England found themselves facing tough, and eventually overpowering, competition in the form of wheat from Pennsylvania and corn from Virginia. Land once used for grain production was converted to other uses,

especially pasture. By the time of the Revolution, New England was well established in a pattern of regional agricultural specialization. Grain was being imported, mostly into the more densely settled areas of eastern Massachusetts, while
such local products as meat, cheese, butter, and horses were being exported to
other areas.

The Middle Colonies   The rapid expansion which had characterized the
Middle Colonies before 1720 continued during the last years of the colonial
period. In fact, this region actually grew a little faster than the colonial average,
increasing from 21 percent of the colonial population in 1720 to 24 percent in
1780. A major force behind this expansion was the remarkable growth of Pennsylvania, whose inhabitants increased more than tenfold during this sixty-year
period. The prime force behind it all, of course, was the international market for
wheat. It was not that the total sales of bread products were growing so rapidly
among North Atlantic consumers, but rather that among the wheat-producing
areas available during that era Pennsylvania was especially efficient. By the time
of the Revolution not only had almost all farmland along the lower Delaware
River and across southeastern Pennsylvania been settled but also the area adjoining the lower Susquehanna and Juniata rivers well into the Appalachian Mountains. Down these rivers and connecting roads (Pennsylvania's highway network
was considered very good by the standards of that time) came the swelling volume of wheat for distant markets. Much of it was collected and processed in
Philadelphia, which by 1720 had become the largest city in the Colonies. (No
wonder ambitious Benjamin Franklin left his native Boston for Philadelphia during this period.)
    Late in the colonial period exports of wheat also gave another American city
a sizeable boost toward prominence. The land of tidewater Maryland, just south
of southeastern Pennsylvania, no longer yielded the tobacco crops which had
become regularly expected from it ever since it was settled. Local farmers turned
to producing wheat, much of which was collected, milled, repackaged, and
shipped out of Baltimore. That city continued to be a major American milling
center until well into the nineteenth century.
    Although it did not grow as dramatically, the colony of New York paralleled
Pennsylvania in its experience during this period. Settlement continued to fill in
along the lower Hudson River below Albany but it also advanced westward
along the Mohawk River, the future location of the Erie Canal, and well into
central New York. The region around New York City was also settled at this
time, particularly Orange County (now resort country to the northwest of the
city) and central New Jersey. The exports of these areas were similar to those of
Pennsylvania; wheat and its derivatives were the predominant products and they
were shipped via—and therefore helped to develop—a large ocean port, New
York City. On the eve of the Revolution, New York City was America's second
largest urban center and was already showing the economic vitality that has
characterized the "capital of the world" in more recent times. Only the existence
of a larger immediate market during this period allowed Philadelphia to remain
first for a few decades.

The Southern Colonies   Contemporary observers, especially foreigners, tended to picture the Southern Colonies as the most successful in America. In the late colonial period that region appeared to be acting as if it wished to prove the assertion. The Southern Colonies continued to be favored by robust demand for their prime products—tobacco, rice, indigo, and naval stores—and by limited competition. No other major subtropical regions were competing with them during this period (unlike the Northern Colonies, many of whose products were identical to those of established European economies). The expansion was obviously evident in the population. The South grew even faster than the national rate and thus increased its already commanding position—42 percent of the total population of the Colonies in 1720—even further. In 1780 one out of every two Americans lived below the Mason-Dixon line. Naturally this striking increase in population led to a substantial increase in the settled area of the South. Most of the land east of the Appalachian Mountains (north of the Savannah River) was developed and some pioneers were even spilling over the mountains into Kentucky and Tennessee by the end of the colonial period.

In 1720 Virginia and Massachusetts were about equal in contention for the title of the largest colony in America. By 1780 it was no contest. Virginia had become twice as large as the slower-growing Bay Colony. In fact, by then, 20 percent of the entire colonial population lived in that single jurisdiction. The explanation was simple and of long standing—tobacco. Continual cultivation of tobacco had worn down much of the soil of tidewater Virginia, but demand for the crop, insensitive to any such difficulties, continued its long-term expansion. The planters simply moved inland, filling in the higher country between the coastal area and the Blue Ridge Mountains to the west. During the last decades of the colonial period intensive cultivation of tobacco also expanded south and southwest of Petersburg (just below Richmond) toward the North Carolina border. These areas, along with coastal Maryland, enclosed the specialized, commercial tobacco-producing regions of the Colonies. Tobacco was also raised as a cash crop throughout the frontier regions of North Carolina and Virginia, of course, but the high costs of delivering it to market reduced net income—and therefore the quantity—from this particular form of cultivation.

To the south, the Carolinas were expanding even faster than Virginia was. Both North and South Carolina registered more than tenfold increases in population during the period. This was particularly impressive for South Carolina which was already a relatively large, established colony in 1720. While some Northern Colonies were searching for a single, obviously profitable export, South Carolina succeeded in finding two during the 1700s. Furthermore, each of the two crops used different, noncompetitive types of land. Rice was naturally adaptable to the swampy coastal areas of the colony. Beginning about 1700 it was grown in fields close to the lower reaches of the rivers and was irrigated from nearby holding ponds. By the time of the Revolution, however, rice cultivators had perfected the technique of "back flooding," in which the high tides of the ocean pushed fresh water at the mouths of the rivers into coastal rice paddies. Rice culture was a striking anomaly in the conventional pattern of colonial agriculture. Whereas colonial farms usually sprawled across the landscape, conserving scarce labor

Table 2-2   Rice Exported from
Charleston (five-year averages)

Years	Barrels
1716–1720	9,000
1721–1725	19,000
1726–1730	31,000
1731–1735	41,000
1736–1740	58,000
1741–1745	68,000
1746–1750	51,000
1751–1755	58,000
1756–1760	69,000
1761–1765	92,000
1766–1770	113,000
1771–1775	120,000

Source: Lewis Cecil Gray, *History of Agriculture in the Southern United States to 1860,* vol. 1, The Carnegie Institution, Washington, D.C., 1933.

and capital by using land extensively, rice plantations were the exact opposite—they were extreme examples of intensive land use. Large numbers of slaves and sizeable investments in the form of clearing, grading, ditching, and diking were poured into an area of only a few square miles in total size. The explanation is simply that this particular type of land was both very limited and very productive. With rice planters in the mid-1700s reporting that they were able to recover all their initial investment in three years' time, they had reason to apply large quantities of complementary resources to those valuable areas. (See Table 2-2.)

Indigo, a plant whose leaves produced the purple dye material we today associate with blue jeans, could be grown in the well-drained, higher soil of the colony. The plant actually produced larger yields in certain warmer climates in the hemisphere. The more productive locations, however, also had better alternative uses, such as in Jamaica where sugar production pushed the price of potential indigo land to prohibitive levels. The plant was eventually to suffer an analogous fate in South Carolina. Cotton, using soil of the type in which indigo was cultivated, began its rapid expansion in the 1790s. In the process it pushed indigo culture into obscurity. But until the Revolution, with its disorganization and removal of the British bounty, the crop was the growth sector of the South Carolina piedmont. Indigo culture was the cutting edge of development moving into the interior during the late colonial period, replacing the earlier extensive cattle ranching with settled, commercial agriculture.

The rapid growth of South Carolina and Virginia can be easily explained by the thriving staple exports they developed. The reason for the expansion in North Carolina, however, is not as obvious. In part the colony succeeded in appropriating some of the prosperous products of the two neighboring colonies. The northern region, particularly the coastal area of Albermarle Sound, adopted the tobacco culture of Virginia, while the southeastern area, around Cape Fear, extended the rice culture of South Carolina. The colony also produced sizeable amounts of tar, pitch, turpentine, and resin (naval stores) which the other Southern Colonies had periodically tried but had never succeeded in producing. Perhaps most important of all, however, was that North Carolina was essentially a frontier area during this time. In 1720 only a thin coastal margin of the colony had been settled, so that as the feasible area of development began to cross its borders and push into the interior, North Carolina experienced an immensely rapid population growth. Its growth was much like that of other essentially frontier areas, such as Georgia and New Hampshire, during this period. North Carolina demonstrated that it was not necessary to have an obviously successful staple export to expand. While those areas that did have such assets grew very well indeed, those that did not still expanded relatively rapidly. The inducements toward expansion—the return on additional labor and land—were so strong that growth was occurring throughout the Colonies. While Virginia, South Carolina, and Pennsylvania were thriving with their special exports, the other colonies, such as Connecticut, New Jersey, and North Carolina, were also expanding rapidly—ever with no such special advantages.

Income in Colonial America

In all this discussion of colonial economic conditions it would be helpful to have some overall measures of the economy within which we could place our observations. It is only natural to ask for some "solid" quantitative estimates, such as average incomes and their variations within the economic performance of the Colonies. Unfortunately such a comprehensive record is not now available, nor is it likely that it will be later. The necessary raw material for such estimates, such as reports of output of various products with their respective prices, does not now exist. Furthermore, it is unlikely that a reasonably complete set of such estimates can be inferred from other forms of surviving data. We have, in short, bumped up against the limit of existing scholarship and we must wait until new techniques or insights (undoubtedly coupled with painstaking reconstruction) can produce such numbers.

While good estimates of the level of income are not available, there are, nevertheless, a large number of qualitative indicators which suggest that per capita incomes were rising during the period. These signs are found in a wide variety of changes in commercial organization, technology, factor-combination techniques, factor movements, and land rents. The weight of such evidence for rising incomes overwhelms any reports of diminishing returns in the economy which might have annulled the increases.

One of the best-documented examples of adaptations in the period which would have led to higher per capita incomes was in market organization, particularly ocean shipping.[1] In that sector the interaction of growing demand and

---

[1] Douglass C. North, "Sources of Productivity Change in Ocean Shipping, 1600–1850," *The Journal of Political Economy,* September/October 1968, reprinted in Robert W. Fogel and Stanley L. Engerman (eds.), *The Reinterpretation of American Economic History,* Harper & Row, New York, 1971. James F. Shepard and Gary M. Walton, "Trade, Distribution, and Economic Growth in Colonial America," *The Journal of Economic History,* March 1972.

decreasing freight rates allowed—and, in turn, reinforced—greater specialization in economic functions. Often individual ships became committed to certain routes and cargoes because the captains and their agents in each port developed familiarity and expertise with them. Then when it came time to order a new vessel it would be specially designed for that particular commerce. Meanwhile, in the ports themselves, wharves, warehouses, and, perhaps most important, those who managed them, split off into trade in particular commodities. Even individual agricultural areas tended to focus on particular products as the colonial period passed. New England, for example, is often characterized as an economy in which an average farm produced a variety of products, mostly for self-consumption, while shipping services constituted the prime source of export earnings for the region. In actuality, each rural area of New England that had access to coastal outlets developed its particular export trade during the 1700s. Coastal New Hampshire and Maine produced lumber products. The North Shore of Boston (Salem, Marblehead, and Gloucester) developed an extensive fishing industry. The lower shore of Cape Cod and the adjacent islands became involved in whaling. Rhode Island specialized in raising horses for the West Indies, particularly Barbados. The hill country of Connecticut and western Massachusetts found its best returns in products of the pasture, such as meat (salted or dried) or cheese. The more fertile valley of the Connecticut River produced wheat until a rust on that crop forced a switch to the second best alternative, onions for the West Indies.

This surprising degree of specialization within colonial New England underlies the assertion that such organization must have been an important source of productivity gain in the period. Producing a particular item in relatively large quantities allows economies of scale—reductions in the cost of providing an average unit. These savings in cost release resources for the production of other goods or, equivalently, increase the total output available in the economy. The constraint, of course, is that these gains from the reorganization of production can be created only if sufficient demand exists for the good in question. Viewed in reverse, this process explains much of the restructuring which occurred in the colonial economy. The expansion of markets, both within the Colonies and in the North Atlantic economy in general, created opportunities for such reorganization. Enough colonists saw the personal rewards in such alterations to implement them, in the process making a sizeable contribution to the growth of the economy.

Another gain in the colonial economy that is easy to overlook came through adaptations of European technology to American conditions. The first immigrants to the Colonies, who generally assumed that America would merely be a replica of the European environment in a faraway location, were distressingly surprised. The Pilgrims, for instance, landed at Plymouth in December. On the basis of a report from a ship which had visited the area in midsummer, the area was believed to be subtropical! This conclusion was understandable on the part of observers fresh from Northeastern Europe. They were accustomed to a climate in which prevailing winds off the Atlantic moderated seasonal temperature changes. If it was hot in the summer they therefore expected it to remain relatively warm in the winter. The Pilgrims paid heavily for their mistaken expectations. Pending the completion of permanent quarters they moved into some nearby empty Indian wigwams. About half the immigrants died that winter from "the great sickness," most likely a combination of exposure and pneumonia. The local Indians considered the Pilgrims' behavior foolhardy. They themselves used the wigwams only for summer homes, and in the colder seasons they moved inland to the longhouses—large, well-insulated dwellings in which they could wait out the winter.

The first settlers at Jamestown were also surprised by the weather. They suffered most, however, from the heat of the summer, particularly because they had chosen a site in an unhealthy swampy area. The early colonists soon found new ways to dress—winter and summer clothing took on more differentiation—new ways to heat their dwellings—fireplaces were modified—and new forms of building construction—the traditional thatched roof from England was soon discarded.

Along with the shock of the new climate the early colonists also suffered through the "starving period." The early food shortages resulted partly from the substantial separation from European supplies and partly from underestimation of how large a reserve would be required until the Colonies could produce their own supplies, but they also resulted from the new settlers' substantial ignorance of agricultural conditions in the new land. The colonists were accustomed to a type of agriculture which was based on small grains, such as wheat and oats, and livestock, such as horses, cows, sheep, and hogs. Wheat did become a major crop in the Colonies, but it was overshadowed by an indigenous grain. Corn was more adaptable to a wide range of climates and soils, and furthermore, unlike wheat, it could be grown on partly cleared or unplowed land. Colonial farming quickly adopted many of the crops of the Indians, such as corn, beans, and squash, and also emulated some of their farming techniques, such as using hoes (rather than plows) to plant and cultivate crops.

European livestock introduced into the Colonies necessitated similar adaptations. They had been selectively developed over a long period for use in an agricultural environment in which farmland was relatively scarce. They had therefore been developed to be restricted to relatively small pastures and to be given comparatively good shelter and supplementary feed in winter. In contrast, American conditions encouraged the use, and therefore the development, of animals which could forage widely for themselves on underdeveloped land, often through a wide range of weather conditions. Colonial livestock, particularly cattle and hogs, tended to become more rangy, hardy, and self-sufficient as the early colonial period progressed. If the Indians had had some domesticated livestock, or even if some not too dissimilar wild animals had existed in North America, the colonists might have started adapting and modifying them to their own requirements rather than "Americanizing" the European imports.

While many of the examples cited above occurred at the beginning of the colonial period, this process of adapting and shaping existing production techniques and products to American conditions continued throughout the entire time. There may or may not have been many new developments in technology that originated in colonial America. Descriptions by contemporaries do not report many such changes. That, however, is not conclusive evidence. Many improvements in technology occur as small, gradual gains in productivity even while the larger techniques and institutions that use them remain unchanged. For example, as an institution for producing goods the factory has now been around for at least two centuries. Yet it would be foolhardy to argue that because factories existed in 1770, and were still widespread in 1970, no improvements in efficiency in them or in the economy in general had therefore occurred. Even seemingly simple machines, such as looms or drills or metal-cutting devices used within production units, can increase in productivity (and have in recent years demonstrably done so) without any change in their basic form or function. Better bearings or stronger steel or faster electric motors can increase the output of the unit while it remains—to an untrained eye—fixed to, and unaltered on, the factory floor.

Thus we cannot reject the possibility of growth in the colonial economy simply because there are no obvious records of such occurrences. That issue must be reserved until evidence of representative productivity trends in the Colonies is available. Even if such indigenous gains in technology are shown to be unimportant, however, we have not yet exhausted the sources by which the Colonies could have acquired new technology. New ideas and techniques can be appropriated from foreign sources, too, after all. During the colonial period, England was the most likely such source. And studies of the British economy during this period—which has so far received much more careful scrutiny than the colonial economy because it is the antecedent of the so-called industrial revolution—have shown important advances in technology occurring then. Americans would be naturally expected to borrow these developments, in the process shaping them to their own special conditions. Hence, the only reasonable conclusion that we can draw is that some gains in productivity must have continued to occur throughout the colonial period. Those advances would not have been as obvious as the adjustments made by the earliest colonists, mentioned above, but however subtle and unassuming their inception was, they still would have increased per capita incomes.

One knowledgeable scholar, while admitting to the lack of comprehensive estimates, places colonial per capita incomes at £6 to £8 (colonial currency) in the period from 1710–1720.[2] If we are sufficiently presumptuous we can translate that figure across the centuries as about $100 in current purchasing power. The next available estimate of American per capita income, while far more credible, is much removed from the early 1700s. Per capita incomes for 1840 are estimated

---

[2] Robert Gallman, "The Pace and Pattern of American Economic Growth," in Lance E. Davis, Richard A. Easterlin, and William N. Parker (eds.), *American Economic Growth: An Economist's History of the United States,* Harper & Row, New York, 1972, pp. 19–26.

at $90 in prices of that period. If the above incomes from the early 1700s are also expressed in 1840 prices they would range from $45 to $60 per capita. This implies a growth rate of from 0.3 to 0.5 percent per year over this entire (long) period. Obviously this coverage extends well beyond the colonial period, and thus, depending on whether growth rates in the latter period (after the colonial period but included in this estimate) exceeded or fell short of the colonial experience, the 0.3 to 0.5 percent estimate would either overstate or understate respectively the growth rate in the colonial period. An annual growth rate of from 0.3 to 0.5 percent (even if understated) seems low in comparison to recent experience in our economy. In terms of the total span of history, however, it is certainly above average and places the American colonists' experience among the more innovative and progressive periods of past economies.

SUGGESTED READINGS

Anderson, Terry: "Wealth Estimates for the New England Colonies, 1650–1709," *Explorations in Economic History*, vol. 12, 1975.

Andrews, Charles M.: *The Colonial Period of American History*, Yale University Press, New Haven, 1934.

Bidwell, Percy Wells and John I. Falconer: *History of the Agriculture in the Northern United States, 1620–1860*, The Carnegie Institution, Washington, D. C., 1925.

Bridenbaugh, Carl: *Cities in the Wilderness: The First Century of Urban Life in America, 1625–1742*, Oxford University Press, New York, 1971.

Bruchey, Stuart: *The Colonial Merchant: Sources and Readings*, Harcourt Brace Jovanovich, New York, 1966.

Davis, Lance E., Richard A. Easterlin, and William N. Parker (eds.): *American Economic Growth: An Economist's History of the United States*, Harper & Row, New York, 1972.

Gray, Lewis Cecil: *History of Agriculture in the Southern United States to 1860*, vol. 1, The Carnegie Institution, Washington, D. C., 1933.

Henretta, James A.: "Economic Development and Social Structure in Colonial Boston," *William and Mary Quarterly*, vol. 22, January 1965.

Jones, Alice Hanson: "Wealth Estimates for the New England Colonies about 1770," *The Journal of Economic History*, vol. 32, March 1972.

Josephy, Alvin M.: *The Indian Heritage of America*, Knopf, New York, 1968.

Morison, Samuel Eliot: *The Oxford History of the American People*, Oxford University Press, New York, 1965.

North, Douglass C.: "The Role of Transportation in the Economic Development of North America," in *Les Grandes Voies Maritimes dans le Monde, XV–XIX Siecles*, SEVPEN, Paris, 1965, pp. 209–246.

———: "Sources of Productivity Change in Ocean Shipping, 1600–1850," *The Journal of Political Economy*, vol. 76, September/October 1968. Reprinted in Robert W. Fogel and Stanley L. Engerman (eds.), *The Reinterpretation of American Economic History*, Harper & Row, New York, 1971.

Robertson, Ross M.: *History of the American Economy*, Harcourt Brace Jovanovich, New York, 1964, chapters 2 and 3.

Shepherd, James F. and Gary M. Walton: *Shipping, Maritime Trade and the Economic Development of Colonial America,* Cambridge University Press, Cambridge, 1972.

U. S. Bureau of the Census, *Historical Statistics of the United States, Colonial Times to 1957,* U. S. Government Printing Office, Washington, D. C., 1960.

Public Finance and Revolution

In the 1500s England claimed dominion over the area along the Atlantic coast from what is now Georgia to Maine. The assertion was tenuous at best, as not a single Englishman lived there. Other European powers, heartened by the prospect that some of the region might someday be part of their empires, countered with claims of their own. Even after a few English settlements had been established along the coast in the early 1600s, the Dutch and the Swedes also erected outposts there without opposition.

England was not indifferent to her claims in North America, but the cost to her of enforcing them would be very high relative to any gains that might be accrued from possession. In this manner governmental behavior paralleled that of private groups who saw this area as unproductive and thus neglected to develop it. America, then, was an orphan—not worth the effort of any European powers to include it in their empires.

Yet even while the region which was to become the American Colonies remained unprofitable for settlement in the sixteenth century, the margin of loss was being reduced. A few English entrepreneurs, either very adventurous (like Sir Walter Raleigh) or foolhardy (like Sir Walter Raleigh) decided to attempt settlements. To do this, they first obtained charters from the royal government, a procedure characteristic of previous major foreign undertakings by English groups and of the establishment of all the American colonies yet to come. The proprietors then received ownership and some local political authority over a section of the unsettled area. In turn, they acknowledged British sovereignty over their colonies. It seemed like a reasonable bargain to both parties. The proprietors received the profits for their efforts and investment in building the new colony, and the British government received recognition of its claims to a region at no cost to itself.

In practice, the settlements proved very unprofitable to their proprietors—even those settlements like Jamestown, which experienced rapid expansion after their founding. Sir Walter Raleigh lost about $180,000 on his ill-conceived ventures, a large amount in those days even for a fellow of his flamboyance. The backers of the Pilgrims finally received an $8,000 settlement for their original $28,000 investment. The underwriters of new colonies in that period were almost certain to suffer a loss. After they had paid labor and capital at the rates required to attract them away from employment in Europe, the remaining returns did not repay their own contribution. However, the process did encourage labor and capital into the colonies, so that the proprietors' efforts sometimes created thriving colonies even as their personal finances degenerated to bankruptcy. The colonies therefore owed their establishment to the subsidies created and borne by the miscalculations of British investors.

In most colonies the proprietors relinquished their claims, which were proving to be of dubious value, to royal authority. Only Maryland, Pennsylvania, and Delaware survived as proprietorships until 1775. In each of these cases the proprietors had avoided much of the cost of establishing a new settlement when they achieved control of the colony. Maryland was merely a northern extension of the tobacco culture already demonstrated to be profitable in Virginia. Pennsylvania, as the second to last colony to be established (1681), was immediately successful as a wheat and livestock region. Delaware, founded by the Swedes, was transferred to the Dutch, then to the English, then into Pennsylvania, until it finally became a separate colony in 1704.

The royal government stepped into the positions vacated by the proprietors and soon found itself facing the conditions which had forced the proprietors out. The British government was not required to make the colonies profitable, of course; it could finance losses through tax revenues. In addition, the colonies were established organizations and royal governments were not required to finance the founding of settlements. But no matter who held the title of the official government of the colonies, the Americans were taking over effective control of the colonial governments. The most symbolic shift of power was not from proprietorship to royal colony, but rather the success of Rhode Island and Connecticut in achieving self-governing status under their original charters rather than submitting to royal colonial governments.

COLONIAL GOVERNMENTS AT WORK

The basic structure of each colonial government was patterned after that of England. Each colony had a governor, appointed either by the King (in royal colonies) or by the proprietor (in Maryland, Delaware, and Pennsylvania). The governors of Connecticut and Rhode Island were chosen in general elections. Each legislature had two houses. The upper house, often called the Council, was appointed by the King or proprietor—except in Connecticut, Massachusetts, and Rhode Island, where they were elected. The lower house was elected in general elections in every colony. Of course, there were also many other officials in every colony, such as judges and sheriffs.

The British assumed that because the Americans were generally considered to be colonists they should defer somewhat to the interests of the Empire. When the colonial governments were established they were designed to incorporate the objectives of the mother country as well as those of the colonists. The governors were expected to be the chief representative of the Empire in each colony. Most were appointed by the King and all had veto power over all legislation enacted by their respective colonial legislatures. In principle the governors would not allow laws to go into effect if they were contrary to the interests of the Empire. But the governors' powers were gradually constrained and reduced and the legislatures of every colony gained extensive control over appropriations. Governors could veto programs to which they objected, but only if the legislature concurred could they obtain funding for the projects they desired. Assemblymen became very adept in structuring appropriations so that the executives had no discretion in spending them. Furthermore, the legislatures provided the governors' salaries and although the colonists usually had little trouble financing other state expenditures, in many colonies the governors' salaries were usually in arrears. The governors were not free to represent the interests of the crown; they were forced to use all the power of their office merely to keep that office viable in the Colonies. The colonists held the ultimate power in civil affairs—the power of the purse—and they skillfully employed it to direct colonial government.

While her local representatives, the governors, were stifled by the colonists, Britain had another level of authority which might have represented her interests in the Colonies. Each of the colonies had been chartered by, and remained subject to, the King. But the King had lost much of his authority during the revolutions in England during the 1600s. He could have exercised decisive influence on the earliest colonies in their first years, but after 1690 his power was reduced to carrying out the directives of Parliament. Most of Parliament's deliberations focused on domestic affairs, however. It had little time for specific rules by which the Colonies should be administered. The King, barely more interested in the matter than Parliament was, turned most colonial matters over to an advisory group called the Board of Trade and Plantations. The Board relayed its recommendations through its immediate supervisor, the Secretary of State for the Southern (mostly Mediterranean) Department, to the colonial governors, who dutifully informed the colonists of the recommendations, who in turn did exactly what they pleased. It was a classic case of buck-passing in which the colonists quickly seized the powers of decision making that the other parties neglected.

Of course, the Americans did occasionally pass legislation which irritated the British enough to arouse them from their lethargy. All laws enacted by the colonists were subject to review by the Privy Council, a board appointed by the King, and it vetoed about 5 percent of them. But even then the colonists were often able to achieve their objectives because the review process was so slow. Once a colonial legislature had enacted a law, it had to be printed, certified, and delivered to England—not a fast process in the eighteenth century even if the colonists had wanted it so. Once in London, the statutes were placed on the agenda of the Privy Council. As befitted its commission as a thorough, deliberate body, the Council considered each law at length. It heard from interested parties, including the appropriate agents retained by each colony to represent itself in London. When the Council had reached a decision, it dispatched its rulings via the next ship to the Colonies. That required several more months and the colonists did not feel bound by any decisions until official notice reached them. Each step in the review process added to the total elapsed time from when the colonists enacted legislation until word of British disallowance reached them. That time averaged a very bureaucratic three years! The colonists were quick to realize the implications of this lag and to use it for their own objectives. Almost every one of their laws would remain in force for a considerable period before it could be vetoed, and, if it were, another law which subverted the intention of the veto could remain in effect for another several years.

Even if the British had controlled local governments in the Colonies, they would have had very little leverage with which to rule them. Colonial governments were relatively small. The colonists either transferred elsewhere or dispensed with many of the traditional functions of government. Potentially, military affairs were the most expensive activity of colonial governments. But the colonists had no established forces—they depended on the British Army and Navy to protect them from other nations. Occasionally they organized military ventures against the Indians or, during the British-French international wars, against the French. Even then, in the latter case Parliament reimbursed them generously. Other functions such as roads, schools, and welfare were consigned to local, often private, responsibility. The largest expenditure in most colonies was the governor's salary. Other state officials, such as judges, the treasurer, and the agent to London, consumed much of the rest of the colony's budget. Massachusetts, just before the Revolution, spent 20 cents per capita each year on colonial government. Thrifty Virginia spent just 10 cents per person. Parkinson's law of governmental growth did not have a chance with the colonists.

In short, the Americans were independent in every way except name. They ran their own colonies in the face of surprisingly few effective constraints by England. The colonists considered this arrangement ideal. They could pride themselves on being English citizens, but otherwise the advantage of being a citizen of the Empire was that it left them alone. Britain also found this "salutory neglect" convenient: it required much less of her resources and energy than an active management would. But this tacit autonomy was fragile and so were the reciprocal benefits which resulted from it. The colonists could ignore the King and his listless bureaucracy with impunity because Parliament was the muscle in the Empire. But if Parliament, or the King acting in response to Parliament, moved against the colonists, then one powerful force would collide directly with another. Until the French and Indian War, Parliament tolerated the colonists' de facto freedom. But for several reasons it became increasingly assertive of its formal powers thereafter until the dispute intensified into war—a war to *abolish* American independence.

THE ECONOMICS OF EMPIRE MEMBERSHIP

Americans were citizens of the British Empire during a period now characterized as being mercantilistic. As spokespersons of that era told it, mercantilism was a philosophy of nation building, a series of economic controls intended to strengthen a country and its colonies against other antagonistic empires. A major tenet of this view was self-sufficiency: sources of supply—raw materials, agriculture, and industry—should be developed domestically, or in colonies, to prevent interruptions by hostile foreigners. A large merchant marine was also deemed important. Cargo vessels of that era were designed to repel pirates and thus could be easily adapted to military roles during wars. Finally, the mercantilists were preoccupied with specie (gold and silver), then a universal foundation of money. Short of possessing gold mines, as Spain did, specie could be acquired with a "favorable" balance of trade, that is, through earning foreign exchange by selling exports that brought in more money than was paid out for imports.

In retrospect this perspective sounds very misguided. It sacrifices efficiency and human welfare for a very narrow view of the national interest. Security and independence are desirable goals, but in the framework of mercantilism only limited amounts of each could be purchased, and those at a large cost to other objectives. Probably for this reason mercantilists paid mostly lip service to their doctrine. If general mercantilistic principles could be cited to support the specific regulations which certain individuals wanted, so much the better. But if the dogma, even when construed very liberally, conflicted with the self-interests of particular groups, the hypocrisy was evident. Pragmatic, specific interests rather than a generally held concept of mercantilism is the best explanation of the behavior of Empire governments during the American colonial period.

Regulation of the economic life of the Colonies in the British Empire centered around the Navigation Acts. As first enacted in 1651, these laws required that goods imported into England be carried by a ship from the nation where the product was produced. The acts were obviously designed to stifle the competition of the Dutch whose efficiency and initiative in ocean shipping in the early 1600s were winning large portions of the world's trade. The laws succeeded, excluding the Dutch from what was then the largest market for shipping services in the world.

The Navigation Acts had mixed effects on the welfare of the Americans. They benefited from the reservation of ocean trade to citizens of the Empire, especially as the mariners of New England were among the most efficient in the Empire. And, compared to other alternatives of the time—trading within another, smaller empire system or competing as hapless independents—membership in the British Empire was certainly a net gain. The Americans also profited from a provision of the Navigation Acts, added in 1660, which decreed that trade in the

Empire had to take place in ships built in the Empire. Again, New England was more productive than any of its competitors under British rule. At the time of the Revolution, one-third of all the merchant ships operated in the Empire had been built in the American Colonies.

Nevertheless, there were disadvantages of the Navigation Acts for the Americans as well. Another amendment in 1660 established a list of "Enumerated Goods," products which the Colonies were required to ship to England before they could be shipped to an intended destination elsewhere. The initial list— including sugar, tobacco, indigo, and certain wool products—was extended throughout the 1700s to incorporate naval stores, rice, furs, and molasses. Certain products which the Americans imported were also enumerated; they had to stop in London before they could be shipped to America. Enumerated goods obviously created considerable waste motion—featherbedding—which had to be paid for, at least partially, from colonial pockets.

Tobacco was the largest colonial export and bore the largest burden from enumeration. A sizeable portion (probably about 80 percent) of the quantity which was shipped to London was destined for customers in continental Europe. Nevertheless, the law required that it be unloaded, inspected, and reloaded before proceeding to Amsterdam. This created employment for customs agents and dock workers in London, but it added to the cost borne through the higher prices paid by continental smokers and lower prices received by American growers.

Since the enumeration of tobacco imposed a cost on the colonists, it also encouraged them to avoid complying with such regulations whenever possible. Some tobacco was smuggled into Europe without passing through customs in England, but the most blatant violations of regulations occurred in the Western Hemisphere, farthest removed from British officialdom. In fact, violations of the economic regulations of the Empire appeared to be the rule rather than the exception in America. In 1733 England enacted the Molasses Act, which placed tariffs on molasses, sugar, and rum imported into the Colonies from any other than the British islands in the Caribbean. Naturally Americans preferred to buy from French and Dutch sources in the West Indies, which were more productive and therefore cheaper. Sometimes custom officials in the Colonies were bribed— the going rate was 2 pence per gallon. Usually, however, molasses was simply smuggled into colonial ports; those violators who were infrequently arrested were seldom convicted by colonial juries.

The Molasses Act was merely one of several British regulations which the colonists generally flaunted. The surveyor-general for the crown traversed colonial woodlands looking for the large white pines which were valuable as ship masts. Each tree found was branded with the insignia of the King, a broad arrow. Broad arrows were supposed to be respected, and to be used only in ways approved by the crown. Colonists found gaining approval cumbersome and not particularly remunerative—and many of the King's arrows disappeared as the trees were sawed into boards and planks.

During most of the colonial period England looked with favor upon American efforts to produce pig iron, which was expensive in England because wood for smelting fuel had become scarce. From 1740 on, however, English iron producers developed the technology which allowed coal to replace charcoal as fuel. Furthermore, the colonists, not content merely to produce pig iron, increased their manufacture of products from it. Viewed from England, colonial iron production began to appear more as competition and less as an asset to the Empire. In 1750 a law was passed prohibiting additional slitting mills (nail factories) in the Colonies, but new mills were erected afterward with impunity.

In 1763, the British defeated the French and acquired all the Great Lakes area that had belonged to them. That territory was inhabited by large numbers of Indians who had been friendly with the French. Some naturally harbored grudges against the English colonists who had pushed them away from the Eastern seaboard. These antagonisms soon caused fighting when frontier people moving west invaded Indian areas, and the skirmishes erupted into a major war when Chief Pontiac led the powerful Iroquois tribes into the foray. England responded with a typically bureaucratic, but seemingly reasonable, program for peace— separate the warring parties. The Proclamation of 1763 forbade survey or disposition of any land beyond the divide of the Appalachian Mountains; that is, the colonists were not to be allowed to move into Indian territory. But the law, no matter its apparent logic in London, did not come to grips with the major forces in the conflict. Nor did it satisfy the colonists. The Empire had given them little assistance in their recurrent struggles with the Indians except when the natives fought alongside the French. Few Americans were eager to initiate warfare with the Indians, but periodically one of those hostile populations became a major detriment to the advancing frontier. Then the colonists organized a major campaign to destroy or displace them.

Only a few colonists had moved across what was declared the Proclamation Line in 1763, but large numbers of pioneers would inevitably follow them. Improving technology, falling transportation costs, and increasing population along the Atlantic Coast all forced the borders of settlement westward. New areas west of the Proclamation Line became productive, and if they had remained unused, colonial incomes would have been lower. There was not much sacrifice because of the law, however. As so often when the colonists found a British edict a hindrance, they simply ignored it. Settlers continued to cross the Proclamation Line on their way west after 1763. In 1768 British officials, recognizing some of the reality of the situation, concluded treaties with some Indian tribes and moved the line farther west.

The colonists prudently obeyed some laws of the Empire, of course, even when compliance imposed some costs on themselves. The enumeration of tobacco, discussed above, was one case. Another was the aborted beaver-hat industry. Beaver hats were very popular in England, and North America was the major source of the pelts from which they were made. (Beaver furs were far more valuable than mink in the colonial period, an indirect verification that only a mink *requires* a mink coat.) Some colonists saw the profit in converting the furs into hats in the Colonies, thereby saving some transportation charges. But this industry caused a major outburst from English hatters who pursuaded Parliament to ban such manufacturing in the Colonies. Unlike other laws, this one was enforced so that this small but profitable colonial industry was destroyed. Parliament similarly prohibited the colonists from exporting wool cloth, even to the other colonies. This also appears to have been enforced, but because most wool cloth made in the Colonies was made at home for home use, the prohibition appears to have been unimportant. The Empire enforced its policies in one other sector, the money supply in the Colonies. This also inflicted some economic costs on the Colonies, but to understand why we must first examine their monetary system.

MONEY IN THE COLONIAL ECONOMY

The colonists frequently complained about "a shortage of money" and many historians writing about money in the Colonies since then have taken them quite literally and uncritically at their word. According to such an interpretation the Colonies did not have enough money—gold, silver, paper money, and so on—to complete all the feasible economic exchanges and hence the economy often experienced hard times. Viewed a little more analytically the complaint might reflect several phenomena. One is simply scarcity. There is always a "shortage of money" in that it represents potential resource capabilities compared to a larger set of desires. Ask you roommate or your wife or the man next to you on the bus and each will undoubtedly tell you that they too suffer from a shortage of money. The colonists were not that much different than we are today in that they also tended to suspect there must be a defect in the system rather than recognizing that their unsatisfied desires were a fundamental fact of economic life.

Undoubtedly one reason the colonists perceived themselves as suffering from a "shortage of money" was that they could see how relatively little of it they used themselves. But this did not result from a shortage in any absolute sense, as the colonists presumed it did. Rather, acting as individuals, they voluntarily restricted the quantity of gold and silver money they used and devised cheaper means of implementing transactions. The primary service of money is as a common denominator, a convenient form of generalized purchasing power by which dissimilar goods and services can be bought, sold, or traded. The more specialized an economic production unit (the more it tends to restrict its production efforts to limited types of goods rather than producing a wider variety for its own consumption), the more useful it will find the services of money. Most colonial economic activity was in agriculture and most colonial farms, especially in the earlier part of the period, were largely self-sufficient. They exchanged a few of their own products, such as grain, meat, potash, or barrel staves, for the limited items they did not provide for themselves, like salt, ammunition, metal articles, and better grades of cloth. This limited exchange naturally led to barter between a farmer and a country storekeeper or peddler, thereby eliminating money and its associated costs. But the savings of the barter in the reduced use of money is offset by the inconvenience of this form of exchange. If a trade is to occur, both parties must be willing to accept the particular goods the other party has, whether they want them or not. A colonial merchant may have been forced to take a farmer's barrel of salted pork knowing that he must undergo the additional expense of retrading it in order to sell his own goods to the farmer.

As a compromise betweeen the respective costs and gains of barter and money, the colonists used "country pay," a form of commodity money. The most common product of an area, such as tobacco in Virginia and Maryland, became accepted as the country pay. Other products were valued in terms of the commodity money, so that a barrel of tobacco might equal three barrels of tar or eight gallons of brandy. The obvious advantage of country pay was that exchanges were not required to take place with commodities in hand. Also, individuals could buy or sell items without having to exchange an unwanted item in return. Sales could be affected by crediting or debiting account balances between parties. A disadvantage of commodity money appeared when individuals wished to settle obligations. If the balance due was three barrels of tobacco, that required actually delivering three barrels to the creditor. Settlement often raised another difficulty with country pay in that payees had an understandable tendency to settle debts with a poor-quality product while creditors demanded high quality in the commodity money they accepted. Massachusetts, which accepted certain commodities in payment of taxes, was forced to issue a directive that no more "lank cattle" could be accepted.

Of course, more conventional forms of money, such as coins, bills of credit, and other private credit documents, were also used in the colonies. Most transactions in the port cities utilized these, but the colonists farther into the interior used them less. They were more apt to use barter and commodity money. They frequently complained about this pattern in which money remained in the coastal areas and believed it discriminated against their regions. Such beliefs build on a misunderstanding of the nature of money as well as reflect elements of hypocrisy; their behavior belied their assertion. Economic activities in the port cities were generally more specialized to particular functions than those in the country. In addition, a large part of the commerce of seacoast towns was with foreign parties in which barter or commodity money was far more unwieldly. Coins and paper money were thus more commonly used in the port cities while the countryside developed cheaper substitutes. But as the Colonies grew, a growing proportion of the exchange used coins and paper money. Higher incomes and reduced transportation costs pulled more of the economy into market activities and the commercialized sector. The monetized area spread inland, replacing the other forms of exchange which were becoming more expensive as the farms and merchants became more specialized.

Probably the most important cause of the "shortage of money" was the relatively high cost of capital in the Colonies. During this period a large part of the money supply of the Western world consisted of gold and silver. Individuals generally distrusted fiat money, that is, money which did not have an intrinsic value in its metallic content or was not guaranteed by a pledge of redemption for such metal. There was good reason to be suspicious. Kings and other public officials were often tempted to issue a little extra money to pay their own expenses, but in the process depreciated the value of the money held by the citizenry. There was no such temptation if money required the backing of precious metals. On the other hand, this assurance that money was "safe and solid" came at a cost to the society which used it. An equivalent amount of resources must be sacrificed to obtain the gold and silver which is used in the role of money, whereas if pieces of paper serve the function of a medium of exchange, those resources can be employed in other ways. This diversion of resources was particularly costly to the colonists because such resources could earn a high return in alternative employments. Money's services were expensive, and understandably the colonists economized on their use of it. The "shortage of money" was thus a rational and voluntary response by the colonists to its relatively high price.

The colonists attributed their shortage of money to a continuing outflow of specie (gold and silver coins) to England. That, in turn, was believed the result of Britain's deliberate mercantilistic policies to sell more to the colonists than she purchased from them. This view contained some elements of truth but was generally misleading. Even if Britain desired a "mercantilistic" surplus in her balance of payments, the actual flows of foreign exchange depended on the net effect of thousands of individual decisions about buying and selling. Particular governmental policies certainly affect the decisions of individuals, or groups of individuals, which, in turn, affect foreign trade transactions. But it is a long, bold, and unwarranted leap to then conclude that England somehow created a mercantilistic surplus in her balance of payments.

Specie did undoubtedly leave the Colonies for Britain at times, but that was only one segment of a larger pattern of foreign exchange flows. The Colonies were simultaneously acquiring specie, for example, by exporting goods to the West Indies and providing shipping services to other nationals of the Empire. Even if the colonists were buying more goods and services from foreigners than they were selling to them, they were not necessarily required to export specie to pay for the deficit. The Colonies were growing and developing relative to the rest of the world during that period and, as usually characterizes rapidly growing regions, were importing capital. This transfer was included in the transactions which entered into the balance of payments. When Americans borrowed money from Europeans, they gave them IOUs, usually in the form of bills of credit. These debt obligations acquired foreign exchange for the colonists just as if they had sold exports of equal value. In fact, this borrowing must have more than offset any deficits the colonists may have accrued. The economy obviously expanded tremendously during the colonial period, as did the total value of transactions and the amount of money used to conduct them. Much of this increase in the money supply was in gold and silver coins which, despite noises of the colonists to the contrary, could have been acquired only through importation.

There were forces at work to ensure that the colonists did obtain the money they required, forces so strong that even a major governmental policy, such as authentic mercantilism, could not have diverted them. The colonists had no standard money of their own; they simply used the coins and currency which they acquired through foreign trade for domestic commerce. Surpluses or deficits in

the colonial balance of payments were settled by transfers of money which therefore increased or decreased (respectively) the domestic money supply. But the
effects did not end there; they reverberated through domestic economic activity
until they returned to affect the sector which had initiated the changes. Increases
in the money supply raised the price level in the Colonies while decreases in the
supply lowered it. The price changes, in turn, affected the attractiveness of buying
or selling with foreign parties. When prices fell, foreigners found it more advantageous to buy in the Colonies and colonists found it less attractive to buy from
abroad. Both responses contributed to a surplus in the balance of payments
which brought money into the economy. If prices rose, the process was reversed:
the balance of payments moved more toward a deficit position and money left
the Colonies. In short, the Colonies' money supply was self-equilibrating. No
matter what feelings the colonists held about the adequacy of their existing stock
of money, its size was determined by certain basic forces—colonial prices relative
to other prices in the world, and the total quantity of money the colonists were
willing to hold when each was faced with the cost of doing so. These parameters
were very difficult to alter, as the colonists discovered when they unsuccessfully
attempted to legislate more money into the Colonies.

The colonists used an amazing variety of assets to fulfill the functions of
money—bills of credit, book credit (accounts payable), tax anticipation notes,
"commodity money," and even barter—but coins were the most important and
were the standard by which the others were reckoned. Surprisingly, it was the
coins from Spanish mints that were the most commonly used. English shillings
and pence tended to move with trade back to Britain while Spanish coins, made
from Spain's large gold and silver acquisitions in the Western Hemisphere, were
diffused throughout world commerce. A heterogeneous assortment of other
coins, including Dutch guldens, French guineas, and even Portuguese "joes" were
also used in the Colonies. The extensive use of the Spanish peso, or Spanish
"dollar" as the colonists soon called it, led to its adoption as the standard denomination for money in the Colonies. Later, when monetary units were established
for the United States, its common name was borrowed for the American dollar.
The colonists also used the Spanish "bit" or "real," one-eighth of the peso, for
smaller change. The name is still used today (two bits equal a quarter, for instance) long after the coin has disappeared. The Spanish dollar was equal to
about four and one-half English shillings by silverweight. (Spanish mints were
neither uniform nor meticulous in their production practices.)

The colonists believed they saw a way to increase their money supply by
altering this ratio between coins. Individual colonies established official exchange
rates of six, six and three-quarters, eight, and even more shillings to the dollar. It
was hoped that this higher valuation of dollars would keep them in America but,
in retrospect, this was obvious folly. Revaluation—raising the price of one currency relative to another—as practiced by the colonists created a deficit, and
outflows of money. The colonists were saved from their own nonsense by their
economic instinct: if the local government insisted on a particular exchange rate,
the traders simply raised the prices of their goods in foreign trade to compensate.

England stopped the exchange rate game in 1704 by establishing what she believed to be a generous official rate of six shillings per dollar. But colonial merchants ignored this law, just as they had circumvented those of their own colonial governments. They continued to vary the effective exchange rate as conditions indicated, in practice employing a flexible, or "floating," exchange rate.

A second major program in the Colonies which sought to expand the supply of money originated as an improvisation to a different problem. As part of the recurrent wars with France, Massachusetts assisted Britain by sending a contingent of soldiers to capture Quebec. It planned to finance the campaign out of the booty which it naïvely expected to capture. The campaign failed, the troops returned home asking to be paid, and in 1690 Massachusetts was suddenly forced to raise a large amount of revenue. It issued bills of credit (which today would be called tax anticipation notes) or notes similar to those used by merchants. The notes were generally accepted and soon were circulating as currency until their redemption dates. Initially Massachusetts followed a conservative policy of gradually reducing the amount of bills outstanding from tax revenues, but in 1702 it did an about-face. The bills had proved popular and many citizens were advocating larger issues as a device to increase the quantity of money in circulation. Other colonies soon followed so that by 1712 all but three had issued bills of their own. Some colonies issued them in modest quantities, but a few (Massachusetts, South Carolina, and especially Rhode Island) issued proliferous amounts. Naturally, prices in terms of the colonial bills increased and the face value of the bills was discounted substantially when they were exchanged for Spanish dollars or English shillings. In 1751 Parliament banned the use of the bills as legal tender and required that the Colonies earmark tax sources to promptly redeem all notes.

It was an unfortunate act of paternalism, unnecessary to protect British interests, and costly to the Americans. The indignation of English merchants about inflation in the Colonies which caused the ban was misdirected; they could have protected their claims against colonists by specifying contracts in terms of English money. Despite colonial abuse of bills as paper money, however, the ban imposed a cost on them. It will probably never be known how much money was in use in the Colonies at any one time; estimates of the period just before the Revolution range upward from $4 million. Any such figure, if obtainable, would probably be misleading because the colonists used a wide variety of assets as money, with varying degrees of success. In any case, a sizeable quantity of capital resources was committed to serve as money and each year it continued in that role while its potential returns in other employments was lost. For instance, if the colonists were using $10 million worth of silver and gold as money, probably a conservative estimate, and the prevailing return on capital was 10 percent yearly, then the real cost of using that money each year was $1 million. If, on the other hand, some of the functions of money were performed by bills of exchange or other assets which did not tie up resources, then the costs to the colonists would be correspondingly reduced. This is precisely the cost which the British ban on paper money imposed; that is, it denied the colonists the possibility of reducing the cost of their monetary services. It is unlikely the colonists would have used this option to full advantage, anyway. Before the prohibition their issues of paper money were often responses to short-term financing needs such as military operations. But even if the colonial legislatures had no such reasoned program to reduce the cost of issuing money in the Colonies, the ban was detrimental in that it prevented actions which might have reduced that cost.

THE NAVIGATION ACTS SUMMARIZED

Americans found living under the rules of the British Empire a mixed, but not uncomfortable, environment. Some of the directives from London hurt colonial interests—the enumeration of tobacco, the restrictions on manufacturing, and the ban on colonial currency. Some provisions of the Empire were beneficial—the large, protected market for colonial shipping, the defense by the British military, and the bounties for indigo and naval stores. And a large part of the formal regulations were either ignored or ineffectual—the proclamation halting western settlement in 1763, the ban on iron manufacture, and the Molasses Act. The colonists could not have borne any major hardships resulting from the Navigation Acts, a judgment verified by two recent quantitative studies of the system.[1] The Americans evidenced that themselves, showing very little discontent with British sovereignty and no inclination to rebel—until the French and Indian War.

THE INCREASED COST OF EMPIRE MEMBERSHIP

For most of the colonial period, England found it either convenient or expedient to allow the Americans to go their own way. North America was a long, unmanageable distance from London and, furthermore, the British believed their colonists to be a feisty bunch. Sir George Walpole reflected this judgment when he counseled against legislation to increase colonial taxes: "I will leave that for some of my successors [as Prime Minister] who may have more courage than I."

At the conclusion of the French and Indian War in 1763, something obviously overcame Britain's reluctance to interfere in American affairs. Certainly the large increase in her national debt resulting from the war and the consequent higher taxes to pay its interest encouraged England to consider untapped revenue sources. Perhaps, as the colonists believed, a new breed of British officials, more

---

[1] The two studies below measure the impact of the Navigation Acts on the Colonies before 1763. They are good illustrations of the power and precision of economic analysis introduced into history by the "new economic history." They are not, however, as each author assumed at the time of writing, a measure of the economic conflicts between Britain and the Colonies which may have contributed to the Revolution. The Revolution erupted out of a new environment and a substantially different set of considerations than the pre-1763 Empire. See Robert Paul Thomas, "A Quantitative Approach to the Study of the Effects of British Imperial Policy upon Colonial Welfare: Some Preliminary Findings," *The Journal of Economic History,* vol. 25, no. 4, December 1965; and Peter D. McClelland, "The Cost to America of British Imperial Policy," *The American Economic Review,* vol. 59, no. 2, May 1969. These two studies have since been examined in Gary Walton, "The New Economic History and the Burdens of the Navigation Acts," *Economic History Review,* ser. 2, vol. 24, no. 4, November 1971.

aggressive than Sir George Walpole, had emerged. But it is certain that the basic relationship of power between America and Britain had changed, and that must have been influencing and altering England's behavior. In their early years the American Colonies stood to gain a great deal from the protection of membership in an Empire. As small and independent settlements they would have been excluded from much of the world's commerce and subject to frequent attacks by hostile nations and even pirates. As the Colonies grew they became more self-reliant, of course, but even during the Revolution it is clear that the British could have defeated them if they had made a total effort to do so.

The colonists had to be associated with an empire, but up to 1763 there were other empires besides Britain. Before her ejection by the French and Indian War, France had certainly not neglected many opportunities to augment her empire in the New World. In fact, Britain's and France's continuing worldwide conflict forced the two empires to contend along the common borders of their territories in North America. On occasion the Dutch and Spanish also competed with Britain for the regions each was to rule in America. The American colonists were by far the largest group of inhabitants north of the Rio Grande, and they found themselves centrally located—right in the middle of the area for which the various empires were contending. Naturally they had some allegiance to Great Britain: many colonists were only one or two generations removed from England and almost all used her language. But while most preferred to be considered English, their own interests as inhabitants of the Colonies certainly predominated. The colonists' frequent violations of the Empire's laws are well known, but an even more pointed illustration of the precedence of their interests over England's occurred during the French and Indian War. Colonists continued to trade with the French, on occasion selling them goods which they must have known would go directly to the French army. The English were understandably upset, but even strenuous efforts were unable to stop the colonists or their governments from trading with the enemy.

By the early eighteenth century the American Colonies had become a valuable asset for any nation which sought an empire in North America. They were a potentially large source of troops, supplies, and military bases in the event of any open warfare for the region. Even their political association with a particular European power gave credence to its claims in the region. There is little evidence that the colonists actively proclaimed the advantage of their membership in an empire, but it was a major asset for them and there is no doubt that it influenced their relations with other nations. In a pinch they could change empires, as in fact was done when they enlisted French aid in their revolution against the British. The colonists were never compelled to brandish that power because England treated them kindly, enforcing only minor restrictions and generally allowing them to manage their own affairs. But the colonists' position vis-à-vis Britain deteriorated as a result of the French and Indian War. With the departure of the French there were no imperial systems other than Britain's to which the colonists could belong. Yet England's attitude toward the Americans had stiffened noticeably, enough so that many historians have distinguished between the "old colonial system" before 1763, and British policies thereafter. Before 1763, for instance, England had dutifully repaid the colonists for any troops and supplies they provided in wars against the French. After 1763, however, she expected them to support any troops which she decided to use against the Indians. Britain had become the only empire in the region and she began to act like it.

PRELUDE TO REVOLUTION

George Grenville, Chancellor of the Exchequer (treasurer), was the first in a series of British officials to suggest legislation by which more revenue could be extracted from the colonists. He proposed what have become known as the Sugar Act (a reduced but enforced tariff on molasses) and the Stamp Act (tax payment certificates affixed to documents and periodicals). In addition, enforcement was to be strengthened by a series of required cargo manifests (papers detailing the cargo and its itinerary) for shippers and the trials of alleged smugglers in admiralty courts. The colonists, of course, took a dim view of these acts but were uncertain as to what position, either in principle or in tactics, they should take against them. To contest the Sugar Act the colonists developed nonimportation agreements among themselves. These proved to be almost 100 percent effective in stopping imports from Britain because the "Sons of Liberty," local vigilante groups which appeared during this period, strong-armed any reluctant merchants into line. The Stamp Act did not take effect until later and by then the colonists had developed their battle plan. Either the individuals appointed by the crown as its stamp agents were unceremoniously harassed out of any such inclination or else the colonists simply refused to use the stamps.

Parliament was not willing to yield to the impudence of the Americans but it found other reasons to repeal the troublesome Stamp Act. The nonimportation agreements hurt the business of English exporters severely and their petitions as members of the electorate encouraged the M.P.s to reconsider. Benjamin Franklin, appearing as spokesperson for the colonists, assured Parliament that they objected only to "internal taxes," not to any "external taxes" for the benefit of the Empire. It was a soothing statement at the time but it led to future problems because the Americans at home were not saying that. They were asserting that Parliament had no right whatsoever to tax them, and that was only a short step of logic away from claiming independence. By a close vote Parliament repealed the act, but as a parting shot passed a Declaratory Act asserting her right to legislate for the Colonies. The colonists were puzzled and unhappy about the intent of the declaration, but since they were accustomed to living with the *actions* of the Empire rather than its official pronouncements, they soon forgot it.

The Colonies were quiet for a brief period, but in 1767 Charles Townshend, the new Chancellor of the Exchequer, proposed further taxes on the Americans. These were to be a number of tariffs on items the colonists imported, such as glass, paint, and tea. These could be heralded as external taxes, a distinction Townshend considered silly. He was unaware that the colonists considered this equally absurd. To enforce the new tariffs he also proposed a new Board of

Customs Commissions, headquartered at Boston (which the English considered the center of dissension). Parliament readily accepted these suggestions, partly because it allowed them to reduce England's real estate tax, but also out of anger at the colonists who had refused to provide the support for English soldiers in America as Parliament had directed.

The Americans had been through this before and they knew exactly how to counterattack. Nonimportation agreements were quickly and effectively reinstated, the revenue which Parliament expected to collect did not materialize, and British merchants were punished again for their government's feuds with its colonists. In 1770, Parliament repealed all of the duties of the Townshend Act except for the tariff on tea which they kept to reassert the principle that they could tax the colonists if they wished. The colonists considered maintaining the nonimportation agreements until, as a matter of principle, the tea duty was also repealed. However, their usual preference for pragmatism over polemics prevailed, the nonimportation agreements dissolved, and trade resumed.

While the colonists were able to dismantle the duties imposed by the Townshend Act, they found that the provisions established in the act to collect revenues were more durable and far more troublesome. The Board of Customs Commissions established in Boston was staffed by experienced, energetic agents drawn from other areas of the Empire. Furthermore, their incomes were earned by commissions out of the revenues they collected. This was in striking contrast to the previous situation where the treasury officials, working for fixed salaries and living in the Colonies, had developed accommodations with the colonists. The new agents undertook their tasks with total dedication. Whereas previously there had been a great difference between the detailed, official laws of the Empire and the conventional practices in the Colonies, now the agents began to enforce laws strictly—not every law on the books, but every law by whose enforcement they could collect either fees for issuing documents or a portion of the fines or contraband seized for violations of the law. This "customs racketeering," as Professor O. M. Dickinson named it, inflicted large costs on the colonists, not only because of the direct payment of fees and damages but also because of the inefficiency which strict adherence to the rules created. The customs agents made it all the more irritating by allowing laws to go unenforced until the colonists became lax in their observance and then sweeping down to punish the violators.

The colonists fought back with the weapons they had perfected in previous conflicts with the crown's representatives. They first tried mobbing—a tactic which had worked well in 1765 against stamp distributors. But the customs agents were operating too lucrative a business to panic. They retired to Castle William, a fortress in the Boston Harbor, until British troops could arrive to protect them.

The four regiments of British troops that arrived could not possibly have misconstrued the colonists' displeasure at their presence. The Bostonians, employing the tactics of the customs agents in reverse, cited them for any possible violation of every law, no matter how obscure or infrequently enforced. (The soldiers were probably the last individuals arrested for walking on the grass of the

Boston Common until the hippies in 1968.) Despite the presence of the provocative Red Coats, no violent clashes occurred for a year and a half until the Boston Massacre in March 1770. But even the shock of that dramatic and (since then) glamorized event subsided during the subsequent period of tolerance established when England repealed the Townshend duties. The customs agents continued their work, however. Then, in 1772 the *Gaspee,* a revenue schooner on loan from the British Navy, had the misfortune of running aground in Narragansett Bay in Rhode Island. The local inhabitants had come to hate the ship and its crew because they had been seizing small boats carrying firewood along the coast without carrying the proper papers, had been stealing cattle, and had been cutting down fruit trees for firewood; as a result, the citizens forcibly removed the crew and burned the ship to the waterline. A commission later appointed to investigate the incident could not find one person in the colony who admitted to knowing anything about it.

Four days after the burning of the *Gaspee* an announcement by the royal governor of Massachusetts further heightened the tension. Hereafter he would be paid from customs revenue, not by the legislature. A little later some court officials were similarly switched to the new paymaster. The colonists had never been enthusiastic about appropriating money to pay royal officials but they realized the control over colonial government that such appropriations gave them. They were not about to give up that small expense because it would undoubtedly cost them much more in the loss of control. The colonists seemed temporarily outflanked, but they were outraged and began to assert their position through the "Committees of Correspondence," town bodies which gave more of an official and seditious aura to their protests. But while the two parties were considering each other, pondering their next move, England took decisive action.

When Parliament passed the Tea Act in 1773, her troubles with the Americans were not a conscious consideration. The East India Company, nearly bankrupt, had come to the government for help and the M.P.s were forced to devise a way to save the company in order to protect British interests in India. The plan was to give the company more of the profits made in distributing the tea it produced by granting it a monopoly in its sale to the Colonies. Ironically, the law might have lowered the price of the colonists' tea, because the company could bypass the merchants in England who were benefiting from enumeration. But the Americans, having grown highly sensitive to such issues, objected to Parliament's presumption that it could legislate such laws affecting their welfare. They had ceased to consider just the specific effect of the law because they were now fighting for a much larger principle in which they felt far more at stake. When the ships began arriving with the tainted tea, the colonists were ready with an organized effort to prevent its admission. Most ship captains faced with the adamant opposition to their cargo prudently returned it to Europe. But in Boston, the presence of the British military emboldened the local officials of the crown to unload it nevertheless. The colonists beat the longshoremen to the task. They dumped it into the bay—and with it went any hope of avoiding open warfare with Britain.

THE ECONOMIC ARITHMETIC OF INDEPENDENCE

By the time of the Stamp Act—their first major confrontation with Britain—the Colonists had sensed the basic issue dividing the mother country and themselves: which of the two parties would control the government in the Colonies? From that time until their stance forced them into war, they consistently adhered to the belief that they should govern themselves. Their public pronouncements to justify their cause shifted during the period as they constructed the philosophy basic to their position. The tactics of their response to British moves also varied. But from the Sugar Act to the first skirmish at Lexington, the colonists' underlying concern was in preserving their de facto independence. "No taxation without representation" was one familiar phrase with which the colonists vocalized their position. In the final analysis, however, they wanted undisputed control over both taxation and representation in the Colonies, and they wanted neither representation nor taxation in the Empire.

The British found the Americans a brash, quarrelsome bunch. Rather than argue their cause through established channels, they seemed always ready to resort to physical coercion or violence to gain their ends. That impression was correct: the colonists were as ready to fight over the Stamp Act as they were over the unloading of tea in Boston. But the British failed to realize just how ominously these seemingly minor initiatives presaged the future actions of the colonists. In retrospect the Americans' instinctive judgment of the question was correct. The cost of yielding to Britain's seizure of colonial government would have been large indeed, large enough to make armed resistance a rational procedure to prevent it.

After 1763, a showdown between Britain and America was inevitable as long as England insisted that she should rule the Colonies in fact as well as in title. Had Britain been content with mere claims of sovereignty, the colonists would have readily assented. But the relaxed days of the "old colonial policy" were over: England was sequentially forcing governments responsive to her interest onto the Colonies.

On the surface the record of the conflict between Britain and the Colonies between 1763 and 1775 might suggest that the colonists were holding their own. After all, they forced England to repeal the Stamp Act and the Townshend Act and succeeded in nullifying the intent of the Tea Act. But while they were winning the battles, England was winning the war. Step by step she was extending her control over government in the Colonies, building a governing system whose structure, incentives, and power were responsive to British desires and resistant to colonial pressures. There could be no compromise. Either the colonists rebelled or they would gradually be made subordinate to the directives from Parliament. Obviously they rebelled—a choice, we shall see later, which reflected their pragmatic character.

Parliament was obviously searching for more revenue after 1762 and the Colonies appeared to be a large, untapped source. Much of the legislation directed at America would not have returned money directly to the exchequer in London, of course, but it would have had the equivalent effect by reducing royal expenditures. The Molasses Act was intended to make customs operations in America self-supporting, the Quartering Act was designed to reduce Britain's expenses from maintaining troops in North America, and the Tea Act was an attempt to avoid the direct appropriation otherwise necessary to salvage the East India Company. Whether direct or indirect, there were taxes nevertheless and the colonists had no desire to pay them. People do accept tax obligations voluntarily if they are convinced the public services they provide justify them, but in this case the colonists knew that any additional taxes they paid would be used merely to reduce those of English citizens and would not provide any additional governmental assistance for themselves. The English felt that the colonists should be willing to accept higher taxes as a part of their "fair share" of paying for the recent war with France. After all, they reasoned, the Americans had gained from the removal of the French from North America. But the colonists were not convinced that the removal was beneficial; in fact, they were increasingly realizing that the loss of the French presence was constraining their own freedom. Furthermore, the consequences of the victory of the British Empire were a thing of the past. The interest on the national debt created by the war was "sunk cost," an obligation to be paid whatever the results of the war. The Americans could expect no more benefit from paying more taxes to Britain than the dubious comfort of knowing that Britons were paying correspondingly less.

From 1763 to 1775, the British continuously attempted to impose more taxes on the Americans who, in turn, were able to frustrate many—but not all—such efforts. It seems obvious that the British would have continued their efforts had not the Americans converted the contest into an armed conflict. It also seems obvious that if the colonists had remained in the Empire beyond 1775, they would have been forced to yield to those tax initiatives. One important question, therefore, when evaluating the economic cost to the Americans of remaining in the Empire is *how much more* they would have been paying. There is no obvious quantitative answer, but certain expected patterns of behavior can provide guidelines. Just before 1775 the Americans were paying far fewer taxes per capita than were the British. It could be argued that while their tax burden would certainly be increased it would not rise so dramatically that per capita burdens on both sides of the Atlantic would be equalized. On the other hand, the Americans were not represented in Parliament and therefore would not have had recourse to the most effective technique for tax resistance—voting against the representatives who imposed them. No matter what intentions Parliament might have held about not imposing taxes beyond some indicated level, there would always have been the incentive for them to do so. The personal cost to each M.P. of taxing the Americans an additional shilling would have been less than taxing his own constituents, so naturally he would be encouraged to impose larger charges on the Americans.

Furthermore, the colonists would probably have paid more per capita than the English, even for equal tax rates, given the usual structure of taxes in that era. Tariffs and excise levies were the predominant sources of government revenues—anything equivalent to the familiar modern income or profits taxes was almost nonexistent. The manner by which taxes were imposed, therefore, made it diffi-cult to equalize personal tax burdens—even if that was intended. Individuals did not pay taxes on their real wealth or income but rather in proportion to the extent that the goods they produced and purchased passed through taxable commerce. At first this might suggest that the colonist would pay fewer taxes: their economy was characterized by substantial self-sufficiency which would be beyond the reach of such taxes. But Britain's economy also contained large elements of noncommercialized economic activity and, looking beyond 1775, the proportion of American economic activity developed outside of market transactions was decreasing. However, American per capita incomes were higher than those of the English, possibly by as much as 50 percent. That implies, other things being equal, up to 50 percent more taxable goods per person in the Colonies. In addi-tion, the general pattern of trade in the Colonies was more susceptible to taxation than was that of Britain. Most colonial commerce—intracolony, intercolony, and foreign—was funneled through a limited number of coastal cities, a very conven-ient vortex for tax collectors. England, though it too had natural commercial concentrations, was less vulnerable to central tax collections and thus less attrac-tive to legislators seeking more public money.

It appears reasonable to predict that if the Americans had stopped their resistance and acknowledged England's sovereignty they would soon have been paying taxes similar to those paid by the English. (Several of the above condi-tions suggest that they would have been paying even more per capita than Brit-ons.) Thus, the excess of British taxes over actual taxes in the Colonies just before the Revolution is certainly a good indicator of the Americans' stake in control-ling their own government. The size of the difference is striking and explains why the colonists considered the principle of control over their own taxation so im-portant. It also indicates that even if England had imposed only a fraction of its own per capita tax burden on the Colonies, it would still have constituted a major cost to the Americans. Table 3-1 gives the estimates (converted to American currency) of per capita tax payments which R. R. Palmer calculated for 1765.[2]

From the vantage of the 1970s, $5.50 per person does not seem a heavy or provocative burden. But such a tax would have come from colonial per capita incomes variously estimated at only $60 to $100 yearly and, whichever estimate is correct, $5.50 of such an amount constitutes a relatively large burden. It ranges upward from a minimum of 5 percent of colonial income to almost 10 percent, if income is estimated at $60 yearly. In terms of our modern perspective, condi-tioned by current incomes, that is comparable to a yearly tax of from $250 to

[2] See R. R. Palmer, *The Age of Democratic Revolution: A Political History of Europe and America,* vol. 1, *The Challenge,* Princeton University Press, Princeton, 1959. The figures for Ireland are very suggestive and lend support to the assertion that Americans would be paying far more taxes as nationals of the Empire. Ireland was under British control and was paying more than six times per capita the taxes of any of the colonies. In addition, Irish personal incomes were probably only about half of the Americans' so that their burden was further doubled (equivalent to about $3.00 per person for Americans). Moreover, Ireland's taxes were substantially increased to $2.22 per capita by 1785 (twice that amount for the American equivalent), an indication that taxes levied on the Americans would probably have also increased after 1765.

Table 3-1 Tax Burden per Capita in 1765

Great Britain	$5.76
Massachusetts	0.22
Pennsylvania	0.22
Maryland	0.22
New York	0.15
Connecticut	0.13
Virginia	0.10
Ireland	1.47

Source: Adapted from R.R. Palmer, *The Age of Democratic Revolution: A Political History of Europe and America 1760–1800,* vol. 1, *The Challenge,* Princeton University Press, Princeton, 1969, p. 155. Adapted by permission of Princeton University Press.

more than $400 for each person. Furthermore, that yearly charge would be repeated each year as long as the colonists remained subordinate to Empire government. They were not, therefore, contending for 5 to 10 percent of the current year's income, but rather for the much larger asset of not paying those charges each year endlessly into the future. Depending on the particular interest rate, that advantage would range up to $100 for each colonist.[3] That maximum value equals the maximum estimate of an average colonist's income for one year. Capitalized tax savings—the value today of not paying that endless series of annual levies to the British—were probably lower than $100 yearly, but then income was also probably less. The colonists would have been justified in equating the elusion of British control with an entire year's income. Even if independence was worth only a fraction of that, it was still a very large consideration. Again, to place the disputed asset in modern perspective, a $100 misunderstanding to the colonists in the 1700s would be comparable to $4,500 taken from each American today.

Groups that we can observe in modern times always resist and contend with any action that threatens as much as 5 to 10 percent of their income. In fact, groups—of individuals, businesses, or localities—usually develop, even if they had not existed previously, when the interests they hold in common are so threatened. (However, the Americans showed surprising unity against the British initiatives, considering how fiercely they had quarreled with each other previously. Ironically, one reason the British felt they should maintain rule over the Colonies was that they feared that otherwise they might degenerate into the chaos of anarchy.) Actually, groups will usually contend for vested interests of much less value than 5 to 10 percent of their income. Thus, the colonists may have been

[3] An asset which pays $5.50 yearly is equivalent to $100 invested at a prevailing interest rate of 5½ percent. Higher interest rates would reduce the value of the investment necessary to return $5.50. Interest rates below 5½ percent, which appear unreasonably low for the colonial period, would value the future tax savings at the present more than $100.

instinctively responding to an economic threat, even if it was smaller than this range of estimates. In addition they may have been reacting to economic self-interest, even if potential tax transfers to Britain would have been small. There were, after all, other economic costs to British domination.

Any system of taxes imposed on the Colonies would undoubtedly have been a collection of specific levies, such as tariffs, excises, licenses, and property taxes. Such selective taxes would have altered and demeaned the economic decisions the colonists would have made. When scarcity confronts people and they find that they do not have enough purchasing power to buy all the goods and services they want, they are forced to choose—and exclude—among the alternatives. These options appear to them in the form of "trade-offs"—the price of each item relative to other possible purchases. The relative prices dictate how they allocate their buying power: a low price encourages them to use relatively large amounts of a good; a high price discourages them and restricts the amount they can buy. Normally the price of a good determined by market forces—expressing the opportunity cost society places on alternative uses of those resources—measures its contribution to human welfare as individuals themselves view it.

When a tax is imposed on a specific good, it simultaneously lowers the return paid for the resources used in its production and raises the price to the consumer. Naturally consumers, faced with the higher price, reduce their purchases. Producers and the owners of the resources used in the good's production shift some of their inputs to other, more remunerative uses. Consumers perceive a higher price for the taxed good than producers do. Consequently, the value to them of the last unit of that product at which they stop buying is greater than the opportunity cost to society of the last unit of output at which the suppliers cease production. This results in a misallocation of resources. The total output of the colonial economy could have been increased if more resources had been used in the production of a taxed good by withdrawing them from less productive (non-taxed) uses elsewhere. The misallocation would have persisted even if the tax revenue going to the British had been counted as a transfer rather than a loss. In other words, the colonists stood to lose more from a system of taxation imposed by the British than the latter stood to gain. Thus, when estimating the cost to the Americans of remaining in the Empire, this difference must be added to the value of taxes they would have paid.

No trustworthy estimates of these costs of misallocation resulting from taxes are available yet. That void is very understandable: the necessary calculations would require a tremendous amount of research and reconstruction of the colonial economy. The burden on the colonists imposed by a specific tax on a specific good or resource depended on the elasticities of that product's demand and supply responses. That side of the market's participants—the consumers or producers—which adjusts its quantity behavior least to the imposition of the tax, bears the largest portion of its effect. Parties with elastic price responses, however, shift to alternate consumption or production possibilities and thus escape the levy's bite. The cost to the Americans of a hypothetical tax on a specific good, therefore, depended on the identity of the buyers and sellers and their respective price elasticities. The British might have intended that the Americans pay the full cost of the imposed taxes, but it would have been very possible for sizeable portions of the burden to be shifted to other economies—their own in particular. In the colonial period the obvious candidate for the imposition of taxes was foreign trade. By its very definition, either the buyers or the sellers of a good in international trade must be foreign nationals. If output of a major American export, such as tobacco, was price-inelastic, for instance, the colonial producers would have borne a large portion of the tax. On the other hand, if European smokers demanded a constant quantity of tobacco, whatever the price, they would have absorbed the higher price created by a tariff. Of course, the colonists would have borne the full damages of misallocation from levies imposed on strictly American markets, such as property taxes, stamp taxes, or license fees.

Even if the researcher had, by a herculean effort, completed the estimates of misallocation costs borne by the colonists from each one of a hypothetical system of taxes, his task would not be finished. The system of taxes we have envisioned the English as imposing would have had too much breadth and intensity for the effects to stop at specific goods. Spanning a major part of colonial economic activities, they would have approximated a very high (by contemporary levels) sales tax in modern America. The taxes would have undoubtedly reached beyond individual goods to affect the colonists' basic behavioral parameters of work effort, saving, and ownership of real property. Thus, although an exact measurement is difficult, distortions in the employment of resources certainly would have been a major cost of British governance to the Americans.

The expected costs outlined above certainly gave the Americans good reason to wish to remain independent of Parliament's effective rule. In addition to taxes and misallocations from taxes, however, there were at least two more potentially large costs implied by British sovereignty. To extract taxes from the Americans, the English would have had to have taken control of government in the Colonies. Of course, they had little interest in the domestic affairs of the Americans, such as building roads in Virginia or operating village schools in Connecticut, but these provincial concerns absorbed a large part of the attention of colonial governments. The British might have been able to decentralize some functions of government, giving the colonists authority over local affairs but retaining control over those powers necessary to assure a flow of funds to the exchequer in London. In practice there would probably have been some conflicts, however. The colonists, working from such local governments, had proven their proficiency at subverting British objectives. For example, the English could have earmarked certain taxes for their own use, allowing the colonists to enact other levies to finance those government activities which they desired. The Americans would undoubtedly have used this arrangement to divert goods or activities from the categories taxed for the British. They probably would also have structured their own taxes and expenditures in such a way as to stifle England's revenues. The British administrators, much like modern internal revenue officials, would have faced a continuous battle of rulings, interpretations, and tax-avoidance innovations with the Americans. Either for convenience or in desperation they would probably have preempted an ever-widening share of domestic colonial govern-ment. That control would also have inflicted losses on the Americans' economic welfare. Empire officials, not accountable to the Americans, would have decided for them what services of local government they should be provided with and how they should be compelled to pay for them. No matter how well intentioned, these British bureaucrats would not have provided government services as effi-ciently as the Americans would have for themselves. Their information and in-centives would have produced different conclusions and decisions than those reached by the colonists when they matched up their own preferences with the costs of such activities. The misallocations would have been exacerbated if Par-liament had insisted, as it tended to do in its struggles with the Americans, on reserving some decisions for London rather than delegating them to its officials in the Colonies. By the time issues could have been relayed to London, passed through the slow, haphazard, and conjecturing decision process there and re-turned to the Americans, the latter could be forgiven for believing that no gov-ernment at all would be a better alternative.

There would be still one more cost to the Americans of being genuine citi-zens of the Empire. One collection cost has not yet been discussed or allocated to one of the parties. If, in levying taxes on the colonists, the British had attempted to obtain a certain amount of *net* revenue, this cost would have been added onto the total paid by the Americans. The agents of the Empire in America had always found some accommodations with the colonists advantageous and even neces-sary. They lived among them as neighbors and were much closer to their society or retribution than they were to their own superiors in London. When it came to the regulations of the Empire, both agents and colonists could gain from arrange-ments between themselves which neglected their enforcement. The agents re-ceived bribes and local cordiality in exchange for lower taxes and less government red tape for the colonists. England, of course, was the loser. If she expected to have her regulations in America enforced, she had to create an envi-ronment in which the local officials responded to her interests and resisted those of the colonists. One obvious solution was an incentive payment system for Em-pire officials, such as the one instituted in 1767 that began the period of "customs racketeering." As that experience demonstrated, the agents could be encouraged, in fact catapulted, into collecting revenue, completely oblivious to colonial pro-tests. That era also proved that such a system of tax collection would cost the Americans considerably, in money as well as annoyance. Had the British sought to collect any sizeable revenues from the colonists, they would have had to resort to such a commission arrangement and the Americans would have paid those overhead charges as one more cost of remaining in the Empire.

Thomas Paine, in a characteristic outburst against established authority, de-clared that "while continents may rule the small islands around them it is absurd to believe that an island should forever rule a continent." The statement is not necessarily true—its impact results from a play on words. We associate "island" with small duchies and "continents" with major world powers. In the 1700s an island (England) was probably more important in world affairs than any of the continents except Europe—of which she was naturally only a fraction—and Asia. Perhaps Paine would forgive us if we restructured his statement to read: "While England might rule America in the latter's infancy, it is absurd to believe that both could ever be ruled effectively by one government." They did have some interests which united them, but the things which divided them—not the least of which was the Atlantic Ocean—were much stronger. Any government which ruled the two nations jointly would be much less successful for either of them than its own autonomous government would be. In other words, there were substantial diseconomies of scale from the government incorporating a wider domain than the efficiency of the geography dictated. Either one or both of the parties jointly would have to absorb these additional costs from stretching the borders of the state too far. Britain tried to do it on the cheap for herself. She attempted to use her home government to rule both areas and thus pass all the costs onto the colonists. The Americans were quick to sense the important issue and they decided to fight for independence rather than submit to the Empire.

THE OCCASIONAL WAR

When the fighting began in 1775 and the two parties came face to face with the consequences of their intransigence, neither showed much enthusiasm for warfare. The British vacillated between a desire to teach the Americans a lesson and a reluctance, as supposed country men, to destroy them. In England there was considerable oppositon to the war, so substantial numbers of Hessian mercenaries were hired rather than committing many nationals to the fighting. Nor did the British generals appear interested in using the troops they did command. Sir William Howe, for example, showed no interest in aggressively pursuing the colonial armies even when they were obviously vulnerable. He preferred the comfort and society of New York or Philadelphia to chasing the rebels across the countryside. Howe's tactics—or nontactics—might have succeeded if the British had sealed off the Patriots' coastline by controlling the six strategic ports of Boston, Newport (Rhode Island), New York, Philadelphia, Norfolk, and Charleston (South Carolina). However, England never committed enough military forces to hold more than three of these locations simultaneously. Had they not evacuated Boston, the British would not have had enough troops to capture New York. To conduct the campaign in the South in the latter part of the war, they gave up all pretense of contesting for the Northeast.

Nor did the size of the American military effort ever indicate complete dedication to prosecuting the Revolution. During the seven years that the Revolution continued, the colonists mustered an impressive total of nearly 200,000 men into regular military units and about that many more into the militia. But the level of effective fighting strength was always much less. At its largest, Washington's Continental army numbered 20,000. Usually, however, only about 5,000 were available. The Patriots' small navy, though spirited, was no match for the much larger British fleet. Only the intercession of the French Navy, for instance, isolated Cornwallis and compelled him to surrender at Yorktown. Ironically the Americans' largest effort in the war was conducted completely independently of the official military organization. Almost entirely in response to their own importunity, individuals or groups of individuals were given public charters as privateers. This entitled them to capture British ships, sell the prizes and their cargoes, and pocket the proceeds. At least 10,000 Americans served each year of the war after 1776 and probably more than 50,000 served at the peak of activity in 1781.

Some of the lethargy in the prosecution of the Revolution by the Americans is explained by the indifference—or even opposition—of major groups of them to it. Approximately one-third of the Americans did not wish to be independent of Britain and natually rooted for an English victory. In some cases they joined the British Army or organized militia units to oppose the Patriots. Tory sentiment was particularly strong in larger towns, such as New York. The occupying British soldiers were welcomed warmly and their officers quickly received into the best social circles. When the British evacuated a port city, boatloads of local Tories usually left with them rather than face retribution by the Patriots. Probably more than 50,000 loyalist colonials left America during the war, most of them for Canada.

The Americans had a much better chance than the British did of getting what they wanted from the Revolutionary War. They had only to hold out and endure to establish their independence. On the other hand, for the British to force the Americans into the Empire they had to conquer and subdue a distant, unruly people. These considerations, coupled with Britain's superiority in naval power, dictated the type of war which ensued. With the exception of the enterprising colonial privateers who sought out English shipping everywhere, all of the war was fought in America and most of it right along the Atlantic coastline. The British, controlling the ocean but short on troops, attempted to subdue the Americans by capturing their important seaports. The colonists usually conceded the waterfront but challenged any armed intrusions from there into the interior. Britain's two major ventures into the American interior were Burgoyne's campaign in upstate New York in 1777 and the Southern campaign from 1779 to 1781. (Significantly, both produced major British defeats: Burgoyne at Saratoga and Cornwallis at Cowpens, South Carolina.)

As a consequence, most of the interior never experienced the disruption and destruction of fighting during the Revolution. The war's effect there was limited to disruption of trading patterns with the central areas. However, that disruption was not unimportant—it decimated the gains the colonists had gradually extracted from a widening market—although, given the relatively high degree of self-sufficiency in the economy of the back country, life proceeded with few discontinuities. Activity on the frontier, in fact, seemed completely oblivious to the war. Settlers made major strides into previously uninhabited territory in western Pennsylvania and North Carolina, Kentucky, Tennessee, and the Ohio Valley. Between 1775 and 1783 the first settlements at the present sites of Pittsburgh, Cincinnati, Lexington, Louisville, and St. Louis were established.

Most of the war may have been fought along the coast, but from most points on the coast during most of the Revolution it would have been difficult to see that a war was going on. The fighting never encompassed as much as half of the colonial shore at any one time, and usually it was much less. Nor was any one section of the coast involved for more than a fraction of the time. As the war progressed, British initiatives kept shifting it southward, probing for weakness and Tory sympathy in the colonial ranks. In 1775, when the fighting began, the British troops were located in Boston, from where, since 1768, they had been attempting to subdue unruly Massachusetts. Lexington, Concord, Bunker Hill—the names strike an immediate association with the Revolution, Minutemen, and armed resistance. But the fighting in New England, although dramatic, was short-lived. In 1776, Washington occupied Dorchester Heights, commanding Boston Harbor, and forced General Gage to evacuate his forces from the port. The British continued their base at Newport, Rhode Island, but its function was limited to protecting Long Island Sound—the flank of the operation in New York—and disrupting colonial coastal traffic. Even that ceased in 1778 when the garrison was withdrawn to bolster the invasion force at Savannah. The land of the proud shrines to American liberty passed most of the war in peace. New Englanders' main contribution to the war effort occurred when the personal gains they reaped from privateering coincided with the substantial damage these efforts inflicted on the British cause. Unlike other colonial ports south of New England, which suffered and contracted during the Revolution, many of New England's coastal cities prospered. The harbors of New Haven, Salem, Boston, Beverly, and Providence were busy building and outfitting privateers. Ironically, the sharpest and most destructive fighting in the region took place between colonial factions when feuds between local Patriot and Tory groups devastated the coastal Connecticut towns of Norwalk and Fairfield.

Most of the war occurred south of New England, and thus the Colonies there suffered most from it. When a particular area was under British control, the regular wartime pursuits of blockage running and privateering were natually stopped. If combat accompanied occupation, additional costs were inflicted in the form of destruction of the countryside. Usually the transfers of power were gentlemanly and perfunctory, but in the campaign through Georgia and South Carolina the British decided to get tough. They razed buildings and crops and captured an estimated 25,000 slaves, hoping thereby to break the Americans' willingness to resist.

THE ECONOMICS OF THE PECULIAR
REVOLUTIONARY MILITARY

When Washington took command of the Continental army, he might have understandably assumed that it functioned just as its name implied—as the major army, by the standards of that day, of a sizeable economy. He could not have held that illusion very long because the constraints pressing down on the army's performance were much too immediate and obvious. When the army was established, it had the understandable shortcomings of inexperience. Most of the troops were new to military life and their typical peacetime experiences as independent farmers hardly prepared them for regimented discipline. There was also a serious shortage of officers who had either the appropriate experience or training. But these problems were mitigated by the passage of time. The raw recruits, like so many American draftees since then, quickly became capable soldiers. The officer ranks were augmented by volunteers from Europe such as Lafayette, Pulaski, and von Steuben. Washington proved to be a good commanding officer, particularly considering his dual role as field commander and Chief of Staff reporting to the Continental Congress. He was a much better general than others who have also subsequently made it to the White House.

One major constraint on the Continental army could not be overcome by experience; it persisted throughout the war. The British Navy controlled the coastline sufficiently so that neither American troops nor supplies could be moved by water. Washington's forces were essentially landlocked and, in the context of colonial conditions, that was stifling and expensive. Land transportation typically cost about 100 times more per mile for longer distances. This meant that the British could move and supply their armies along the coast at only a small fraction of the cost of equivalent movements to the Americans. Thus the British could put more military forces into combat, out of any given supply of military resources, than could the Americans. The English were handling muskets on the battle lines while the Patriots were driving wagons, caring for horses, and filling the deepest potholes in the supply roads. In practice this led to a regionalization of the colonial military and a reduction in its effective fighting strength. Washington did not have a standing army as such; a large part of his forces at any one time was composed of militia from the area within which the army was operating. When the Continental army was operating in New England, a good part of its membership consisted of militia from Massachusetts, but when the army, parrying British moves, shifted to the Middle Atlantic Colonies, the New Englanders returned to their farms and replacements for them had to be sought among the militia of New York and Pennsylvania.

The army was also bedeviled by another constraint beyond its control throughout the Revolution. The Continental Congress had no power to tax and it could not market long-term loans to pay the expenses of conducting the war. The states had magnanimously given it the right to *request* funds from them, but they showed almost no cooperation until near the very end of the Revolution. Its only recourse was to issue short-term debts, such as bills of credit, certificates of indebtedness, and loan-office certificates, hoping that its creditors would accept these in payment despite their obvious drawbacks. There was the obvious risk, especially early in the Revolution, that the new government would be destroyed and that, as a consequence, these debts would be repudiated and worthless. In addition, the bills of credit circulated from hand to hand as money, so that each new issue of debt increased the quantity of money in circulation and thus also increased the level of prices. The "continentals" depreciated in value and the process accelerated as quartermasters found it necessary to issue larger and larger quantities of bills to obtain given supplies. The value of debt issued by the Continental government in 1775 was $6 million; in 1776, $19 million; in 1777, $13 million; in 1778, $63.5 million; and in 1779, $90 million.

Washington and his army were caught in the middle of this inflation. Frequently the soldiers were paid late or not at all, but when they did receive their wages they discovered they had depreciated to a fraction of their original expected values. To attract soldiers, enlistments had to be shortened and salaries continually increased. Even then inflation was still rapid enough to cause widespread grumblings and desertions in the ranks. The supply agents for the army had similar problems. Despite the productiveness of agriculture in the areas within which the army operated during most of the war, food and horses were often difficult to obtain. Local farmers were understandably reluctant to accept depreciating continentals for their produce. Sometimes the quartermasters were forced to resort to seizure and compulsory payment to obtain required supplies—obviously not a good public relations technique. In that bitter winter at Valley Forge, Washington complained that while local farmers would not provide food or firewood to his army, they readily sold them to the British in nearby Philadelphia. That revered moment in American history could have been avoided by a modest amount of trustworthy money.

Profitable Patriotism at Sea

America's little navy acquitted itself well during the Revolution but there was never any question that it could match Britain's naval power. England was much too large and experienced in maritime affairs to be checked by the upstart Americans, even given their skills as sailors. But the Patriots quickly discovered a major weakness in England's naval defenses which they exploited with devastating effectiveness. Privateers (armed private ships legally chartered to raid commerce of enemy nations) have an aura of the unreal and unethical about them today. Americans of the eighteenth century, however, viewed them as conventional, ethical enterprises and were willing and even eager to use them against the British. The crew and the owners of a privateer divided the value of all prizes—both ships and cargo. How fortunate for the American cause that personal rewards and national war objectives coincided so perfectly!

Privateers were neither built nor operated as warships. They were sufficiently powerful to subdue lightly armed commercial vessels, but few were large enough to have held off a British man-of-war. Therefore, their objectives were to locate vulnerable merchant shipping but to avoid warships. By this criterion, one of the most famous battle cries in American history should be looked upon as evidence of failure, not as courageous defiance of the enemy. Privateer Captain John Paul Jones's statement, "I have just begun to fight," came when the British warship *Serapis* had caught up with him. The statement was literally and ironically true. Jones had been easily subduing commercial ships so that when the *Serapis* challenged him he had a fight on his hands for the first time.

The English, of course, tried to prevent privateering by blockading the American ships in their home ports. The effort was only partly successful and collapsed completely when the evacuation of Newport in 1778 opened all New

England ports to privateers. The British were able to check most privateering on the high seas by strengthening their navy and instituting protective convoys on major shipping routes. But this defense was offset when England's major European rivals were pulled into the war on the American side and part of the British fleet was confined at home to protect the British Isles from the French Navy. Friendly, convenient ports opened up in France, Spain, and the Caribbean where the privateers could acquire supplies and sell their prizes. Meanwhile the privateers improved their weapons and their tactics even as they used them. Their original ad hoc collection of fishing boats, coasting vessels, and modified cargo ships was replaced by specially constructed, fast, heavily armed, and low-silhouetted sloops. The officers and crews of the privateers became highly adept at cowing English captains into surrender and delivering their vessels to a friendly port. Whereas in the early part of the war three or four prizes were considered good work for a voyage, productivity increased toward the end of the Revolution to the point where six or more captures were necessary to credit a voyage as successful.

The American privateers sought out English shipping wherever it sailed— along the North American coast, in the Caribbean, around the British Isles, and in the North Sea. They were so persistent in seeking out prizes that insurance was taken out on the ferries plying between England and France for fear that they too would be captured. Although some were subsequently recaptured, the privateers seized about 2,000 ships and 12,000 English sailors during the war. One English authority put the value of Britain's total loss of ships and cargo at $80 million. The impact of these operations is also reflected in insurance rates on English vessels which, at times during the war, exceeded 25 percent of value—which suggests that insurance underwriters expected one out of each four ships to be lost on any given voyage.

The American economy—and some conspicuous American entrepreneurs— clearly benefited from privateering during the war. It served as an outlet for shipping resources otherwise idle because the peacetime pursuits of fishing and foreign trade were restricted by the fighting. It brought many captured goods into American ports at a time when imports were curtailed (although goods captured at random often do not match a conventional shopping list). It also provided a source of foreign exchange earnings to replace that lost by the reduction of such traditional exports as tobacco.

Obviously, as the above evidence underscores, privateering brought havoc to Britain's water commerce. It, probably more than any other American venture, forced England to conclude peace. When a merchant of Salem organized a privateering venture, the uppermost consideration in his mind was likely to be that, given a few successful expeditions, he, too, could have a big house on Chestnut Street. Little did he realize that his efforts, much more than those at Concord, Valley Forge, and Philadelphia, were responsible for American independence.

Foreign Commerce during the War

When the fighting began in 1775, the Continental Congress in the first flush of patriotic indignation prohibited all trade with Britain. England, feeling at least equally offended, returned the compliment. America's international trade was substantially reduced and this, coupled with the nonimportation agreements the colonists had been maintaining since 1774, in the aftermath of the Tea Act, led to very high prices for goods which had normally been imported. Congress relented somewhat to allow trade which brought in military supplies—the Patriots were especially short on guns and gunpowder during the early part of the war.

Such exceptions became the rule as the war progressed. When it began, many contemporaries in the Colonies believed that it would develop as a political showdown with Britain which would be quickly over. But as the fighting continued, it became increasingly obvious that the colonists had best prepare for a long struggle. In 1776, in a move that demonstrated how complete the break with England had become, Congress removed all restrictions on foreign trade except the prohibition of commerce with Britain and the British West Indies. Extensive trade then developed between America and France, Spain, and Holland, who, although officially neutral at that time, were obviously antagonistic toward Britain. Traders from these nations brought some goods directly to America; for example, French ships came directly to New England between 1776 and 1778. More frequently, however, foreign trade was routed through intermediate ports to legitimize it and protect it from hostile powers. Technically France was neutral, but the English understood perfectly well that goods carried in French vessels were going to England's enemy, the Americans. They consequently harassed, intimidated, and contested legalities to try to stop such trade. If, however, goods were sent to the port of a third and neutral nation, where they could be relabeled and mixed in with the unquestionably neutral commerce, the risk of interference with that trade could be prevented. Amsterdam, Bermuda, and the Bahamas, and various West Indies ports served as such intermediate entrepôts.

Intermediate ports were kept additionally busy after France (in 1778), then Spain (1779), and finally Holland (1780) joined the war against England. More of the commerce on the North Atlantic was converted from neutral to belligerent status and thus subjected to attack by some of the warring parties. The effect on American shipping was not as pronounced, however. When France entered the war, its navy excluded the English from some areas and, in effect, freed those areas for use by American shipping. The French fleet also forced the English to commit more of its navy to the defense of other locations and thus reduced the number of warships available to hinder American commerce.

The reciprocal gains which individuals made by participating in international trade were much too large to be sacrificed for a mere war. Trading parties, even those residing in hostile nations, devised alternate arrangements so that business could proceed (almost) as usual. For example, one of the largest volumes of trade during the Revolutionary War developed between Britain and her rebellious colonies. When British forces occupied an American city they considered it part of the Empire and allowed it all the trading privileges that conferred. New York City, for instance, was occupied for most of the war and its residents traded with England during that period. The demarcation of the areas controlled by the British outside the city was not clear, however, so it was only natural that goods imported from Britain would be distributed throughout New York's market area in the interior, much of which was clearly in the hands of the Patriots. English merchants traded with Americans in unoccupied regions by means of intermediate neutral ports. Amsterdam, for example, was busy receiving both British and American goods and applying the necessary cosmetic procedures to affirm them as neutral cargo. Not that many Americans or English were deceived by this procedure. One well-known English commentator stated that large quantities of British goods came to America via Nova Scotia and the West Indies. Some Americans made almost no effort to conceal their illicit trade. At least one importer is known to have sent his payments directly to a merchant in London.

As a consequence, the volume of America's international trade was not reduced substantially during the Revolution. It was certainly reorganized and redirected, but the amount of goods exchanged did not fall precipitously below what it would have been if the North Atlantic nations had been at peace. The largest declines in foreign commerce occurred at the beginning and at the end of the war. It took some time after the fighting began for traders to restructure their activities and for governments to acknowledge that trade was permissible while pursuing the war. Oddly enough, the British imposed one of the largest disruptions of the war on American trade during 1782—after they had surrendered at Yorktown and while peace negotiations were proceeding at Paris. Freed from protecting the flanks of maneuvering land forces, English vessels suddenly concentrated on attacking American shipping. Operating from the ports of New York, Charlestown, and Savannah, which they still controlled, they dramatically reversed their previous behavior of usually ignoring colonial shipping. In 1782, Boston's merchants reported that their trade with the West Indies had its worst year of the war.

Although a large part of American foreign trade continued during the war, it was not as much as there would have been if the Colonies had been at peace. The fighting increased the cost of using foreign commerce. Some shipping usually available for trade was diverted to military uses, some was destroyed or captured by privateers, and that which continued in trade had to take longer and riskier voyages to deliver cargo. Freight rates rose dramatically, and Americans became less willing to buy the same amount of imported goods as they had before. One would have expected, as the accounts of the period unquestionably verify, that the Americans would have compensated for this reduction in trade in at least two ways. First, they would have increased their own output of the goods, usually characterized as manufactures, which they had previously imported. Thus, during the war there was a notable expansion in American output of cloth, paper, salt, and finished metal products, among other items. Second, with the increased cost of using one segment of market activity (foreign trade), they would have reduced their use of market organization for their economic activities. Colonial households, for example, would have increased their output of "homespun," shoes, tools, and furniture.

Recurring conventional patterns of economic behavior also suggest another adjustment which the colonists would have been expected to have made. Contemporary reports frequently remarked on the abundance of imported luxury goods in port cities during the war, an observation often linked with condemnations of the lavish expenditures of their inhabitants. As the war pushed freight rates up, the colonists stopped importing those lower-valued goods on which freight charges substantially raised the delivered price. (This was a temporary regression of the long-term process operating in this era in which decreasing freight rates had incorporated successively lower-valued goods into international trade.) What happened, then, was not that more luxury goods were imported, but that a higher proportion of imports were characterized and seen as luxuries and were more conspicuous to observers.

The wartime rise in freight rates had another important effect on American foreign commerce: the quantity of exports decreased much more than that of imports. During this period Americans typically exported bulky commodities whose value was low relative to the shipping space they required—products such as tobacco, rice, wheat, and fish. On the other hand, imports, such as manufactures, were typically high-valued goods relative to their requirements for cargo space. As the rising freight rates forced the colonists to reappraise which goods were worthwhile to continue in trade and which were not, exports dropped off the cargo manifests much more quickly than imports did. This adjustment paralleled, and was directly related to, changes in available shipping capacity. Because exports usually required more shipping space than imports, ships during peacetime usually arrived in the Colonies with partial loads but left with full ones. As the number of voyages of cargo ships was reduced by the war, space available for exports was directly curtailed. Space for imports was also reduced, but since some of it had not been used before anyway, the quantity of imports was not as severely curtailed.

In ordinary circumstances this reduction of exports relative to imports would have led to a deficit in the balance of payments with a resulting fall in domestic prices and increased unemployment. This pressure would have been accentuated because the war decimated another important source of foreign exchange for other nations. The Revolution cannot be considered as "normal circumstances," of course, but then it was not an ordinary war either. Three extraordinary sources of foreign exchange appeared—unlikely even for wartime conditions—which offset the loss of exports and shipping earnings. First, privateering obviously brought substantial revenues into American pockets from abroad, probably as much as would have been earned in peacetime by selling shipping services. Second, France and Spain gave gifts and loans totaling nearly $10 million to bolster the Continental Congress's resistance against their common enemy, England. Third, both England and France committed sizeable elements of their armies and navies to their conflict in America. They placed orders locally with the delighted colonists for large quantities of food and supplies. Thus the American market for imports was able quickly to adapt to, and avoid major damage from, the dislocations caused by the war.

In sum, it was an unusual war. Large portions of its military operations developed into bizarre patterns and its impact on the economy was equally peculiar. A large percentage of Americans never saw warfare and their impression of what was happening along the coast was formed from word-of-mouth accounts, a few dated newspapers, and some changes in goods and prices in the village store. Other colonists were surprised to hear that they were living in a war zone because they saw so little fighting. Military operations, like thunderstorms, passed through very quickly and life returned to its usual tranquil state. Colonists in those areas which were occupied by British troops usually found them to be accommodating visitors. They spent more foreign exchange—in prized gold coins—than would have any group of tourists that a local chamber of commerce could have hoped to attract. International trade went through wrenching changes. Peaceful commerce was restricted and some merchants went bankrupt, but privateering was very profitable and it created numerous personal fortunes and bustling ports. Incorporating a few adjustments, economic life in America went ahead little disturbed by the war. It is ironic that, while making such a dramatic and effective assertion of their independence, the Americans focused most of their attention on routine, peacetime activities.

SUGGESTED READINGS

Dickerson, Oliver M.: *The Navigation Acts and the American Revolution,* Barnes, New York, 1963.

McClelland, Peter D.: "The Cost to America of British Imperial Policy," *American Economic Review,* vol. 59, no. 2, May 1969.

Nettles, Curtis: *The Roots of American Civilization,* Appleton-Century-Crofts, New York, 1938.

Shepard, James F. and Gary M. Walton: *Shipping, Maritime Trade and the Economic Development of Colonial North America,* Cambridge, New York, 1972.

Thomas, Robert Paul: "A Quantitative Approach to the Study of the Effects of British Imperial Policy upon Colonial Welfare: Some Preliminary Findings," *Journal of Economic History,* vol. 25, no. 4, December 1965.

Walton, Gary M.: "The New Economic History and the Burdens of the Navigation Acts," *Economic History Review,* ser. 2, vol. 24, no. 4, November 1971.

Weiss, Roger W.: "The Issue of Paper Money in the American Colonies, 1720–1774," *Journal of Economic History,* vol. 30, no. 4, December 1970.

Chapter 4

Economic Shocks and Growth: 1783-1815

As a small, yet relatively developed economy at the end of the Revolutionary War, America was irresistibly enmeshed in the international commerce of the North Atlantic. Just as irresistibly, all the developments affecting those trading patterns reverberated back into the American economy. From 1783—and the birth of the new nation—to 1815 such events were especially dramatic and traumatic. Americans were constantly adapting their economic behavior to new conditions imposed from outside—exclusion from the British Empire, a new form of government, a major war between European powers, and, finally, another war with the mother country. The normal condition of the economy during this era was the abnormal. Yet while the Americans rolled with the punches of foreign events, they pursued a large part of their day-to-day economic activities oblivious to external events. These domestic efforts had the by-product, largely unrecognized by their instigators, of gradually modifing the major contours of the economy. From the complex of decisions reached by individual Americans in the pursuit of their personal objectives there emerged a larger and redistributed population, a larger capital stock, improved technology, and better market organization. With or without a boost from abroad, the United States was growing on its own.

CONFEDERATION PERIOD

In 1783 the Thirteen Colonies became the United States of America, complete with a new national flag, and Americans might well have congratulated themselves for having repelled the threat of taxes and inefficiency implied by rule from London. However, independence was not an unmitigated gain. Some groups of Americans suffered losses by their exclusion from the British Empire, and all suffered some inconvenience in adjusting to new conditions. Most citizens spent some effort in the following six years in devising a government to replace the one they had so unceremoniously kicked out.

Hardest hit was the ocean shipping sector, particularly the New England ports, which had freely plied the extensive trade routes within the British Empire before independence. Contemporary accounts are filled with citations of idle ships, shuttered warehouses, and unemployed sailors. The gloom spread back from the docks as sail makers, insurance agents, and nearby farmers saw the shrinking demand for their supporting services. Naturally the Americans made the best of these setbacks by seeking out new areas for trade, such as China, and by shifting into other activities, such as domestic commerce and small-scale manufacturing. Yet the gloom was barely dissipated; ocean shipping was such an obvious use of that large sector of resources that second-best solutions appeared as disasters. Complaints and moans of despair continued until 1790 when fortuitous developments (at least for the Americans) pulled the maritime sector into exceptional prosperity.

American suppliers, such as those of naval stores and indigo, who had formerly received British bounties for their products, also suffered withdrawal symptoms upon leaving the Empire. Taxpayers found their assessments higher, not only to pay for the recent war, but also to finance those functions of government formerly assumed by the Empire. Foremost among these was national defense, particularly a navy. The Americans discovered how important and expensive that could be when, with independence, they were forced to deal with the Barbary pirates on their own. Some groups found it advantageous to be free of the Empire. Tobacco commanded a higher price in the upper South because it could be shipped directly to its intended destination rather than having to make the previously required featherbed stop in England. Other Americans benefited more from independence than they realized. They mistakenly assigned some of the transitory costs of adjusting to the end of the Revolution to burdens of independence—a forgivable confusion since (at least some) historians have continued to do so ever since.

During the War for Independence the influences and constraints which international trade normally imposes were absent from the American economy. Understandably, when the war ended and free trade resumed, the existing pattern of economic activity in America was in for a traumatic realignment. After a lapse of more than seven years regular trade resumed in late 1782 when the United States and England signed a provisional peace agreement. By this time the Americans had developed a lengthy shopping list for replacements for goods which had worn out but had not been replaced by either smuggling or domestic manufacturing. They imported more than $26 million worth of goods from England in 1784 and 1785, very large purchases for a nation of its size and income. The imports ranged widely from textiles through housewares to playing cards, but usually were among the best in quality of their particular category. The Americans noted the apparent extravagance of these imports and naturally blamed it for a group of interrelated developments which were troubling them— an outflow of specie, falling prices, and rising unemployment—although in actuality the events simply reflected the adjustment of the economy to a postwar state. During the war, as we noted earlier, the Americans received loans and subsidies totaling nearly $10 million from the French, Dutch, and Spanish. Consequently, when peace returned, far more gold coin was circulating in the domestic economy than was customary before the war, and the average level of prices was correspondingly higher. The natural foreign exchange balancing act then took effect. Americans found foreign prices lower than their own and bought large amounts of imports. Foreigners, on the other hand, bought few of the relatively high-priced American goods. A balance-of-payments deficit developed in which gold coin left the country to pay for the net inflow of goods.

Unconstrained, a deficit sets up the conditions which reduce and finally eliminate it—it self-destructs. The outflow of gold reduced the domestic money supply and, in turn, the prices. Foreigners increased their imports of American goods, and Americans reduced their imports of foreign goods. But Americans appeared unable to comprehend or stoically accept this self-adjusting process. Their contemporary communications were filled with complaints about the brutal nature of the adjustment—again, unemployment, falling prices, and lackluster sales. They blamed their woes on almost every possible cause except the actual one—the necessary transition to peace. It is no wonder, then, that some commentators have been persuaded to characterize the confederation period from 1783– 1789 as one of depression. All those complaints by eye witnesses must serve to demonstrate that. Other scholars, however, believed they detected a few hopeful signs of growth and expansion in the despair of the moment. Some, especially those who focused on the period after 1785, when much of the adjustment to peace was completed, saw the difficulties of 1783 to 1785 as merely a short detour from the usual "high road of American progress."

As usual, the tone of these evaluations varied much more than the underlying conditions they were attempting to describe. Commentators tend to fasten onto specific changes or forces and blow them up into unwarranted generalizations, while an economic system demonstrates the resilience and interia characteristic of a motley collection of self-seeking units. The true situation was undoubtedly a mixed picture falling somewhere between the extremes of full prosperity and deep depression. There was a strong undercurrent of indigenous growth in the American economy in the 1780s, yet the blows delivered to its external relations certainly restricted economic activity. An exact appraisal, which is not available now (and therefore explains the diversity in proffered answers), requires a comprehensive, quantitative picture of the economy. The only available such record of the economy in the 1780s details its foreign trade sector.[1] It shows the upper South, with restrictions on its tobacco exports lifted, increasing its volume of trade over prewar levels. The Middle Atlantic states presented a mixed picture, and the lower South and New England regions showed absolute losses in trade volume. Nationally, trade was about equal to that before the Revolution, but since the population had increased, it represented a per capita decline, possibly as much as one-third. Because this record is the only available evidence, there is a strong temptation to extrapolate its pessimistic implications onto the entire economy. However, less than 10 percent of the yearly output of the American economy was funneled through international trade in the 1780s. A small change in the rest of the economy could more than offset a relatively large shift within the trade sector. For instance, had trade declined by a full one-third per capita from 1775 to 1790, a gain of 4 percent in the remainder of the economy would have more than compensated for the loss. Such figures are highly suggestive as to what must have happened in the American economy in that period. Given the prevailing (favorable) environment for innovations, a gain of at least 4 percent in the economy in those fifteen years seems likely. Thus, an average American probably experienced an increase in real income over the period, despite all the much publicized, adverse events.

ECONOMICS AND A NEW GOVERNMENT

At about every third chamber of commerce meeting a speaker rises and suggests something approximated by the following: "The success of American society and its economic system is explained by its system of free government, codified by the Constitution, which has energized the natural initiative and ingenuity of its people." The argument is not as simple as it first appears. It necessarily builds on several asserted (and presently unproven) relationships. One obvious implication of this interpretation, however, is that in the absence of the Constitution, the American economy would have developed very much differently. Viewed in this light, the proposition is not as obvious. Before the Revolution, the American Colonies had prospered and grown under the formal authority—but de facto independence—of the British Empire. As we saw above, the Americans were not doing poorly in the period after the Revolution but before the Constitution. Many traditional accounts of the confederation period have subtly begged the question by blaming its alleged economic troubles on the existing form of government. However, if the problems were exaggerated, then the confederation need not be the scapegoat. Its image has suffered from that very common human trait of assuming that governments have more power—for good or for bad—over their respective economies than they actually do have. The confederation was actually not a bad form of government insofar as the American economy of the 1780s was concerned. It has been a victim of bad press.

[1] Gordon C. Bjork, "The Weaning of the American Economy: Independence, Market Changes and Economic Development, *Journal of Economic History,* vol. 24, no. 41, December 1964. See also the subsequent discussion by Albert Fishlow.

Whatever the merits of the confederation form of national government, the Americans were preoccupied with one glaring defect that government had evidenced during the war. The congress of the confederation had the authority to borrow money or to request it from the states, but it had no power to levy taxes. To finance the military in the recently completed war, the government had therefore resorted to a variety of borrowing schemes, all of which increased the money supply and raised prices. The memories of dislocation and hardships caused by that wartime inflation—in effect, a form of taxation—were still fresh in many minds. In addition, a number of contemporary events causing concern were being attributed to the confederation. Foreign powers were playing the individual states off against one another, and the confederation gave the chagrined citizens no collective arrangement to resist. Shay's rebellion in western Massachusetts, although unsuccessful, convinced many of the "law-and-order" set of the period that stronger powers should be available to resist such anarchy.

When the constitutional convention convened in 1787 there was no initial agreement as to whether the delegates had met merely to patch up weaknesses in the Articles of Confederation or to devise a completely new government. The question was answered de facto, if not directly. The convention developed into a sequence of compromises and innovations which, when specified in the Constitution, established the outline of the new government. Historians have since spent considerable time conjecturing about and debating over what the participants in the convention were up to. It is not clear whether they themselves knew; that is, it is unlikely that they had given much thought beforehand to the specific issues which the proceedings of the convention threw out to them. The question of the background and motivation of the delegates is an interesting one, but it is probably not the most important one to ask about the Constitution. Its aftereffects on the economy were more important—and were, to a large degree, divorced from its origin. Intentions, no matter how benevolent, are frequently not realized. Those which are implemented often produce unexpected and even contrary results. The delegates, who came together to rectify the perceived faults of the confederation, left after bravely structuring an untried government to supersede it. It was a whole new ball game, but since it brought in an entirely new set of rules, players, and paying spectators, it was not immediately clear that it was a better ball game.

The changeover from the condederation to the Constitution obviously affected most parts of the economy. With some thought and considerable effort we could trace out the net impact on each individual sector. But we can make a suggestive approximation if we examine the four areas—public goods, international trade, domestic trade, and monetary matters—where the switch from one form of government to the other had its greatest impact. One clear advantage of the Constitution was its giving to the national government the *explicit* power of taxation. Taxes are not necessarily a virtue; governments have been known to abuse them. But under the confederation the costs of government could be financed only through the devious procedures of borrowing and printing money. Since the confederation had been prohibited from levying taxes, and therefore the money could never be redeemed nor the bonds repaid, those assets rapidly depreciated in value. The purchasing power which slipped away from the individuals who owned them financed the Revolution. It worked as an ad hoc system of tax collection, but it imposed extra costs on the exchange mechanism and decision processes of the economy that direct taxes would not have done. Score one for the Constitution.

When issues concerning international trade arose, the delegates, still feeling the recent cuffs from foreign governments, were determined to prevent any such recurrences. Thus the Constitution prohibited the states from exercising (their relatively weak) control over international trade and reserved all such authority to the stronger, centralized hand of the federal government. Ironically, no matter how much these new regulations bolstered the Americans' collective ego, they reduced their net economic welfare. The British and other aggressive national powers had been doing the Americans a favor by squeezing concessions on imports from them. When a nation buys imports in a competitive world market—that is, when its buying power is not large enough to affect world prices—tariffs on the imports reduce its available economic output. The higher costs borne by domestic consumers exceed the gains to protected local producers. Characteristically, Americans have purchased their imports in markets approximating competition, so that these regulations have reduced economic welfare ever since.

But the Constitution limited this power to imports. As a concession, to win the support of the Southern states, any constraints on exports from the United States were prohibited. And in the perverse way that well-intentioned edicts so often turn out, it was in exports that Americans could have used tariffs to improve their welfare. A large part of our sales abroad have been in categories, such as tobacco, cotton, and commercial jet transports, where American output constituted a large part of the world market. Here optimal export taxes[2] could be applied to exploit this market position and increase the total quantity of output available to the economy. Score one for staying with the confederation.

Discussion of international trade naturally overlapped aspects of domestic trade, and here some troubling events had occurred. Although their incidence was still minor, individual states had imposed some restrictions on products entering from other states. The most publicized example was New York's tariff on imported agricultural products, a particularly incongruous law because natural waterways linked New York City with the farmlands of Connecticut and New Jersey into a natural market area. Removing such maleficent powers from the states would seem to have been an attribute of the Constitution much like the elimination of tariffs on goods in competitive international markets produces a net gain. But the Constitution did not stop there. In prohibiting such actions by individual states it reserved them to the federal government. That has since allowed the growth of a series of regulations and regulatory bodies which, although originally conceived to foster competition, had developed into cartel coordinators

---

[2] Optimal tariffs are a complex topic, expounded adequately only by a series of graduate seminars in international economics. But basically they consist of a tax on items in which the nation has some monopolistic power in foreign trade and accompanying taxes and redistributions in the domestic economy to offset the losses.

to suppress it instead. It is not clear whether New York's tariffs on imported tomatoes or the ICC's control of freight rates is symptomatic of the worst behavior. In the absence of an inning-by-inning score, we will call this sector a tie.

In any case, by this point the delegates began to recognize that they were devising, de facto, a new government. Naturally they asked how the important monetary sector would fit into the scheme. The delegates were showing reluctance to delegate power over economic affairs to states. No doubt the behavior of some of the colonies in issuing large quantities of state currency, thus depreciating its value, reinforced this tendency. Therefore, the Constitution prohibited the states from designating anything other than gold or silver coin as legal tender and from issuing their own paper currency. It also reserved to the federal government the right to mint coins.

Some writers have hailed these actions as unifying the nation into a single marketplace, bringing with it all the gains from specialization and exchange that such a consolidation would imply. Clearly, widening markets have been a source of such benefits in the history of the American economy. It does not follow from that, however, that a nationwide market in market services would have been an improvement over existing arrangements in 1790—or in any other period, for that matter. In fact, at least up to the Civil War, the historical record suggests that it would have been worse. Markets can be too large in that the added transaction, information, and transportation costs from the larger dimensions can exceed the marginal returns from specialization. Participating economic units, either buyers or sellers, find it in their self-interest to divide such markets into regional, or local, entities. Consumers can make their purchases more cheaply from local than from national suppliers, and naturally they tend to do so. (Producers are prodded by analogous incentives.) A national market for credit of any significance did not develop until after the Civil War. Most individuals used private bank notes rather than federal currency until 1863, and switched then only because Congress placed a prohibitive tax on private issue. In the period immediately after 1790, monetary markets of national scope would have been a costly undertaking. Americans, by their collective behavior, were demonstrating that they believed they had a better way to make the most of their existing opportunities.

Even if a national monetary market had been desirable in the period around 1790, federal actions did not create (or would not have created) one. Besides prohibiting states from issuing currency, and establishing a national mint to provide coins, the only other important act emanating from the new government was an effort to monetize the national debt. Federal securities and interest obligations were to be paid in gold coin. So guaranteed for value, it was hoped the notes would circulate from hand to hand as money. The size of the national debt, however, has never responded in any useful way to the monetary requirements of the economy. It has always increased sharply during war years and generally declined slowly from peacetime budget surpluses. In the mid-1830s it disappeared entirely and the chagrined federal government redistributed surplus funds back to the states. If you need a new market, do not ask the federal government to design it for you.

Thus the government did not develop any monetary markets to supplement existing ones and it restricted such options available to other groups. Credit one to the passive, but at least not counterproductive, confederation. Final score: confederation two, Constitution one, and one tie. Not bad for the disparaged underdog.

One could easily extend the list of new institutions established by the Constitution and the new government which have been alleged to have aided America's subsequent development—the national bank, the patent laws, the court system. . . . Each may have contributed somewhat. No analytic evaluations have been published yet. The justification for a specific institution's importance, however, usually assumes that alternative channels were less attractive or were not available and—crucially—that substitutes would not have been developed elsewhere in the economy. Furthermore, the possible offsetting costs arising from rigidities in the structure of the acclaimed institution are also commonly ignored. So far, most of the harrahs for the Constitution have merely been assertions of its virtues. Its net contribution to American economic life, however, depends on an evaluation of how much better it worked than other arrangements might have, which people could reasonably have been expected to develop in its absence. It may have worked far better, but until we have a clear demonstration—which hardly seems possible—the weight of evidence appears to favor the skeptics.

THE NAPOLEONIC WAR PERIOD, 1790–1812

In the summer of 1789 the most frequent topics of conversation among Americans were, as usual, the weather, the price of corn, and the difficulty of obtaining reliable help. The newspapers gave coverage—and exchanges in village stores occasionally turned to—the adoption of the Constitution, the election of Washington as first president, and the establishment of the routine functions of the new government. Most Americans had also heard of the Revolution in France, although except for some intellectuals who heralded it as a harbinger of worldwide democracy, few spent much time discussing it. Ironically, that "small disturbance across the large ocean" was to have far more impact on the American economy for the next twenty years than its new government was, and was to dramatically affect the price of corn and the availability of reliable help.

The conflict beginning with the Revolution spread, embroiling most of Europe in what is now commonly called the Napoleonic Wars. It also overflowed the confines of Europe and seized the attention of the Americans when its effects began appearing in their port cities. European nations financed most of their wartime expenses by borrowing, so domestic prices in their respective economies increased. Warfare disrupted food production and imports from traditional nearby sources, so food prices increased. Military operations commandeered some commercial vessels, destroyed others, and harassed still others out of their traditional supply routes, so shipping rates also increased. And the Americans, finding these higher prices very remunerative, eagerly moved into the role of suppliers.

Europe's most pressing demands, for agricultural goods and ocean transportation, fortuitously dovetailed with America's most productive capabilities. The spur to ocean shipping was particularly welcomed, as that sector had been in the doldrums since the War for Independence. These added demands for domestic goods and services had widespread effects in the economy, reaching all the way back from the port cities to some of the least accessible farms. With a few interruptions, almost all the nation experienced exceptional prosperity in the period from 1790–1810. Contemporary accounts were filled with references to flourishing trade, new fortunes, and busy harbors. Some of America's finest architectural landmarks, such as Chestnut Street in Salem, Massachusetts and Nathaniel Russell's house in Charleston, have remained as memorials to that affluent era.

In one sense, however, the prosperity was not universal. Because it arrived through commercial trading channels it stimulated the monetized, exchange segments of the economy at the expense of the self-sufficient areas. Farmers increased the percentage of their crops that they sold, but then bought—rather than made for themselves—a larger proportion of their household items. Crafts workers, merchants, and shippers tended to become more specialized in either products or locations and cut down on some of the wide range of activities they had typically engaged in previously. Major urban centers, where specialized activities naturally congregated, grew much faster than rural areas during this period. The proportion of the population in cities of more than 2,500 increased from 5.4 percent in 1790 to 7.8 percent in 1810. While these values appear small, they indicate a percentage growth of more than 50 percent. The three largest cities in 1810, all Atlantic seaports, grew especially rapidly. While the national population grew by 80 percent, Philadelphia expanded by 120 percent, Baltimore by 175 percent, and New York by 190 percent.

Napoleon's prosperity came to America in two basic forms: an increase in the demand for shipping services, and an increase in the demand for agricultural products. The worldwide increase in the demand for shipping opened up opportunities for the Americans in several ways. As a neutral nation their ships were not, at least in principle, subject to attack and capture by the warring nations. Some combatants found it advantageous, indeed sometimes necessary, to allow the Yankees into trade previously prohibited to them.

One special variant of this role of neutral trader was that of the reexport trade. American ships were nominally free from attack, but because the goods they carried obviously came from, or were destined for, one of the warring nations, they received considerable harassment from their respective opponents. One way to minimize such badgering was to reduce the provocative visibility of the cargo. Products destined for Europe were often detoured to America. There they were mixed with domestic products, repackaged, issued new shipping papers, and generally disguised as native exports. Then they were sent on their way to their intended destination, smugly camouflaged as neutral American goods. The tactic was so successful that in some years during these two decades the quantity of reexports exceeded the volume of domestically produced exports (see Figure 4-1). Naturally this additional activity contributed to the general prosperity by keeping stevedores, coopers, and merchants—as well as American shipping—busy.

The demand for American shipping also appeared in the form of a reduction in the percentage of American foreign trade carried in foreign vessels. Measured by value, Americans carried 40 percent of their foreign commerce in 1790, 80 percent in 1793, and more than 90 percent in 1805 and 1807. This larger share of the shipping market came on top of an approximate fivefold gain in total shipping activity. Thus, in its best years, Americans were providing about ten times as many shipping services as they had in the period just before.

The period from 1793–1807 was particularly prosperous. The only interruption came in 1803 when the European conflict momentarily eased and the demand for shipping fell accordingly. A far more serious disruption coincided with the end of the best years in 1807. Both the French and the English, but especially the latter, continued to harass American vessels throughout the Napoleonic War. Reaching a point of exasperation, Thomas Jefferson embargoed all United States foreign trade. His rationale was that if other nations would not respect our ships we would punish them by ceasing to trade with them. This stopped the harassment, but also a sizeable part of the American economy. Unemployment, almost unheard of for the previous fifteen years, increased dramatically. Farm prices fell, ships were laid up, and port storefronts were covered with foreclosure and bankruptcy notices. Fourteen months later Jefferson rescinded his misguided measure.

Europe's misfortunes from 1790 to 1810 unquestionably rebounded to America's benefit. In the absence of warfare among the Europeans, American output and incomes would have been less. The conflict offered the Americans the chance to keep some of their most productive resources busy and they made the best of the opportunities confronting them. Higher incomes for the present—that is, until the Europeans settled their differences—were certainly an asset to the United States. The wars and the windfall gain they brought with them inevitably ended, however. It is only natural to ask, then, what long-term effects they had

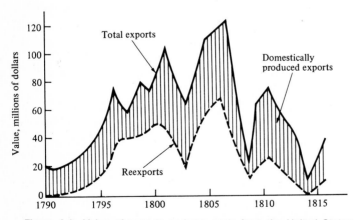

Figure 4-1 Value of exports and reexports from the United States 1790–1815. *(Source: Douglass C. North, The Economic Growth of the United States, 1790–1860, Prentice-Hall, Englewood Cliffs, 1961, p. 26. Reprinted by permission of Prentice-Hall, Inc.)*

on the American economy. One is tempted to quickly expound the concrete achievements during the period: new piers and buildings, an expanded and improved road system, an increased stock of other forms of capital, accumulated experience, and wider market areas. Some, but not necessarily all, of these acquisitions could augment the future capacity of the economy. Each of the investment commitments, whether in physical capital, people, or new knowledge, that was made during the Napoleonic War period emerged from the conditions prevailing in that period. When those wars, and thus their influence on economic decisions, ended, the investments which Americans then found feasible shifted dramatically. Ships, piers, warehouses, which were obviously attractive to construct during the time of intense demand for shipping services, were shunned when it ceased. Existing facilities were used, when possible, but no new facilities were constructed to replace them as they wore out. The stock of maritime capital was whittled down to peacetime requirements and the war's heritage in that sector was reduced to mere memories.

The above example does not necessarily demonstrate that the wars had no lasting impact on the American economy, however. The ships, piers, warehouses had very specific functions. Given a decline in demand for their services there was little else to which they could be profitably converted. Some assets attributable to the war had more general capabilities. Traffic on roads built to carry farm produce to seaports for export could be reversed to carry settlers inland and away from the now depressed coastal economy. Improvements in brickmaking, building design, and horticulture, which developed under the impetus of war-inflated demand, could also be turned to postwar projects.

The boom in the economy probably also increased learning by doing, that type of improvement in technology which is the by-product of the level of production. The higher level of output during the period probably increased the rate of improvement in technology correspondingly. This gain would be a "one-shot" advance which would cease along with prosperity. It would, however, shift the level of all future productivity upward by the amount of this one-time gain. Of course, that advance is subject to discount. Only those parts of the improvement applicable to the postwar economy constitute net gain from the war.

UNDERLYING FORCES AT WORK

The postrevolutionary adjustment, the new government, and the wars in Europe had their effect on the American economy. Almost universally commentaries on this era emphasize these forces, although they do not agree on the exact nature or amount of their impact. In fact, these developments come to mind so easily that they tend to obscure the gradual, subtle, but more powerful forces at work in the economy. It was more than thirty years from 1783 to 1815, and even small changes each year could have accumulated into a larger change by the end of that time than a major shock to the economy could have created. An increase in average productivity of one-third of 1 percent a year—a very low rate by current standards—compounds to a gain of more than 10 percent by the end of thirty years. It would be extremely unlikely that a single external force could increase the value of the output of an economy by a net 10 percent.

There were undoubtedly a large number of gradual, unobtrusive forces at work during this time. Two of them, increases in population and productivity, played central roles in reshaping the economy, however. Today, population growth is suspect. In industrially advanced countries it is viewed as an ecological liability; in lesser-developed nations it is viewed as a dissipation of hard-won increases in output among more consumers. Most experiences of population growth, however, have coincided with periods of growing output per capita.[3] In the past, increasing population has heralded expanding opportunities, not diminished prospects. Societies have typically used some of their widening choices to expand their own numbers—an attribute sizeable numbers of individuals considered affordable then.

A look at the growth of total population during this period is illuminating. The federal census was taken each ten years beginning in 1790, when it counted 3,929,000 Americans. By 1800 the national population had increased more than 35 percent to 5,297,000. In the next ten years it grew even faster, 36 ½ percent to 7,224,000. By 1820 it had increased another 33 percent to 9,618,000. This growth is even more striking when it is broken down on an annual basis. It implies a yearly increase of 3 percent, almost all of which must have come from natural growth because there was very little immigration during that time. If the contemporary death rate was twenty per thousand inhabitants each year—it was certainly no lower than that—birth rates must have been at least fifty per thousand inhabitants annually. Such rates would be among the highest ever documented, well above the recent maximum levels of thirty to thirty-five which horrify development planners in underdeveloped countries today. Clearly most Americans were not preoccupied with establishing an all-time record when they considered the size of their family. They were responding to much more powerful forces— the forces of an expanding, labor-short economy strong enough to intrude into their private decisions on the number of their children and to influence them to increase that number to a typically large level.

A look at the composition of this growth—examining the increase by state— shows the characteristic internal shifts. Frontier areas showed dramatic gains, well above the national average. Settlement moved north and south as well as in the familiar westward direction. Northern New England, initially very sparsely populated in 1790, developed rapidly. Maine's population tripled by 1820. Vermont, the first state to be added to the original thirteen, more than doubled the number of its inhabitants. On the southern frontier, the rapid expansion of cotton farming initiated a large movement into the up country. South Carolina's population doubled and Georgia's increased more than fourfold in the thirty-year period.

The western frontier showed the largest relative gains. (See Table 4-1.) In 1820 there were nearly 1,200,000 inhabitants of the East South Central region

---

[3] Simon Kuznets, *Six Lectures on Economic Growth,* Free Press, New York, 1959.

Table 4-1   Population for States: 1790—1820

	1820	1810	1800	1790
East North Central	792,719	272,324	51,000	
Ohio	581,434	230,760	45,365[1]	
Indiana	147,178	24,520[2]	5,641[2]	
Illinois	55,211	12,282[3]		
Michigan	8,896[4]	4,762[4]		
Wisconsin				
West North Central	66,586	19,783		
Minnesota				
Iowa				
Missouri	66,586	19,783		
East South Central	1,190,489	708,590	335,407	109,368
Kentucky	564,317	406,511	220,955	73,677
Tennessee	422,823	261,727	105,602	35,691
Alabama	127,901	9,046[5]	1,250[5]	
Mississippi	74,448	31,306[6]	7,600[6]	
West South Central	167,680	77,618		
Arkansas	14,273	1,062		
Louisiana	153,407	76,556		

[1] Territory northwest of the Ohio River.

[2] 1810 includes population of area separated in 1816; 1800 includes 3,124 persons in those portions of Indiana Territory which were taken from Michigan and Illinois Territories in 1805 and 1809, respectively, and that portion which was separated in 1816.

[3] Illinois Territory.

[4] Michigan Territory as then constituted; boundaries changed in 1816, 1818, 1834, and 1836.

[5] Those parts of Mississippi Territory now in the present state.

[6] Those parts of the present state included in the Mississippi Territory as then constituted.

Source: Adapted from U.S. Bureau of the Census, *Historical Statistics of the United States, Colonial Times to 1957*, U.S. Government Printing Office, Washington, D.C., 1960, p. 13.

(Kentucky, Tennessee, Alabama, and Mississippi). In 1790 there had been less than 110,000 in Kentucky and Tennessee together. In 1820 there were nearly 800,000 residents of the East North Central region (enclosing Ohio, Indiana, and Illinois). In 1790 there had been too few to justify an official report. Altogether there were more than 2 million people west of the Appalachian Mountains in 1820, more than 20 percent of the nation's populace.

Among the established states along the Atlantic coast, population growth varied considerably. The number of Pennsylvania's residents increased more than two and one-half times while New York's population quadrupled. Both these states extended far enough into the interior so that their western regions were just being settled during this period. In addition, each possessed a large, rapidly growing port city. Both New York City and Philadelphia had passed the 100,000 mark by 1820. Other areas, such as the southern states of New England

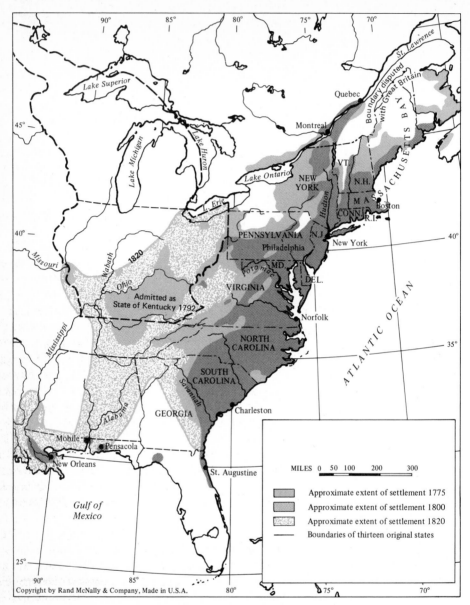

Figure 4-2 *(Source: R. R. Palmer (ed.),* Historical Atlas of the World, *Rand McNally and Company, New York, 1965, p. 20. Copyright © 1970 by Rand McNally and Company, Chicago, and reprinted by permission of Rand McNally College Publishing Company.)*

(Massachusetts, Connecticut, and Rhode Island) and the northern states of the older South (Virginia, Maryland, and Delaware) experienced only modest growth. Some of their major products—tobacco in the upper South, and the diverse collection of crops found in the generalized agriculture of southern New

England—were meeting intensifying competition from other suppliers. Understandably some of the residents of these areas found other, faster-growing regions of the country more attractive and migrated to them. Naturally, these two regions then grew more slowly than others and their natural population growth became less than would otherwise have been indicated. Even in this early, generally prosperous period of American history, the pressures of growth were at work, pushing resources toward uses perceived as the most productive and withdrawing them from products society now designated as expendable.

GROWTH IN PROGRESS

Explosive population growth was one indication that America was experiencing economic growth from 1790 to 1820. There are a large number of other qualitative manifestations of improving technology, also, so that the case for increasing productivity and rising incomes in the period is very persuasive. Unfortunately, however, aggregate measures of income or productivity are not available for this time span. It is unlikely that enough basic information—the raw material from which such estimates could be constructed—is obtainable. Nevertheless, the daily work-a-day activities of the Americans provided numerous examples of the spread of improved techniques.

Around 1800 there was not much activity in the United States that could be classified as formal R&D—the specialized, organized search for new knowledge. The agricultural improvement societies, formed between 1767 and 1811, came closest to that function. Their membership tended to be restricted to wealthy farmers, merchants, and professional men, including such luminaries as President Washington. The societies collected, disseminated, and encouraged efforts to develop new information about farming methods. Some of their efforts were dissipated into—for that time—misguided recommendations to farm managers. For example, they advocated deep plowing, crop rotation, application of fertilizers, and other comparable advice implied by their vision of what constituted efficient farming. They made the common mistake of equating economic efficiency with contemporary, but capital-intensive, technology. While such methods would raise the output from a given average, they would not provide as much increment as comparable effort would in bringing more land into (nonintensive) production.

Other activities of the agricultural societies were much more productive, however. They encouraged their members to experiment with livestock, crops, and farming methods, and to report their findings. Members discussed current work and aided each other in planning experiments. Prizes were frequently given for the best efforts on an issue of particular concern. The societies published journals of their findings and disseminated those results widely through local newspapers and pamphlets. From them, American farmers learned such things as how to exterminate the Hessian fly, what new farm implements had been developed, and what new varieties of clovers, hay, grasses, and fruit trees had become available.

Local newspapers were anxious to print reports from the agricultural societies because some of their agrarian readers were anxious to read them. During this period the farmers' patronage was also instrumental in establishing what has since become an American tradition, the county fair. Starting in 1811 in Pittsfield, Massachusetts, such gatherings rapidly became ubiquitous yearly occurrences in rural America. Like most fairgoers in any age, the farm families went to see the color and the contests and to listen to the patter of the pitchmen. But they also brought their best animals, fruits, vegetables, and handicrafts, hoping to best their neighbors for the prizes offered. As they strolled by the exhibits they pondered how they could put to use on their farms all they saw and learned and how they might produce next year's winning entry.

This quickening interest in new developments in agricultural techniques suggests that farm families were finding such knowledge useful. The pattern bears a close resemblance to the activity in English agriculture in the last half of the eighteenth century, just before this era. There the wide diffusion and interest in agricultural innovations coincided with rapid improvements in productivity. It seems plausible to assume that when substantial numbers of a population engage in an activity they must find it worthwhile, and the developing network for encouraging and reporting new agricultural techniques in America strongly suggests that the opportunities and rewards for such activity were increasing. Almost certainly the annual improvements in agrarian productivity would increase also.

A new or rapidly expanding industry is a likely place in which to expect to see a high rate of productivity increase. It is usually accompanied by burgeoning demand and innovative efforts in production, which is required to adapt technology to new, specific uses. Internal transportation was obviously a rapidly expanding sector—and therefore a likely candidate for large gains in efficiency—during this period. Americans could move into the interior in large numbers only if they had some reasonable method of getting there and then of continuing to conduct trade with the established coastal areas.

During this time the countryside was busy with road-building projects. An extensive system of turnpikes was developed that connected major coastal cities and extended inland along the primary trade and migration routes. They were built by private companies under state charter with reimbursement coming from tolls, hence the name—a *pike* (pole) barring the road, and *turned* only when the required toll was paid. The network of local, or feeder, roads was also expanded and improved. Although these farm-to-market roads were neither used for, nor intended to be used for, heavy traffic, their condition would often have been judged appalling by modern standards. With no paving, they were trails of mud in rainy seasons and layers of dust in the summer. The roadbed—using the term charitably—was often merely a forest trail widened by years of use. With very little grading, it rose or twisted with every variation in the terrain. Only the most obstructive objects, such as trees or large rocks, were removed. Both Indiana and Ohio found it necessary to prohibit leaving stumps that were more than a foot and a half high in the roadbed.

Yet the roads worked. They performed the admittedly minor functions expected of them and did so with a miserly expenditure of resources. If a heavy rain made the road impassable one day, it would certainly dry out within a week. If the road was specked with rocks and stumps, a wagon with large wheels could maneuver over and around them. And while the 2 miles to the village and the beginning of the improved road was a time-consuming, tedious trip, a few such difficult excursions each year were preferable to spending several months improving a road so little used. Early road systems, like most social institutions, developed to reflect the interests of the people they served.

In early America, when a road came to a river, it simply stopped. If the water was shallow, traffic forded it. If it was deeper and business supported it, a ferry was made available—for a fee, of course. In any case, these water crossings slowed traffic and made overland commerce more expensive. Beginning in the late 1700s the growth of such trade made these bottlenecks increasingly expensive. Americans began to "think bridge," essentially in economic terms a capital investment (bridge construction) used to reduce operating costs (labor, time, and inventory size). Many of the early projects were crude, ad hoc structures of stone and timber, obviously assembled by amateurs. But as the demand for bridges grew, their design and workmanship became more professional, imaginative, and diverse. A class of professional bridge architects emerged, one of whom, James Finley, developed the basic structure now embodied in the modern suspension bridge. Many of his projects in Pennsylvania and Maryland used metal chains suspended between stone piers to support the bridge roadway. Other designers began to use iron supporting beams, and some even experimented with floating bridges. Perhaps the most noted design adopted in this age, however, was the covered bridge. Originally roofed over to keep the roadway clear and dry in winter, they have since been shown to have a special aesthetic appeal to millions of photographers and viewers of calendar reproductions.

Over these new bridges came the bizarre, heterogeneous streams of traffic which were becoming increasingly common in interior America: wagons, carts, buggies, stagecoaches, pack animals, and the Conestoga wagons, usually pulled by four to six horses, which were the most common mode of inland freight cartage. Although its distinctive silhouette has become a stereotype of pioneering on the great plains, the Conestoga wagon was a dominant freight vehicle well before the frontier reached the grasslands. It was developed in the 1780s, probably in the well-settled Pennsylvania Dutch country.

Of course, people also traveled along the roads and over the new bridges in growing numbers. When not otherwise busy as teamsters or livestock drovers, a sizeable proportion of individuals went by stagecoach. The famed Concord stage, since "subject" to thousands of robbery and Indian attacks, was not invented until 1828, but its forerunners were gradually modified and improved during this period. One major advance was the invention of the curved coach spring in 1804. This allowed for smaller wheels—now practical as major roads improved—and reduced the weight of the vehicle. To early nineteenth-century coach passengers perched 6 feet above the roadway, however, its prime virture was in mercifully reducing the sway from each bump in the roadway.

The growing road traffic demanded a parallel expansion in services for travelers. Inns were built along major routes and even at many less-traveled cross-roads. Some were welcome oases of good food and lodging after a long, bumpy, dusty day on the road. But quality varied greatly, so that often, in those days before the AAA and the Mobil Travel Guide, a traveler found the stopover as uncomfortable as the journey. Stables were commonly erected nearby, and beyond them frequently were the animal pens, where livestock drovers could buy food and water for their charges and a night's reprieve for themselves.

SUGGESTED READINGS

Bjork, Gordon C.: "The Weaning of the American Economy: Independence, Market Changes and Economic Development," *Journal of Economic History,* vol. 24, December 1964. See also the accompanying comments by Albert Fishlow.

Jensen, Merrill: *The New Nation: A History of the United States during the Confederation, 1781–1789,* Knopf, New York, 1950.

Nettles, Curtis P.: *The Emergence of the National Economy, 1775–1815,* Holt, New York, 1962.

North, Douglass C.: *The Economic Growth of the United States, 1790–1860,* Prentice-Hall, Englewood Cliffs, N.J., 1961.

Westward Expansion to 1860

When the Europeans formally recognized the independence of the United States in 1783, they naturally looked upon the new nation as a far-ranging entity. It comprised all the present-day eastern third of the United States from the Atlantic coast to the Mississippi River (except for Florida), or about as far as from Berlin to Moscow. Furthermore, there were only 4 million inhabitants in all this space, most of them clustered along the Atlantic coast. There was 600 miles of wilderness between the frontier outpost of Pittsburgh and the Mississippi River, a distance equal to that between London and Berlin.

One might have expected that this large area would have contained the Americans' economy for a long time to come. After all, had it not taken several centuries for the Europeans to settle and develop their own (smaller) regions during the Middle Ages? Those expectations were badly out of date, however. The forces causing change and geographical expansion had quickened considerably in the preceding years and America's original borders could not enclose the geographical limits of its economy for long. The potential rewards from adjacent, unappropriated territory were growing so rapidly that political expansion would soon be irresistible. In 1803, only twenty years after independence, the Louisiana Purchase was negotiated.

This rapid expansion was primarily caused by substantial gains in transportation efficiency. (These will be discussed in more detail later.) To individuals living at that time the most suggestive indicator of such a change would appear when they traveled or shipped goods; the bill for transportation services was going down. This made it feasible to ship items farther than before. Within a given area it encouraged the interchange of a wider range of goods. And it allowed the shipment of products into or out of previously unsettled areas—the pushing back of the frontier.

This transition is illustrated in Figure 5-1 where D_B is the demand at some distant location, say Boston, for a good which can be produced in what was initially a frontier region, say Ohio. S is the supply curve of the product in Ohio, while S_B is the supply curve of that product delivered in Boston. The vertical distance between S_B and S expresses the cost of delivering the product to Boston, or the average freight charge per unit. In Figure 5-1, S_B exceeds D for all quantities, which means that it is not feasible to send any products to Boston from Ohio under these circumstances. If this situation is typical for all products in Ohio, there is very little reason for anyone to settle or develop the area.

Suppose, however, that transportation costs are substantially reduced, such as by the opening of the Erie Canal and as shown by the downward shift of S_B to S_B'. This reduces the price at which goods can be feasibly delivered at Boston. Middlemen now begin to find it profitable to purchase, ship, and generally mobilize such goods from Ohio for the New England market. Consumers in Boston begin to purchase some of the goods as they discover that they are competitive with established supplies in their locality.

Meanwhile, the development of this export trade has created a new source of income for resources in Ohio. This is illustrated in Figure 5-2, which contains the same supply curve, S, isolated from Figure 5-1 for the sake of clarity. Q' is the quantity of the product exported from Ohio and P' is the net unit price which suppliers in Ohio receive for it. (The difference between P_B and P' in Figure 5-1 is the portion of the Boston selling price received by the transportation sector.) The total revenue received by the Ohio producers is therefore represented by P' times Q'. Of this amount, the part "under" the supply curve labeled a is the

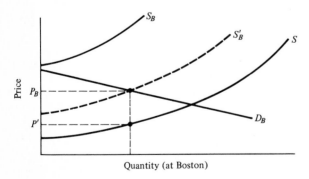

Quantity (at Boston)

Figure 5-1

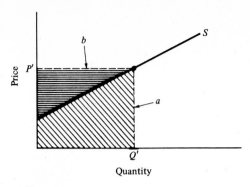

Figure 5-2

remuneration necessary to secure production of the amount Q'. It represents the opportunity cost of the resources used in this production and is the minimum payment necessary to command their employment away from alternative uses. In the case of the early development of Ohio, for example, these payments would be primarily to labor and capital, as these are the basic attractions which bring immigrants and investments into the region.

The area b between the supply curve and the level of the price P' is the economic rent resulting from this line of production. It represents extra—or greater than necessary—payments to resources particularly productive in this specific line of production. In this example of Ohio, these payments would go primarily to land. That is the input which cannot be increased by the importation of similar resources even when the payments for its use exceed its opportunity cost. The extra returns become capitalized, or captured, in the price of land and thus become a measure of the net value of the region, abstracting from the value of any mobile resources which could be moved into or out of the locality.

The area b, therefore, represents the direct economic gain in acquiring a new area at any given time. From 1790 on those values for most regions within or next to the United States experienced a long-term increase. Rising incomes and population tended to pull the demand curves up, and improving technology worked to push the supply curves of locally produced goods down, all of which expanded the respective b area. Regions which had been beyond the frontier and unsettled in 1790, because their net economic value was zero at that time, later became feasible for development and settlement. Potential immigrants and landowners in the established United States naturally took notice and very soon, in turn, their government did also.

THE ECONOMICS OF TERRITORIAL ACQUISITION

The science of economics has not yet provided us with a good explanation of how economic interests influence the behavior of a society's basic institutions. We cannot, for example, place much confidence these days in our prediction about the response of the government to an increase in the price of coal. To go one

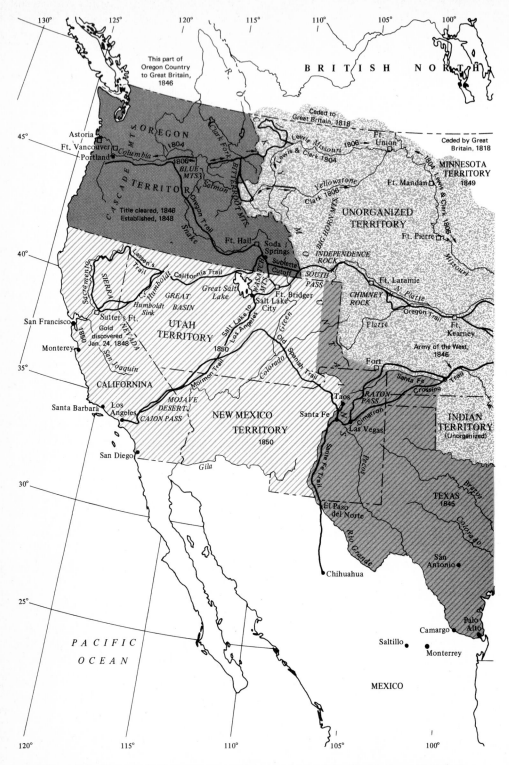

Figure 5-3 *(Source: R. R. Palmer (ed.),* Historical Atlas of the World, *Rand McNally and and reprinted by permission of Rand McNally College Publishing Company.)*

95° 90° 85° 80° 75° 70° 65°

A M E R I C A

Quebec

Boundary
adjusted
with
Great Britain,
1842

MAINE
1820

Montreal

St. Lawrence

45°

Lake
Superior

VT.

N.H.

Ft. Snelling

Louisiana Purchase, 1803

M I C H I G A N

Lake
Huron

NEW
YORK

Boston

Hudson

WISCONSIN
1848

Lake Michigan

MASS.

1837

CONN.

Lake Ontario

Buffalo

R.I.

Detroit

Lake Erie

IOWA
1846

Milwaukee

40°

New York

Chicago

INDIANA

OHIO

Philadelphia

Ft. Arkinson

1816

Pittsburgh

N.J.

Mormon Trail

1803

Baltimore

Nauvoo

Road

DEL.

St.
Joseph

ILLINOIS

MD.

Ft. Leavenworth

1818

Cumberland

Washington

Independence

St. Louis

Cincinnati

Council
Grove

Ohio

Louisville

VIRGINIA

35°

MISSOURI
1821

KENTUCKY

A P P A L A C H I A N

Arkansas

Cumberland

ARKANSAS
1836

TENNESSEE

NORTH CAROLINA

Ft. Smith

Mississippi

Tennessee

SOUTH
CAROLINA

A T L A N T I C

Red

O C E A N

MISSISSIPPI
1817

ALABAMA
1819

GEORGIA

Charleston

30°

Sabine

LOUISIANA

1810

1813

1812

New Orleans

West Florida
seized

FLORIDA
1845

Annexed
1819–1821

Galveston

85°

80°

75°

G U L F   O F

WESTWARD EXPANSION 1800–1850

0   50 100   200   300   400

M E X I C O

	U.S. Territory 1783	IOWA 1846	States admitted 1800–1850
	Louisiana Purchase, 1803		Western Trails
	Texas, 1845		Railroads of 1850
	Oregon Country		Major Canals of 1850
	Mexican Cession, 1848		

95° 90°

complicating step further, we cannot now specify how changes in the economic system cause adaptations in society's institutions. Our understanding has been aided somewhat in recent years by some imaginative efforts on the question,[1] but the basic relationship remains elusive and unspecified. It will certainly enhance our ability to explain the past when such a framework is developed. At any time one might treat the structure of social institutions as given and work out the consequences of economic change in isolation. Over the longer term—and that perspective encompasses most of the important questions in economic history— institutions can no longer be considered exogenous. Governments, businesses, and the other arrangements society uses to mobilize resources, themselves become variables which must be adapted to the broader shifts in the system.

The federal government of the United States is an obvious example. The size and nature of its major functions have changed dramatically since its founding in 1789. Certainly one of the primary forces behind that metamorphosis has been the growth and development of the economy with which it was linked. The aspect of this transformation that interests us here is the geographical expansion of the country. (See Figure 5-3.) Almost everyone knows that a westward migration of the American population occurred, because everyone is familiar with the stereotypes associated with that moment—covered wagons, cattle drives, Indian raids, and so forth. Very few people, however, have critically asked *why* the existing American government was extended to incorporate the new areas. Most people have simply assumed that there was cheap, empty land to the west and, therefore, Americans naturally settled on it, bringing their government with them.

It was not that simple. The land had never been entirely uninhabited. And while it may have been cheap in terms of the selling price per acre—at least until major settlement began—it was not a bargain in terms of the returns obtainable from it. Finally, there was no reason that the American government was required to take over its administration. It could have remained under the colonial rule of various European powers, or been annexed to a neighboring state such as Canada or Mexico, or adopted the solution which Texas tried for a while, and become an independent nation. These options were never adopted, and the very fact that they were not tells us something about the considerations shaping institutional arrangements in these new lands.

Ever since Columbus, various European powers—England, France, Spain, Holland, and Russia—had claimed areas that are now included within the United States. In the early years these claims tended to be ill defined, meagerly justified, and frequently in conflict with one another. This vagueness began to disappear as exploration, settlement, and adjudication of claims matched each area more precisely with its owners. All these refinements were the results of a more basic trend, namely, that the areas in question were generally becoming more productive. As with any other resource, as land became more expensive it was investigated more fully, used (or settled) more intensely, and the general

---

[1] Lance E. Davis and Douglass C. North, *Institutional Change and American Economic Growth*, Cambridge, New York, 1971.

rules defining its use—property rights—were defined more carefully. In other words, as the benefits obtainable from an area increased, it tended to move from a state of ambiguous common property to one of well-specified operation. This type of transition can be seen in the areas that were incorporated into the United States during the first seventy years (1790–1860) after independence.

During the 1790s large numbers of Americans moved westward through the Cumberland Gap into what is now Kentucky and Tennessee. The migration developed so rapidly that the former was qualified to be admitted as a state in 1792 and the latter in 1796. This rapid settlement was prompted by the availability of good farmland in the central zones of these two states, land which at that time was much more productive than most of the undeveloped acreage east of the Appalachian Mountains.

The advantages of the soil per se, however, were dampened by the relative inaccessibility of the region to the established markets. The only form of direct commerce with the eastern seaboard was over the mountains by wagon or pack animals, which was so expensive that only high-valued products were carried by that route. A cheaper, but more roundabout path, was to use the water transportation provided by the extensive river systems in the interior of the continent. Most of these funneled into the Mississippi River which provided an outlet to ocean transportation at New Orleans. That city, however, was not controlled by the United States at that time, a factor which turned the simple economics of transportation into an aspect of political economy.

The Louisiana Purchase, 1803

For most of the period between its exploration by white men and 1800, the land to the west of the Mississippi River—then commonly known as Louisiana—was controlled by the French. They had not settled the area extensively, however, and there were only two areas of note—the trading center at St. Louis and the sugar-cane region along the lower Mississippi, established by 1800. In fact, until 1800, the territory of Louisiana had been treated much like an item in a pawnshop; that is, as being valuable—and hence useful as collateral—but as having little current return to its owners. In 1762, the French had bartered Louisiana to the Spanish in a treaty package. In 1800, in another settlement, it was given back. This latter development bothered the Americans—especially those living west of the Appalachians—because they knew the French had more military muscle to back up their position than the departing Spanish had. France had effective control over the only economic trading channel for the (then) western United States, and hence over its prospects for development. She was in a position to extract all the economic rent, or net gain, that the Americans could receive from developing the trans-Appalachian West.

In 1803, President Jefferson sent a delegation to Paris to negotiate the purchase of—or, if necessary, merely the right of—unencumbered transit through New Orleans. The American representatives were authorized to offer up to $10 million for the passageway to the Gulf. The French countered by offering the entire territory of Louisiana for $15 million. Their response was entirely understandable in that if the Americans gained control of the single outlet to the ocean, then any French land west of 'the Mississippi River would be landlocked and exploitable in the same way that the American's land on the east bank of the Mississippi was when the French controlled New Orleans.

The Americans' acceptance of the offer is a standard item in accounts of the history of the nation. Most modern Americans also "know" that the agreement was a bargain for the United States—imagine acquiring a large part of the present area of the United States for only $15 million! This reading overlooks the fact that the purchase took place in 1803, however—not yesterday. The Americans may not have been so fortunate, nor, by implication, the French as naïve, as has been assumed. While the midwestern section of the United States would sell for much more than $15 million dollars *today*, even in dollars of the same purchasing power as of 1803, it probably would not have been worthwhile to buy it for that amount *in 1803* in anticipation of those future gains. After all, that would have committed resources for a very long time, and each year that passed would see the loss of opportunities to invest those resources elsewhere. And compounded, those alternative returns would be huge. For example, $15 million yielding a yearly return of 7 percent would be worth about $2 *trillion* today, and it would therefore require such a value on the unimproved land *alone* to have justified the purchase of the region in 1803. Any improvements that have been made in the land subsequently are additional resource costs that must be recognized. Obviously, a complete postmortem on the Louisiana Purchase would be more complicated than the above example suggests. Costs and benefits scattered across the intervening years, for instance, would have to be incorporated. But however the amplifications and modifications are worked in, one factor always remains dominant in such decisions: the passage of time imposes progressively larger charges against purchased territorial acquisitions. The land is usually sparsely settled when it is first acquired and some time elapses before a sizeable part of it can be effectively brought into the economy. In the meanwhile, the value of the resources sacrificed by the purchase is growing each year so that their possible alternative uses are lost. By the time substantial development has been achieved the real cost of the territory has become much larger than the initial price.

The territory of Louisiana was a prime example. After its purchase in 1803 there was no immediate rush to claim land in the area. In fact, for the next thirty years development was mostly limited to two areas—the rich, alluvial cotton and sugar land along the lower Mississippi River, and the area adjacent to the Missouri River westward from St. Louis. These patterns of settlement were simply a continuation of trends already well established before the Americans purchased the area.

Thus Americans had to wait quite a while for their investment in Louisiana—that is, the land, as distinguished from the city of New Orleans—to begin yielding returns. This should not have been surprising. In 1803, Americans had very little interest in the land west of the river because it did not appear productive. They were much more concerned about assuring free access to the Gulf of Mexico. Because they were willing to pay $10 million for that privilege, the true cost of the area that we commonly think of as the Louisiana Purchase was only $5 million. The other two-thirds of the total price was actually purchasing sovereignty for an area that was officially already a part of the nation.

In part the Americans were encouraged to purchase Louisiana by a peculiarity of geography. In the early nineneenth century, water was by far the cheapest medium of transportation. Rivers, therefore, naturally dictated the major trade network across large land areas. Thus the Mississippi River and its tributaries forged the central part of the present-day United States into a common economic region with a single outlet to the ocean and to markets elsewhere.

When the Americans started moving west over the Appalachian Mountains in the late 1700s, they were unwittingly forcing an all or nothing choice as to the administration of the entire interior. The ad hoc arrangement of two sovereign governments sharing authority over an economically unified region was headed for a crisis. The settlers probably did not realize this, at least not immediately. They were innocently taking up good farmland in what was at that time clearly a part of the United States. But they shared the trade routes which could make settlement successful with another (hostile) jurisdiction. Because the potential number of Americans who could benefit from the area greatly exceeded that of the French, it was logical for the Americans to take over control of the entire interior. This is what the Louisiana Purchase represented in economic terms. The Americans found it worthwhile to buy out the French, while the French found it worthwhile to sell out rather than pay to develop the wild and distant area they held west of the Mississippi.

Florida, 1810–1819

While the Louisiana Purchase expanded the American border well to the west, enough to take care of the aspirations of American settlers in that direction for the next several decades, another chunk of real estate controlled by a foreign power stood directly in the path of American migration. At the turn of the century (1800) Spain owned "Spanish Florida," which included all the present-day state of that name plus an extension called "West Florida," a narrow strip which ran westward along the Gulf Coast all the way to the Mississippi River. Today West Florida is subsumed within the state of Louisiana (the portion lying east of the Mississippi River) and the southernmost extensions of the states of Mississippi and Alabama. It was this part of Spanish-held Florida which was attractive—indeed was becoming a roadblock—to development by the Americans in the early 1800s. The land of eastern Louisiana, especially around Baton Rouge, would very soon be producing good crops of sugar and cotton. Mobile Bay, where the Alabama River reached the Gulf, controlled access to the excellent cotton lands of central Alabama. Spanish ownership of this outlet retarded the development of that land in the same way that French ownership of New Orleans had retarded economic activity in the Mississippi basin.

There would be very immediate benefits to the Americans, then, from gaining this territory. Spain's relative weakness as a military power in the area made the task easier, and much less expensive, than the acquisition of Louisiana, where the formidable French had to be bought out. Many Americans argued that the part of West Florida included in present-day Louisiana had already been acquired in the Louisiana Purchase—borders had not been carefully specified. When some of the local Spanish subjects rebelled against the local officials of their Empire, the Americans simply annexed the area by an act of Congress. Spain offered no response beyond muted complaints. In the War of 1812, Andrew Jackson, in a display of the individual initiative that propelled him into national prominence (he was disobeying a directive of the President), seized the remainder of West Florida and the Spanish fort at Pensacola in East Florida as well. After the war the Americans gave Pensacola back, but retained all of West Florida. It was one of the least expensive and most brazen acquisitions in American history and it illustrated a cardinal law of international relations: when one nation has a major military advantage over another, it creates a strong, often irresistible temptation for the stronger to use that advantage to achieve its aims. In short, why bargain with the Spanish when it was much easier to push them out? In 1819 the Spanish accepted $5 million for East Florida and pulled back into Latin America.

Meanwhile, Back at the Economy

By now it would appear that the economic development of the nation was shaping its territorial acquisitions. Thus, a brief pause to consider how the economy was evolving in this period should provide some illumination about the changes in its borders.

When the War of 1812 ended in 1815, four states west of the Appalachians, Kentucky, Tennessee, Ohio, and Louisiana, were members of the Union. Ohio had been admitted in 1803; the southern part of the state bordering the Ohio River had already been settled by the same migration that filled in Kentucky and northern Tennessee. Louisiana was one of the few areas which already had a sizeable non-Indian population when it was acquired by the United States. The additional influx of American planters after 1803 soon made it qualified for statehood, which was granted in 1812.

Thus the "American West" was clearly a growing area in the years immediately before the War of 1812. The conditions propelling that expansion were repressed but not altered by the war so that, when hostilities ended, expansion picked up again. An unusually high price for cotton caused farmers in the South to buy large areas of land and to begin to develop them into cotton acreage. Sizeable regions were settled all across the South: central Georgia, central and northern Alabama, Mississippi, western Tennessee, and eastern Arkansas. Mississippi was admitted as a state in 1817 and Alabama in 1819. Another pattern of expansion followed the river system to the North. Again the primary objective was agricultural land, but in this case it was based on corn, pork, and small grains. In the decade after the end of the war, the parts of southern Indiana and Illinois that bordered the Ohio River were settled, as was Missouri where it bordered the Mississippi and Missouri Rivers. A rudimentary specialization began to emerge in this area. Cincinnati grew to be the largest city by virtue of the meat-packing operations which concentrated there. It processed the region's pork output that was destined for export to distant markets. It was commonly packed in salt brine, in barrels, a process that both economized on transportation costs and was one of the best-known methods of preservation of that day. One of the important factors that caused this development at this time was the introduction of the shallow-bottomed steamboat. Its appearance substantially reduced the cost of transportation over the rivers, "the highway system" around which this area was developing. (We will examine this development in more detail later.) The influx of new states into the Union in this period gives an indication of how rapid the expansion was. Mississippi was admitted in 1817 and Alabama in 1819. In the North, Indiana was admitted in 1816, followed by Illinois in 1818 and Missouri in 1821.

Texas, 1821–1845

In 1821, an American named Moses Austin obtained a charter to settle in the Gulf plain in what is now the state of Texas. This was foreign territory to Austin's group and to the other Americans that followed them. In 1819, in the treaty that had obtained Florida, the United States had officially recognized the area to be the property of Spain. Spain's imperial power in the Americas, however, was falling apart at this time, and control over the area in which the Americans had settled passed to the forerunner of the present government of Mexico—New Spain. American settlers continued to come into the area until 1830, attracted by the productive land available for cotton production. But in 1830 the Mexican government stopped the immigration of any more Americans and banned slavery—then an integral part of cotton production. Over the next five years additional constraints were imposed. In 1836 the settlers openly rebelled and won their independence in a series of well-publicized encounters.

Texas was another case in which the political institutions proved to be inappropriate for the economic system that was developing within it. This time, however, unlike the Louisiana Purchase, it was not in the geographic scope of the government that the mismatch occurred. The nation of Texas could have been adequately governed by sovereign authority of Mexico's or New Spain's size, as its independence from 1836 to 1845 demonstrated. This time it was the particular set of controls imposed on the province of Texas which created the conflict. Had Mexico followed a policy of local federalism, in which the Americans in Texas effectively ruled their own territory, there would have been little motivation for revolt. But national preferences overruled the local environment. The Mexicans disliked slavery so much that they imposed a nationwide ban on it. They also (rightly) mistrusted the tendency of the immigrants to "Americanize" Texas and thus stopped any further influx of them.

One can appreciate the objectives of the Mexicans, particularly in view of commonly held views today, and yet recognize that they wreaked havoc with the prospects for economic development in the region of Texas. There was a growing distaste for slavery at that time in much of the Western world, but it was an established—and defended—fact in the economy of the Southern United States.

Texas was merely a western extension of that agricultural region, particularly the eastern section of the state that was being developed at that time. Eventually slavery was eliminated from the Southern United States, including Texas, but at a very great cost. The Texans foresaw similarly large costs in forgoing the use of slaves when they were being used in adjacent areas to produce crops directly in competition with those of the Texans.

The ban on further immigration could also have proved very expensive both for potential immigrants and for the residents already there. At that time there were large amounts of land in the area that could have been expected to be developed into profitable cotton acreage, but there was only a small amount of labor available so that new hands would have made a large contribution to the output of cotton. This would have made the area attractive to potential immigrants, such as residents of the United States, and they would have sought ways to come—such as applying pressure to their government to open up the region to them. The residents of Texas could also have gained from additional newcomers. If there were economies of scale or gains to be realized through agglomeration, the established residents could share through the reduced unit costs in such activities. For example, the added output from new farms could encourage a reorganization into larger, more efficient processing and transportation facilities for agricultural products. Additional citizens could also support more specialized consumer services and—in this the interests of the locals diverge from those of the Mexicans—provide more military and political power to protect Texan interests.

The Americans in Texas saw the likely costs of getting out of this arrangement as less than the costs of remaining in it. So they declared their independence—and successfully enforced it. It is natural to suggest that this move toward self-rule is something one might expect of Texans. After all, independence and self-assertion are reputed to be particularly strong traits of individuals in that region. There are a number of indications, however, that it was a change in circumstances rather than a special propensity to quarrel that explains their reaction. Most of us probably would have done the same thing in the circumstances. The first Texans—who were probably as fiercely individualistic as any—readily consented to live under another nation's authority. They started making noises about freedom and independence only when the host government drastically altered its treatment of them.

The Northern Border, 1812–1848

A revealing contrast had occurred just before this time on the northern border of the United States. Before the War of 1812, when western New York State was being settled, a number of American settlers had continued westward past Niagara Falls to settle in southern Ontario, then under British rule. When the war began it was assumed that these individuals would support (at least tacitly) the American cause. They did not. They were satisfied with the system in which they were living and they made no move to change it.

These cases illustrate an important fact about the role of local government in the North American experience. The local residents have had a good deal to say about the form of authority to which they will subject themselves. Usually this power has not been obvious because it has not been brandished to alter the status quo. But that probably indicates that generally the locals were able to achieve changes within the existing system or were reasonably content with the way things were. The local residents have, on occasion, demonstrated that they will use power when they believe it necessary. The step is not taken lightly, and only when the expected benefits of a different government exceed the (frequently disruptive) costs of jettisoning the existing one. This cost of shifting to a new form of government explains why the American immigrants in Ontario were not interested in annexation by the United States. They did not consider it worth the trouble that they thought the transfer might create.

This choice in Ontario illustrates why the border between the United States and Canada has been stable and peaceful from the earliest phase of development. The Americans and Canadians pushed their respective frontiers westward at about the same pace because the expansions in both nations were governed by common economic factors, and both nations were receptive to the changes in economic conditions, such as transportation, which made the Western lands attractive.

Thus the citizens of each country tended to take up their frontier land at about the time it became economically feasible, which was just the time that potential settlers in the other nation would have found it attractive also. This eliminated the reason for the citizens of either nation to look covetously over the border and nudge their own government to incorporate the other. Once an area had been settled by a society with a similar economic environment, all the potential economic rent of settlement would be dissipated and the incentive for acquisition evaporate. Thus Canada (or its British forerunner) and the United States could begin on the East Coast of North America, grow westward side by side across the continent, and then settle into peaceful coexistence. This factor explains a situation that has puzzled some observers—Americans, at least—for a long time: Why would Canada, strung out as it is along the northern American border, not find it desirable to incorporate itself as part of the United States? One can foresee gains in a consolidated market and a common system of laws, money, and government. While such advantages probably do exist, they are small in relation to what the gains of consolidation might have been if the two nations had started out with markedly different levels of economic proficiency. They did not, of course, and with the added costs of a transition the Canadians have preferred to retain their independence, thank you.

The Mexican Border, to 1853

The independent status of Texas from 1836 to 1845 suggests that the territorial ambitions of the United States were not insatiable. Throughout the period the Texans wished to be accepted into the United States as a state. One motivating factor was that the Mexicans had never officially accepted Texan independence and periodically made threatening military moves against their southern border.

They would have been much less likely to pressure Texas if it had been part of the United States. The Americans, however, resisted statehood for the same reason. They rightly saw annexation of Texas as a move that would prompt a war with Mexico. In addition, there was a growing antislave constituency in the North that feared that the admission of Texas would strengthen the slave forces nationally, perhaps by the division of the territory into four or five slave states. So for those nine years, Texas conducted its affairs much like any other independent nation, establishing diplomatic relations and commercial treaties with the major nations.

By 1845 the Americans' receptiveness to Texas' request for statehood had undergone a noticeable change. It was not so much that they saw the desirability of admitting Texas into the Union differently, but rather that that step was becoming enmeshed within a broader pattern of conditions that was unfolding on the Western frontier. About 1842, Americans began to settle in two areas in the West that were beyond the borders of the United States. One was the Willamette Valley in Oregon and the other was central California. Both of these were reached over the fabled Oregon Trail, which ran westward from the last river port at Independence, Missouri. It took the settlers a good part of a year to make the trip—at the rate of 15 to 20 miles a day in covering 1,500 miles—but the land at their destination was so good that they considered the time well invested. The promise of these areas was so good, in fact, that by 1845 the number of wagons moving west each summer was increasing dramatically. And the prospects for future migration were seen to be even better,[2] so that the American government began to take some notice of the territorial implications.

For a number of years before 1846, the United States and England had agreed to joint ownership of the Oregon Country—roughly the current states of Washington, Oregon, and Idaho. This had allowed both nations to postpone the painful process of negotiating a permanent solution for government of the region. The arrangement worked well as long as only minimal settlement, such as that for the fur trade, took place there, but in the 1840s the influx of Americans began to force the issue. The Americans and the British began to propose permanent solutions to the problem, including the one which was finally adopted in 1846, extending the existing boundary between the United States and Canada (the 49th parallel) westward to Puget Sound.

In the process of the bargaining over Oregon, the British stirred up the Americans' interest in Texas. England hoped to divert and spread out American commitments by using her influence to strengthen Texas as a buffer state on America's southern flank. The Americans responded by admitting Texas into the Union. This, in turn, aroused the ire of Mexico, but that was not entirely unwelcome to the United States. The Southwest—California, Nevada, Arizona, Utah, and New Mexico—which was held by Mexico at that time, was becoming much more attractive and the Americans were looking for a way to appropriate some of

---

[2] In retrospect, these predictions turned out not to be rosy enough. In 1847 the Mormons moved into the Salt Lake Valley and in 1848 gold was discovered at Sutter's Mill in California.

it. The United States sent a delegation to Mexico with the authority to offer up to $40 million for the entire Southwest. The Mexicans flatly refused. The American Army was then moved into the disputed area between the Nueces River, which runs into the Gulf of Mexico at Corpus Christi, and the Rio Grande River. That almost guaranteed a military encounter. The results of the war, in which the Americans had a decided advantage in military proficiency, are well known. The Mexicans ceded the entire Southwest area that the Americans had previously sought to purchase, but this time for only about $18 million in compensation.

In 1853 the United States bought an additional area from Mexico—below the Gila River in what is now southern Arizona and New Mexico—for $10 million. This became known as the Gadsden Purchase after the American envoy who negotiated the deal. The acquisition was believed to provide a better route for a transcontinental railroad, a possibility that was gaining more attention now that the population of California had been swelled by gold-seeking "49ers." The Gadsden Purchase completed the area of the continental United States as it still stands today.

Thus, in exactly fifty years (1803–1853), the Americans acquired one of the largest areas of real estate ever added by a nation in such a short period of time. (See Figure 5-4.) Even more striking was that, unlike other great territorial acquisitions in history—the Roman Empire, the China of the Khans, the Islamic caliphates, and Spain in the New World—they took over territory as they were ready to settle it as an intergral part of their established economy. They did not acquire new sections of land to hold idly. While large areas of land, particularly in the arid West, were neglected for long periods after American acquisition, they were simply the marginal components of larger parcels. The United States never made a territorial acquisition which it then failed to develop in its entirety. Nor did the Americans take over much land that had already been developed by comparable economic systems. While they did displace most of the native American Indians in their expansion across the continent, they then applied vastly different techniques of production to the natural resources. Their settlement supported a much larger population at a much higher per capita level than did that of the indigenous people they replaced.

The "American conquest" was unusual and unparalleled. Its essential characteristic was economic, the adaptation and development of new technology to turn a major portion of a continent into an economic resource for the first time. It probably would not make a good movie, but in some ways it was a more powerful and enduring conquest than others achieved by political or military power. The American expansion was more peaceful—and less noticed—because, rather than take over a niche held by others, it created a new one for itself. Indeed, the "conquest" took place with the active cooperation of the subjects. The Americans brought their economic system and government with them as they moved west, and their most common complaint was that this system of social overhead was not following fast enough to support their efforts.

It has been common for historians to picture a later period, around 1900, as the "Age of American Imperialism." The United States did acquire a number of

Figure 5-4 (Source: Ross Robertson, History of the American Economy, 3d ed., Harcourt Brace Jovanovich, New York, 1973, p. 114. Copyright 1955 © 1964, 1973 by Harcourt Brace Jovanovich, Inc., and reproduced with their permission.)

overseas possessions at that time. And the aggressive, rather callous procedures used to acquire such places as the Canal Zone and the Philippines were noticed, both then and later. Nevertheless, they had far less net impact on the American economy than did the territorial acquisitions made in the sixty years preceding the Civil War. The acquisitions at the turn of the century tranferred the government of a few relatively unimportant areas from one power to a stronger one. The previous expansion across the North American continent had not attracted as much attention, but it had created an entirely new, far more important economic entity.

DOMESTIC TRANSPORTATION, 1815–1860

Underlying much of what we have said about the American territorial expansion from 1815 to 1860 is the premise—sometimes stated, sometimes implied—that transportation costs fell drastically during this period. While this was obviously not the only force contributing to the major migration of this time, it was undoubtedly the most important one. It was the sizeable reductions in the cost of getting "out there" or getting products back that made these large areas of land economic for the first time and attracted settlers to them.

This explanation natually raises another question: What caused the dramatic gains in the technology of transportation? It would take more than one factor to explain the entire change. Part of the improvements were attributable to developments outside the American economy. For example, the British had pioneered important innovations in railroads and canals as part of what is commonly called the industrial revolution. But a sizeable number of improvements were worked out locally. Americans, obviously being on the scene, could most readily see where improvements might be made. They were also more likely to be able to see the potential personal rewards from such innovations and were therefore more likely to undertake them.

Around the year 1800, for example, an American observer could see that there was an enormous area of good, undeveloped land to the west of the Atlantic seaboard. Some of it was being settled, but far more of it would become accessible if some cheaper method of reaching it could be developed. Whoever succeeded in developing such transport, therefore, would be in a position to reap some of the sizeable increase in economic resources that it created. Accordingly, during the antebellum period Americans put considerable effort into the quest for more efficient transportation, just as an economy usually does in the early, expanding phase of a particular sector.

The Steamboat on Inland Waters

The steamboat, devised for American interior waterways, is a good example of this environment of invention. Today almost every kid in grade school knows the name of Robert Fulton, its successful inventor. What is much less commonly appreciated is that the *possibility* of such a device had been recognized for more than a hundred years, ever since the steam engine had successfully pumped water out of a coal mine. Only in the last twenty years before the steamboat's invention, however, had the *conditions* existed which encouraged the necessary level of effort to create it.

Two wealthy American brothers-in-law, John Stevens and Robert Livingston, combined their talents in an attempt to develop a functional steamboat after the Revolutionary War. In the 1790s, residents of New York City became accustomed to seeing their experimental models plowing along the Hudson River. They made some improvements, but not enough for the boats to be commercially successful or to qualify for the monopoly on service between Albany and New York that the state of New York offered to the first successful steamship.

Then Robert Livingston went off to Paris where he headed the American delegation that negotiated the Louisiana Purchase. While there he met an American named Robert Fulton, who had acquired a reputation as an innovative genius while designing canals in England and submarines in France. Livingston persuaded him that there was an immense potential for steamboats on the rivers of America. When Fulton returned to the United States, he built the successful *Claremont* within one year's time.

Other Americans quickly recognized the value of Fulton's invention and they praised him for it, but they did not let esteem stand in the way of appropriating its design. Within a few years steamboats were used throughout the economy, wherever a minimal waterway allowed them. By 1820 they were regularly working along the eastern seaboard, on the Great Lakes, and on the western rivers. Each area began to learn how to adapt the vessels to its own particular conditions and to make them more productive in the process.

Along the Atlantic coast there was an extensive, long-established network of water transportation that used sails for motive power. Water was such an inexpensive way of moving goods and people that not only were coastal routes used as much as possible but sailing ships struggled well up such major rivers as the Hudson, Connecticut, and James as well. In this environment the steamship was actually at a disadvantage in carrying most types of cargo. While it was faster and more dependable, it was also more expensive, in that, unlike sailing vessels, it had to pay for its fuel. Thus, in Eastern waters the steamboat was forced to develop into a specialized vessel in order to survive. Primarily it carried passengers or their express cargo, for which they were willing to pay premium fares in exchange for speed and dependability. And very quickly the design of the steamboat began to be shaped to emphasize these qualities. It became longer, a characteristic that tends to increase speeds, and more plushly appointed, obviously intended to attract passengers, not bulk cargo. A steamship must have presented a very rakish appearance cruising across Long Island Sound in the 1850s. Except for its side paddle wheel and a conspicuous smokestack, it might have been mistaken for a modern ocean liner.

No one would have confused an antebellum steamboat on the Western rivers with a cruise ship. That area presented conditions substantially different from Eastern waters and the boats were designed accordingly. One major difference was that the Western steamboats carried considerable cargo. Sailing vessels could not operate economically in the cramped confines of the interior rivers. Before the steamboat, the most common medium for moving Western cargo was by flatboat down the river system to New Orleans. That leg of the voyage, in itself, was inexpensive, but rather than haul the boats back up river, they were simply broken up at New Orleans for lumber. Thus the total cost of flatboating was quite high: one new boat for each trip.

The Western steamboat was more of a workhorse than its Eastern counterpart. Relative to its length, it was much wider. This sacrificed speed but more than offset that loss through larger cargo capacity. The greater width had an additional advantage in the river system that these boats were working. It allowed them to have a shallower draft. By 1840 many Western steamboats were designed to operate in only 3 feet of water. This allowed them to bypass snags and sandbars and to extend their operating season well into low-water periods. After 1840, steamboats which could operate in as little as 2 feet of water became common and some captains claimed that they could operate their vessels any-where on mornings with heavy dew.

This process of reducing the draft of Western steamboats so that they could operate in progressively shallower water was not an isolated development. It was merely one example of a more general process of learning to get more productiv-ity from boats in the antebellum period. When they were first introduced to the rivers, in about 1815, their builders simply added a steam engine and paddles to an existing boat hull. As time passed, they developed a design more appropriate to the particular conditions these ships encountered. The hull was made longer and broader, and the deep, sharp keel of seagoing vessels was dropped. The weight of the boat—necessarily heavier for seagoing vessels in order to provide hull strength—was reduced by using lighter wood and moving most machinery and passenger facilities up on the deck. By 1860, the effective capacity of a steamboat of a given official tonnage had increased three times the 1815 level.

The wide, flat decks also aided the loading and unloading of cargo, another improvement that was working to raise steamboat productivity. The average number of days that a ship spent in port during a given round trip fell from about sixty around 1815 to about ten in 1860. Part of this gain in turnaround time can certainly be explained by enlarged and more specialized port facilities as the area served by the ships developed and became more densely settled. In addition, the speed between ports increased so that from 1815 to 1860 average trip times were reduced by one-half to two-thirds. Together, these changes allowed a typical steamboat on the Louisville to New Orleans run to make twelve round trips by 1860, while only about three had been typical in 1815.

A recent study[3] incorporating all these factors showed that productivity gains in Western steamboating from 1815 to 1860 averaged 4.5 percent to 5.5 percent each year, a very rapid rate of growth for such an extended period of time, even compared to recent years where average gains have tended to become higher. Another indication of the dramatic improvement in transportation in the interior, which the steamboat caused, can be seen in Figure 5-5. It shows up-stream river rates declining by more than 90 percent from the time of the intro-duction of the steamboat to the beginning of the Civil War. Even downstream rates dropped by more than 50 percent—which is noteworthy because they oc-curred in competition with the flatboats, which had already reduced downstream rates considerably before the steamboat appeared. All this evidence helps to explain why the steamboat was adopted so quickly and universally and why the area it could reach experienced such rapid development during this time.

Turnpikes

During the same period that Americans were working on the steamboat, consid-erable effort was also being put into the development of better transportation services of a much more traditional type—the road system. The period from

[3] James Mak and Gary M. Walton, "Steamboats and the Great Productivity Surge in River Transportation," *Journal of Economic History,* vol. 32, no. 3, September 1972.

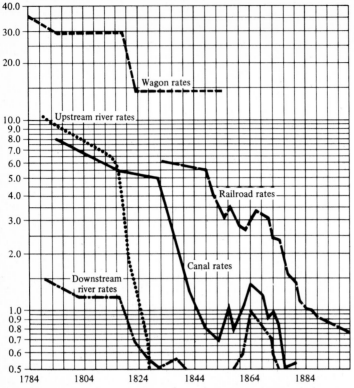

Figure 5-5 Inland freight rates, 1784–1900. *(Sources: Douglass C. North,* Growth and Welfare in the American Past, *Prentice-Hall, Englewood Cliffs, 1973, p. 108; and Douglass C. North, "The Role of Transportation in the Economic Development of North America", paper presented to the International Congress of the Historical Sciences, Vienna, August 1965, and published in* Les Grandes Voies Maritimes dans le Monde XVe-XIXe Siecles, *SEVPEN, Paris, 1965.)*

1790–1825 is rightly known as the "turnpike era." Some of this development was discussed earlier in Chapter 4. The effort continued after 1815, however, with some turnpikes still being constructed in the 1830s. Thus for the first half of the period we are considering (1815–1860), highways were considered a viable form of long-distance transportation. For the entire period, of course, roads were an integral part of the total transportation system in that they provided for the local collection and distribution of goods even when more efficient forms of long-distance transportation became generally used. And the road system contributed to general growth of productivity, as a glance at Figure 5-5 will show. While wagon rates remained well above those of other types of transportation, they nevertheless improved, which reduced their cost by at least 50 percent.

In 1815 the most intensely developed section of the eastern seaboard was served by an extensive system of local roads and turnpikes. Most localities in southern New England, New Jersey, eastern New York, and Pennsylvania were within a short distance of a good road—good, that is, by the standards of the day. Interest in providing an adequate road system extended well beyond this Eastern zone, however. Good roads were naturally desired by those areas which did not have them yet, particularly frontier areas where they made the difference between development and isolation.

For much of the antebellum period, considerable pressure had been focused on the federal government to institute a national program of better roads. In 1808, Albert Gallatin, Jefferson's Secretary of the Treasury, had proposed such a system. In 1817, Calhoun and Clay had jointly sponsored the "bonus bill," intended to use the expected profits from the Second National Bank to finance such roads. There was considerable dispute as to the constitutionality of such projects, but ultimately all major federal efforts in road construction were stopped because of the unevenness of the regional benefits they would provide. New England, for example, consistently opposed federal road programs. Not only would most of the construction have been done elsewhere, but it would also have reduced rents and profits in the New England area by improving the accessibility of competitive resources. In the early years New York and Pennsylvania supported such programs, but as their western regions became settled their support was transformed into opposition.

Hence the "turnpike era" was primarily the result of local initiative. Local governments frequently provided financial backing, but the actual projects were usually conceived and organized by private entrepreneurs. After 1815, the road projects divided into two major categories. One filled in local connections as an area developed. The other—of more direct interest here—provided the longer road links between major areas where alternative transportation systems had not developed. In this context, the main gap to be filled was across the Appalachian Mountains, which formed a natural barrier between the developing West and the established markets of the East. About 1815, a series of turnpikes was linked together to provide a through road from Albany to Buffalo, New York. This paralleled the route which was to be opened by the Erie Canal in 1825. Another series of turnpikes crisscrossed Pennsylvania, providing a (rough) connection with the Ohio River system around Pittsburgh. Probably the best-known turnpike was the Cumberland, or National, Pike, which was the western extension of a good road originating at Baltimore. It was one of the few major roads receiving federal aid during this period, and even then the aid was often provided in roundabout ways to blunt potential criticism of such sponsorship. In 1818, its western terminus was Wheeling, (now West) Virginia, which then provided access to the steamboat network on the Western River.

In the fifteen years after 1818 the National Pike was extended across Ohio and Indiana to Vandalia, Illinois. This section was not as productive as the basic stretch, however, and is symbolic of the fortunes of turnpikes in that period. In 1825, the Erie Canal was completed across New York State. In the 1830s canals were completed through parts of Ohio and Indiana, thus providing a direct, cheap, all-water route from the Ohio River to the eastern seaboard. The brief, but productive era of the long-distance turnpikes was over. While they were clearly inferior to the transportation modes that replaced them, the turnpike era emphasized just how valuable the new lands must have seemed, considering the length to which Americans went to develop them.

Turnpike construction died out in the 1830s as better transportation became available in most parts of the economy. This is not to say that road building ceased, however. If anything, the development of better methods of long-distance transportation increased the return from good local roads. The greater specialization and higher incomes resulting from an emerging national market made the trip to the local river port, general store, or mill all the more important—and frequent. The process of extending and improving the local road system went on throughout the entire antebellum period.

During the 1840s and 1850s that local road-improvement program went through a phase that was characteristically American. The Russians had experimented with plank roads in the 1830s. These were roadways whose surface was constructed out of heavy boards laid crosswise to the road. The idea had been picked up by the Canadians and then been introduced to New York State in 1844. While these roads deteriorated faster than the traditional ones, that were commonly built with minor grading and a topping of gravel, they had some marked advantages. They did not become hopeless bogs in the muddy season, which comprised a good part of the spring in the Northern states. Nor were they nearly as dusty in the dry spells. They did, of course, require a good deal of lumber, so that their construction was sensitive to both the price and proximity to timber. Thus, it is not surprising that most plank roads were built in the Middle Atlantic and Great Lake states. Lumber was relatively inexpensive in those areas in the 1840s and 1850s, because extensive areas were being cleared for cropland. This also explains why virtually no local roads were constructed of planks after 1860. By that time most of the easily accessible timber had been used and settlement was then moving into the grasslands of the upper Midwest.

Although we might not recognize it as such, the basic principle of the plank road survived in two special uses to the end of the nineteenth century. Both cases were particular examples of the set of conditions which made the original roads desirable. The first was the wooden sidewalk, an American innovation that was used widely, as its stereotype in western movie sets indicates. While it may not have paid to pave the entire street with planks, it was worthwhile to get the much smaller pedestrian corridor out of the mud. Before the introduction of concrete and asphalt at about the beginning of the twentieth century, wood was cheaper than such alternatives as stone or slate in many parts of the country, even if it had to be replaced periodically.

The plank road also survived in logging operations up to the end of the nineteenth century. Planks or timbers were obviously cheapest and most readily available near the cutting operations. A plank path, usually greased to reduce friction, made it much easier for horses or oxen to drag the logs out of the woods. These "skid roads"[4] were used until such devices as the donkey (steam) engine introduced more versatile forms of power into logging operations.

---

[4] The common meaning of "skid row" as a sleazy district of town is derived from the logging term. In early Seattle, Washington, such a section of the city developed right where the logging road reached Puget Sound, hence the designation of the road was transferred to that type of area.

Canals

For a long time it has been generally known that transportation by water is usually cheaper than that by land. That this pattern held true in the antebellum period can be verified by comparing wagon (or railroad) rates with those of canals (or steamboats), again using Figure 5-5. As a consequence, goods are usually shipped by water rather than over land, when the opportunity is available. Given the cost difference, it is often cheaper to use a longer, more circuitous water route than a shorter, more direct land one. The difference in shipping costs also strongly influences the spots where economic activities are initially established. A brief glance at a map is sufficient to verify that almost no settlement in the colonial period was far from either the coast or the waterways that were connected to it. It was only after the most accessible land had been settled (and its locational advantage capitalized in its price) that immigrants moved into areas farther removed from water routes. This factor explains a seeming paradox about American development. The soil of southern New England, for example, yields much less corn than that of Illinois, and land in Virginia is not as productive in wheat as that of North Dakota, yet the former were settled 200 years before the latter. The explanation is simply the cost of getting *to* each area. It is not the direct cost of farming that is the relevant measure, but rather the total economic cost of the "package"—the output. Crops in the interior can be grown using fewer resources, but if that advantage is more than offset by the higher costs of getting them to consumers, society will naturally opt for the package—including, in this case, the land that is "less productive"—that requires the least in total resources.

Finally, the cheapness of water transportation encourages its development where it does not already exist. (The creation of the steamboat, which we examined above, can be considered a variant of this process. It created a new network of water routes—capable of transporting large quantities of people and cargo—from what was previously a restricted avenue for communications.) A more direct approach is simply to build a new waterway—commonly called a canal.

In 1815 the United States had a total of less than 100 miles of canals and only three individual projects of any appreciable length. This was in sharp contrast to the experience of England where a network of several thousand miles of canals and improved river channels served most parts of that (much smaller) economy. The difference is instructive. It helps to demonstrate the basic conditions that make canals productive—or otherwise. In contrast to the United States, England (excluding Wales and Scotland) has very little land at higher elevations. Only a tiny fraction of cultivated land is at elevations above 500 feet and only a few "mountains" reach 1,000 feet. Yet a good part of the trans-Appalachian West undergoing development in the antebellum period was at elevations exceeding 500 feet. Most of the Great Lakes states and the sites of Chicago, Cincinnati, Detroit, and Nashville were so included. In addition, England's coastline was very irregular so that every point in the interior was not more than 100 miles from an inlet of sea. Chicago was 1,000 miles from either the Atlantic Ocean or the Gulf of Mexico. Naturally, England made good use of the opportu-

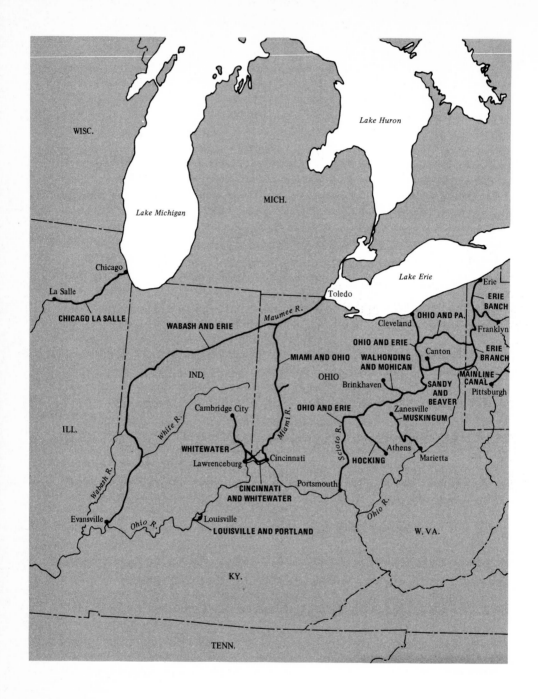

Figure 5-6 *(Source: George Rogers Taylor,* The Transportation Revolution, *Harper Torch-and reprinted by their permission.)*

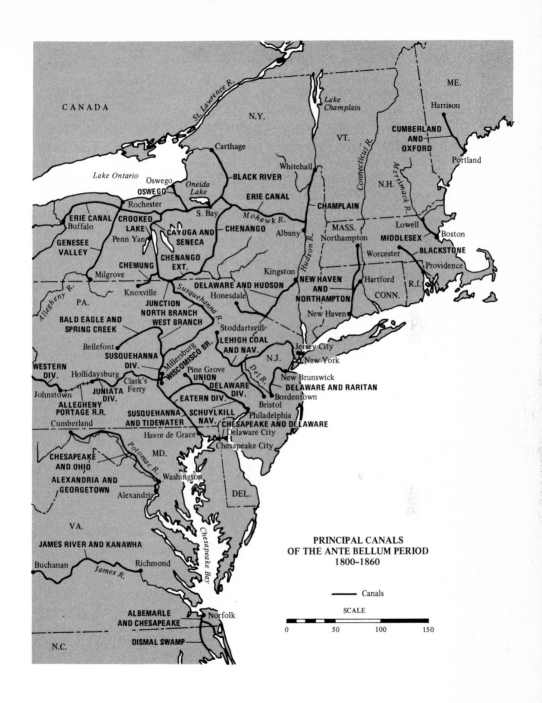

CANADA

St. Lawrence R.

N.Y.

Lake Champlain

ME.

Harrison

VT.

CUMBERLAND AND OXFORD

Carthage

Whitehall

Connecticut R.

N.H.

Portland

Lake Ontario

Oswego

Oneida Lake

BLACK RIVER

OSWEGO

Rochester

ERIE CANAL

S. Bay

Mohawk R.

CHAMPLAIN

Merrimack R.

ERIE CANAL
Buffalo

CROOKED LAKE

Penn Yan

CAYUGA AND SENECA

CHENANGO

Albany

MASS.

Northampton

Lowell

Boston

MIDDLESEX

GENESEE VALLEY

CHEMUNG

CHENANGO EXT.

Worcester

BLACKSTONE

Providence

Milgrove

Allegheny R.

Kingston

Susquehanna R.

DELAWARE AND HUDSON

Honesdale

NEW HAVEN AND NORTHAMPTON

Hartford

R.I.

CONN.

Knoxville

JUNCTION NORTH BRANCH WEST BRANCH

Hudson R.

New Haven

PA.

BALD EAGLE AND SPRING CREEK

Stoddartsville

Bellefont

SUSQUEHANNA DIV.

Millersburg

WISCOMISCO BR.

LEHIGH COAL AND NAV.

Jersey City

N.J.

New York

WESTERN DIV.

Hollidaysburg

Clark's Ferry

Pine Grove

UNION

Del. R.

New Brunswick

Johnstown

JUNIATA DIV.

DELAWARE DIV.

EATERN DIV.

DELAWARE AND RARITAN

Bordentown

ALLEGHENY PORTAGE R.R.

SUSQUEHANNA AND TIDEWATER

SCHUYLKILL NAV.

Bristol

Philadelphia

Cumberland

Havre de Grace

CHESAPEAKE AND DELAWARE

Delaware City

MD.

Chesapeake City

CHESAPEAKE AND OHIO

Potomac R.

Washington

DEL.

ALEXANDRIA AND GEORGETOWN

Alexandria

Chesapeake Bay

VA.

JAMES RIVER AND KANAWHA

Buchanan

James R.

Richmond

PRINCIPAL CANALS OF THE ANTE BELLUM PERIOD 1800–1860

———— Canals

SCALE

0   50   100   150

ALBEMARLE AND CHESAPEAKE

Norfolk

N.C.

DISMAL SWAMP

books, Harper & Row, New York, 1968, p. 35. Copyright © 1968 by Harper & Row, Publishers nity for cheap transportation that canals and improvement in rivers provided. It allowed her to avoid the larger investment in steamboats that the Americans had to make to overcome the distance and elevation of their vast interior.

Surprisingly, then, from 1815 to 1840 the Americans undertook a major program of canal construction. (See Figure 5-6.) Not surprisingly, in aggregate, it was a failure. That irony requires a little clarification. In 1815 there was one site in the United States that was a logical candidate for a canal. Ever since Gallatin had suggested it in his 1806 report it was widely known that northern New York provided a low elevation bypass of the Appalachian Range. The project was much too large for a private construction venture at that time, so efforts turned to the governmental level. DeWitt Clinton pushed through state sponsorship in 1817. (As usual, in that period, the federal government was avoiding such projects.) Very early in the construction work it became clear that the Erie Canal was going to be successful. The first sections finished attracted considerable local traffic, even before distant connections were foreseeable. By 1825, when the canal was completed, the traffic was generating so much revenue through tolls that it was being used to finance a series of branch canals to the mainline.

The success of the Erie generated considerable enthusiasm for canals elsewhere in the country, which was, for the most part, unfortunate, because the conditions behind that success were quite specific to that project. While the Erie did open up a cheap route between the Great Lakes and the Atlantic coast, most of the traffic originating west of Buffalo developed later. Local traffic, that generated by the canal in the process of making the nearby good land accessible, was much more important to its immediate success. For another canal to be as successful as the Erie, it would not only have to have the favorable terrain and water supply that its forerunner enjoyed, but it would also have to open up a new area of good, but otherwise unexploited land. It was a subtle consideration and in the rush to imitate the Erie after its 1825 opening, it was usually overlooked.

By 1840 more than 3,300 miles of canals had been constructed in the United States at the then immense cost of more than $125 million. Most of the construction had taken place after the opening of the Erie Canal in 1825. Most, also, had been initiated and largely financed by individual states. Some of the latter canals appeared to have been successful. The Ohio Canal, for example, connected Lake Erie with the Ohio River, thereby completing an all-water route from the East Coast to the interior river system. The Oswego and Champlain Canals were branch lines of the Erie and successfully opened up Lake Ontario and the northeast New York–northwest Vermont regions, respectively. A number of short canals in the vicinity of the Delaware River were profitable in carrying anthracite coal from northeastern Pennsylvania to the urban markets of Philadelphia and New York.

Beyond that there was a long list of also-rans, ranging from the marginal to the total disasters. The former included the Cumberland and Oxford Canal, which connected a section of the interior of Maine to the port of Portland, and the Chesapeake and Delaware Canal, which provided a shortcut between the two great bays of those names. Among the latter were the Indiana Canals, most of which were never completed and whose large cost pushed the state government to the edge of bankruptcy. Another notable failure was the New Haven and Northhampton, which attempted to provide a water route up the Connecticut Valley in western New England. It was plagued by frequent malfunctions and was often unusable because of lack of water in the summer months.

The ultimate disaster, however, was the canal system undertaken by the state of Pennsylvania. Presumptuously titled The Main Line of Pennsylvania Public Works—commonly shortened to The Main Line—it was an enormous undertaking, absorbing more than 15 percent of the total spent on all canals in the United States up to 1840. The Main Line was planned in imitation of the Erie's success and also out of the fear that the Erie would cause eastern Pennsylvania to lose the resulting commerce with the developing West to New York. But implementation proved more difficult to achieve than intention. The eastern and western sections of The Main Line were relatively straightforward projects. Canals were built paralleling the major river channels that ran east and west. However, the center of the state is bisected by a series of mountain ranges whose lowest passes are all above 2,000 feet. Even the optimists of Pennsylvania could not foresee the construction of a canal over that barrier. They devised a series of inclined railroads to bridge the steepest sections. While some traffic did move over this route, it proved very slow and expensive. In addition to the loading and unloading from canal to rail and back, there were lengthy delays in the canal sections themselves. Even with the railroads for the steepest sections, the canals were still built over steep terrain. As a consequence, 174 time-consuming locks were encountered in a trip over The Main Line.

The unfortunate example of the Pennsylvania canals demonstrates an important generalization about the canal experience in the United States. The nation was an unlikely candidate for canal transportation in the antebellum period. Not only were distances great and elevations high, but the traditional resource endowment of the United States is just the opposite of that which canals emphasize. They are capital-intensive operations, achieving low operating costs by virtue of an initial, extensive construction project. In addition, given the available technology of that day, the building itself was labor-intensive. The common method used to construct canals was hard labor—shovels and wheelbarrows. The most mechanized technique was a horse-drawn scrapper. Thus it is easy to understand that only a few canals, such as the Erie or the short coal waterways, could have succeeded in the United States. It required a rare combination of elevation, markets, and lack of available alternative transport possibilities. Contemporaries failed to recognize the special success of the Erie was just that—an unusual case that was not likely to be reproduced in many other locations.

Railroads

By 1830 the combination of developments in roads, steamboats, and canals had substantially reduced the costs of transportation in the United States. Of course, that process was far from being completed. Yet it should have been clear to any contemporary observer who stopped to examine it that ongoing changes in the technology of transportation were substantially enlarging the economic dimensions of the nation. There was a discordant omission in this development, however.

American labor had always been relatively scarce and, accordingly, it had been used with circumspection. The general contemporary growth in productivity made labor's time all the more valuable. While the improvements in transportation efficiency had substantially lowered the costs of moving cargo, they had not reduced the time required to complete a given trip by nearly as much. Gains in cost reduction, much more than speed, had been the trend until 1830. This is not to say that no savings in time had been achieved, of course. The steamboat obviously moved both goods and people much faster over inland waters than its predecessors had. The new turnpikes were also faster than the country roads which they bypassed. Yet while passengers on the Erie Canal reported that they enjoyed the smoothness and the quiet of their ride, it took a long time to complete most journeys at an average of 1 ½ miles an hour. For large parts of the eastern seaboard an overland trip was no faster in 1830 than it had been in the late 1700s.

What the country needed was a new form of transportation that could move cargo, particularly passengers, faster. Speed was the important factor as a method of economizing on time. If it could be achieved at no more cost, so much the better. But even a higher cost was acceptable. A higher charge per trip could be more than offset by the return from the savings in labor and inventory time.

Like most major inventions, the railroad was not suddenly invented. It evolved out of a series of innovations and problem-solving adaptations. For example, the advantages of a fixed track in reducing the friction of hauling had been recognized for a long time before 1830. Mining operations, in particular, had readily adopted some form of this device because they moved large quantities of material through and out of the mine shaft. Steam engines had been used to pump water out of English coal mines as early as 1700. As their efficiency was improved in the eighteenth century they were applied to a widening list of other uses in the mines. One was to move the mine cars, usually by means of a stationary steam engine providing power through a set of cables. Around 1800, the high-pressure steam engine developed by Robert Evans (the flour-mill innovator) and John Stevens (the steamboat entrepreneur) was sufficiently powerful to move several times its own weight. For the first time this allowed a mobile power source which could venture far beyond the former confines of such devices as cables. By 1830 this basic possibility had been developed into working railroads in both the United States and England.

The railroad was an immediate success in both the United States and England. By 1860 more than 30,000 miles of track were in use in the United States with large parts of the Northeast and Great Lakes states covered by the new rail network. The railroad had captured a large portion of intercity passenger traffic and was beginning to carry sizeable amounts of freight as well. It was generally more expensive than its rivals, except for such competition as stage traffic on parallel roads (as a glance back at Figure 5-5 will show). It was, however, faster, and usually the form of transportation that inflicted the least damage on the cargo it carried. These characteristics explain its success in attracting passenger traffic and also those goods in which safety or value relative to freight costs were important.

In this way the railroad paralleled the experience of the steamboat in Eastern waters. While it was not as cheap as its competitors, it could capture that traffic which valued better service—which also explained the regional pattern of rail investment. For the railroad did not tend to "open up" new territory as much as previous innovations, such as the steamboat. Obviously a new rail line aided local settlement and raised property values along the right-of-way, but most railroads before 1860 were built in areas where substantial settlement was already under way. The majority of railroad mileage was built in the densely settled Northern states which were already evolving into the urban core of the nation. In contrast, the South in 1860 had much less railroad mileage. Large areas of the region were not even yet connected to the national network.

The railroad was obviously a growth sector of the economy from 1830 to 1860. (See Figure 5-7.) Track mileage was less than 100 in 1830, increased to more than 3,000 by 1840, and grew by about 200 percent in each of the next two decades. Accompanying this rapid expansion were the technological innovations which usually occur in such an emerging sector. Developers naturally started with what was available. In 1830, that meant mounting an existing steam engine on a flat platform with four fixed wheels. Passenger cars were simply stagecoaches with railroad wheels. The trains ran on tracks which were composed of wooden rails with strips of iron strapped on top for additional strength. The iron had the unfortunate habit of working loose, curling up under the pressure of the passing wheels, and knifing up through the botton of the lightly constructed coaches. That, coupled with frequent boiler explosions[5] on the earliest engines, made the job of those charged with public relations for the railroads very difficult.

The early, ad hoc methods soon began to be replaced by more systematic and productive techniques, however. Firms and technology especially adapted to locomotive production appeared. The first such manufactures began in England, but while English locomotives were safer and more productive than homemade models, some of their features were not well adapted to American conditions. The Americans had more land and less capital than the English. Thus, when they built a rail system they naturally spent less on the construction of the roadbed and substituted more track length and more-frequent and sharper turns for the excavation required to build straighter, more-level rail lines. British-built locomotives, designed with carefully prepared track in mind, tended to derail on the sharp curves and uneven track in the United States.

To counteract these problems the Americans devised two innovations. One was the swivel truck which allowed the wheels to turn right or left beneath the engine. This gave better stability and traction on sharp curves. Another device, the equilizing beam under the engine, kept power flowing evenly to all drive wheels despite uneven tracks. Such innovations were quickly adopted partly because of their obvious utility and also because a number of American locomotive

---

[5] Several engine explosions were caused by naïve train crews who jammed the safety valve shut because they did not like the whistle of the escaping steam. Southern railroads sometimes pulled a car loaded with cotton bales directly behind the engine to shield passengers in the event of a boiler blowup.

Figure 5-7 Major railroads built by 1860. *(Source: Albert W. Niemi, Jr.,* U. S. Economic History, *Rand McNally and Company, Chicago, 1975, p. 76. Copyright © 1970 by Rand McNally and Company, Chicago. Reprinted by permission of Rand McNally College Publishing Company.)*

manufacturers had been established to build equipment especially designed for American conditions. The firms emerged as spin-offs of textile machinery manufacturers, who, by that time, had achieved the highest level of engineering capability in the country. By 1840, these new companies were turning out locomotives which also incorporated such American innovations as the enclosed engine cab and the cowcatcher.[6] They were also being gradually adapted to such conditions as longer average trips and lower fuel costs.

The old stagecoach cars disappeared also. The swivel truck allowed for much longer, more-comfortable passenger cars. By 1840 the basic car structure,

---

[6] The conspicuous cowcatcher was also, oddly enough, a reflection of conditions in the United States. With more capital for fencing and less undeveloped area along the right-of-way, English trains were much less likely to encounter animals on the tracks. Actually, the name is somewhat of a misnomer. The purpose of a cowcatcher is not to save the cow, but rather the engine. It should more properly be called a cow *deflector*.

which has persisted up the the present, had been widely adopted. Underneath the rolling stock, equally dramatic changes were being made in the railbed. At first rails were laid on granite blocks, but these were too easily pushed out of place by the vibrations of a passing train or even frost. Some lines also attempted to use wooden pilings, but that proved even less satisfactory. The omnipresent system of wooden crossties used today was discovered by accident. They were used as a temporary expedient on one occasion when granite was unattainable. They proved to be so resilient under the weight of passing trains that not only were they more lasting but they provided a smoother ride as well. The problem of "snake heads"—the iron strips on the rails that curled up and smashed through the carriage floors, spearing passengers like marshmallows—was solved by improved rails. The rails became progressively heavier, and by 1860 the use of wood had been almost entirely discontinued. In 1831 the familiar T-shaped rail, which provided close contact with the flagged wheels, was invented. Like so many of these innovations it was quickly adopted throughout the industry.

The sum of the advances described above, and a large number of gradual ones not mentioned, explains the drop in rail rates seen in Figure 5-5. These show rail charges per ton/mile falling by 50 percent from 1830 to 1860. Another way of saying this is that it took only half as many resources in 1860 as it did in 1830 to provide the same transportation services. Since rail travel was faster and more dependable in 1860, this is an understatement of the gains to the economy.

There is an old American joke about the tourist who asked the local town drunk how to get to a nearby town. The poor fellow made several bungling attempts and finally gave up, telling the questioner: "You can't get there from here." In many ways that story explains the difference between the America of 1800 and that of 1860. In 1860 one could get to a much wider range of places than was possible in 1800. To be precise, it was not that one could not get there physically in 1800—as Lewis and Clark had demonstrated—but rather that the cost of doing so was prohibitive. The effect was about the same, however. By 1860 the dramatic improvements in transportation that we have reported had substantially expanded the economic size of the nation. That had made it inevitable that the United States would acquire a large contiguous area to the west, and that a substantial number of residents would move in to develop it. Within that massive expansion, however, there were many repercussions as well. In the next several chapters we shall see how some of those adaptations worked their way out in major sectors of the economy.

SUGGESTED READINGS

Davis, Lance and Douglass C. North: *Institutional Change and American Economic Growth*, Cambridge, Cambridge, England, 1971.

Haites, Erick F. and James Mak: "Ohio and Mississippi River Transportation, 1810–1860," *Explorations in Economic History*, vol. 8, no. 2, Winter 1970–1971.

Hunter, Louis G.: *Steamboats on the Western Rivers*, Harvard, Cambridge, Mass., 1949.

Mak, James and Gary M. Walton: "Steamboats and the Great Productivity Surge in River

Transportation," *Journal of Economic History,* vol. 32, no. 3, September 1972.

North, Douglass C.: "The Role of Transportation in the Development of North America," paper presented to the International Congress of the Historical Sciences in Vienna, August 1965, and published in *Les Grandes Voies Maritimes dans le Monde XVᵉ-XIXᵉ Siecles,* SEVPEN, Paris, 1965.

Ransom, Roger L.: "Canals and Developments: A Discussion of the Issues," *American Economic Review,* vol. 54, May 1964.

————: "Social Returns from Public Transport Investment: A Case Study of the Ohio Canal," *Journal of Political Economy,* vol. 78, September/October 1970.

Taylor, George R.: *The Transportation Revolution, 1815–1860,* Holt, New York, 1951.

Industrialization and Growth

One wag once remarked that the first thing a small nation does when it becomes independent is to start a national airline, and the second is to build a steel mill. Of course the statement is overdrawn—that underlines its humor. Yet it does express a common conception about the manner in which economic development occurs. Growth is associated with highly visible forms of modern technology, particularly industrialization.

This view was vividly illustrated in the early 1960s. Walt W. Rostow wrote a book entitled *The Stages of Economic Growth*, which he rather presumptuously subtitled, *A Non-communist Manifesto.* The study saw all successful, long-term experiences of national growth as fitting into one basic pattern. Each economy went through a long period of preparation which then broke into sustained growth during a period called the "takeoff." The takeoff consisted of a sharp dramatic increase in the average growth rate, fueled by a large increase in saving and the emergence of a "leading sector"—most likely an expanding industry. Rostow's theory received a rough going over within professional circles. When the model was checked out against the experience of most developed countries, it seldom fit. Unfortunately those reports did not get back to most of the policy makers, particularly in the lesser-developed countries, and, as a result, a lot of resources were wasted.

In retrospect, it was not very surprising. *The Stages of Economic Growth* merely articulated and certified the preconceptions that many people already held. Each of the three major components of Rostow's model expressed a commonly held view about the growth process. Specifically, (1) growth is essentially a modern phenomenon, occurring in the last 200 years or so since the industrial revolution, (2) growth is caused by increased quantities of capital, created by saving; and (3) growth is triggered by dramatic innovations which create new industries around themselves.

It is an appealing explanation, partly because it can be readily grasped and the implications for policy are so obvious. If you want growth, you assemble capital, either through foreign aid or by squeezing it out of the peasants, use it to build modern factories, and the rest will fall into place. Unfortunately, it seldom works that way, as so many development plans and aid programs have sadly demonstrated. Had the proponents of this view of economic development stopped to examine the American experience, it is much less likely that they would have adhered to the Rostow theory. The record of the United States is a counterexample, a demonstration that industrialization is merely a part of a larger process of productivity increase.

Growth, after all, is the process of learning to squeeze more output from available resources. This can be done by modification of existing production techniques, creation of new resources out of previously unfeasible materials, and changes in the organization of production. Industrialization is merely one example of the last category, that is, one arrangement which provides goods that meet some demands or desires of consumers. It can be roughly described as a centralized form of production which can achieve large economies in the use of certain resources. Compared to alternative arrangements—handicrafts, for example—it uses more of certain other resources, such as capital and transportation, however. Thus, whether or not its use constitutes a net gain to a given economy depends on the relative importance of such costs in that society. A factory might, for instance, be able to turn out a certain product much more cheaply than alternative methods, but it might also more than lose that margin of superiority to locally produced goods when the cost of delivering them to the final consumer is included. Such modern business operations as breweries, tire retreading, and printing could achieve lower unit costs at volumes larger than the ones at which many of them operate, but the restricted size of their markets precludes such gains.

Implicitly, at least, a society is constantly reviewing the range of possible forms of production it could use to provide its goods, choosing the best combination from among them. When an economy makes a major shift to that type of form which we now call industrialization, it suggests a substantial revision in the costs which the various forms of organization emphasize. Consider the experience of the United States relative to that of Britain. In the late 1700s and early 1800s the average income of the Americans was almost certainly higher than that of the British. If industrialization was a necessary step in a fixed path toward higher incomes, the Americans would have been expected to have undergone the process first. Just the reverse occurred, however. England was the first to experience the widespread industrialization now commonly called the industrial revolution. In 1770 England's economy was more compact and unified than that of the American Colonies. That meant that it was cheaper to ship a manufactured product from, say, Manchester, England—the early cotton textile center—to points throughout the British Isles than it was to ship goods from Watertown, Massachusetts—an early American textile center—to most American consumers. Other things being equal, the more compact market in England would have dictated a turn to centralized factory production there, with its associated gains in production costs, sooner than it would have in the United States. Another factor which probably contributed to the adoption of factory production was that capital was more abundant in Britain. It seems plausible that factories are more capital-intensive forms of production than the alternatives they supplant. Thus the economy in which capital was the least expensive would—again, other things being equal—be the first to switch to industrial methods of production.

Finally, the adoption of factory methods would also be influenced by the scarcity of particular natural resources used in production. Professor Rosenberg has made a convincing argument that the industrial revolution came first to England as a response to developing bottlenecks in certain raw materials in that economy.[1] By 1700, wood was becoming very expensive in England so that activities which used large amounts of it for fuel, such as pig iron, were faced with sharply increasing costs. In the mid-1700s Britain was importing a sizeable portion of her pig iron from such faraway sources as Russia and the American Colonies. The search for substitute fuel—which developed coke, a coal derivative—to replace charcoal in iron refining can thus be understood as a response to an increasing scarcity of wood. Similarly, the pioneering efforts on the development of the steam engine, undertaken primarily by the English, can be seen as a response to another developing scarcity—mechanical power. England did have several good locations for providing water power, but by the eighteenth century many of these had already been developed. In addition, some processes where the application of additional power was becoming more desirable simply could not be moved to where the water power was. In the eighteenth century the growing demand for coal and various metal ores was encouraging deeper and larger mine shafts. As a result, the effort involved in extracting material and draining water from the mines was taking on major proportions. One avenue of attack on this emerging problem was the steam engine. Eventually it was used for a variety of power applications, but one of its earliest uses was in pumping water out of mines and, oddly enough, into reservoirs that powered water wheels. All these innovative efforts were peculiarly English before 1800. With a much larger supply of wood and water, Americans were occupied with efforts to extend other, more expensive resources. Industrialization was postponed for a while on the west side

---

[1] Nathan Rosenberg, *Technology and American Economic Growth,* Harper & Row, New York, 1972.

of the Atlantic. The resources that it would have saved in the American economy before 1800 were among its least valuable, while the ones that it would consume more of were among its most valuable.

A LATE, BUT FAST, START

From 1815 to 1860 the quantity of products manufactured in the United States increased about twelvefold. Even the total value of these goods, a measure whose growth was retarded by sometimes-dramatic reductions in their average prices, rose eightfold. Even allowing for some roughness in these estimates, the amount of manufactured products available to an average American must have grown dramatically in this forty-five-year period, probably about tripling. By any historical precedent this was a very rapid increase for such a large sector over such a lengthy period. Yet, it is not unexpected, given other developments of the time. A good part of Chapter 5 was spent in detailing the substantial reductions in transportation costs that occurred in this period and some of their consequences, such as regional expansion. Industrialization is another major result. Lower freight charges increase the extent of the market for particular suppliers. Both the distance over which they can sell their product and the net price they receive for it (after deducting transportation charges) rise as freight rates decrease. Such a development encourages factory organization as a means of providing goods. Larger markets allow the larger scales of production that often yield reduced unit costs of production. The substantial improvements in transportation that occurred during this time do not entirely explain the industrialization that accompanied them, but they were an important factor in developing the necessary conditions that allowed it.

Another, frequently overlooked, condition in the United States gave an additional boost to industrialization as it reached major proportions after 1815. Before then, high transportation costs had fostered a considerable degree of self-sufficiency in local villages. A large percentage of the goods consumed locally were also produced locally, most within the radius of a few miles. This self-sufficiency should not be taken as implying a limited supply of goods, however. American incomes were high by the standards of that time, which allowed a relatively large portion of their incomes to be spent on items other than food. A good part of the productive time of the work force of a typical locality was spent in providing nonagricultural goods and services. For example, in 1815 *Niles Register* described Mt. Pleasant, Ohio, a town of about 500 people, as having: three saddlers, three hatters, four blacksmiths, four weavers, six boot- and shoemakers, eight carpenters, three tailors, three cabinetmakers, one baker, one apothecary, two wagon makers, two tanneries, one shop for making wool-carding machines, one wool-spinning shop, one flax-spinning shop, one nail factory, and two wool-carding establishments. In addition, within 6 miles of town were nine merchant mills, two grist mills, twelve sawmills, one paper mill, one woolen factory, and two fulling mills. In other words, such items as cloth, hats, shoes, clothing, iron-wares, and furniture were already being turned out in large quantities by local production in 1815. Rather than producing goods that were new to Americans, therefore, factory organization merely represented a cheaper way of providing products for which a market was already established. Viewed in this context, industrialization was not a very revolutionary development in the United States. In good part, it was merely a cheaper method of providing goods, most of which were already well established in the American economy. Rather than being a major break or watershed in the economic history of the United States, industrialization was merely one—albeit widely publicized—example of behavior that occurred through its entire course: devising new ways to meet human desires while consuming fewer of society's limited stock of economic resources.

INDUSTRIALIZATION BEFORE "INDUSTRIALIZATION"

The period after 1815 saw a widespread adoption of factory organization in the United States, but that form of organization was not entirely novel to the economy. Throughout the colonial period the particular advantages of centralized mass production had already caused it to displace handicraft methods for selected products. We know that high transportation costs were an important factor in delaying the introduction of factory organization in the United States. In certain cases, however, where the manufacturing process significantly reduced the weight of the materials to be transported, it was undertaken *in response* to high freight costs. For example, flour mills, lumber mills, and iron furnaces all use weight-reducing processes—that is, the weight or bulk of their *products* is much less than that of the *raw materials* from which they are made. The higher the cost of transportation, the stronger the incentive to locate such processes near the source of the raw materials. It is noteworthy that America had large numbers of such establishments well before 1815, and some of them were then among the largest of their type in the world. Similar considerations explained the use of factory-type organizations for several other products to supply the national market before 1815. For example, sugar mills in Louisiana, tar kilns in the Carolinas, saltworks in the Middle Atlantic states, and distilleries in New England for rum and in the Northwest for whiskey, all demonstrated that large-scale production methods were recognized and adopted where they were profitable.

Even those industries which are commonly characterized as not adopting factory organization until after 1815 showed a tendency to centralize some processes before that. About 1790, improvements in the spinning of cotton yarn began to move that activity out of households and into local mills. By 1815 many of the now picturesque—and very labor-intensive—spinning wheels in southeastern New England had been relegated to other fibers, such as linen or wool. As a result, the organization of cotton textile production went through a phase that also appeared in a number of other developing industries at that time. The "putting-out system" broke the production process into its individual components, centralizing those steps where savings were possible from larger operations and parceling out the other stages to households. In cotton textiles this took the form of centralized spinning (converting the loose fibers into thread or yarn) in village mills, while weaving continued to be carried out in households. Soon a group of specialized merchants appeared who bought the yarn, parceled it out to individual householders, and collected the finished cloth. In smaller, or less accessible, areas, this role was often carried out by the local storekeeper.

Before 1815, the domestic form of organization also developed in the production of certain other goods. For example, most shoes in colonial America were made by local crafts workers as custom projects; that is, they were made to order for a particular customer. In the latter half of the eighteenth century, cobblers in eastern New England and some large cities such as Philadelphia began producing ready-made shoes for distant markets. Soon thereafter certain elements of shoemaking began to be taken out of its traditional household location. First to be centralized was leather cutting, because of the savings in material which that allowed. Later, other steps, such as sewing and final trimming, were brought under central control in order to provide better quality control. Despite the continued growth of the market, however, factory production was not adapted to total shoemaking until after 1840, when techniques of cutting and sewing leather by power machinery were developed.

The production of hats also underwent centralization before 1815. This did not seem to be compelled by any changes in technology, but rather by the growing demand for certain types of hats, which allowed economies in their production through a finer division of labor. In a larger operation, people could be slotted to such specific tasks as cutting or blocking, whereas previously one crafts worker would have performed all such steps, wasting considerable motion in the process of moving between them. (A parallel specialization was emerging in the shoe industry, where individuals were increasingly paired with such finely divided processes as cutting and sewing.) As the number of steps in a given type of production increased, the costs of distributing and collecting the materials-in-process through a domestic system also increased and eventually offset any other advantages it offered. Thus, the production of hats and shoes tended to be consolidated in one enterprise, even though the large power requirements that dictated factory organization in other products were not yet present in these industries.

There was one notable exception to the tendency toward centralization in the production of hats, however: those made out of straw or palm leaves. This industry became important and was organized into a "putting out" form only in the 1820s, after centralized production was well under way in other forms of hats. This deviation from the usual pattern is understandable, however, in the context of the specific advantages of the domestic system. Around 1820, palm leaf or straw could be woven only by expensive hand labor. The task was relatively simple and could be mastered by almost anyone, including small children, within a short time. Furthermore, it could be started or stopped at almost any point without the necessity of redoing previous work. In short, it was an ideal task to fit in around a household where it could be picked up between chores or in front of the fireplace in the evening.

Often merchants who specialized in that line of work collected the assembled hats. In the case of those of palm-leaf construction, they were probably the same individuals who passed out the palm leaves to begin with—obviously an imported raw material in New England. The final shaping, bleaching, and trimming were completed in a central shop. This arrangement succeeded in capturing the gains that are possible in a domestic system. Cheap labor was employed in those functions where there was no advantage to centralized production, while the other steps in which such economies were important were efficiently split off. Furthermore, the costs of transferring work between separated steps was not so large as to offset all the gains from decentralization. In straw- and palm-leaf hat production, all the steps which gained from factory organization (in the early 1800s)—bleaching and shaping, for example—were performed after the hand-weaving was completed. Thus, only one transfer, from home to central shop, was necessary. And as a consequence, this segment of hand production continued to thrive in the form of a "putting-out" system well after the movement of production into factory organization was generally well under way.

THE FACTORY COMES TO AMERICA

While the use of a factory as a method of production was perfected in—and has even become a symbol of—the American economy, it originated elsewhere. The English first worked out its basic components in the cotton textile industry in the late 1700s. That process of development has been recounted numerous times since then as a description of what is believed to be a key sector of the industrial revolution. We have been told of the invention of the "mule" which mechanized spinning and the power loom which did the same thing for weaving. We also know that these machines required so much power to operate them that they were collected together at a water-power site. Within a few years this package of improvements, subsumed under the name of factory organization, had substantially reduced the costs of producing cotton cloth. That made acquisition of those techniques attractive to a number of other economies, including that of the Americans.

It is hard to keep a valuable idea secret for long, as the English soon discovered. They banned the export of textile machinery and prohibited the emigration of mechanics who were familiar with its construction. All this, of course, was to forestall foreign competition and protect the rapidly growing export market for cotton cloth. Soon, however, thinly disguised ads for textile mechanics began to appear in English newspapers, promising generous rewards for the appearance of such skills in America. Some English artisans went so far as to conceal themselves in barrels to make the trip to America—and also to earn large bonuses. Samuel Slater, the most famous emigré of this group, memorized the complete design of a new textile mill and then quietly slipped aboard a ship bound for Philadelphia.

Slater is commonly given credit for establishing the first factory in the United States, a year after his arrival in 1789. He took over management of the faltering cotton mill of Moses Brown in Providence, Rhode Island. (Brown more than fulfilled any expectations of gain which Slater had probably held in coming to America. He gave him all the net profits of the firm.) The enterprise was only marginally successful, however. Slater found the existing locally made equipment obsolete beyond redemption and was forced to replace all of it with new pieces of his own design. While they embodied the best techniques then available in England, they were handicapped by an orientation toward British, not American, conditions. Slater, for example, was proud to point out how much better his employees were paid and generally provided for than were those in English textile mills. He apparently failed to recognize that American labor was generally rewarded better than its English counterparts, so that his "benevolence" toward his employees grew more out of the necessity of acquiring employees than his personal generosity toward them. In any case, if one uses as much labor as English producers do, while paying them more to turn out the same quantity of cloth, the cost of the finished product will necessarily be higher. Consequently, Slater's enterprise had tough going for its first two decades, often being undersold by imported cloth. While he and a few other American manufacturers ran their operations carefully and made a number of innovations, the factory production of cotton cloth was still a marginal operation in the United States in the twenty-five years after 1790.

America's first obviously successful cotton textile factory was opened in Waltham, Massachusetts in 1814. Three years previously a Boston businessman, Francis Cabot Lowell, had taken a trip to England to regain his health. Unlike most other tourists, however, who spent their time recuperating at a hot springs or in the green countryside, Lowell found it rejuvenating to stroll through the English mills around Manchester. He observed their construction and operation very carefully, and then, in the seclusion of his hotel room, made careful drawings of them which he smuggled out of the country. Upon his return to Boston, Lowell joined with several other business people to raise the then enormous sum of $300,000 to build a large factory.

Perhaps even more important to his ultimate success than the capital he raised was the mechanic, Paul Moody, whom he enlisted to help turn his sketches into a concrete operation. Moody was not only able to reproduce the English processes, but he went well beyond them, introducing substantial modifications which made the factory much more suitable for American conditions. He was able, for example, to speed up the rate at which materials were moved through the factory and also to make the processes more automated than contemporary mills had done in England. These innovations saved resources, particularly labor, commonly the expensive input in American calculations. In this way Moody overcame the barrier that had stifled Slater's earlier efforts, namely, adapting the advanced technology of England to the resource costs of America.

By 1820 it was clear that the factory production of cotton textiles in the United States had reached the status of a growth sector. Existing mills were making sizeable profits, other forms of production, such as household weaving, were being driven out of business in market-oriented areas, and quite a few potential entrepreneurs were looking for a way to get into the industry—and its profits. For the next forty years cotton textile production grew rapidly, averaging a hefty annual gain of 15 percent. In 1860 it was the largest manufacturing industry in the United States, as measured by the value it added during the production process. (See Table 6-1.) By then it had spread well beyond the original successful mill at Waltham to include numerous large establishments along the Blackstone River (which ran from Worcester, Massachusetts to Providence, Rhode Island), the Merrimack River (which came through New Hampshire and ran through northeastern Massachusetts), the Connecticut River, Philadelphia, and Patterson, New Jersey. Twenty percent of the output of the industry was provided by one company, The Boston Associates. They were an expanded continuation of the group that had underwritten Mr. Lowell's first effort at Waltham. The most noted of their projects was the construction of a major—entirely new— town on the Merrimack River. After buying out the local canal company that bypassed the falls near the junction with the Concord River, The Boston Associates erected a major dam. It supplied power for one of the largest textile factories

Table 6-1   New England Cotton Industry Output, 1805—1860

Year	Yards of Cloth (000's)	Value Added ($000's) Cloth	Year	Yards of Cloth (000's)	Value Added ($000's) Cloth
1805	46	2	1830	141,616	7,435
1806	62	3	1831	161,566	8,482
1807	84	4	1832	205,836	10,806
1808	181	10	1833	231,486	12,153
1809	255	13	1834	238,260	12,509
1810	648	34	1835	250,773	13,166
1811	801	42	1836	283,182	14,867
1812	1,055	55	1837	308,079	16,174
1813	1,459	77	1838	315,440	16,561
1814	1,960	103	1839	317,605	16,674
1815	2,358	124	1840	323,000	16,958
1816	840	44	1841	353,111	18,538
1817	3,883	204	1842	373,895	19,629
1818	7,216	379	1843	369,565	19,402
1819	9,941	522	1844	395,762	20,778
1820	13,874	728	.	.	.
1821	22,292	1,170	.	.	.
1822	30,171	1,584	1850	596,867	31,336
1823	41,459	2,177	.	.	.
1824	55,771	2,928	.	.	.
1825	69,677	3.658	1855	634,200	33,296
1826	84,349	4,429	.	.	.
1827	95,005	4,988	.	.	.
1828	111,187	5,837	1860	857,225	45,004
1829	128,779	6,761			

Source: Adapted from Robert B. Zevin, "The Growth of Cotton Textile Production after 1815," in Robert W. Fogel and Stanley L. Engerman (eds.), *The Reinterpretation of American Economic History,* Harper & Row, New York, 1971, Table 1 (New England Cotton Industry Output, 1805—1860), pp. 123—24. Reprinted by permission of Harper & Row Publishers, Inc.

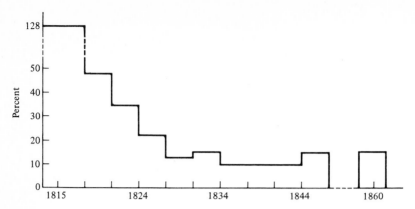

Figure 6-1 Average annual increase in cotton cloth production in the United States, 1815–1860. *(Computed from Robert B. Zevin, "The Growth of Cotton Textile Production after 1815," in Robert W. Fogel and Stanley L. Engerman (eds.),* The Reinterpretation of American Economic History, *Harper & Row, New York, 1971, Table I (New England Cotton Industry Output, 1805–1860), pp. 123–124. Reprinted by permission of Harper & Row Publishers, Inc.)*

constructed as of that time, with nearly 1,000 looms for weaving cloth. The dam had sufficient extra power to operate other mills as well, including one of the largest woolen mills built in the United States by the 1830s. Appropriately enough, the town that emerged out of all these factories, with the necessary auxiliary housing and commercial facilities to service them, was named Lowell.

The production of cotton cloth continued to grow at a brisk pace until the Civil War (Figure 6-1), although, as is inevitable in all new industries, the rate of increase gradually slowed down. One obvious source of such gains, improvement in technology, continued to contribute to the advance. For example, in the late 1820s several improvements culminated in the introduction of "ring spinners"—essentially a modification which took the pressure off the spindle and placed it on the bobbin during spinning. This allowed the operation to be run up to three times faster than before and also produced a finer thread. The impressive total effect of such improvements can be seen in the cost of producing a yard of standard cotton cloth. In the forty-five years before the Civil War it fell from 18 to 2 cents!

Recent investigations have established, however, that the traditional emphasis on technological advances does not explain the predominance of growth in textile output. A careful examination of the sources of the increase in sales of cotton textiles shows that about half of it can be explained by various factors which increased demand,[2] such as the growth of the domestic population (which was expanding at the rate of 3 percent a year), the fall in transport costs, and the increase in per capita income. These factors would have caused a large increase in the output of cotton textiles even in the absence of any improvements in

[2] Robert B. Zevin, "The Growth of Cotton Textile Production after 1815," in Robert W. Fogel and Stanley L. Engerman (eds.), *The Reinterpretation of American Economic History,* Harper & Row, New York, 1971.

technology! This is a surprising finding—at least in the context of previous accounts—and illustrates an argument presented in the introduction to this chapter: Industrialization is not likely to be the initiating force in economic growth. It is partly a response to growth already occurring. Furthermore, the improvements in technology which do occur in the developing industry are also partly a reaction to the increase in demand for that product. Potential inventors would probably try to devise a better process of spinning and weaving if the likely rewards appeared to justify the effort—and even if the demand for cotton cloth were not growing. If it were growing, however, they would be more likely to notice the opportunity, and the increasing demand would make it appear worthwhile to put additional effort into devising more productive techniques. Thus the industrial revolution that has been held to be so important to modern growth begins to take on the appearance of a result as much as a cause. A good part of it is simply innovation induced by growth in demand.

Beyond Cotton Textiles

Most previous accounts of the development of the textile industry have focused on cotton textile factories. Perhaps that is understandable, as they were the first and the largest part of the textile industry to undergo transformation (and one can expound at length about the operation of textile machinery). Yet cotton was only one fiber and cloth was only one product to which this new technology was applied in the antebellum period. In addition to the improvements in the use of cotton fibers in cloth there were parallel advances in wool, silk, linen, felt, and mixtures thereof. Besides textile manufacture major gains were also scored in the manufacture of lace, canvas, carpets, bagging, and knitted goods.

One obvious example of this broadening scope of technology occurred in the composition of the products themselves. Before industrialization, cloth was fairly homogeneous: cotton was cotton and wool was wool, without much variation. When different fibers were mixed together, such as linsey-woolsey, they were usually segregated by warp and woof (that is, lengthwise and crosswise) to obtain the desired mixtures of strength and softness. The new textile machinery, however, began to provide opportunities for mixing and extending the available fibers within the thread or yarn itself. The first mechanical spinning machinery could handle only long-staple cotton (which, in the United States, could be raised only on the coastal islands of Georgia), but operators soon learned how to dilute it with the more abundant short-staple fibers. Later they learned how to mix in cotton waste as well. In the 1830s they were devising mixtures of cotton and wool. Soon afterward they developed a combination of hemp and cotton waste to replace the former "negro cloth" made out of wool. This material brought the word "shoddy" into common use, although its present connotation is misleading in that the material was highly serviceable for its extremely low price of 15 cents a yard. Just before the Civil War, a method of mechanically shredding flax (formerly a laborious, back-breaking job of hand flailing) was devised. This allowed the mixture of cotton and flax fibers to form an imitation linen cloth. By 1860, therefore, the existing boundaries between different types of cloths were becoming blurred as the industry continuously sought new combinations to obtain a better balance of costs and fabric characteristics. Synthetic fibers might yet be a thing of the future, but "synthetic textiles" were well established.

Wool

The production of woolen textiles did not increase as rapidly as that of cotton. Part of this slower pace is explained by the introduction of cotton itself. In an economic sense it was effectively a brand new competitor in the fabric markets and therefore naturally displaced other materials from some of their traditional niches. Wool also took somewhat longer to adapt to the mechanical processes of factory production. This was ironic in that it had actually preceded cotton in the use of mechanical power in one of its stages of processing. Before 1790—and the opening of Slater's cotton-spinning mill—water-powered wool-carding mills were in operation in the United States (carding consists of drawing the shorter wool fibers through comblike "teeth" to align them for spinning). The development of the power for wool in the 1820s ran about a decade behind that of cotton. The 1820s also saw the introduction of the Goulding condenser, a device which automatically transferred the wool fibers from one stage of carding to another and then directly into the spinning equipment.[3]

Another distasteful step of hand labor was eliminated in the 1830s with the introduction of equipment to crush and filter out the burrs from the raw wool. Still another element of hand labor was displaced in the 1850s when a system of mechanically combing wool (the counterpart of carding, for long-fiber wool) was devised. Observers touring the woolen mills at Lowell in the late 1850s noted that except for the exterior of the building, the factory had been effectively rebuilt since its original construction some twenty-five years earlier. These ongoing efforts to increase productivity were reflected in the cost of wool cloth, which fell to less than half of its initial level during that same period. In terms of its market share, woolen cloth was certainly not a growth industry—but it was nevertheless experiencing large improvements in technology comparable to those in the cotton textile industry.

These gains in productivity through the adoption of mechanized processes appeared throughout the woven-fabric industries. Knitting machines were first used in New York State in the 1830s. Soon thereafter, knitted underwear, once the exclusive possession of the rich, became commonplace. Power weaving was adapted to silk in the 1830s, but it never became a large industry because of the high cost of the raw material. (And, one should add, the continued cheapening of competing fabrics.) Americans never succeeded in raising silk domestically so they relied on imports of the raw material whose cost tended to confine it to such accessories as ribbons. Mechanization was also applied to the manufacture of

---

[3] The invention of the Goulding condenser provides a counterexample to the frequent equation of the rise of child labor with industrialization. Before the introduction of the condenser, children frequently performed the simple task of transferring wool from one machine to the next. But although child labor is cheap, it is also likely to be used for more routine steps and is therefore more susceptible to displacement by mechanical innovations.

heavier fabrics, such as the bagging constructed from hemp. By the time of the Civil War, the border states of Kentucky and Missouri were producing nearly 10 million yards of the material annually. That volume of output is one measure of the progress in the fabric industry; without the preceding improvements in technology, that quantity of material—which was primarily used to wrap raw cotton—would have been prohibitively expensive and an alternative form of packaging would necessarily have been used.

Up from Homespun

When the price of a product drops relative to that of most other goods, as that of textiles did in the period before the Civil War, the quantity of the product used per capita normally rises. In addition, consumers tend to desire a somewhat higher quality of the product. In 1800 most Americans, most of the time, were dressed in homespun. It was slow work turning out such cloth by hand. It took a full week's labor to perform all the tasks involved in producing a few yards of material. As a consequence, most individuals processed only a limited number of items of clothing which they wore, then patched, repaired, and handed down until all conceivable wear had been squeezed out of them. Furthermore, most clothes were rather drab affairs, dyed in simple natural colors and with little else in the way of decoration.

As the price of textiles began to fall, Americans began to modify their clothing habits. They typically held a larger number of clothes in their closet with several noticeable effects in the way they used them. Clothing was discarded sooner, and one incidental beneficiary was the paper industry, which collected rags. Clothing also became more differentiated. Individuals could earmark particular clothes for work, for Sunday, or for evening wear; whereas before, one outfit had often had to do double duty. Clothes became more richly colored and decorated. The first cotton textiles had been given patterns by hand-block printing, but by the 1830s rotary printing machinery which performed this task had been perfected. Weaving also became more sophisticated in that manufacturers learned how to dye yarn and weave more elaborate patterns into the cloth. In addition, a whole range of woven decorations, such as laces and ribbons. became cheaper as the new technology was applied to their production. In the 1850s the sewing machine came into general use, a logical innovation in that it saved on the expensive American labor time devoted to sewing this increased quantity of fabric into clothes.

THE IRON INDUSTRY

The traditional explanation of the industrial revolution has it that the key sectors were textiles and iron, perhaps with coal and steam engines acting as important auxiliaries. If that indeed were so, then—so the story goes—the United States batted only about .500. For while textiles were an obvious growth sector in the antebellum period, the American iron industry appeared to be backward and noninventive. For example, while English blast furnaces had, early in the 1800s, been almost entirely converted to coke for fuel (coke was derived from coal), American operations persisted in using charcoal almost up to the Civil War. Again, American ironmasters continued to use the older hammer-and-reheating methods of refining pig iron long after the English had adopted the new puddling-and-rolling process (a method of heating and shaping the pig iron without bringing it in direct contact with the fuel). Americans appeared to be stubbornly clinging to older methods when new, more productive ones were available.

Some writers have attempted to explain the Americans' persistence in using charcoal by reference to the fact that wood was cheaper than coal in the United States. That observation is correct but it is not important in this case. Although charcoal was derived from wood, most of its total cost was accounted for by labor. It took considerable time to cut the wood, prepare the fire pits, turn and wet down the material over the period of a week or so, and finally gather the finished charcoal out of the fire pits. Charcoal was very demanding of labor, just the type of process which Americans would *not* be using—if things were equal.

Other things were not equal, however. The alternative to using charcoal was using coal as a fuel, but only a particular kind of coal, bituminous or soft coal, was usable at that time. It contains methane gas which was necessary for the burning process in the furnaces which had been devised up to 1833.[4] There were large quantities of bituminous coal at hand in the northeastern United States, but almost all significant deposits discovered before 1840 contained sulfur, which produced a poor grade of iron.

A demonstration that the Americans' continuing use of charcoal was not merely a result of their interia occurred in the 1830s. In 1829 the English developed the "hot blast" method for blast furnaces. This replaced the picturesque bellows which had forced air over the burning coke and ore to make it burn faster. The "hot blast" channeled the escaping warm exhaust from the furnace back into it, thus increasing the temperature of the burning process, making it more efficient, and thereby saving on fuel. It also opened the possibility that anthracite, or hard coal, could now be used. Entrepreneurs on both sides of the Atlantic saw the opportunity almost immediately and almost simultaneously in 1833 the technique was perfected in both the United States and Wales. From that time on, American iron manufacturers east of the Allegheny Mountains—where it was available—began a rapid shift to anthracite.

Then there was the case of the Americans' "backwardness" in continuing to use the older method of reheating and hammering pig iron into finished iron. Until some refinements were made in blast furnace design in the 1830s, wrought iron (that is, the hammered product) was generally superior to the rolled variety. It was, of course, also more expensive, but in most forms of employment in the United States up to 1830, the additional expense was justified. A good portion of iron consumed in the United States in the first decade of the nineteenth century went into such things as tools, stoves, kitchenware, and building hardware, in

---

[4] Ironically, it is the methane gas that aids the burning process in certain uses of coal which makes underground coal mining so dangerous. It is the chief culprit in coal-mine explosions.

general, items which did not use large amounts of iron but in which quality and dependability were important characteristics. This pattern of use was in contrast to that of England, where a larger proportion of iron went into engineering or construction applications, and therefore the cheapness of the rolled iron was more attractive. The Americans, of course, were more likely to use wood in larger items, such as bridge supports and machinery frames, for the same reason.

Between 1830 and 1860 continual refinements in technology and its modification to particular American conditions caused the American iron industry to appear more like its "modern" English counterpart. The improvements in blast furnaces and rolling mill design tended to make that format of production more efficient compared to alternative techniques. The mills also tended to become larger as their designs evolved, in order to take advantage of economies in the use of materials and labor. With larger size they moved toward serving larger geographical markets and thus became more free to locate where transportation costs were least. In the period just before the Civil War this often meant Pennsylvania, where the river system cheaply joined the coal of the eastern and central parts of the state with the iron ore from the Great Lakes areas. Thus the mills began to concentrate on the Delaware River at Philadelphia, the Lehigh at Bethlehem, the Lackawanna at Scranton, and—already the clear leader in 1860—the Ohio at Pittsburgh.

The conclusive demonstration that iron was, in fact, a growth sector in the antebellum period appears in the production estimates for the period. In the four or five decades preceding the Civil War, the output of iron increased by a factor of 5 per capita. (Total production increased twentyfold.) This equals a long-term average yearly growth of about 4 percent per capita, which is quite high compared with the trend of other economic aggregates of that era. This quantitative record refutes any impressionist evidence that the American iron industry was backward in any meaningful sense in the period.

Iron as an Input

Oscar Wilde once said that you can make an economist out of a parrot by teaching him to recite the words "supply and demand." The statement provides levity but, alas, is misleading. The essence of economic analysis is not in naming categories of behavior but rather in applying them to particular situations in order to improve our understanding of how and why they occur. Simply repeating the words "supply and demand" provides no more insight into economic behavior than memorizing the words "hypertension and cardiovascular system" makes one a doctor.

A good illustration of such a discrepancy is found in most previous accounts of the American iron industry before the Civil War. Developments on the supply side of the industry have been treated in considerable detail. Technological improvements and changes in the organization of the firms were expounded upon at length, but little notice was given to where all this growing output of iron was going. It must have been assumed that the demand for iron was always there as long as improved technology reduced its price sufficiently. While demand curves do slope down—that is, more output can be sold at lower prices—that does not seem to explain the vast increase in iron consumption that took place.

Iron is what is termed an intermediate good. It is not bought in the supermarket and carried home to be consumed with pork roast or tomatoes. It is used as an input for various products which in turn provide the final services to the consumers. The demand for iron, therefore, is derived from the demand for the products within which it is used. And a good part of the expansion in the use of iron in this period can be explained by changing patterns of demand for service in response to the general evolution of the economy.

In the first decade or so of the 1800s most iron was produced by relatively small enterprises, scattered across the countryside, in conjunction with the predominantly rural markets they served. Their products consisted of such items as nails, kettles, toolheads, horseshoes, and, in general, a variety of near-custommade items to serve diverse local demands. A few larger items, such as anchors, cannon, or nail rods,[5] were made in specialized foundries, but these were still the exceptions. However, forces were at work in the economy which would soon overwhelm this localized pattern.

The development of cities is a phenomenon which appears to be more typical of later years in United States history. Indeed, it would be several decades after the Civil War before the absolute numbers of city dwellers would approach that of rural areas. Yet the antebellum period of 1820–1860 is the one in which the percentage of the population living in urban areas increased the fastest. Furthermore, some of the cities became quite large then, even by modern standards. New York City had more than 1 million residents by the beginning of the Civil War. The nation remained predominantly rural for a while, but the urban sector was growing rapidly and, with it, the demands for products particularly useful in urban areas.

One of these products, interestingly enough, was the cast-iron stove. Actually, Americans were already familiar with it in the early 1800s, as its use had been increasing ever since the mid-1700s. Ben Franklin, for example, devised one model which still bears his name. This trend had been prompted by increasing prices for fuel—especially when it had to be transported any distance—and labor. (Compared with fireplaces, stoves economized on both fuel and labor.) Urbanization encouraged this trend by shifting the population even farther from its rural supplies of wood. At the same time, coal (delivered in urban areas) was becoming cheaper because of the construction of the canal system serving the Northeast urban area (see Chapter 5). In the 1830s stoves were developed which would burn the anthracite coal being brought into production for the iron industry. By the 1840s the cast-iron stove industry had taken on many of the characteristics of well-established sectors. Specialized foundries, such as those at Philadelphia and Albany, New York, were turning out large quantities of major stove parts. To save on transportation cost, these were shipped to major transportation hubs,

---

[5] "Slitting mills" cut iron sheets into stips which were then hammered into nails by local blacksmiths.

such as New York City, where they were assembled. In the years before the Civil War more than half a million stoves were being sold yearly. In relation to the population, this made them as common as refrigerators or air conditioners are today. In effect, it meant that a sizeable portion of the increase in antebellum iron production was providing cooking and heating services in the economy. Ultimately, therefore, iron was becoming a substitute for bricks (in fireplaces), trees (in cordwood), and labor (in wood chopping).

The public sector of the expanding urban areas also consumed sizeable amounts of iron. The most important needs were for cast-iron pipe to build the major water and sewer systems which the urban centers demanded as they became more densely settled. Street-lamp poles and water hydrants were also necessary. Privately owned buildings serving the general public also found uses for iron. As stores, business offices, and tenements became larger they increasingly used iron beams to span the longer distances and support the larger loads. More iron was also used to decorate the fronts of public buildings with cast-iron fronts and pillars. This introduction of iron as ornamentation was only one part of a general trend to use the new material for decoration. Every new private home of any consequence in Northern cities "had to have" wrought-iron railings and a cast-iron fountain.

Iron for Transportation

Almost everyone knows that the railroad became a large consumer of iron products. W. W. Rostow in his *Stages of Economic Growth* even made it an important element in his "takeoff" of United States growth. Actually the railroad was a relative late comer in the antebellum period. Before 1840, not only stoves but also steamboats consumed more iron than did the "iron horse." Steamboats, of course, grew very rapidly in the twenty years from 1810–1830, before the railroad was even begun. By 1830 there were engineering firms located on the upper Ohio River at Pittsburgh, Wheeling, and Cincinnati, and along the Northeast coast, which specialized in producing steamboat engines. These were quite large items, with engine cylinders 6 feet in diameter and 10 feet deep being common. Along with such engine blocks went all the correspondingly large accessories: boilers, shafts, gears, and mountings. A single steamboat engine used a lot of iron. As late as 1840, probably more than twice as much iron was going into steam engines for steamboats as was going into railroad locomotives.

There were, of course, a number of other uses for steam engines, such as in coal mines, rolling mills, and sugar mills in the antebellum period. In the 1850s steam engine manufacturers began turning out small, standardized, "off-the-shelf" models. These were made like sewing machines or clocks, using interchangeable parts, and were designed for smaller businesses such as farms or machine shops. With the appropriate attachments they could perform such varied tasks as grinding corn, or powering a lathe or a drill press. Yet, as measured by total horsepower, the steam engine was predominantly employed in transportation. By itself, the steamboat accounted for more than half of the existing steampower in the United States in 1860, and it, combined with railroad locomotives, accounted for more than 80 percent of rated horsepower in existing steam engines.

This predominance contrasts with England, where steam engines were used extensively to power factories, mills, and mining operations. Once again the Americans were not being obstinately backward, however. They had a cheaper source of power in the form of falling water, which the English lacked. So the Americans used waterwheels to provide much of the stationary power required for their factories and mills. In the 1840s when most of their feasible sites for the waterwheels had been taken, Americans began replacing them with water turbines. These were a recent French innovation which extracted more of the potential energy from a given volume of falling water. They were more expensive per unit of energy produced than the older waterwheels, but were still cheaper than installing steam engines with their large capital and recurring operating costs. Water power continued to be the most important source of stationary power in the United States for another four decades after 1840.

It also determined much of the geographical pattern of industry as well. Most heavy industries in the decades before 1860 were located in Pennsylvania. The object was to minimize transportation costs—which could be a major expense to the sector, given its consumption of large quantities of raw materials. New England attracted the majority of light industry, however, primarily because of the availability of water power sites in that region. Clearly this was the motivating factor in textiles, but it was also evident in the hundreds of mills and factories erected in the river valleys to produce such items as knives, axes, tin pails, wire, pins, and clocks. Typically these products benefited from some, but not large amounts of mechanical power in their production. In addition, they did not incur large transportation costs in either bringing the necessary raw materials into the area or shipping out the finished products. That was an important consideration because New England generally had higher labor, transportation, and fuel costs than much of the rest of the nation. If some of these costs had been large, they would have wiped out the region's advantage in cheaper (water) power—as did indeed happen after the Civil War,[6] but as of 1860 a regular, year-round precipitation rate, and plenty of hills for water to run down, gave New England a distinct advantage as a location for light industry.

On Track

One use of iron was becoming readily obvious in the two decades before the Civil War. A dense, interconnecting network of railroad lines was rapidly being completed in settled areas of the United States. In effect, that meant a lot of iron rails needed for the track. The railroads had experimented with almost every conceivable combination of materials before they finally adopted the familiar, T-shaped

[6] New England suffered as a "declining" region for the first half of the twentieth century largely because the shift to electricity destroyed its natural advantage in power. In recent years its relative recovery has been accomplished by shifting its economic base to activities in the "knowledge" sector, such as electronics, medicine, and education, where its traditional cost handicaps in the national market are again minimized.

iron rail. Iron, it seemed, was the only material generally available that combined strength, resilience, and relative cheapness. This last criterion was probably the major factor which at first caused railroad managers to search so diligently for alternative forms of track. When they were first adopted, iron rails were relatively expensive. The promise of a large future market for them, given that railroads were obviously going to use them, however, set off considerable effort to devise ways to produce them more cheaply.

The first American mills which produced only iron rails began to operate in the mid-1840s. These were quite large by previous standards. The capacity of one located in Pittsburgh was equal to the entire output in the state of Pennsylvania two decades earlier. The overall design or hardware of these rolling mills did not seem to embody many improvements in productivity, however. They were merely scaled up in size compared to those constructed previously. One measure of the relative inefficiency of these mills was that, until 1860 at least, a large portion of the iron rails used to construct American railroads was imported from Britain. The advantage of English ironmasters in rolling cheap iron was sufficient to allow them to pay the additional freight charges across the Atlantic and still be able to compete with the domestic product.

That margin of superiority was in part due to the rather surprising discovery that iron ore and coal had distinct local personalities. When the Americans attempted to use refining techniques which the British had successfully employed, they usually did not work. At that time chemistry had not yet advanced to the point where it was recognized that such properties as acidity and certain trace elements were crucial—and could be manipulated—in the making of iron. So the Americans were forced to proceed on a trial-and-error basis to find specific combinations of local minerals which would yield iron economically—a form of ad hoc metallurgy. In the period before the Civil War the American iron industry learned to recognize and build around such specific properties of local minerals. One major example of success was the discovery and development of the sulfur-free bituminous coal near Connellsville, Pennsylvania. One by-product of this localized learning curve was that the American iron producers narrowed the margin of superiority which the English industry held over them. Imports of British iron rails began to taper off and, after 1860, were mostly confined to very prosperous periods when the domestic industry was operating at its maximum capacity.

One problem which ad hoc metallurgy did not solve was that the existing rails were simply not strong enough to withstand long-term use, and gradually flattened and became misshapen. While some progress was made in increasing the strength, and thereby the average life, of iron rails, the problem was not effectively solved until steel rails supplanted them after the Civil War. In the meanwhile the iron-rail industry was compelled to serve two functions. The first function was to supply new rails to construct additions to the existing railroad network, and from 1845 to 1870 that was an important demand because the network was being extended rapidly. The second function required little new iron but consisted instead of rerolling the used, misshapen rails back into their original form. The demand for this service was substantially independent of the construction of new facilities. It was determined by the volume of traffic and hence the depreciation of the existing rail network. Total traffic also increased very rapidly in the decades after 1840, however, so that the amount of rerolling increased rapidly as well. The Americans quickly captured the rerolling sector of the iron-rail industry because of their natural advantage of location. That by itself was a sizeable amount of production activity, given the magnitude which the total iron sector quickly obtained.

Beyond Transport

Like the cast-iron stoves, the steam engines, locomotives, and iron rails were only intermediate products on the way to satisfying human demands. *Directly,* iron in these products was providing transportation services. The steamboat and the railroad were obviously major improvements over wagons and pack trains for hauling a wide array of goods. At the level of basic physics, iron on iron (in the case of the railroad), or iron moving through water, had a much lower coefficient of friction than that of wagon wheels, or hooves on a hard surface. *Indirectly,* iron was reducing that cost of moving goods from place to place, thereby allowing new forms of production to compete with local self-sufficiency. In essense, the use of iron was growing rapidly because it provided an attractive substitute to the services of the local blacksmith, hand loom, and cobbler. One could list a large number of other functions which were absorbing increasing quantities of iron in the antebellum period. We have not, for example, detailed the growth of nails, wire, or barrel hoops. The underlying motivation would be quite similar, however. Iron was a basic material which was becoming cheaper and, as such, was being substituted for existing materials—and, given its own specific properties, was creating new ones as well.

THE AMERICAN SYSTEM OF MANUFACTURES

The English who saw American production facilities in the antebellum period were not particularly impressed with the nation's cotton textile mills or blast furnaces. Such things were commonplace at home and sometimes even more advanced than the American models. They were, however, impressed with the organization of a number of American manufacturing industries which produced relatively intricate products such as clocks, firearms, and sewing machines. They noted how machinery was extensively used to reduce even minor steps of labor, how stages of production were coordinated to eliminate delays in the flow of materials, and how products and their parts were standardized to minimize fitting and adjusting in assembly.

Two incidents illustrate this contrast between the two economies. One was carefully staged, and the other was comically inadvertent.

In the early 1850s the British were so intrigued by American-made rifles that they sent a Parliamentary committee to the United States to find out how they were made. In a routine marked by a bit of early-day show biz, the Americans selected ten muskets made in ten different preceding years, disassembled them, and mixed the parts up in a box. They then borrowed a worker from the armory work force who, in a short time, reassembled the ten guns, using only a screwdriver. The British were flabbergasted. In England it would have taken a skilled crafts worker the better part of a day to hand-file and finish the parts of one musket into a workable unit. The committee was so impressed that it paid the Americans the ultimate compliment of buying their machinery to make its own muskets.

In the late 1830s a Connecticut manufacturer began producing cheap "24-hour" wind-up clocks by stamping many of the parts out of sheets of brass. Searching for a possible market, he sent a consignment to England. The English customs officials bought the clocks for their declared price, an option they were given in order to forestall underdeclaration of value and hence underpayment of tariff charges. The American producer, however, was delighted. He had received what he believed was a good price for his merchandise and he quickly sent another shipment. The customs agents bought these, also, so the American producer sent a third and even larger consignment. The British officials—presumably by now well supplied with "24-hour" clocks—gave up, allowing them to enter the country without challenge.

Indigenous Technology

Probably what surprised the English observers the most was that they had thought of the Americans as followers rather than leaders, insofar as knowledge concerning production techniques was concerned. They had adapted English innovations in textiles and iron production to their own conditions and admittedly shown considerable ingenuity in doing so, but as for developing new methods—well, that was something else. In retrospect, however, the American advances are not surprising. Developing new techniques is, in principle, no different than modifying existing ones. Both practices require innovative effort. As long as the British were doing the difficult work in developing such sectors as textiles, it was reasonable for Americans to merely modify, then use any improvements for their own purposes, rather than independently creating a separate new technology. In other areas, where the returns from innovation appeared to be higher for the Americans than for the English, however, it was logical for the former to take the lead. One such obvious category was in labor-saving innovations, because that resource (labor) was more expensive in the United States. And indeed, those processes where American technology was considered to be superior in the antebellum period were universally characterized by a saving on labor, often at the cost of using somewhat more capital or natural resources.

Consider, for example, the principle of interchangeable parts, the technique which so impressed the British Parliamentary committee and probably became the most widely recognized American contribution to technology of the period. Its essential idea is to standardize the various component parts of a product so that they are completely interchangeable; that is, it does not make any difference which part of a given kind is used in a product—any one will work equally well.

This saves labor in two important ways. First, it eliminates the labor involved in fitting or matching individual parts in the assembly process. This can make a huge difference, as the British committee must have noted. Whereas American workers could easily assemble fifty rifles a day, their British counterparts considered two muskets a good day's work. That differential of twenty-five times in productivity is explained by the English workers being forced to shape, file, polish, and generally modify each part they worked with, while the Americans merely snapped them together and tightened the screws. Second, it greatly reduces the labor involved in repair. If a part becomes defective in a product manufactured with interchangeable parts, it can be readily replaced by its exact counterpart. Otherwise, each replacement involves the same fashioning and fitting required to put new pieces together.

The adoption of interchangeable parts can be a major gain to an economy, even one in which the savings of labor would be less than in the United States. While it is almost inevitable that some individuals in an economy will notice such potential gains, certain conditions must nevertheless be met in order to capture them. First, the adoption of standardized manufacture requires a reasonably large market for the product. Interchangeable parts imply a much finer degree of production specialization than had generally been possible until the early 1800s. In the Springfield Armory in the late 1820s, for instance, shaping wooden gun stocks took sixteen separate machines, each devoted exclusively to its particular function. It takes a considerable volume of output—and a market to purchase it—to justify the large cost of acquiring such a stock of capital. It is not an accident that interchangeable parts became common for the first time in the United States. While high American labor costs encouraged it, the growth of the domestic market past a certain level allowed that degree of specialization for the first time in history.

Second, the adoption of interchangeable parts requires new forms of technology, including much finer tolerances in production methods than are otherwise necessary. This requires both new machinery and new methods of measurement beyond those available in 1800. The antebellum period witnessed the introduction of such measuring devices as the vernier caliper—a small hand tool which allowed individual workers to check machined tolerances to within less than one-hundreth of an inch—and wire gauges—necessary in the manufacture of clock springs. The total collection of such improvements allowed parts to be cut accurately enough so that they fit and then functioned with little further hand finishing. In essence, that expresses the principle of interchangeable parts—substituting machine accuracy for hand labor.

The American Contribution

Eli Whitney is credited with introducing the concept of interchangeable parts, but he was not the first to suggest it. The French military had used the principle in producing cannon carriages, for example. They had had some success with the method because the tolerances in that product had been rather large. In general, Europeans who experimented with the technique in the late 1700s concluded that it was "visionary." It simply was noneconomic yet, given the prevailing conditions in the economic systems. Whitney's contribution is probably best summarized by observing that he was the first to actively seek to implement the technique in circumstances where it would be productive. Nor was Whitney entirely successful at the beginning. Still basking in public admiration—but not remuneration—for devising the cotton gin, he succeeded in obtaining a contract from the federal government to produce 10,000 muskets at a little more than $13 each, an unbelievably low price in the early 1800s. Whitney did make some progress in standardizing and improving the efficiency of the production process. He constructed forms and jigs, for example, to guide the hand shaping of his workers and to eliminate later fitting. He also devised the first milling machine, by which sharp teeth, on a gearlike wheel similar to a modern power saw, cut metal. He failed to meet the terms of his first contract, however, and the government granted him another only after extensive negotiation. Whitney's problem was simply that the technology necessary to make his (conceptually solid) methods work was not yet developed.[7]

What Whitney failed to achieve in a surge of inspired effort in the first decade of the 1800s was gradually achieved in a series of evolutionary improvements in the antebellum period. The basic problem of shaping wood—that ubiquitous American material—into irregular forms took a major step forward with the invention of the Blanchard Stocking lathe, in 1818. The lathe was originally conceived to cut gun stocks, but its basic design was modified to turn out such other shapes as wheel spokes, shoe lasts, ax handles, and oars. The task of cutting metal, both accurately and rapidly, was advanced by the evolution of the milling machine, which culminated in the standard Lincoln model in the 1850s. By that time various modifications of the basic model were used in producing sewing machines, textile machinery, hardware, knives, firearms, and locomotives. During the Civil War a further model, the universal milling machine, was devised. It was originally conceived to sharpen drill bits by machine, but it proved to be able to machine all types of spiral designs—including the cutting of gears.

Other basic machine operations were also perfected about this time. The turret lathe, generally available after 1850, capped a series of improvements in mechanical drilling techniques. It allowed a number of boring operations to be performed by one piece of equipment by using a bank of tool attachments. A later refinement "automated" these operations through the use of a series of cams. Hand finishing of metal was greatly reduced by improvements in grinding and polishing equipment, and advances in the presses and hammers used in foundries substantially increased the ability to bend and shape sheets of metal—what today we know as stamping. Thus, by 1860 a good number of the basic steps involved in fashioning materials into finished products had been adapted to machine functions.

All the while, managers in almost every industry in the economy were learn-

---

[7] Whitney's first experience with musket manufacture is an early example of what we today have begun to call military "cost overruns." He, like Lockheed with the C-5A cargo plane, expected to be able to develop technology to meet his contract at certain costs. The failure to achieve those advances in knowledge dictated older, less efficient methods of production and therefore increased the anticipated costs.

ing to adapt these new methods to the production of their products. Sometimes this meant simply replacing hand operations by power machinery, as in the furniture industry's extensive adoption of saws and lathes. At other times it involved more basic changes in production methods or materials, as in the button industry where hand-cast pewter buttons were superseded by those mechanically cut out of sheets of brass. Admittedly this diffusion of new techniques was incomplete by 1860, yet there had been very few economic processes in the antebellum United States which had not been touched by it. Even in activities which were still characterized by hand labor as of 1860, such as cigar rolling or jewelry manufacture, some mechanized steps were being used.

Continuous Processes, or the Assembly Line

Industrial engineers have invariably noted how much labor is spent in transferring materials between—or in setting up—various production steps compared with that spent in performing the steps themselves. Thus it is no surprise that a good portion of energy Americans spent on innovation was directed toward reducing the labor employed in shuttling and arranging materials in production. After all, labor was a valuable resource, and savings were desirable wherever they could be achieved.

Of course, the incentive to economize on labor had always been particularly strong in the American economy, even before the technological advances of the antebellum period came along to facilitate the task. The flour mill Oliver Evans designed at Philadelphia in 1784 was generally recognized for its savings on labor. He devised a series of elevators and conveyors which unloaded the wheat from boats, moved it through the stages of filtering, grinding, and shifting in the mill, to the final step where it was funneled into barrels. Evans' emphasis on labor-saving automation continued to characterize later American flour mills as they grew larger and moved westward, following their suppliers, before the Civil War.

This effort to save on labor was most obvious in the processing of agricultural commodities before the Civil War. This is understandable, however, in that such products were generally low in value relative to their bulk so that labor costs in transferring them could be large compared to their final price. It would take more labor to move a dollar's worth of corn or wheat, for example, than it would to transfer the same value of clock or firearm parts the same distance. This judgment—that the bulk of a product, compared to its value, affects the amount of effort made to reduce the costs of labor involved in moving the product—appears to be confirmed if one looks at nonagricultural materials. Those whose value was lowest compared to their volume, such as lumber, coal, and ore, showed much the same emphasis on labor-saving methods.

The hog-slaughtering and packing industry was probably the most obvious example of organization designed to reduce the labor costs of transferring material. The industry was centered at Cincinnati, around which the major American hog-producing region developed after 1815. Contemporary observers marveled at how ordered and routine the process had become. In a typical factory, the hog carcasses were hung on a moving overhead track which moved from one station to another. At each station workers performed a specific task, such as removing the heart or cutting off one hind quarter. The operation moved fast enough so that workers barely had time to complete one operation before the next one was upon them. In effect, all labor time was directed toward production steps; none was being diverted in preparing the material for them.

While the hog operations of Cincinnati represented the ultimate saving of labor by assembly-line organization in the antebellum period, they did not, interestingly enough, use any form of interchangeable parts. In this type of operation—actually a form of disassembly—that would have involved the use of specialized machines to make particular cuts, which was ruled out (as it still is even today) by the irregularities of animal carcasses. It is one of those processes, like haircuts, doctor's diagnoses, or serving a meal in a restaurant, where the variations in the individual product—and thus the necessity of compensating judgment—rule out mechanized production. Yet that does not rule out the possibility of increasing labor productivity, as the Cincinnati packing plants demonstrate. If one can develop techniques to "concentrate" the particular activities which require labor, then the remaining functions, otherwise performed by labor, can be produced by substituting less expensive resources.[8]

Henry Ford is usually given credit for devising the assembly line in his quest for a better means for putting automobiles together. Indeed, his reported contribution is almost a stock item in American folklore. Yet, as the above examples suggest, that innovation is not as unique or dramatic as is commonly assumed. Assembly-line methods of manufacture were clearly visualized and used at least a century before Ford appeared on the scene. In general it was not the lack of the appropriate technology which prevented the use of assembly-line methods—the specific problems encountered were usually solved within a short time. Usually it was relative economic costs, particularly those of labor vis-à-vis capital, which were most important in deciding when assembly-line methods would be adopted. Such methods generally increase the productivity of labor by using large quantities of capital per worker. Thus assembly-line methods became more attractive (compared with such labor-intensive forms of production as custom projects or batch processing) as the price of labor rose relative to that of capital.

And precisely that shift toward an increasing scarcity of labor has been characteristic of the long-term development of the American economy, which explains the continuing tendency to move to automation or assembly-line forms of operations. In this context the automobile factory can be seen as simply a rather dramatic example of a longer-term trend in production methods. It in no

---

[8] This is undoubtedly what has been happening in medical services in recent years. Despite the widespread belief that such services, being labor-intensive, cannot be improved in efficiency, all careful studies of them have found them to be undergoing respectable gains in productivity. In doctor services this has undoubtedly taken the form of more screening of routine matters by nurses, and the use of more tests. It also explains the recent drive to use more paramedics in standardized medical operations such as giving inoculations, and treating wounds and sprains. Another example of this process has been the demise of house calls. It may be more convenient for a patient if the doctor comes to him, but during the same time the doctor can treat five patients in the office or hospital.

sense marked the climax of the movement. In the typical American automobile factory in the 1920s there were still numerous stops in the flow of materials on the assembly lines as well as the use of labor off the lines. Since that time the production process has been made more automated, but only as a matter of degree. A wide range of specific steps continues to be performed by laborers because that method is cheaper than the substitution of machines for those tasks. In the future, if the price of labor continues to rise, more of those steps will undoubtedly be automated. Even then, however, it will be merely a continuation of the process obviously under way in the American economy since before the Civil War.

The Machine Tool Industry

One result of the increasing mechanization of production processes before the Civil War was the development of a new industry to produce those machines. Before 1815 most machinery had been custom made—that is, turned out for a specific use, usually at the site where it was to be employed. Equipment which was particularly complicated or novel was often imported. The "machine tool industry" before 1815 was actually a subsector of the activities of such local crafts workers as carpenters, blacksmiths, and masons. Equipment such as water-wheels, plows, cotton gins, and cards for wool were commonly put together where they were to be used.

This ad hoc system of providing capital equipment began to be displaced after 1800. One factor working against it was the familiar force of expanding markets. As transportation costs fell and the use of particular types of machinery increased, it became feasible for some enterprises to specialize in machine production. Another factor was that some of the advantages which were making the use of machines more attractive also carried over to the machines themselves—an obvious example being the use of interchangeable parts. The milling machines which were turning out standardized parts for various products in the 1840s were themselves constructed in just the same way.

The first specialized machine tool firms in the United States emerged, under-standably enough, out of the first industries to use large amounts of machinery. The most important early case was the textile industry. When the Waltham Mill was constructed in 1814, it was forced to construct its own equipment on the spot. As the mill continued to expand, in the face of increasing demand, a sepa-rate workshop was established within it to make textile equipment. Soon it turned to selling that equipment to other mills as well and, by the 1830s, several of these in-house operations were being split off on their own as independent firms.

The independent machine tool industry also had its roots in the firearms industry. While the textile industry was important in establishing companies which specialized in producing machinery, many of the techniques that subse-quently proved applicable throughout industries undergoing mechanization were developed in the firearms industry. Most of the specific steps of manufacture were actually variations on a few basic processes, such as cutting, drilling, and guiding. All of these were necessarily used in the then rather sophisticated manu-facturing sequence worked out for firearms. And those improvements became available to other industries through the medium of the emerging machine tool industry. In fact, that industry came to play a central role in the creation and dissemination of new technology before the Civil War. It was soon supplying machinery to numerous industries, and its representatives naturally heard of the problems each was having with its own particular processes. Many of these bottlenecks began to sound familiar, however. Certain elements developed a pattern of recurrence. And the machine manufacturers began to apply the knowledge they had gained in developing machinery for one industry to similar circumstances as they appeared in other industries. In this role they became a focus for developing and disseminating technological knowledge throughout the industrializing sector.[9]

INCOMES DURING THE EARLY PERIOD OF INDUSTRIALIZATION

The traditional assumption that growth resulted from industrialization carried over into prevailing views about a close corollary, changes in per capita income. Industrialization has been seen as the cause—and therefore the beginning—of rapid, sustained increases in income per person. Sometimes this was implicit in the term "modern growth," used to differentiate the period of industrialization from the time preceding it. The latter was considered to be a time when per capita incomes rose only very slowly, if at all. Again Rostow's conception of the "takeoff" probably best illustrates this association. He saw economies breaking out of a traditional period of no growth and a preparatory period of slow growth into a high, sustained increase in output per capita. This breakthrough was caused by the emergence of a leading sector which was usually thought to be a new manufacturing sector.

The main thrust of all the above discussion, however, suggests that such a view of growth is selective and misleading. Higher incomes result from increased productivity which can—and undoubtedly does—occur in all branches of economic activity. Manufacturing has experienced increases in productivity but it is not the only source of them and is probably not even the most important source at that. Industrialization's elevation to its esteemed position was probably a coincidence. It was an obvious growth sector in the economy during the time which later observers credited with being the beginning of modern growth. And besides, manufacturing is tangible and obvious. A new textile mill or iron furnace is very noticeable, even when it may not be much of an improvement over the traditional forms of production it supplants. In contrast, a major increase in the productivity of wheat or corn is much less likely to be noticed. The plants appear to be the same, growing in a field, and are unlikely to call for a new form of economic organization, such as a different type of farm, to produce them.

And there was at least one more, coincidental reason for looking to industrialization as a likely beginning for growth. In both the United States and Britain

---

[9] Here again we defer to the authority on this aspect of American technology, Nathan Rosenberg. See his *Technology and American Growth,* Harper & Row, New York, 1972, Chapter 4.

it began at about the same time, a time at which numbers to measure aggregate output began to be recorded. So it was very tempting to assume that because available measures of growth began with the beginning of industrialization, that that time must also mark the beginning of growth. Of course, there is no more compelling logic in that deduction than there would be in the assumption that sex became important only after Kinsey surveyed it and Johnson and Masters began to investigate it therapeutically. Indeed, if one takes a more careful look at the available numbers and filters them through some elementary economic logic, just the opposite conclusion emerges.

The important point to keep in mind here is the special characteristics of a growth sector of which industrialization in the antebellum United States is obviously an example. Both the output and the productivity of such a sector increase faster than that of the remainder of the economy. That, after all, is almost a definition of the case. As a consequence, an individual growth sector is almost universally small relative to the economy within which it is located. (This is to be expected because such a sector consumes a disproportionately high share of the resources a society has available for innovation. The faster its growth relative to the average of the remainder of the economy, the larger the domain it must draw upon to sustain its own pace.) For example, during the decade from 1830–1840, the period during which it has often been argued that rapid industrialization speeded up national growth, the manufacturing sector was still quite small, reaching only 10 percent of gross national product (GNP) in 1840. (See Figure 6-2.) Even though it maintained a faster rate of growth than agriculture for the next fifty years, it was not able to catch up with the *total output* of the latter until the end of that time.

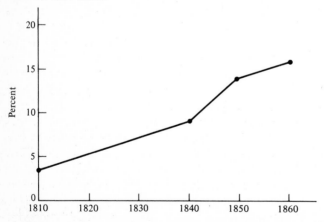

Figure 6-2 Manufacturing output as a percentage of the GNP, 1810-1860. *(Sources: The estimates of 1810 to 1840 are based on the proportion of the work force engaged in manufacturing and are taken from Stanley Lebergott, The American Labor Force, McGraw-Hill Book Company, New York, 1964. The estimates from 1840 to 1860 are of commodity output (assumed to constitute one-half of the GNP) as reported in William N. Parker (ed.), Trends in the American Economy in the Nineteenth Century, Studies in Income and Wealth, vol. 24, Princeton University Press, Princeton, 1960, p. 24 and adapted by permission of the National Bureau of Economic Research.)*

An important corollary of this relatively small size in its early years is that industrialization would be unlikely to explain national growth single-handedly. Suppose, for purposes of discussion, that no increase in output per worker occurred in any sector of the economy except manufacturing. Then the national growth rate would simply be the increase in output per worker in the industry weighted by the latter's share in the economy. Further suppose that before the Civil War productivity in industry had increased by something like an average rate of 5 percent per year, exceptionally high by long-term historical standards. Given its relative small share of the economy, however—17 percent of the GNP in 1860 and, for most of the period, much less than that—industrialization can explain only a fraction of the growth in the period. In 1840, for example, a productivity incease of 5 percent, diluted across an economy ten times as large as the originating sector, would yield an economywide average of 0.5 percent. This would explain less than 40 percent of the growth in the economy at that time. Furthermore, as we noted above, as a sector such as manufacturing grows relatively larger in an economy, its rate of growth, both of output and productivity, is likely to slacken toward the average of the economy. Thus, while the increasing relative size of the "leading sector" causes its contribution to be diluted less as it grows, the strength of its contribution still tends to slacken. In short, the traditional explanation of growth as being primarily caused by industrialization simply does not square with the facts. Growth must be explained by a broader increase in productivity than that contributed by that dramatic, but small, sector. Only significant increases in productivity in all major sectors of the economy during this period can explain the expansion of its total output. In early nineteenth-century America, that necessarily includes agriculture, which consituted well over half the output in the economy at that time. (We will examine the contribution of agriculture in this period in more detail in Chapters 8 and 9.)

If industrialization cannot explain growth in the antebellum period, neither can it be the cause of a sudden acceleration to rapid growth. It was simply not a large enough part of the growth during the period at all. If growth was coming from the total spectrum of economic activity, rather than a single new sector, it is not obvious what might have prompted such a sudden change. Some new force—economywide—would have had to occur, causing economic units to substantially increase the part of their resources that they devoted to innovative activities.

The above intuitive impression received strong confirmation in an imaginative study by Paul David.[10] Lacking the aggregate economic data for the economy before 1840 that is usually used to construct national income estimates, he devised a method he preferred to call *conjectural estimates.* It made use of a simple identity of economic production, namely that output per capita in an economy is the product of the proportion of the population actively engaged in the labor force times the productivity of an average worker. Such partial measures of economic change could be scrapped together, and although they would not in themselves provide any information about the absolute level of incomes,

[10] Paul A. David, "The Growth of Real Product in the United States before 1840: New Evidence, Controlled Conjectures," *Journal of Economic History,* vol. 27, no. 2, June 1967.

they would provide a consistent measure of its change. David's results were striking, even seen in the context by which we have approached them here. The increase in output per capita in the first half of the antebellum period (1800–1835) was, at 1.22 percent per year, almost as high as that in the latter part of the period (1835 to 1860), at 1.3 percent annually. The economy grew almost as rapidly before it had any significant amount of industrialization as it did during the time when it began to acquire it. And even that small increase in the rate of growth could be attributed to things other than industrialization. There has been a long-term tendency for the growth rate of output per person to increase over time, basically because the return on innovative activity has increased relative to that on current output. One such force has been the widening of markets which has made the potential return to any given innovation increase accordingly. The period from 1800–1860 was certainly one of the most dramatic in American history in terms of rapidly expanding markets. It is conceivable, therefore, that the small increase in the growth rate in the antebellum period was caused by the widening scope of markets rather than the appearance of factories.

And so we state a proposition which we have reported before and shall be forced to repeat again because of its importance. Industrialization is not the prime cause of economic growth. Indeed, it does not explain any growth except when it is adopted in place of less productive alternative methods of production—circumstances which are far from universal. Industrialization occurred in the United States after increases in productivity were already an established pattern. In fact, it was some of those previous advances, such as in transportation, which provided the conditions that made industrialization feasible. Thus, while it contributed to growth by increasing productivity, industrialization can be viewed as a result of growth as well. Its proper role in American economic history is probably best seen as one example of a nearly universal process of ongoing improvements in efficiency which were already indigenous to economic behavior by this time.

SUGGESTED READINGS

Clark, Victor S.: *History of Manufactures in the United States, 1607-1860,* Carnegie Trust, Washington, D.C., 1916.

David, Paul: "The Growth of Real Product in the United States before 1840: New Evidence, Controlled Conjectures," *Journal of Economic History,* vol. 27, no. 2, June 1967.

Fogel, Robert W. and Stanley L. Engerman: "A Model for the Explanation of Industrial Expansion during the Nineteenth Century: With an Application to the American Iron Industry," *Journal of Political Economy,* vol. 77, May/June 1969. Also reprinted in Robert W. Fogel and Stanley L. Engerman (eds.), *The Reinterpretation of American Economic History,* Harper & Row, New York, 1971.

McGouldrick, Paul F.: *New England Textiles in the Nineteenth Century,* Harvard, Cambridge, Mass., 1968.

Rosenberg, Nathan: *Technology and American Economic Growth,* Harper & Row, New York, 1972.

Temin, Peter: *Iron and Steel in Nineteenth Century America,* M.I.T., Cambridge, Mass., 1964.

Chapter 7

Easily Slighted Intermediaries: Finance and Commerce before the Civil War

Will Rogers is reported to have said that the three greatest human inventions were fire, the wheel, and central banking. That always drew an appreciative chuckle from the crowd because they shared his bewilderment and suspicion about the financial system. How, they asked, can an industry which handles no tangible goods and merely exchanges pieces of paper, mostly of its own creation, be contributing to human welfare? Of course, banks, paper money, shares of corporations, and mortgages have often aroused the suspicion of people of eras well before Will Rogers articulated the issue. And this attitude has carried over to accounts of various aspects of the financial system which historians have provided in retrospect. Yesterday's collection of banks and currency has frequently been pictured as somehow in isolation from the economy within which it was evolving, merely playing a kind of sideshow role in the struggle between debtors and creditors, or speculators and farmers, or sound-money advocates and "wildcatters."

Notwithstanding public opinion, the financial system does play a positive role in the economy and how this function has evolved is an important element of American economic history. The industry provides such services as aiding in the exchange of goods and services, and assembling and transferring capital. And it uses some of society's scarce stock of resources in the process of doing so. To the extent that it can improve on the services it provides, or reduce the resources necessary to do so, it contributes to economic growth. Given our finding that growth probably occurred in all major sectors of the economy during the antebellum period, we would be very surprised not to find some evidence of productivity increase and changes in organization in finance before the Civil War.

THE BEGINNING OF AMERICAN BANKING

Mention the rather abstract term "financial system" today and most people immediately think of banks. That is not too misleading an association because banks do play a central role in the financial industry and they were a particularly important component of it in the period before the Civil War. Somewhat surprisingly, banks were rather novel in the antebellum era. There were no commercial banks, at least as we understand the term today (in the United States), before 1780. So while commercial banks constituted a growth sector of the American economy at this time, they were quite new as far as familiarity with major social institutions usually go.

This is not to say that Americans did not use banking services before 1780. They did, as we noted in Chapter 3. It is just that they were provided through other channels, such as the merchants of the major port cities. British authorities might have offered some resistance to chartering colonial banks before the Revolution. They did place restrictions on the issue of state paper currencies when some of the states appeared to abuse that opportunity. Even in the absence of such barriers, however, it is unlikely that many private banks would have been started in what is now the United States. The major disincentive to a potential business unit which specialized in providing only financial services at this time was undoubtedly the limited market for its services. The volume of economic activity in the largest local markets, which were the major port cities, could not have generated sufficient deposits and/or found sufficient customers for their loans to depend solely on banking activities. Instead, the pre-1780 economy found other means of handling its financial requirements—somewhat more costly per unit of service provided than commercial banks could have achieved, but less costly overall. Before 1780, Americans got some of their monetary services from merchant's bills of credit, that is, promissory notes by major merchants which circulated until their redemption date. They also used relatively large amounts of money substitutes, such as barter and trade credit. When it came to making final settlements of accounts or handling small day-to-day transactions, however, the colonists were forced to fall back on specie. While that medium was expensive— the domestic stock of coins had been obtained in a dollar-for-dollar exchange for exports—it was the best alternative available.

One way to view the changes in the financial system after 1780 is that the Americans were devising better alternatives. The most obvious change in the next fifty years, that is, from 1780 to 1830, was the rapid growth of commercial banking. The Bank of North America was established in Philadelphia in 1781. Within a decade there were banks in all the major port cities. By 1800 there were banks in every state except for the least-populated areas, such as Vermont. A tabulation for the year of 1836, probably incomplete, showed more than 700 banks operating in the United States. Their note issues and loans outstanding totaled about $200 million, or more than $10 for each person in the economy.

Commercial banking was clearly a growth sector in this period in that it quickly took over the provision of a major part of the financial services in the economy. There was considerable misunderstanding and distrust of its role, but the advantages of the new form of organization were so substantial that ways were quickly devised to implement them throughout the economy. The prime driving force was that commercial banks were more efficient in providing a large component of financial services than were existing alternatives. One advantage of the banks was that they used only fractional reserves; that is, they issued bank notes and loans in some multiple of the quantity of specie reserves they held to guarantee them. This entailed some risk, but it took advantage of the normal condition that only a fraction of bank customers would exercise their claims on the bank's specie stock at any given time. If large numbers of depositors were to convert their deposits or notes into specie withdrawals at the same time, however, the bank would be forced to suspend convertibility—that is, the immediate payment of coin upon demand. Such a risk was real enough, and it occurred periodically throughout the antebellum period, often during depressions or what contemporaries then called "panics."

Many participants of the period thought it was worth the risk, however. The leveraged money it provided cost less per dollar to use because there were correspondingly fewer resources tied up in supplying it. To the potential bank customer this appeared in the form of lower interest rates on loans from a commercial bank (which issued its own bank notes for the debt obligation) than on a direct loan of specie. Commercial banks also had the advantage of economies as middlemen in the capital market. They could consolidate the individual deposits of small savers into the desired larger sizes for loans. In addition, by handling a larger volume of such transactions they could reduce their average unit cost below that which individuals would experience.

It is no surprise, then, that commercial banks had become a universal part of the American landscape by 1830. They provided services which consumers found particularly attractive and were therefore profitable for entrepreneurs to provide. Within a little more than one generation, the occupation of banker, now recognized as a somewhat conservative type, was created literally out of nowhere. The first bankers were often merchants, a natural spin-off from their traditional role of providing credit along with the merchandise. Within a short time, however, bankers were being created out of the ambitious element in almost every existing occupation. Banking in the early 1800s illustrated an axiom recently evident in such occupations as Xerox repair people, recreational equipment salespersons, and managers of fast-food outlets: aptitude and qualifications are readily created for a given occupation when the returns are sufficient.[1]

---

[1] This tendency to attract the ambitious and innovative—true of almost all growth sectors—is one of the factors which gave early banking the unethical aura it has often been associated with during the antebellum period.

Early Bank Creation: Social Innovation

Recruiting the necessary bankers was only one of the obstacles to be overcome in establishing early banks. There was also the frequently frustrating task of obtaining legal authorization for such an enterprise. In the antebellum period, as today, banks were an incorporated form of business. Unlike more recent times, however, there was no routine, established procedure by which such incorporations were granted for banks—or for any other major types of business, for that matter. Consequently, each bank had to obtain its charter by a special act of its state legislature. (The exceptions were the very few banks which were granted national charters, a special feature we shall discuss later.) This brought the creation of individual banks into the tugging and pulling of the political arena. An application for a charter called into play the support from those members of the electorate who believed that they stood to gain from the proposed banking services, and rallied the opposition of those who distrusted banks in general and those—such as existing banks—who stood to lose most directly from the new competition. These conflicts have been given considerable coverage in the traditional historical accounts of early banking. We are assured, through the citation of numerous examples, that these legislative battles were marked by vote trading, intensive lobbying, and even outright bribery. In short, they represented all the behavior patterns which the general public generally and disdainfully associates with politicians.

In a less dispassionate view, however, such behavior is to be expected, given the circumstances. Beyond their philosophical positions, both the supporters and the opponents of a particular bank charter stood to reap (or lose) tangible gains (or losses) from the decision. The recipients of a bank charter did not quite have the power implied by the vernacular expression "a license to print money" (their own bank notes had to earn adequate public confidence, otherwise they would be subject to substantial—and debilitating—discounts in circulation), but it was a valuable asset nevertheless. It allowed them to issue their own bank notes, which served as quasi-legal tender in an amount several times that of the value of the monetary assets they actually owned. In these early years the dividend rate on established banks was quite generous, and bank stock commonly sold for substantial premiums over the amount indicated by its paid-in capital. This markup was the economic "rent," or return above potential alternative earnings, which capital invested in banking was capturing at this time. It also showed the value of winning a bank charter, because that was the determining factor as to whether one could capture those above-normal returns or not. Thus it is quite understandable that applicants for a bank charter would consider bribing officials. It also explains why they sometimes paired early-day applications for a charter with promises to provide such publicly desired services as water systems or roads. It was a way of winning the necessary approval by sharing some of the rent with the decision makers.

The opponents of bank charters also stood to make tangible gains by winning the vote. Their opposition was based on more than the superstition of uninformed rustics. While an expansion in the quantity of monetary services in the economy from a given stock of resources benefits the economy in general, the gain is unequally distributed. The issuance of new bank notes obviously causes a relative depreciation in the value of the existing supply of currency. Each new dollar created causes a depreciation in the value of the existing money supply vis-à-vis any given amount of goods and services exchanged.

This observation helps to explain a marked difference in regional attitudes toward the creation of banks and the freedom with which they were allowed to issue bank notes. Generally, the Western or frontier states were most liberal in granting charters and allowing the issuance of notes. In contrast, Eastern states, or those with relatively developed financial systems, such as Louisiana, were commonly more restrictive.[2] Historians have usually attributed this difference in the degree of freedom which banks were given to arrange their operations to differences in philosophy. The West and newly developed areas in general were said to have placed more emphasis on freedom and "openness." The regions with a longer-standing record of development had become more conservative. Actually these regional contrasts expressed the best economic solutions for the different areas, given their respective circumstances. The West at this time was growing rapidly and thus was a substantial net importer of capital. Liberal banking rules allowed such areas to obtain borrowed funds at lower interest rates than they would have been required to pay otherwise, a fact that some observers of that era duly noted. More established regions, in contrast, had less in the way of new capital requirements and more to gain from protecting the value of their existing assets.

Wildcat Banking

American antebellum banking has often been denoted as having been chaotic, risky, unregulated, unstable, and inefficient. Often this characterization is summarized under the single heading of "wildcat banking." The source of the phrase is subject to some disagreement. Some authorities say that the term originated from the known habit of some bankers to freely accept deposits and issue bank notes but to be as scarce as wildcats when customers returned to redeem their claims. Others argue that the phrase was merely coined to suggest bankers who set up operations where only wildcats lived. In any case, the widely used characterization conveys the picture of a banking system with a marked tendency toward dishonesty and fly-by-night operations. Most commentators who use the term also advance a corollary—namely, that it had adverse effects on the stability and efficiency of the economy as well.

The wildcat view of pre-Civil War banking is overdrawn and misrepresentative, however. While there were some banks which fit the wildcat description,

---

[2] There are some significant exceptions to this pattern, however. Some of the most leveraged (or "wildcat," as the term will come to be understood below) banks were located in major Eastern financial centers, New York City being the most obvious example. They were able to operate on a smaller base of assets because they had access locally to markets for liquid assets which they could use to bolster their reserves on short notice.

they were a very small minority. Most banks operated safely and conscientiously by modern standards. There was, of course, some variation, as one would expect within any sector. And the range of variation was larger than it has been in the economy more recently. This larger diversity undoubtedly explains a good part of the wildcat legend. Commentators have readily assumed that this wider range of banking behavior necessarily indicated carelessness and detrimental activity on the part of the unrestrained bankers, but this judgment overlooks the fact that the bankers were still subject to at least one set of constraints and that their behavior was undoubtedly still conditioned by that.

The constraint was that of the customers for banking services. Many historians have assumed, though usually not explicitly, that the customers were readily deceived. That seems unlikely, if for no other reason than that the individuals involved with the banks had a lot more assets at stake and therefore more reason to examine the merit of a particular bank than the historians did. There is no evidence that the population was consistently and universally surprised by banking manipulations. Rather, they appeared to recognize the risks involved with particular banks, but they used their services nevertheless because of compensating associated returns.

The Arithmetic of "Risky" Banking   Nowadays it is unusual to hear of a bank having serious trouble in meeting its obligations to its depositors. That possibility is substantially reduced by banking regulations specifically designed to minimize such risks. Besides, when the possibility of such troubles does arise, regulatory officials are there to lend money or arrange a merger and generally repel the threat to "the confidence of the financial system." In the antebellum period this elaborate system of precautions did not exist and banks could—and sometimes did—place themselves in conditions which exposed them to such risks. The compensating returns they anticipated from such vulnerable positions sometimes make it appear foolish for them *not* to have done as they did. For example, consider the experience of two hypothetical banks, Security Bank and Income Bank, deliberately drawn to illustrate this point. Assume that both institutions begin operations with an initial paid-in capital of $1,000 in specie. They then begin to grant loans, issuing their own bank notes in exchange for the promise to repay. Each bank recognizes, however, that some of these notes will certainly return for redemption in specie, so that the loans they can issue are limited by their specie reserves. At this point the difference in bank behavior becomes noticeable. Security Bank writes fewer loans than Income Bank because it deems it more important that it will be able to meet the demands upon it for specie. Table 7-1 provides a quick summary of the positions of the two banks.

It is quickly apparent that Income Bank is supporting twice as many loans and notes for a given value of specie than Security Bank, and is therefore less likely to be able to meet demands for specie. In such shortfalls, it would not be able to honor its notes and their value in exchange would be subject to discounts. Those who held them would suffer losses accordingly.

Table 7-1   Balance Sheets of Two Banking Styles

Security Bank		Income Bank	
Assets	**Liabilities**	**Assets**	**Liabilities**
Loans $2,000	Notes outstanding $2,000	Loans $4,000	Notes outstanding $4,000
Specie $1,000	Net worth $1,000	Specie $1,000	Net worth $1,000

It takes a little closer examination to illustrate the advantage which comes from doing this, however. Assume that the prevailing interest rate on loans for borrowers with comparable credit ratings is 8 percent. Income Bank would receive $320 in income (omitting operating expenses) while Security Bank would take in only half that amount, $160 annually. Even if Income Bank were forced to reduce the interest rate it charged on loans to below that of Security Bank—because the notes it issues in exchange for loan agreements are riskier and therefore subject to discount—it could charge a rate only half as large (4 percent) and still receive the same net income. Thus, it would not be at all unreasonable for a potential borrower to find the Income Bank an attractive source of capital. Its notes might be subject to more depreciation than those of other banks, but the lower cost of borrowing could easily more than offset it. Judging by the behavior of Americans in the antebellum period, that was often what happened.

Perhaps it was even more surprising that savers could find it attractive to entrust their hard-earned assets to such a recognized, risky enterprise. The reason, however, is basically the same as that influencing borrowers from wildcat banks. While the risk of not being able to obtain one's money on demand—or even of losing it entirely—is greater in a wildcat bank than it is in that of a more conservative institution, the potential return is greater. The Income Bank stretches each dollar of deposits it receives into a larger number of dollars loaned out and therefore into a larger potential return of earned interest. Thus the riskier bank can afford to pay a higher return on its accounts in order to attract (and compensate) depositors. In this context, wildcat banking in this era was not much different from the varied array of financial assets exchanged in modern times. Corporate bonds, for example, are systematically ranked by very fine gradations, according to their perceived risks. The most secure obligations are ranked AAA, those of decreasing quality AA, A, and so on down to the *b*'s (of the independent oil-drilling companies and the buggy-whip factories) which are assigned a good chance of not being able to repay their obligations. There is a corresponding structure of prevailing interest rates on these securities. The bonds considered most secure sell at the lowest rate while those of increasing risk sell at progressively higher interest rates. In this context, wildcat banking is a perfectly understandable phenomenon. It was the *b*-grade part of the banking spectrum which existed at that time.

Perhaps we can concede a positive role for wildcat banks in the day-to-day functioning of the economy, but other possible adverse effects come to mind. Did they not make the total economy less stable and therefore impose the costs of depressions and inflation upon it? Obviously an individual wildcat bank would create more money during prosperous times and be more likely to go bankrupt during depressions, relative to its more conservative cousins. However, this does not necessarily add up to more instability at the aggregate level. Wildcat banks would provide a larger stock of money than a group of comparably financed "conventional" banks and could also provide a larger absolute increase during periods of expansion. That does not, however, necessarily mean that the *relative* change would be greater. The size of the variations themselves—measured in dollar amounts—are larger, but there is no reason to believe that the percentage changes would be any larger (or smaller) than such changes in an economy serviced by more conventional banks.

It is true that the more highly leveraged banks operating in the antebellum period did run into trouble more often. It was not usually the calamitous event that bank failures are considered today, however. Most of the "failures" consisted of a suspension of payments; that is, the inability to redeem bank notes or deposits in specie. Such suspensions usually lasted for only a day or so, however, until the bank was able to borrow or exchange some of its assets for coin. While bank notes would be subject to a discount during the suspension, they could—and would—continue to circulate nevertheless. Thus contemporaries of the antebellum period learned to live with bank "failures." Indeed, because suspensions were relatively commonplace and expected, they arranged their affairs to minimize the effect of such disruptions when they occurred. They probably viewed the problem much as modern citizens consider the possibility of electric power outages during thunderstorms. They would prefer not to have them but, since they do exist, remembering to have a few candles on hand and to open the refrigerator very sparingly goes a long way toward ameliorating the discomfort.

Of course, this is not to say that there were no costs to the highly leveraged banks. Banks did experience troubles beyond that of temporary suspensions in specie redemption. Some went bankrupt (no pun intended), taking down the assets of depositors and note holders in the process. And because of the tendency to assume risks greater than those shouldered by modern banks, rates of failure were correspondingly higher. Yet in the broadest sense, contemporaries of that period were arranging their economic affairs to compensate for those losses. The services provided by the banking sector were somewhat less predictable and complete than we might expect today, but then they required correspondingly fewer resources. This was the compensating gain which made wildcat banking tolerable. The stock of capital saved from the financial sector allowed Americans to have more housing, roads, barns, improved farmland, and store inventories. Thus, wildcat banking was an understandable adaptation in the American economy. When capital is scarce—and consequently existing opportunities for using it are productive—it pays to cut corners to obtain it wherever possible, including in the financial sector.

First Attempts at Central Banking

One of the best known instances of American antebellum history is the conflict between Andrew Jackson and Nicholas Biddle, President of the Second National Bank of the United States. Jackson—and a good number of historians since then—pictured the bank as a financial monster, exercising its monopoly power to the detriment of working people, small farmers, and merchants. In contrast, Biddle's role has been defended by those who saw a central bank as being crucial in instilling stability and confidence into the banking system. Obviously the issue was larger than the two dominant personalities themselves. Jackson and Biddle did personify very different styles (which their respective supporters found it readily easy to identify with) but in large part they were the symbols, rather than the substance, of the question. The key issue was the appropriateness of a central bank in the antebellum economy. Both sides saw such an institution as having sufficient power to make itself felt. Proponents of such a bank emphasized the use of its power to smooth out the ups and downs of the business cycle and to improve the quality of the banking system. Opponents stressed that such power also created the likelihood that economic diversity would be suppressed—especially that of smaller economic units which were viewed as having less power to defend themselves. There was some truth to both forecasts, as we shall see, but first we must take a more careful look at the nature of the situation—which differs somewhat from that which has often been pictured.

Central banks perform numerous roles in modern economies, but their prime responsibility is almost invariably that of monetary policy. They are charged with dampening the fluctuations in the aggregate economy, thereby reducing some of the associated costs of inflation and unemployment. In actual implementation, however, this objective has proven much more difficult to achieve than the simple act of establishing a central bank and instructing it in what to do. Economic analysis still does not sufficiently understand the role of money and financial assets in the functioning of an economy to be able to fully predict the timing and magnitude of the changes necessary to carry out policy goals.

If one occasionally sympathizes with the difficulties of the modern Federal Reserve Board, consider the plight of the poor antebellum central bankers contemplating undertaking monetary policy. There were no existing aggregate indicators of the economy's performance such as the GNP, or unemployment, or even the money supply to guide them. They might have drawn some casual impressions on the state of the economy from personal reports of merchants or shippers, but these could easily be misleading. At that time, the economy was much more segmented than it is today so that reports from one locality (even if correct) could be a misleading indicator as far as the total economy was concerned. A report that receipts at New Orleans from up-river had fallen off, for example, might or might not call for an increase in aggregate spending in the Northeast.

Being able to detect that the economy needs some remedial attention is a necessary condition if one is to conduct an effective monetary policy. By itself, however, that provides no more than academic enlightenment. Another requirement is that there must be some way to implement that policy. And here the First and Second Banks of the United States also fell well short of the capabilities possessed by the modern Federal Reserve Board. They did not have the legal powers of a true central bank to set reserve requirements or otherwise restrict by edict the behavior of individual banks in the economy. They were basically private—albeit relatively large—banks which could affect monetary conditions only by their impact on the financial markets. The only special power which they held by virtue of their national charters was as fiscal agents for the federal government. But even that was mitigated in that while the banks were given all the government deposits, they also conducted all its fiscal transactions *free*. So, for example, when Andrew Jackson withdrew federal deposits from the Second Bank in 1833, it became for all practical purposes a large private bank. After that the political noise generated in the fight over the renewal of its charter was inconsequential. It made no difference in its effective power in the monetary sector whether it operated under the authorization of the United States or the state of Pennsylvania (as it did after its United States charter expired).

The banks had two channels whereby they could affect the financial affairs of the economy. Because of their large size, and also their role as the federal fiscal agent, they became a natural clearinghouse for all the diverse, circulating bank notes. They could put considerable pressure on individual banks which they felt were overissuing notes by presenting all the notes they received from that bank back for redemption. Or, if they wished to expand the money supply of the economy, they could delay presenting notes for payment, which in effect provided a form of loan to the banks involved. The other avenue of influence which the two national banks had on the American economy was through specie dealings. Gold and silver coins were the medium of international exchange. They moved in and out of the economy depending on the balance of payments, affecting the level of spending in the process. The national banks had by far the largest holdings of such specie, and they could cushion the economy against such international effects by adding to or drawing down their own holdings.

These policy tools were not all-powerful, however. They were limited by the private assets of the two banks. If, for example, the banks were to protect the economy against the effects of specie outflow by selling off their own stock, there would be less left to support their own bank notes. (This was a real constraint in that other private banks, chaffing under the banks' ability to restrict their notes, sometimes presented the notes of the national bank for redemption in order to constrain their influence as much as possible.) Or if the national bank allowed the float of state bank notes to increase in order to put more money in the economy, that amounted to an interest-free loan from them to the local banks. As a rule the activities the national banks carried out to help the aggregate economy were not the most profitable actions for them as private banks. Any altruism of the two national banks in stabilizing the economy, therefore, came from their own wealth, and ultimately out of the pockets of their shareholders. This conflict of interests was evident when Nicholas Biddle was president of the Second Bank of the United States. His stockholders were constantly pressing him to raise the dividend rate above the prevailing 6 percent or 7 percent rate on paid-in capital. Most other banks, they noted, were paying rates well in excess of that level. Biddle's dilemma, however, was that he could not try to stabilize the economy and still make a competitive return on the bank's capital. So, in the long run, central banking attempted by private groups with private resources faced a difficult choice. If they persisted in their attempts to stabilize the entire economy, their own wealth would decline relative to that of the remainder of the banking system. In short, the longer they persisted in attempting to regulate the economy the less power they would have to do so. This sobering fact became evident in 1841 when Biddle's organization went bankrupt trying to aid the economy by holding cotton prices artificially high.

Thus, antebellum Americans did not have an effective central bank in the modern sense of the word. There were some individuals who had a surprisingly good understanding of how monetary policy might work, but that by itself was not sufficient. The major bottleneck was the lack of a mechanism to implement such a policy. The financial system was simply not yet sufficiently developed—nor would the political climate yet allow the necessary monetary controls, for that matter—to conduct an effective monetary policy. It was almost another century before a true central bank, with the necessary power, perception, and endurance, appeared in the economy.[3]

As a consequence, most of the effect of the two central banks which did exist in the United States before the Civil War (from 1791 to 1811, and from 1816 to 1836) was on aspects of the economy other than its business cycle. Their main influence was actually in controlling the quality of the stock of currency in use in the economy. As we noted, the two national banks had considerable power in this regard because of their role as clearinghouses for the diverse bank notes. They effectively imposed a limit on the amount of notes an individual bank, and, by extension, the entire banking system, could issue relative to its established capital base. In the context of our above discussion, it was a choice for safety in return for somewhat higher costs of operating the banking system.

Now the reasons for the dispute over a central bank in this era are more apparent. The bank would impose "safe" or conservative practices on the nation's entire banking system. Obviously this would primarily affect the more highly leveraged banks in this economy, which would explain the position of the frontier areas—the wildcatters—in supporting Jackson, for example. It also explains, however, the opposition of the more innovative New York Wall Street financial interests to the Second National Bank. Such a policy would also benefit creditors and holders of existing financial assets (stated in dollar amounts) rela-

---

[3] This emphasis on the relative weakness of the antebellum central banks differs somewhat from that developed by Peter Temin in his *The Jacksonian Economy,* Norton, New York, 1968. It is not inconsistent with his findings, however, and actually supports one of them; namely, that international monetary developments rather than the disappearance of the Second Bank caused the substantial price changes of the late 1830s.

tive to debtors and potential borrowers. Thus it is no surprise that the question of a central bank generated so much political dispute and that the parties tended to divide along economic and regional lines. It also explains why, with the demise of each of the National Banks—in 1811 and 1836—there was a rapid increase in the number of banks, particularly highly leveraged ones, in rural and Western regions.

Beyond Central Banking: Other Means of Control over the Financial Sector

Those who have argued that a central bank in the antebellum United States was or would have been an asset to the economy have generally based their case on the improvement in stability and efficiency they believed it would bring. Our above discussion suggests, however, that both these objectives were illusionary. A central bank could not feasibly contribute much to aggregate stability and any improvements it made in the safety of bank assets was generally made at the *cost* of efficiency. The policy of the bank(s) was merely an extension of the economic trade-off evident in the question of wildcat banking. Thus, rather than looking at the central bank as an innovation to increase the net output of the economy at this time, its primary effect was probably to affect the distribution of income within the economy.

That kind of collective intervention into the free-working economy was by no means exceptional in this era. The antebellum period has often been labeled by historians as one of laissez faire. Relative to more recent American experience that may be so, although it would require a far more careful investigation than has so far been conducted before much confidence could be placed in that characterization. If the period was one of limited intervention in the economy, however, it was because participants found it advantageous *not* to intervene rather than because of any philosophical reluctance to do so. When favorable opportunities presented themselves, Americans showed little hesitation in grasping them. One dramatic example occurred right in the financial sector.

In the 1820s an arrangement which became known as the Suffolk System (after the bank which pioneered the arrangement) was worked out between the banks of Boston and those of the surrounding rural market area. It guaranteed the acceptance of the notes of participating country banks in Boston at par if they would agree to keep a minimum balance in an account in a specified Boston bank. The Suffolk System operated until the Civil War, at which point private notes were severely restricted and almost disappeared. Variations of it were adopted in other large cities of the time, such as New York and Philadelphia. It appeared to solve a problem which had troubled urban banks and merchants since the establishment of the first rural banks. Bank notes issued by the country banks naturally followed the lines of commerce and, therefore, were constantly being presented for payment in such urban marketplaces as Boston. City merchants were reluctant to accept them at face value because it was expensive to redeem them and, moreover, the country banks frequently failed to honor them when they were presented for specie. As a result the notes were discounted—their going exchange value was some amount less than their face value—depending on the distance and reputation of their issuing bank. The city banks did not like to deal in these notes, which they often disdained as "funny money." More concretely, the country notes competed with those of the city banks and it was thus in their self-interest to hinder their use. For this reason, a good part of the trade in rural notes in the major cities ended up in the hands of specialized money dealers who had no competing loyalties.

The Suffolk System supplanted this network of discounted individual bank notes. Historians have generally lauded the step as a movement toward monetary stability and uniformity. It did remove the variable discounts on bank notes so that all of them circulated interchangeably at very close to their face value. It is not clear that it was designed to benefit all participating parties, however. Most of the country banks joined the system only after all the city banks had banded together in a common front and threatened to present all "nonguaranteed" country notes which they could get their hands on back to the (nonparticipating) bank. They were required not only to keep a balance in their account at the Suffolk Bank sufficient to redeem all their notes presented in the city, but to keep an additional specified balance (commonly $5,000) as well. In effect, these minimum balances constituted a charge on the country banks because they were forfeiting the interest they could have earned from using these funds otherwise.[4] This meant that the country banks were being forced to hold a higher proportion of capital, or reserves, against the bank notes they issued than they would have held in the absence of the Suffolk System. It also meant that the voluntary coalition of Boston banks was imposing much the same financial solution on the eastern Massachusetts market area which the Central Bank of the United States had sought to impose on the national economy during its tenure. It was a triumph of the groups who gained from the safety and protection of existing financial assets over those who stood to benefit from cheaper borrowing and inflation. In this sense it is not surprising that an arrangement like the Suffolk System was successfully enacted in Massachusetts, and to a lesser extent in other developed Eastern areas during the period, but not in the more rapidly growing Western areas. The gain to such conservative institutions was relatively higher (vis-à-vis the costs of forgone alternatives such as more expensive credit) there than in the rest of the economy. One indication that the conservatives were successful in Massachusetts during this period was that the price level in the state tended to decline in contrast to most other states where increases were common.

The Safety Fund System   By the 1830s it was becoming clear that New York City was destined to become the largest city in the East Coast—or, for that

---

[4] When the country banks overdrew their minimum balances, the Suffolk Bank charged them interest on the deficit. In time these overdrafts became a standing practice and often several times as large as the minimum balance itself. In effect they became a vehicle for intraregional lending, whereby capital available in the major cities was lent to rural users, a function previously performed by mercantile relations.

matter, in the United States. It had emerged as the leading innovator in both commerce and finance, two growth sectors of the economy at this time. One of the financial institutions which originated there was known as the Safety Fund System. It was a compulsory insurance program for private banks enacted by the state of New York. It operated much like the present Federal Deposit Insurance Corporation by collecting a small portion of each participating bank's assets to pay off the claims upon any banks which failed. The advantage of the fund was that it allowed an economy to collectively guarantee the safety of its banks without incurring the expensive constraints imposed by enforcing conservative banking—such as in neighboring Massachusetts. The cost of banking security purchased through the Safety Fund System amounted to at most 3 percent of a bank's assets, while the imposition of conservative banking policies commonly reduced a bank's effective asset base by 20 percent to 40 percent.[5] The arrangement appeared successful enough so that Michigan and Vermont copied it to provide security in their banking systems. Although the Safety Fund System was able to withstand moderate contractions, it was not designed for a catastrophe. In the major, nationwide contraction of 1837, bank failures overwhelmed the accumulated reserves of the fund and bankrupted the program. So the state of New York was forced to go back to the drawing boards to try to find another arrangement to provide security while maintaining its competitive position in the financial industry.

Free Banking   In 1838, New York State inaugurated a new system of bank control[6] which was subsequently widely copied and even more widely discussed (the latter by historians). The arrangement was called *free banking*. The name has since aroused considerable confusion. It does not mean that banking services began to be provided free nor does it imply that it was costless to establish a bank. Rather, it represented a major change in the method by which banks were established. Formerly each new bank had required individual approval by its state legislature to begin operation. That mechanism made each new charter a political decision and aroused considerable public distrust of the method in the process. In addition, the number of new bank applications was becoming overwhelmingly large, especially after the demise of the Second Bank of the United States in 1836.

The free in free banking meant that any group which could meet certain conditions was allowed to establish a bank. Some of the requirements, however, were more restrictive than the hurdles erected by legislative chartering of banks. For example, banks were required to deposit a certain proportion of their paid-in capital in state-designated depositories. There were also limits on note issues

---

[5] This differential is overstated somewhat because the state of New York was forced to place some restrictions on banking practices to reduce what insurance agents call "moral hazard." Because banks are protected somewhat against failure they have less incentive to conduct their affairs to avoid such a possibility. So the state found it necessary to proscribe certain high-risk activities.

[6] Actually, the state of Michigan had enacted a free banking policy in the previous year, but the system had been so loosely administered that it amounted to a nonpolicy.

relative to assets and on the types and maturities of loans which the banks could make. Ironically, after receiving their charters, the free banks were probably less free in terms of operations than those established by legislative decree.

Free banking proved to be by far the most widely adopted method to regulate state banking in the two decades before the Civil War. It appeared to be about the right balance in the continuing conflict between safety and efficiency. The state rules prohibited the practices which the populace collectively believed posed a threat to their banking systems, but otherwise allowed the banks to work out their own accommodations with their customers. Free banking did not solve one major problem of antebellum banking, however. Banks were required to maintain reserves with a designated central depository, but these provided no assistance to the bank if it suddenly needed liquid assets to meet the demands of depositors. A bank basically had to depend on its own holdings to meet peak demands for withdrawals. The troubled bank might be able to sell some of its less-liquid assets, such as bonds or mortgages, for specie in the financial markets, but because other banks were usually under pressure to raise liquidity at the same time it was a costly and difficult means of providing short-term liquidity. Basically, the only means to assure such an economywide reserve of liquidity is some central agency in the economy (most likely, a central bank) with sufficient reserves to do so.

That was not to happen in the American economy for another full century. In the meantime the banks had to prepare to meet the worst by themselves, whatever the cost. One of the major costs of such precaution was the severe restriction it imposed on the types of financial assets in which the banks could place their resources. In fact, throughout much of the nineteenth century there was a continued controversy in banking circles on just this issue. It took the form of a debate between the proponents of the "real-bills" doctrine and those who advocated "accommodation." The former held that bank lending should be restricted to financing commercial inventories which would be short-term and self-liquidating. This—so the argument went—would automatically make bank credit correspond to the needs of the economy and would also ensure that banks would always have liquidity close at hand to meet short-term demands for specie. There were some severe drawbacks to this position, such as the lack of financing for long-term capital investments, but if it were followed conscientiously, it would make banking safer.

The advocates of accommodation stressed that most business credit requirements were longer-term than that. Even inventory funding had to be renewed if businesses were to continue in operation. Thus they favored short-term loans but with the recognition that they could be renewed if conditions warranted. While the debate continued in banking circles, in the economy it was largely academic. Whatever the general guidelines to which the banking profession gave verbal support, the question was actually decided in their day-to-day allocations of bank funds. In aggregate, the real-bills doctrine tended to be the dominant result, whatever the public proclamations. The banks were forced to keep their funds close at hand to protect themselves against sudden influxes of insistent depositors. To be precise, one should say that the banks tended to practice accommodation until the crunch came, and then switched to the real-bills doctrine. (In actuality it is difficult to tell the difference between issuing a new loan when the old one expires or simply renewing the old one.) Thus, when a bank restricted lending in a period of tight credit, it might have appeared to be following real bills but more likely was merely protecting its assets.

Other Financial Intermediaries

From 1780 to 1830, commercial banking was obviously a growth sector of the economy. In the thirty years after 1830, however, its expansion slowed down so that its increase in deposits and other measures of bank activity only kept pace with the rest of the economy. At the same time a number of other financial intermediaries—some of them new but others long established—began to grow quite rapidly. In part they seemed to be providing services which the commercial banks were failing to deliver. One common element of these institutions was their ability to loan capital on a longer-term basis than the liquidity-conscious commercial banks.

There was, for example, the rapid growth of savings banks from deposits of only about $10 million in the mid-1830s to more than $150 million by the time of the Civil War. The first savings banks had been established in the decade from 1810–1820 for the express purpose of encouraging thrift among the poor. They soon lost interest in that objective, however, when they discovered that the potential for savings among that group was quite restricted. It was not the lack of an appropriate institution but rather the lack of spending power which kept the poor from doing much saving. The savings banks found the predominance of their depositors among the middle class. (While the rich did make some deposits in savings banks, they often had other investment opportunities available.) Deposits in savings banks were typically for a longer term than those in commercial banks. Funds deposited could therefore be placed in less-liquid, longer-term assets, such as stocks, bonds, and mortgages. A good portion of deposits in New England savings banks were loaned to textile mills. Those in other major Eastern cities went heavily into state bonds which, in effect, were contributing to expansion of the transportation system.

A very high proportion of savings banks, much larger than proportional representation by population or income would indicate, were located in the four largest American cities of that time—New York, Boston, Philadelphia, and Baltimore. This is not surprising when we note that the savings banks were serving a specific—and hence somewhat restricted—portion of the spectrum of financial services. They were accepting the savings of individuals who were willing to set them aside for reasonably long times but did not wish to invest them directly themselves. The banks, therefore, were acting as specialized middlemen between long-term savers and borrowers, and they could operate only in localities where the volume of funds was sufficient to support their function. The rapid growth of savings banks in the economy undoubtedly reflected the growth of the domestic marketplace at this time (which we have already noted). There were advantages (in the form of economies of scale) in splitting financial services into such specialized functions, but they could be realized only if the market for them was large enough to support them as separate units. The volume of savings in the larger cities was apparently sufficient to do so after 1830. It had also become large enough to support—and thereby gain from—a range of other specialized financial institutions as well.

The Appearance of a Bond Market Another example of domestic market growth was the beginning of an active trade in bonds. The term *bond* has had many meanings in history but today we commonly take it to mean a debt instrument which is designed to be negotiable; that is, it can be traded between parties until its date of redemption. Other things being equal, this makes it somewhat more attractive to hold as a financial asset than mortgages, or personal loans, in that it is more liquid. This means that lenders should be willing to accept a somewhat lower return (interest rate) on their investment, given this compensating advantage. It also suggests that borrowers who can avail themselves of this medium might be wise to do so. Typically, it is worthwhile for only a small minority of borrowers to borrow money by issuing bonds. Bonds can be exchanged only if potential buyers are generally assured of their security, or at a minimum that a trusted rating agency (such as modern day Moody's or Standard and Poor's) certifies their worth. In contrast, there would be no advantage to Uncle Willie's corner grocery store issuing bonds, because each potential purchaser would need to conduct an extensive credit investigation—much like a bank considering a mortgage—before buying the bonds. In such cases it would probably be more efficient for a specialized financial institution, such as a bank, to make the loan and borrow on its own name if it found it necessary to raise additional capital.[7] Thus, at any given time there is a logical division between borrowers who obtain capital directly from lenders, and those who find it advantageous to go to a financial intermediary.

Before 1830 there were very few private American companies of sufficient stature to be able to sell their own bonds. Most of the existing bonds had been issued by the federal government, one of the few economic units in the economy whose good credit was generally acknowledged. About 1830, however, the market changed drastically, both in size, and in the groups who participated. The federal government gradually disappeared from the scene as it paid off the national debt. (In fact, in the 1830s it faced the then embarrassing problem of having extra money in the treasury, which it finally gave out to the states—the first revenue-sharing plan.) Its place as a borrower was taken by several other groups. Some private companies of sufficient size to merchandise their own debts began to appear. The most obvious were the railroads, who necessarily assembled large chunks of capital to put their networks together. Municipal governments

---

[7] The bank's first line of adjustment to changes in its credit resources, of course, is to expand or contract the number of new loans it makes. Selling off its existing mortgages is usually less common a step, even though there are modern institutions which are specially designed to create a market for such assets.

began to rely heavily on the bond market to finance the water and sewage systems and roads which the rapidly growing large cities were building. One of the largest and most interesting collections of new borrowers was the state governments. A good portion of the funds they acquired, especially in the 1830s, were for canal projects. In this function they appeared to be using their financial standing to raise the large quantities of capital necessary for such projects, and which private firms were not yet conditioned to undertake.[8]

Bonds, being the most readily exchanged and presumably the most trustworthy of existing debt instruments of that time, tended to be traded over the widest distances. Before the Civil War that meant that about 50 percent were held in England. The British still had an incentive to lend to the Americans, as they had in the colonial period, because the return on capital remained generally higher in the United States than it did in England. However, the traditional arrangement whereby credit was advanced through the network of trading merchants was becoming less workable as the importance of such trade between the two economies was decreasing. Besides, once the market became large enough to support a trade in such a specialized asset, the bond market was undoubtedly a more efficient technique for transferring capital internationally.

Foreign dominance in the antebellum bond market led to considerable ill feeling on both sides of the Atlantic. In the United States the cry was often raised that the British were gaining control of the economy. (This concern was also evident in the debate over the renewal of the charter of the Second Bank of the United States.) In fact, the proportion of the American capital stock owned by foreign nationals was probably decreasing. The bond (and to some extent stock) market was simply the particular segment of the market for that resource where foreign ownership was most convenient, and therefore where it tended to concentrate and be noticed. The British disappointment in the bond market came in the late 1830s after the banking panic of 1837 had caused widespread failure of financial obligations in the economy. Surprisingly, among the groups with the worst rates of default on the bonds they had issued were the state governments. Part of the difficulty was that most of the canal projects which the states had financed were economic failures so that they did not produce the anticipated revenue to redeem the bonds when they came due. Nor did the state governments seem to feel obligated to make up these deficits out of general tax revenues, an attitude that British investors found surprising and certainly ungentlemanly. Many of them vowed that they would never buy American bonds again. In a few years, however, they began to come back into the market. The yields were better than they were elsewhere, and bonds were a convenient way to invest capital, and those American governments must have learned more about fiscal responsibility and so . . .

Insurance   Insurance had actually been one of the largest and best organized of American financial activities during the colonial period. Most of it, however, was directed to two dominant features of colonial life—fires and ocean

---

[8] This argument was developed in Lance E. Davis and Douglass C. North, *Institutional Change and American Economic Growth,* Cambridge, London, 1971.

shipping. After 1815, fire and marine insurance continued to be important in absolute size, but their relative importance declined. The segment of the insurance market which grew the most rapidly, especially after 1840, was life insurance. In the early 1800s life insurance was mostly a sideline of trust companies (who themselves were an important source of longer-term capital). Most of their policies were limited term insurance—that is, they were written only for a designated period of time and there was no refund or dividend when the policy expired. They were insurance in its purest form.

Beginning in about 1840, some major innovations appeared in antebellum life insurance, forms which have continued in extensive use up to the present. One of these was the agency system whereby local representatives sold the insurance issued by a distant underwriter. This type of organization allows a firm to expand the size of its business without the necessity of increasing all the administrative aspects needed to handle the increased volume. It is similar to modern franchising, such as is practiced by such well-known enterprises as MacDonald's and Howard Johnson's. The advantage of such an arrangement is that it allows a firm to devote its attention to those aspects of the business where it can make best use of its effort while splitting off the more routine functions for others to operate. For the antebellum insurance companies it probably offered the advantage of increasing the size of the investment portfolio they managed, an activity which was likely subject to increasing returns. After 1840 they were making large long-term investments in the form of mortgages, bonds, personal loans (which usually were to business people and therefore, in effect, to businesses), and stocks. Thus, they were also becoming an important medium whereby capital was provided for long-term uses in the economy.

Another innovation in life insurance was the introduction of "whole life" policies. These provided coverage over an individual's entire working life, unlike the previous term-insurance plans. They also incorporated saving and retirement provisions into insurance plans for the first time. Such a new financial plan suggests that consumers were finding it attractive to provide for several dimensions of their economic security in one package. This indicates that the income of at least a significant subsector of the economy was increasing. In addition, the package plan was a convenience in time and decision making for the buyers and therefore suggests that such features were also becoming more valuable to them. The large increase in spending on insurance suggests, too, that, as of then, people were able to provide some security against contingencies which they had previously tolerated as "just part of life."

Another appeal to the consumers of the new insurance plans was probably that they offered some of the advantages of participation in the emerging financial markets which they could not undertake alone. Insurance companies could acquire assets which yielded relatively high returns and they could, by diversifying their holdings, eliminate much of the risk that an individual buyer would face. They also reduced the transaction costs to the individual by spreading operating costs over a large volume of holdings. Insurance companies could pass these savings back to their customers in the form of attractive terms on their insurance policies. Thus, in some ways, their operations were similar to the other financial intermediaries which developed at this time. They mobilized capital into those uses in the economy with the highest return and they relayed some of those gains back to their customers, thereby encouraging them to direct their resources into those channels.

COMMERCE

By this point in the examination of economic conditions in the antebellum period, it is clear that a major transformation was under way in the economy as was previously exemplified in transportation, industry, and finance. It is difficult to specify original causes, but it is certain that a combination of forces, some of which overlap, were at work. These would certainly include improvements in technology, rising incomes, population growth and redistribution, and the increase in the nation's capital stock from cumulative saving. Not surprisingly we shall now see that a comparable reorganization was also at work in commerce.

An exchange of goods and services between people is hardly new, of course. It has appeared—often independently—in every society as far back as available evidence goes. The advantages of trade are usually so large that individuals of almost any temperament readily adopt some form of it. It was not, therefore, that commerce per se was new in the antebellum period, which made it interesting, but rather the changes that took place within it—and one of the most noticeable changes was the increase in its size relative to the economy. At any given time people have some choice as to whether they buy a particular product from someone else or make it themselves. For example, even in modern America, which is sometimes considered the epitome of commercialization, there is considerable private production in the form of house painting, home improvements, clothes sewing, home vegetable gardens, and car repairs. Whether one is likely to buy or do-it-oneself is obviously influenced by the relative cost of each method. Items commonly purchased are those in which large economies or specialized knowledge are involved, such as in automobile production or brain surgery. Those where the skills are easily learned or the equipment used is simple are more likely to be done at home. During the antebellum period the net effect of the ongoing changes in the economy was to cause a decisive shift *toward* buying goods outside the home and *away* from self-production. This included food production and preparation, cloth and clothes, as well as a good portion of tools, hardware, drugs, and furniture. The market was replacing self-sufficiency and commerce was becoming a growth sector as a result.

The Colonial Inheritance

In the first two decades of the nineteenth century the commercial structure of the American economy was still much the same as that which had developed in the prerevolutionary era. The center of that mercantile network was formed by the major (often called sedimentary) merchants of the major port cities. They served a number of functions, including retailer, wholesaler, banker, shipper, and commodity dealer. Their services were supplemented, especially in rural areas, by smaller (general-store-type) merchants and peddlers. In the larger cities a certain amount of specialization had been developed by the merchants in those commodities which were most heavily traded; but basically the commerce of the economy was conducted by generalists rather than specialists. The reason, of course, was that the effective marketplace for most goods in the economy was still quite small. The relevant demand for a product is determined by available incomes, population, and transportation costs. All of these worked to curtail local marketplaces until about 1800. All of them, however, began to work in the direction of expanding it after 1800. The result, which will be worked out in more detail below, was a complete reordering in the structure of American marketing. This is perhaps best illustrated by looking at the evolving market structures of two important emerging sectors of this period, textiles and cotton.

Textiles: Mass Distribution to the Consumer

When Samuel Slater began turning out cotton yarn in quantity in the early 1790s, he found a market for his product which was accustomed to much more modest efforts. The older spinning mills had not been too concerned about marketing their wares. Local weavers usually took most of it, sometimes in exchange for flour or raw cotton (which they must have in turn acquired through some previous barter). The output of the Slater mill quickly overwhelmed the local weavers, however, so that he was forced to look for more distant customers. The existing trade network would have forced him to send the yarn to the nearest large city (Newport, at that time), from where it could be redistributed to weavers in the hinterland. Slater, instead, sent the material directly to country storekeepers on consignment; that is, he kept ownership of it and paid the storekeeper a commission upon completion of the sale. This basic form of commission sales was to be very important in marketing textiles. For Slater, it had several specific advantages. The storekeepers were already functioning as collecting agents in the "putting-out" system so the arrangement required little extra effort on their part. Also, the typical store could handle a large enough volume of yarn so that shipments to individual merchants were a cheaper form of distribution than a roundabout route through the port merchants.

By the time the Waltham Mill came into production in 1814, however, the volume of individual mills had grown well beyond the capacity of nearby markets to absorb. The mills began to rely on commission merchants who specialized in textiles. The latter had begun to set up shop a few years earlier in the larger port cities when imports of British-made textiles first became sizeable. These enterprises did not buy and then resell the cloth, but rather, like modern real estate brokers, located buyers and arranged shipments and payments. The commission merchants received a percentage on sales and they were generally not responsible for any bad debts of the buyers.

This took some of the burden of marketing off the textile manufacturers, but apparently it was not enough, because during the second decade of the 1800s the larger mills created a new institution known as the *selling house* to handle all such matters. The selling houses not only took over all marketing, but they also provided credit advances to the manufacturers on the basis of goods in process, and in addition advised on the demand for particular grades, sizes, and patterns of cloth.

One thing this intermediary still did not do, however, was to actually, physically, take over the cloth. It arranged for the sale and shipment of the goods at a price set by the manufacturer (presumably influenced by the reports of the selling house on market conditions). If unsold inventories piled up, they were simply disposed of at auctions in the larger cities. This type of procedure generally economized on working capital and storage facilities, but usually at the loss of some revenue through forced, untimely sales. These irregular auctions—as distinguished from organized exchanges which trade regularly—are usually used where markets are "thin" and imperfect in order to set prices and dispose of goods. If trading is infrequent, an appropriate price may not be known, and it is usually not worthwhile to keep such rarely purchased items in stock. The solution is an auction, which solves both pricing and inventory problems simultaneously.

The market for textiles was one of the largest in the economy in terms of finished goods so that "thin" markets seem unlikely to explain the resort to auction. Actually, only a small portion of textiles were sold in open public bidding; most were exchanged at listed prices. In this context the auction system probably played a useful function of providing information about market conditions and establishing new prices when the existing ones were becoming inappropriate. (It may also have provided a way for the manufacturers to check up on the information that the selling house was providing.) Furthermore, it was unlikely that the manufacturers would be hurt by distress selling through the auction system because there was another group of merchants, the jobbers, who maintained inventories of textiles and thereby cushioned such influxes of supply.

The jobbers, a kind of junior wholesaler, supplied the smaller retailers in the economy. They were virtually forced to carry inventories of goods by virtue of that clientele. The small retailers bought textiles in lot sizes smaller than the minimum that the selling houses would ship. So the jobbers commonly broke wholesale lots into smaller quantities. In addition, the country retailers did much of their buying on semiannual trips to larger cities where most of the jobbers were located. The latter understandably kept the supplies on hand rather than forcing the storekeeper to wait around town until the next auction. Thus, the jobbers were the logical ones in the distribution network to look to for inventory needs.

There was also another reason that this function should have fallen to the jobbers. We noted in the first section of this chapter that funding new enterprises in this period was constantly calling forth new innovations in financial arrangements. The trick was to provide reasonably secure long-term financing, yet provide enough liquidity in the asset structure to protect the system against short-term demands. One common practice was to link the extension of credit to trade or inventory holdings which usually had a fast turnover. The distribution system in the cotton textile industry is an example of that concern. The jobbers typically could borrow on their inventories or on the bills of credit they advanced to their customers, thereby obtaining the capital necessary to finance inventory holdings of cotton textiles. The selling houses might have undertaken this function but they advanced most of the credit they could raise by themselves back to the mills. This, of course, was a partial substitute for the long-term capital which the mills generally found difficult to acquire. Hence the jobbers seemed the best people to create the necessary financial assets so that capital could be injected into the industry.

In the process, the jobbers performed the other typical functions of merchants in this period.[9] They, of course, were the middlemen, buying goods in large quantities and distributing them in smaller lots to retailers. They were also bankers and loan officers. Most retail merchants bought their supplies on credit, and therefore the jobbers became minicredit bureaus, constantly evaluating who should be issued what amount of credit and on what terms. In settling such accounts they often acted as bill brokers and money dealers, accepting paper drawn on distant sources or even payment to their accounts at correspondent merchants in other cities. Often the jobbers acted as the country merchants' personal errand-runners in town. Porter and Livesay (see Suggested Readings) report that typical drug jobbers in the antebellum period obtained textbooks and medical periodicals for their doctor clients and also relayed their questions on medical practice to other suppliers.

The jobber system became the common form of distribution before the Civil War. It included not only textiles but also shoes, clothing, foodstuffs, drugs, hardware, and household furnishings. It was not universal, however. Where the advantages of such middlemen were not compelling, means were quickly devised to bypass them. For example, in the 1850s, when the ready-made clothing industry developed on a large scale, its buyers soon circumvented the cloth jobbers who attempted to maintain distribution control. Within a short time the cloth buyers were buying in quantity direct from the selling houses—and telling the manufacturers how to make their cloth as well!

The sales of the railroad and industrial-equipment industries reached sizeable levels in this period but the number of their customers remained relatively small and readily identifiable. In such industry structures, the manufacturers were much more likely to retain control of the distribution network by sending out their own representatives. Usually there was also less need for inventories, because goods, such as locomotives, were apt to be produced on order for a particular customer. In this system the company salespeople played particularly useful roles in that they relayed product specifications and requirements from buyer to manufacturer.

Raw Cotton: Collection of a Raw Material en Masse

In the middle of the nineteenth century the United States dominated the production of raw cotton in the world. Not only did the American planters supply

[9] An excellent description of antebellum marketing in general and the textile and iron industries in particular is contained in Glenn Porter and Harold C. Livesay, *Merchants and Manufacturers,* John Hopkins, Baltimore, 1971.

enough of the prime input to make the cotton textile industry the largest domestic industry of the time, but cotton was by far the largest export of the economy as well. It was clearly the most widely traded raw material in the economy. (The total value of corn production in the United States may have been greater during this time, but much of it was consumed in the farm sector near where it was grown and thus it never became a participant in formal trading.) The marketing of cotton serves, therefore, as an example of how developed and sophisticated trading in a raw material could become in the antebellum economy.

Almost everyone has heard of the cotton factors. They are usually given a major role in accounts which commonly picture the antebellum South as a somewhat unusual and colorful society. The cotton factors were actually variants of the commission merchants (who today would be called brokers) who were so common before the Civil War. They not only arranged for the sale of cotton to distant buyers but they also advanced credit and acted as bankers and purchasing agents for the growers as well. This central position in the distribution network is the basis for so many of the judgments by historians that the factors held a stranglehold on, and were commonly able to exploit, the planters. If one had asked the factors about their "power," however, they would have been astonished at the suggestion. From their daily dealings in the cotton trade, they were keenly aware of the alternatives to their services. First of all, there were a lot of other factors who stood ready to take over if the occasion arose. In each of the major port cities of the South, such as Charleston, Savannah, Mobile, and New Orleans, there were factors who constantly solicited new business.[10] There were also others who were permanently settled at interior cities, such as Montgomery, Macon, and Atlanta, where major quantities of cotton were assembled. While factors sometimes bought cotton on their own account, their usual practice was to ship and sell the planters' cotton for them. The factors naturally tried to get the highest possible net price for their consignments. They might sell it in the local market or ship it on to distant markets, such as New York or Liverpool, for sale. In addition, they could store the cotton in anticipation of getting a better price later. From the correspondence of the factors, it is obvious that they spent considerable energy watching events which could influence the price of cotton.

Cotton growers who distrusted the judgment of their factors could order them to sell at a particular time and place. Thus, factors could be almost entirely bypassed. Country storekeepers commonly took cotton in exchange for merchandise. They were particularly active as dealers for small farmers whose output was too small for the factors to profitably handle. There are reports of storekeepers who handled transactions as small as 25 pounds, less than one-tenth of a bale (a factor's commission on that sale at prevailing rates would have been about 15 cents), and combined them into regular bales for resale. There were also itinerant cotton buyers. In the earlier years these were often peddlers who stood ready to accept cotton for either cash or merchandise. As an area became more densely

---

[10] A comprehensive account of the cotton marketing system is contained in Harold D. Woodman, *King Cotton and His Retainers,* University of Kentucky, Lexington, 1968.

settled, general stores usually drove the peddlers out of business, but traveling cotton buyers continued to roam the countryside. They would buy cotton right out of the barn—or even in the field for future delivery. In short, there were numerous means by which cotton growers might market their product and it is extremely unlikely that only one individual, or group, could maintain monopolistic control over its outlet.

Part of the reason for the general skepticism about the role of the cotton brokers in the Southern economy grows out of a general misconception and suspicion about middlemen in general. It is unlikely that they would be the parasites they are sometimes pictured. Economic systems generally find ways to bypass nonproductive agents simply because some parties gain by doing so.[11] If the middlemen are not providing services commensurate with the costs they add to the final product, they will be bypassed by another arrangement. Middlemen are usually used when there are economies of scale in certain services. The marketing of cotton beyond the farm is a good example. Individual farmers would need to arrange for the transportation, insurance, storage, grading, and sale of their crops if they carried out the marketing on their own. They would also have to arrange for financing, unless they could pay for all these services out of their own funds and then wait for the proceeds from the sale of the crop to arrive. Some of these functions might be arranged by mail, although that would often involve long delays. Inevitably there would be some adjustments or problems which would force the planters to leave the farm and follow the cotton along its course to expedite it. Almost universally they found it better to pay someone else to carry out those tasks, particularly when that other person—read *factor*—could perform them for a number of other planters at the same time. The factors spent their full time arranging insurance, shipping, sales, and so forth, by virtue of being in close and nearly constant contact with the agents and businesses who performed those services. The gains from their constant attention to these affairs were all the trips, letters, and frustrations that the planters avoided, and which would have been necessary in the factors' absence. Their roles also had the effect of greatly economizing on the acquisition and use of information. They knew at any given time, for instance, the cheapest—or fastest or safest—way to ship any type of cotton to market, things it might have taken the planters several seasons to learn (by which time the situation might have changed). They also had numerous contacts in the financial sector, by which they were able to tap the most desirable sources of credit, including some in the North that the planters would not have access to. In sum, the cotton brokers provided a number of services for the planters more cheaply than the planters themselves.

The cotton factors were simply the most dramatic example of the general category of middlemen which expanded so rapidly in the antebellum economy.

---

[11] Many innovations can be introduced without resorting to political or legal changes, and when they cannot it is often possible for the gainers to compensate the losers for a given modification. The former have more to gain—and therefore more to bargain with—than the latter have to lose. An example of this type of bargaining was indicated above in the chartering of antebellum banks.

As the amount of specialization and the volume of trade increased, numerous opportunities for specialized intermediaries developed. And because these potential middlemen used less of the economy's resources to carry out their functions than other arrangements would have, customers soon came to them. In the process of tooling up to supply these services, commerce became a growth sector and—by the resources it saved in the process of the changeover—contributed to that growth as well.

The Retailer in the Antebellum Era

Ultimately, the aim of this whole system of distribution we have been discussing is to provide goods for consumption. The last step, to the consumers—and a very important one in terms of the total resources it consumed—was usually through the local storekeepers. In one major way, antebellum retailing maintained a noticeable characteristic of storekeeping before 1800, namely a lack of specialization in the sales format. The prime model continued to be the general store, especially in rural and Western areas. Such enterprises were not just in the business of selling goods to final customers, but they were also operating as commodity dealers, bankers, bill dealers, post offices, credit bureaus, and social centers. In fact, the country stores were performing many of the functions for their market areas which the factors were handling in the cotton belt.

The importance of the general store was gradually declining in this period, however. One major force behind that trend was the increase in urbanization. Cities provided larger markets for the retailers located there and encouraged a move toward finer specializations in their product lines. Thus the designations of dry goods, grocer, shoe store, and butcher shop became familiar. As a rule, the city retailers could also operate on a much smaller inventory than their rural counterparts. The major channels of supply of goods converged in the major cities, and many of the jobbers who were organized to redistribute them naturally located there also. So the urban retailers could usually restock their stores in a day or so, while it took the country merchants several weeks at least. One obvious result of this difference between town and country merchandising was that the urban customers had much better access to such services. The average city retail store was smaller, but there were three times as many of them relative to the population as there were in the rural areas.

The advantage to the retail stores of being located in the large cities in the East, particularly Philadelphia and New York City, can be appreciated if we note the lengths to which rural storekeepers were willing to go to avail themselves of the same opportunities. According to Lewis Atherton,[12] many country store operators in the 1830s and 1840s in such Western states as Illinois and Missouri traveled to New York and Philadelphia once each year to purchase most of their merchandise. They did so despite the fact that numerous wholesalers and com-

---

[12] Lewis E. Atherton, *The Frontier Merchant in Mid-America,* University of Missouri, Columbia, 1971. The book contains numerous colorful examples of frontier merchants, which have been gathered in the course of a good part of Professor Atherton's life work.

mission merchants were soliciting their patronage from Western cities such as St. Louis and Cincinnati, and that the trip to the Eastern centers cost at least $400 (out of gross sales of an average of about $10,000 per year) and took them away from their stores for about two months. The Western storekeepers had often found through sad experience that they could not acquire their goods through mail orders. All too often sizes or quality or styles proved to be wrong. Some country merchants were able to use agents in the buying center, much like Southern cotton factors, but most found there was no good substitute for choosing the goods themselves and then making sure they were packed and on their way home.

There were some exceptions to this pattern. Western merchants found that coffee and sugar could usually be bought most cheaply in New Orleans, coffee because of its proximity to South America, and sugar because of local production. For the same reason, storekeepers commonly stopped at Pittsburgh for ironware on their return from their Eastern trips. They also often picked up paper, whiskey, rope, and flour at the river ports of Cincinnati or Louisville. Thus, it was not snobbery or habit that caused them to bypass Western wholesalers for the much longer trips to the East. Rather, they found that the majority of goods in those local centers commonly sold for up to twice the price of those in the Eastern markets. The Western storekeepers may not have realized it, but they were responding to an early example of what urban authorities today call agglomeration. Cities have higher costs than rural locations in some ways, such as the costs of land, but they also have some offsetting advantages. One of these is the gains from concentrating related or complementary business activities in close proximity so that they reinforce one another. New York City vividly illustrated this phenomenon. Philadelphia was also important, but declined somewhat over the period. Storekeepers visiting in New York City in the 1830s or 1840s, for example, would find not one but several jobbers who carried dry goods, and all would have particular specialties in which they were well stocked and well versed. Within a few close stops, the visiting merchants would be able to see, buy, and have packed up for shipment all the goods they expected to need for the coming year. They were so well served because the network of jobbers, wholesalers, auctioneers, and commission merchants serving them had developed so extensively in the city.

In (Not So) Old New York

In 1800 Philadelphia was recognized as America's leading city. It served a thriving hinterland and also dominated the large back-country trade of the South and what areas were then the West. If market areas alone were to determine size, however, Philadelphia was destined to become number two. In 1825 the opening of the Erie Canal made New York City the prime outlet of East-West domestic trade. In addition, the city became the focus of the cotton trade in the country. It served as the major outlet for textiles from the New England mills. More important, it became the trading and financing center for the raw cotton trade in the nation. Cotton was usually shipped directly to New York from the South, even when it was almost certainly going on to Liverpool. (Later in the antebellum period, cotton dealers developed a way to bypass this stop when possible. They sent samples of the cotton to New York when the shipment went to sea. If the New York agents wished to buy that particular lot, they could divert the ship into their port. Otherwise it went on to Europe without stopping.) The advantage of this intermediate stop, which at times might seem unnecessary, is again that of the specialized middleman—or, to be more precise in this case, the specialized intermediary location. New York was the major raw cotton market where buyers and sellers were almost always trading the commodity. The cost of a stop in New York City might be more than offset by the possibility of obtaining a better price there. The city was also the financing center for raw cotton where one could almost always obtain an advance on shipments. Furthermore, New York City was also the major American port for both exports and imports in the late antebellum period. As a result, there were frequent ship sailings into and out of the harbor. This meant that the opportunities for sending cotton on to another destination were better, but—and probably more important—it also meant that the guarantee of return traffic into the port spread the costs of a round trip and therefore tended to lower the cost of the outward trip (the one carrying cotton) as well.

Enter the Railroad

New York City continued to hold its preeminence in commerce right up through the Civil War. Ironically, some of the forces in the economy which were helping to decentralize most kinds of economic activity acted to strengthen the city's role as a mercantile center. The railroad network which was laid down in the 1840s and 1850s was a major example. It reduced the risk and time involved in acquiring goods over long distances—particularly those goods typically handled by retail stores. One would naturally expect this to have reduced the costs of Western wholesalers in such cities as Chicago and St. Louis. It would have allowed them to lower their prices vis-à-vis the Eastern suppliers and thereby capture a larger share of the purchases of retailers in their respective areas. Some of these reductions in costs did occur, but the large Eastern centers held on to a substantial share of the wholesale business nevertheless. For one thing, the reduction in shipping barriers allowed the rural retailers better access to the Eastern markets. Their trips to town took less time and there was also less delay in receiving goods upon purchase. Even more important, however, was the innovation which the Eastern jobbers and wholesalers introduced into marketing. They began sending out agents to call upon the rural storekeepers. Thus, that American institution, the traveling salesperson, was born. It is easy to visualize them climbing down from the trains and dragging their sample cases to the local stores. In making their rounds, however, they would be performing the important function of providing physical examples of the goods which the merchants would otherwise have bought in New York or Philadelphia. This saved the storekeepers their long yearly trips to the big city, as is evident in the rapid decrease in this yearly migration by the time of the Civil War. The salespeople also reduced the problem of the storekeepers' complaints of not being able to buy what they wanted at a distance. The agents were expected to handle gripes, make adjustments, and generally expedite the delivery of the items the retail merchants desired. By their forbearance, the Eastern centers had extended and maintained the advantages they had developed through agglomeration.

SUGGESTED READINGS

Atherton, Lewis E.: *The Frontier Merchant in Mid-America,* University of Missouri Press, Columbia, 1971.

Davis, Lance E., Richard A. Easterlin, and William N. Parker et al.: *American Economic Growth,* Harper & Row, New York, 1972, Chapter 10.

Hammond, Bray: *Banks and Politics in America from the Revolution to the Civil War,* Princeton University Press, Princeton, 1957.

Johnson, E. R. et al.: *History of Domestic and Foreign Commerce of the U.S.,* 2 vols., Carnegie Institution, Washington, D.C., 1915.

Kross, Herman E. and Martin R. Blyn: *A History of Financial Intermediaries,* Random House, New York, 1971.

Porter, Glenn and Harold C. Livesay: *Merchants and Manufacturers,* John Hopkins, Baltimore, 1971.

Rockoff, Hugh: "Money, Prices and Banks in the Jacksonian Era," in Robert W. Fogel and Stanley L. Engerman (eds.), *The Reinterpretation of American Economic History,* Harper & Row, New York, 1971.

Temin, Peter: *The Jacksonian Economy,* Norton, New York, 1968.

Woodman, Harold D.: *King Cotton and His Retainers,* University of Kentucky Press, Lexington, Kentucky, 1968.

Chapter 8

Northern Agriculture before the Civil War

This text has already examined a number of individual sectors in the antebellum period—such as transportation, manufacturing, finance, and commerce. From that sample it might appear that all parts of the economy must have been growth sectors. Such a situation is impossible, of course; all the components of an economy cannot grow more rapidly than the aggregate economy itself. Our sample of sectors discussed so far is specifically biased because the pace of adaptations is most likely to be the fastest (and therefore of most interest in recounting historical changes) in the growth sectors of the economy. Now we turn to a sector which would be conventionally termed a declining industry—agriculture.

It would be difficult for agriculture not to be a declining industry, given its initial position. At the beginning of the nineteenth century, it dominated the structure of the economy; some authorities have estimated that it comprised as much as 90 percent of total economic activity. That figure is misleading in terms of modern conceptions, however, because although up to 90 percent of the population might have been classified as farm people by primary occupation, they devoted a good share of their time to activities which today would be in other sectors. The self-sufficiency of that era meant that the farm family devoted a large part of its average day to functions which would now be classified under food processing, cloth and clothing manufacture, medicine, and education. As the economy became more specialized and interdependent after 1800, many of these functions moved off the farm. Thus, the reported share of agriculture was bound to fall simply because the sharpness of occupational categories was increasing. Even so, agriculture still remained relatively large. It was not until after the Civil War that it lost its place as the largest single sector. As a rule of thumb, large sectors generally grow more slowly than smaller ones as the economy they are a part of expands. That tendency is given particular reinforcement in the case of agriculture by Engel's law. If per capita incomes are rising—as the above discussion of this period has certainly indicated—the share of income spent on food in the economy must decline. The long-term prospects of the position of agriculture in the American economy, therefore, were downward.

A declining sector is not necessarily a stagnant one, however. While the relative position of agriculture was decreasing in terms of total output, the efficiency with which it used resources was increasing. This may sound like a paradox, but it comes close to being a necessary condition for rapid growth in the economy as a whole. Suppose the agricultural sector did *not* show any significant increase in the efficiency with which it used its resources. This would mean that that large component of the economy was acting as a drag and diluting the gains made by the rest. Fortunately, the agricultural sector appeared to be just as innovative and progressive as the others. Although the output of farms was not growing as fast as the output of the rest of the economy—its *absolute* size was increasing, however, because the *total* output was increasing so rapidly—agriculture underwent a substantial transformation which changed its organization nearly as much as any other sector in the antebellum period.

PREDICTABLE ADAPTATIONS

If one knew absolutely nothing about Northern agriculture in the antebellum period, other than the above discussion about changes in other sectors in the economy, it still would be possible to make some reasonably confident predictions as to what must have occurred in that sector. For example, we already know that transportation costs in the period fell dramatically so that specialization in economic activities was greatly encouraged. In agriculture this would most likely take the form of regional specialization by types of crop to take advantage of the differing natural properties of soils, temperature, rainfall, and so on. The tendency would then probably lead to another predictable adaptation. As particular areas began to concentrate on certain types of crops, they would soon produce quantities well in excess of local consumption, which would require the expense of additional processing which local consumption could often avoid. All crops are perishable to some extent, so shipping them longer distances often dictates some form of preservation. And it is desirable to process some crops near where they are grown even though they are not particularly perishable. Livestock, for example, loses substantial weight when it is converted to food products, so it is desirable to slaughter and process near where it is grown rather than after it has been shipped to where it is to be consumed.

Then there would be other manifestations in agriculture of the general growth and change taking place in the economy as a whole. One of these would be an additional result of Engel's law; that as incomes increase, people not only reduce the proportion of their incomes which they spend on food but they also upgrade the quality of the food they buy. That commonly takes the form of shifting away from lower-priced starches, such as bread or macaroni, to more attractive items, such as fruit, fresh vegetables, and meat. As a corollary, one would expect this to result in corresponding shifts in agriculture, with a decline in the production of grains for human consumption—such as wheat—and an increase in such enterprises as orchards, truck farms, and dairy farms.

Agriculture would also be forced to adapt to another by-product of the national growth process—the tendency for labor to become increasingly scarce compared to the major factors of production, especially capital. This would manifest itself in a more extensive use of capital items, such as machinery, buildings, livestock, and improvements to farmland. Finally, it would be surprising if the improvements in technological knowledge which were taking place throughout the remainder of the economy at this time did not extend to agriculture. This sector was operating with much the same incentives, opportunities, and people as the rest of the economy. It would be almost impossible for some improvements in technology not to filter through.

REGIONAL SPECIALIZATION

In the early 1800s the frontier of Northern agriculture was still relatively close to the Atlantic coast. In central New York, for example, the rich wheat-producing area of the Genesee Valley south of Rochester was just beginning to be brought into production. Farther west there had been some settlement along the Ohio River in the states of Ohio and Pennsylvania, the latter around the Pittsburgh area. The region had been able to develop an outlet for pork and flour at New Orleans, and some of its cattle were driven overland to Eastern markets. Economic activity was severely dampened by isolation, however. It would be a few more years until the steamboat, canal system, and railroads had their combined explosive effect on the area. (See Figure 8-1.)Almost all agriculture in New England was confined to that small section in the three southern states of Connecticut, Rhode Island, and Massachusetts. Some of the best farmland in the region—one of the few areas still actively farmed today—was the potato country of northern Maine, but at that time it was still an inaccessible wilderness. Actually, the farthest inland extension of agriculture was in the border states of Kentucky and Tennessee. This fact had been prompted by the excellent locations for raising tobacco and cattle in those states. We shall postpone our discussion of that development until the next chapter, on Southern agriculture.

Even in the first decade or so of the 1800s, however, it was becoming clear that Northern agriculture, like the other major sectors of the economy, was already in the process of growth and restructuring (see Chapter 4). The new wheat-, cattle-, and tobacco-producing areas were intensifying the competitive pressures on some of the older areas and forcing them to modify their efforts. After 1815,

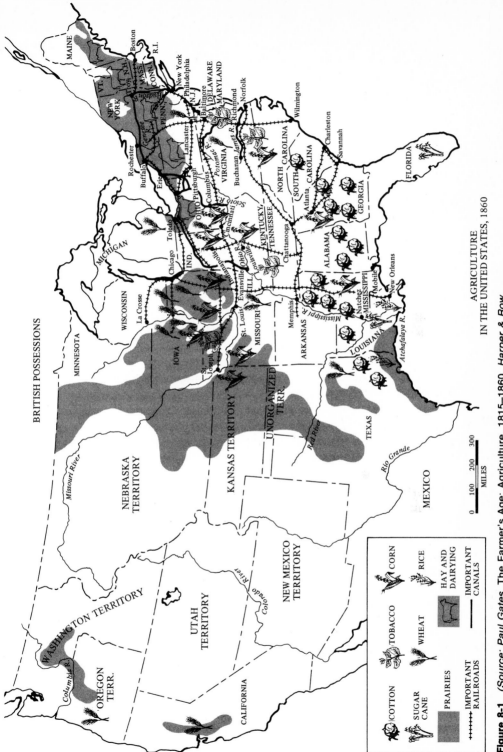

Figure 8-1 (*Source: Paul Gates, The Farmer's Age: Agriculture, 1815–1860, Harper & Row, New York, 1960, frontispiece. By permission of Harper & Row, Publishers, Inc.*)

AGRICULTURE
IN THE UNITED STATES, 1860

BRITISH POSSESSIONS

MAINE
VT.
N.H.
MASS.
CONN.
R.I.
NEW YORK
PENN.
N.J.
DELAWARE
MARYLAND
VIRGINIA
NORTH CAROLINA
SOUTH CAROLINA
GEORGIA
FLORIDA
ALABAMA
MISSISSIPPI
LOUISIANA
ARKANSAS
TENNESSEE
KENTUCKY
MISSOURI
ILL.
IND.
OHIO
MICHIGAN
WISCONSIN
IOWA
MINNESOTA
NEBRASKA TERRITORY
KANSAS TERRITORY
UNORGANIZED TERR.
TEXAS
NEW MEXICO TERRITORY
UTAH TERRITORY
WASHINGTON TERRITORY
OREGON TERR.
CALIFORNIA
MEXICO

Boston
New York
Philadelphia
Baltimore
Richmond
Norfolk
Wilmington
Charleston
Savannah
Atlanta
Chattanooga
Louisville
Evansville
Cincinnati
Columbus
Pittsburgh
Lancaster
Rochester
Buffalo
Erie
Toledo
Chicago
La Crosse
St. Louis
St. Joseph
Memphis
Natchez
Mobile
New Orleans

Hudson
Genesee
Potomac R.
James R.
Scioto R.
Ohio R.
Mississippi R.
Wabash R.
Red River
Missouri River
Rio Grande
Colorado River
Columbia R.
Atchafalaya R.
Buchanan

0 100 200 300
MILES

COTTON
SUGAR CANE
TOBACCO
WHEAT
CORN
RICE
HAY AND DAIRYING
PRAIRIES
IMPORTANT RAILROADS
IMPORTANT CANALS

215

however, this began to occur at a faster and hence more noticeable pace. Probably the most noticeable change was in the development of the Ohio Valley. Helped in no small part by the introduction of the steamboat, the population of Ohio, Indiana, and Kentucky increased from 660,000 in 1810, to 1,300,000 in 1820, to 1,900,000 in 1830. Most of this increase took place within the upper reaches of the Ohio River, but by 1830 large numbers of immigrants were spilling over into southern Illinois and eastern and central Missouri as well. The common denominator of the region and the asset which was bringing it into the economy so rapidly was corn. After some of the dense, natural forest had been cleared away, the underlying soil was more productive than much of that which was in use in the East. Most of the corn was used for feeding hogs, in order to produce pork. Unlike cattle, those pigs which were usually grown in the Ohio Valley were not hardy travelers[1] and could not be driven to distant markets. As a consequence, local packing industries developed at central points along the major rivers which naturally served as the primary trading routes of the region. The leading packing center was Cincinnati—or "Porkopolis" as it was referred to in less-than-formal terms—but there were other important centers in St. Louis, Missouri; Alton, Illinois; and Louisville, Kentucky. Until the 1830s most processed pork was directed down the Ohio–Mississippi River route to New Orleans and beyond. After that time, however, an increasing amount was shipped directly by canal and, somewhat later, by railroad to Eastern markets.

During the antebellum period, the transportation system serving the river ports improved. And the volume of processed pork moving over it to market increased dramatically, pushed along in the 1840s and 1850s by the rapid development of packing facilities at Chicago. This joint happening prompted the development of a complementary industry based on the by-products of slaughtering. When a hog was butchered on the farm, much of the animal was discarded as waste. In the packing plants such trimmings accumulated in large quantities and created a major disposal problem. Thus, the plants eagerly sought uses for their waste products. Some were eventually processed into such traditional items as lard, tallow, candles, and bristles. These products were being turned out in sizeable quantities by 1840, as witnessed by their prominent place on the manifest of cargoes leaving the river ports. The packers also had some success in developing a lighting oil distilled from animal fat. In an era when whale oil was becoming more expensive, and kerosene and the widespread use of gas for lighting were still in the future, this item proved quite salable. Actually, such efforts were not unique to this period—they merely reflected the usual incentive to find ways to satisfy demands by using cheaper, more common materials. An example of this continuity is reflected by the two lard dealers named Procter and Gamble who formed a partnership in the antebellum period. At that

---

[1] The "poor traveling" hog was partly cause and partly effect. Given that they were to be butchered locally, the animals were selected for meat and cost considerations, which usually came at the expense of endurance. Those areas from which hogs continued to be driven to market, such as northern Ohio and western Pennsylvania, had animals which looked much more like the traditional wood hog.

time they were interested in developing markets for pork fat, but the organization they established still seeks to devise new ways of satisfying old demands under such familiar labels as Tide, Crest, Pringles, and Pampers.

Wheat

For thousands of years, well before the discovery of the Western Hemisphere added corn to the list of opportunities, small grains have been a basic element of Western agriculture. And for at least the last thousand years the basic small grain has been wheat. Of course, today it plays a much smaller role in the economy than it did in the antebellum period. (Its importance within the food sector has declined, as has the agricultural sector itself.) As of the early 1800s, however, wheat was still a primary, nearly universal crop. That is not surprising, given its characteristics and the conditions of the times. Wheat requires less of a growing season than either corn or cotton, the other two major crops of the period. It can also be grown on land which for other crops would be marginal, in terms of fertility and rainfall. In addition, its value relative to weight is high—several times that of corn, for instance—so that it can be grown in fairly isolated areas and profitably shipped to distant markets. This last factor was particularly important in the antebellum period. As of 1800, the most important wheat-producing area of the nation was in the states of Virginia, Maryland, and Pennsylvania, centered around Chesapeake Bay. The region had assumed this position of leadership in the late colonial period when its more southern parts had begun shifting away from tobacco and emulating southeastern Pennsylvania, which had by then been exporting sizeable quantities of wheat for over a century.

In the first two decades of the nineteenth century the Chesapeake Bay region began to feel the competition of the developing areas of western New York and northern Ohio. This was intensified after 1825 when the Erie Canal and the development of shipping on the Great Lakes brought the output from such locations as southern Michigan and northern Indiana to the Eastern markets. By 1830, the production of wheat in the Chesapeake Bay region had begun to contract, as had that of most other remaining areas of wheat cultivation on the eastern seaboard. They were being undercut by the unbeatable combination then operating in Western lands—higher fertility, lower land prices (initially, at least), and reduced costs of moving the produce to market.

On to the Prairies

The major wheat-producing regions continued to shift westward with the frontier after 1830, but they began to move into a very different landscape which created a new set of problems and adaptations. In Ohio and Indiana the settlers had sometimes found small clearings in the natural forest. These they understandably welcomed as a reprieve from the arduous task of clearing away the oak trees. When they reached the edge of the great prairie in northwestern Indiana or Illinois, however, their response was just the opposite.[2] They preferred to settle

---

[2] An extensive and interesting account of the movement onto the prairies is contained in Allan G. Bogue, *From Prairie to Cornbelt,* University of Chicago Press, Chicago, 1963.

among the woods which bordered the rivers of the region. The prairies were covered with a dense, almost impenetrable mat of sod, the roots of which often went down 6 feet. Then there was the horrifying prospect of fire when the grass dried up in the fall, and also the absence of wood for buildings and fences. The latter were particularly important in the early years because without general cultivation the best alternative use of the land was as open range.

Such problems notwithstanding, the soil under the frustrating turf was excellent—indeed, among the best in the world—so that there were strong incentives to find ways to bring it into cultivation. The first step was the use of the "breaking plow," a variation of the special plow which had been devised for the first plowing of old pasture land in New England. The plows were very large by contemporary standards, and often had to be pulled by as many as twelve oxen. This is obviously the type of specialized production task which encourages the creation of correspondingly specialized production units. Such enterprises developed quickly on the prairies in the form of custom breaking teams who traveled from farm to farm in the plowing season. Within two or three days a good team could open up about as much new acreage as an individual farmer could normally expect to bring into production in one season. Subject to the variability of the weather, a single breaking team could normally expect to get from fifteen to twenty-five plots of grassland started in cultivation in a year.[3]

Soon after substantial settlement was under way on the prairies, the pioneer farmer was given another useful weapon to deal with the new soils. An Illinois blacksmith by the name of John Deere is commonly given credit for devising a strong, light, steel plow. Actually, he was only one of a large number of innovators who were working on such a device. But the development of the plow, like other inventions such as the steamboat and the cotton gin, fulfilled a widely recognized need. A good number of farmers, blacksmiths, and tool manufacturers had been adding steel plates to existing plows and generally experimenting to improve their design. So instead of devising any *particular* technical innovation, Deere probably assembled the first total organization to design, produce, and market such an implement.

In any case the steel plow soon became a nearly universal tool in prairie farming. One of its prime advantages was in scouring; that is, it did not accumulate or cake soil when the ground was wet, which was a good part of the plowing time on the prairie. (With earlier plows, the packed dirt had to be knocked off frequently, slowing down plowing and creating an irregularly plowed field as well.) The steel plow could also be used as a partial substitute for the larger breaking plows. Pulled by two strong horses, it could break prairie sod if the

---

[3] The length of the breaking season represented a trade-off which the farmers of the prairies became quite adept in calculating. On the one hand, there was the desirability of using the specialized plows and plowing teams as long as possible in order to reduce their average costs. On the other hand, there were diminishing returns to plowing in certain periods of the year. Most of the breaking was carried out between early May and late June. If the plowing was undertaken before that, the native prairie grasses had a good chance of reestablishing themselves during the growing season. But if breaking was carried out too late in the year, the up-ended sod did not have sufficient time to decompose and presented the farmer with a tangled mat of obstructions the following year.

native grass had been grazed down by livestock, as it often had been since that was one of the most productive uses of prairie land before cultivation.

The pioneers also began grappling with the problem of fencing material, another major drawback in the treeless terrain where livestock and field crops were commonly interspaced. The first settlers had usually taken homesteads which included some of the woodlands that paralleled the rivers.[4] Soon, however, these limited local supplies were exhausted and a search for substitutes began. One early method was a combination of a ditch and the mound of dirt thrown out alongside it as it was dug. This esoteric device was effective in keeping cattle out of the fields—too effective. Farmers grew tired of pulling animals out of the ditches and gradually abandoned the entire technique. Another common approach was to plant hedgerows, much like those crisscrossing England. Literally scores of different plants were tried, with the most common variety finally adopted being the Osage orange shrub. It could withstand the gophers and the winters and could be pruned into a thick hedge whose thorns discouraged cattle from venturing through it. Its main drawback, however, was that it required considerable labor to maintain, so, considering the large amount of fence required per working person, it was not surprising that the pioneers continued to search for still better alternatives. One technique came in with the railroads. They allowed relatively cheap lumber to be brought in from the forests of upper Wisconsin and Michigan, and, in the 1850s, board fences began to appear alongside those made of rails, pickets, and Osage orange trees. Farmers were not entirely satisfied with any of these, however, as witnessed by the general shift to barbed wire when it became available after the Civil War.

Chicago and the Coming of the Railroads

Today northern and central Illinois, southern Wisconsin, and eastern Iowa are part of a larger agricultural area known as the Corn Belt. That designation came after the Civil War, however. In the two decades before 1860 it was clearly the fastest-growing wheat-producing area in the nation. In the 1850s, for example, national output of wheat increased by 70 percent and all of that increase came from this rapidly growing, three-state area. The three states also accounted for almost one-quarter of the total population increase of the nation during that decade, with Illinois registering the largest increase of any state. Not all this growth came in the rural areas, of course. The cities of Chicago, Milwaukee, and Davenport also acquired sizeable populations. Yet much of the growth of these urban centers can be attributed to the rapid development of commercial agriculture in the rural areas they served. It was the cities which provided the farm machinery, grain storage and transfer facilities, marketing and financial services, and supplies which such specialized agricultural operations required.

[4] Understandably, the ability to make the most out of those increasingly scarce local wood supplies was a socially valued trait. Thus the term "rail-splitter," seemingly rather mundane to folks outside the area, became a local slogan of approval—as witnessed by the most famous one of all, Abraham Lincoln. A good rail-splitter could fashion enough fence rails in one day—say 150—to construct 200 feet of fence which was "horse high, bull strong, and hog tight."

And it was the railroad that allowed this rural area to reach such a high degree of specialization. In 1840, the area had been served by the (then) same low-cost water transportation which generally characterized the Great Lakes region. Even so, the cost of hauling wheat by wagon to the nearest water port made sizeable areas of otherwise good land not feasible for commercial agriculture. The railroads ended that isolation and enticed most of that good-quality soil into production for the marketplace. Within the fifteen-year period from 1845–1860 this new wheat-growing area was covered with a dense network of railroad lines. Nine separate lines were built across Illinois from east to west, and four similar lines were built in eastern Iowa. These tracks were obviously laid down in anticipation of the farm produce they could carry, and it was not long before it was forthcoming. The most important cargo was wheat, of course, but a large amount of livestock also began to be delivered. Much of this outpouring was funneled through the natural outlet at the foot of Lake Michigan where the rail lines converged on a crossroads of water routes. Thus Chicago became the fastest-growing large city in the economy at this time.

The Dairy Industry

At the beginning of the nineteenth century the typical American cow was a rather pathetic creature. Most were general-purpose animals, better adapted for survival on limited care and foraging than for the production of dairy products. Visitors from England, touring the economy, marveled at how neglected and emaciated American cattle were. This general characteristic was not the result of callousness on the part of the farmers, however. Only those animals which they truly valued, such as horses and sheep, could be given careful care, and most dairy animals were treated casually because they were marginal in the operation of American farms. Only limited amounts of fresh milk were consumed on the farm—Americans then had a distinct preference for such drinks as cider, tea, or whiskey—and most farms were far enough removed from potential urban customers to prohibit the delivery of milk while it was still fresh. Surplus milk in rural areas was usually turned into rather low-quality butter or cheese. Most farmers did not have either the patience or the skill to turn out good cheese. A commonly quoted term for it in urban markets of the time was "soft country," which is to say that it had not been properly cured. Butter was a similar story. Some of it was sold fresh at weekly farmer markets, but the usual practice in areas still further removed from large cities was to save it for periods of up to three months and then exchange it for merchandise at the general store. The storekeepers commonly consolidated these individual contributions rather indiscriminately into large barrels and shipped them off to distant markets. Needless to say, quality sometimes suffered.

Nevertheless, there was a market for dairy products in the major cities before 1840, so human ingenuity went to work on the problem. The problem obviously was that *milk* could not be shipped very far, given existing transportation and refrigeration techniques, which meant that the *cows* had to be situated near the customers. This converted the problem into one of finding relatively inexpensive feed for the cattle in the face of relatively expensive urban land. One common practice was to feed the cows the residue of the grain from the local breweries, but many people objected that milk from such sources was contaminated and sought to ban the practice. Although the health of the cows may have suffered, it is not clear that the practice affected the milk, and it was, also, a typical solution to what would otherwise have been a major problem of disposing of large quantities of garbage. But other sources of local fodder were still actively sought, and two likely ones were the parks and commons of the cities where the livestock were located. There are frequent references in the city council records of the early 1800s to the question of pasture privileges on city lands, a practice which was viewed not unsympathetically by the city officials. Dairy people were usually willing to pay for the pasturing and, furthermore, it solved the problem of mowing the grass in an era before a successful mechanical lawnmower had been developed. One ironic example was that Boston found it desirable to sell permits to pasture cows on its common in the 1820s—some fifty years after it had fined British soldiers for walking on the lawn!

Railroads and the Expanding Milk Sheds

The introduction of the railroads drastically changed the organization of the dairy industry by expanding the effective distance from which cities could draw fresh milk products. After 1840, the farms supplying milk to the urban areas began to locate along the rail lines emanating from them. The common distance was usually from 10 to 40 miles from the city center. This allowed the farmers to use somewhat cheaper forms of feed for their livestock although they still practiced more land-intensive agriculture than was common in most of the rest of the economy. Dairy farmers located near urban areas, for example, were among the first to adopt the use of corn silage for cattle feed. It not only increased their yield of fodder per acre but also allowed them to supply a more even year-round supply of milk. The milk was shipped directly into the city by railroads whose schedules were often arranged with that purpose in mind. In warm weather it was kept in large cans immersed in cold water. Once in the city it was distributed quickly by neighborhood deliverers who ladled it into customers' containers out of their own large pails. Nowadays the milk deliverer is somewhat of an anachronism. With refrigeration nearly universal, both in the home and the store, customers can pick up milk whenever they want to. In the antebellum period, however, the milk deliverer was an important link in the distribution of a commodity in which speed was crucial for product quality.

Similar drastic reorganizations were also taking place in the supply of the other major dairy products, butter and cheese. The new rail lines allowed these products to be delivered relatively quickly from much wider areas. One result was that some areas, such as Vermont and upstate New York, became commercial dairy areas for the first time. This regional specialization also allowed the development of specialized processing facilities, such as creameries and cheese factories. This took advantage of the economies of scale in such larger operations and allowed much better quality control of the products as well. The latter was becoming an important selling point in the urban markets. Consumers were placing a sizeable premium on quality, and the processing agencies were seeking to satis-fy it. Such products as butter from Orange County (in the Hudson Valley) and cheese from Oneida County (Utica, New York) came close to being used as generic names for quality products because the processing firms in those areas took special care to ensure that only quality products went out under their names.

As a result of these innovations in the supply of dairy products, their real price fell and per capita consumption increased accordingly. But there were influ-ences operating on the demand side, also. Per capita incomes were rising in this period and they were probably highest in the larger cities. This effect showed up on both the type and the quality of food products which urban residents desired. As we noted, there was an obvious demand for quality in dairy products. This carried over to most other types of food items as well, and it was primarily the result of spontaneous consumer demand rather than of government regulation. Thus, changes in the organization of agriculture were responding to changes in the overall economy and were initiating such changes as well.

Fruits and Vegetables

Other examples of the adaptation of agriculture to increasing incomes and urban-ization can be readily seen in sectors supplying other crops. For example, before 1820, most fruit grown in farming areas was used for local purposes. Some of it was converted into alcoholic drinks, such as cider or brandy, and sizeable quanti-ties were fed to the livestock. Some fresh fruit was sold in local markets, but only a small percentage of total production was shipped any real distance. By the 1830s, however, some orchards were being developed with distant markets in mind. Upper New York began to export large amounts of apples and the states of New Jersey and Delaware began to be known for their peaches. In the last decade before the Civil War, Virginia and Georgia also began exporting large quantities of fruit. The prime market for this new flow of produce was the large Eastern cities, particularly New York and Philadelphia. New Orleans was the principal market in the West—until 1850 anyway, when cities such as Chicago became large—and northern Ohio became its major source of apples. As farmers began to specialize in particular types of fruit, they began to pay much more attention to the tree stock than they did during the older, more casual days of fruit culture. The merits of particular varieties became commonplace conversa-tion in orchard country. Another, more tangible bit of evidence of this new specialization was the appearance of commercial nurseries that advertised in their yearly catalogs the hundreds of varieties of fruit trees which were available. Fruit trees were too valuable a resource at that time to be taken for granted; any random apple tree was no longer a good substitute for any other.

In the summer of 1837, the *New England Farmer* reported on the fresh vege-tables being sold in the central Boston market.[5] Most of the *Farmer*'s readers were interested in the prices being paid for such produce, but the description

[5] As quoted in Paul W. Gates, *The Farmer's Age: Agriculture, 1815–1860,* Harper & Row, New York, 1968, p. 267.

provides modern readers with a striking example of the availability of fresh vegetables at such an early date—that is, when urban populations were still small compared to what they would be later in the century. In July, one could buy string beans, cabbage, lettuce, carrots, onions, turnips, peas, radishes, early summer squash, new potatoes, cucumbers, strawberries, cherries, currants, blueberries, gooseberries, raspberries, tomatoes, shell beans, green corn, celery, cauliflower, melons, thimbleberries, pears, peaches, grapes, apples, and plums. In short, except for tropical products, the choice was not too dissimilar from that offered in a modern supermarket. Most of the vegetables on this list had undoubtedly come from gardens on the edge of the city. By 1840, such specialized farms existed around all the major cities, including New York, Philadelphia, and Baltimore, as well as Boston. Not only were there farms concerned primarily with turning out vegetables or berries for the nearby cities, but others appeared with specialties in more exotic fare, such as flowers and ornamental shrubs.

Another product which was produced in large quantities around cities was hay—the equivalent of gasoline in 1840. While the per capita use of horses in the cities was not as large as that in the countryside, the total number used increased along with that of the population of the cities, which was becoming quite sizeable. Furthermore, there was little or no pasture in the city so that horses there had to be fed hay and oats all year round, unlike their rural counterparts who required supplementary feed only in the winter. Thus, the demand for hay in urban centers grew along with their population and farmers took steps to meet it. One obvious example of these efforts was the development, after 1835, of a series of devices to compress hay. Loose hay was an extremely volume-consuming item and thus ran up huge transportation costs if shipped over any distance. The continual efforts to improve hay presses in the late antebellum period ensured that this problem would be surmounted and that cities could afford to continue to use horses.

EXPANSION WITHIN A DECLINING SECTOR

This picture of vitality and growth within the dairy, fruit, and vegetable industries may come as something of a surprise. After all, before 1860 most of these industries were in the Northeast and it is almost an axiom of American history that Eastern agriculture was in headlong retreat before Western competition during this period. Indeed, the aggregate amount of agriculture did decrease in some of the larger Eastern states in the years just before the Civil War. However, within that total decline, the picture was mixed. Those products which were in direct competition with the exports of the new Western regions, such as wheat and preserved meats, underwent heavy contractions. Once transportation costs came down sufficiently, the superior resource endowments of the new lands could not be matched and the land in the Eastern states which was best adapted to those specific products was hit hardest. In practice this meant the lands devoted to extensive-type agriculture, which in 1820 and 1830, on the eve of the imports of Western foodstuffs, were for the most part marginal operations anyway.

These included upland acreage—as distinguished from the valleys—of New England, New York, and Pennsylvania, as well as such low country as that bordering Chesapeake Bay.

While *extensive* agriculture was contracting in the East, however, those farming operations which typically use land more *intensively* were expanding. The same complex of changes which was making some Eastern lands noneconomic was also, surprisingly enough, making other acreage in the region more productive and, therefore, more expensive. Part of the explanation was that although lower transportation costs made importing some agricultural goods cheaper, it also encouraged changes in the organization of the economy which increased the demand for other products that still could not be imported from any great distance. The important factor here was the lack of any means of keeping food products fresh beyond their natural lifespan. Thus, the fresh items, such as milk and vegetables—of which the Eastern cities were rapidly increasing their total consumption—had to be produced close enough to these markets to be able to reach the customers in a short period of time. Good-quality land in proximity to urban markets, therefore, became a valued resource. And, as a natural consequence, it began to be used more intensively, not only in the types of products to which it was devoted but also in the farming techniques used upon it. For example, one of the best areas of farmland near the larger Eastern cities was the lower Connecticut River Valley in southeastern New England. By railroad it was only a few hours from Boston and the major textile centers in eastern New England. New York City and the developed market area of Long Island Sound were directly accessible to small boats going down the river. The valley had produced a variety of crops in its two centuries of cultivation, such as wheat, onions, broom corn, and tobacco. Then, in the second decade of the 1800s, it developed a new technique—the stall-fattening of cattle. This was obviously in response to the demand for higher-quality, fresh meat which could be provided only by slaughtering animals near the market. Furthermore, the costs of shipping fat cattle in from the West was so high that good-quality fresh meat destined for Eastern cities had to be finished nearby. Shipping livestock by railroad before the Civil War was costly, and cattle that came East by the cheaper route—walking on their own feet—normally lost considerable weight and had to be refinished in Eastern feedlots anyway.

The fact that Eastern farmers were using the technique of stall-fattening also illustrates another trend in local agriculture. Confining an animal to close quarters increases the efficiency with which fodder is converted into meat, and often the quality of the meat as well. This gain is counteracted by an increase in the amount of labor required—bringing the feed to the livestock instead of letting the livestock forage for it—as well as of capital, in the form of barns and feedlots. In short, it illustrates the increase in the value of good Eastern farmland by the corresponding application of larger amounts of labor and capital to it. Hauling the food to the cattle rather than having them forage for it in the pasture increased the yield per acre. It also indicates how much the cost of land had risen relative to other resources since the colonial days when the livestock had been turned out into the woods to fend for themselves.

Stall-feeding was only a small example of a much larger shift in agricultural techniques which was taking place in the East. As the price of land rose there was a major move toward restoring and raising its productivity. As early as 1800, farmers near the large Eastern cities of Boston, New York, and Philadelphia were applying gypsum, a cheap though often less effective substitute for lime, to their soil. Such practices became more common and spread into wider areas as the antebellum period passed.[6] Gypsum was by no means the only supplement added to the soil. American farmers quickly developed a wide variety of them in response to local costs and conditions. For example, gypsum was generally displaced by lime in the 1830s and 1840s when improvements in the use of anthracite coal allowed the lime to be burned out of limestone. The shift was gradual, however, occurring first in such areas as eastern Pennsylvania and New York, near limestone deposits, and much later in distant areas where supplies of cheap substitutes were locally available. Shore areas of New England and Long Island used fish and seaweed for fertilizer. In the Chesapeake Bay region, crushed oyster shells were used.

American farmers also changed their attitude toward manure. In the colonial period it was considered a nuisance, something to be disposed of as cheaply as possible. Whenever possible, farmers built their barns alongside waterways so that they could pitch the residue into the current and be done with it. Farmers without access to running water often found it easier to move the barn periodically rather than the piles of manure which accumulated around it. After 1800, however, this attitude began to change in the East, first in the areas around the larger cities, and then in those farther afield, until by the Civil War most agriculture east of the Allegheny Mountains had been altered. Manure had become a valuable resource. It was painstakingly redistributed back over the farmland. One indication of this newfound value occurred in the cities. Before 1800, stable owners had considered the disposal of dirty straw as one of their most difficult and persistent problems. In the antebellum period, the problem was turned into an asset. Nearby farmers were not only willing to cart it away free, but often were even ready to pay for the privilege. Farmers also practiced similar ingenuity on their own acreages in seeking all possible sources of organic additions to the soil. Many Eastern farmers established a compost pile for which all the available kitchen scraps, garden trimmings, and spoiled produce were carefully set aside.

There were also numerous other indications that Eastern farmers were giving more concern to the future fertility of their soil. Most farmers began to use some system of crop rotation. The traditional sequence of wheat/wheat/wheat or corn/corn/corn began to disappear and in its place appeared more complicated

---

[6] A complete account of this transformation in land practices is contained in Clarence H. Danhof, *Change in Agriculture: The Northern United States 1820–1870,* Harvard, Cambridge, Mass., 1969, Chapter 10. The book also contains extensive, interesting discussions of other aspects of agriculture in this period.

patterns in which grasses, such as clover and timothy, played an important role. By plowing under such cover crops as grass or red clover, rather than using them as fodder, Americans were even able to restore some lands which had been abandoned as totally exhausted. Much of the former wheat and tobacco lands of Maryland and Delaware came back into production as livestock areas in this way. Overall, it is quite clear that large numbers of Americans saw that it was to their advantage to drastically change their use of agricultural land. Formerly, land had been treated casually because available virgin land was a cheaper substitute than the additional resources required to maintain the existing stock. Now that the alternatives to certain types of land were severely restricted, however, it was treated much more carefully. And with that shift in behavior went the former stereotype of American farmers as short-sighted, dull-witted characters. Americans began to handle their land in a more provident and respectful manner.

SOURCES OF HIGHER PRODUCTIVITY IN AGRICULTURE

The American farmers who were considered so careless in the use of land before 1800 were also often construed as somewhat noninnovative, tradition-bound characters. They were reported to be skeptical of new farming methods or crops and to ridicule their neighbors who were so bold as to experiment with newfangled ideas. Some of this characterization was undoubtedly true, and yet such attitudes were not unreasonable in light of the typical quality of prevailing suggestions. Nor did they necessarily foreclose the possibility of increasing productivity either. One can sympathize with the inertia of the colonial farmers if one examines a list of the advice they were typically offered. Much of it was well intended but counterproductive. A good portion, for example, sought to emulate the widely praised "high farming" which developed in England in the latter half of the eighteenth century. Although that was a modern system in that its techniques had been perfected only recently, it was designed for specific English conditions which tended to use both labor and capital quite lavishly. That was one of the worst types of arrangements for most American land before 1820. Thus, if farmers were to implement all or even a random selection of the suggestions given to them in those days, they would in all probability decrease their output rather than increase it. In this context, the "backwardness" of American farmers is perfectly understandable. It is best seen as a rejection of the flow of bad advice they were receiving under the presumptuous label of "enlightened agriculture."

Caution toward new techniques, however, does not necessarily eliminate the possibility of improving productivity. Before 1800, or 1840 in the areas not immediately adjacent to the major cities, some farmers initiated changes which did increase efficiency, and other farmers were convinced by observed good results. Successful techniques—even when pioneered by a few idiosyncratic individuals—were copied and spread throughout the areas where they were profitable. And many small improvements came about merely from random variations in farming operations, or marginal changes in techniques. Farmers who noticed that a particular patch of corn did well in one year might save seed from it for next year's planting. If it continued to perform better than the others it would continue to be planted and to be adopted on nearby farms as well. In this way, by the time of the Civil War literally thousands of specific varieties of plants had been developed to make the most of local variations in soil, moisture, and temperature. Advances also came from minor experiments. Farmers might introduce variations into the way they plowed a field, or blacksmiths might try changing the angle of the moldboard of a plow when they assembled it for local farmers. If these minor experiments added nothing, they would be forgotten. If they were successful, however, they could be extended further in later practices. Thus, the early American farmers were not necessarily an obstacle to progress per se, despite their image and their public statements. Rather, they screened new ideas carefully and rejected those suggestions which did not have any convincing evidence of practicality, because they knew from experience that the odds were against such a priori advice being productive. The American farmers' conservatism, therefore, is best seen as a strategy for implementing new knowledge in the light of a pattern of costs and benefits of doing so, rather than as a blanket rejection of progress. This should not surprise us when we consider that it is not dissimilar to the evaluations of potential new products and major investments carried out by many modern American corporations. The difference is mostly in appearance. Few companies advertise that they are opposed to progress, and most of the intense scrutiny and naysaying given to suggestions goes on internally and is much less subject to public notice.

The Changing Framework for Technological Diffusion in Agriculture

Until at least 1800, farmers pretty much had to fend for themselves when it came to screening and implementing ideas. After 1800 the importance of help received from outside sources gradually increased. The main reason for this shift in channels was probably the same one affecting so many other activities in the economy—specialization. As transportation costs fell and the economy became generally more interdependent, it became more advantageous to split off functions—such as that of collecting and screening information—into specialized enterprises. This tendency clearly was under way in American agriculture before the Civil War. We have alluded to some of the earliest efforts, such as county fairs and agricultural societies (in Chapter 4). Undoubtedly the most important general source of information about new developments was the agricultural periodicals which appeared in this period.[7]

   In modern times not many people would recognize such periodicals as *Rural New Yorker, American Agriculturist,* or the *Cultivator,* but by the middle of the nineteenth century these were household words—in country households, at least. The farm journals spent most of their linage describing new or successful varie-

---

[7] Again, an excellent description of this aspect of agriculture is contained in Clarence H. Danhof, *Change in Agriculture: The Northern United States 1820–1870,* Harvard, Cambridge, Mass., 1969, Chapter 3.

ties of crops or animals, implements, and farm management procedures. They collected this information from European publications, government reports, letters from farmers, local correspondents, and the travels of their own staff members. The staff members became increasingly important as time passed and the periodicals became larger. They developed writers who became expert in particular aspects of agriculture, in answering readers' questions, and in evaluating current developments in regular columns. Needless to say, in such a role they not only relayed reports of agricultural developments but also sought to assess their merits. The screening of suggestions for improving agricultural productivity was passing from the individual farmers to a somewhat more prepared intermediary. This did not relieve the farmers of making judgments on their own but the ideas and the reasoning behind certain recommendations were spelled out much better and helped them to make decisions.

The Search for Better Methods

Ironically, the specialized dissemination of knowledge in agriculture by such means as the agricultural periodicals was encouraged by the growing specialization of agriculture itself. When farming was primarily a self-sufficient operation, there was less incentive for an individual farmer to seek to improve a particular type of activity. For example, a commercial dairy would be interested in higher milk yields because they would be directly translated into larger revenues, whereas one self-sufficient farmer with one cow would have less to gain from an increase in milk production. It might even prove of very little value. The one cow might provide as much in the way of dairy products as the household wished and the off-farm market for such products was often sharply limited. In such an environment the farmer would still seek to increase the family income but more likely through such avenues as obtaining livestock which were capable of fending for themselves—in economic terms, reducing operating costs—and which could serve several functions. Indeed, if one examined the typical livestock in use in the United States in 1800, this was the obvious common denominator. A newborn calf might become a source of milk, meat, leather, motive power, or some combination of these. There was little differentiation among types of cattle.

This pattern began to break down when agricultural units began to specialize. A dairy farmer was interested in cows for their milking potential, a rancher for their ability to put on weight cheaply, and the teamster for their endurance and strength in pulling loaded freight wagons. Since one such attribute usually comes at the cost of the others, the logical tactic was to develop particular strains, or breeds, which emphasized the desired qualities. Exactly this type of selective breeding program had been going on in England on a major scale since at least the middle of the eighteenth century, when commercial agriculture began to become important there. Naturally, one response of the Americans when they first turned to commercial agriculture on a large scale in the early nineteenth century was to try out the existing British breeds. It was at that time that such provincial English names as Hereford, Jersey, Guernsey, and Ayrshire became commonplace in the American vocabulary.

While foreign stock was an improvement over the native stock for some purposes, it also fell considerably short of what Americans seemed to expect from it. Thus, after 1820 the Americans undertook extensive breeding operations to develop new varieties of livestock. These efforts were primarily undertaken by breeders who specialized in raising specific types of livestock. These enterprises not only imported foreign cattle and developed new strains but they also undertook to advertise and sell their particular breed. The result was a competitive environment in which breeders sought to show that their animals offered the traits which farmers desired and also attempted to develop those qualities in subsequent livestock through selective breeding efforts.

Out of this nineteenth-century system of competition through product improvement evolved a completely new spectrum of livestock. They were adapted to specific niches in the agricultural sector and were also more productive than was the native stock generally in use at the beginning of the nineteenth century, and which they superseded. For example, consider the transformation of the old family milk cow. In the early 1800s the British breeds of Ayrshires, Guernseys, and Jerseys were imported.[8] They were subsequently modified so much to suit American conditions, however, that they effectively constituted new breeds. There was a long-standing debate among American dairy folk during this period as to whether it would be better to try to modify native cattle or to work with the imports. In effect, both parties won their points. The cattle which evolved out of the repeated cross-breeding of the period had both the hardiness of the native stock and the larger milk and cream production of the British breeds.

Similar efforts were going on with beef cattle, hogs, sheep, horses, and even poultry. Sometimes the name of the imported breed, such as the English Shorthorn, continued to be used for beef cattle. At other times a distinct American species became recognized, such as the Chester Whites (a type of hog still very popular today, named after the county near Philadelphia where it was developed). Whatever the nomenclature, however, the animals were a new species, or at least subspecies, adapted to American conditions. Most of the working inventory of livestock in the economy was slowly but persistently upgraded by the farmers' natural tendency to keep and breed their best animals. In the areas that specialized in raising livestock, however, the average quality of the animals was brought up to the best current levels very quickly. Often the quality was better than that of the original English stock on which the animals were based. This was reflected in the reverse migration of livestock buyers across the Atlantic. There were often as many English buyers at American auctions as there were Americans at British auctions.

As in most historical trends, the change was far from complete at the time of the Civil War. The process of upgrading and diffusing the new animals was itself

---

[8] Some Ayrshires are still in use in the United States today. Their coloring varies through different shades of brown, sometimes with a reddish hue. Guernseys are more common. They are easily recognized by patches of light brown on white. The Jersey is also common. It tends to be among the smallest of the dairy cows and has light brown coloring, much like a deer. Indeed, it is not unheard of for deer hunters from the city to return with a Jersey cow proudly tied to their fender.

incomplete. Furthermore, the increased specialization and commercialization of agriculture which was encouraging the trend was itself still going on—as can be seen in the remaining reluctance to adopt some of the most common varieties of cattle found today, such as the most common milk cow in the United States, the black and white Holstein. It is an excellent milk producer but sacrifices other attributes, such as cream output and slaughter value, for that marked specialization. The market for butter and meat were still too important to most dairy farmers on the eve of the Civil War to shift away from the more familiar (milking) Shorthorns and Guernseys. Similarly, the red and white Hereford, now the most common American beef animal, was used in mixtures but generally not as a pure breed before the Civil War. The animal is a good forager on grasslands and converts corn into steak at a very high rate but does not do well if it is driven 500 miles from the range to the feedlot. Its present popularity had to wait until the development of the railroad network and the Midwestern Corn Belt. Until that time farmers raising beef preferred a somewhat less-productive but more general-purpose animal.

Innovations in Farm Equipment

Around 1800, typical American farmers possessed a motley assortment of hand implements, such as shovels, rakes, hoes, sickles, and so on. Their largest implement was usually an all-purpose plow which was used for cultivating or hilling row crops, as well as for plowing. This state of affairs was likely to change in the antebellum period, however, for at least two reasons. First, the incentives for innovation which seemed so generally prevalent would almost certainly reach into agriculture. Second, the rising price of labor relative to other resources, particularly capital, would encourage farmers to use more equipment per capita. This incentive to adopt additional implements would be most likely to appear first in those peak periods of farming in which the low labor supply became a bottleneck. Probably the most important such instance in the beginning 1800s was the early-season activities of plowing and seeding. The amount of acreage a farmer could handle in the planting season determined his maximum yearly crop, so the more he could speed up the planting step the more he could raise his yearly output.

In this context it is easy to understand the American farmers' continual preoccupation with improving the design of plows. Any gains there lowered a barrier which allowed them to use their time more productively throughout the remainder of the growing season. Around 1800 the typical plow was a cumbersome, wooden model. It had several drawbacks, including a very high coefficient of friction which necessitated a large team to pull it through the soil. It wore out easily, and this was costly in several ways. First, the yearly maintenance was often a large fraction of the purchase price. Second, most malfunctions occurred when it was being used, namely, in that part of the year when delays were most costly. Third, it was very difficult to replicate parts exactly, so that if a particular design turned out to be an improvement it was often very difficult to reproduce. In short, there was considerable incentive to find a better model.

Traditionally, the improvement of the plow is ascribed to two major steps, the invention of the cast-iron plow by Jethro Wood and the later development of the steel model by John Deere. Actually, the process was much more evolutionary. The successful iron plow was really the summation of at least three lines of attack on separate problems of plow design. One was to achieve more quality in the casting process in order to reduce the incidence of plow breakage. A second was to solve the rather complicated problem of designing the shape of the moldboard (which Thomas Jefferson attempted to solve through the use of mathematical simulation). On the one hand, it is desirable to have a smooth cut and a furrow which turns over neatly, but on the other hand, it is also desirable to minimize the offsetting cost of friction. A third problem was to design interchangeable parts so that wrought iron could be substituted for cast iron where strength was most important, and broken parts could be easily replaced on the farm.

These innovations had been carried out over a period of two decades before Wood's famous model put all the components together in 1817. Even then adoption of the plow was slow, requiring another two decades to win over most of the farmers in the East. One reason was that wooden plows were much cheaper. The premium was only gradually reduced as improvements in metallurgy and manufacturing techniques worked to reduce production costs. Another drawback was that, unlike the older wooden plows which were usually put together by the local blacksmiths, the cast-iron models were produced at distant factories or foundries. This meant not only establishing a distribution system but also convincing the farmers that if their plow were to break down in the middle of plowing, spare parts would be available locally.

The design of the cast-iron plow also underwent literally hundreds of variations before the Civil War. One of the largest manufacturers listed about 150 different models. These were not merely cosmetic differences but were attempts to match the plow design to particular soils, crops, terrains, and plowing functions. This latter function was evident in the proliferation of plows for specific uses. There were plows for breaking sod, for light cultivation of loose soil, for planting, or for deep plowing for those who were using that new method (primarily in the East) to get more out of their acreage. There were also special plows for cultivating, hilling, and making shallow ditches. In this context the famed steel plow is merely another example in a broader process of matching plows more closely to local uses. It was successful in wet, heavy soils. It did not replace the cast-iron plow generally, however, until improvements in steel technology eliminated its price premium after the Civil War.

Harvesting Equipment   As the improvements in plowing developed during the antebellum period, the bottleneck in the farming season shifted to other phases of crop growing. In wheat and hay, this meant the harvesting season. Mature wheat rapidly lodges (falls over) and loses much of its grain if it is not cut soon after reaching maturity. Hay suffers severe quality loss if it is caught in the rain after it is cut. Before 1850, inventors spent considerable effort trying to devise a machine which could handle both of these problems successfully. Ultimately the differences in the cutting functions for small grains and for grass forced them to devise separate machines. (For example, with grain it is not important to cut right along the ground, as it is the head of the stock which constitutes most of the useful product. With hay, on the other hand, failure to cut closely along the contour of the ground can result in the loss of a sizeable portion of the potential crop.)

The development of the horse-drawn reaper was another invention from which a large payoff was generally foreseen, and considerable effort was therefore put into devising one. The process was slow and frustrating, however, because a successful reaper ultimately proved to be a complex device. One major problem was that if it was to compete successfully with hand labor, using scythes, it had to be able to cope with the many harvesting conditions which human skills could handle. These included variable thicknesses in the standing grain, and also blow-over, or matted, stalks. It took considerable time and experimentation to build such adaptability into mechanical equipment. Another major problem to be overcome, as with the plow, was the dependence on improvements in the materials out of which the reaper was built. To reduce the likelihood of breakdowns, the early reapers were beefed up with large castings and shafts. This made for a very heavy machine, however; one which exhausted several large teams of horses in the course of a day's work. It took some time before engineering design and developments in metal technology reduced the weight of the reapers to that where typical farmers could expect to operate them with their own resources.[9] The net result of these delays was that it took a full thirty years (around 1820 to 1850) before widespread work on a reaper was translated into a unit which was economical for a sizeable fraction of grain farmers.

During the same period parallel improvements were going on in the task of cutting grass for hay. A simple, inexpensive hayrake was developed around 1820. A successful mower took nearly as long to develop as the reaper, however, and did not become a generally specialized piece of equipment—as distinguished from the reaper, pressed into double duty cutting hay—until just before the Civil War. Another parallel development was that of a mechanical thresher to separate the grain from the cut stalks. This was not a rush job, however, as was reaping. Once the grain had been cut and bundled, it could be kept in the stalk for some time without significant loss. In fact, farmers had commonly reserved this task for the slow winter months when they had extra time on their hands anyway. There were costs of waiting, however. Grain in the stalk was bulky to store, so the opportunity costs of delaying threshing was in erecting some rather large barns to store the sheaves . Besides, threshing was hard, tedious work so that farmers often found it difficult to hire laborers at prevailing wage rates.[10]

---

[9] Here again is a historical parallel to modern problems, namely, the recent efforts of automobile manufacturers to reduce the weight of their vehicles in order to save on gasoline. In antebellum times, savings in weight could be translated into lower operating costs through the use of fewer horses—not too far from the very words engineers would use to describe their task today.

[10] These wages were undergoing a long-term increase during the antebellum period, and one of the benefits the workers seemed to wish to buy with their higher income was more desirable working conditions. Thus, near the end of the period they shied away from hand threshing, even though around 1800 it was considered "just part of the job."

Like the other pieces of farm machinery, the thresher was a combination of specific innovations, for specific functions, which were eventually successfully put together. These included a power source, a beating device to break the grain out of the stalks, a device to separate them, and a winnowing device to blow the chaff from the grain. The development of this total package was long and complicated. Suffice it to say that it represented the same combination of trial-and-error efforts, numerous minor refinements, coupled with the aid of better metals evident in the development of the other implements of the period.

Simultaneously, development was going ahead on the remainder of the wide range of large implements which contemporaries thought might be useful. These included grain drills (a device to speed the planting of small grains, such as wheat), corn planters and shellers, grinding mills, harrows, and cultivators. These last two implements were important for the expansion of the corn crop. Unlike wheat, corn does not have to be harvested soon after maturity. It can be left standing in the field and be plucked off when convenient. Once the productivity of plowing was increased, however, the time-consuming factor in raising corn was in keeping down the weeds in the first half of the growing season. Good antebellum farmers generally estimated that it took at least four cultivations before the corn was tall enough to dominate the weeds. In the early 1800s when most of the work was done with a hoe, about six days of labor were needed per acre. Thus, in the two-month early phase of the growing cycle, a single person could handle only about ten acres—and little else.

There was probably more variation in the cultivation of corn than in any other major crop in the period. Some hoeing was nearly universal, but in the last decade or so before the Civil War farmers in the Midwest, in an effort to eliminate hand weeding altogether, began to experiment with horse-drawn cultivators which tilled very close to the plants. Typically, the major thrust of efforts throughout the period was to devise methods of mechanical cultivation to reduce hand labor. One common practice was running a simple shovel plow between the rows. On some larger fields the farmers carefully planted their corn in squares so that cross-plowing could eliminate all weeds except those immediately around the plants. The most common effort was to devise better cultivators. These came to include models which could encompass several rows in one pass, had steel-spring teeth which were strong yet would not hang up on obstacles in the soil, and had wheels and a seat so that the tiresome task of trudging all day behind the cultivator in the fresh-turned soil could be eliminated. The net result was that a properly equipped laborer could cultivate ten times as many acres of corn in 1860 as he could have done with a hoe in earlier days.

PUBLIC LAND POLICIES, 1790–1862

Through most of its history, the American federal government has had just the opposite problem concerning land from the one it has had in recent years—namely, to get rid of it. During the confederation period the individual states decided that one way they could resolve their competing claims over Western lands without losing face was to turn them over to the federal government. Later, massive additions of acreage were periodically added to this domain, beginning with the Louisiana Purchase in 1803. The federal government had little interest in developing most of this frontier land, but private parties could almost always see ways in which it could be put to use.

It became, therefore, a problem of how to transfer large amounts of land from federal to private ownership—and it was not always a simple matter. On the one hand, there was the obvious objective of making the program easy to administer. On the other hand, there was the desire of seeing to it that any system of transfer would bring in enough revenue to avoid the need of imposing large taxes elsewhere. Then there was another entire set of issues concerning the distribution of benefits among the different groups in the economy. These latter concerns occupied much of Congress's attention to land policies over the nineteenth century—and a large share of historians' discussion of them since then.

When the federal government began disposing of lands with the passage of the Land Ordinance of 1785, it had only one model to go by—the earlier experiences of the Eastern states. For the most part they had minimized the mechanics of such programs by simply auctioning off large blocks of acreage to syndicates of private investors who, in turn, undertook the greater detail of retailing them in smaller parcels. The first federal land program was a step down from such a policy of limited involvement but was still conservative by later standards. Land was to be sold at auction, but at no less than $1 per acre. Furthermore, the minimum-size lot was to be a section (640 acres equal to a square mile) in alternative townships, while the townships which comprised the other half of the land were to be sold at auction in their entirety, that is, all 36 square miles as one unit. And the conditions of sale were cash. As the antebellum period progressed, these terms were gradually softened. The minimum-size sale was reduced to 320 acres, then 160, then 80, and finally, in 1832, to 40 acres. In 1800, credit terms were introduced but were repealed in 1820 because of frequent defaults. The minimum price per acre was raised to $2 in 1800, but dropped to $1.25 in 1820, where it remained until the passage of the Homestead Act in 1862.

There was admittedly a loosening up of the requirements to obtain public land but many individuals then—and since—have argued that during most of the period a significant group of potential land buyers was excluded. And this, it was felt, further caused the distribution of income to be turned in favor of the rich who were the only ones able to take advantage of such opportunities. That conclusion can be reached, however, only if the chain of reasoning is worked out much more carefully than we have outlined above. Probably the most important distinction which needs to be drawn is that between the *initial access* to land and the *pattern of ownership* which is likely to develop as a longer-term arrangement. While it is true that restrictive terms might limit the initial purchase of land to those individuals or groups able to assemble sizeable amounts of capital, in the longer run the land is likely to be subdivided into smaller plots in accord with the prevailing pattern of use in the economy; before the Civil War that was primarily family-sized farms.

The important question, therefore, is how much the initial distribution of land affected the final pattern of use. Many commentators have argued that the connection was important and have suggested several ways by which the initial ownership would have provided leverage over how (and when) the land was eventually used. For example, it has been frequently argued that the initial land purchasers could have held land off the market until the price was forced up to the level they desired. This, however, is a confusion between "relatively few" purchasers and a complete monopoly. If all land had been controlled by one agency it could have regulated the rate at which land was made available. But although the number of purchasers of federal land was small in relation to the total population in any given year, there were still thousands of them. Furthermore, the federal government followed a policy of auctioning off land in new areas as soon as sufficient interest in it seemed to develop. To corner the land market, one would need to have coordinated thousands of individual landowners as well as to have purchased all land opening up on the frontier as well.

Another argument runs that even though large landowners might not have been able to monopolize power, they could have inflated the cost of land considerably when they subdivided and resold it to smaller holders. Again, such a pattern of behavior depends on the absence of competition. If buyers are able to choose among alternative parcels of land, owned by different sellers, the price of any plot will tend toward the initial purchase price plus the cost of any productive improvements. Private owners could indeed have charged more per acre for the small subdivisions than they paid initially for the larger parcel, but only to the extent that they had incurred costs which made the units they were selling correspondingly more productive. The question then naturally arises whether these costs would have been avoided if the federal government had been the agent to subdivide and sell the acreage to begin with. The answer is that it, too, would have required additional resources to undertake such a finer division and sale of property. Unless the government had some natural advantage in efficiency in the real estate market—which seems unlikely—it would have cost society an equivalent amount in resources either way. And the net price to buyers would finally work out to be about the same either way. The difference would probably show up on the initial auction price. If the government had already gone to all the effort to prepare the land in plots appropriate for final use, then the price would be higher and would tend to approximate the final price which private developers would charge if they were to undertake that task themselves. In the program which was followed where the federal government often sold land in lots larger than those used by a single farming unit, however, the initial price per acre would be less. The first buyers would be forced to anticipate the development costs they would have to pay to resell the land. Either way, the price paid by the ultimate user would be the same.

The tendency of the federal government to dispose of land in larger parcels than could be used by individual economic units, therefore, simply amounted to a tactic to reduce the size of the government's involvement in the land sector. Either the government or the private sector could have sold the land to individuals, but in characteristic early nineteenth-century practice, the government decided to pass the task along.

Probably more important to the economy than the *initial size* in which land was distributed to the private sector was the *speed* with which it was made available. By either speeding up or slowing down the rate at which it sold off public lands, the government could make a sizeable difference in the price of land generally and, therefore, the way in which it was used. For example, if the federal government had followed a policy of allowing land to come to auction only very slowly—for instance, so that it commanded $5 per acre instead of the near-minimum of $1.25 to $2.00, which was common—it would have made it much more difficult for anyone, rich or poor, to begin a new farm on the frontier. It would also have tended to raise the price of all developed land, and probably to increase the price of land relative to that of labor as well. This would have led to a shift in the distribution of income in favor of landowners and away from labor. Such a "go-slow" policy would have undoubtedly led to much hardship on the poorest segment of the population, but so long as the government continued to sell land near the minimum price, just as soon as people were willing to buy it, it would tend to remain cheap and generally available for everyone.[11]

One force which was encouraging a relatively liberal land policy was the uninhibited behavior of the American frontier folk. They were not easily restrained by federal regulations about property rights when they could see large quantities of good, vacant land just ahead of them. For example, there was the common practice of *squatting*—that is, using and occupying land before they had any legal claim to it. Sometimes they would simply abandon their location when settlement and land sales encroached, but more often these people were constructing permanent homesteads which they fully expected to keep—or, at the least, to reap some gains from when formal ownership became general in an area. To this end there grew up a whole body of informal and extralegal practices to translate such unofficial practices into accepted procedures. The main concern of squatters was that someone else could appropriate the improvements they had made to their property by buying the land at public auction. They would then be forced to buy back the value of their improvements in order to retain their claim. Alternatively, another buyer would obtain the property at less than its fair market price. Either way, the squatters were out the value of their improvements.

But the squatters soon found ways to protect their acreages. Local "protective societies" began to appear at auctions to dissuade nonowners from bidding on land which was already occupied. In some country areas the local courts

---

[11] It would have been to the federal government's advantage to have followed a slow, or restrictive, land policy insofar as it would have probably led to a large increase in its revenues. It would be an interesting question of economic interests as funneled through the political decision-making process to examine why it followed the policy which it did in the face of such a seemingly strong temptation to the contrary.

recognized the rights of squatters to sue for the value of improvements if their land was bought out from under them. These informal efforts became so well established that Congress finally recognized them by writing them into the land acts. The Log Cabin Bill of 1841 granted squatters the right to purchase their property at the minimum price when it was put up for auction. With such provisions, it became difficult to sell land at much above the minimum price.

SUGGESTED READINGS

Bogue, Allan G.: *From Prairie to Corn Belt,* University of Chicago Press, Chicago, 1963.

Carstensen, Vernon (ed.): *The Public Lands,* University of Wisconsin Press, Madison, 1963.

Danhof, Clarance H.: *Change in Agriculture: The Northern United States, 1820-1870,* Harvard, Cambridge, Mass., 1969.

Fogel, Robert W. and Jack Rutner: "The Efficiency Effects of Federal Land Policy, 1850-1900: A Report of Some Provisional Findings," in William Aydelotte et al. (ed.): *Dimensions of Quantitative Research in History,* Princeton, Princeton, N.J., 1972.

Gates, Paul W.: *The Farmer's Age: Agriculture, 1815-1860,* Holt, New York, 1960.

North, Douglass C.: *Growth and Welfare in the American Past,* Prentice-Hall, Englewood Cliffs, N.J., 1974, Chapter 10.

Robertson, Ross M.: *History of the American Economy,* 3d ed., Harcourt Brace Jovanovich, New York, 1973.

Williamson, Harold F. (ed.): *The Growth of the American Economy,* 2d ed., Prentice-Hall, New York, 1951, Chapters 8 and 9.

Chapter 9

The Antebellum South: Conventional Behavior among Peculiar Institutions

To a traveler in modern America it must sometimes seem that the entire country is becoming homogenized. The signs for Holiday Inns, Kentucky Fried Chicken, and Exxon gasoline along interstate highways are so regular that you are forced to catch the names on the exit signs to tell whether you are in Connecticut or Tennessee. Yet local and regional identities do survive, or at least our conceptions of them continue to prevail. If one were to conduct a Gallup poll as to what are the distinctive regions of the United States there would probably be frequent references to "the West" or "New England," but there would almost certainly be answers of, "Well, of course, the South."

The South has a special identity in the minds of many, partly because of such standing associations as magnolias, pecan pies, and Spanish moss. But even more important to its distinctive image is the prevailing image of its past. No locality seen through the stereotypes of plantations, slavery, and Robert E. Lee can be easily forgotten.

Understandably, this identity carries over to historical coverage of the

South. The South is believed to be best understood by reference to its special features, its departures from the usual pattern of the rest of the nation—particularly before the Civil War.

Of course, if we work hard enough at refining the classification procedure, every region can be shown to be unique in some sense. But its differences can be far less important than the continuities they are allowed to overshadow. We can focus on unimportant differences while overlooking very basic similarities. This certainly appears to have been true in many of our previous discussions of the antebellum South. That economy did have a number of unusual features, such as slavery or a low level of urbanization, which appear to have distinguished it from the rest of the nation. Yet it is not obvious that such features were examples of eccentric behavior on the part of the South. Indeed, they may even have been reasonable adaptations to particular conditions which the South faced. As we examine the economic behavior of the antebellum South, some examples of the latter form of behavior will become evident. Sooner or later we will be forced to ask whether the traditional "peculiar institutions" might not be better labeled "ingenious adaptations."

THE UPPER SOUTH IN 1815

In 1815 the bulk of the South's population and its economic activity was positioned along the Atlantic coast east of the Appalachian Mountains. The large migrations which were to pull its center of gravity westward in the later years had not yet achieved much cumulative effect. Virginia was still the most populous state in the South, although its economic base appeared to be becoming a little threadbare. (New York had only recently surpassed it as the largest state in the country.) Virginia and the upper South were synonymous with tobacco, but the once-bright prospects of that crop had dimmed considerably by 1815. American tobacco had lost a large portion of the foreign market by this time and was becoming progressively constrained to domestic consumption. When its production characteristics are considered, it is surprising that the American product was able to dominate the world market for as long as it did—two full centuries. Tobacco uses a large amount of labor—that relatively expensive American resource—and it was only a matter of time until the production techniques were mastered in a moderately warm, cheap-labor economy, such as Turkey.

By 1815 a sizeable portion of the best soil of Virginia and North Carolina had at some time been devoted to tobacco culture. The usual cropping practice had been to cultivate the land intensively for a short but very destructive period. For a long time thereafter the land was only productive in the (then) much less remunerative crops of wheat, corn, or pasture. By the early nineteenth century, a sizeable portion of Virginia's farmland had passed through this pattern. In some areas, particularly those settled earliest along Chesapeake Bay, all efforts at farming were being abandoned and the land was returning to its natural state of shrub pine forest.

Virginia's woes in the early nineteenth century can be overplayed, however.

The decline of tobacco cannot be entirely attributed to exhaustion of the soil.[1]
There was still enough good, underdeveloped acreage in Virginia in 1815 to have
supported production for some time to come. Rather, it appears that the Old
Dominion was being priced out of the market by rising labor costs. Until 1790
tobacco production was the predominant employment of slave labor in the economy. Furthermore, importations of slaves tended to keep their cost down until
the trade was banned in 1808. Then the relatively fixed supply of slaves, coupled
with the meteoric rise in cotton and its resulting demand for labor, forced their
prices up sharply. By 1820 slave prices were at least twice the level of the late
colonial period and the incentive to use them in tobacco was correspondingly
reduced. The decline of tobacco production in Virginia cannot be seen as an
unmitigated loss, however. Tobacco had become less profitable, but the value of
the slaves had increased. As Virginians sold their chattels in the subsequent years,
they came to recognize and appreciate those offsetting capital gains.

In any case, whatever problems Virginia was having with tobacco, that crop
was also becoming less important to her. In 1815 the state extended well to the
west beyond the declining tidewater regions, including at that time all that is now
the separate state of West Virginia. This was a newly developed, prosperous area
(current perceptions notwithstanding), which was part of a larger mountainous
region encompassing eastern Kentucky, Tennessee, and western North Carolina.
The region was laced with rivers which had built up fertile valleys at such locations as Lexington, Kentucky; Nashville and Knoxville, Tennessee; and Charleston, (now West) Virginia. These areas yielded a variety of crops, of which cattle
and tobacco were among the most important. Another crop which was to become
progressively important as the antebellum period progressed was hemp. It was
processed into rope and bagging to package the cotton from the lower South. The
fibrous part of the hemp plant was contained in its stalk so that the seeds were
sown very thickly to force the plants to grow tall and shed their lower leaves in
competition for sunlight. This would appear a curious practice to the modern
individuals who search the countryside of Kentucky for the wild descendants of
the plant. They smoke the leaves and throw the stalks away.

In the hilly countryside surrounding these valleys a less intensive form of
agriculture developed. The principal product of this region was also cattle, but
they obtained a good part of their own fodder by foraging in the woods rather
than being more carefully pastured as in the valleys. Some of these animals were
slaughtered locally, packed in barrels, and exported via the Ohio, Cumberland,
Tennessee, and Mississippi Rivers to New Orleans. Some of the more hardy

---

[1] Soil exhaustion is a term which is readily used but frequently misunderstood. The "common-
sense meaning" to most people is that the physical quality of the soil has been worn down so that it
no longer produces as much of a given crop as it once could. However, there are numerous cautions
to bear in mind when using such a term. An important one is that soil fertility can be increased or
decreased by the deliberate efforts of the farmer. When soil is suffering erosion or depletion it is
usually because it appears no longer profitable to maintain at its previous level. Thus it is usually an
indication that it has become unprofitable to farm a given piece of land and that it is being phased
out—not vice versa.

animals, however, especially those raised in western Virginia and North Carolina, were simply driven overland to markets along the eastern seaboard. This region also produced large amounts of the ubiquitous American staple crop—corn. Some was eaten at the dinner table and some was used to tide livestock over the winter, but even so there were still large surpluses potentially available. But because it was not valuable relative to its weight, corn was not profitable to ship to distant markets—so the local farmers distilled it into liquor, which was remunerative to ship and for which the area is still famous.

By 1815 this mountainous, inland area of the upper South had already become an important segment of the nation's economy. More than 15 percent of the country's population lived there, testifying to how quickly the area had been developed. It had been the first major area in the United States to be developed west of the Appalachian Mountains. Kentucky and Tennessee had been the first two Western states to be admitted to the Union before 1800.

THE LOWER SOUTH IN 1815

In 1815, the coastal area of South Carolina and Georgia appeared very much as it had in the late colonial period, a tightly ordered economy of large rice plantations. In contrast, the up-country of these states had undergone a drastic transformation in the same period. Before 1790 the region had been mostly pine woods, devoted to ranching and lumbering and interspaced with occasional cleared areas that produced indigo. Then the fortuitous combination of Eli Whitney's practical genius and rising per capita incomes produced the explosive growth of cotton.

Until 1790 the basic textile material in the North Atlantic economies had been wool. Other fabrics, such as linen and silk, were available but were relatively expensive. Cotton introduced into the wardrobes of the common family clothes that were light, soft, washable, and, given the substantial improvements in cotton textile technology pioneered in England in the late eighteenth century, comparatively cheap.

Cotton was also a benevolently simple crop to raise. It required only sufficient warmth and rainfall, and adequately drained soil—criteria met by most of the interior of the lower South. Unlike tobacco or rice it could tolerate considerable mistreatment in planting, weeding, and thinning. Cotton was ready for picking by the first of September and continued to produce until the second or third frost, usually in December.

In short, cotton was an almost perfect opportunity for the lower South. From 1790 to 1820 its price remained almost consistently above 10 cents per pound, a level which yielded most farming operations in the region good profits. In these thirty years, settlers swarmed into the piedmont area of South Carolina and Georgia to establish cotton farms, sweeping away the cattle, the indigo, and the pine trees. By 1815, the potential cotton planters were moving into lower Alabama in force. At this time entire townships in central North Carolina were being depopulated by "Alabama fever."

Prospective farmers were also settling on the extremely productive land along the lower Mississippi in the present states of Mississippi and Louisiana. Here they were extending an economy already well established by the French, who had developed a major sugar industry in southern Louisiana. Americans went into cotton as well as sugar production, all of which made the lower Mississippi into one of the most prosperous regions in antebellum America. This wealth supported the huge mansions at Natchez and the sophisticated social life of New Orleans, the latter being enhanced by the French influence, one of the few foreign societies enveloped by the advancing American frontier.

SLAVERY

Tobacco, America's first and most important colonial growth industry, was a Southern product. So was cotton, the country's dominant export for much of the nineteenth century. Both crops required large amounts of tedious, routine labor—and this in an economy generally characterized by the lack of an unskilled labor force. If free workers could have been hired to tend tobacco or cotton, they would have been both expensive and underused resources. A much more suitable source of labor was close at hand, however. In the seventeenth century there was a well-established Negro slave trade centered in West Africa. By 1619, when an enterprising Dutch trader sold the first Negroes to the colony at Jamestown, the trade had already been extended to points farther south in the Western Hemisphere. Slaves were imported continuously thereafter until 1808, when the trade was legally stopped, but even afterward a few were smuggled into the South through Florida. In the colonial period most slaves were employed in Maryland and Virginia, in the area adjacent to Chesapeake Bay. Rice production in South Carolina, although constricted within a very small area, also employed a sizeable number of slaves by using them intensively.

Between 1800 and the Civil War, slaves were increasingly concentrated in the South.[2] The slave population, primarily restricted to its natural population growth, was shifted to its most productive uses. In the antebellum period that could be expressed in one word—cotton. With the exception of sugar in southern Louisiana, slaves were being systematically removed from other crops, such as tobacco and rice. They were moved into the cotton belt, which ran southeast from central South Carolina, across Georgia to Alabama, and westward through Mississippi, southern Tennessee, Arkansas, Louisiana, and eastern Texas.

The regional concentration of slave-holdings was paralleled by a sharpening of regional attitudes on the propriety of slavery. Although most slaves were held in the South in the colonial period, there were a few in Northern colonies as well. These Northern holdings subsequently disappeared, however, as many of the colonies (later as states, of course) placed restrictions, even prohibitions, on slavery. Some commentators have attempted to explain the viability of slavery in the

[2] A good discussion of this process of interregional transfer of slaves, as well as what is probably the best overall discussion of the economics of slavery, is contained in Robert W. Fogel and Stanely L. Engerman, *Time on the Cross,* Little, Brown, Boston, 1974.

South and its demise in the North as owing to a difference in climate. The warmer South had a longer growing season in which slaves could be kept working, while in the North they had to be idle in the winter but still required food and shelter.

Two observed conditions suggest that the difference in climate is not an important factor. While the South did have a longer season each year in which the slaves could work outside, the important constraint on the use of their labor, particularly in cotton, was labor requirements at peak periods of activity, such as planting and harvesting. While the earlier spring and later fall might allow the slaves to produce more of some items in the South, the maximum output of the primary products, such as cotton or tobacco, was effectively set by how much the entire labor force could manage during the busy periods. Thus, the growing cycle of Southern crops made the South's longer season of secondary importance.

The "longer-season" thesis is also contradicted by another characteristic of Northern activity. While the North stopped using slaves, it continued to acquire indentured servants, who also had to be fed, clothed, housed, and generally provided for, no matter how long the work season lasted. This contrast—using indentured servants while eschewing slaves—points to what is probably the strongest force excluding slavery from the North. Fundamentally, slavery is a property right, the legal authority of one person to demand, direct, buy, sell, lease, hire, or exchange the future labor services of another person. And to be viable, property rights must be enforceable. They must have the consent of the general populace and be upheld by the established political system. In the North, large numbers of individuals had doubts about the morality of one man owning another; a few had emphatic objections. In the face of these reservations the value of slavery as a device for providing labor was weakened compared to other means of obtaining a labor supply. Eventually, in most of the Northern states, a collective decision was made that slavery did not provide enough benefits to outweigh its socially objectionable aspects. It was then either banned outright or restricted and ostracized into oblivion.

In the South, opinions swung the other way. Slavery was too valuable as an economic institution and too many Southerners had too much wealth committed in slaves to entertain many doubts about its ethics. Various spokespeople in the South began to offer justification as to why slavery was just, or in accord with Christian principles, or in the best interests of the Negro. Perhaps the average free Southerners believed the arguments, or perhaps they only gave them lip service. In any case, their economic significance is discernible. It reflected the social support and approval necessary to uphold slavery as an institution, that is, as a viable property right buttressed by the sympathy of the society it served.

Slavery: For Fun or Profit?

The debate continued within the historians' profession for a long time, sometimes dying down, but only to erupt again because the basic issues remained unresolved: Was slavery profitable? Was slave ownership in the best interests of an individual Southerner? Did slavery impose a straitjacket on the Southern economy which stifled (or would eventually have stifled) its growth and development? As is quickly apparent, one reason the controversy lasted so long is that the issues were broad and poorly specified. Scholars could easily talk around each other and investigate different aspects of the issue while reporting, within this broad, fuzzy context, diametrically opposed answers.

The relation between slavery and the economic development of the South is too important and interesting a question to neglect, so we will return to that issue later. For the present, however, let us focus on whether slave ownership was profitable to an individual slaveholder; that is, whether in committing some of his resources to slavery he was forgoing other opportunities which would have yielded larger returns. Historians who have taken the position that slavery was not generally profitable have usually offered one of two general justifications. First, slaves were held, even while not profitable, for defensive reasons. Whatever Southerners might have hoped for and expected during the development of slavery, they simply would not tolerate the destructive effects they anticipated if the slaves were to be freed. Southerners were alleged to be keeping slaves, then, not to maximize profits, but to minimze losses by absorbing the smaller operating deficits of retaining the slaves rather than facing the enormous costs of chaos if they were freed. That seems unlikely, because under such circumstances the individual slaveowners would have had no incentive to keep their own slaves. They could have cut their own losses by freeing them, and the personal cost to them of their ex-slaves' freedom in the Southern society would have been negligible. Had this condition been prevalent, one would have expected the slave states to have enacted legislation to compel owners to retain their slaves. And beginning in the 1820s manumission *was* made increasingly difficult, especially in the states of the lower South which had the highest proportion of slaves. Such restrictions seemed to be more difficult, especially in the states of the lower South which had the highest proportion of slaves. Such restrictions seemed to be more symptomatic of conditions, however, rather than having much net impact of their own. The states which made the freeing of slaves most difficult were also those in which such rates were generally low, both before and after the tightening of the requirements on manumission.[3] It was much like the Puritan colony of Massachusetts Bay banning gambling. Most of the residents agreed that such a law should be enacted, but it did not much affect the amount of gambling.

If slaves were, in fact, liabilities to their masters, one would have expected owners to discourage births and childrearing among their charges. Just the reverse occurred. Potential mothers were encouraged by such inducements as generous maternity leaves (from their usual assignments), medical care, and special food allowances. Many slaveowners were obviously seeking, and including in their business calculations, the capital gains from the natural increase in their

---

[3] The percentage of slaves freed in any given year was always highest in the border states, especially Delaware and Maryland, where rather severe doubts developed about the propriety of slavery and consequently the institution declined in the antebellum period. Manumission rates did tend to decrease but this seems to be entirely explainable by the increasing concentration of slaves in states where such doubts about its morality were not entertained.

slave-holdings. They behaved as if they believed their stock of slaves was an asset, salable if and when they desired. That is just the opposite of how the "slave-control" hypothesis would have expected them to perform. Another group was also contradicting the explanation of the "slave-control" hypothesis. Professionals in the South, such as doctors and lawyers, purchased slaves in the antebellum period, not expecting to employ them in their own practices but rather to rent them out to others. Had slavery been unprofitable, such owners would have lost money out of the necessity of containing the slaves without even providing the purported social services of slave retention.

Other scholars have argued that slavery was also unprofitable, but for exactly the opposite reason. They believed that slaves were held for conspicuous consumption; that is, that Southerners valued them in much the same way as they did art objects, for the increased social status believed to come from their possession. It is understandable how someone examining the antebellum South could have arrived at this explanation. Immediately before the Civil War, slaves were the most important form of nonhuman wealth of free Southerners. This was particularly true in the deep South where the ratio of slaves to the free populace was the highest in the region. To a citizen of the antebellum South, slave ownership served much the same function that corporation stock ownership plays in modern America. It was a common asset in which current purchasing power was invested, from which reasonable returns could be expected, and for which an established market existed.

Slave ownership, however, was not an asset in which one could invest small amounts of money, such as one can today by buying a few low-priced shares of stock. The minimal investment, one slave, required well above the average income of that day. For example, a slave selling for the not unusual price of $1,000 in the 1850s had about the same value as an average home would to a modern American family. A Southerner who had twenty to thirty slaves would be a millionnaire by contemporary standards. No wonder slave ownership carried such an obvious connotation of wealth. Owning even one slave represented far more in assets than an average citizen held.

The key to distinguishing whether slavery was profitable or merely a form of consumption, therefore, is whether Southerners valued slaves per se or whether those slaves were primarily a manifestation of the wealth implied by their ownership. Larger numbers of slaveowners acted as if the latter consideration was the important one. The economy of the antebellum South has frequently been pictured as consisting of a few wealthy citizens, all of whom owned big plantations with large numbers of slaves, and of large numbers of small, independent (yeoman) farm operators. Clearly, inequality existed among the economic positions of Southerners, although whether there was an unusually large divergence is currently a debated quantitative issue.[4] Yet while most slaves were held within

---

[4] See, for instance, Lee Soltow, "Economic Inequality in the United States in the Period from 1790 to 1860," *Journal of Economic History,* vol. 31, no. 4, December 1971, pp. 822–839. See also Gavin Wright, "Economic Democracy and the Concentration of Agricultural Wealth in the Cotton South, 1850–1860," *Agricultural History,* vol. 44, no. 1, January 1970, p. 63.

relatively large groups (in 1860 each slaveowner *averaged* more than ten slaves), the *majority* of slaveholders held five or fewer slaves, and fully 20 percent owned only one. Thus, most slaveowners could not justify hiring an overseer to direct their slaves, so if they intended to use them in their own businesses they had to supervise them themselves.[5] It was not unusual for individuals crossing the South to report seeing farmers toiling in their cotton fields next to the slave or two they owned. Clearly, not all Southerners thought of their slaves as a form of conspicuous consumption.

The Arithmetic of Profitable Slavery

That was where the basic historical issues rested in 1958, although the basic arguments contained far more variety and vocabulary, of course. Then in one of those classic studies which irrevocably shifts the course of future scholarship, Alfred H. Conrad and John R. Meyer took a look at the arithmetic of slave ownership.[6] Ironically, some of their estimates slipped off target and required additional formulation later, but their basic conclusion emerged unscathed and has only been reinforced by other studies since then. Slavery was profitable; the net returns from typical slaves' labor and their natural increase over time returned as much to their owners as existing alternatives would have. Some individual owners may have found ownership unprofitable or may have held slaves as household servants or ornamentation, but that was not necessary to explain the retention of slaves. Owning a slave was sufficiently profitable in and of itself, and that motive is sufficient to explain antebellum slavery.

When it came to a decision on an individual farm, a slave was profitable to own because he (and she, subject to some additional considerations below) produced enough cotton to pay for their room, board, and a competitive return on their purchase price. Table 9-1, citing figures from Conrad and Meyer's paper, shows the yearly percentage return on the ownership of a prime (male) field hand. Return rates are computed for various combinations of slave prices, at an output of 400-pound bales per hand, and at net prices received for cotton at the farm.

Conrad and Meyer also performed comparable simulations in an effort to show why Southerners were also willing to purchase female and child slaves—at lower, but nevertheless substantial prices. Females were not as productive as males at many field tasks, but a slave mother who produced healthy children yielded her owner compensation in another way. Children were an expense only in their early years, of course. Within a few years, however, they were capable of handling enough simple chores to pay for their upkeep and soon thereafter they

---

[5] Fogel and Engerman, in *Time on the Cross,* have demonstrated that a good portion of the supervision on large farms was carried out by the slaves themselves, either via "drivers" (stewards) chosen from among the dependable slaves, or by the gang system, where the pace of all workers was controlled by that set by certain select teams. See Fogel and Engerman's Chapter 6.

[6] Alfred H. Conrad and John R. Meyer, "The Economics of Slavery in the Antebellum South," *Journal of Political Economy,* vol. 66, no. 2, April 1958.

Table 9-1   Simulating the Profit to Slave Ownership

Current slave price	Cotton bales per hand	Net farm cotton (in cents)	Rate of return (percent)
$1,350–1,400	3.75	7	4.5
1,350–1,400	3.75	8	5.2
1,350–1,400	3.75	9	6.5
1,600	4.50	7	5.0
1,600	4.50	8	7.0
1,600	4.50	9	8.0
1,250–1,300	3.00	7	2.2
1,250–1,300	3.00	8	3.9
1,250–1,300	3.00	9	5.4
1,700	7.00	7	10.0
1,700	7.00	8	12.0
1,700	7.00	9	13.0

approached maturity and adult prices. Conrad and Meyer believed that these slave "products" outside of crop production could explain certain features of antebellum slavery which have previously baffled historians and caused them to suspect that slaveholding was not motivated solely by profits.

Persistent Price Differentials

One of the features that Conrad and Meyer sought to explain was that the price of slaves in the developing Gulf States was persistently above that prevailing in the older slaveholding areas along the Atlantic coast. That differential continued despite the movement of large numbers of slaves from the older South, such as the states of Virginia and North Carolina, to the newer states, such as Mississippi, Louisiana, and Texas. Thus, those slaves who remained in the older (lower-priced) regions were apparently paying their owners less than their opportunity costs, that is, what they could have been receiving in the lower South. In the absence of extenuating factors, this seemed to support what many historians had suspected all along; namely, that the slaveowners were not particularly closely attuned to economic maximizing. Conrad and Meyer thought they found the reason, however. The composition of the slave population differed between the two regions in that the proportion of female and younger slaves was higher in the old South. If one were to add the gains accrued to owners from the increasing value of children in their holdings, then the returns would equalize between the two regions. In short, the finding confirmed the historical observations that the older South was engaged in "slave breeding." Or, in the terms of modern economics, the old South was making up its deficit in operating income by producing capital goods to be used, not as final products, but as inputs in the production of other products.

The slave-breeding thesis was accepted for a decade or so, but not without reservations. While the extra increment of capital gains might make up the deficit of operating earnings in the old South, there seemed no reason why it had to be conducted in that specific location. If those slaves were moved to the newer South they could still breed and earn higher incomes from field operations as well. This was confirmed by Fogel and Engerman when they measured the realized gains from increases in slave prices.[7] At most, such gains could have amounted to only a few percent of the yearly average return from slaves. The reason was not that the wealth capitalized into slave prices did not amount to much; on the contrary, it accounted for a good part of the national capital stock in the antebellum period. It was simply that the planters had to wait so long—and incur expenses in the meantime—before slave children reached the age where they began to yield labor services equivalent to those of an adult. In essence, raising slaves in anticipation of increases in their selling price is a form of capital investment. And the expenditures on children before they approached the proficiencies of adults was money which could be put into other forms of investment which would begin to pay returns in the interim. Raising young slaves primarily for appreciation in their price was made a poor investment by the law of compound interest. At an interest rate typical of the period, say 7 percent, an invested dollar would be worth twice as much ten years later if the interest were plowed back onto the principle. Thus, if a planter were to spend $100 on an infant male slave and then have to wait until he was twenty to sell him, the opportunity cost of the initial investment would have increased to $400.

Fogel and Engerman found that the major factor explaining the difference in slave prices between the regions was a consideration in which historians had traditionally not placed much credence: that is, a regard for the feelings of the slaves themselves. It has been customary to argue that slavery was a dehumanizing institution in that it tended to tear apart black families. Accounts of mothers being separated from their children, or husbands from their wives, have been sometimes dramatically played up. Fogel and Engerman's exhaustive study of slave transfers, however, demonstrated that such family-dismantling moves were the exception—indeed, the very rare exception. The reason was not necessarily that slaveowners were concerned about the emotions of their slaves, but rather that their productivity could drop drastically if they became distraught or resentful. Members of broken families would often run away in order to see each other, or simply withdraw into sullen, slow-paced passivity. Most owners soon understood that the costs of such disruptive trading commonly outweighed the profits.

Accordingly, most relocations or sales of slaves took place in groups, the minimum size being the nuclear family, and the quite-frequent maximum size being that of the entire plantation population. And this tendency to move complete collections of slaves intact explains the persistent difference in slave prices between regions. Slaves were, in fact, moved to the lower South in response to the higher returns on their employment there. But the majority of those shifted were

[7] *Time on the Cross,* pp. 78–86.

moved along with the entire organization of plantations from the old South to the new. And such a move was no small matter. It involved not only transferring the slaves but also closing out the operation of a going farming concern, transplanting the owner's family and assets, and usually fashioning a completely new plantation out of land still in its natural state. In short, if we consider the total costs involved in moving slaves between regions, the differential in prices is understandable. It reflects the costs of the one-time transfer that planters had to anticipate regrouping through higher earnings in the future in order to make the move worthwhile.

Profitability: Again

From the comfortable vantage of retrospect we can say that it should have been obvious that slavery was profitable. Labor has always been a scarce resource in America, and even the lowest grades of labor, reasonably employed, have been able to generate output of more value than the cost of modest room and board. And the economic essence of slave prices is simply the conversion of those streams of labor services, less the associated expenses, into capital commodities. The price of a particular slave represented—or capitalized, in the economic jargon—the net earnings expected in the future from the services of that particular individual. This is vividly evident if we compare how slave prices vary with such attributes as age, sex, skills, disabilities, and vices, which clearly would have affected productivity. Notice, for example, the relation of prices of male slaves to their ages, as shown in Figure 9-1. (Figure 9-1 is only one of a wide range of such profiles of slave prices, correlated with their specific attributes, assembled by Fogel and Engerman.)[8]

The figure shows that prices displayed a bell-like curve relative to age, rising rapidly until they reached a sharp peak at about age thirty and declining rapidly thereafter, but tending to fall more slowly as the slave grew older. The shape of the price curve fits very closely with that of expected future earnings at each phase of the slave's life, much like that predicted by the modern theory of the returns to human capital. See Figure 9-1. The profile rises until about age thirty because slaves were acquiring maturity and skills during that period which increased the present value of the product they would provide for the remainder of their lifetimes. At about age thirty this learning function slowed and was more than offset by the combination of lower productivity resulting from aging and the falling life expectancy in which that yearly product could be realized. The slower rate of decline in the advanced years reflects the fact that although aging reduced the slave's productivity, the expected lifespan, having reached that age, was still a couple of decades. Most older slaves were kept busy as household servants, or in lighter farm tasks such as gardening, handicrafts, or child care, and thus were generally able to provide a positive return for most of their years.

This hardheaded appraisal of slave prospects as shown in their prices was also evident in the premiums paid for special skills. Blacksmiths, carpenters,

---

[8] *Time on the Cross,* pp. 67–78.

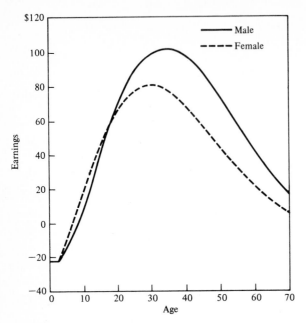

Figure 9-1   Prices of slaves by age and sex about 1850, Old South. *(Source: Adapted from Robert W. Fogel and Stanely L. Engerman,* Time on the Cross, *vol. 1,* The Economics of American Negro Slavery, *Little, Brown, Boston, 1974, p. 76.)*

wheelwrights, and other trained blacks commanded prices averaging perhaps 50 percent above those for unskilled slaves who were otherwise comparable (depending on their individual proficiencies). As one might expect, the peak of prices for skilled slaves came at a somewhat later age than for unskilled slaves, reflecting the fact that the payoff from their training began at a later age. Similar differentials appeared by sex. Females commanded lower prices, except for a short period in late childhood when expectations of gains from their childbearing added to their otherwise lower daily earnings. Prices also clearly reflected the discounts applied for disabilities. Crippled, deaf, or tubercular individuals were exchanged at correspondingly lower prices, as were those who had previously run away or were known drunkards.[9]   Altogether, this comprehensive pattern of prices should dispel any doubt that economic returns were the basic force underlying slaveholding. Ironically, slave prices were so clearly and finely differentiated that they provided an unusual verification of the theory of human capital itself. Scholars generally have had access only to modern labor markets where most forms of servitude which could provide capitalized or asset prices of labor

---

[9] When slaves were sold on organized exchanges it was common for the seller to certify that the slave was free of certain categories of vices. Such declarations were enforceable in courts so that misrepresentation was grounds for damages. In this manner the larger slave markets, such as those at New Orleans or Charleston, resembled the sophisticated trading by grade now practiced on major commodity exchanges.

were prohibited.[10] Thus, the peculiar institution of slavery which allowed such lifetime earnings to be traded allowed a rare empirical verification of the factor.

Profitability in the Long Run Slavery was profitable during the antebellum period because the prices of slaves reflected, and were reimbursed by, their productivity. There is another question, however, as to whether slavery would have continued to survive as a longer-term arrangement. This is reflected in the argument sometimes made that the Civil War was unnecessary in that slavery would have withered away anyway.

As an institution, slavery was subject to legal, political, and moral considerations so that its economic underpinnings were a necessary but not sufficient condition for its survival. Insofar as its economics was concerned, slavery would survive if it were able to cover its costs in the long run. This is much the same criterion applied in the short-run question of profitability except that the relevant costs are somewhat larger. It would be worthwhile to retain a slave whose current output covered the current costs of maintaining him or her, such as room and board. For slavery to be viable—that is, for it to continue indefinitely—it was necessary to cover these operating costs as well as the longer-term costs of raising young slaves until they became productive and self-supporting. Another way to distinguish between profitability and long-term viability is that the former requires only that current operating costs be covered, but the latter requires reimbursement for the full, lifetime costs of a slave.

It took something like the Civil War to destroy slavery because it certainly would not have self-destructed for economic reasons. The economics of slavery was self-renewing all through the antebellum period, and the margin that perpetuated its existence was growing larger. The productivity of slaves was such that they produced enough not only to cover all the expenses of their maintenance and upbringing, but a sizeable net return as well. Furthermore, that margin of rent per slave steadily increased.

It comes as a surprise to many people that the returns from slavery, cushioning their viability, increased during the antebellum period. Part of the surprise is undoubtedly because slavery was such a controversial institution during the latter part of the period. Its political problems did not carry over to its economic functioning, however—indeed, as we shall see, its economic success naturally stiffened the South's defense of it and thereby intensified the conflict. We shall return to this rather lengthy—and ironic—discussion of the economic performance of slavery later.

One additional factor which was driving up the returns on slaves was the restrictions on their number. After 1808, when further importation was banned, the available supply was restricted to the natural increase of the population already in America. While this increase was relatively rapid, about 25 percent to 30 percent per decade, the sectors in which slaves' services could be profitably used

---

[10] Occasional glances of lifetime earnings of labor are provided in such arrangements as professional sports, or entertainment contracts, or in insurance settlements for death or permanent injury.

grew even faster. The worldwide increase in demand for cotton cloth, and thus for cotton, was even faster than the increase in the population of American slaves. Additional land and capital could be attracted into Southern farming, but with their supply restricted, slaves became ever scarcer as a resource for cotton production. Naturally, they were used along with larger quantities of other factors in such a way that their contribution to output rose along with their relative scarcity.

Each of these factors contributed to the long-term increase in the net returns from an average slave. This made their ownership more valuable, and slaveholders bid up their prices in attempts to acquire them. A prime field hand selling for about $600 in 1800 would have commanded $1,800 by 1860.

This rise in prices has baffled many previous observers who assumed that a slave must always be a slave. Therefore why would anyone want to pay more for one unless it was for extraeconomic reasons? So the rise in prices was heralded as evidence that Southerners were holding slaves for defensive purposes, not for their inherent productiveness. This position was frequently backed up by numerous reports of individual slave-holdings which appeared to be only marginally profitable. Paradoxically, all these reported characteristics could have been anticipated if one had asked how profit-seeking Southerners would have reacted to the increasing productivity of slaves. Consider a potential slave buyer calculating how much to pay for a young male slave who can be expected to produce $40 of net revenue each year over his lifetime. (For the sake of simplicity, we shall not factor in disability, aging, and death.) Suppose the prevailing return on alternative investments is 5 percent; that is, capital committed to investments such as railroad bonds, real estate, or crop advances would repay a net 5 percent on the original investment each subsequent year. The purchaser would then buy the slave for any price up to $800, upon which $40 is a 5 percent return, but not for a larger amount because the rate of return would fall below 5 percent. Competition among buyers would force the price of a slave such as this one up to $800, because at lower prices the net return is higher than 5 percent and potential purchasers would transfer capital from alternative uses. On the other hand, at prices above $800, owners of slaves would sell them in order to transfer the capital to alternative investments paying the going 5 percent. Consequently, the price of slaves would fall until buyers had no further reason to sell—which would occur, of course, when prices fell to $800 and the net return rose to 5 percent.

Not only did prices tend upward in the antebellum period, but they would have continued to do so after 1860 if extraeconomic considerations had not destroyed slavery as a social institution. The reason is the same one which caused them to rise before the Civil War, namely, the increasing productivity of slave labor which the rising price of slaves was reflecting. Fogel and Engerman recently calculated these forces which affected productivity and found that they would have been sufficient to increase the price of an average slave another 52 percent in the thirty years after 1860.[11] Thus, the Civil War—or something equivalent to

---

[11] *Time on the Cross*, pp. 94–97.

its effect on slavery—was "necessary"; slavery could have continued indefinitely after 1860 insofar as the economics of the institution were concerned.

PRIVATE INTERESTS AND SOCIAL RESULTS IN A DISDAINED INSTITUTION

Today slavery is almost universally regarded as undesirable. (It is easy to forget that such a public outlook has become prevalent only in the last two centuries, however. Most people of earlier times would think of it as normal and find our dislike for it peculiar.) That attitude is understandable in the context of the changing alternatives which have allowed a greater emphasis on human freedom and dignity in recent times. In one way, however, it has been misapplied and has tended to hinder our understanding of how slavery actually operated. It has been widely assumed that because slavery is considered a decadent institution, it was inefficient as an economic arrangement and was used by economies which in themselves were backward. That is not necessarily true, however, any more than current activities which society deems bad—often more in word than deed—such as gambling, prostitution, or loan sharking, are necessarily run inefficiently or by the poorest segments of society. Indeed, a little examination of media accounts of such activities suggests that their operators are quite ingenious in running their operations efficiently and devising new arrangements to increase their profits and security.

In the same light, the best way to understand the operation of slavery is to set aside our aversion of it for a moment and ask what behavior would be in the best self-interest of the individuals involved with it. For example, we have already noted the incentive which owners had to try to maintain slave families and even plantation groupings intact in order not to undermine productivity. Or another common view is implicit in our colloquial expression "to be treated like a slave." Slaves are often pictured as receiving poor food, clothing, housing, and medical care, as well as frequent whippings and hazings. Yet if we stop to consider the owners' interest in their slaves, such treatment seems unlikely. Slaves represented a large investment on the part of their owners and one which could be maintained only if the slaves were to remain productive—which implies being strong and healthy. Owners would be foolish to forgo a $1 doctor visit for a sick slave who was worth $1,000. (Avoiding doctors in those days, however, was not necessarily a sign of foolishness; the amount of help a doctor could provide was much less than it is today.) Similarly, it was to the owners' advantage to maintain the slaves' productivity by providing adequate, nutritious food, functional clothing, and warm, clean housing. Fogel and Engerman found that by the standards of the day, slaves generally were well provided for in these categories.[12] Instead of the old stereotype of slave drivers, it might be better to picture the owners as more like a modern football coach. They were probably as concerned about the condition of their slaves as a coach is about that of the starting quarterback.

[12] *Time on the Cross,* pp. 107–126.

INCENTIVES UNDER SLAVERY FOR THE LONG RUN

We might acknowledge that there were reasons not to mistreat slaves in order to avoid compromising their productivity, but even so there was another group of incentives within which the slaves operated. And here, again, the environment of slavery has commonly been seen to have produced undesirable results. After all, the argument goes, slavery is essentially a negative system. Slaves were forced to work and had no reason to try to do a better job. Nor did slavery provide much incentive for owners to try to improve their circumstances. Slave labor may not have been motivated to be efficient, but it was cheap, and that worked against searching for alternative techniques.

Once again the self-interest of the individuals involved overruled such stereotypes of behavior. For example, owners found that a mix of incentives which included positive as well as negative inducements seemed to work best in motivating the slaves. Slaves were given bonuses for meeting quotas or for exceptional performance. These varied considerably, but common rewards were cash, special food or clothing, a larger house, time off from usual duties, or permission to go to town on Saturday evening. These were handed out for the best performance by a hoeing team or for meeting a quota in picking or ginning cotton. Sometimes these rewards were announced in advance, sometimes they were spontaneous. On the sugar plantations it was common to declare a holiday for a day or two when the sugar harvest was completed.

The slaves also operated under a system of incentives which influenced how they allocated their efforts over time spans longer than a year, as well. There was a recognized hierarchy of status and perquisites within the slave society. At the bottom were the field and mill hands who spent the frequently sultry days at hard physical labor. Above them were the household servants, chosen for their dependability, who could reap some of the comforts and leftovers of the "big house." Also esteemed were the positions of the skilled crafts workers—the carpenters, millwrights, and blacksmiths. With such jobs went greater rewards, responsibility, and independence. They also offered some opportunity to escape to the wider world outside the farm. Particularly capable crafts workers were often rented to other parties for special construction projects. Many were sent into Southern cities and even took up permanent residence there, reporting only infrequently to their absentee owners. Skilled crafts workers' positions also offered some of the best possibilities for slaves to win their independence. Most free Negroes living in the South before 1861 were skilled workers who had served their former owners well, thereby providing some assurance that they could manage their own affairs well in freedom.

The important point about this environment in which the slaves operated is that there were rewards for superior service and innovation. While, obviously, slaves did not have the full spectrum of opportunities which might be available to a free individual, there was, nevertheless, a wide range of living standards and degrees of personal freedom within the slave system. Slaves may not have been able to reach the upper limits available to free men, but they still had a large range—in relative terms probably as large as that of *most* free men—within which they could improve their personal welfare.[13] Thus, slaves *could* gain from conscientious and innovative work. Not only could they increase their current income and privileges, but they could also move up in the working hierarchy, each level of which moved them to a higher base level of such perquisites.

An easily unappreciated by-product of this system of internal incentives was that the slaves could gain nearly as much from innovative efforts as could their owners. For instance, a slave who devised a better cultivator or an improved method of transplanting tobacco plants stood to gain if for no other reason than that it reduced the effort required to carry out such tasks in the future. Probably the most important source of reward for inventive slaves, however, was that their owners found it desirable to set them up in that form of business in which they excelled. Blacksmiths who were good at devising repairs or modifications for machinery were usually set to work as full-time blacksmiths, serving not just their own plantation but also the market provided by the neighboring farms. In that capacity they were usually given considerable freedom in organizing their work and were often given housing near their work—removed from most of the other slave quarters—as well. It is not easy to show how important such incentives were to the slaves—but then, we can show little more for the free population, although we shall later show that the aggregate gains in productivity in the Southern economy were quite respectable in the antebellum period. One concrete example that we have on record is that of a Louisiana slave who devised major improvements in the vacuum process of refining sugar. Of course, that was an atypical record but the invention itself was unusually important, and there are few similar accounts of such major successes by free inventors in Southern agriculture.

Now we have a better picture as to why slave prices increased in the antebellum period. Not only were slaves restricted in number because of the prohibition of their importation, but the average slave was becoming more productive as well. Some of this greater efficiency resulted simply because of acclimation. The slaves had an opportunity to adapt to the American climate, food, and organization. The second generation was stronger, healthier, and more familiar with tools and farming techniques than the first. Much of that advance would have come through normal acclimation with little more effort on the part of the slaves than abstaining from resistance. Another component of the increasing productivity, however, came from the active and self-interested efforts of the slaves themselves. Slavery may be a backward institution which we have long ceased to tolerate as a social arrangement, but there was still room within it for the normal economic interests of all involved parties to operate.

This leads us to one final paradox—another striking contrast between what is generally believed about slavery and what its influence actually was when examined carefully. Slavery is understandably considered an institution which

---

[13] Fogel and Engerman found that variations in the real income of slaves by a factor of as much as 7 existed and that differences of several times that were common. See *Time on the Cross,* pp. 149–152.

operated to the long-term detriment of blacks in the United States, both past and present. From our above discussion we can say that the institution did exploit blacks while they were slaves. Each year, part of their net earnings were transferred to their owners. At the same time the slaves were being exposed to a system of incentives which caused their marketable skills to be upgraded, much like those of the contemporaneous free population. Thus, when the slaves finally were freed in the 1860s they began to receive the full amount at which their services were valued in the economy. As of the 1860s those services reflected much the same upgrading of experience and training as they would have if the slaves had been free citizens before that time. In other words, the *burden* of slavery fell almost entirely on the blacks who were actually slaves. Since the 1860s, blacks have been subject to many constraints which have retarded their economic progress—an issue we shall return to later—but slavery per se has had little economic impact on blacks today because their starting point in the economy as of emancipation was much the same as if they had been free up to that time.

(NEGLECTED) GROWTH IN THE ANTEBELLUM SOUTH

In recent years average incomes in the South have been noticeably below those of most of the rest of the nation. Some rather unsympathetic commentators have suggested that the South should be considered an underdeveloped economy whose lagging growth can be traced to a long history of backwardness. Such judgments have been given credence by the common practice in history of picturing that region before the Civil War as developing in an unusual and backward manner. The antebellum South had all the characteristics which go with the stereotype of underdevelopment. Its agricultural sector was relatively large, and in the amount of urbanization, services, and transportation facilities it seemed well behind the rest of the economy.

Some of these reported characteristics are, indeed, correct, but when one takes a look at the record of performance of the aggregate Southern economy before the Civil War there is no indication of stagnation or of falling behind. Southern per capita income appeared to grow just about as fast as that of the other states before the Civil War[14] (with or without adjustments for the slave sector). The sharp break with the pace of the rest of the economy developed in the two decades beginning with the Civil War, not before 1860. Thus, the appearance of backwardness which has been used to characterize the South in recent times is a comparatively modern development. (This retrogression on the part of the South seems to be explained primarily by the Civil War, a development we shall explain in more detail in the next chapter.) Before the Civil War the South-

---

[14] A summary of the results and conclusions of this work is found in Fogel and Engerman, *Time on the Cross,* pp. 247–257. The derivation of such income estimates is a difficult and painstaking task and, not surprisingly, some doubts have been raised about certain of their results. Even though the author of this text has been among the critics, it still appears reasonable to now conclude that when such outstanding issues have been resolved, the South will appear to be growing and responding to its economic possibilities in much the same way as the rest of the nation before the Civil War.

ern economy was (literally) developing with the best of them, in that it was growing as fast as the larger American economy—which was undoubtedly one of the most successful in this period in terms of increasing per capita incomes.

Moreover, if one takes a closer look at those characteristics which have often been advanced to illustrate the South's backwardness, it becomes much less obvious that they are really harbingers of poor performance. For example, consider the South's concentration on agriculture, a phenomenon one readily associates with underdeveloped economies which must devote a high proportion of their resources to acquiring food. The South was supplying most of its own food before the Civil War, but its farming operations were far from being structured for that purpose alone. Southern agriculture was quite specialized; that is, individual farms were organized to earn a large part of their income from the sale of a limited number of crops in markets off the farm.

The South had an advantage in certain types of agriculture. It had the proper combination of soil, temperature, and rainfall so that it could efficiently produce certain crops which were very much in demand in world markets, namely sugar, tobacco, and, above all, cotton. And, as introductory economics textbooks have so often propounded, an economy should specialize in those activities in which its advantage lies. Southern entrepreneurs were quite quick to grasp opportunities that implemented that concept. To devote maximum effort to, and reap maximum benefit from, specialization, an economy should import or hire out those activities in which it does not have an advantage. In the case of the South that meant relying on other areas, mostly the Northern United States, for such services as transportation, finance, and manufactured products. In short, rather than reflecting backwardness, the economic organization of the antebellum South showed a calculated ability to organize in a way, however novel, that made the most of existing resources and opportunities at that time.

Actually, the fact that the South was specialized in agricultural exports is somewhat misleading because most of these were not used for food even if they were grown on a farm. These exports are perhaps best classified as what we now call primary products, or raw materials. In that context the South was merely an early example of what has since become recognized as a common form of economic specialization, the primary-product exporter. Since World War II there has been a good deal of discussion—much of it adverse—about the wisdom of developing economies specializing in a few primary exports. It was often assumed that the demand for such products would deteriorate and that the economies involved would be subject to severe dislocations when external forces disrupted the specialized trade patterns.

Thus, as so often is the case, the American experience provides another counterexample to the usual rules of thumb offered to achieve economic development. The South was developing quite successfully by concentrating on the production of a few primary products which were sold out of the region. It is true that this strategy was upset by the Civil War, but that was basically an extraeconomic interruption. (Some sectors which did not specialize in the export of agricultural commodities, such as the textile industry of England and New England, were also severely disorganized by the war.) In the absence of that conflict there is every indication that the South could have continued to grow at a relatively high rate for at least several decades after 1860.[15] And that would have meant a per capita income in 1880 or 1890 of perhaps one-third more than there actually was. Much of the increment would have been carried along in the form of higher incomes up toward the present time, because the higher productivity of resources and larger amounts of capital and land held per person would have tended to perpetuate themselves. In that case the income of the modern South would be closer to that prevailing in the rest of the economy and there would have been much less effort wasted in attempts to pin down the sources of Southern "backwardness" before the Civil War.

In the absence of the Civil War, the South would have continued to grow much as it did during the antebellum period because the basic forces supporting that growth would have continued much the same. For example, the output of cotton continued at a rapid pace between the Civil War and World War I, even though slavery had been destroyed. Production was increased by opening up new lands to cultivation in the West, and to the north of the antebellum cotton belt— the latter made possible by the development of new varieties of cotton adapted to cooler weather and shorter growing seasons—as well as continuing to increase the productivity of farming on existing lands. Probably the most important reason for the continuation of growth, however, would have been the usual impact of self-interested human ingenuity at work. Probably one of the least appreciated but strongest historical forces is the imagination and resourcefulness of people in making improvements—usually quite minor, but large in their cumulative effect—to their economic position. Slavery is a good example of this in that it is widely assumed to be so far out of the range of normal arrangements as to be debilitating in economic performance. Yet on closer inspection it seemed to function well within the usual range of human responses. The lesson here for underdeveloped nations today is that the basic source of growth is to be found in encouraging and freeing the human tendency to innovate, not in making specific arrangements of the economy. It was not so much whether the South did or did not have a particular form of organization, such as an export base in primary products, which determined how well it would grow, but rather whether it would identify and develop the opportunities that it did have.

THE COMING OF THE CIVIL WAR

Millions of college undergraduates have sat through classes while the professor droned on listing and explaining all the possible frictions which might have led the North and the South to go to war with each other. Some lecturers advocate a particular cause, but in recent years many have tired of looking for *the* cause and resigned themselves to assigning a paperback anthology of noted opinions on the

---

[15] This judgment that growth would continue for several decades after 1860 should not be read as implying that growth would cease after that time; merely that the forces capable of propelling growth for that duration could be foreseen, but projections beyond that become more difficult.

question and moving quickly on to the next period. Some have despaired of ever finding an answer, noting that each generation tends to interpret the problem in terms of its own interests.

Some commentators have argued that the cause of the Civil War is a particularly complicated and intractable problem but that explanation in itself does not help much. Any problem which has not, after so many years, yielded to attempts to solve it appears complicated and difficult. Indeed, such words as "the richness or the diversity of history" are often evoked because historians have not succeeded in devising any good overall explanations for particular patterns of past events. Moreover, the inability of practicing historians to find or even narrow down the cause of the Civil War is not specific to this particular question. There are many issues in the history of almost all periods on which scholars have not been able to achieve any general consensus, despite major efforts.

Unless one wishes simply to argue that history is generally a difficult discipline, there must be another explanation. In most cases history has far more ideas and facts than it seems able to assimilate into a consistent account. This in turn suggests that the most likely starting place for raising the quality of historical study is in the framework where facts are fitted *together,* rather than in the facts themselves. In essence, what is needed is some method of posing questions so that alternative explanations can be evaluated, the weaker hypotheses discarded, and follow-up efforts focused on the more promising ones. To be more specific, let us take the question of the Civil War as an example of how such an attack could be mounted.

Innumerable suggestions have been made as to specific factors which might have caused a Civil War. That is a necessary, but far from a complete, specification if the question is to be answered. What is required is not only to show that friction existed, but also to show that it was sufficiently powerful to cause the involved parties to resort to war. This latter step is the one which is almost universally missing from the scholarship on the Civil War and what has made it so correspondingly indecisive. We can sympathize somewhat with such a general omission, however, when we see what it entails to construct such an estimate. The *size* of the friction necessary to explain the resort to war must obviously be larger than the expected cost of the war itself. Moreover, it must also be less costly than other methods of dealing with the conflict, which in this case would be either some form of peaceful accommodation or the costs to the parties involved of simply ignoring or putting up with the friction.

Even then, one further step is required. Having identified the "cause," the foreseen cost of going to war, and the relevant alternatives to war, it is still necessary to show that the former is greater than each of the latter. This requires some form of measurement, or method of comparison—however crude—which is something most historians have shied away from, at least until recently. That is one predilection which will have to be laid aside, however, if history is ever to be significantly better at explaining patterns of past events than it now is. Practicing historians could—and sometimes it seems that they do—argue endlessly as to which particular hypothesis best explains a particular event. The only way to curtail such endless talk is to have some way of demonstrating that a particular force was stronger than others—in short, some way of ranking historical forces by their strength in a particular situation.

To make this generalized, abstract procedure a little more concrete, we can follow through an actual example. So far only one possible friction between the North and the South, as of the 1860s, has been shown to be sufficiently great to explain the Civil War—and that is slavery. Slavery is readily recognized as one of the prime candidates for a cause of the Civil War, but exactly how that institution produced such a conflict has, until recently, been left quite vague.[16] The South's stake in slavery is the most straightforward and most easily understood of the two. By 1860, slaves, by the standards of that day, represented a huge stock of wealth to their owners. All those incomes expected to be produced by slave efforts in future years had been capitalized into the prices of the slaves. If slavery were to be compromised—which meant anything that would reduce the income expected to come from slave ownership in the future, as well as the more dramatic step of emancipation—that wealth, in the form of their prevailing prices, would be correspondingly reduced. By 1860 that wealth was not only large in itself but it also represented a large part of the income expected each year in many of the slave-holding states. This is vividly shown in Table 9-2 where the percentage of prevailing income which free citizens of the slave states would lose from noncompensated emancipation of slaves is developed.

The first obvious feature of Table 9-2 is how large a portion of income the slave states, particularly those of the deep South, were receiving from their holdings on the eve of the Civil War. For all slave states combined it amounted to about 20 percent, but for the states of the Deep South it exceeded 30 percent. For such selected states as Alabama and South Carolina, the vested interest in slave income was even higher. In this context it becomes more understandable why such vocal supporters of slavery and Southern self-determination as Calhoun and Yancey could maintain their home bases in such states well before they were accepted elsewhere as anything more than extremists.

The large amount of income which Southerners had tied up in slave-holdings also helps to explain their general vigorous reaction to any group which they saw as posing a threat to that institution, such as the Republican party. That self-interest was much larger and more direct than that implied in alternative explanations of their behavior, such as those based on regional identity or "precapitalism." The proportion of their incomes invested in slavery was much higher than that at which they could reasonably be expected not to oppose threats to its continuation. For example, the per capita American income nowadays is around $5,000 per year. The amount represented by the value of slaveholdings for the entire South in 1860—about 20 percent—would be comparable to $1,000 per person per year today. Suppose that some prominent public official or political

---

[16] Much of the remainder of this section builds on the author's study of "The Origins of the American Civil War," *Journal of Economic History*, vol. 34, no. 4, December 1974. The fact that slavery is at present the only demonstrated cause of the Civil War does not necessarily mean that it *is* the only one. There may be others of sufficient potency which await work necessary to detect them.

Table 9-2   The Loss of Income to Free Citizens of the Slave States from Noncompensated Abolition of Slavery in 1860

State	Per capita income	Percent slave	Slave earnings per free citizen	Earnings other than from slaves per free citizen	Percent reduction in income of free citizens from abolition
Alabama	$ 75	45	$ 50	$ 70	42
South Carolina	80	57	57	102	36
Florida	89	44	48	95	34
Georgia	84	44	40	96	29
Mississippi	125	55	74	179	29
Louisiana	131	47	54	175	24
Texas	(100)	30	26	108	24
Above seven states	$ 97	46	$ 50	$113	31
North Carolina	79	33	21	87	19
Tennessee	75	25	17	76	18
Arkansas	95	26	21	100	17
Virginia[1]	88	32	20	100	17
Above eleven states	$ 91	38	$ 35	$100	23
Kentucky	83	19	10	88	10
Maryland	(90)	13	6	94	6
Missouri	(90)	10	5	93	5

[1] Excludes counties which later formed West Virginia

group were to propose a law which would reduce the real incomes of everyone in the economy by that amount, or even a fraction thereof. Then suppose that the proposal reached the point where it was given serious consideration. One would confidently predict that organized, concerted resistance would begin to form. This is very close to what happened in the South in response to Lincoln's election. The slaveholders who felt threatened by that event were concentrated in one area and, therefore, political secession to form a government more congenial to their interests was a logical step. (In certain ways the effect of the dramatic step of forming the Confederacy was merely to formalize the de facto division of the nation into the slave and nonslave regions which had always existed, right up to 1860.) While the Southerners did not view Lincoln as a total abolitionist—emotional rhetoric of the 1860 election notwithstanding—they did correctly perceive his position as leading to the long-term erosion of wealth held in the form of slaves.[17]

Another interesting characteristic of Table 9-2 is the correlation between each state's vested interest in slavery and its behavior in the national crisis of

[17] The calculations performed in "The Origins of the American Civil War" indicate that Lincoln's election was expected to lead to a reduction of about one-fourth the value of those slaves who continued to be held in the Union after 1860. This is far from the result an abolitionist would advocate, but nevertheless it was still a loss of more than three-quarters of a billion dollars in wealth.

1860–1861. The states are listed by decreasing order of their relative dependence on slave income. Remarkably enough, that also is an exact ordering of how drastic their responses were to Lincoln's election. The first six states on the list—whose solidarity in response was recognized with the name of the "Gulf squadron" by contemporaries—seceded from the Union almost immediately after the election. Texas, the seventh state, joined them several months later but before the War began. The next four states, North Carolina through Virginia, decided not to secede in response to Lincoln's election, but did join the Confederacy when fighting began in April 1861. The final three states, with the lowest vested interest in slavery among the slave states, chose to remain in the Union even though that meant contributing to its war effort and furthering the demise of slavery. It is noticeable that when the crunch came, each state went to that particular course which best corresponded with its own position rather than with any regional identity. For example, both Virginia and Kentucky had obvious pro-Southern sympathies and both had sought ways to develop a compromise and avoid a war, but when such alternatives were voided by the beginning of fighting, Virginia went with the South and Kentucky went with the North in exact accord with their vested interests in income from slaves.

The North Looks at Slavery

The interests of the South in maintaining slavery are fairly direct and obvious. They come down to a matter of dollars and cents. The North's dislike of slavery and the costs it was willing to bear to remove it are much harder to pin down and measure, however. In the South there were organized markets for those who wished to deal in slaves, but there was no such organization in the North for private citizens who found slavery distasteful and were willing to contribute some of their resources to futher its demise. Their only recourse was to work through the political arena. (It was the appearance of just such sentiments in the political field which prompted the animosity of the South.) If we are to decipher the strength of the North's dislike of slavery, therefore, it must be inferred from actions in the sector of government.

Few who are familiar with the antebellum North in the last few decades before the Civil War would deny that some antislavery feeling existed, and it was not confined to just the small minority who were vocal abolitionists. The important question, however, is how large was that preference and how did it compare to other objectives which might have impelled the North to go to war. For example, the motive attributed to the North most often—other than slavery—is probably that of preserving the Union. The problem is that *all* parties, including the South, agreed that preserving the Union was laudable, but they certainly differed on what tactics would best achieve it. Moreover, when a given group advocated more than one objective, such as the North, which clearly favored both the elimination of slavery and the maintenance of the Union (if both came at no cost), it was simply good public relations to advertise the objective that others also desired. So, for example, Lincoln proclaimed that he wanted to preserve the Union and he would be willing either to destroy or to retain slavery, depending on whether it contributed to that goal or not. At first hearing that might sound like a strong stand, but until we know what his definition of the Union involved, there is still ambiguity. Would he have been willing to accept slavery to perpetuate the existing Union, or did he have a slave-free union in mind—or even a society in which a majority of the people could decide to end slavery at any time through the usual channels of government action? Thus, the only objective way to determine what the North actually wanted is to look at what it did and not at what it was saying.

There were a number of situations where the North had to make a collective choice which expressed a trade-off between its two goals. One such declaration was made in the presidential election of 1860. By a somewhat complicated process of interpolation, it is possible to demonstrate that the North was predominantly motivated by antislavery feelings in the national crisis of the 1860s.[18] In one respect this should not come as a surprise; the election of Lincoln was implicitly a vote to diminish slavery while increasing the likelihood of rupturing the Union. Yet it takes some method of objective measurement to reach this conclusion; more than one century of debate over what Northerners were "really saying" or "really thinking" failed to yield any substantive conclusions.

Thus the North, like the South, was primarily motivated by slavery in going to war. And that raises another important question. One can see that the South's interest in defending slavery would have existed for as long as it owned slaves, but the North's objection to their holding them was only a relatively recent phenomenon. Until the American Revolution, slaves were held in all Northern colonies. Over the next half-century, however, all states north of Maryland restricted slavery in various ways so that by the time of the Civil War it had completely disappeared from the North. What makes this development even more momentous historically is that slavery had already existed for thousands of years and the morality of it had very seldom been seriously questioned.[19] While this shift in preferences was unique in time, however, it was common to much of the North Atlantic world in the century before the American Civil War. Whatever forces were propelling this new desire to rid society of slavery were common responses in similar circumstances and were not just an American idiosyncrasy. But unlike the economies of northern Europe, where slavery had never been widespread, the Americans in the Northern states had a large slave population right next door so that they alone were forced to go to war to destroy it in their own locality.

Today it surprises many people that slavery was ever considered a normal and accepted institution. We would not think of tolerating it now, and we would go to great lengths to eliminate any elements of it in our society. What is easy to overlook, however, is that modern Western economies have a much greater capacity to eliminate slavery if they wish to than did those which existed before the

---

[18] See, "The Origin of the American Civil War."

[19] David Brion Davis received the Pulitzer Prize for the book in which he articulated this problem (but failed to resolve it). See his *The Problem of Slavery in Western Culture,* Cornell, Ithaca, N. Y., 1966.

nineteenth century. Slavery can be destroyed in several ways: one can prohibit it, one can buy the slaves' freedom, or—like the North—one can wage a war to destroy it. All require resources of some sort. Prohibiting slavery or establishing a program of gradual emancipation imposes the cost on the owners of the slaves at the time that the legislation is enacted because the wealth which they hold in the form of slaves is destroyed. Buying the slaves and then freeing them shifts the cost of emancipation to the taxpayers. And, of course, freeing them through force of arms creates its own set of costs. One obvious trend in most of the Western economies during this time was rising average incomes, which is another way of saying that the number of amenities which an average individual could command was increasing. The common tendency is to think of higher incomes as allowing people to buy more goods, such as appliances or larger homes, but if one careful-ly examines changing patterns of spending it becomes apparent that people also spend some of their larger purchasing power on such items as street cleaners, aid to the poor, and larger public libraries. In short, they spend, collectively or indi-vidually, to improve the general environment in which they live, as well as to increase the goods they possess. It seems reasonable, therefore, that they would also choose to devote some of their increased incomes to the elimination of that social arrangement which deprives certain members of their society of much of their freedom.

Another factor which probably prompted a growing uneasiness about slav-ery in the American economy was that, in effective terms, it was coming closer to citizens of the non-slave-holding regions. In the antebellum period transportation costs fell so that people traveled more widely than before. In addition, communi-cation became faster and more comprehensive. The telegraph made the transmis-sion of major news events almost instantaneous, and cheap newspapers and periodicals—made possible by the sizeable reductions in printing costs as a result of the rotary press—disseminated it much more completely. Americans not only had more income with which they could choose to end the unwholesomeness they saw in slavery, but they were reminded of it far more often as well.

In one sense, therefore, the Civil War was the result of an ongoing process of growth in the economy. It was not growth of the form conceived by some past historians who saw the war as a necessary step to remove the handicap which a backward South imposed on the nation, however, but rather a conflict of values brought on by changing preferences resulting from the rising incomes of the North focusing on an institution in which much of the growing wealth of the South was being reposited. The North's growth was not being held up in any significant way by slavery in the South, but it was causing (and allowing) the North to object to a particular form that growth was taking in the South. Thus the Civil War is a specific example of the adverse effects which many people have begun to associate with economic growth in recent years. It is not at all clear that the war is an example of a common characteristic, however. (Besides, it did destroy slavery, which most moderns would say was good, even if it had to come at that price.) For reasons which we shall spell out below, the Civil War was an exceptional event in American history. Even so, it is a reminder that while growth allows societies to satisfy certain wants which they deem important, there are always other wants which emerge to become the problems of the next period.

The Calculus of Going to War

We have taken a close look at slavery and identified it as the basic friction responsible for the Civil War. A complete specification of the War's cause, however, requires one more element. Military efforts were not the only way to deal with such a disagreement. Two other major options implicitly available were some form of peaceful compromise or—the "common-cold" strategy—simply living with the problem. To provide a complete explanation of the cause of the Civil War we must show why war appeared preferable to the other alternatives. With the advantage of retrospect we know the values of those alternatives somewhat better than the parties making the decisions did at the time. For example, we can calculate that the actual cost of the war to each side was in excess of $2 billion. Both sides expected the conflict to cost them considerably less, probably a half-billion dollars at the most. They badly underestimated on this point, but the bad judgment is understandable in retrospect—a point we shall consider in Chapter 10. In any case, they had to decide their course of action with the information they had at the moment. One alternative to fighting was to put up with the situation. We can see why the South found that undesirable; in its estimation the cost of a war would be less than half a billion dollars while the cost of the loss of slavery would be more than three-quarters of a billion dollars. We have no such direct measures for the North's valuation of eliminating slavery, but from its behavior we can infer that they considered tolerating it less desirable than going to war.

The cost of a general program of peaceful compromise is less uncertain because all the elements could be anticipated. The most likely form of such an accommodation would have been for the federal government to buy the slaves at their going market price and free them. The huge amount of revenue necessary for such a program would have been raised by increased federal taxes. There is evidence that at least some of the participants in the decisions of 1860–1861 were aware of both the possibility and the cost of such a program. In any case, the more they considered it the more likely they would be to reject it. If the tax burden of compensated emancipation through federal purchase were distributed equally per capita (including the now freed men), the pro rata share of the South would have been $0.9 billion while that of the North would have been $1.8 billion. No wonder the two parties would rather fight than switch. To the South the cost of peaceful compromise was nearly twice that of the foreseen cost of a war so that unless its chances of surviving such a conflict were rather dismal, fighting appeared to be the cheapest alternative. (Actually, the judgment of most objective observers at the time the war began was that the South had a good chance of winning. That judgment seems to have been supported by the actual experience of the war. If it had been of only the magnitude originally expected, the South certainly would have survived.)

The North's incentive to choose war rather than peaceful emancipation was greater. Its tax burden would have been about four times larger than the expected costs of the war. War would have appeared the better strategy unless the estimate of achieving its goals had been seen as quite poor. In short, both parties went to war because it appeared to be the cheapest alternative. The basic reason was that military action—even allowing for some possibility of defeat—seemed cheaper than buying out all the slaves. Here again the profitability of slavery came into play. By 1860 the slaves in aggregate were so productive, and hence so valuable, that buying them was by far the most expensive way to settle the conflict they had created. It was simply cheaper to go to war.

This finding runs headlong into a large body of thought, which was common several decades ago about the cause of the Civil War. The argument was that the war was a mistake. The leadership of the era was weak and irresponsible and bungled itself into unnecessary conflict. There is little direct evidence for that view. Leadership of that time appeared to be no less (or more) effective than in the rest of American history. In fact, the blundering which occurred was on the part of the historians who failed to recognize that war was not necessarily always a poor course of action. Sometimes it just might be the best way to go. (If that is not the case, the frequency of wars in human history suggests a rather broad pattern of failure.) What was involved in this crisis was an unusually large conflict of interest, one which the routine framework of the society was simply not designed to handle. What was called for, consequently, was action outside the usual range, and it would have been blundering on the part of that generation if it had not had the vision and adaptability to find exceptional solutions to exceptional problems. In that sense, the citizens of that time were doing their task well. If the Civil War is the great American tragedy, it is the circumstances and not the participants which made it so.

SUGGESTED READINGS

Conrad, Alfred H. and John R. Meyer: "The Economics of Slavery in the Ante-Bellum South," *Journal of Political Economy,* vol. 66, April 1958.

Fogel, Robert W. and Stanley L. Engerman: *Time on the Cross: The Economics of American Negro Slavery,* and *Time on the Cross: Evidence and Methods,* a supplement, Little, Brown, Boston, 1974.

Golden, Claudia: "The Economics of Emancipation," *Journal of Economic History,* vol. 33, March 1973.

Gray, L. C.: *History of Agriculture in the Southern United States to 1860,* Carnegie Institution, Washington, D. C., 1933.

Gunderson, G.: "The Origin of the American Civil War," *Journal of Economic History,* vol. 34, no. 4, December 1974.

Parker, William N. (ed.): *The Structure of the Cotton Economy of the Antebellum South,* Agricultural History Society, Washington, D. C., 1970.

Storobin, Robert S.: *Industrial Slavery in the Old South,* Oxford, New York, 1970.

Wright, Gavin: "New and Old Views on the Economics of Slavery," *Journal of Economic History,* vol. 33, June 1973.

Chapter 10

The Economic Impact
of the Civil War

In the initial burst of enthusiasm in response to the firing on Fort Sumter, almost everyone in both the North and the South wanted to get on with the war. Local regiments were hurriedly formed and mayors urged their townspeople to join the great cause. Everyone seemed to be in a hurry to start fighting except the professional military officers who were in charge of getting the armies in motion. General Lee was struggling to assemble enough percussion caps to outfit the troops he had on hand and was asking the rest of the militia of the South to stay away from Richmond until he could outfit them. The problems of the federal authorities seemed even greater. They were having major difficulties getting their troops through unsympathetic Maryland to Washington, D. C., let alone organized to face the hostile territory of Virginia to the South. It seemed that bureaucracy was up to its usual tricks of slowing down the important business of the nation. And yet, the military planners were to be the ones proven right by subsequent events. This war was going to be more than the short-term, flag-waving jaunts which Americans seemed to believe characterized such efforts.

That message began to sink in when the fighting began in June of 1861. Neither Northern nor Southern military leaders considered themselves ready for fighting, but exhortations from the civilian leadership, prompted in turn by cries for action from the electorate, forced them to move. They first met at an otherwise insigificant creek named Manassas, which is now commonly known throughout the North as Bull Run. As Bruce Catton was later to observe, it would not have been so bad if it had not been Sunday. With the battlefield only a comfortable carriage ride away from Washington, a sizeable contingent of congressmen and their families came out to watch the event. They clustered together on a pleasant grass knoll, too far away from the battle site to see much but a nice spot for a picnic—and right in the line of retreat. The battle that day was hardly one to record in the textbooks as an example of well-executed maneuvers. The South won because its field officers (including a brigadier general named Thomas Jonathan Jackson who won the sobriquet "Stonewall" for holding the line that afternoon) were somewhat more successful in coordinating their still-inexperienced troops in battle. The Union troops began to pull back, a maneuver which to them in a few months' time would become almost as instinctive and ordered as breathing. In their inexperience, however, the battle quickly disintegrated into a rout, with men, horses, and wagons stampeding back toward Washington, sweeping up the congressional delegation along with them.

As the officers gathered up their troops and hurriedly threw up defenses for the city in the next few days, it became more apparent that—as the congressmen had literally discovered—this war was not going to be a picnic. The generals went back to drafting plans and the civilian leaders started procuring the larger quantities of resources which the conflict was beginning to demand. Any misperception about the conflict not becoming a huge affair was completely dispelled a little over a year later. The two armies of the Eastern front met head on at a place called Antietam Creek, just north of the Potomac River in Maryland. More than 23,000 Americans died in that single day—nearly as many fatalities as had occurred in all American wars combined up to that date. Moreover, the battle was not decisive, except insofar as it finished any hopes that the war might be concluded in 1862. The only thing it clarified was that this war was turning into an enormous consumer of men and materials and the end would likely come only when one side or the other ran completely out of either resources or motivation. The days when a war went to the side that captured the field in a bayonet charge were over.

THE ECONOMICS OF TOTAL WAR

In retrospect, all major parties involved in the Civil War underestimated how large it would ultimately become. Recent interpolations indicate that it was expected to be from 10 percent to 40 percent of the size which it actually became.[1] We should not be too harsh on the judgment of the contemporaries of that period, however. They were not predicting a small war; judging from their behavior they expected a conflict several times larger than any which had so far oc-

---

[1] Gerald Gunderson, "The Origin of the American Civil War," *Journal of Economic History,* vol. 34, no. 4, December 1974.

curred in American history. Nor were they deceiving themselves that a war was unlikely. The choices of all the parties suggest the recognition that there was a high probability—at least 85 percent—that war would occur as a result of their actions. Even with the advantage of hindsight we are still not sure what caused the Civil War to become such an enormous conflict. We do know, however, that it marked the first of what are now recognized as "modern" or "total wars." The American Civil War was a milestone not only in American history but also in the history of warfare generally. It was not just larger in *degree* than previous wars, but clearly larger in *kind.* It was a quantum jump upward in the scale of warfare in that it consumed a much larger portion of the resources of the economies within which it took place than had any previous wars. We can be somewhat more sympathetic with the underestimation of the size of the Civil War by its contemporaries. They looked for just another run-of-the-mill war like all the others they had known. They had no idea they would be the victims of a historical first.

No one has yet completely succeeded in showing why warfare suddenly became so much larger an operation at the time of the Civil War. There are, however, some likely reasons. An obvious place to start looking would be for changes in military technology which might have made warfare considerably more expensive. There had been some dramatic gains in the military arts since the last major war (the Napoleonic Wars in the early 1800s), as one might expect in an economy where innovations were occurring in almost every sector. Probably the most important of these was the introduction of rifling into the classic infantry musket. That increased the effective range of fire from less than fifty to several hundred yards and forced a complete overhaul of battlefield tactics (that is, the introduction of trench warfare).[2] Similar increases in firepower occurred in larger guns, such as field artillery and naval weapons. Yet when all these new weapons were put together in the test of battle, it did not seem to make warfare that much more equipment- or capital-intensive. The Civil War was basically a struggle between foot soldiers. The improvements in the individual firearm seemed to make the individual infantryman sufficiently more versatile and powerful to offset any gains from the use of more hardware and equipment in fighting.

More likely the important changes took place in the organization behind the front lines rather than in them. It was not so much that the act of fighting had become so expensive in itself, but rather that the cost of mobilizing and delivering resources to the combat zone had fallen so drastically. It is now very clear that the antebellum period witnessed a drastic fall in interior transportation costs (see Chapter 5). This meant that a much larger part of a military budget could be used for securing fighting resources rather than consumed in delivering resources to the battle area. The contrast with the Revolutionary War vividly illustrates this

---

[2] Rifling is a technique of metal working which imparts a spiral shape to the inside of a gun barrel. This produces a spin on the bullet which gives it a truer trajectory, much as a spiral does for a thrown football.

factor. The American effort in that conflict was comparatively small—but who can blame the patriots? A large part of each dollar they allocated to the war effort was consumed in simply getting the resources to the fighting zone (especially when the British Navy controlled the coastal waters and forced all transport to use the much more expensive overland routes). In contrast, the fraction of each dollar consumed in moving Civil War supplies was much smaller compared with the amount left over for direct military use. This is illustrated by the size of the armies the two sides mustered for battle. While not all were regular soldiers, and not all served for the duration of the war, nevertheless about 2 million men served in the combined armies. This was probably the largest military force ever assembled up to that time. European observers marveled at such numbers but they were even more impressed by the facility with which such large armies could be moved about. Late in 1863 a Union Army, advancing into northern Georgia, was defeated and came very close to being decimated in a battle at an otherwise insignificant small creek called Chicamauga. The Union high command sent several divisions of reinforcements from the army of the Potomac—some 3,000 miles away by railroad. Most of them were on hand within two weeks, an astonishing feat of mobility to European observers. They naturally compared it with Napoleon's retreat from Moscow, which had taken a good part of the winter to cover only half the distance.

Thus, part of the reason that the Civil War grew so large was that more net fighting could be procured from each dollar spent. In addition, however, there were more dollars per capita which could *be* spent. The same process of economic growth which was evident in the improvements in transportation was also greatly increasing the total amount of resources which the economy had available for war. An economy can never engage in a war effort larger than the flow of current output available to it, unless it draws down its capital stock, but even that is only a short-term solution. All nations are subject to this basic reality when they organize their military efforts, and most seem to recognize it when they sit down to plan for a war. The civilian economy must have sufficient resources to provide some minimal level of food, fuel, clothing, and shelter if it is to persist in its effort to support the war effort. That, for example, means leaving enough of a work force on the farms and in the factories to produce the output deemed necessary in such "essential" sectors. Economic growth changes these calculations by increasing the pool of resources an economy has to work with. It also tends to increase the proportion of resources deemed "nonessential" but which can be diverted to military purposes (although what is considered "essential" probably also increases somewhat as a result of growth). By way of example, the South during the Civil War drafted all men (with only a few exceptions) between the ages of eighteen and forty-five. Most of these were taken off farms and their missing services were partly made up for by workers who, in peacetime, would be considered marginal, and partly by simply turning out less farm output. While living standards in the South were substantially reduced during the War, most civilians survived and the Army received necessary, albeit meager, supplies. It is hard to imagine the Southern colonies being capable of making such a major effort during the Revolution, especially for the full four years which the wartime South endured.

Thus, growth provides a kind of double leverage in increasing the amount of resources, and therefore the size of military effort, which an economy can muster. Not only does the total amount of output available (for a given population) increase, but the proportion of total output available for military purposes rises as well. This appears to be another of those paradoxes of growth. It was suggested earlier that growth was a prime underlying force in bringing on the Civil War. Now there is some evidence that it was a contributing factor in making it so surprisingly large. This is not to condemn the growth process as being necessarily bad—which would be such a futile gesture anyway, considering the remote possibility of suppressing the basic behavior from which it springs—but simply to emphasize what it implies when considered in objective terms. Growth increases the quantity of resources available to meet human wants, but it imposes no particular constraints on what those wants must be. A society can choose to spend its augmented income on better grades of steak, or on more trips to the South Seas in the winter, or on aid to nursing homes—or on warfare. It seems only reasonable that individuals would choose to have assurance of their own freedom, or of congenial political arrangements in neighboring states, as well as more satisfied palates or warmer winters.

TO THE BITTER END: THE SOUTHERN ECONOMY DURING THE WAR

One of the examples most commonly used in introductory economics classes to illustrate the gains from trade and specialization is to picture two economies, one whose strength lies in producing guns, and the other whose strength lies in turning out butter. The instructor carefully shows how each society would have more total output if each specialized in that product where its advantage lay, and traded some of its output for the produce of the other economy, than if it tried to produce both products by itself. Then the instructor points out that there is a certain risk to this tactic. If war should develop between the two economies the gun producer will be in good shape, but the butter producer will be reduced to throwing half-pounds of processed butterfat back at the advancing foe.

The South was the great "butter producer" of the Civil War. In the antebellum period it had succeeded in earning good incomes by specializing in a limited number of agricultural staples. Unfortunately for the South, cotton, tobacco, rice, and sugar were not the critical items in equipping and supplying a large army of that day. That in itself was not such a surprise to the South, but even the leverage they expected these exports to have in enlisting the support of foreign powers to their side failed to materialize. The South was therefore forced to fight the war pretty much on its own resources.

The North spent a good part of its military resources during the war making sure that that indeed was the case. After the first few months of warfare passed and most people recognized that the conflict was probably going to be a long one, the North settled down to a basic strategy of isolation and attrition. An extensive naval blockade was established along the entire coastline of the Confederacy and was gradually tightened by capturing major ports and coastal enclaves. This obviously interdicted the South's international trade, but another—often overlooked—effect was that it seriously handicapped internal trade with the South as well. The South had a good system of natural waterways, and because water transportation was cheap it had already learned to use them extensively. But most of them emptied into the Atlantic Ocean or the Gulf of Mexico so that they were vulnerable at those points and thus Southern shipping was soon confined to serving strictly local traffic during the conflict.

The effects of the blockade were soon obvious in the Southern economy. An extensive list of formerly imported items, such as iron, machinery, textiles, salt, leather, and almost every kind of household utensil, soon became scarce or nonexistent. The South had only one iron foundry, the Tredegar Works in Richmond, and naturally everything it could turn out was taken by the priority claims of the military. That left almost no new supplies for such users as the railroads and agriculture. When the railroads wished to replace or build new track, their only recourse was to dismantle some mileage elsewhere. Over the course of the war, the efficiency of the Confederate rail system steadily deteriorated, particularly after guerillas and Union cavalry learned how vulnerable it was and tore up a few lengths of track. By the end of the conflict those trains which were running were seldom averaging better than 2 or 3 miles per hour (a dubious achievement not equaled for another century, until the Penn Central came along). Similarly, there was nothing to replace agricultural implements when they wore out. For something like plowshares, which were expected to wear out and to be replaced periodically, much like saw blades, there was no substitute except much greater hand labor. One had the unenviable choice of filing the share by hand or hitching up more animal power to pull it through the soil. Either way it took more of other resources—all of which were becoming increasingly scarce in the hard-pressed Confederacy.

The disruptions in trade within the South also took a heavy toll in economic welfare. While the average prices of goods tended to move up in unison throughout the South,[3] certain items at certain places became particularly scarce. Before the war the South had been a net importer of salt, whose prime use in those days was for the preservation of meat. Saltworks were established in Alabama soon after the blockade went into effect, but transportation was inadequate to distribute the output throughout the rural South where it was needed. As a result, meat used in local consumption had to be eaten fresh, which meant at the additional cost of keeping the livestock on hay and grain into the winter. Meat produced for off-farm use often deteriorated rapidly because of inadequate salting. There are frequent accounts of bacon spoiling in army collection centers, while at the same

---

[3] The best quantitative study of the Southern economy during the Civil War had been performed by Eugene Lerner. Two of his reports are reprinted in Ralph Andreano (ed.), *The Economic Impact of the American Civil War,* Schenkman, Cambridge, Mass., 1967.

time front-line troops were receiving only half-rations, and often meatless ones at that. Another understandable response to the higher transportation costs—and partly also to the disruption in supplies from the upper border states—was the widespread appearance of distilling in the Confederacy. Government officials strongly objected to this practice and frequently laws were promulgated to mini-mize it, because it used up grain which was in short supply. Distillers countered with the argument that it was necessary for hospitals, particularly with the sharp-ly increased numbers of patients resulting from the war. (Liquor was indeed the most commonly used anesthetic of that day, but it was difficult to determine where pain killing left off and social withdrawal began. Booths selling liquor quickly appeared around each hospital and officials usually objected. However, with the chances of coming out of a hospital being as poor as they were in those days, one can understand the ready resort to drink.) The more compelling reason was that distilling was a logical adaptation to an economy in which the cost and disruptions of shipping goods took a large part of the final price one could obtain for bulky commodities.

The disruption of the South's transportation system became especially no-ticeable in the spread between the price paid for commodities in rural areas and that quoted in the larger cities. Residents of Richmond, for example, complained that the prices they were paying for food was often five to ten times as high as that prevailing in the country areas from which it was coming. Such a large spread is understandable, however, when we note that virtually all railroad traffic into the city was commandeered by the military so that almost all civilian goods were forced to come by wagon. That raised transportation costs considerably, particularly because the population of Richmond more than doubled during the war and food supplies had to be hauled in from an even wider area than in peacetime. Hauling goods into the city was made even more expensive by the high cost of animal fodder and by the common habit of the Confederate commis-sary agents of seizing both the teams and their cargoes and paying their owners only a fraction of the true market value. Richmond's situation became even worse beginning in early 1864 when Sherman's campaign began destroying sources of supply farther south. The screws continued to tighten until, in early 1865, when, after extensive destruction in the Shenandoah Valley to the west and in interior North Carolina to the south, the Southern Army simply could not obtain enough food to feed its troops. The immediate cause of Lee's abandon-ment of Richmond was not so much Federal military pressure as that the Army was quickly vanishing, as hungry troops deserted in search of food. The Union learned its lesson well: that it was engaged in a total war, and that the enemy was likely to be defeated only when its necessary resources were completely de-stroyed.

Profitable Gaps in the Blockade

During the middle of the war cotton was selling for about $1 a pound in the textile centers of New England and Manchester, which was about ten times its normal peacetime level. Similarly, the prices of those goods which the South had obtained almost exclusively outside the region before the war were about five times higher (adjusted for changes in prices) during the war. The cause, of course, was the Federal blockade which sought to make the normal exchange of such items impossible. It also established an environment where anyone who could find a way to evade that barrier could make immense profits. People who bought traditional Southern imports in the North at prevailing prices, succeeded in getting them into the South, bought cotton with the proceeds, and then succeeded in getting that back also, could increase their original investment fifty times over. There were extremely difficult obstacles to surmount, but with possible rewards like that there was no shortage of people who were willing to try.

Nassau, now that well-advertised hub of the Bahama Islands, was for the most part an unknown quantity out in the Atlantic Ocean—except for one brief, intense period. During the Civil War it was the chief port for blockade runners attempting to reach Confederate ports. Their usual destination was Wilmington, North Carolina, which was well protected by Fort Fisher at the outlet of the Cape Rear River and was not taken by Federal forces until just two months before Appomattox. As befitted the potential rewards of their trade, the blockade runners spent considerable money and ingenuity to get through the screen of Union ships. At first they used the oldest, cheapest boats they could find, on the theory that they did not want anything valuable to be lost to the Union patrols. As the Federal forces became more proficient, however, they found it worthwhile to use the best vessels that money could buy. The English shipyards were soon filling orders for specially designed blockade runners: fast, low-silhouetted steam vessels, painted gray, burning smokeless anthracite coal to reduce visibility, and sometimes even equipped with smokestacks that could be cranked down to deck height to camouflage the ship's profile even more. They were unusual and expensive vessels, but the owners could recover their investment in two voyages, and each successful circuit after that would provide enough profit to retire comfortably for life. A load of 500 cotton bales reaching Nassau could bring a profit of more than $100,000. One skipper made more than $2,000 on a carpetbag of corset stays—in addition to his regular salary which commonly ran to about $5,000 per voyage.

Such huge incentives for contraband trade naturally caused potential participants to search for any other channels where they might start such commerce. One place where the two parties were close together was the battlefront itself, and it did not take long for traders of both sides to open up exchanges around and even through the front lines. In 1862 the cities of New Orleans, Nashville, and Memphis were captured by the Union forces. Right behind—or sometimes even a little ahead of—the troops came merchants anxious to sell Northern goods and buy cotton and sugar. Within a short time they were shipping sizeable quantities of cotton back to Northern buyers and selling large quantities of salt, bacon, cloth, shoes, and leather. Such trade was supposed to involve only citizens of Federally controlled territory, but cotton bales did not have any birthmarks— even for those who were looking for them. Trades were supposed to be registered with authorized representatives of the Treasury to ensure that no enemy personnel or material were involved, but the agents were not so altruistic as to be above accepting a "gift" for their sympathetic expedition of commercial deals. Besides, failing that, suspect commerce could always occur through third parties whose loyalty to the Union—if not their business ethics—was unquestioned.

Government officials on both sides of the lines were not so naïve as to overlook what was happening, if for no other reason than that certain well-placed officials complained about it. General Sherman, for example, fumed that such cities as Memphis were more valuable to the Confederates when they were in the hands of the Union forces than they were when they controlled them themselves. He was not too far wrong. The bacon and shoes the Confederate armies were receiving through the lines were probably just as necessary to them as the arms and ammunition they used in battle. Sherman and Grant—who was also conducting military operations in the Mississippi Valley during 1862 and 1863 in the midst of contraband trading—could see the nature of the war they were engaged in and understood that such trading was prolonging it by providing the enemy with needed resources. The officials back in Washington realized this also, but in a way they were being torn by the same strong forces that were appearing in more concrete form to the battlefield merchants. True, trading with the enemy might prolong the war, but the war looked like it was going to be a long one anyway—which meant one had to maintain sufficient domestic support for the long haul. The Federal government remarked that it needed the cotton to make uniforms and tents for the Army, but it might well have added that it also eased the pressure on New England textile mills and Northern consumers. The Confederacy was more candid: by early 1863 it was admitting that it would have to trade with the enemy if it was going to continue to conduct the war over any sustained period. Both sides had discovered that the rather large gains which can be made in peacetime specialization are not lightly abandoned in wartime. While there were some gains in cutting off trade with the enemy insofar as prosecuting the war was concerned, there were also some benefits in continuing it. The supplies one side received from the other seemed to do the supplying foes more damage than the goods which might be withheld from them.

Confederate Finances

The Confederate government had been officially established for only a few months when it found itself fighting a major war, one which was larger in relation to the economy which supported it than most of the wars in previous human experience. At first the new government attempted to assemble the resources it believed it needed for the war effort through conventional means. It ordered a nationwide assessment of property to prepare for some form of tax. It also issued a war loan, which, in the first burst of enthusiasm, was oversubscribed. It was going to take more than enthusiasm and yearly property taxes, however, to keep the war machine supplied. The war very quickly developed into an enormous consumer of people and materials—probably using about half of the total yearly income which the region had been producing before the war. (During the war, the military effort probably used up an even higher percentage of current income

because the disruption imposed undoubtedly reduced real output.) The traditional means of raising revenue simply were not going to yield the huge amounts
which were required immediately. Therefore, the Confederacy resorted to some
less orthodox methods to gain control of those necessary resources. The first was
simply to print large amounts of paper money, far more than the economy could
use at the initial level of prices. The natural result was that prices began to rise
and those who held such currency were subject to losses in its buying power.
During the first three years of the war (after January 1864 the statistics dissolve,
along with the Confederacy) the total stock of money in the area controlled by
the Confederacy increased eleven times.[4] Had the money supply been composed
entirely of government issues the increase would have been even faster. More
than $800 million of Confederate notes were issued, but private bank notes in-
creased by less than three times in the period, thus slowing the growth of the
aggregate supply. In the same period, however, the average price level in the
region rose by more than *twenty-eight* times. The difference is partly accounted
for by speedup in velocity, that is, the rate at which the money changed hands.
With the value of Confederate currency depreciating by about 10 percent per
month, holders soon found it to their advantage to pass it on as soon as possible.

Prices were also going up faster than the money supply, because the area
within which it could circulate was steadily shrinking. Residents near the front
lines were particularly reluctant to accept Confederate money because it would
become worthless if the Union forces advanced past them. People in such areas
preferred gold or even—heretically—Northern greenbacks. Actually, the response of individuals in the border areas was not too different from that of those
in the interior of the Confederacy. When an asset such as paper money depreciates so severely and predictably, substitutes will be developed. One of these was
barter. Employers began to pay their employees in so much cash and so much
flour. Firms began to swap commodities with each other rather than selling them
for cash. Forms of commodity money began to appear. Storekeepers began to
charge their customers' accounts in so many units of leather, for example, rather
than in dollars.

Even by taking a good portion of the medium of exchange in the form of the
"inflation tax," however, the Confederate government was unable to raise the
real resources it needed. (Of course, the money substitutes the public devised to
protect themselves from inflation reduced the return from that tax and made
resort to other sources of revenue even more necessary.) Finally, the Army's
commissary units simply began seizing the materials they needed. Owners were
supposed to be reimbursed at fair market prices but the official valuations of
most items lagged well behind their current prices. As a result, most owners
received only about one-third to one-half of the real value of the goods they gave
up to the military. Sometimes it was even worse, as when the commissary agents

---

[4] Again, the best record in regard to this aspect of the Confederacy has been compiled by
Eugene Lerner. See his "Money, Wages and Prices in the Confederacy," *Journal of Political Economy*,
vol. 42, February 1955, reprinted in Ralph Andreano (ed.), *The Economic Impact of the American Civil
War*, Schenkman, Cambridge, Mass., 1962.

paid for their requisitions in debt instruments rather than cash. Such paper was less negotiable and was likely to end up being completely worthless as the authority of the Confederacy slipped away. Some Southern citizens complained—and rightly—that these expropriations were discriminatory in that some areas were hit much harder than others. That was true, because the Army naturally tended to seize those supplies most useful to itself. That generally meant provisions either near the combat areas or, farther back from the front, near the railroads. Farm products from less accessible areas were often overlooked, because bringing them out would have required large numbers of horses—which were themselves one of the items the Army was seizing, as they were constantly in short supply. One of the areas which suffered the most under these policies was the Shenandoah Valley of western Virginia. It was a convenient source of supplies for Lee's army, which spent most of the four years of the war within 100 miles of it. For that very reason it was also a favorite target for Northern scorched-earth tactics. General Sheridan, who completed the task of destruction in the valley in late 1864, remarked that if a crow were to fly over the area now it would have to carry its own lunch with it. Such was the disadvantage of being a productive resource in the midst of a modern war—to be expropriated by its own forces and destroyed by its enemies.

Real Incomes during Destruction and Turmoil

Southerners, and many outside the South as well, view Sherman's march through Georgia and South Carolina as wanton institutionalized destruction and brutality. Such widespread damage to helpless and unresisting civilian property seems heartless, especially when carried out according to Sherman's own seemingly callous orders. But if Sherman scored poorly on public relations, he understood quite clearly the harsh reality of the war he was conducting. In the first year or so of the conflict, most of the destruction was the usual by-product of fighting and marching armies. For example, the most damaging form of destruction was probably the innocent result of soldiers trying to keep themselves and their suppers warm. Most of the developed agricultural land in the fighting zone was enclosed by Virginia rail fences (the zigzagging patterned type often known as worm fences). These were essential if the predominant form of agriculture, a mixture of cattle and crops, was to be successful.[5] It was also a handy form of cut, dry firewood. Many a soldier bivouacked in a farmer's field for the night fought back the chill by sleeping near a fire made of fence rails. It was an expensive form of heating, however. The extensive network of fences in farming areas had been painstakingly pieced together over many years and by the time of the war represented a large and productive capital resource. Without them—which was exactly

---

[5] In speaking of the South as being highly specialized in the export of a limited number of agricultural staples, it is important to remember that these were not necessarily its only products. Actually, most farms in the antebellum South were largely self-sufficient in foodstuffs. They raised large quantities of such items as corn, hogs, and horses. This was a logical form of organization in that much of the effort devoted to the nonstaples could be carried out between the peak work periods of the staple crops.

the state of much of the South by the end of the war—cattle had to be either herded or individually tethered each day, a very labor-intensive method of livestock culture. But such were some of the costs of the widening war.

During the last two years of the war, the destruction moved from casual to systematic. The soldiers from the North, and a good many of the civilians at home, had come to realize that this war was different from all others which had gone before and that it therefore required some changes in military practice. Ultimately it came down to this: every resource in the Confederacy was a part of its war potential. If a given resource could not be denied the enemy permanently by holding the area, then it must be destroyed. That obviously meant factories, railroads, bridges, warehouses—preferably full of supplies—and wagons, but in practice it also came to mean city buildings, fences, livestock, and even crops in the field. When any hostility was shown the passing troops, it could also mean private homes. This kind of sweeping destruction was practiced mostly in the last year of the war which, in effect, meant the area which the Confederacy still formally claimed at that time. (There is a big difference between a *formal* and an *effective* claim, as Sherman's march, completely independent of Federal supplies and contact, proved.) Thus, the Southeastern states, running from Alabama through Virginia, experienced the worst battering during the war. The destruction of Sherman's march through Georgia is common knowledge, but the most destructive phase of that campaign was in South Carolina, where the troops had both more experience and a special grudge against the first state to secede from the Union. Western North Carolina was continuously raided by Union patrols and local unionists from eastern Tennessee during the last year of the war. Northern Alabama was singled out for a special cavalry operation to destroy the military manufacturing facilities at Selma. On the way, of course, the troopers inflicted considerable damage on the weakly defended countryside.

WARTIME LOSSES AND POSTWAR INCOME

Wartime destruction in the South is not a neglected subject, of course. History books have commonly given it considerable coverage. In recent years, however, there has appeared a kind of minirevisionist school which has argued that the casualties were not nearly as bad as has been reported. The reports of widespread deaths among the civilian population, particularly among the freed—but inexperienced—slaves have been downplayed. If one makes a careful count of the population both before and after the fighting, the death rates during the period could not have been much above normal, so that deaths from starvation and disease could not have been widespread. Or consider the reports of widescale destruction. Even in 1865, when the fighting did not end until mid-April, the cotton crop was already back up to half the prewar level. Within a year after the war the railroads were running regularly, and within two years they were fully restored and some had even resumed paying dividends to their stockholders.

This recent trend to downplay the damages wrought by the war has been beneficial if for no other reason than that it has forced commentators to distinguish between physical and economic destruction. Burned-down factories and collapsed bridges are very tangible evidences of loss, but if the return from their services remains high they will soon be rebuilt. Societies can experience immense losses in both population and material and yet recover quickly if the basic productivity and incentives are not changed, as witnessed by much of Europe's recovery from World War II. Yet there *are* losses which persist beyond the initial program to repair most of the physical damage of the fighting. Some scholars have rightly pointed out that if an economy like the South, which had experienced severe destruction, can profitably operate the facilities which are to be replaced, it pays that economy to borrow the money to do so. In other words, it is not necessary for the devastated region to gradually build its capital back up by slowly saving out of its depressed income. It can borrow enough to buy those investments and repay the credits out of the earnings. But the catch is that while the economic productivity of the area may be restored, the income of the residents *of that area* will not regain its prewar level because part of the total product representing the opportunity cost of the borrowed capital is owed to outside creditors. In other words, the wartime destruction is a permanent cost; it may be restored in physical terms, but it nevertheless imposes a long-term loss equal to the opportunity cost of the dissipated resources.

Thus, wartime destruction should be included in any explanation of the severe setback received by Southern per capita incomes during the two decades from 1860–1880. At the end of those twenty years they had barely regained the level at which they began. This meant that they had fallen well behind the level of the rest of the nation, which had resumed growth at about its prewar pace. The Civil War seems to be the predominant explanation for this lag, as almost all the retardation occurred between 1860 and 1870 (those being the two closest benchmarks for which we have evidence on incomes).

Of course, physical destruction was not the only reason for Southern income to fall behind that of the rest of the nation. There was immense destruction of human capital also. Military casualty figures available for the Confederacy are of poor quality at best, but it is not unreasonable to use the estimate of a quarter of a million men either killed or severely disabled. This would amount to a little less than 5 percent of the white population of the Confederacy or slightly less than 3 percent if the freed slaves are included also. By this measure the loss does not appear to be more than marginal. However, this particular segment of the South's labor resources represented far more productivity to the civilian economy than any group of average composition. Almost all of them were men between the ages of eighteen and forty. As such they embodied a considerable investment in education, training, and experience which had prepared them—had the war not come along—to take on the most responsible and productive niches in the economy. In short, they represented a considerable portion of the investment in human capital in the South which had not yet been recouped and depreciated. So if the loss of labor resources is scaled upward by its relative contribution to the economy, it appears to be somewhat greater than the percentage might indicate.

There was also another major change in labor services in the South as a result of the war, namely, the abolition of slavery. On the face of it, the end of slavery should not have made that much difference in net output, merely in the distribution of the rewards from labor. While former owners would lose the wealth representing the future income they would otherwise have earned from slave labor, the freed slaves could now reap the complete returns for themselves. The conversion was more complicated than that, however, because the basic decision of how and when the freed slaves would work was now also shifted to them. Under slavery, the owners had reason to keep the slaves working extended hours as long as it did not severely reduce their productivity. In addition, they could impose forms of labor or organization distasteful to the slaves, such as the team system, if it resulted in higher productivity. The amount of free time and the types of conditions under which they worked made a difference to the slaves, of course, so that when they gained their freedom they made such considerations part of the package of benefits they bargained for when going to work. One predictable result was that when the freed slaves did resume work they generally worked fewer hours than they had before. This was particularly noticeable in the working patterns of recently freed black families. Under slavery the owner had an incentive to use the labor of all slaves, down to the least productive. To do so, elaborate systems of assignments were created so that the old, young, handicapped, and new mothers were all kept busy. After emancipation, this complete system of participation declined noticeably, especially among children and women. Liberation for the black women took the form of getting out of a job and into the home, not vice versa.

ECONOMIC CHANGE IN THE WARTIME NORTH

The Civil War was so large an event in the economy that it would have been difficult for any sector to have escaped its effect. The Northern economy did not experience the severe dislocation which the South did, but in certain ways it felt the conflict very keenly nevertheless. The primary impact on the North—as in the South—was that the war consumed large amounts of resources which would otherwise have been available for civilians. It might have been possible for these expenditures to have been made up out of initially untapped reserves. If considerable unemployment had existed at the beginning of the war, as it did at the onset of World War II, the output necessary for war could have come through fuller employment of resources and not from the existing civilian sector. Or a sizeable increase in productivity might have allowed a greater total output so that the civilian portion could have been maintained. But neither of these possibilities developed,[6] so the cost of war had to come out of the civilian consumption.

This opportunity cost of the war is so basic and inevitable that it is hard to deny its existence. Yet it has been frequently overlooked. For example, some scholars calculated real civilian incomes in the North during the war and, not

---

[6] Even if these escape routes from civilian sacrifice were to have developed, the war would still have been a net cost in that it would have reduced civilian consumption by that amount below what it otherwise would have been.

surprisingly, found that they fell. But from that point they jumped to the unwarranted conclusion that profits, or the income of other nonwage sectors of the economy, must have risen. This, of course, is assuming that the total amount of income available to the civilian sector was constant—which it was not. The reduction in the output available for civilians was so large and so general that both wages and profits were undoubtedly reduced. There have been accounts of individual fortunes made in the wartime industries but that is not necessarily representative of the average returns on all capital. One could readily contrast the profits of the munitions factories with the depressed condition of all the Northeastern cotton mills idled by the almost complete disappearance of their prime raw materials. As usual, the ambitious and the innovative can devise ways to improve their personal situation, but the average return to all resources in the economy is determined by the total output available to them.

Another comparison which seems to have masked the fall in real incomes in the wartime North has been the frequent and obvious one with conditions in the South. The fall in per capita incomes in the Confederacy was probably about three times as large as that in the North simply because the size of the war effort of both sides was about the same (if the damage to the civilian sector of the South is taken into account), but the South had only about one-third the populace among which to spread the burden. The contrast between the living standards of the two regions was particularly evident in the resources which could be made available to the respective armies. The Southern Army was habitually short of food; the soldiers were constantly supplementing their rations by gathering corn and apples from nearby fields. Many of the troops wore either the clothes they brought with them from civilian life or the discards they could pick up on the battlefield. The men often went without shoes and blankets. The mobility of the Army was restricted by a shortage of horses to pull field guns and wagons, and even those animals which were available were often weak from lack of forage. In short, it was war conducted on a shoestring.

Union soldiers griped about their field rations—as have apparently all armies—but by the standards of the day they were quite well fed. The Northern quartermasters took full advantage of that new form of preserving food, canning. The troops undoubtedly had more fish and shellfish and out-of-season vegetables than any land-based army before them. They were also well supplied with uniforms, blankets, and tents, so much so that Union officers frequently had difficulty in compelling them to take care of their equipment. They tossed aside blankets at the first sign of spring weather—and a long march—knowing that the quartermaster would supply them with replacements when it was necessary. One can make a good case that the Confederate army could have lived off the discards of its foe—and to some extent it did.

All this seeming abundance of available material does not mean that the economy which was supporting it was doing so effortlessly. Part of the Army's extravagance simply reflects any bureaucratic organization's tendency to consume all resources made available to it and not economize on them according to their true social value. In any case, the Northern war effort did come out of the real incomes of Northern consumers. The best available study of incomes in the wartime North indicates that during the peak of the war effort, from late 1862 to early 1865, real wages fell short of their immediate prewar level by about 15 to 20 percent.[7]

FINANCING THE NORTHERN WAR EFFORT

The North extracted the resources it needed to conduct the war out of the civilian economy in much the same way that the American government has usually financed its wartime operations: it borrowed the necessary purchasing power. It did impose a series of excise taxes and raise the tariff, but for the most part it raised revenue by printing money and issuing more debt. Since neither of these techniques directly diverts the real resources from civilian to military use, the process must take place indirectly. This was accomplished by the inflation which the enormous increase of these financial assets created. As prices rose, the real purchasing power of existing dollars fell, and therefore the civilian sector of the economy could not command as many goods and services as it had previously—thus releasing some of them to the war effort. Or to say it another way, while prices charged for goods and services rose by an average of 125 percent over the course of the war, the dollar value of average income rose by only about 80 percent to 90 percent, and therefore the amount of goods which could be purchased fell correspondingly. The North did *look* quite prosperous during the Civil War. There was full employment, buoyant demand, and little of the dislocation which plagued the Southern economy. Yet the usual signs of prosperity can be deceiving. The best measure of economic welfare is real income, and despite appearances to the contrary, it fell during the conflict.

THE WAR AND POSTWAR GROWTH

The Civil War has often been treated as a great watershed in American history. According to common reports, it instituted major changes in the financial, industrial, and social organizations of the economy. One must be careful in accepting such judgments, however. Changes were already taking place at a relatively fast pace even without the war, and therefore the question should be posed as to how much *net* difference the war made other than that which would have occurred anyway. For example, it was during the Civil War that the American merchant marine clearly lost the competitive advantage which it had held for nearly two centuries in transporting goods between nations. It is easy to blame the war for this transition in that a good many American ships were destroyed during the fighting, and domestic shipbuilding activities were preempted by military construction. At the end of the war much of the American component of internation-

[7] Ruben A. Kessel and Armen A. Alchain, "Real Wages in the North during the Civil War: Mitchell's Data Reinterpreted," *Journal of Law and Economics,* vol. 2, October 1959. Reprinted in condensed form in Robert W. Fogel and Stanley L. Engerman (eds.), *The Reinterpretation of American Economic History,* Harper & Row, New York, 1971.

al shipping had disappeared, and ever since it has failed to retake most of the share it lost.

Yet it seems unlikely that the war performed the shift all by itself. If shipping had continued to be as profitable for the Americans as it had been before the war, they could—and undoubtedly would—have simply resumed buying and operating ships in the international trade. That they did not indicates that something more basic had been altered. Actually the transition was evident well before the war began. Ocean shipping was undergoing a major transformation as such new technologies as metal hulls and steam propulsion, and changing relative costs such as greater capital intensity, worked their way into the pecuniary decisions of potential shipowners. In terms of costs, the decline of America's position in international shipping had been evolving for several decades before the Civil War. For a while this had been masked by the dramatic appearance of the clipper ships. These might have appeared as the ultimate in American technology and competition, but actually they were only a specialized, rearguard action in a losing war. The clipper ships were graceful and fast, but at the cost of much higher unit costs in carrying cargo. In this sense they were the counterpart of air freight today: an expensive means of shipping goods, which is only justified for that limited range of products where speed or high value (which would be felt in inventory costs) are particularly important. But even this niche of American shipping in the international market eroded as other types of ships gradually came to supply faster and safer services. The Americans' ability to compete in this market was waning well before the Civil War and would have disappeared even in its absence—which is another way of saying that the war did not really make any difference in the long run.

This examination of the effect of the Civil War on the economy could be extended by going through numerous other examples, some of which will be considered in other chapters concerning banking and retailing. However, the important point in each case is that it is not gross changes which matter but rather the net effect of the war on underlying economic trends. The war dominated the economy for more than four years. During that time there were numerous changes in technology, spending patterns, and the investments which implemented them. Many of these developments would have occurred with or without the war. Some took place in response to the fighting and would not have happened otherwise. Others—which we obviously cannot observe directly—would have occurred in peacetime but were suppressed when conflict developed. The net effect of the war, therefore, is the difference between these last two eventualities—what actually did occur compared with what might have otherwise occurred.

We can see this type of analysis in operation if we examine one more—and the most important—example of the war's possible impact on the economy. The Civil War has often been advanced as the great catalyst which permanently speeded up the long-term growth of the economy. The war effort, so the argument goes, developed a large market for certain manufactured products, thereby encouraging the creation of the production and marketing facilities to handle them. Many of these facilities continued in operation after the war was over, so it is easy to assume that the conflict was solely responsible for them. It is, however, possible to make a fairly objective test of this thesis. Thomas C. Cochran undertook this test by comparing what happened in the economy in the decade of the war with what happened in it both before and after that decade.[8] These adjoining periods do not provide exactly the precise contrast we need to make our comparison, but they do seem to provide a good approximation to it. By comparing the wartime decade with the established trends both before and after it, one should be able to obtain a pretty good measure of its impact.

A short look at Cochran's results, however, is enough to dispel any doubts about the adequacy of this substitute measure. His estimates clearly show that the economy grew in the decades both before and after the Civil War at a significantly higher rate than it did during the war decade. The latter decade stands out as a glaring, retarded exception to the established pattern of growth. It says that not only did the Civil War not speed up the long-term growth of the economy but it actually set it back—which is really not so surprising in retrospect. A good portion of the innovations and arrangements created during the war were created in response to special wartime conditions. Some of those advances might have been transferred to civilian or peacetime uses, but by their very design some would necessarily be lost when the conflict ended. Thus, the postwar economy would gain to some degree when the Union Army compiled a profile of the clothes and shoe sizes of its troops because manufacturers and merchants could use the profile for civilian requirements. But the resources the Army spent in measuring those men could have been used in peacetime by civilian entrepreneurs to acquire much the same information, but with the added advantage of learning what people would actually buy, as opposed to merely whatever the Army felt they needed and therefore issued to them. This example captures much of the essence of the impact of the war on the economy. Yet that portion of the gains which could be appropriated by the civilian economy was small, or at least less than it could have created on its own if left at peace. Thus, the war was a costly undertaking in any total accounting. Not only did it consume a large quantity of resources during its course but it left a legacy of reduced output in future years as well.

SUGGESTED READINGS

Andreano, Ralph (ed.): *The Economic Impact of the American Civil War,* 2d ed., Schenkman, Cambridge, Mass., 1967.

Cochran, Thomas C.: "Did the Civil War Retard Industrialization?" *Mississippi Valley Historical Review,* vol. 48, Spetember 1961.

Engerman, Stanley L.: "The Economic Impact of the Civil War," *Explorations in Economic History,* ser. 2, vol. 3, Spring 1966, reprinted in Robert W. Fogel and Stanley L. Engerman (eds.): *The Reinterpretation of American Economic History,* Harper & Row, New York, 1971.

[8] Thomas C. Cochran, "Did the Civil War Retard Industrialization?," *Mississippi Valley Historical Review,* vol. 48, September 1961.

Gilchrist, David T. and W. David Lewis (eds.): *Economic Change in the Civil War Era,* Eleutherian Mills-Hagley Foundation, Greenville, Delaware, 1965.

Kessel, Rubin A. and Armen A. Alchain: "Real Wages in the North during the Civil War: Mitchell's Data Reinterpreted," *Journal of Law and Economics,* vol. 2, October 1959, reprinted in Robert W. Fogel and Stanley L. Engerman (eds.): *The Reinterpretation of American Economic History,* Harper & Row, New York, 1971.

Industrialization, 1865–1914

Economists often view an economy as being composed of three major sectors: the primary sector, which includes agriculture and basic raw materials; the secondary sector, which consists of industry and turns out goods; and the tertiary sector, which consists of services—economic output which is not in the form of goods, such as education, medical care, or military activity. This system of classification is generally used to describe the changing composition of an economy as it develops. The usual pattern is to begin with a large primary sector, which then shrinks first as the secondary sector increases, and later as the tertiary sector also begins to expand. This characterization glosses over a good deal of the economic change within the sectors, however. For example, the primary sector is a composite of those activities in the economy which supply basic materials, some of which are foodstuffs and some not. Thus, although the consumption of wheat could be expected to decrease as income rose, this does not necessarily hold true for other materials, such as coal or copper ore.[1] The experience of a particular resource

---

[1] Indeed, the dividing line between raw materials and foodstuffs is not entirely clear. Some of the most important products of agriculture, such as cotton, flax, hemp, and the oils from soybeans and corn, compete more directly with other raw materials than they do with other agricultural products.

depends on the complex interaction of such forces as demand, technology, and location. Not infrequently growth enhances the importance of a particular raw material, including some rather esoteric and seemingly unlikely ones, as the following discussion will illustrate.

From 1830 to 1860 the amount of American shipping engaged in the whaling trade increased more than fivefold, from about 35,000 to almost 200,000 tons. The driving force behind this expansion was a growing demand for the various components which a whale yielded: whale oil for high-intensity lighting, such as street lights, railroad headlights, and lighthouses; sperm oil for making a good-quality lubricant which could withstand the heat and speed of operations of much of the new machinery coming into use at this time; and whalebone for providing both strength and flexibility for such varied uses as buggy whips and corset stays. But whatever their virtues in providing useful raw materials, whales had the distinct disadvantage of being limited in supply. Perched at the top of a complex pyramid of ocean life, their population was closely restricted by the size of the ocean itself. For a while the whalers were able to increase their yearly catch by simply expanding the area they patrolled. In the colonial period this meant such coastal waters as Nantucket Sound, where careless whales could be picked off close to port. By the early 1800s the search had expanded to much of the Atlantic Ocean. In the three decades before the Civil War, the ships from such ports as New Bedford and Nantucket were making voyages of a minimum of six months into the Pacific Ocean to locate their catches. Just before 1860 this territory was extended to the extremely cold and remote Bering Sea off the coast of Alaska. With this move, whalers were literally going to the ends of the earth to find their product—a 20,000-mile round trip from the American ports of the northeastern United States. Hence, whale products were an almost classic example of diminishing returns in operation. The demand for the product was making it increasingly scarce and therefore expensive. This, of course, was illustrated by the ever-greater distances whalers found it feasible to go for their product. It also set off a predictable search for substitutes for the increasingly expensive whale inputs. The most important of these efforts probably was the one devoted to finding a better form of illumination. In the 1840s a Polish scientist devised a type of lamp which could burn kerosene for fuel. This finding was pushed toward commerical feasibility in 1855 when a Yale chemistry professor, Benjamin Silliman, Jr., showed that petroleum could also serve as a lubricant. In that function, and in illumination as well, it was clearly competitive with existing alternatives. Oil was not difficult to find because for some time it had been a messy nuisance in mining operations, especially in mining for salt. It took nearly four years, however, before drilling techniques improved enough to produce the oil at commerically feasible levels.

Within two decades after 1860, kerosene had largely supplanted the pre-Civil War coal and animal oils. The notable exception to this trend was in the lighting of streets, or larger public buildings. There gas proved to be the most popular fuel because it did not require the extensive hand labor of filling and adjusting which the kerosene lamps did. Part of kerosene's popularity can be explained by the major gains in its production and distribution methods, which substantially lowered its cost. When Edwin Drake drilled the first successful oil well in 1859, it took several months—and considerable impatience on the part of his financial backers—before he hit oil at the depth of 69 feet. Clearly, drilling technology has been improved considerably since that time. (See Table 11-1.) The original up-and-down motion of the drill, much like a pile driver, was replaced by the rotary drill in the late 1800s. The bit and the well casing were improved as better grades of steel were developed. There proved to be tremendous economies in the distillation and transportation of petroleum products, a realization which helped to make John D. Rockefeller so successful in organizing the original Standard Oil Company. By 1880, deliveries from the fields to the refineries and from there on to the major markets had been shifted to specially constructed pipelines. These replaced the cumbersome initial method of hauling oil in barrels, with all the loading and unloading which went with it. They also drastically lowered the cost of transportation, in most cases by more than 80 percent.

At the same time economies were being achieved in the distillation of crude petroleum into usable products. It was not until the twentieth century that engineers learned to "crack" crude oil—that is, to rearrange its component molecules into new, more productive combinations—yet considerable progress was made in distilling it into its various natural parts. At first refiners were concerned only with obtaining kerosene, the so-called middle of the barrel, and considered the lightest distillate (naptha) and the heaviest ones (heavy oil and paraffin) as little

Table 11-1   Production of Crude Petroleum, 1859–1904 (quantities in thousands of 42-gallon barrels)

Year	Production	Year	Production	Year	Production
1904	117,081	1888	27,612	1873	9,894
1903	100,461	1887	28,283	1872	6,293
1902	88,767	1886	28,065	1871	5,205
1901	69,389	1885	21,859	1870	5,261
1900	63,621	1884	24,218	1869	4,215
1899	57,071	1883	23,450	1868	3,646
1898	55,364	1882	30,350	1867	3,347
1897	60,476	1881	27,661	1866	3,598
1896	60,960	1880	26,286	1865	2,498
1895	52,892	1879	19,914	1864	2,116
1894	49,344	1878	15,397	1863	2,611
1893	48,431	1877	13,350	1862	3,057
1892	50,515	1876	9,133	1861	2,114
1891	54,293	1875	8.788	1860	500
1890	45,824	1874	10,927	1859	2
1889	35,164				

Source: Adapted from U.S. Bureau of the Census, *Historical Statistics of the United States, Colonial Times to 1957*, Government Printing Office, Washington, D.C., 1960, p. 36.

more than trash. By 1880 much of the lighter grades were being converted into lubricating oil, which was particularly valuable as faster and heavier machinery outpaced such traditional lubrication materials as animal and vegetable fats. The refiners also found that the heavier distillates could be converted into heating or fuel oil, which proved to be particularly salable in those areas which were farthest removed from coal supplies. By 1900 a large part of the railroads and much of the home heating in California and the Southwest had switched to oil for fuel. This conversion was given further impetus after 1880 by the introduction of electricity, which began to erode the demand for kerosene and encouraged refiners to shift to progressively lighter grades of oil for fuel.

INDUSTRIALIZATION AS A PROCESS OF INNOVATIVE SUBSTITUTION

Most previous accounts of American industrialization in the latter half of the nineteenth century have tended merely to enumerate and describe the new industries of that period, supplying little in the way of explanation as to why those specific sectors, among the much wider range conceivable, emerged. Yet our above description of the oil industry suggests that this may be leaving out one of the most important elements in the story. New industries do not develop in a vacuum but must ultimately be based on being able to meet some human demand, and that in competition with alternative desires for the limited stock of resources which can be applied to them. Thus the rise of the oil industry is not explained by the sudden desire of people to have more petroleum per se. Most individuals would find that sticky, dirty liquid useless in itself, simply a nuisance to be disposed of. Petroleum *is* useful, however, for the services it can be manipulated to provide. In the period in question this included light, the demand for which was growing rapidly because of the increasing number of economic activities which were being moved indoors in response to industrialization and urbanization. Moreover, the general increase in incomes and communication had caused a large increase in the readership of newspapers, books, and periodicals, which led to a corresponding increase in the demand for home lighting by which to read them. Petroleum was also in demand because of its superior lubricating properties which allowed a given amount of machinery to turn out larger amounts of goods. Similar considerations applied to its use as heating oil. In some localities it was cheaper than coal because of the transportation resources it saved. And, as so many homeowners and janitors have learned since that time, it saved a lot of work in that—unlike coal—it did not have to be shoveled into the furnace.

These accounts of the whaling and petroleum industries suggest that it might be helpful to consider the other important growth industries of the post-Civil War period in the broader context. This is not to deny the traditional observation that considerable innovation and technological advance occurred in these sectors, but rather to look beyond that to see why it occurred. In retrospect it is not surprising that particular clusters of innovations developed, given the amount of effort which was put into devising them. In some cases, such as that of the electric light, it was widely recognized that a certain type of invention would be valuable, and numerous individuals went to work to try to develop it. Thus a complete explanation of industrialization in this period needs not only to account for the important sectors which developed, but also to explain why those sectors seemed so promising. Or to say the same thing in another way, this period of industrialization has often been associated with a number of well-known entrepreneurs, such as Carnegie and Rockefeller. (We shall have more to say about their roles later in this chapter.) Even if we grant such individuals a great deal of credit for developing the industries with which they were associated, the question remains as to why they did not apply their talents to other industries instead. Thus, whichever way we choose to approach the subject of industrialization after the Civil War, it is helpful to recognize the broader forces which were at work.

STEEL

By 1860 iron had become a sizeable industry in the economy and had captured a good portion of the market for construction materials once supplied by such items as wood and stone. Yet though iron was an improvement over traditional materials, contemporaries could still see ways in which it could be improved further. It was stronger than most forms of wood and more easily fashioned than stone, but it was also brittle and thick sections were necessary where strength was required. The alternatives available in this latter case were either to use tool steel, a very strong specialty metal used in cutting edges or silverware and produced only in small batches, or wrought iron, a form of processed iron in which strength was acquired by laboriously hammering out the carbon. Either method was expensive, and thus there was considerable experimentation in the 1850s to devise a strong, cheap grade of iron. These efforts led to a number of parallel breakthroughs almost simultaneously. In 1854 an American ironmaster, William Kelly, and an Englishman, Henry Bessemer, independently discovered that pig iron would burn and purify itself without exposure to further heat if air was forced through the molten metal. Kelly was ridiculed and ostracized when he reported his discovery,[2] but Bessemer was lauded and supported, so that today the familiar round converter of steel mills which embodied the principle he discovered is commonly known by his name. In 1858 another method of making steel, the open-hearth process, was developed. It looked much like a large bathtub which could be filled with molten metal. It had an advantage over the Bessemer converter in that the chemical composition of the steel could be controlled more precisely. Toward the end of the nineteenth century it came to be the dominant

---

[2] When Kelly told his wife of his finding she told him that he was mad, that iron obviously could not burn. She then called the doctor but that man, being more of an empirical type who believed what he could see, thought Kelly to be quite sound and the invention impressive. Nevertheless, the neighborhood generally ridiculed Kelly's work and forced him to conduct his experiments in the seclusion of the woods which, of course, seriously restricted his ability to make refinements in his apparatus. After a few frustrating years he committed suicide. The moral of the story is that if you have a good idea, take it to a place where they recognize it as such and give you the support to implement it.

form of steel production in the United States because of the control it allowed over the composition of the alloy steels, which were becoming common then, and because it used a larger range of ores than the Bessemer process could.

The steel these new methods produced combined the best qualities of wrought iron and tool steel. It was strong, but it had enough resiliency to bend while under pressure and then spring back. And it was substantially cheaper than available alternative materials. Part of this competitiveness came from the immediate gains in the introduction of steel making itself. A large part, however, came from refinements in other stages of the metal industry. The basic blast furnaces which converted the iron ore into pig iron were gradually made larger. In 1860 a blast furnace which turned out 100 tons a week was considered large. Two decades later furnaces were routinely turning out ten times that amount each week. And by World War I, output of 1,000 tons *per day* had been reached. (See Figure 11-1.) Some of these gains were accounted for by simply increasing the size of the furnaces, but a sizeable portion came from speeding up the flow of materials. Powerful fans were installed to recirculate the heat of the exhaust fumes and raise the temperature inside the furnace—which reduced the time it took to "cook" a batch of material. The movement of materials into and out of the furnace was speeded up—and considerable labor saved as well—by the extensive introduction of conveyers and hoists. The total result was that a furnace could turn out more processed materials over time and the cost per unit went down accordingly. The rolling mills which converted the hot steel ingots into the basic finished shapes, such as sheets and beams, were also enlarged and made more automatic. The "three high" mill, which allowed the rolling to be conducted in either direction— that is, back and forth without repositioning—became standard after the Civil War. Not only did it speed up the production of such routine products as rails but it also allowed more complex designs—such as the framing for bridges and large buildings—to be rolled rather than going through the laborious process of individual casting.[3]

To these gains at the mills should be added the improvements in the mining and transportation of the raw materials themselves. One of the most important trends in the period was the development of the Lake Superior ore beds. These beds replaced most of the scattered local supplies, such as those in Pennsylvania, which the industry had depended upon before the Civil War. At first, mining tended to exploit the more southernly ore deposits (in Wisconsin, as distinguished from the more recently used Minnesota deposits). These deposits had the advantage of being close to the lake ports but were deep enough in the ground to necessitate tunnel mining. The locus of mining tended to shift north, however, as the industry learned how to develop the ores of the Mesabi range, which lay close to the surface. This included the technology of strip mining the ore, as well as techniques of suppressing the huge amount of dust that the operation naturally created.

Whether the ore was taken from deep mines in Wisconsin or strip mines in

---

[3] A good discussion of these improvements can be found in Peter Temin, *Iron and Steel in Nineteenth Century America, an Economic Inquiry,* M. I. T., Cambridge, Mass., 1964.

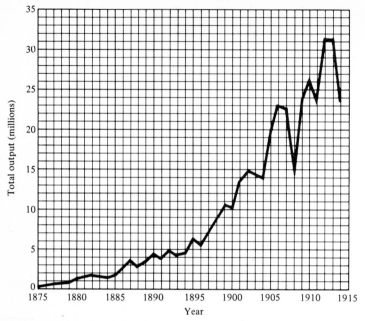

Figure 11-1 Physical output of steel ingots and castings, 1876–1914. *(Source: Adapted from U. S. Bureau of the Census,* Historical Statistics of the United States, Colonial Times to 1957, *Government Printing Office, Washington, D. C., 1960, p. 416.)*

Minnesota, however, it was carried to the mills on what was evolving into an extremely cheap system of transportation—the Great Lakes ore trade. By 1860 it was becoming evident that ore carriage from the Superior ranges was going to be both permanent and sizeable, and as a result shippers began constructing boats which were specially designed to handle that trade. What soon emerged was the classic design of the Great Lakes ore boat, now generally recognized by its distinct silhouette. The boats not only could carry large cargoes but were also built, in conjunction with the port facilities, to be able to load and unload them very rapidly. One measure of their efficiency was that by 1900 freight rates on ore had fallen as low as $1 a ton, which is to say only about one-tenth of a cent a ton/mile. Another measure of the strength of this effect was the tendency to relocate the steel mills to the edge of the Great Lakes. The late 1800s witnessed the establishment of the hugh mill at Gary, Indiana as well as major new facilities at Cleveland and Buffalo.

The Steel Eaters

There was no problem in selling the steel which began to come out of the new Bessemer facilities in the 1870s. Ever since the mid-1850s the railroads had been struggling with the dilemma that the increasing weight of the rolling stock which they found most profitable to operate was outpacing the strength of the track to support it. The iron rails then in use became flat and bent in a distressingly short time; in the case of the heavily traveled main lines that was as little as three years.

If someone could develop a stronger, durable rail, the railroads would be willing to pay a premium for it in order to avoid the replacement and inconvenience costs which the iron rails were imposing. Thus the American railroads purchased a large part of the output of the Bessemer mills in its first twenty years of operation; indeed, they also imported large quantities of steel rails from England both before and during the period when American mills began to turn them out.

By about 1890, however, a subtle shift in demand had begun to take effect. The demand for steel rails began to taper off because nearly all the rail network had been converted to steel track, and new construction slowed down because most of the promising markets for rail services were now served by established lines. Nevertheless, the total demand for steel continued to grow rapidly because other uses for it picked up even as the demand for rails slowed down. The new impetus was coming from sectors which are best summarized under the all-purpose category of *construction materials,* but which included two main groupings— stationary structures, and equipment. The former included office and factory buildings, bridges, tunnels, and utility systems. One can readily see the effect of urbanization in these items, particularly for the rapidly developing central business districts. (We shall consider this sector in more detail in Chapter 14.) The other major group consisted of machinery comprising the wide array of implements being devised to increase the output of products, particularly new ones. These included cranes, excavating and dredging equipment. elevators and conveyors, mining equipment, oil drilling and refining equipment, and electrical machinery.

Paralleling this increase in structural steel was a rapid expansion in production of steel wire which was used to make barbed wire and nails. The former was the cheap and durable solution to the problem of farm fencing which we discussed earlier (in Chapter 8). The latter was obviously a replacement for the square-cut nails made from iron sheets which had been used throughout the entire nineteenth century. The new model had the advantage of being cheaper to manufacture and, because of their shape, they yielded more nails per pound of material as well.[4]

After the turn of the century, another noticeable trend appeared in steel consumption, namely the widespread use of sheet steel as a construction material. It was first used extensively in the railroad-car industry. About 1880 steel began to replace wooden parts in freight cars, first in the frame and then in the body and doors. Passenger cars, which were so ornate in this period that they were frequently cited as examples of garish decoration, resisted the switch to more utilitarian materials until, after 1900, more attractive comparative costs caused them to begin to use more of the material. This conversion was reflected in railroad advertising for passenger traffic which began to neglect the status of travel and to emphasize the safety of steel coaches and their resistance to fires and wrecks. This shift from materials such as wood to steel was obviously moti-

---

[4] The steel nail was not an unmitigated improvement over the older square cuts. Their round shape made them easier to drive and less likely to split wood, but at some sacrifice in holding power. Such trade-offs were enough to fuel lunch-hour discussions among carpenters for decades.

vated by the decrease in the price of the latter. In 1880 engineers estimated that it would cost three times as much to build a steel car of a given weight as it would to build one of lumber. By the eve of World War I, however, the costs had become approximately equal so that the advantages of steel—such as greater durability and a greater net carrying capacity—proved to be decisive.

Similar considerations were at work in the other sectors which were also beginning to use large amounts of sheet steel. Office-equipment manufacturers were observing that the falling price of steel made it desirable to use more of that material in such items as filing cabinets, desks, and chairs. The new electrical-appliance industry found that steel was the best material to build such large items as washing machines and stoves, as well as the new smaller appliances, such as irons and fans. Just before World War I the rapid growth of the motor vehicle industry made it a major consumer of sheet steel. Its consumption of fenders, axles, panels, frames, and other assorted parts has continued to grow since that time, enough so that today it is the single largest user of steel products. The common element in all these adoptions of steel is that they are the end product of the complex productivity-increasing innovations in the industry which produced it. As the cost of producing steel fell—and soon thereafter the prices charged to consumers for it—the range of uses in which it was profitable to employ it increased dramatically. Cheap steel obviously supplanted some of the prevailing uses of such materials as wood, stone, iron, and clay. But it also had more far-reaching and less obvious effects, such as its effect on the spatial distribution of economic activities. The introduction of relatively cheap steel played a major role in encouraging such developments as high-rise office buildings and large water and sewerage systems in the big cities. This, in turn, allowed a compact concentration of people who could reinforce each other's productivity by sharing their skills. As a consequence, the density of people per acre in the central business districts of major cities during working hours rose to unprecedented levels. And, at the same time that cheaper steel was concentrating people in certain urban areas it was also making a good part of rural America even less populated. The twentieth-century outpouring of automobiles, trucks, buses, and tractors decimated the market for horses, and with them the market for hay, oats, and pasture. Probably one of the things that was least on the minds of the people who were working to devise cheaper methods of producing steel in the latter half of the nineteenth century was the spatial distribution of the population. But their efforts affected that important parameter just as surely as they did the things which were probably near the top of their concerns, such as capturing some of the markets—and profits—of existing materials.

THE ELECTRICAL INDUSTRY

The most obvious association with the term *electrical industry* is Thomas Edison and his light bulb. Like so many symbols of economic change, however, it oversimplifies the complexity and continuity of the actual situation. Electricity had been usefully employed long before Edison patented his light bulb in 1880. It was, of course, the basis of the telegraph introduced in the 1840s. It was also the transmitting agent of the telephone, which preceded the incandescent light bulb by several years. A major distinction between the electrical system developed to operate the light bulbs and its predecessors was the sudden, dramatic increase in the power required for lighting. The telegraph, and to a large extent the telephone, could be operated on storage batteries. Electric lights required a continuously operating dynamo which, in terms of the economies of operation involved, effectively required a central generating station and a system of wires to distribute the output.

Edison is best known for inventing the light, bulb, but in terms of the creativity involved, it was not one of his most original contributions. The possibility of creating an electric light had been generally recognized for some time before 1880, especially because so much effort was being spent in searching for improved forms of lighting. There was a series of major technological barriers which had to be cleared away first, however. The most obvious one was that almost every conceivable material which had been tested as a filament for the light oxidized; that is, it soon burned up in the presence of air. This problem was partly bypassed by the development of arc lighting, in which the light was created by the spark of an electric charge between two electrodes. Arc lighting was developed in 1810 but its immediate use was almost entirely confined to special attractions, such as expositions. It required a huge lamp, and its glare and flickering made reading by it unnerving. But by the 1860s, sufficient improvement had been made in the generators and arc units so that they began to be installed to light the downtown areas of big cities. They caused such a large increase in evening shopping that would-be inventors doubled their efforts in the search for a better form of lighting for what was by far the biggest market of all—indoor lighting.

Around 1870 an efficient vacuum pump was developed and that, probably more than any other single innovation, paved the way for the incandescent light, because with the oxygen removed from the light bulb the problem of oxidation was solved. This possibility had been generally recognized and had set off a widespread search for the materials and configuration which would work as a light bulb. Edison had a marked advantage at this point, not so much because of superior talent, but because of the large-scale facilities he had at his laboratory in Menlo Park, New Jersey. On the basis of his previous successes and royalties[5] from such inventions as the phonograph, and his major improvements to the telegraph, stock ticker, and telephone, he had been able to erect a complete research center and to staff it with nearly a hundred assistants. Edison simply solved the problem by sheer force of effort, testing at least 6,000 carbon materials before he found one that was satisfactory.

A working light bulb was only the beginning of the solution, however. Much like the story of the man who invented the tin can but then was in trouble until someone invented a can opener, Edison was compelled to develop a complete

[5] Edison was so highly regarded even before his invention of the incandescent bulb that when the word got out that he was working on the project, the stocks of gas-lighting companies dropped by large margins.

electrical power system in order to operate his new lights. Actually, he was well aware of this when he was searching for the material for the bulb filament, and had sketched out the elements of a total system including the generating plant, the power lines, and even the electric meters. Even so, there was still a great deal of improvisation to do as the first systems were installed. For example, consider the most basic part of the new system, the light bulb itself. While Edison had "invented" it, there still remained an enormous range of potential improvement in its operating characteristics. The first bulbs cost about $1.25 each to produce, but Edison estimated that in order to compete with established forms of lighting they would have to be offered at no more than 40 cents each. To offer them at that price he kept control over their production and absorbed the loss himself while he worked on reducing their cost to a profitable level. In the second year of production he pushed costs down to $1.10 a unit, in the third year to 50 cents, and in the fourth to 37 cents. When he had worked costs down to 22 cents each, he sold the manufacturing operation to concentrate on other research interests.

Edison's experience with the production of light bulbs illustrates the common "learning curve" in operation. There is usually a large amount of yet-unexploited potential improvement in new innovations, and the early work in developing them for commerical use usually taps sizeable amounts of that potential. Another example of this influence was the early design of electric circuits, a case where Edison came off rather poorly. His first power plants had delivered power by means of direct current, which unfortunately dissipated so rapidly in the friction of the lines that a power station could not deliver electricity for much more than a mile. If this state of affairs had continued it would have denied electricity to all except the larger cities, where customers were concentrated in a tight radius. This disadvantage caught the attention of George Westinghouse, who had already established a national reputation as the inventor of the railroad air brake and natural-gas delivery systems. Westinghouse knew enough about electric current to understand that a given level of power could be provided by different combinations of amperage and voltage, and that certain ranges of these suffered much less loss over a given distance than others. By taking advantage of transformers recently invented in Europe, he could vary the current over the line to reduce the loss of power, and yet operate at the appropriate level for either the production or the use of the current. This system saved large amounts of electricity and therefore the correspondingly large amounts of capital equipment it would take to produce it. It did, however, require a switch to alternating current in order to make the transformers work, and this prompted the "battle of the currents" between the Edison and Westinghouse systems. Westinghouse's methods soon dominated because of their marked advantage in costs, but not before some bitter comments had been leveled against them.[6]

While electricity was pioneered primarily to provide a better form of light-

---

[6] In one of his least laudable moments, Edison attacked alternating current as likely to cause death and injury through unspecified side effects. It was an incongruous attack on a new invention by a man who had done so much to create it himself.

ing, it was soon extended to a wide variety of uses. The small incremental cost of adapting it for other purposes, given that the electric lines were in place, encouraged a widespread search for such ways of using this new power source. The 1890s saw it being applied to a wide range of tasks in the household, including cooking, washing, ironing, cleaning, and refrigerating. This was to mark the beginning of the end for such picturesque but burdensome American institutions as the iceman, the washboard, the rug beater, and the starting of morning fires in the kitchen range. Outside the home, electricity's advantage in providing small, decentralized power sources was readily recognized. Electric motors could be used for those isolated applications where the then usual water- or steam-power systems would be too expensive to install. They also freed the layout of business enterprises from the tight strictures dictated by such centralized power sources so that they could be planned to facilitate the flow of materials or the organization of work, and not merely planned to cluster operations in such a way as to have access to the motive power.

One of the almost immediate applications of electric power was in urban transit. This was another of those pressure areas, such as lighting and railroad tracks, where the problem had become so obvious that numerous people were looking for a solution and some partial adaptations were being tried. Rapid urban growth was creating the need to move large numbers of people around quickly in the major cities. Horsepower, the traditional means of transportation, was just not up to the task. If everyone were to have traveled by carriage or coach, the volume of hay and oats consumed in the cities would have become immense and the traffic congestion debilitatingly severe. The horse-drawn trolley car was a marginal improvement but not a basic solution. The obvious next step was the railroad, but it had some severe drawbacks. If it were operated on tracks laid on the street like the trolleys, it would create a major noise and safety problem. If elevated lines were erected—as the famous Chicago El—the pedestrians were safeguarded, but the problems of noise were joined by the advantage the height conferred in depositing soot and smoke over the city. Another possible solution was to go underground, that is, to create a subway system. (This method looked particularly attractive to cities like New York, where Manhattan was surrounded by water and bridges were very expensive because they had to be high enough to clear the shipping on the rivers.) Tunnels, however, have their own problem of ventilation. Electricity seemed to be a good solution to all these handicaps. It was smokeless, noiseless, and sootless, and it did not require feeding, watering, currying, doctoring, and hitching up 100,000 horses every morning. Within a few years it had been adapted to trolley lines and elevated trains as well as to subways.

FURTHER REPERCUSSIONS

The effects of the introduction of electricity were not merely limited to a substantial reorganization of economic activities but went beyond that to affect the very basic materials which were available to them. Before 1880, copper had been a minor metal; its use was confined primarily to cases where its special ability to resist corrosion was important, such as in roofing or ship sheathing. But the demand created for it by the new electrical industry was enormous. Two and one-half miles of a single power line used a ton of copper,[7] and there were literally millions of miles of wire erected within a few decades, not to mention the large quantities installed in all the dynamos, transformers, and motors. These demands, coupled with those of the new telephone system, and later the automobile industry, created a major new industry. Copper output increased from merely 25,000 tons in 1880, to 130,000 tons in 1890, to almost 1 million tons annually by World War I. (We shall discuss the technological improvements which allowed this rapid expansion in the section which deals with mining.)

While demand for inputs by the electrical industry almost single-handedly created the copper industry, its output was, in turn, the crucial input in creating another new industry. All the major metals developed up to 1890, except aluminum, had been economically and successfully refined by either heat or mechanical processes. Aluminum alone remained stubbornly locked into its ore until, in the 1890s, it was discovered that electricity was able to pry it free cheaply. This was the key to a new industry, because once the material was economically available, the properties of the metal naturally identified its own markets. It was corrosion-resistant, lightweight, and readily worked into thin or fine configurations. As such it soon began to replace steel in those applications where weight reduction was an advantage, such as in motor vehicles or railroad cars. Its ductability made it particularly useful as a packaging material, as evidenced by the number of beer cans and foil wrappers that are so immediately obvious in any American landfill these days.

PAPER

The rapid, widespread adoption of the electric light intensified one of the pressures which had encouraged that new form of lighting in the first place, namely, the growing demand for reading material. The number of newspapers, periodicals, and books turned out in the economy grew rapidly in the nineteenth century, particularly after 1840. The decades before the Civil War witnessed the introduction and rapid expansion of the "penny press," named for the usual price of a newspaper designed to appeal to a much larger market than the older, more expensive papers. The larger circulation and lower price were the joint product of a major innovation in printing newspapers. Before 1840, printing had been done by hand, with each sheet requiring a separate impression. A skilled pressperson, stopping to ink the press periodically, could turn out perhaps 1,000 single-page copies in a day's work. The simple arithmetic of labor costs and production runs dictated that such newspapers would serve a relatively limited clientele. But then the rotary printing press was devised, which was able to turn out large numbers

---

[7] That was the consumption rate for the first few years of the electric power industry. In later years, the usual learning process had achieved much more productivity in the use of that material by squeezing more current flow out of each wire.

of copies in a short time. (In the process the newspaper not only moved to serve a larger audience, but it also shifted more toward coverage of recent news. Earlier reporting had covered longer periods, much like a modern news magazine.) By 1860 the best presses were capable of turning out 25,000 copies of a paper in one hour.

One generally unappreciated effect—except possibly by the newspaper purchasing agents—of this transformation of newspapers was a huge increase in the demand for, and the price of, paper. In those days the prime input in the production of paper was cloth rags, and the price of rags soon increased. This tended to make Americans somewhat better dressed in that it increased the payment they received for their discards and thus encouraged them to trade up to newer clothes more often. That slowed, but did not reverse, the upward pressure on paper prices, and predictably it encouraged individuals to begin to look around for substitutes. The major success among these efforts was the invention of the sulfite process in the 1860s, which was a technique of making paper out of wood by breaking down and rearranging the fibers. After refinements made this process commercially feasible, it created a major increase in the economic resources which could be used in the paper industry. Before, inputs had been limited to whatever portion of the textile industry output survived depreciation in its original, intended function. Afterward, the paper industry was capable of converting a good portion of the forests into its raw material.[8]

THE CHEMICAL INDUSTRY

The sulfite process in the paper industry symbolized another important emerging industry, that of chemicals. A good example of this new emphasis is common salt, which for thousands of years had been used mostly as a meat preservative. Then, beginning in the late 1700s, individuals began to realize the possibilities of using its individual components sodium and chloride, separately. This process was encouraged considerably in the 1860s when the Solvay process was perfected. It was able to make soda ash, an important input into both soap and glass, out of common salt. This, in turn, created a much larger demand for salt and fostered new techniques of acquiring it beyond the traditional methods of mining and the evaporation of sea water. The most important of these was a method whose basic principle was adopted in the mining of several other chemicals about this time. It consisted of pumping steam down into the salt beds so that the heat

---

[8] There is an interesting parallel between the experience of the paper industry in the nineteenth century and that which occurred about 600 years before. In the earlier case the causation was reversed but similar forces seemed to be at work. About the twelfth century there were some substantial gains in textile production, which lowered both its cost and that of paper also. Soon thereafter eyeglasses were invented, which greatly enlarged the market for reading material, especially among the elderly. The pressure then shifted to the book industry, where by far the largest cost of production was the labor of the scribes, who copied the books by hand. Predictably, considerable effort was put into devising methods of mechanical copying, of which Gutenberg's printing press is the well-known result. A very knowledgeable account of these events, among others in the period, are recounted by Lynn White, Jr., in his "Technological Assessment from the Stance of a Medieval Historian," *American Historical Review,* vol. 79, no. 1, February 1974.

and pressure it created would force the salt—in molten form—back to the surface. The only drawback was that this system required large amounts of heat so that only those locations where cheap fuel was available could be considered. As it happened, nature had been fortuitously kind in that salt domes were often located near petroleum deposits—indeed, that is how the latter were often discovered. It was doubly lucky in the fifty-year period after the Civil War in that fuel oil was often a marginal product of petroleum distillation and thus was generally cheap.

The other major chemical to come into prominence in this period was sulfur. Its primary use was in sulfuric acid, which in turn was important in a host of products which were rapidly expanding, including fertilizer, petroleum, paper, rubber, and insecticides. Until the late 1800s, most sulfur was obtained from sulfur pyrites, usually imported from such distant sources as Spain. When exploration for petroleum got under way along the Texas and Louisiana coasts around the turn of the century, however, large deposits of relatively pure sulfur were found. Unfortunately, almost all of it was well below ground level where the use of conventional mining techniques was much too expensive.[9] But then engineers devised a variant of the salt-recovery method which worked for sulfur. It consisted of forcing both hot water and air pressure down into the sulfur beds through a pipe which also had a separate channel by means of which the molten material returned to the surface. The new technique became known as the Frasch process, after one of its most important originators. Its success reduced the cost of sulfur and encouraged the widespread adoption of sulfur derivatives in industrial processes.

THE MINING SECTOR

The Frasch process and the parallel developments in the extraction of salt were actually only a small part of a general effort under way in this period to increase the supply of minerals. This is perhaps not so surprising in that many of these raw materials were important inputs into some of the most important growth industries. Yet in terms of the value of output, the mining industry grew even faster than the manufacturing sector itself. The explanation is that not only were the mineral supplies being used in the new industries, but they were also carving out a good share of certain established markets as well. For example, by far the most important raw material in the American economy before the Civil War was wood. It was used both as a building material and as fuel. In 1860 the majority of homes were heated by firewood and the majority of railroad locomotives were still fueled by it. Even by this time, however, coal was obviously capturing an

---

[9] Notice the parallel here between the development of sulfur, which initially was a nuisance in the way of petroleum drilling, and that of petroleum itself—which was at first a substance which ruinously seeped into salt mines. Materials which at one time were noneconomic (or worse, if they required the use of other economic resources to get them out of the way) have often been converted into economic resources at a later time. The incentive to do so is heightened by the element that the innovation not only gains the services of the resource but eliminates the cost of disposing of the otherwise troublesome item as well.

increasing portion of these markets. It provided much more heat content relative to the volume of space it occupied and thus tended to become the favored fuel when it had to be transported any distance. (And this latter circumstance was just the situation which was developing in much of the economy after 1860—namely, the location of wood supplies and the population were generally moving farther apart.) Similarly, the use of lumber as a prime construction material in buildings, machinery, and bridges was being eroded by the increasing use of such materials as iron and steel. Its output barely kept up with growth of the population in the period between 1865 and 1914—a time when the total volume of economic output was expanding at several times that rate.

The explanation for this twofold expansion of the mineral sector can be found in the same basic cause. There was considerable innovation in the industry during the period, which substantially raised its productivity and made its products more competitive with existing alternatives. Part of this surge of development was undoubtedly encouraged by the rising demand for these raw materials by the emerging industries, and the prospect of the larger opportunities which they created. But then some of this innovation would undoubtedly have occurred in the absence of any rapid surge in the demand for raw materials. Some of the new techniques were simply the application of general improvements, such as power sources or mechanization, to this specific industry.

Although it may be difficult to sort out the precise motivation for the improvements in mining, its resulting form and impact are more obvious. Before the Civil War most minerals were taken out of the ground by what was called *open-pit mining,* a process of digging large holes in the ground. Today we might be tempted to call such operations *strip mining,* but the earlier operations were generally so much smaller that they were different in kind. They lacked the massive application of mechanical power which characterizes most modern operations. In the mid-1800s most of the digging, loading, hauling, and lifting were done by hand labor. Steam power had been successfully applied to some operations, such as drainage and hoisting, but it was generally a cumbersome and inflexible medium for mining purposes. Its drawbacks at that time, for example, accounted for the limited use of tunnel mining.[10] It was much too dangerous to use a steam engine inside a mine because the boiler would ignite mine gas any time it reached a critical level. The alternative of operating the engine at the mouth of the mine and transmitting the steam through pipes was prohibitivly expensive because of the large losses of heat by the time it could reach the working area. Thus, steam power was confined to the face of the mine and tunnel mining was correspondingly restricted compared with modern operations. Improvement in the situation

---

[10] The choice between tunnel mining and strip mining is strongly influenced by the relative costs of the two operations. Surface mining generally requires the removal of more overburden, or waste earth; the tunneling method is more selective in that it can directly follow the veins. It is more expensive than open-face mining per ton of burden removed, however, so that mining engineers are always comparing the two costs when deciding which method to employ in a given situation. For example, the general switch from pit mining to tunnel mining of bituminous coal after the Civil War can be explained by the faster decrease in the cost of tunnel mining during that period.

came in the 1880s with the introduction of compressed air, which used much the same principle that was then being applied to making railroad braking safer. For the first time it provided mechanical power to drill and haul ore at the working face of the mine, some distance removed from the entrance. The mechanization was further aided by several other developments: the invention of the Ingersoll rock drill, improvements in the drilling bits (largely because of better alloys of steel), and the replacement of black powder by dynamite.

Mechanization of underground mining operations received a further boost near the turn of the century when electricity was adapted to mining uses. It was somewhat more flexible as a power source in that it did not require the extensive system of pipes, hoses, and compressors to supply the air-driven equipment. It also had the advantage that it allowed the introduction of a better spark-free lighting source in the mines, a seemingly constant problem in mining history until then. With electricity in place in the mines, efforts were soon under way to utilize it to take over the full range of strenuous tasks involved in mining. This included cutting, loading, transporting, and lifting the material, as well as the traditional tasks, such as draining and ventilating. In the process, the productivity of these operations increased so much that most raw materials became cheaper (for a more detailed treatment of this process, see Chapter 15). And that, in turn, explains how an industry such as coal was able to grow even faster than industry in general. It not only was able to improve the delivery of its product sufficiently to keep up with the demands of the growing manufacturing sector for raw materials, but also—overpowering any diminishing returns in operation—to increase its sales at the expense of traditional materials, such as wood.

The Special Challenge of Copper

While considerable progress was being made in the process of getting ore out of the ground more efficiently in this period, special problems had to be solved in processing certain kinds of ore once they were above ground. Copper ore is a notable example. Unlike coal and iron ore, which were available in relatively pure form, most copper ore was relatively dilute. Ores which contained concentrations of greater than 5 percent were rare and were soon exhausted in the nineteenth century. There were sizeable supplies of ores in the 0.5 percent to 4 percent range but these were noneconomic unless someone could devise a better way of extracting the copper. The bright idea appeared in the form of the flotation process, which seemed to defy the usual laws of physics. Normally, heavier elements—the copper component of the ore in this case— work their way to the bottom of a mixture, if they are somehow agitated. The flotation process forced them to the top of a water bath by mixing the ground ore with oil and then blowing air bubbles through it. The copper ore could be skimmed off in sufficiently high concentrations to make the last step of refining by roasting worthwhile. By World War I this step had been sufficiently perfected so that ores as low as 0.5 percent copper could be economically processed.

Another major improvement in the copper-mining industry was the adoption of open-pit mining, much like that being simultaneously developed for iron ore. This was almost imperative if the industry was to handle the low-concentrate ores which were becoming its prime input with the flotation process. The net cost of copper would have become prohibitively expensive if 50 tons of material (at prevailing tunnel rates) had to be hauled out of the shaft for each ton recovered. The copper industry solved the problem by adopting a cross section of the heavy machinery which was being developed at this time. This included large steam shovels to scoop up the ore, special railroad trains of hopper cars which ran right into the pits to receive the ore directly from the steam shovels, and huge crushers to grind the ore into a fine consistency for flotation. With the exception of the crushers the operation was very similar to that adopted in iron-ore operations of the Mesabi range.

Thus, it is fairly clear that major strides were being made in both surface and underground mining in this period. If we recall the advances in the various forms of liquid mining, such as oil and sulfur, which we discussed earlier, it becomes fairly certain that these advances were occurring across the board in the extraction industries. At the same time that some industries were finding ways to use more of these minerals, the industries which were supplying them were finding ways to increase their supply. The net result was that in most cases, despite the rapid increase in the consumption of these minerals, the quantity available for future use actually increased. This, in turn, brings us to the final, important point to be drawn from the experience of the mining sector. It seemed to be responsive to the same incentives for improvement which characterized the manufacturing sector; indeed, it was even more successful than the latter in this regard. This reaffirms a point we noted in our discussion of the antebellum period. Growth results not necessarily from industrialization, but rather from the more basic and universal motive of people wanting to improve their position, whatever their activity. The mining sector demonstrated this by outgrowing the major growth sector, manufacturing.

MEANWHILE, BACK IN THE OLDER SECTORS

Much of the above discussion focused on the newer industrial sectors which emerged in the fifty years after the Civil War. Certainly a fair amount of interesting economic change occurred in those sectors, and yet that should not blind us to the important developments which were simultaneously going on in the remainder of the economy. There was, for example, the experience of the textile industry, the economy's well-known growth sector of the antebellum period. While it no longer commanded as much attention as an example of the changes which were under way in the economy, it still continued to behave in much the same way as it had when it was in the spotlight. Textile managers continued to improve their positions through the usual variety of approaches—reducing production costs, devising new products, seeking a better location for the factory, or changing the organization of the marketing system. The net result of this total collection of efforts was an increase in productivity just as surely as if the industry had been in its earliest years.

There was, by way of example, continuing improvement in the basic spinning and weaving processes. Labor productivity was increased by continual mechanization and automation of the mill operations. The most dramatic of these steps was the introduction of the Northrup automatic loom in 1890. It completed the system whereby the weaving machinery ran completely by itself unless something went wrong, in which case it shut itself off and waited for an operator to correct the problem and start it again. This tripled the number of looms attendants could cover—as well as their productivity—in that it was no longer necessary to be within an arm's length of a loom to prevent a mass of tangled yarn when a thread broke.

Similar changes were occurring in the products of the mills. The long-term shift from woolen to cotton fabrics that was initiated in the antebellum period resumed after the interruption of the Civil War. Even within the woolen sector itself the shift toward lighter material was evident, with an increasing proportion of the industry's output going into worsteds. The influences causing the shift toward lighter-weight clothing—which undoubtedly included the shift away from outdoor and heavy manual work—were also evident in the increase of materials such as silk and knit goods.

At the next step closer to the consumer, where the cloth was converted into apparel, changes were also underway. In the decade before the Civil War the sewing machine had been introduced, and some progress had been made in establishing a ready-made clothing industry. Most of such earlier products, however, were obviously inexpensive, utilitarian, and bought for heavy manual labor or for slaves. After the war, the industry gradually turned toward products of greater variety and quality until it had taken a good share of the clothing market away from home sewing. This was particularly true of men's clothing, where nearly 90 percent of production was commercialized by World War I. A large portion of women's and children's clothing also was shifted to commerical production, although the conversion in these sectors was not as rapid, possibly because these forms of apparel were somewhat more individualized.

These last-mentioned adaptations of machinery in the industry were a large part of the reason for the increase of productivity and the consequent ability to capture a sizeable share of the market from household sewing. The diffusion of the sewing machine, which had been introduced before the Civil War, continued, and its rate of output was considerably increased by the introduction of power units to replace the original foot treadle. And, as usually happens to a major innovation such as the sewing machine, its applications were gradually widened and specialized. Special models were developed for such specific operations as making buttonholes and sewing on the buttons. Other labor-intensive steps of production, such as cutting and pressing, were also mostly mechanized in this period. Direct comparisons of labor in clothing are difficult to make for this time because of variations in the product itself. In shoe manufacturing, however, where the product remained fairly uniform and a similar pattern of mechanization occurred, the amount of labor spent on a single pair of shoes fell by about 90 percent.

Obviously, there is a good deal more we could say about industrialization in this period. We have not given any detailed consideration to the machine-tool industry, which continued in much the same pattern of growth and innovation as we recounted in Chapter 6 for the antebellum period. Nor have we considered such important individual inventions as the camera or the typewriter. Yet we have examined enough of the individual sectors in enough detail to grasp some of the important ongoing changes. And that, rather than any encyclopedic coverage of the subject, is the important aspect. The intended function of history to provide illumination by identifying the important relations in past events in detail is helpful only if it contributes to that end. We shall leave the task of compiling the total description to the archivists.

INDUSTRIALIZATION: THE TOTAL RECORD

In 1859, on the eve of the Civil War, agriculture accounted for more than half of commodity output[11] in the United States. Manufacturing had come a long way since the beginning of the century but was still a distant second at 32 percent. (Construction at 12 percent and mining at 1 percent completed the commodity sector.) Forty years later, in 1899, the positions of these two major sectors were almost exactly reversed. Manufacturing commanded 53 percent of output while agriculture contributed 33 percent. (The rapid growth of the mining sector is shown by the more than fourfold increase in its commodity share to 4.6 percent.) This gain in the relative share of output by manufacturing clearly indicates its status as a growth sector, but this is even more evident in the total value of manufacturing output—which increased from $860 million in 1859 to $6.26 *billion* in 1899.[12] This sevenfold gain in the value of manufacturing output occurred in a period when the total population of the economy increased by only about two and one-half times. Thus the output of manufactured goods per person rose by a factor of almost 3 during these four decades. (This gain in output per capita did not take place at the expense of other sectors; all major groups, including agriculture, increased their output faster than the population increased.)

The changes which were taking place in the industrial sector were not unique, of course, but rather were symptomatic of an economywide increase in the output per person. This can be seen in the measures of per capita income which are available for this period. For the forty years from about 1870 to 1910, per capita incomes rose from about $225 to $600 per year. Even manufacturing's

---

[11] Commodity output consists of "countable" physical goods, such as bushels of wheat or tons of steel. It does not include service output, such as that provided by barbers, school teachers, or the government. It is used to approximate GNP in earlier years when records of service output were not kept. Commodity output averaged about 40 percent to 45 percent of total GNP over the period so that our comparison of the positions of agriculture and manufacturing within the commodity sector would seem to be reasonably representative. It can overstate the relative importance of the commodity sector—or a portion thereof—to the extent that the service sector grows at a faster pace.

[12] These values are all in 1879 prices. They were compiled in *Historical Statistics of the United States, Colonial Times to 1957*, Government Printing Office, Washington, D. C., 1960, p. 139. Like a good portion of the estimates of nineteenth-century American output, they were painstakingly constructed by Robert E. Gallman.

rapid rise in the economy could account for only a fraction of this total increase. The source of this growth had to be something more than just the act of industrialization.

Our above discussion of manufacturing suggests that much of that augmenting influence probably occurred in the form of technological improvements in production. Indeed, that was an important factor, as many of the recent studies investigating the sources of growth have tended to indicate. And yet one of the more traditional explanations has also staged a comeback in recent years. Classical economists commonly considered capital to be the prime explanation of growth. Since about 1950 this factor has been downgraded because of a series of studies showing the primacy of technological improvement and improving markets in modern growth. But many of these studies were made for recent periods when growth rates were quite high by historical standards, so it is possible that other sources of growth might be overshadowed, even though they could appear to be larger in periods when the total growth rate was lower. Capital is one such candidate, and in a recent, sophisticated study, Jeffrey G. Wiliamson shows that its role has been very much underestimated in the period we have been considering.[13] He examined the notable increase in the savings rate during the Civil War decade and demonstrated that it had lasting effects on the growth and composition of the economy for the remainder of the century. For reasons not yet adequately explained, the rate at which income was saved—out of total gross output—suddenly shifted upward to a new level half again as large as the rate of about 15 percent which had seemed to be well established before 1860. Whatever its origin, Williamson was able to simulate its consequences, which proved to be surprisingly persuasive. The higher rate of saving was directly translated into a larger yearly flow of capital into the economy, which in turn began to make it more abundant in relation to the other major categories of resources—land and labor. It was against this latter group that the effects were most obvious. The increased flow of new capital encouraged a greater use of mechanization, or what today is commonly called automation. Equipment was more frequently substituted for labor simply because the cost of capital goods appeared favorable to the individual manager. If we look back over our above account of developments in the industrial sector with this in mind, we can see that such a trend did seem to be under way. While it is natural to attribute much of the new machinery put into use to the objective of getting the new technology in operation, it may also be reflecting the relative attractiveness of using large quantities of that item. Some new investment may have been inevitable, given the rate at which the new innovations they embodied were occurring, but the speed with which they were put into place was certainly affected by the cost of capital. A good example of this distinction is probably seen in the adoption of open-pit mining in the copper and iron-ore industries. While this pattern was obviously possible only with the development of heavy equipment—which is to say, such inputs as cheap steel and

---

[13] Jeffrey G. Williamson, *Late Nineteenth Century American Development: A General Equilibrium History,* Cambridge, London, 1975, Chapter 5.

efficient steam engines—it was also undoubtedly encouraged by the cheaper cost of using such equipment as compared with hiring thousands of men to toil away with shovels and wheelbarrows.

One other important trend has received new attention as a result of Williamson's investigation of the effect of higher savings rates after the Civil War. Some scholars had previously noted that although the growth in per capita income slowed down somewhat in the two decades or so before World War I, the increase in the return to the average worker held up somewhat better. Williamson's analysis now explains this effect. As larger quantities of capital were used in conjunction with each worker, the latter's product tended to rise faster than the general increase in productivity in the economy. A corollary of this effect was that the return on capital tended to decrease during the period as its marginal contribution to output was gradually driven down by the use of progressively larger amounts of it. This tendency for the return of labor to rise relative to that of capital in the period from roughly 1880 to 1910 is interesting for at least two reasons. First, this was the period during which the largest amount of immigration into the economy occurred, with entrants topping 1 million in several years. This was more than 1 percent of the then current population and, given the slowing down in the natural rate of increase of the domestic population, accounted for a sizeable share of the total increase in the economy as well. This influx into the national labor supply was coming at a time when the returns to labor were generally rising and was undoubtedly at least partly a result of it. It was also accompanied by a rising chorus of domestic protest to such unlimited immigration as, it was often worded, "a threat to American labor." Actually it was not so much the earnings of domestic workers which was threatened as the extraordinary gains they stood otherwise to reap because of the increasing capital intensity of the economy's production structure.

This period was also marked by increasing protests against the "trusts, monopolies, and exploiters of the public" who were seen to be imposing heavy costs on consumers and the working class. (We shall return to this issue shortly.) Such charges still remain to be verified—after almost a century of trying to do so—but if there is substance to them it comes with an ironic twist. The period of the "trusts" was marked by a shift in the division of income toward labor and away from capital. If the monopolists were indeed taking some of labor's fair share away from them, it would have had the effect of shifting the share of labor income back toward its "pretrust" level.

ROBBER BARONS

In 1934 Matthew Josephson wrote a book whose title, *The Robber Barons,* has become almost a household name. He was attempting to characterize a number of prominent, wealthy businesspeople who dominated their industries around the turn of the century. His title was certainly meant to include such individuals as Andrew Carnegie in steel, John D. Rockefeller in oil, J. P. Morgan in finance, and a host of railroad operators such as Jay Gould, Edward H. Harriman, Collis

P. Huntington, and Cornelius Vanderbilt, among others. The title clearly conveyed Josephson's view of the economic role these men played in the economy. They were robbers in that they were taking something other (or something more) than that which rightly belonged to them, and they were barons in that they held unchallenged sovereignty over their realms. Needless to say, the phrase has become so commonplace because it articulates a theme which has commonly appeared in historical accounts ever since the time when the "robber barons" were themselves active.

Yet when one attempts to examine the role of these individuals in a detached, analytic way, the issue is neither simple nor obvious. One major problem is that such terms as power, exploitation, or monopoly have seldom been carefully defined and different commentators have tended to use them in quite different ways. Another barrier to fruitful investigation is that the dimensions of the question have never been spelled out precisely. Who, for example, *is* a robber baron (and, implicitly, who is not), and within what time period is their influence confined? We cannot pretend to answer all these questions here; that will require considerably more diligent work by scholars of the subject, but we can put the issue into a more rigorous framework and that, by itself, will make the dimensions of the question more intelligible.

Underlying much of the previous discussion of the robber barons is the concept of economic power. It is central to any assessment of their roles and yet has usually been used only implicitly. A good many accounts of the robber barons assume that such individuals possess vast power as a direct result of either their wealth or position. Thus, if Carnegie owns a steel company whose market value equals $200 million, or if J. P. Morgan and his associates sit on the boards of directors of eighteen large companies, that is taken as prima facie evidence of their power. But it is important to distinguish between *size* (or management thereof) on the one hand, and *power* on the other. The former does not necessarily dictate the latter. Presumably, power means the ability to choose between a number of alternatives. One can be formally in charge of many assets and yet not have much effective choice as to how they can be deployed.[14]

The prime constraint on the operations of economic units in America is, of course, the markets within which they operate. No matter whether it is steel, or canned peas, or contemporary posters, if a product cannot command enough for its sales to repay the going rates on the resources it requires, it cannot survive for long. In short, profitability is the basic constraint on economic power in the marketplace. Unless an entrepreneur operates within the range in which his activities meet that basic test, his ability to operate at all within the economy will soon be reduced. Losses mean direct losses in the assets with which that unit has the ability to maneuver—or to exercise its power—in the next period.

---

[14] Robert Solow (of M. I. T.) has told the story of the young couple who allocated decision-making responsibilities in the household. He was to make the "big decisions" and she the "little ones." The big ones concerned such questions as whether China should be admitted to the U. N. and whether underground nuclear testing should be banned. The small ones concerned how the family money should be spent and how the children were to be raised. This lighthearted account illustrates the point that *formal* and *effective* power can be very different things.

This point is quite important, enough so that it deserves further amplification. The story about John D. Rockefeller's tactics in gaining dominance in the oil industry has become almost a stock item of folklore. He is reported to have cut prices in those areas where he encountered competition, to drive the competition out of business, and to have made up the losses by raising prices in those areas where he had already eliminated the competition. Thus, the common account goes, he was able to systematically gain dominance of the entire industry by virtue of the presumably large stock of capital he held when he started this predatory behavior. Few listeners seem to have ever stopped to examine the logic of this account, however. If they had, it is doubtful that it would have ever gained such widespread currency. While it may be possible to drive out the competition through systematic price cutting, it is another thing to keep it out. Unless Rockefeller had some special device to prevent competitors from returning to "cleared" areas, he would have incurred losses which he could not expect to recoup, even if he was making above-normal profits in other locations.

In fact, when scholars looked at the price behavior of the early Standard Oil Company, they found active price cutting to be the exception. Sometimes the prices of the Rockefeller organization were below those of their competitors, but that did not mean that they were losing money on those sales; in the formative stages of the industry they were often producing and delivering oil products at lower cost. Historians who have looked at the industry during this period have also noted that Rockefeller bought out many of his competitors rather than drive them out and, interestingly enough, many of those competitors came to Rockefeller to *ask* him to buy them out without any noticeable pressure on his part. This behavior is understandable on the part of both parties—if Standard Oil had a cost advantage. Independent owners would be ahead if they turned their facilities over to the superior Standard organization instead of losing their assets in a long, pointless struggle. Similarly, Standard Oil stood to gain by buying out competitors rather than duplicating their facilities and forcing them out of business through an extended period of competition.

Hence, Rockefeller, one of the most noted robber barons, seemed to follow our above guidelines that economic power must obey market realities. He did not use his productive holdings in frontal attacks on competitors or other wealth holders. Rather, he used his assets to make the most of his own position and although this would inevitably damage competitors sooner or later, it was basically a defensive strategy. It would be very surprising if he had not followed that basic approach. Earning power—which is synonymous with, and the source of, wealth—of that magnitude could be amassed only if the return on the economic assets used was above the prevailing rates. The exception to this statement is that capital can reach large cumulative levels if it is allowed to compound for long periods. In the case of the robber barons, however, their typical fortunes grew faster than that course would have allowed.

John D. Rockefeller, for example, often advised his associates to save 10 percent of their income each year, making their families wear some of last year's clothes if necessary. That might be a prudent guideline for household finance, but it would not acquire wealth on the scale associated with the robber barons.

Almost all of them, including Rockefeller, acquired the bulk of their assets through a different mechanism.

The typical course was to acquire—and hold—wealth in the form of ownership of a limited number of companies. Sometimes these began as small proprietorships, but usually they were converted into corporations with some stock offered to the public after they reached a large size. Thus, most of the wealth of the robber barons was created by increases in the market values of the companies they commonly managed and in which they held large positions of ownership. Their wealth came predominantly in the form of capital gains or huge increases in the going valuation of their companies.[15] Such increases are often considered somehow intangible and illusionary and are often dismissed as being merely "paper profits." They represent the quite tangible force of a claim on future profits, however, and are no less solid than the income one can reasonably expect from owning an apartment house—whose tenants might all move out of town— or of a civil service job—which could be cut out in the face of a taxpayers' revolt.

Thus the robber barons created most of their wealth—and, hence, whatever power they came to possess—by drastically increasing the flow of earnings of the companies they managed.

The question turns, then, to the issue of how these people could have created such large quantities of wealth within the constraints of a market environment. Economists recognize a variety of sources whereby an enterprise might make above-normal profits, but basically they fall into two major categories. One is the profits earned by providing a product which is more attractive, that is, the same item at a lower price or a better product at the same price. These might be considered "positive profits" for superior service in that, although the producers can make a larger profit, they do so by providing the consumer with a better package of goods. Such profits can come from pioneering methods which reduce the cost of producing a good, devising ways to extend its lifetime or range of functions or convenience (all of which are, in effect, ways of providing more goods at the same price), or improving the methods of merchandising and delivery. So, for example, Carnegie is primarily known for reducing the cost of producing an existing product—steel; Rockefeller is better known for innovations more toward the distribution and marketing end of petroleum products; and Henry Ford is remembered for introducing a new product (even though that admittedly involved innovations in production as well). The "negative" side of the road to wealth is earning extra profits through monopoly positions or market rigging. As economists have demonstrated—and the general public knows intuitively—monopolies, or trusts, make above-normal profits at the expense of the

---

[15] This process of capitalization is essentially the same thing that Adam Smith captured a few years ago in his book *Supermoney*. He pictured the creation of instant wealth when a privately owned, promising young company placed some of its shares of ownership in the public security markets. This allowed the initial owners much greater discretion in tapping the earning power they had created. One should note, however, that it is not "going public" per se (creating "supermoney," in Smith's terms) which creates the wealth, but rather it is a step which makes the enhanced earning prospects of the company more obvious and convenient to exchange. See Adam Smith, *Supermoney*, Random House, New York, 1972.

consumers (relative to a more competitive market environment). Firms, whose output is a sizeable fraction of the market, can alter the price in the market[16]—and thereby their profits—by changing the amount of output they offer for sale in a given period. The logical behavior for a firm with some monopoly power in a product line is to push up the price of that item in the market, thereby establishing a higher price (and a lesser quantity) relative to a competitive industry structure. This is the source of both the higher profits and also the loss to the consumer.

The question, therefore, is, Which is the dominant source of a robber baron's wealth: socially productive or nonproductive profits? Unfortunately, the issue is complicated in that both forms of profit often appear inseparably. Consider, for example, the often-cited case of John D. Rockefeller in the early petroleum industry. Historians now generally acknowledge that he played a positive role in the economy insofar as he devised more efficient methods of producing and distributing oil products. In one sense, however, he might be said to have been too successful as a competitor. Standard Oil, in its formative years, was able to destroy a large number of its potential competitors. Ironically, the more effective the competition became, the more likely it was to destroy the competitors.[17] While substantial innovations in economic affairs increase the total output available to society, they are likely to make a good part of the existing industry obsolete. It takes some time to copy and adopt new innovations, so that while the established economic units are trying to catch up with the new methods, the innovators may run off with a sizeable share of the market. This advantage is compounded by the predictable phenomenon that during the time the hard-pressed units are learning to catch up, the innovators are not standing still. They are usually able to refine and extend their original improvements, which, of course, tends to perpetuate that initial advantage. Thus, it is not surprising that firms which grab a dominant position in an industry can often maintain that position for extended periods of time. And the robber barons embodied in such firms as U. S. Steel (Carnegie), Standard Oil (Rockefeller), and Anaconda (Guggenheims), are by no means exceptional in this regard. Such antebellum innovators as the Boston Associates (textiles) and the Baldwin Locomotives Works were able to maintain a sizeable long-term lead position in their industries. Similarly, modern observers are familiar with the staying power of such firms as IBM, Xerox, and Procter and Gamble.

Hence, while we would still like to find out whether the robber barons were particularly dominant in their period, we can be assured that they were hardly unique. Depending on one's interpretation, they were either the most notable—or

---

[16] The price can be influenced as long as the demand curve has some elasticity, which is to say that as the price rises (falls), less (more) will be purchased. The primary detriment of this shift is the availability of substitute products, but the effect of price changes on an individual's real spending power will also have an effect.

[17] This is misleading wording, perhaps, in that the fact that they are being driven from the market suggests that they are not really effective competitors after all. The failure to recognize this distinction underlies much existing legislation, such as fair-trade laws, which attempt to promote competition by protecting noncompetitive competitors.

noted—phase of a process which has continued throughout much of American history. Individuals continually came upon new techniques which were more efficient and thus superseded existing economic arrangements. This created a repetitive process which might best be termed "creative destruction." Better methods were adopted and average per capita incomes increased, but older arrangements and the resources and firms which embodied them were pushed out and penalized.

One can readily see that this creates new monopolies, but it is frequently overlooked that it is also likely to erode existing monopolies in the process. For example, Standard Oil soon came to dominate the American petroleum industry in the late nineteenth century. By itself, this lessened competition in the oil industry, of course. That sector is only part of the relevant spectrum of competition, however. As of the later nineteenth century, petroleum served several quite distinct functions, such as lighting, lubrication, and heating fuel. In the first of these it competed with not only whale oil, electricity, and fireplaces, but also early bedtimes and illiteracy. While Rockefeller's emergence lessened the direct competition in the oil industry, it *increased* the competition felt by economic units within the whaling, firewood, and coal industries. Thus it is by no means certain that the overall effect of the robber barons was to reduce competition. To the extent that they may have succeeded in reducing it for themselves, they intensified it for others.

This tendency to overlook the total effect wrought by the robber barons on competition in the economy reappears in discussions of concentration. This is a measure which has been devised in an attempt to relate the structure of an industry to the intensity of the competition it displays. (A fully successful indicator has yet to be found, because the common gauges of concentration—such as the share of industry sales held by the four largest firms—are mitigated by other factors—such as the range of substitute products from other industries, transportation costs, and various pricing interactions among firms.) Usually it has been assumed that the era of the robber barons marked an increase in the level of concentration in the American economy. The impetus for this conclusion is the obvious density of concentration of the industries in which the robber barons were operating. As the above discussion has suggested, however, that view is probably too selective. These people were associated with industries in which the level of concentration was higher than that prevailing in most of the economy at that time. That, in itself, does not demonstrate that they heralded an age of higher concentration, however. There have always been some sectors in the economy—characteristically the newly developing ones—which exhibited a high degree of concentration. At the same time there has always been an accompanying pattern in other sectors in which concentration was less, or was in the process of being reduced simultaneously. The robber barons were generally in the industries which were developing most rapidly, causing them to be doubly obvious, not only for their own personal visibility, but also because it would be easy to surmise that the sectors which they dominated were in the process of swallowing up the entire economy as well.

To someone who has generally accepted the theory of the robber barons as being a reasonable explanation of the developments in American business organization during the last part of the nineteenth century, the above discussion may be a bit unsettling, but at least it is plausible. The usual response at this point is to grant that some concentration has existed at all times (accompanied by the common rising and ebbing of individual sectors), but to argue that the increase during this particular period was especially large and dramatic. With so many industries coming under the sway of dominant entrepreneurs during this era—so goes the argument—concentration must have intensified. Yet even this view of intensification is subject to much of the same types of reservations as we have laid out for the general problem of the robber barons above.

The first important item to note is that the absolute size of the firm, whether measured by sales, profits, or number of employees, is a deceitful index of concentration. Certainly the enterprises of Rockefeller and Carnegie were much larger than anything which had ever existed previously in American history, but then the total size of the economy was also growing rapidly so that in a relative sense they did not represent quite so dramatic an appearance. As the size of the demand for individual products in the economy grew, so did the size of an individual firm which the market could support at a given level of competitiveness increase correspondingly.

Even that measure of firm size, relative to total demand, can be misleading, however. The element of location intervenes because transportation and handling cost become necessary whenever the producers and customers are not concentrated at one point. And as all service-station operators know, distance is a substitute for monopoly in that the farther motorists have to travel to get to the next station, the higher the premium the operators can charge without forcing them to drive on down the road. High transportation costs tend to shield local sellers from competition and thus increase the effective concentration in the market for a given product. The important point to note in the context of the nineteenth century is the large reductions in transportation costs which preceded the period of the robber barons. This must have had a strong influence in reducing the effective levels of concentration during the period, independent of any other forces which were operating. We know that most economic units of the antebellum period were small, at least by current standards. Most commentators have implicitly assumed that such a restricted scale implied that most firms must be subject to the competition of numerous other small firms. Yet the number of potential competitors was sharply reduced for any product line in which transportation costs were important. There may have been large numbers of producers and dealers in certain lines of merchandise, but the cost of moving the item between them restricted the number of those units which could effectively compete with each other. In the early nineteenth century, high transportation costs made numerous small firms into local monopolists. Thus the concentration in each relevant market in the economy was much higher than the total number of firms with a given specialization would suggest. Indeed, it is quite possible that the effective level of competition was less than that which prevailed in the latter period of the robber barons. We can entertain that as a serious possibility simply because of the long-term fall in transportation costs mentioned above. As these decreasing costs lowered the barriers which protected localized monopolies in trade, services and some kinds of manufactures were swept away. This was most noticeable in those lines of activity where transportation costs tended to become a large portion of total costs if the goods were carried any sizeable distance. Obvious items which were included in this category were firewood (which encountered severe competition from coal after railroad lines were completed) and retailing (which the railroad also affected in that it sharply reduced the cost of comparison shopping in adjacent communities). Ironically, this process of breaking down local monopolies has received little attention in historical discussions, and most of the efforts devoted to examining the competitive effects of the railroad have focused on the tendency of the networks to consolidate and generally reduce competition among themselves. Such efforts certainly were not lacking, but the paradox of railroad consolidation is that, even if railroads did not compete much among themselves, they could well have intensified competition in other sectors by more than any amount which they suppressed in their own sector.

The Long-Run Dynamics of the Robber Barons

As became evident above, a clear-cut appraisal of the role of the robber barons is complicated by the intermingling of their positive (innovative) and negative (monopolizing) roles. The creation of new products or processes aids the consumer, but this is often done by carving out new niches which are shielded from existing competition. This is hardly surprising when we consider that the prime objective of the robber barons, or any other managers for that matter, must be to make profits. (If they do not meet that minimal test for survival, they will not be in a position to achieve many other objectives either.) One tactic which seems likely to generate profits is to devise products which are sufficiently novel so that they create new markets which do not compete head-on with existing goods. This difficulty of distinguishing between these two avenues to profit carries over to the issue of whether the robber barons operated primarily in a socially productive manner; that is, did most of their earnings come from devising more efficient ways of using society's resources, or did most of their earnings come from creating and exploiting socially costly monopolies? One could not tell directly from their activities, because they would be expected to grab either kind of opportunity when it came along. The fact that they became wealthy is consistent with their performing either a socially productive or a counterproductive role, or a mixture of the two. Money, in this case, does not prove much.

There is another way of asking the question, however, which seems to shed more light on the role of these people. It is to look at their behavior as it appears to be ordered over the span of their business experiences. One important observation is that although a typical robber baron would likely take advantage of possibilities for monopoly profits at any stage of operations, these were much less likely to occur during the first years in business. After all, small operations have much less chance to dominate particular markets than larger ones do. This judgment is confirmed when we examine the activities of the robber barons in their formative years. All demonstrated a marked capability to innovate and to create profitable enterprises almost entirely on their own. Perhaps even more important, almost all of them began on a shoestring; that is, with little or no personal or family wealth to bankroll their initial operations. Thus, it seems safe to say that a creative capacity—of a socially productive gender—is a necessary attribute for a potential robber baron to begin amassing wealth.

It is undoubtedly a necessity in order to continue to increase wealth as well. The wealth they created in the early years might also create some monopoly positions which could be exploited later. Without infusions of further improvements, however, profits from such positions would level off and soon erode. (Profits higher than those earned in existing alternatives encourage potential competitors to devise ways to capture some of these monopoly profits, sooner or later driving the leaders down to their competitive level.) Thus, for the robber barons to achieve the long-term, sustained increase in wealth which was typical of them, they must have been effecting improvements in the efficiency of their organizations on a fairly continuous basis. They may have been exploiting their monopoly positions all along, but without the innovative inputs these opportunities would never have been available to them.

The Robber Barons: An Overall Appraisal

Probably the best way to view the total contribution of the robber barons to the economy is as a kind of package plan; that is, their good and bad contributions came tied up together. There was—or for that matter, still is—no way by which their socially beneficial attributes can be split off and captured separately from their monopolizing attributes. One naturally then asks if they were truly beneficial or not. The way to evaluate this question is to try to compare the actual events in the economy during that period with those which might have occurred if the individuals we choose to call robber barons had never existed at all. The question is obviously easier to answer conceptually than in elaborated detail. However, the major elements are not too difficult to discern. The major loss in the absence of the robber barons would have been the innovative edge, or margin of efficiency, they gave to the economy. This is not to say that such advances would have been lost forever. Obviously, incentives existed for others to develop such improvements so that they, or some substitute for them, would eventually have been devised. The robber barons' positive contribution, therefore, is the gain to society from making these improvements available at an earlier date.

The cost, of course, is the monopoly profits they are able to squeeze from the position they have established by positive innovation. There is good reason to believe, however, that the cost would be less than the accompanying gains. The costs are possible only given the gains, so that if they were to exceed them, consumers could improve their own positions by simply ceasing to buy the item in question. So, for example, if Carnegie had attempted to charge more for steel than its margin of superiority (which he created) would allow, consumers would simply have reverted to traditional materials, such as wood or iron. Thus, although all the activities of the robber barons in the economy are not unambiguously positive, their net contribution appears to be beneficial. This judgment is at variance with much of the traditional literature, but we can place somewhat more confidence in it because it draws on the total context of their activities, not merely emphasizing certain partial aspects. It again illustrates the basic axiom of economic history; namely, that as long as some wants remain unsatisfied—the universal experience—individuals tend to focus on the costs of particular circumstances. The monopoly costs of the robber barons are easy to recognize and to protest. However, the gains in consumption possibilities which allowed them to come about are readily absorbed into the prevailing conditions of life and forgotten.

SUGGESTED READINGS

Falkner, Harold U.: *The Decline of Laissez-Faire, 1897–1917,* Holt, New York, 1951.
Kirkland, Edward C.: *Industry Comes of Age, 1860–97,* Holt, New York, 1961.
Rosenberg, Nathan: "Technological Change in the Machine Tool Industry, 1840–1910," *Journal of Economic History,* vol. 23, December 1963.
Williamson, Harold F. (ed.): *The Growth of the American Economy,* Prentice-Hall, New York, 1951, Chapters 24 and 25.
Williamson, Jeffery G.: *Late Nineteenth Century American Development: A General Equilibrium History,* Cambridge, London, 1975.
Wilson, Mitchell: *American Science and Invention, A Pictorial History,* Simon & Schuster, New York, 1954, Part 5, *The New Era.*

Chapter 12

The Intermediaries

Economists are sometimes accused of using theory which abstracts so much from the real world as to be useless, or, even worse, misleading. The charge is not unique to economics, of course, because any science that uses generalizing models sooner or later runs into such limitations. Central unifying themes can be isolated only at the cost of some simplification of detail so that minor variations often remain inexplicable.[1] Scholars persist in such activities, however, because there are often tremendous economies to be gained in organizing knowledge in this way, more than enough to tolerate the lack of detail which accompanies it.

Nevertheless, some important qualifications can be overlooked in the search for generalized themes. For example, until recently many economic models have assumed that the world was frictionless, that is, that goods went directly from the producer to the consumer without any intervening costs; no additional resources were consumed in buying, financing, or transporting them. Today we realize that that premise is so abstract as to be very limiting indeed and have since elaborated the basic frameworks to include such costs. (Interestingly enough, the improve-

---

[1] This is merely one reason for which theorizing is attacked. Another common objection is a "lack of realism," which really boils down to the proposition that the critic believes that the answers of the exercise do not correspond to the real "state of the world" as the observer sees it.

ment has been achieved by an extension of the concepts of the basic model, not by jettisoning the original formulation in search of one which is more "realistic.") In doing so, we have discovered just how important such intermediary activities are. When they are included, many of the attributes of economic behavior which we had previously found puzzling become understandable. We have simultaneously discovered that these important intermediate sectors have created a good deal of interesting economic history along the way as well.

TRANSPORTATION

Transportation, pushed by dramatic improvements in technology and pulled by the commercialization of the economy, was a growth sector in the antebellum period. It continued to grow at a respectable rate after the Civil War although, like any major sector, it showed the inevitable tendency to slow down over time. The particular component of transportation which had grown most rapidly in the immediate pre-Civil War period was, of course, the railroad. From 1840 to 1860 the total number of miles of track in place increased more than tenfold, from about 2,800 to 30,000 miles, as shown in Table 12-1. Over the next thirty years, growth was not quite as rapid by comparison but, with a more than sixfold increase, to about 190,000 miles of track, it was still a very fast rate of increase by any usual standard. Beyond 1890 the increase continued at a slower pace. In the next thirty years (until 1920), track mileage almost doubled. (It reached its maximum in the early 1930s and has declined since that time.) Thus the railroads, which were the largest single form of transportation during the period between the two wars, went through the complete cycle of growth and maturation typical of that of most industries in a developing economy. This progression seems to be a good framework around which to organize our study of postbellum transportation because it inevitably includes the alternate transportation techniques available in the economy, as well as the shifts in the more general economy which shaped the organization of the transportation sector.

Refining the Rail System

As we have illustrated a number of times before, "inventions" almost never burst on the scene full-blown but rather *evolve* by incorporating improvements gradually and fairly continuously. The railroad is certainly an example. The railroad which existed in 1860 would be considered obsolete and little more than amusing by individuals who were accustomed to the rail system as of the eve of World War I. One obvious difference was the substantial increase in the size of equipment in use. Around the time of the Civil War, for example, a single freight car could carry a maximum of 10 to 12 tons of cargo. By 1914 the typical unit was designed to handle loads of up to 70 tons. The amount a single train could carry increased even more dramatically: a typical locomotive of about 1860 could pull twenty-five or so cars, while one built around 1914 could pull fifty to one hundred cars.

Table 12-1   Railroad Mileage
in Operation 1830—1950

Date	Mileage
1830	23
1835	1,098
1840	2,818
1845	4,633
1850	9,021
1855	18,374
1860	30,626
1865	35,085
1870	52,922
1875	74,096
1880	93,262
1885	128,320
1890	166,703
1895	190,094
1900	206,631
1905	236,855
1910	266,185
1915	291,231
1920	296,835
1925	299,593
1930	303,182
1935	294,846
1940	287,113
1945	280,544
1950	277,313

Note: Mileage figures do not include yard tracks and sidings.

Source: Adapted from U.S. Bureau of the Census, *Historical Statistics of the United States, Colonial Times to 1957,* Government Printing Office, Washington, D.C., 1960, pp. 427 and 429.

   This approximate fifteenfold increase in the cargo capacity of a single train was possible because of a series of reinforcing inventions. The freight cars could be larger because of a shift in materials from wood to steel, and because of the use of stronger trucks (wheels and axles) and tracks to carry the growing loads. The number of cars could be increased primarily because of the greater power of the locomotive which allowed them to draw heavier loads. Part of this gain represented improvements in boiler design and power-transmission devices, but part was attributable to the increase in the size of the engines. This in turn can be partly accounted for by the increase in the strength of the track. The first steel rails introduced in the 1860s were known as 65-pound track, which is to say that one foot of rail weighed exactly 65 pounds. By 1910, however, rail weights had reached 100 pounds, consequently allowing the track to bear correspondingly heavier traffic.

But increases in physical capacity were not the only reason that railroads could move more goods. Westinghouse's air brake, introduced in the late 1860s, not only increased the safety of railroading but allowed a large increase in the number of cars a single train could handle by converting braking from a hand operation to one controlled as a unit from the engine. The movement to longer trains got a further boost when Westinghouse devised the improved car coupler, which allowed a long series of cars to be started up gradually without severely jarring either them or the cargo in the process. And apparently just to prove that his early innovations were simply routine, Westinghouse then devised the basic system of block signals and switches which is still in use today. These also made railroading safer, but their primary purpose was to improve the efficiency of train operations as, by this time, traffic patterns were becoming heavier and more complicated and hand directions were cumbersome and slow.

Accompanying these improvements in the basic hardware of the railroads were other refinements which made them more productive. One noticeable change was the shift to specialized rolling stock. The all-purpose freight car gave way to special designs for such cargoes as cattle, fresh meat, petroleum and chemicals, and coal and other minerals. And along with these car configurations went the evolution of specialized loading and unloading facilities for the specific cargoes, facilities such as icehouses, cattlepens, oil tanks, and coal docks, all built next to the rail lines to reduce transfer costs as much as possible.

Probably the ultimate example of specialized design and function in railroad cars, however, occurred in the case of the passenger trade. In the 1840s, after an extended trip on the American railroads, tourist Charles Dickens was moved to write that "to tell you that these beds are perfectly comfortable would be a lie." Actually, as befitted a gracious visitor, Dickens was being polite. By more recent standards, travel by train was, at that time, a sequence of hardships and ordeals. The ride was bumpy, the heating was inadequate, the food service was often left to the initiative of local vendors or railroad stations, and sleeping facilities consisted of a series of hard, narrow wooden bunks which were often overbooked.

There was clearly a market for a better grade of services, however, because rail was the most convenient form of travel for any distance overland. And entrepreneurs were soon working on the problem. In the 1850s, Theodore T. Woodruff devised the first convertible sleeping car in which the daytime couches could be folded into beds for the night. The arrangement had the obvious advantage of using the same space for both daytime and nighttime purposes. Otherwise, nearly twice as many cars would have been required to provide the same amount of service. Woodruff became a millionaire within two years, making a number of his financial backers—including a young man named Andrew Carnegie—wealthy along with him.

Another man by the name of George Pullman also became involved with railroad travel at about this time. He rode overnight on a train, did not like the experience, and made a mental note that it would almost certainly be profitable to devise a more comfortable form of travel.[2] After accumulating some capital in several other ventures, he attempted his first "Pullman." It was little better than a converted boxcar—from which it had in fact been made—and was not successful. A few years later, however, a second model, redesigned from the ground up with the comfort of the passengers in mind, was very successful. It had more space, luxurious furnishings, and a smoother form of suspension which used rubber cushioning in the springs. Pullman was now selling a luxury good and he merchandised it as such by hauling prominent citizens and newspaper reporters on special free excursions. He scored a special coup when Lincoln was assassinated and the government sought the best existing car to transport his body back to Illinois. Millions of spectators saw a Pullman car for the first time and, possibly more important, bridges and stations had to be modified very quickly to accommodate its oversized dimensions. (The car was larger than the existing rolling stock in order to provide for "the convenience of the passengers, not that of the railroads," as George Pullman put it.) The sleeping car went through further modification and ornamentation in the remainder of the nineteenth century, and finally became what is now recognized as an American institution. Among those further modifications were the additions of the vestibule, that is, the bellowslike hall which connected cars together and prevented passengers from being knocked off the moving train, and that standard of American culture, the dining car.

Improving into Decline   The effect of the total cumulative improvement in railroad efficiency, of which the above examples comprise merely a small sample, was to lower further the transportation costs after the Civil War. In the middle of the period, 1870–1900, for example, real freight rates fell by about one-third. This is not as dramatic as the reductions before the Civil War, but it is sizeable nevertheless. It does suggest, however, that the railroads' days of rapid growth were over and that they were now becoming vulnerable to the appearance of newer, more efficient substitutes.

In the late 1800s the railroad seemed to be the dominant and largely unchallenged transportation medium of the economy. Competition was closer at hand than was generally supposed, however. Long-standing alternatives, such as water and wagon carriage, had been driven out of many markets, but they had not disappeared. Innovators were surprisingly successful in introducing improvements into them (as we shall demonstrate) while waiting in the wings for further opportunities. In addition, a number of new competitors were appearing in some rather surprising forms.

When the oil companies began to move sizeable amounts of kerosene to market, they soon discovered that it was cheaper to move it by specially constructed pipelines than by the labor-consuming method of barrels and railroad cars. The first lengthy pipeline, between the Pennsylvania oil fields and the East

---

[2] Pullman is far from being the only entrepreneur who conceived a profitable new business in response to a misgiving about existing travel services. A noticeable modern counterpart is the Holiday Inns, which pioneered many of the features of modern motels. They were initiated when their founder spent a miserable week attempting to locate accommodations for his vacationing family.

Coast, was completed in 1878. By World War I more than 10,000 miles of pipe were in place and the new Texas oil fields were rapidly being joined to the network. Bolstered by the improvements which were being effected in pipeline technology, such as larger pumps and techniques of handling a number of liquids in rapid succession, this network by 1914 could carry a large volume of products which would otherwise probably have gone to the railroads.

Another unlikely railroad competitor was electricity. It introduced an alternative technique of distributing such services as lighting, heating, and power for manufacturing operations by allowing for a different spatial pattern of resource use. One could, for example, locate a power plant near the source of fuel and distribute the energy through wires, rather than shipping the coal or petroleum more widely over the market area. Costs were obviously a prime consideration in the decision of where to locate a power plant and one would naturally expect planning committees to include the delivered cost of fuel in those considerations. Thus, if transportation charges could be saved by converting coal into power at the electric plant, rather than distributing it physically throughout the countryside, that saving would encourage the former method of distribution—and reduce the demand for transportation services.

There was also considerable action going on within that traditional competitor of the railroad, the road and highway system. The rise of the motor vehicle after the turn of the century is well known, but probably of more immediate importance in the period before 1914 were several other less widely recognized developments. For instance, the most complete adoption of bicycles in the United States occurred in the 1890s. A number of improvements were introduced in their construction at that time[3] and bicycles began to be used much more widely, both for practical transportation and for pleasure excursions. They served as a substitute for railroad services to some degree but they also stimulated another trend which was to undercut the market of the railroads even further.

Almost as soon as the cyclists began traveling away from their own neighborhoods, they noticed what many rural residents of the nation had known for some time—namely, that the condition of most roads outside the central business districts was miserable. The cyclists soon added their sympathy to the "good-roads" associations which were forming in the decade. These were voluntary, private groups, something like informal chambers of commerce that lobbied for, and publicized the cause of, improved highways. The good-roads groups also received strong support from the postal system, which had instituted rural free delivery in the 1870s and was having considerable difficulty reaching mailboxes on a regular basis.

The good-roads effort also received support from that considerable portion of the population which continued to use horse-drawn transportation. After 1890,

---

[3] One noticeable improvement was the adoption of equal-sized wheels both in front and in back. Before this time the common design had a very large front wheel which made it susceptible to "headers"—that is, for the rider to be thrown over the handlebars whenever the wheel encountered uneven ground. The introduction of the modern wheel structure opened up the bicycle as a pleasurable form of travel for women and children as well as more cautious males.

horse-drawn trolleys rapidly disappeared from use as public transit in larger cities (primarily in response to the introduction of electric power, with which the horses simply could not compete). For individual conveyance, however, the horse and buggy was still the prime means of travel. And it was not a bad means of getting around either, by the standards of that day at least. Contrary to the current popular idea of such transportation, as implied by the phrase "horse-and-buggy days," horse-drawn carriages had actually become quite a stylish and comfortable means of travel by 1900. They were another of those frequent examples in economic history in which a particular product, or device, continued to be improved even while it was pushed into obscurity by some competing arrangement. During the nineteenth century, the horse-drawn carriage was substantially improved by better suspensions, improved lighting, and better upholstery and seating. Despite the railroad's dominance of longer-distance passenger traffic, carriages were the choice of most individuals who could afford them for local trips. They were, in fact, the contemporary equivalent of the automobile in that they provided the most convenient, comfortable, and private form of transit for their day.

In this context it is easy to see that the carriage users would add their voices to the good-roads movement. It also helps to sort out the basic forces which were at work in the American transportation sector at this time. Probably the most striking fact is that the good-roads movement preceded the introduction of the automobile, which means that even before 1900 there was a growing market for the specific attributes which an improved road system could provide. Looking at the innovations which seemed to prompt this drive (bicycles, mail service, and improved carriages), these attributes would seem to include such things as convenience, smoother rides, and a saving of time; in short, things which a society whose average income was rising would be expected to want. These, in turn, help to explain the efforts put into inventing the forms of powered travel which culminated in the automobile. There was a strong and growing demand for the very combination of services which the automobile provided. Of course, the motor vehicle became an important addition to the economy, but that relationship can also be reversed. That is, although it contributed to a more productive use of society's resources, there was considerable pressure in the economy to devise something approximating it for just that reason.

The "Indispensable"(?) Railroads   In the last part of the nineteenth century the railroads dominated the transportation system. This happened at a time when the nation completed the last, great phase of regional expansion and when there were both obvious growth and large structural realignments occurring in the economy. It was only natural to link the two and, indeed, in many historical accounts the railroad had begun to be assigned an important role in the development of the late-nineteenth-century economy. Just how strong that feeling was began to be evident when the question was examined more critically and analytically in the 1960s.

In 1964, Robert W. Fogel published a book entitled *Railroads and American*

Economic Growth.[4] The volume actually contains several essays on the role of the railroad in the nineteenth-century economy but the one which set forth to measure its contribution to national output received by far the most attention. In fact, it received *so* much attention that the work became a kind of methodological symbol of the changes which were taking place in the study of economic history in general. The debate about the essay often took such a high level of abstraction (and emotion) that the important details of the specific study which started the dialogue were overlooked. That has been unfortunate in that, properly presented and qualified, the study offered some important implications about the process of growth.

Fogel began his study with a seemingly unassailable premise: if one argues that the railroad was indeed "indispensable," or, somewhat more cautiously, "important," to American growth, it follows that in its absence the economy would have produced less in any given year during that period. An equivalent way of stating the proposition is that in the absence of the railroad, the regular yearly growth in output which the economy experienced would have been set back for a number of years because it would have to have started from a much lower base. A number of critics contended that such a way of stating the proposition was absurd; after all, the railroad did exist and therefore to perform such exercises was a form of "hypothetical history" which had no relevance to the actual past. In a very narrow sense, these critics were correct. Such events did not occur and therefore they are not part of the known pattern of events which comprise the raw material of history. What most critics overlooked is that no historian who is considered at all useful practices history in that manner. The essence of historical explanation is interpretation, and interpretation requires judgments about relationships which existed between past events. Conventional folklore notwithstanding, the facts do not speak for themselves. Even the critics of Fogel's work did not adhere to their proposed guidelines in offering counterexplanations to his study, or even in the procedures which they practiced on their own projects.

If one wishes to determine the importance of a particular invention, or arrangement, such as the railroad, one must examine the available alternatives to that device. The fact that the railroad was used extensively at a given time shows that individuals found it more attractive than alternative methods, but that does not tell us *how much* more attractive they found it. Yet the size of that advantage is the important factor in determining its *net* importance. If close substitutes were at hand—alternatives which would do the job with little increase in cost—then the item could be given up without much impact on the economy. But if no close substitutes were at hand, that lack of good alternatives could make the item quite important. Note that because it is the *largely unseen* distance to the next best substitute, rather than the *absolute amount* of the item being used, which determines its historical importance, some interesting paradoxes can occur. For example, an innovation which seems to play only a small role in some obscure

[4] John Hopkins, Baltimore, 1964.

corner of the economy could well have more *net* importance than one which is universally used and very familiar.

The Analysis of the Railroad's Contribution Thus, to assess the importance of the railroad to the economy at some time in the past, it is necessary to determine its advantage over existing alternatives. For several reasons, that is a deceitfully difficult task. First, because the alternatives were *somewhat* less attractive, they were not used—at least not in the way that would make a comparison with the innovation in question feasible. That makes it difficult to simulate exactly how much they would have cost. Indeed, because they did not exist as such, it sometimes makes it difficult to even conceive what they might have been. (This last problem seems to underlie many of the objections to such a comparison being valid at all; that is, because observers have trouble picturing the economy without the innovation, they reject such an exercise as being totally unhistorical.)

Second, alternatives are seldom perfect substitutes, even if we overlook the difference in unit costs. The next best substitutes for the railroad, for example, would have been a combination of water and wagon transportation. The former was generally cheaper in direct costs but was slower, more likely to damage the cargo, and more subject to seasonal interruptions, such as freezing weather. The latter was more expensive on a direct cost-per-ton/mile basis but offered the advantage of more flexibility and decentralization in local freight haulage.

Third, complications arise from the fact that in order to gauge the contribution of a particular innovation we must "pull it out" of the economy in question. Yet because, up to that point, the economy has developed around, and with the aid of, the innovation, if we were suddenly to withdraw it (only by simulation, of course), our subsequent measurements would overstate its contribution. In the true absence of the innovation, the economy would have devised and constructed substitutes that would have filled some of that void. Thus the usual measurement procedure leads to an overestimate of the contribution of a particular innovation because it does not allow for the predictable act of human adaptation in its absence. This is not a difficult problem in a measurement for a single year because in such cases the investigators are usually concerned with obtaining a maximum estimate of the innovation's contribution anyway. For calculations over longer periods, however, it can become quite an important element. If one does not allow for the normal acts of substitution and innovation over such a span, the calculations will probably overstate the net cost of a specific device.

With these considerations in mind, we can retrace some of the main steps in calculating the role of the railroad in the economy (and in so doing, follow one of the most well-worn paths of economic historians in recent years). In Figure 12-1, the cost of the railroad is depicted by a supply curve, S_r, which shows the amount of railroad services that railroad operators would find it profitable to provide on a long-term basis at various prices. The cost of providing comparable services by the next best alternative(s) is shown as S_a. This curve is above S_r, indicating that the increase in cost implied by shifting to alternative forms of transportation makes them somewhat less desirable than the railroad. These sup-

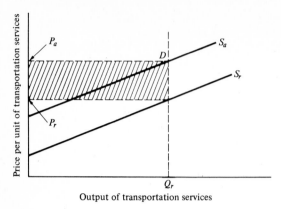

Figure 12-1

ply curves have been drawn parallel to each other, an assumption that makes calculations easier in that the difference in unit costs at the margin (those observable in the market) can be used to calculate the cost difference for all the other units of output (to the left of the equilibrium quantity in Figure 12-1) as well.[5]

The demand curve for transportation services is shown as D in Figure 12-1. It is drawn completely inelastic, or vertical, a configuration which also makes calculation somewhat easier.[6] The cost to society of using the transportation services provided by the railroad can be inferred from the figure. It would be the quantity of railroad services in a given year (Q_r) times the cost of a unit of service (P_r). The cost to society of forgoing the use of the railroad would be the increase in the cost of using the next best alternative to provide the same amount of output (Q_r). This would be equal to the difference between the unit cost, P_a less P_r times the quantity of output Q_r, which is shown by the shaded area. This "social saving," as Fogel dubbed it, shows an upper-bound measurement of the contribution of the railroad to the economy's output at the time of the calculation.

While the foregoing describes the essential core of the method, there were the inevitable complications of any major research project to surmount, of course. One of these was the characteristic mentioned earlier—namely, that wagons and canals do not provide equivalent transportation services, and thus differences other than those in direct freight costs must be taken into account. Fogel

[5] This assumption can overstate, understate, or not affect the measured contribution, depending on the slope of the supply curves to the left of the equilibrium quantity. For a more complete discussion of such fine points of these calculations, see this author's "The Nature of Social Saving," *Economic History Review,* August 1970.

[6] The assumption of completely inelastic demand allows one to use the observed market quantity, in the case of the railroad, for the alternative transportation sector as well. This assumption is one of those constraints on human adaptation which we mentioned above. It does not allow individuals to use fewer transportation services as their prices rise. Normally one would expect the curve to have some elasticity, that is, to "tilt backward" from its intersection with S_r, thus intersecting S_a at a lower quantity. The effect of this assumption is to overstate the measured contribution of the innovation to the economy.

looked first at canal rates and found, somewhat surprisingly, that direct canal rates were actually below those of the railroads. In this case the "nonprice" items must have been making the crucial difference because with shippers generally preferring to use railroads rather than canals, the nonprice advantages in railroad services appeared to be more than enough to offset the price differential. This is not too surprising when we examine the items which made up that implicit advantage. Water transportation was slower, so that on the average the economy would have to hold larger stocks of goods at consuming points to offset the slower distribution of new supplies. The increase in stocks would tie up more capital and thus impose the opportunity cost of denying its use elsewhere. A second cost was the higher damage rate characteristic of water transit, which could be directly inferred in the differential between insurance rates charged the respective shippers. A third, nonprice advantage of railroads was that they were much less subject to interruptions, such as during the colder seasons, which immobilized canal traffic with frozen waterways. This cost is equivalent to adding a longer waiting period to delivery, much like the slower delivery factor, and is reflected in the capital costs of holding larger inventories to fill in during the delays.

In those areas where the waterways could not be developed to make up for the disappearance of the railroads, wagons were the next best alternative. They were also the logical substitute for much of the local traffic carried by the railroads which the canals would have found impractical to carry over such short distances. The railroad's advantage over wagons in direct costs was quite large, without even looking at the more subtle nonprice factors. (Unlike the case of the canals, the nonprice factors were not a very important element in the comparison between these two modes of transportation.)

Thus most of the railroad's net contribution to the economy in the late nineteenth century came in those areas where it substituted for wagons rather than canals. Furthermore, much of this gain came in local traffic in the relatively settled areas of the economy. While there were areas where no feasible water substitutes existed, and which would thus have entailed long wagon hauls to replace the services of the railroads, these generally did not add up to much in the context of the total economy. It is ironic that while the railroad is generally thought of as a form of transportation whose primary function was long-distance transportation—the transcontinental railroad is often the first example most individuals mention—its major contribution was in serving relatively short connections.[7]

In one way, however, this is not surprising. Our discussion has noted the extent to which relatively short-term travel, especially in and around cities, was becoming a major pressure point in the late nineteenth century. Although railroad services within urban areas were not satisfactorily meeting this demand,

[7] This is an example of the difference between the gross, and more obvious, effects of an innovation and the net effects which we mentioned earlier. It also illustrates our earlier caution that the net contribution of an innovation may diverge significantly from its positioning in the delivery of final output.

they were providing one of the closest then-existing substitutes to it and this was noticeable within the calculations of social savings for the entire railroad sector. A more tangible indicator of this pressure for a better form of transportation for short distances is seen in the rapid appearance of the "interurbans" from 1890 to 1910. (Fogel's study was calculated as of 1890 and thus did not include this new variant of railroad services.) These were electrified urban trains designed almost exclusively for passenger traffic. In a span of only twenty years, nearly 20,000 miles of such track was constructed. On the eve of World War I, all major American cities as well as many medium- and small-sized ones were served with interurbans or close substitutes for them. And on an average weekday, about 50 million passenger trips were made—that is, the equivalent of a quarter of the national population was using them for a round trip each day. Yet despite the rapid rush to build urban electric railways, and the large patronage they quickly built up, a good portion of the industry dissolved within a decade or so after the automobile became commonplace. The entire history of the interurban sector is a strong testimony to the strength of the demand for convenient, local transportation. The sector was obviously a response to that demand, grasping the opportunity of the new source of power, electricity, to perform that function somewhat better. It also illustrated in a kind of backhanded way, however, how much it—and other improvisations—fell short of completely solving the problem. When the automobile did make a major step in that direction, the electric street-railroad industry nearly vanished within a very short time.

Adding Up the Railroad's Contribution   When Professor Fogel had completed his calculations, he found that the total contribution of the railroad was surprisingly small. Depending on how much flexibility one gave the economy to adapt to its absence, it came to a mere 1 or 2 percent of gross national product in 1890. In absolute terms this is not a small amount (by comparison with recent years it would amount to at least $15 billion, for example), but it is much below any level implied in most previous discussions of the railroad. For example, it has been argued that without the railroad the growth of the United States would have been penalized significantly. Fogel's results, however, suggest that the pace of the economy would be set back by only about three or four months. That would be equal to the size of the calculated contribution of the railroad to the economy relative to an average year's growth—that is, 1 to 2 percent a year compared with a long-term average increase in the GNP, during the last half of the nineteenth century, of 4 to 6 percent. Thus, if the railroad were to have been absent from the economy over that period, the reduction in output would have been equivalent to a postponement of growth by about one-quarter to one-third of a year, hardly a major upheaval.

These results went far beyond simply demonstrating that the railroad was not all it was touted to have been in American history. They suggested that portrayals of economic history which were built upon major turning points in the form of "big" inventions or institutions were generally suspect. Here was an innovation which had been commonly viewed as having played a key role in the economy and yet, when it was examined carefully, it turned out that there were

reasonably good substitutes for it all along. If it had simply vanished, the economy would not have functioned significantly differently. Furthermore, there did
not seem to be any compounding or cumulative effects from that superiority,
either. At the time the railroad's contribution was measured, in 1890, it had long
since driven many of its next best alternatives into disuse. Yet when their costs of
operations were estimated in place of the railroads, also in 1890, they obviously
had not stagnated during disuse. Innovations and increases in productivity had
been continuing in these alternatives as well as in the railroads. This suggested
something which other recent investigations have tended to reinforce: that productivity increases tend to be more gradual and dispersed than had previously
been commonly assumed. Thus, while innovation was going on in the railroad—
which could be fairly obvious because it was being introduced and used conspic-
uously—it was also going on in the alternative inventions which would be the
"back-up" techniques in the absence of the railroad.[8] Therefore, instead of the
railroad steadily widening its advantage as soon as it displaced the alternate
means of transportation, the entire range of substitutes moved along within a
not-too-distant range of one another. This provides us with one more example of
our premise that growth does not depend on the development of particular inventions, or forms, such as industrialization, but is more the result of a general
environment in which increases in productivity are feasible and encouraged. In
this context, the railroad was simply the result, or end product, rather than the
basic cause of economic growth.

Neglected Passenger Cars   In one sense, Fogel's study of the railroads was
quite limited—which is ironic given that it succeeded in answering some very
important questions. But it was concerned with only freight—not passenger—
traffic. Recently the passenger component was filled in by Royd and Walton.[9]
They found that the social saving in this function was several times that of
freight. In retrospect this is not surprising. We saw above that in the antebellum
period the railroad was not such a dramatic improvement over the existing canals
and steamboats in terms of the direct costs of delivering goods. Rather, its particular advantages were those of speed and convenience. Thus, it quickly picked off
much of the passenger and express cargo trade but was able to take over only
slowly the majority of the bulk cargo during the rest of the nineteenth century.
Similarly, our examination of the railroad's contribution near the end of the
nineteenth century suggests that its advantage over straight freight-hauling competitors was not very large. Again, its advantage was in shorter urban hauls where
the savings to passengers seemed to be becoming an important element. This is
another illustration of a characteristic we examined earlier. Innovations typically

[8] Notice that it is not necessary for inventors to continue work on improvements specifically
in those techniques which are not being used. Indeed, why should they, without any likely prospects
of foreseeable payoffs? Many improvements are more general, however, and occur outside the industry in question but have applications to many such sectors. Wagon technology could be improved, for
example, by the development of better wheel bearings, wood-forming devices, and road systems, all of
which could take place independently of any incentives (or lack thereof) in the wagon sector.
[9] J. Hayden Royd and Gary M. Walton, "The Social Savings from Nineteenth Century Rail
Passenger Service," *Explorations in Economic History,* vol. 9, no. 3, Spring 1972, pp. 233–254.

are not direct substitutes for one another, but generally differ somewhat in the specific combination of services they provide. The railroad's most advantageous attribute was not cost, but speed and convenience. That is why we would expect it to be most successful against stagecoach service over longer distances, which it almost completely destroyed, and least successful against the automobile, which has destroyed much of it.

The Strange, Suspect Economics of Railroad Finance

Some of the most notorious "robber barons," like Jay Gould, Jim Fisk, and Daniel Drew, made their reputations in railroad operations. Their particular forte was financial arrangement, which made their activities appear all the more dubious to the general public and to subsequent historians. Financial operations, especially the rather unusual ones of the railroads in the latter half of the nineteenth century, have generally been puzzling and therefore a bit suspect. And when one hears of construction companies which did not build anything, stock which was sold below its stated value, and large giveaways of federal land, it certainly arouses curiosity as to what was going on.

Accounts of railroad financing in the period 1860 to about 1890 are filled with references to "watered stock." In fact, some Wall Street brokers once erected a statue of Commodore Vanderbilt with a watering can as a jest at his reputed tendency to produce watered stock. Actually there is nothing mysterious or particularly unethical about "watered stock"; it has existed in every economy in some form and includes many of the most widely known securities today, such as those of IBM, Xerox, and Sears Roebuck. In nineteenth-century terminology the "water" of a stock was simply that part of its selling price which exceeded its "par," or book, value. Par value—that is, the value of the original investment in the company—was considered the true value of the enterprise. Anything above that amount was considered unearned, or speculative, and therefore "watered." Today we recognize that the true value of a company, and therefore the valuation placed on its shares of ownership, is determined by its *expected* earnings which may be greater than, equal to, or less than, the initial capital put into the firm.

While future expected earnings determine the market value of a stock, par value is nothing more than the opportunity cost of capital in uses outside the company. In other words, if, in nineteenth-century terminology, a stock was "watered," it simply meant that it was expected that the company would be able to earn more by using those assets than would a typical manager elsewhere in the economy. In modern parlance, a watered stock is a growth stock, one whose earnings are better than average. Any growing economy will have some "watered" stock, some which sells near its "par," or alternative cost level, and some which is "concentrated." (It seems strange that popular accounts of nineteenth-century finance seldom mentioned this latter possibility—that stock could also become "dewatered.")

This clarification of "watered" stock, using modern terminology, explains a good many of the financial dealings which have puzzled (or at least misled) generations of historians. For example, railroads in the 1860s and 1870s could sell watered stock because they were growing and could reasonably anticipate making returns on that investment that were greater than the average for the rest of the economy. Similarly, investors were willing to pay the premium on that investment because they expected that the growth of future earnings would compensate for the higher immediate current return they could make on other investments. Investing in railroad stocks in the 1860s—strange as it may sound today—was the equivalent of buying electronics or computer stock in the 1960s. It should not be surprising that if individuals were willing to pay a high price-earnings ratio in the 1960s for such securities (that is, a high current price relative to current earnings in the expectation that future earnings would increase much more rapidly), that contemporaries of the railroad era would value their ownership similarly.

Or there were cases where new stock was issued in exchange for that of the older companies as part of a railroad merger. Sometimes the total value of the new stock was larger than the sum of that which it replaced, leading observers to conclude that this exchange also was merely a device to puff up values by watering the stock. If we note, however, that "water" is created in stocks whenever the future returns of an enterprise (or the parts thereof) are increased, then the process seems much less ephemeral. A merger could indeed make the anticipated profits of the railroad larger than that of its combined antecedents. The new organization might achieve economies in certain operations denied to the smaller units, or it might be able to increase its bargaining power for more favorable rates with adjoining railroads (a factor of some importance which we shall return to). Whatever the source, the new "water" was justified and was a predictable result of the merger. Moreover, it was not merely the concoction of the financial reorganizers. Had they consummated the merger and then simply reissued the stock pro rated to the old price, other investors would have bid the market price of the new issue up to a higher level as soon as the higher profits became recognized.

The "Construction" Companies When the Union Pacific built the Eastern segment of the first transcontinental railroad in the 1860s, it used a financial subsidiary called the Crédit Mobilier to arrange the construction of the rail system. The name later became a kind of byword for fraud after a special congressional investigation turned up a whole raft of unseemly practices involved in its operations. The Crédit Mobilier was one of the first of what were known as the railroad construction companies, a misleading label in that they were not directly involved in actually constructing new rail lines but were simply legal bodies to handle the funds during incorporation. Yet despite the bad image they acquired from the Union Pacific experience, construction companies continued to be used in forming new railroads for several decades thereafter. This suggests that there was something more advantageous about them than merely perpetuating fraud. Investors had sufficient opportunity to be aware of their dangers; when they continued to purchase the stock of such enterprises, it must have been because the construction companies added something to the profitability of the enterprise.

The construction company was really devised to get around another of the obstacles put up by the contemporary misconception about the par value of stock. Because it was considered unsound for stocks to sell for more than their par value, some states enacted laws to that effect. As we saw, however, stocks will be traded above their par value whenever expected profits exceed the going rate on capital—which was true of many of the railroads up into the 1880s. Thus, a new railroad company which scrupulously offered its new stock at par value was giving a windfall gain to its buyers. They could immediately turn around and sell it for the higher price which capitalized its expected future returns. The construction company was merely a legal device to sell stock at its market value rather than at the lower par value. (One good indication that this was indeed the companies' prime motivation was that after 1890, when the market value of railroad stock generally fell to or below their par values, the construction companies disappeared.) The normal railroad company offered regular issues of stocks and bonds to the public at their par value. It then gave the cash plus any proceeds (such as that of land given as grants by the government) to its construction company. That organization, in turn, gave its own stock *at a discount* to the railroad company. In effect, the construction company became the real company and the railroad corporation merely a dummy organization. Thus, selling stock at a premium above its par value could be done legally.[10]

Historians have been quick to interpret this form of organization as merely a device to defraud the stockholders by siphoning off a good portion of the investment into profits of insiders. They have correctly noted that the management of the construction company was usually identical to, or at least strongly overlapped that of, the official company. Furthermore, these officials often received a good share of the stock of the construction company, which was not given back to the regular company in exchange for cash, bond, and land contributions. This was not necessarily irregular, however; much the same thing would have occurred if the companies had gone public in the securities markets if there had been no restrictions on the market value of the stock rising above its paid-in capital. When new, promising companies offer their stock to the public, they often initially price the shares at a level which they believe will make them attractive to buyers. This means that the anticipated returns must be near the rate that investors can make on capital elsewhere in the economy. However, because the money which the new stockholders pay into the company can earn more there than in other investments, this leaves some "surplus" which the organizer(s) of the firm can capture in the form of some of the initial offering of stock. In essence, the founders, or organizers, of the company are capturing some of the expected excess profits they have created in forming the enterprise.

Similarly, the incentives for the board of directors and officers of the corporation to violate the interests of the stockholders is no different in the case of the construction company than it would be without it. If the executives of the two

---

[10] This is far from an isolated case in economic history. In modern times most Americans are familiar with "key" or "redecorating charges" which one must pay a landlord to obtain an apartment in a rent-controlled city, such as New York City. This is simply a device to adjust the official controlled price of the service to the real level which the market would set on its own.

organizations were identical—as they often were—then they were accountable to stockholders for their actions just as they would have been in the absence of the intermediate financial company. Of course, some directors of the construction companies appeared to abuse their positions at the stockholders' expense, but that happens in regular corporate firms. The construction company did not make any real difference in the incentive for a corporate official to defraud the shareholders. In either case, the stockholders could be persuaded to invest in the enterprise only if they saw a reasonable—that is, in light of existing alternatives—return on their investment. Whether the operations of the company are run through a dummy organization is of no major consequence to them. They are simply looking for the appropriate return on their share of stock.

The Economics of Railroad Reorganization   Between about 1890 and 1914 a good part of American railroads went through financial difficulties which often culminated in insolvency and reorganization. Most previous historical accounts have advocated the view that this was not surprising. After all, their argument went, because of such flimsy foundations as watered stock and income diverted through construction companies, it was only expected that the railroads would experience financial difficulties as soon as hard times came along. We have argued above that this view is mistaken, that railroads were reasonably funded in terms of the profits which seemed to be forthcoming from them. Consequently we shall look elsewhere for an explanation of the railroads' financial troubles after 1890. We do not have too far to look. By 1890 most of the basic rail networks had been completed. Some construction was still continuing, but at a much-reduced, marginally profitable rate, which simply filled in and often competed with the existing lines. The predictable result was that the average profit rates on railroad operations fell as it ceased to be a growth sector.

This had some strong ramifications for the capital structure of the railroads. During their earlier years, when profits on invested capital were higher, it was worthwhile for them to rely heavily on bonds to finance their investments. If, for example, the going rate on capital in the economy was, say, 8 percent and the expected return on additional rail investment was about 12 percent, then a railroad could make a "profit" of 4 percent on the money it borrowed. By 1890, however, this advantage had largely disappeared. Further competition and investment in the transportation sector had eliminated most of the above-normal profits. Thus bonds ceased to be such an attractive form of borrowing capital for railroads. In fact, at times they became downright burdensome.

Railroad operations are characterized by many resources which are fixed and are not, therefore, easily converted to other uses when the demand for their services falls off. Tracks, bridges, terminals, and switching yards have very few alternative uses. As a consequence, railroad profits tend to fluctuate considerably, thereby affecting the ability to meet a series of fixed yearly charges, such as that of the interest on bonds outstanding. When a slowdown in the economy occurred after 1890, one could have confidently predicted that some railroads would not have had enough cash flow from operations to meet their debt obligations. The result would be defaults on those obligations and forced receivership by anxious debtors who were protecting their own positions.

Under the impetus of receivership, or the immediate threat thereof, most railroads went through reorganization in the three decades before World War I. The process—sometimes called "Morganization" after J. P. Morgan, who was so prominent in such activities—restructured the financial assets of the railroads to the new realities of the situation. This consisted of calling in all existing obligations, such as stocks, bonds, and equipment debts, and paying them off with the proceeds of a new issue of securities. The significant characteristic of this new financial structure was that it relied less on debt financing and more on equity capital. Thus the company was much less subject to unavoidable claims on its cash each year. And much of the variability was shifted back to the stockholders who could expect to absorb a good portion of it through changes in their dividends.

Land Grants to the Railroads

In 1850 the federal government gave some of its land to the Illinois Central Railroad. This was recognized as a precedent-setting action but it was considered justifiable in the public interest because it sped up the construction of certain rail lines which were then deemed especially important to national development. Actually, it was not such a dramatic break with past policy; numerous state and local governments had previously made grants of various sorts—including land to railroads, in order to induce them to build lines which they considered particularly favorable to their jurisdiction. Such efforts seemed small in comparison to the land grants authorized in the 1860s, however. During that relatively short period—short in terms of the total Western movement, anyway—the federal government agreed to give designated railroads certain amounts of land upon completion of tracks that ran parallel to it.

Most of these land grants were in the Western territories, which is not surprising, given two considerations. First, and almost trite, was that almost all the land the federal government owned and therefore could give away was in those regions. (It might have bought land in the developed East but that did not seem likely for reasons which we shall elaborate below.) Second—and most necessary—was that it was in these areas that the policies which the government wished to carry out could be effected. By far the largest portion of the land given to the railroads was to encourage the construction of four transcontinental railroads. This objective of bridging the continent seemed to be motivated by several goals. First, although the northern and southern borders of the United States had been formalized with England and Mexico, there was still some uncertainty as to whether all parties considered those lines immutable. One way to solidify such perceptions was simply to develop the area by moving in large numbers of people who gave concrete support to the formal claims.

A second goal was the link between transportation systems and the economic development of any area, a relation which was obvious enough so that contemporaries of the mid-nineteenth century had no difficulty in accepting it and using it in support of the land grants. The entry of railroads into an area which was not then served by developed transportation facilities drastically lowered transportation costs and led to a correspondingly large increase in the amount of worthwhile economic activity in the area. But the process was somewhat circular in that the amount of traffic which a railroad could hope to attract was closely related to the volume of economic activity which was operating in the area. Thus, the usual argument went, if a railroad could be enticed into any area by special provisions—such as a land grant—then the profitability of the enterprise would be self-fulfilling. The railroad would attract settlers, and the settlers would provide enough business to make the initial investment in the railroad profitable.[11]

(Not) for Sale, Cheap   If one examines maps of the United States that show the extent of federal land grants to railroads, it appears that they were given a sizeable part of the West. Or, as a few historians in their less guarded moments have been known to say, the railroads stole the country blind. This impression comes from the fact that maps show a broad band paralleling each of the transcontinental routes as well as some of the major branches. It looks as if a large portion of the most developable land in the West was simply handed outright to the railroads.

Yet the maps are deceiving for several reasons. First, the apparently wide bands of grant land were not complete parcels but were in most cases the maximum possible width from the tracks within which *some* of the land was given to the railroads. To be more precise, the government gave *alternate* sections of the land to the railroad within the specified corridor so that only one-half of the apparent size was actually deeded. This produced a checkerboard pattern within the grant which the government expected to sell, thereby recouping the losses it suffered in giving up the railroad's share. (Later, of course, this expected federal revenue was ceded to potential settlers with the passage of the Homestead Act.) Thus, the land-grant policy was not the obvious giveaway it was pictured to be. The government, not unreasonably, expected to make more by selling one good parcel of land served by good transport than by selling two which were inaccessible. The effect on the railroads, of course, was to cut their potential sales in half, and perhaps by even more in that under the Homestead Act, or the prevailing policy of early land auctions, the settlers would naturally take these least-expensive options first.

The railroads found that land-grant acreage was not so valuable for other reasons as well. The federal government placed a ceiling on the price per acre at

---

[11] This argument will be readily recognized in its frequent modern forms. It has been used to urge such projects as the Apollo missions, the Saint Lawrence Project, and the SST. The difficulty with the idea is that it can be used to justify almost anything since it provides no way of testing whether the resulting benefits have any chance whatsoever of recouping the costs. In most such cases, private evaluations are probably a good guide. Private investors are certainly smart enough to know that their actions will generate demand and they can incorporate that factor into their plans. Thus, the fact that no private group seems willing to undertake the project is usually a good indication that it is not socially profitable and that the special government aid advocated is usually a way of subsidizing the special interests involved.

which it could be resold. This prevented the railroads from capturing the rents on land which was particularly productive, or convenient to the railroad stations (such as town building lots), unless the railroad wished to operate such properties itself. Then there were the problems with the certification process. To take title to the grant land, the railroads had to physically build the rail line and the federal surveyors had to chart the mileage. Sometimes the surveyors were a little slow, and even when they were not it did not take too much imagination on the part of a new settler to pick out a parcel of land which was in the path of the oncoming rail line. Until the land was actually turned over to the line, it remained in the public domain—which meant that it could be appropriated until the moment that the surveyors drew it onto the public maps. There was a provision in the land-grant legislation that if the land otherwise belonging to the railroad should be already occupied, the railroad would be granted alternative land of equal acreage outside the bounds of the specified grant. The catch, of course, was that such land was much less accessible to the new transportation system and thus less valuable.

Undoubtedly the factor which tended to reduce the value of grant land to the railroads the most, however, was the economic productivity—or, more precisely, the lack thereof—of much of it. The total amount of land given the railroads was very impressive, about 200 million acres. That amounts to about one and one-half times the area of the state of Texas. Yet, as we have often noted, physical resources are not the same as economic resources. Land is valuable only in relation to the existing technological base, which includes such important factors as the ability to use agricultural and mineral resources. In the 1860s much of the West was surprisingly unattractive in these terms. Farming was being developed in certain localities, such as California, Oregon, and the eastern slope of Colorado, but the predominance of acreage offered to the railroads under the land grants would not be productive for several decades at least. Similar considerations applied to such activities as mining and forestry. While they made certain areas valuable, their total contribution to the potential value of land grants in the 1860s was relatively small. One measure of this cheapness of grants to the railroads was that, of the total amount authorized by Congress, less than two-thirds was actually claimed. The rest reverted to the public domain after the railroads failed to construct the necessary track during a twenty-year authorization period. Even some of the major transcontinental grants, such as that for the Northern Pacific, were not completed until after more than a fifteen-year delay. The same phenomenon can be seen in the land accounts of many of the grant railroads. Large unsold acreages were common until the 1900s. The railroads advertised extensively and allowed generous credit terms in order to encourage new settlers to develop the land, but concessions did not seem to help much. During periods of drought or low prices for farm products, the settlers simply abandoned the land without losing much investment. In some years it was quite common for land returns to equal sales so that the railroads sometimes found themselves with as much acreage for sale at the end of a decade as they had at the beginning.

The basic factor underlying all these shortfalls was simply that the land grants were trying, by fiat, to make an economic resource out of lands which were not. It did not work, of course. While much of the land involved eventually did become economically productive, it had to wait until the true determinants, such as transportation costs and agricultural technology, were developed. This underlying factor is important for two reasons. First, it says that much discussion about what a valuable public resource the federal government gave away to private interests is vastly overdrawn. Common perceptions notwithstanding, the government was not really giving up that much.

Second, because the land involved was not particularly valuable, it did not play a major role in the decisions of the railroads as to when, and how large, a rail system should be built. Clearly, the land grants had some net value at the time they were received, but the important question is how important they were in relation to the size of the investment projects involved. With the exception of the first transcontinental line, the value of the grants to individual lines probably did not exceed more than 10 percent of the capital cost of the line. This difference was small enough so that it was probably dominated by the other basic factors which determined the profitability—and hence the timing—of the rail line. For example, an improved variety of wheat (which encouraged expansion into the Plains states), or reductions in the cost of railroad freight costs (and therefore expansion of the feasible area of railroad operations), probably had more effect on the timing of railroad construction than the land grants did. In the final analysis, the extensive attention the land grants have attracted has been for exactly the opposite reason it should have been for. In a historical context they are significant not because of their *importance* but because of their *unimportance.* In a kind of backhanded way, they suggest that the determining forces behind the development of the Western part of the United States were much more basic and stronger than the mere transferring of ownership of land could effect. The land grants demonstrate that it takes much more in the way of net resources and incentives if economic development is to be fostered in a particular area.

Railroad Rates and Regulations

Railroads are one of the cheapest forms of transportation yet devised, but they have very special cost characteristics. They can achieve low-unit carrying costs only when they carry relatively large loads of cargo. This implies that a railroad cannot afford tracks to every farm gate or village in order to solicit and deposit traffic. Cargo and passengers must be more consolidated for loading and unloading. This, in turn, implies that a certain degree of monopoly is likely to exist on local lines. The economics of their operations simply does not allow a dense enough complex of lines to encourage anything approximating competition except in densely populated areas. This is most likely to be noticed in rural areas, and in the period immediately after the Civil War the agricultural area most obviously affected was that of the upper Midwest, particularly such states as Illinois, Wisconsin, and Iowa. The farming areas of the East and South also seemed to be affected, but they had some mitigating factors. In the East there were relatively large urban centers scattered among the rural areas, and they seemed to blunt such local isolation. The South, on the other hand, continued to use its traditional advantage of natural waterways as an effective backstop to local railroad monopoly. (Indeed, the combination of local waterways and efficient coastal navigation succeeded in keeping the railroads entirely out of certain parts of the South for several decades after the Civil War.)

The railroads naturally exploited what local opportunities they had and these were readily seen in the structure of tariffs which they posted for freight. Cargo over well-traveled trunk lines went at rates which were much below those (by mile) charged for local lines. Sometimes the difference was so marked that it was cheaper to ship to a distant market, if it went over a main line much of the way, than to a local one. As early as the 1840s, not too long after the first railroads were operating, states began establishing railroad commissions. Most of these were advisory and were relatively weak in terms of conteracting any policies of the railroads which were deemed insalubrious. In the Midwestern states, however, the commissions were given legal power to regulate the rates charged and, furthermore, the authority to set such other charges as warehouse and storage charges to prevent such directives from being circumvented.

One result of these state regulatory commissions was fairly incontrovertible. They did remove much of the differential between long- and short-haul rates in the states where they operated. The longer-term effects of such policies is more difficult to evaluate, however. While charges on unregulated local lines tended to be much higher than those on long hauls, costs were also higher. The amount of cargo hauled over a given mile of track was less, and therefore the overhead—in the form of track and stations—which had to be absorbed by each load over the useful lifespan of the roadbed was higher. Whether these higher costs fully justified the higher (unregulated) costs on a given line is not easy to determine. However, for all such local lines taken together, prices were sufficiently high to make some monopoly profits over and above a normal return on the invested resources.

The immediate effect, therefore, of regulating rates (presuming that it is done carefully) is to reduce some of the monopoly profits on local railroad operations and to lower the cost of shipping goods. The longer-term effect, however, is somewhat less obvious because, although it would encourage more settlers, particularly farmers, to move into areas served by only limited rail connections, it would also encourage railroads not to go there. If rate regulation were a sufficiently precise science so that it could cut away the monopoly fat from local rates without damaging the muscle of normal profits, then it should not discourage the construction of any local lines which would have been built in the absence of regulation. On a case-by-case basis, however, it is very difficult to allocate costs among the specific functions of a railroad. How should the costs of running a train be divided between the time it spends on a branch line and that that it spends on the main line, for example? Such decisions can make considerable difference between the amount of profit charged to local versus long-distance traffic. And thus the rulings by the regulatory body can have a major effect on profits of a railroad even if decisions are made carefully and evenhandedly.

Given this area of ambiguity—and admitted range within which parties might reasonably differ—it is likely that some branch lines which would otherwise be constructed, never will be. Hence, the irony of railroad regulation in such states as Illinois and Wisconsin was that, although it benefited the farmers in those states, it probably discouraged potential farmers who were considering establishing new farms in Nebraska and the Dakotas.

Profits and Coordination on the Trunk Lines As so often happens in such situations, while the regulators were busy perfecting their guidelines to control the railroads, the railroads were busy devising new forms of creating profits outside the boundaries of the regulations. By 1870 the railroads were working out arrangements to share and control traffic on the major interstate lines. At first the efforts had simply taken the form of jointly setting rates which all agreed to follow. These tended to erode quickly, however, in that not only was it easy to cheat on the agreement by offering rebates, but effective rates could be varied considerably by such methods as altering storage costs and delivery schedules (as the state regulators were already discovering). The railroads soon turned their attention to planning arrangements in which such incentives to cheat were eliminated, or at least controlled. The most common form of these was the "pool," in which the railroads divided their total revenues by some agreed-upon formula, thus eliminating the gain an individual railroad could have made by secretly diverting some of the traffic over its own line. Some of the pools, such as the Chicago to St. Louis agreement which lasted for fifteen years, were quite successful. The majority of agreements tended to fall apart much faster and had to be constantly renegotiated if they were to work at all. And despite the pooling provisions, individual railroads still had a wide latitude in which to violate the spirit of the agreements, if not the letter. An even more important problem was that the agreements were not enforceable in the courts, and thus an individual company could gain by threatening to withdraw from the pool unless concessions were made. This was a powerful bargaining weapon. One company acting independently could shade prices and divert considerable traffic from the cartel group, thus cutting their profits substantially. The alternative was to allow them a larger share of the profits in order to keep them within the pool.

The railroads, of course, attempted to circumvent all these problems. They came up with a number of arrangements to reduce the potential instabilities in the system, but most involved controlling the behavior of customers. In the coal areas of Pennsylvania and West Virginia, for example, some of the railroads sought to stabilize their traffic by gaining control of the coal mines. This ran into considerable local opposition[12] and was effectively stopped by the state govern-

---

[12] This local opposition was probably warranted. If the railroads did use such control to control rail rates, then it would have inflicted real resource costs on the locality. The railroad might well have found itself with somewhat of a split personality, however. To the extent that freight rates were higher, rail profits would be higher, but then the return on their investment in coal properties would be lower. Also, the coal properties could well become strong advocates of lower rates, and the railroads would then find a party attempting to break the pooling arrangement right in their own boardroom. Ah, the problems of running a monopoly!

ments, which wrote prohibitions on such operations into the corporate charters of railroads. Besides, the railroads found that operating coal mines was much more difficult than they had anticipated. The best-known case of railroads attempting to control freight charges through the customers was that of the South Improvement Company. This operation was prominently attributed to John D. Rockefeller, but in fact it was created mostly on the initiative of the railroads shipping oil out of northwestern Pennsylvania. The arrangement called for the cooperating shippers to place their oil on the various railroads in such a way that certain agreed-upon shares were maintained among them. In return, the shippers would receive discounts on their own cargoes equal to some agreed-upon percentage of the total fares charged.[13] The function of the shippers in this arrangement was to guarantee the railroads their agreed-upon shares of the market. This eliminated the possibility of the shippers breaking the pool, which was usually the important incentive which was harnessed to force price cuts. The rebates to the shippers were, in effect, sharing some of the monopoly profits in order to forestall this major threat to the pools' existence.

The Continual Erosion of Competition   Even when the railroads were able to keep their pools intact and functioning, they suffered under the bane of cartels, namely, the tendency of outsiders to devise substitute services which eroded their market. The most obvious example of this in the railroad sector after 1870 was simply the construction of additional rail lines. Sometimes this involved creating lines which paralleled existing routes. This occurred, for example, in 1873 when the Baltimore and Ohio extended its western terminus to Chicago and set off a rate war with the other major carriers by offering an additional route to East Coast ports. At other times the construction efforts were more modest, but they still contributed to competition. When the Chesapeake and Ohio and the Norfolk and Western extended their lines (which had originally been designed to carry coal from the Appalachian fields to the tidewater ports) over the mountains to the Ohio River and the Great Lakes, they effectively began to compete with some of the traffic on the main east-to-west trunk lines. Shippers now had the option of shipping cargo by water part of the way east, and then relying on the shorter rail lines to complete the task. As time passed, these alternative routings became more common and consequently became more effective in promoting competition.

The broadening network of competition was clearly visible in the repeated improvisations of the railroad pools. Whenever a new outsider appeared and was able to capture a significant share of the existing traffic of a cartel, the group was forced to take him into the club and reallocate the shares. This meant that ex-

---

[13] The common story has it that Rockefeller forced the railroads not only to give discounts on his cargo but also on that of his competitors as well. This is more a semantic than a substantive distinction. If, for example, Rockefeller shipped one-half of the oil, it made no difference whether he was given 20 percent off his own freight bill or 10 percent off everyone's. There is the additional complication that these were discounts off list prices which can be very arbitrary anyway if shippers and railroads frequently bargain over rebates, and hence over real rates.

isting pool members had to give up some of their share of traffic or profit to accommodate the newcomer. If this process were allowed to continue, the income of the initial firms in the pool would gradually shrink. To forestall this erosion, the member railroads sought to maintain or even increase their share of the traffic, which tempted them to engage in much the same tactics as the new outside competitors. This struggle for the traffic in a given market went on both within and without a pool as long as there were any above-normal profits to tempt such behavior. Thus, whatever their ability to create short-term profits, the experience of the pools was that it was next to impossible to retain them over the longer term.

Railroad Consolidation While the pools were struggling to retain some monopoly profits over some of the major freight routes, the railroads were competing among themselves over another source of potential monopoly profits within the system. In an integrated system comprised of independent rail lines, such as in the United States, freight often moves over the tracks of several different companies to reach its destination. Thus, the railroads are not only dealing with individual shippers when they transport goods, but also with each other. And it should come as no surprise that the rates which one line charges another are influenced by the availability of alternative routes. To cite one example, when the northern transcontinental route to the West Coast was completed in 1882, the Northern Pacific, which comprised most of the route, joined up with a short line operated by the Oregon Railroad and Navigation Company, which ran along the Columbia River to Portland and from there had a branch line to Seattle. The OR&N had an alternate route to the East in the form of the Oregon and Salt Lake Railroad, which ran from its eastern terminus southeast to the Union Pacific lines in Utah, but it held the single outlet of the Northern Pacific to the West Coast. Thus, this small line was in the enviable position of being able to set rates on through traffic which extracted a good part of the monopoly profits being earned on the Northern Pacific's route. The latter's response was typical. As fast as it could, it built a branch line from its western terminus to Seattle.

The monopoly position of one railroad vis-à-vis another was not limited to this one example in the distant Northwest but was found to various degrees throughout the national rail system. And, like the North Pacific, other lines were frequently seeking ways to circumvent the monopolies which controlled the outlets for the traffic they carried. One of the most direct and common methods was to consolidate adjacent independent lines into longer networks, thus ensuring that traffic was "internalized," which is to say that it did not have to be turned over to a neighboring carrier which might expose its monopolistic pricing. This process of consolidation was one of the best-known and most colorful phases of American railroad history. One of its earliest practitioners was Commodore Vanderbilt, who had acquired his initial wealth and title by developing ferries and steamship lines along the East Coast. Vanderbilt put the New York Central together out of nine local lines. In the process he doubled the face value of the total amount of outstanding stock, at which point he was tagged with the lasting reputation of watering stock. The doubled market value was probably warranted, however, in that traffic flowed more smoothly and efficiently over the new line. (Vanderbilt was more than a mere manipulator. He followed up his acquisition with modernization of the physical facilities and management of the new line.) He also assured his operations free access to the large New York City market by acquiring the Harlem and Hudson River lines.

When he sought to gain access to outlets farther west, however, by taking over the Erie Railroad, he ran up against some of the most ingenious and uninhibited management in the industry in the persons of Daniel Drew, Jim Fisk, and Jay Gould. Vanderbilt, therefore, failed in his attempt with the Erie,[14] but he later acquired controlling interest in the Lake Shore, Michigan Southern, and Michigan Central Railroads. The Erie management itself was no stranger to such tactics. Gould, for example, owned a sizeable share of the Union Pacific. To protect his routes he had bought into the parallel Kansas Pacific, and to safeguard that investment he, in turn, acquired shares in the Missouri Pacific. The process of consolidation reached its dramatic climax around the turn of the century when a good portion of the nation's most important routes was controlled by only about a half-dozen lines. These included Gould's holdings in the Southwest, with extensions to San Francisco and Pittsburgh, Edward Harriman's far-ranging system of Western railroads, the Vanderbilt and Pennsylvania networks which dominated the traffic between the East Coast and the upper Mississippi valley, and the newly formed Southern Railroad.

The Evolution of Railroad Regulation   The state regulatory commissions established by the Midwestern states in the 1870s have often been touted as the beginning of effective regulation for the public interest in the United States. Yet the Granger Laws, as these attempts to regulate rail charges were often called, failed to establish any long-term pattern of control. If anything, they might be termed abortive attempts because they proved substantially ineffective for the next three decades. Soon after such states as Illinois, Wisconsin, and Minnesota enacted regulatory commissions, the railroads began to challenge them in the courts. This appeared to be good strategy on their part because they were generally successful. In addition, the states tended to soften the powers of the commissions, apparently in response to a general public appraisal that they had been unduly harsh on the railroads.

Federal regulation of interstate rates began in 1887, after a court ruling that states could not legally prescribe rates on shipments beyond their own borders. The Interstate Commerce Commission, established in that year, had the power to

[14] Vanderbilt's attempt to gain control of the Erie developed into a bizarre and almost "Keystone cops" sequence. He knew that the current management would resist attempts to take over the railroad by any means possible, so he obtained a court injunction to prevent one obvious tactic—namely, increasing the number of shares. Drew and company got around this ruling, however, by issuing convertible bonds which they immediately converted into new stock. They fled to New Jersey—just escaping the sheriff at the ferry dock, by some accounts—until they could persuade (read *buy*) the new state legislature to legitimize their actions and prohibit a merger of the Erie and New York Central.

rule on the reasonableness of existing rates, but not the authority—or so held the courts—to dictate future ones. Again the railroads used the court system to retard, and to a considerable degree negate, the ability of the regulator to effectively set prices. Federal rate setting finally received a strong weapon in 1903, with the passage of the Elkins Act. This act prohibited the practice of rebates, that is, discounts from listed rates granted to selected shippers (usually those that moved large quantities of goods and therefore had stronger bargaining power). The law was necessary in that unless railroads could be held to their posted rates, there was no possibility of making regulation effective. Yet the regulation had a curious effect and some surprising advocates. The law was, of course, supported by smaller business people and farmers who were usually the ones unable to win rebates. If discounts could be eliminated and—this was crucial—overall rates set on the basis of some allowed rate of return on capital, then rates to smaller shippers would be reduced. The law also received almost unanimous backing from the railroads. This might seem surprising at first, because it was a form of regulation upon them, but their response is perfectly understandable when we remember that it accomplished something which nearly five decades of pools had failed to achieve. Eliminating discrimination might be a desirable goal, but the tactic which attempted to do it had the unfortunate effect of destroying the prime channels through which rates in general could be forced down.

In 1904 and 1905 legislation was enacted which created much of the basic regulatory control over the railroads which still exists today. The railroads generally opposed this control but they soon found that, ironically, like the Elkins Act, it could work to their advantage. For one thing, it eliminated another problem they had been struggling with for half a century. One line could no longer exercise its monopoly powers over adjacent carriers. (Of course, this was not good news to those railroads that had such power.) The possibility of using this power had been dampened by the recent phase of mergers in the rail system, however—which appears to have been a good part of the motivation for them.

The ultimate irony of the beginning of regulation is that it finally came when the possible gains from its use were fast declining and the likely costs of imposing the regulations were rising. As of 1905, railroading had moved well beyond the growth phase. The total mileage of track was near a peak, and thereafter investments were made simply to replace depreciating facilities, albeit often with more productive ones. Soon after 1905 the decline of railroading became obvious to even the casual observer. This meant that from then on profits would, at best, be at the normal level and would very likely fall below that level if left unregulated. Furthermore, the special monopoly powers which the railroads held over local shippers seemed especially vulnerable to new, emerging forms of competition. The truck and the automobile did far more than the ICC could have hoped to achieve in injecting competition into local transportation markets. Thus, regulation which was generally intended to ensure that the railroads did not make profits which were too high was enacted at a time when the basic problem was shifting to one in which profits were too low. And the methods established to ensure that the rail lines made only a fair profit ended up by protecting them against the retrenchments which the market would soon have forced upon them. Railroad rates were setting those charges which provided a "fair return" on capital. For most of the time after 1905 that was more than the railroads would have earned if left to fend for themselves, unregulated. To compound this paradox of regulation, this had been possible only because regulation removed from the railroads the very mechanisms of adjustments in prices and services which they would have naturally followed, thus effecting such a course.

THE FINANCIAL SECTOR, 1861–1914

When the Civil War began to reach the unprecedented size that has become clear only in retrospect, the Northern economy was not prepared for the struggle. One of the ways in which its inadequacy was apparent was in the financial area. The nation had always financed its major wars by creating debt, but because this struggle was so large the task took on new and more difficult dimensions. At first the Treasury (with the consent of Congress) attempted to sell bonds to cover expenses. But even at a comparatively high interest rate of more than 7 percent, these debt instruments did not sell very well. (This showed good foresight on the part of the public because inflation and much higher interest rates soon made these bonds quite unattractive by comparison.) Thus, somewhat under the gun, Congress began to look for other sources of revenue.

In early 1862 it authorized the issuance of nonredeemable notes which, because of the distinctive coloring on their reverse side, became popularly known as "greenbacks." These notes circulated from hand to hand just like money, but with one important distinction. They were not redeemable in gold coin. This was necessary if Congress intended to issue large amounts of greenbacks—which it soon did—because there simply was not enough gold in the economy to back such amounts—a situation that soon removed the United States from the gold standard prevailing among the major economic powers of the day, however. In effect, the Northern economy shifted to a two-tier monetary system. The older gold-backed notes, or gold coins themselves, continued to circulate at the prewar exchange rates with other world currencies. The greenbacks were treated as a separate currency and, with Congress continuing to issue large quantities of them, they circulated at a growing discount from the gold currency. The economy, then, had two sets of prices, those for greenbacks and those for gold— although either could always be converted to the other by the current premium paid on gold over greenbacks. The discount on greenbacks increased over the course of the war as more were issued to finance the conflict, and the premium rose to about 100 percent near the end of the war, indicating that the real value of a greenback dollar was only half that of a gold coin of the same nominal value. This inflation in greenbacks was the prime force which accounted for the near doubling of average prices in the wartime North.

The issuance of large amounts of fiat money in the form of greenbacks was one method devised to finance the war. Another involved changes in the nation's banking system. There had always been some discontent with the decentralized arrangement of banks and banknotes which prevailed throughout the antebellum period. Part of this sentiment for a stable and uniform currency had been apparent in the interest in the two central banks which had been established in the period. Thus, when Congress was struggling with the problem of financing the war, it was only natural that it would consider ways by which the banking system—which was the prime candidate for handling financial assets such as government debt—could be reorganized and could absorb war debt at the same time. In short, it would be a way of killing two birds with one stone. (Although in this case killing two birds with one stone was certainly desirable, it was also extremely difficult to do. This perspective of the analogy will appear more relevant as we look at the actual implementation of the legislation.)

In 1863 Congress approved the establishment of the National Banking System. The title is slightly misleading in that it did not establish anything like a coordinated national system of banks but rather established a procedure whereby, for the first time, federal charters would be issued to ordinary banks. One requirement for such a charter was that the bank must deposit government bonds equal to at least one-third of its paid-in capital with the controller of the currency, after which it could then issue federal notes to its customers equal to no more than 90 percent of that paid-in amount. This arrangement was obviously designed to create a demand for both government bonds and notes by converting them into common financial assets in the banking system. The only problem was that it used too many government securities; that is, it was such an expensive way of conducting banking that relatively few banks found it attractive. Most of those that did were new, generally small banks. Almost none that already held state charters found it desirable to convert to the new federal system. (See Table 12-2.)

Congress noted this reluctance and decided to apply the force of a strong stick where a shriveled carrot had failed. In 1864 it passed a tax of 10 percent on the face value of bank notes issued by state banks *each time* they were paid out by the bank. In effect, this amounted to a prohibitory law. About three-quarters of the nation's banks converted from state to federal charters within a year's time. Some writers have praised this step as one which brought a unified national financial market to the United States and therefore improved the allocation of resources within the economy. That is a mistaken evaluation, at least in the way it has usually been portrayed. It is not the existence of a *common denomination* of currency so much as the cost of transferring resources between different areas, or uses, which makes financial markets more integrated. If, for example, the cost of shifting capital from one area to another equals 15 percent of the value of the resource, then rates of return can differ by 15 percent (or 15 percent spread over the time that the resource is expected to be used), whether both are held in the same currency or not. Common denominations of currencies make transactions somewhat easier, but by themselves they cannot repeal the real costs of moving resources among markets.

In fact, the National Banking System probably made the capital markets in the economy work somewhat less efficiently and therefore provided fewer resources for it to use. The federal regulations made the banking system use larger

Table 12-2 Number and Total Assets of National, Nonnational, and State Banks, 1863–1940

Year	National Banks		Nonnational Banks[1]		State Banks
	Number	Assets (millions of dollars)	Number	Assets (millions of dollars)	Number
1863	66	$ 17	1,466	$ 1,192	1,466
1865	1,294	1,127	349	231	349
1870	1,612	1,566	325	215	325
1875	2,076	1,913	1,260	1,291	586
1880	2,076	2,036	1,279	1,364	650
1885	2,689	2,422	1,661	2,005	1,015
1890	3,484	3,062	4,717	3,296	2,250
1895	3,715	3,471	6,103	4,139	4,369
1900	3,731	4,944	9,322	6,444	5,007
1905	5,664	7,325	13,103	10,186	9,018
1910	7,138	9,892	18,013	13,030	14,348
1915	7,597	11,790	20,420	16,573	17,748
1920	8,024	23,267	22,885	29,827	20,635
1925	8,066	24,252	20,986	37,980	19,573
1930	7,247	28,828	17,026	45,462	15,798
1935	5,425	26,009	10,622	33,942	9,752
1940	5,164	36,816	9,912	42,913	9,238

[1]Nonnational banks include state commercial banks, mutual, and stock savings banks, private banks, and loan and trust companies.

Source: Adapted from Albert W. Niemi, Jr., *U.S. Economic History,* Rand McNally, Chicago, 1975, p. 199. Reprinted by permission of Rand McNally College Publishing Company.

amounts of resources to provide a given number of banking services. This would have had the effect of increasing the cost of such services—such as the interest rate on business loans and mortgages—to the public. Thus, fewer of these services would have been used compared with the antebellum period, and the amount of resources transferred—which could reduce differentials in the return on capital among regions—would have been reduced accordingly. Thus the National Banking System did not kill two birds with one stone. It killed one, in that it did force the financial sector to absorb a larger portion of the national debt, thereby easing the task of funding the war effort. However, when it came to the second bird, in the form of a better banking system, it missed. In fact, the better analogy might be that it not only missed but it made the bird more watchful so that it would be even harder to hit next time. The effect of the National Banking System on the economy is best summarized by calling it a tax on the financial system to make the funding of the national debt easier, thereby benefiting the taxpayers.

The Long-Term Erosion of the National Banking System

The federal government forced the majority of state banks to convert to federal charters as of the mid-1860s, by using punitive legislation. For much of the next fifty years, however, the number of state-chartered banks grew faster until at the end of the period, in 1914, there were more than twice as many as those with federal charters.[15] The shift is quite predictable once we recall that federal chartering generally imposed costs of operations which were higher than those of the states. Thus, if a bank could find a way of operating with a state charter but without the taxed bank notes, then it would have an important advantage in costs over the national banks. This device came in the form of demand deposits, or what today we call checking accounts. The switch of payments from cash to check, however, was only partly related to the differences in cost on the supply side. Part of the impetus was coming from changes in the economy which made the advantages of that particular system of payment more attractive. The volume of financial transactions was increasing not only as both total and per capita incomes rose, but also as economic units became more specialized and interdependent. Under these conditions, consumers would undoubtedly wish to shift from cash to check payments irrespective of the bank's incentives in the situation. The fact that under the existing regulations checks were actually a cheaper method of payment further encouraged the shift.

The Price Level, 1865–1914

Between the Civil War and World War I, the average price level in the American economy went through a V-shaped cycle. For the first thirty years, from 1865 to 1895, prices fell rather steadily. Then for the last twenty years they climbed back up. The reason for this pattern is easy to see. Throughout this entire period the nation's money supply was tied to gold. The average price level, therefore, was simply a reflection of the amount of gold in circulation *as money* compared with the total output of the economies which used gold as money at any given time.[16] For the first thirty years after the Civil War the world economy grew faster than new additions of gold and, therefore, to accommodate the additional activity, average prices had to fall. About 1895, however, there was a series of gold discoveries—the important of which were in Alaska and South Africa—which led to a large increase in the monetary stock of gold and, therefore, to increases in prices.

One demonstration that changes in the gold supply were, in fact, the underlying force behind price shifts occurred in the fifteen-year transition period after the Civil War. As we noted, the United States had gone off the gold standard in order to finance the war through inflation. To reestablish that parity, prices in greenbacks had to be brought back down to the gold level, which is just what the federal government set out to do by gradually retiring some of that fiat money from circulation each year. This, combined with the normal expansion in nation-

---

[15] Starting from the initial position in 1865 where there were nearly four federally chartered banks to one of the states, this shows a growth by the state banks that was eight times that of those with federal affiliation. This perspective makes the growth of the state banks all the more dramatic.

[16] Under the gold standard which existed before 1920, changes in the general price levels were shared among all participating nations. If one nation's prices rose above those of the others, its exports would become less attractive and other foreign goods more attractive. This would result in a balance-of-payments deficit and an outflow of gold from the economy leading to a fall in prices. Thus, whatever the initial distribution of gold discoveries or holdings, they would be apportioned according to the average levels of the various economies already in effect.

al output, was sufficient to bring the two price levels back together in 1879. But while this realignment was taking place, prices in gold units were themselves going down. Thus the fall in prices was more than merely the usual deflation at the end of a war. It reflected a trend—given the monetary system in use—which was so basic that it would have occurred in the absence of the war, or of most other major disturbances, for that matter.

Thus, for a thirty-year period, 1865 to 1895, falling prices were a normal part of life in the American economy (see Table 12-3). This seems surprising today because we readily associate falling prices with depressed conditions. There were, of course, such cyclical downturns within this period but the trend toward lower prices continued right through the prosperous periods as well. Deflation was well established as a basic trend, and the short-term functioning of the economy seemed oblivious to it and proceeded normally. The rate of increase in real output and per capita income was just as fast as in the late antebellum period or the two decades before the Civil War. Here again we see American history providing an interesting counterexample to some of the generally held views about the prerequisites for growth or prosperity. One obvious example is the Phillips curve, that much-discussed relation between the level of employment and that of the rate of increase in prices. It is generally assumed that the higher the rate of inflation, the lower the level of unemployment. The period between 1865 and 1895 casts considerable doubt on this relationship and says, at a minimum, that it is the rate of change of prices from their normal trend rather than any given absolute increase which changes employment. Thus, if the average trend in prices is a 4 percent reduction, a 2 percent decrease in a given year is, relatively speaking, a 2 percent inflation, and thus might be able to force a short-term fall in unemployment.

Most historical accounts have considered this long-term decrease in prices after the Civil War in terms of its effects on the relative positions of debtors and creditors. There was considerable agitation by such groups as the Grangers, the Greenback party, and the Populists to increase the money supply in order to stop deflation. Their direct concern was the adverse effects which they believed it was having on debtors. If a man were to borrow money—a typical example would go—and prices were to fall thereafter, then he would be paying back his obligation in dollars which were worth more than those he borrowed. Thus he would lose through deflation and the creditor would make a windfall gain of that amount. Steady deflation, therefore—goes the argument—would lead to continuous losses by debtors.

This argument is a little shortsighted and it certainly underestimates the capability of borrowers to be able to protect their own interests. One could understand that if borrowers agreed to take a loan with terms which were based on stable prices in the future, and were surprised when deflation began, that they would suffer a loss. However, to continue to agree to such terms once a fall in prices becomes well established suggests that the borrowers are a little naïve or befuddled. Once deflation becomes a recognized pattern, borrowers would understand that the real interest charge that they could expect to pay would be the

Table 12-3 Cost-of-Living Indexes (Federal Reserve Bank of New York)

Year	1913 = 100 Federal Reserve Bank of N.Y.	Year	1913 = 100 Federal Reserve Bank of N.Y.	Year	1913 = 100 Federal Reserve Bank of N.Y.
1913	100	1895	73	1877	80
1912	102	1894	73	1876	81
1911	96	1893	75		
		1892	77	1875	86
1910	96	1891	76	1874	88
1909	91			1873	88
1908	91	1890	78	1872	90
1907	95	1889	78	1871	89
1906	90	1888	78		
		1887	76	1870	91
1905	87	1886	76	1869	95
1904	87			1868	98
1903	88	1885	75	1867	102
1902	84	1884	77	1866	103
1901	82	1883	81		
		1882	86	1865	102
1900	80	1881	83		
1899	77				
1898	75	1880	80		
1897	75	1879	79		
1896	74	1878	80		

Source: Adapted from U.S. Bureau of the Census, *Historical Statistics of the United States, Colonial Times to 1957,* Government Printing Office, Washington, D.C., 1960, p. 127.

stated, or nominal, rate on the loan agreement *plus* the decrease in prices. Even if lenders doggedly continued to charge the same rates as they did before deflation became a recognized fact, the higher cost of borrowing would reduce the amount which borrowers would choose to use. This, by itself, would tend to lower the nominal, or stated, going rate of interest on loans.

Even if borrowers are naïve, however, and continue to accept the same nominal rate as unchanged in real cost despite the deflation, lenders are under a strong incentive to lower the rate themselves.[17] When they see that the real cost of funds to them has fallen by the rate of the deflation, they recognize that the net margin of return on their lending activities has risen accordingly. They are then in a position where each additional customer they attract would increase

[17] This line of logic has several applications to important contemporary issues as well, especially those which deal with safeguarding the interests of consumers. One important implication is that it is not necessarily true that poorly informed consumers will be cheated and therefore must be protected by some independent body. Competition among sellers is sufficient to protect the interests of the buyers in that it is in their self-interest to offer the consumer the best possible deal.

their net profits all the more. And the logical way to attempt that is to reduce their loan rates below those of their competitors. In the short run this leads to an increase in their profits, but it soon forces their competitors to follow suit. Rate cutting will continue until the rate has been driven down to the level at which only normal profits are being made. Note that this is simply the predeflation level minus the rate of deflation, which in real terms is exactly the same rate which prevailed before the deflation began. When the inevitable adjustment has taken place, either on the initiative of the borrowers or that of the lenders—or most likely on that of both—the changes in prices will have been discounted and the real costs maintained at their same real level. So if, for example, the prevailing rate of interest before deflation began had been 6 percent, and prices then began to fall by 4 percent a year, the nominal rate of interest would be adjusted downward to 2 percent. At this level the real rate would still be 6 percent—the 2 percent money charge plus the 4 percent annual appreciation in the value of each dollar.

Thus, the concern over the position of debtors during this extended period of deflation is almost certainly overdone. Any likely scenario of human behavior suggests that people would have largely compensated for this phenomenon as soon as it became established. The record of interest rates for the time indicates that this certainly occurred. As we noted (in Chapter 11), interest rates fell substantially throughout the period. While part of this decline reflects the diminishing marginal product of capital resulting from a higher savings rate, there also appears to be a sizeable drop attributable to price adjustment. The question then naturally arises as to whether the various protest groups, such as the Populists, were mistaken in their efforts to stop, or even reverse, the fall in prices. Not necessarily, because even while they (presuming they represent the debtors) would not gain from stable or rising prices, once those trends became recognized, they would benefit during the one-time transition to them. If prices were to level out, for example, then the 2 percent nominal interest rate would become a bargain 2 percent real interest rate as well (admittedly short-term). And, besides, the protest groups did not necessarily have to take their own complaints too seriously anyway. It makes much better public relations to say that one is being hurt by a policy and relief should therefore be provided than to advertise that the "relief" itself is really what one wishes, and the distress is nothing more than a cover story.

The National Market for Capital Resources

Ironically, all the while that such protest groups as the Grangers and the Populists were complaining about the excessive cost of credit, the interest rates charged in their regions were falling dramatically. In 1870 the real farm mortgage rate in all the upper Midwestern states of Illinois, Wisconsin, Nebraska, and Iowa exceeded 16 percent. By 1900, however, the real rates in all these states had fallen below 5 percent. (See Figure 12-2.) In Wisconsin they averaged less than 3.5 percent. In one sense the protesters were getting their way, but not because they were protesting and not in the way they were advocating. Changes in the financial markets were occurring so fast that much of the dissent was outdated by the time it was organized.

The development of the capital market in this period was hardly unique in the economy, of course. The manufacturing, agricultural, and commercial sec-

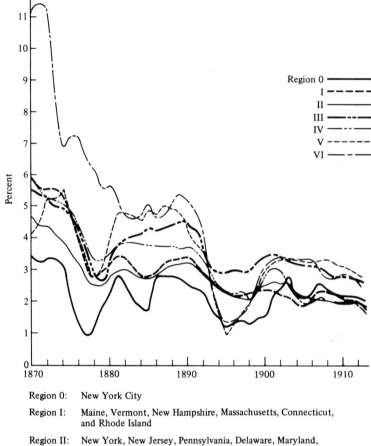

Region 0:   New York City

Region I: Maine, Vermont, New Hampshire, Massachusetts, Connecticut, and Rhode Island

Region II: New York, New Jersey, Pennsylvania, Delaware, Maryland, and the District of Columbia

Region III: Virginia, West Virginia, North Carolina, South Carolina, Georgia, Florida, Alabama, Mississippi, Louisiana, Texas, Arkansas, Kentucky, and Tennessee

Region IV: Ohio, Indiana, Illinois, Michigan, Wisconsin, Minnesota, Iowa, and Missouri

Region V: North Dakota, South Dakota, Nebraska, Kansas, Montana, Wyoming, Colorado, New Mexico, and Oklahoma

Region VI: Washington, Oregon, California, Idaho, Utah, Nevada, and Arizona

Figure 12-2   Three-year moving average net returns of city banks. *(Source: Lance E. Davis, "The Investment Market, 1870–1914: The Evolution of a National Market," Journal of Economic History, vol. 25, September 1965. By permission of Lance E. Davis and the Journal of Economic History.)*

tors, along with others, were going through a similar process of restructuring. The improvements in the financial sector took numerous forms, but they all had one element in common. Each contributed in some way to reducing the cost of shifting financial resources among locations, or among different types of uses. As these transactions, or overhead costs, were reduced, capital moved more readily to its highest prevailing return. The net result was that differences in returns among the various uses of capital were reduced and the economy was able to make a higher return on its existing capital stock.

Consider, for example, the long-term problem of transferring capital from East to West. Generally, the Western areas were developing faster and thus could profitably employ a larger amount of new capital relative to the local supply—that is, saving—than those of the East. Thus, interest rates, which reflected the cost of capital, were generally higher in the West than in the East. This, of course, encouraged investors, or intermediaries who handled their funds, to transfer some of the funds from the East to the West in order to capture some of those higher earnings. The barrier to this reallocation of resources was the complex of costs involved in making the transfer. Before the Civil War these were often quite large. They consisted of much more than simply the physical costs of moving the financial assets. The important elements were the more difficult steps of evaluating credit ratings, collecting payments, and running down deadbeats at a distance of 1,000 miles or so. Before the Civil War it seldom paid to undertake such a task as a specialized function. Most of the capital transferred to the West was tied onto some other economic function. The most important channel was probably the mercantile system. Eastern merchants borrowed funds to finance their operations and, in turn, advanced credit to Western merchants who then usually channeled some of it to their customers in the form of credit sales. It was a roundabout and expensive arrangement but it was still cheaper than using a specialized financial channel to transfer that small an amount of capital.

Such differentiated institutions became more advantageous—and therefore more used—after the Civil War as the volume of financial resources which they could handle continued to increase. One good example is the appearance of the mortgage company. The high returns on mortgages on Midwestern farms in 1870, which we cited above, were an almost irresistible temptation for some entrepreneur to create an organization which gathered up funds in the East and parceled them out in the West. Such companies became a common feature of Midwestern agriculture in the late nineteenth century. The farmers, who tended to look on them as the personification of the exploiting middlemen, resented the high rates they charged. Even so, mortgage rates were lower than they otherwise would have been.[18] The operations of the mortgage companies were the essence of simplicity. They raised funds in major Eastern cities by selling loans to individuals who were attracted by the high rates being paid. These funds were then shifted to Western offices where they were used to buy local mortgages. Often the mortgage companies did not actually write such contracts themselves but merely repurchased

[18] Another Midwestern group that resented the the mortgage companies was that formed by the local bankers. Their dislike was more understandable, however, in that this extralocal competition reduced the rates they could otherwise have charged.

them from the local banks. In this function they acted like another type of financial intermediary which was becoming more common at this time also—the commerical paper broker. These individuals traveled throughout the Midwest, South, and those areas in general where sophisticated financial services had not yet developed, buying up the short-term promissory notes of merchants. The brokers usually did not retain most of the paper they bought but resold it to established holders in larger cities, particularly in the East. These traveling buyers, then, became the purest example of the process of transferring capital. Their charges, in the form of the premium they charged final buyers over that which they paid for the commercial paper, represented the net costs of making the transfer. Just like the differential in interest rates, which tended to express that same category of costs, these declined over time.

The effects of this homogenization and integration of the national capital market have been widely noted in recent years but some seem less appreciated than others. The narrowing of interest rate differentials now seems generally appreciated, as is its logical implication that this improved the aggregate return on capital in the economy. Some other implications of this process require a little more investigation before they can be visualized, however. For example, the same process which reduced the cost of borrowing in the developing areas also raised the return on saving in the capital-exporting regions. While this was partly offset by some decrease in the return on local saving in the capital-importing areas, the overall effect was to increase the interest rate paid to savers. This encouraged a shift toward saving and away from current consumption. In addition, the development of financial markets also probably tended to cause the apparent, or measured, saving rate to increase. The improvements of such markets would naturally encourage consumers to shift to more formalized methods of saving and away from the informal methods they had had to use in the absence of such markets. For instance, modern savers can salt their funds away in such specially designed institutions as savings banks, or in corporate bonds. In the absence of these, saving would be more likely to take the form of investing in land or collecting gold coins. The point for our purposes is that despite care in estimating such *informal* methods, the *formal* ones (in the economy with differentiated financial institutions) are the more likely to be detected. Thus the appearance of specialized institutions is likely to increase the measured rate of saving in two ways, one in a real sense that it increases the return on savings, and the other illusionary in that it makes the savings more noticeable. Both of these influences were probably present in the large jump in measured saving which occurred in the Civil War decade. It is not likely that they are the total explanation, however, in that they are likely to occur more gradually along with the growth of the financial institutions themselves. Nevertheless, they constitute an eligible hypothesis in the attempt to account for that still-unresolved question of why the rate took such a dramatic jump up in that relatively short period.

Markets for Corporate Securities   Ever since its existence became generally recognized, a good portion of Americans have distrusted the stock market. It is admittedly difficult to visualize what kind of a positive function it might play.

Unlike agriculture or coal mining, it does not provide a tangible product which would contribute obviously to human needs. And besides, it seems to encourage the worst kind of human behavior. Many accounts of trading on the stock market suggest that the deceitful and aggressive make money while the more honest "little" guy tends to lose. Moreover, the period between the Civil War and World War I seems to be the one where these characteristics were most exaggerated. This was the era in which financiers such as Jay Cooke could start a business panic when his highly leveraged empire collapsed, or when J. P. Morgan held enough power over the market so that he could personally intervene to stop such a panic.

Or was it? Many of these characterizations have been repeated often enough so that they are now widely accepted as reasonable approximations of the period. Yet when one looks at the specific happenings out of which such accounts have been built, they begin to look much less certain. For example, let us start with the rather basic question of what was the driving force behind the stock market. Most accounts of the market over this fifty-year period tend to focus on the panics and the troubles they brought upon the economy. (That is the tenor of many accounts in general histories of the United States, anyway. More specialized histories tend to be somewhat less accusatory.) We are often told, for example, that there were panics in 1884, 1890, 1893, and 1907. By implication, this is offered as evidence of some basic defect in the system. Yet one might also note that there were twenty-four years from 1884 to 1907, inclusive, and there were no reported panics in twenty of them. Besides, if one looks at the record since World War II, there have been as many major declines in stock prices since then, when the market was presumably safer through tighter public supervision than it was in the nineteenth century.

Then, if we look at the basic function of the stock market, it is no surprise that stock prices go down as well as up, sometimes dramatically so. They reflect the income expected from the future operations of the companies they represent. Thus it is hardly surprising that when economic conditions take a turn for the worse, as they periodically do, that the average prices of a large number of stocks should be written down accordingly. Thus losses in some years are an expected part of owning stocks (if you want a more regular return, buy bonds), yet that does not mean that over a period of time they are not profitable investments. Their prices go up in good years, down in bad ones. At any given time it is not difficult to find individuals—or enterprises—who have lost considerable money on the stock market. Overall, however, there is no evidence that ownership of stocks has been any less profitable than ownership of any existing alternative investments would have been.

Nor is there any convincing evidence that a single individual could manipulate the entire stock market alone. Undoubtedly a single investor, or, more commonly, a syndicate of them, did rig the market in a single stock from time to time, but that is a far cry from manipulating the entire economy. Consider, for example, the frequently recounted tale of Jay Cooke and the panic of 1873. He is credited with starting the panic when his effort to sell the securities of Northern

Pacific Railroad failed. His operation was so highly leveraged that when he was unable to persuade other investors to buy the securities he had agreed to underwrite, he did not have sufficient capital either to hold them or to sell them at enough of a loss to move them onto the market. When Cook's company failed, it then put pressure on all its creditors, who were forced to absorb the losses. Some could not, and the result was a chain of bankruptcies—which in those days came under the catchall heading of *panic.* It sounds much like the classic tale of the battle which was lost for the want of a horseshoe nail. Yet if one considers the situation which must have existed for this sequence to have taken place, it seems much less likely that Mr. Cooke could have done it all by himself. It is not enough for a company to suffer *some* bad debts to drive it out of business. If its general prospects are good, then it will be to someone's advantage to lend it money or to buy into it in order to keep it going. Thus, when firms go down domino-style it does not indicate only short-term financial straits. More likely a large number of them would be vulnerable to bankruptcy anyway, and the credit crunch merely serves to hasten the process. Thus it was not so much Jay Cooke who caused the panic of 1873, but rather a severe financial test which touched off a series of sudden business failures which would otherwise have been spread out (and much less noticed) over a far longer period of time.

The Social Function of Securities Markets The first substantial issues of stocks and bonds were made to raise capital in the transportation and utility sectors. In fact, before 1870 the vast majority of bonds outstanding were issued for such large-scale investments as railroads, canals, turnpikes, and municipal utility systems. The obvious common characteristic of most of these projects was their *indivisibility,* that is, they had to be built all at once to make the investment worthwhile. In such circumstances a firm could not begin with limited capital and build up its operations through retained earnings and borrowed funds if it proved to be profitable. It had to begin all at once, capital included, and since there were few such collections of ready capital just waiting for such opportunities, it had to be somehow assembled. And that, of course, was probably one of the best reasons for the appearance of the corporation as a major form of business organization in the American economy.

It was not the only reason, however, and after 1870 it seemed to become less important. A quick glance at a list of major incorporations in the latter part of the nineteenth century indicates that many of them occurred *after* the companies had already become large, established, profitable enterprises. These companies were not going public merely to raise capital. To a large extent they had already solved that problem. Instead, it appears that the greatest attraction to taking the incorporation step at that time lay in the advantage it offered to the existing owners of retaining the wealth they had already created. The corporate form has several advantages over the proprietorship, which is the form in which most of these large companies had been held before incorporation. One is that fractional portions of ownership can be readily bought and sold in a market organized for just that purpose. This makes the wealth held in the equity of the company much more liquid than it would be if it were retained in the proprietorship. It also opens up a much larger potential market for ownership of the shares, one that includes that vast majority of possible shareholders who would find ownership, but not direct management, attractive. The sum of these advantages of corporate organization results in a higher valuation being applied to the earnings of that form of organization than to a proprietorship, which is comparable in all other ways. A rule of thumb in the late nineteenth century was that a large, successful company under individual ownership could be sold for about three times its current annual earnings. If, however, it was converted to a corporate form, its shares would trade in security markets at a price which would make the valuation of the company worth several times that amount. So, for example, a company earning $1 million a year might be sold through a private transaction for a price of $3 million. If, however, the company were incorporated and its shares released to the open market, it would soon be trading at something more like $8 million of valuation.

It is such advantages of incorporation, reflected in such large differential appraisals, that encouraged much of the shift to that form of ownership. In one sense it was simply another example of the gains to specialization which were becoming increasingly common in the nineteenth century. In this case the advantage was created by separating the functions of ownership and management. In proprietorships they tended to be inextricably linked. Owners might hire managers to take over some of the burdens of supervising, but it was difficult to convert the wealth represented by the future earnings expected from the operation of the firm into spendable assets. If the owners wished to sell their enterprises outright, they had to find someone who not only had access to sufficient resources, but who also had adequate experience and talent to continue to operate the company successfully. Instead of merely selling some shares of ownership when they wished to convert them into cash, proprietors would be forced to resort to something like a specialized industrial property broker who was familiar with the limited range of potential buyers for such a going operation.

Incorporation allows individuals with no time, talent, or interest in management to still participate in the returns from ownership in such an enterprise. In essence, it creates a specialized division of managers who need not have substantial positions of ownership in the firms they direct. In recent years there has been a good deal of public concern over whether the corporate division of management and ownership is a good thing. The danger, it is argued, is that it creates such a wide division between the two that the managers are given a dangerous degree of discretion concerning the use of the vast amount of assets under their control. Such ends are likely to be shaped—so goes the argument—toward the preservation of the managers' own power and prestige, not that of the stockholders or of society. The critics are probably correct that management has somewhat more freedom under the corporate form than it does under a proprietorship[19] but

---

[19] One should be suspicious of any argument which simply asserts that because stockholders do not supervise the day-to-day operations of the company that managers can necessarily operate the

that is not necessarily an unmitigated disadvantage. As a matter of fact, it is precisely that characteristic which also creates its advantages. Individuals can participate in the ownership of the enterprise without being compelled to participate in the management as well. For most typical shareholders, the relevant alternative to the existing arrangement is not more participation, but rather no participation at all. In other words, the separation of management and ownership in the corporate organization may allow a larger amount of control from the outside by encompassing a larger clientele than something like a proprietorship. There may be less control per owner but the potential range of ownership is so much larger that it can offset the lower intensity of control. This appraisal is supported by the prices paid for ownership positions in the two forms of organization. We noted that there was a substantial premium paid for the earnings forthcoming from the corporate form vis-à-vis that of the proprietorship. This difference stems from the advantages that individuals see in receiving such income through the corporate form, which suggests that the separation of corporate management would have to reduce the earnings on the company's assets by quite a bit before it would offset those advantages.

The Investment Subsector in the Investment Market   Whenever a new industry develops into a major sector in the economy, as was the case with the market(s) for financial securities during the late nineteenth century, various subsectors inevitably grow up to supply some of its specialized inputs. One such subsector which almost always appears is those firms which produce the required capital goods for the new industry. With stock and bond markets, that would simply be the firms which specialize in creating new securities—commonly known as the investment bankers, or underwriters. Investment bankers are not bankers in the usual sense of accepting deposits and issuing loans. They are more like brokers who arrange agreements between buyers and sellers of new stock. But even that characterization is not completely accurate because while brokers usually work on a fixed commission, investment bankers usually take a proprietory position in the new issues they sponsor. This means that their profits on a given offering depend on the success of their sales. Often they take some of their proceeds in the form of some of the shares themselves.

This puts investment banking in a different league from regular security trading. In the latter, the market is well established. The *price* at which shares trade changes, of course, but at any given moment the *terms* on which an exchange will take place are easily known. In contrast, there is far more uncertainty when an issue is brought to market for the first time. (And that helps to explain

enterprise exclusively for their own ends. Shareholders—or their representatives on the board of trustees—can create incentive systems which make the rewards of management coincide with the interest of the shareholders. Nor should one assume that the failure of the shareholders to intervene each day in the operations of the firm implies that they are neglecting their duties and allowing management to run the organization however it sees fit. Rather, as in most other such organizational forms, the interests of the two probably coincide most of the time. A better index of management's independence would most likely be that the shareholders *never* intervened rather than that they were left alone most of the time.

why the marketing of new issues is split off as a separate operation from that of trading existing securities.) The price at which a security can be traded can only be estimated, which in turn leaves unsettled what specific type of security (such as common stock, preferred stock, bonds, convertible bonds, or warrants) are best issued and, indeed, when they should be offered, if at all.

Investment banking is perhaps best characterized as a balancing act. To be successful, it must find a combination of terms which is acceptable to both potential investors and the managers of the enterprise who are issuing the security. One can talk to the prospective issuers directly, but the potential purchasers are likely to be much more diffuse and identifiable. Thus it is very understandable that underwriters seek to obtain information and to develop markets for their issues by building contacts with managers of major financial institutions, such as banks, insurance companies, trust and pension funds. Often it is the commitment of a group of such buyers for a sizeable share of a new issue that determines whether it will be offered to the public. There are also other ways in which investment bankers seek to identify and create markets for new securities. One method involves finding ways to assure the consumer that the security will continue to retain its value. This can be furthered in a variety of ways. One—which we shall see developed in the late nineteenth century—was for individuals of the underwriting firm to take positions on the board of trustees of some of the corporations whose stock they issued.

A Short History of Late Nineteenth-Century Underwriting   During the Civil War the Northern government created several billion dollars' worth of new debt obligations. This was far more in the way of financial securities than the economy had ever seen in such a short time before. Not surprisingly, the Treasury failed when it attempted to sell them in the usual prewar method—that is, to individuals who came into their offices to buy them. They readily agreed, then, when a syndicate headed by Jay Cooke offered to take on a national subscription. Cooke's syndicate organized a campaign which took on many of the trappings of modern marketing. The securities were issued in relatively small denominations and were peddled throughout the country by an army of 2,500 salespeople who contacted every possible investor, even those of very limited means. The interest terms on the bonds were arranged to capture the attention of the public (the return on one issue yielded exactly 1 penny a day), and they were touted extensively as a way in which all patriotic Americans could avail themselves to save the Union from rebellion.

In the decade after the Civil War there were three major investment banking houses in the United States, that of Cooke, another headed by Anthony Drexel, and still another headed by J. S. Morgan, who was soon to be overshadowed by his son, John Pierpont Morgan. The younger Morgan had begun his own securities firm in 1860 at the age of twenty-three. By the mid-1870s his organization was widely recognized as the leading innovator in corporate securities in the economy. Morgan used all the tactics of an investment banker and pioneered a few more. He not only placed his own representatives on the boards of some corporations he organized, but in some cases he stipulated that all the voting stock of the new enterprise be placed in his own trust for a period of years to ensure that the assets of the new investors were safeguarded. This device is sometimes cited critically because it gave Morgan extensive, unchallengeable power. Potential investors, on the other hand, found it acceptable and, indeed, desirable. Stock issued and guaranteed by Morgan usually was readily sold in the security markets. Ironically, despite the fact that he is often pictured as a financial manipulator and one of the robber barons, Morgan is a convincing example that stockholders can, indeed, assure that a company is operated for its own self-interest. Morgan's iron hand was welcomed because investors knew that he would prevent the type of internal manipulations which were being ascribed to such individuals as Jay Gould and Daniel Drew at that time.

The "Money Trust" By the turn of the century, Morgan's successes had extended over several decades and his name had become a household word. During the time he had come to know most of the major business and financial leaders in the economy. He had negotiated deals and sat on corporate boards with many of them. The turn of the century, however, was also a time in which the concern over trusts, robber barons, and the power of the economic elite in general was at its peak. As a preeminent symbol of that elite, Morgan began to be ascribed a central role in that coalescing conspiracy. In fact, he soon became the central figure in what was to be a special department of the robber barons—the "money trust." This community was alleged to consist of that group of bankers, financiers, underwriters, and trust managers who generally worked together to promote the joint interests of the fraternity. The alleged money trust was so widely criticized that Congress organized an investigation to see what substance there was to the charges. The famous Pujo Committee, named after its chairman, held hearings and issued a report in 1912. They found no obvious joint coordination of financial affairs in the economy, although a strong community of interest did exist. This seemingly ambiguous result did not dispel the common belief that such a group did, in fact, exist, and that opinion, although mellowed somewhat by the perspective of time, is still widely accepted in many histories of the period.

Like so many other topics of history, the concept of the money trust has lingered on in a kind of no-man's-land of being neither confirmed nor rejected because the question has never been precisely defined and examined. Consider, for example, the Pujo Committee's finding that there was a "community of interest" in the top echelons of the financial sector. What exactly does that mean? Presumably it suggests that the included people had similar objectives. Left at that generalized level, however, it does not help much in distinguishing what effect that quality might have had on the rest of the economy. Suppose the "community of interest" was one which most people would find plausible—namely, to make as much money as possible. But that common objective may or may not require the individuals involved to work together in some form of joint action. The acid test would come, for example, when it came time to submit bids for underwriting a particular security issue. Could J. P. Morgan and company refrain from raising their offer slightly in order to avoid capturing business from other investment firms, thereby forgoing the profits they could have had on that particular issue so that some overall maximization would occur? If so, then something approximating a money trust might have existed. If not, then the dominance of a few large groupings in the financial area did not have any substantial effect on the way that sector functioned compared with the way it would have functioned if numerous small enterprises had provided these services instead. In essence, the situation confronting the money trust was no different from that faced by a potential cartel or monopoly. Unless it is able to jointly decide on output and prices and—most important—has some way to compel all firms (current or potential) to abide by those collective rules, its power will erode. For all the evidence that American investment bankers around the turn of the century cooperated, fraternized, and generally intermingled, there is much less indication that they systematically divided up the market.

Most accounts of the money trust have also been careful to note the extensive amount of interlocking directorships among the financial community at this time. The Pujo Committee reported, for example, that Morgan and his close associates held more than 300 directorships in more than 100 major corporations. Such numbers are almost always taken as prima facie evidence that the money trust was operating. Yet here again we run up against the difficult distinction between *similar* interests and *coordinated* interests. On the face of it, it is not surprising that Morgan and his "close associates" were on so many corporate boards. Generally it is considered advisable to include some members with financial expertise on such boards because that expertise is often important in corporate affairs. Nor is it surprising that Morgan or his associates would be picked so often. After all, his organization was widely acknowledged as one of the best in the field. Then there was the further problem of what constituted a "close associate." Because of his working relations with a good part of the industry, that could easily be taken to include most members of the financial sector, which is to say that almost every financial specialist on a board who was not a working member of the corporation could have been lumped together with Morgan.

Even if someone were linked closely to Morgan in terms of a working association, however, it still is not at all clear that such a relation would represent control over a given corporation. Corporations select their own board members, so it seems unlikely that they would choose those who did not benefit their own operations irrespective of what benefits those representatives brought to their own outside associations. Even in those cases where Morgan "forced" his representatives onto a given corporation as a part of a financial reorganization, the sum of the entire arrangement must have been preferable to the alternatives (although admittedly those alternatives might have consisted of only the dismal end of bankruptcy). The presence of Morgan's representatives assured potential security holders, thereby allowing the company to raise capital more cheaply. Of course such board members influenced the policy of the corporation, but, in general, their interest in protecting the capital of security holders in the company coincided with the interest of the stockholders. After all, the best way to ensure that bondholders would receive their agreed-upon interest and principal was to make sure that the company was profitable. In short, the presence of Morgan or his "close associates" on a corporate board would not necessarily indicate that that company was being held subservient to some all-pervasive money trust. It could simply mean that the organization was tapping what appeared to be the best possible advisors—which, of course, would suggest that they were attempting to run the company as profitably as possible.

SUGGESTED READINGS

Davis, Lance: "The Investment Market, 1870–1914: The Evaluation of a National Market," *Journal of Economic History,* vol. 25, September 1965.

Fishlow, Albert: *Railroads and the Transformation of the Ante-Bellum Economy,* Harvard, Cambridge, Mass., 1965.

————: "Productivity and Technological Change in the Railroad Sector 1838–1899," in National Bureau of Economic Research Conference on Research in Income and Wealth, *Output, Employment and Productivity in the United States after 1800,* National Bureau of Economic Research, New York, 1966.

Fogel, Robert: *Railroads and American Economic Growth: Essays in Econometric History,* John Hopkins, Baltimore, 1964.

Robertson, Ross M.: *History of the American Economy,* 3d ed., Harcourt Brace Jovanovich, New York, 1973, Chapter 16.

Royd, J. Hayden and Gary M. Walton: "The Social Savings from Nineteenth Century Rail Passenger Services," *Explorations in Economic History,* vol. 9, no. 3, Spring 1972.

Sylla, Richard: "American Banking and Growth in the Nineteenth Century: A Partial View of the Terrain," *Explorations in Economic History,* vol. 9, Winter 1971–1972.

Chapter 13

Agriculture: 1860–1914

At the time of the Civil War, westward settlement had reached to about the 95th meridian, which approximately divides such states as Iowa and Missouri on the east (which are therefore, by this measure, within the settled area) from states like Kansas, Nebraska, and the Dakotas on the west. There were some deviations from this pattern, of course. At the northern end of the frontier, settlement had not yet reached this far west. The northern half of the state of Wisconsin had yet to be developed (more specifically, the timber had not been cut). Only the southeast corner of Minnesota had yet to be settled to any significant degree. On the other hand, the westward movement had proceeded well beyond the 95th meridian in the states of Nebraska, Kansas, and Texas, farther to the south. Some settlers had even gone past this frontier and developed areas well to the west of the line. In the 1840s immigrants had begun moving into the Oregon and Utah territories, the former because of its agricultural productivity, and the latter because of its isolation from the non-Mormon or "gentile" world. Development of California received a big push from the gold discoveries which began in the late 1840s. The most important impetus to settlement of the area, however, came after the returns from gold petered out and some of the prospectors discovered just how good the valley soil was at producing crops like wheat and fruit. A similar development occurred along the eastern slope of the Rockies, in Colorado. There the miners who started out for "Pike's Peak or bust" and ended up "busted, by gosh" discovered that the rivers coming off the Rockies provided a steady supply of water in an otherwise arid land. In addition, they found a growing market for foodstuffs in the West, comprised of Army bases, Indian contractors, miners, railroad construction camps, and newer immigrants who were passing through or had not been in the area long enough to supply their own food requirements.

The enormous gap between the 95th meridian and the Pacific Ocean would be substantially filled during the next fifty years. This does not mean that most of it would ever approach the population density already reached in the Northeast. It still contained a very large amount of acreage, however, a good portion of which would be used for products in the agricultural sector. This large increment of new land was bound to cause some reorganization within that sector if for no other reason than that it would substantially change the quantity of certain kinds of agricultural land in use. This impetus for change and reorganization would be reinforced by the filling in of much of the Midwestern land which was officially classified as being settled in 1860. Even though such states as Iowa and Missouri were considered inside the frontier by that date, sizeable amounts of the good farmland in that area were still unoccupied. The working definition of *settlement* adopted by the census bureau was two people per square mile, which was far less population than the soil of such states as Iowa could support in full-time farming. Furthermore, that figure could be easily reached by a county or other area if a moderate-sized town was built to serve as a rail center or supply depot for pioneers traveling west. Thus there was considerable geographical scope for agricultural expansion in the 1860s, and it would inevitably reshape that sector.

REGIONAL SPECIALIZATION

One of the most obvious signs of the reorganization of agriculture after 1860 was the development of a new ordering of crop specialization among regions. In 1860, for example, the single most-important wheat-producing area in the economy was in northern Illinois and southern Wisconsin. It was not likely that that condition would last, however. Wheat could be grown on soil which was much less fertile and received far less rainfall than that of this region, and thus it was almost inevitable that it would be pushed out by crops which yielded more per acre and thus could justify such high-priced land.[1] Wheat culture continued to ride the frontier outward, using land as long as it remained relatively cheap. The special feature which marked the shift in this period, however, was that wheat cultivation moved into areas where it has remained relatively permanent. The distinguishing characteristic of these new areas was that their physical endowments made them incapable of growing anything better than wheat even when they had become fully integrated into the economy. See Figure 13-1.

---

[1] Wheat cultivation generally requires less labor per acre than the crops which replaced it, in this case primarily corn. Thus this transition of crop specialties helped the filling-in process within the frontier which was described earlier.

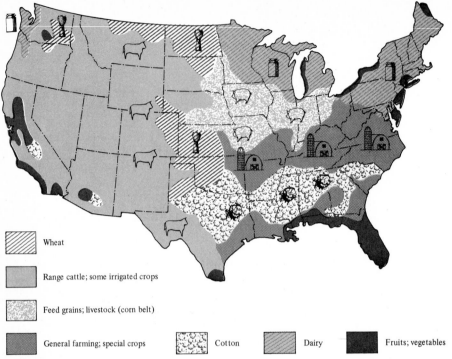

Wheat

Range cattle; some irrigated crops

Feed grains; livestock (corn belt)

General farming; special crops   Cotton   Dairy   Fruits; vegetables

Figure 13-1 *(Source: Ross Robertson,* History of the American Economy, *3d ed., Harcourt Brace Jovanovich, New York, 1973, p. 300. Copyright 1955. © 1964, 1973 by Harcourt Brace Jovanovich, Inc., and reproduced with their permission.)*

The Northern Spring-Wheat Belt

As the frontier advanced northwest in the 1870s and 1880s, wheat production followed it out of northern Illinois and into the Red River Valley of Minnesota. This was also excellent land and for a while it gave rise to one of the more widely reported forms of farm organization of the period. These were the bonanza farms which cultivated tens of thousands of acres (10,000 acres comprises almost 16 square miles) and used hundreds of laborers and machines to handle its crops. The farms were short-lived, however; there seemed to be no special economies which made such organizations especially profitable. In fact, wheat cultivation in the valley was also soon displaced. The land was converted to producing corn and hogs much like it has been previously in Illinois.

In the 1880s and 1890s wheat cultivation moved westward from the Red River Valley into North and South Dakota and the northeastern corner of Montana. This area is far from the most hospitable land for farming. The average annual rainfall decreases as one moves west so that much of the region receives only 10 to 15 inches a year. Moreover, the winters are long and cold; temperatures in January average about 20 degrees and spring is not really established until late May or early June. Nevertheless, the soil is fertile and when people's ingenuity had figured out ways to work around the other drawbacks, it became productive wheat country. The limited supply of moisture was overcome by using a technique which has been practiced since ancient times, namely, plowing the fields each year but allowing them to lie fallow every other year or so, so that they could accumulate moisture for the planted years. The short growing season was overcome by crossbreeding hardy Russian wheat with native American varieties. This allowed it to mature within the limited growing season but produced a complication in that the resulting grains were too hard to mill with existing machinery. This problem solved (of which we shall provide a little more detail later), the way was open to complete the transformation of the region into the major wheat-producing area, which it remains today. A final section was added to the spring-wheat belt in the first decade of the twentieth century when the Columbia basin of eastern Washington was brought into production. Its climate was a little more benign and its top soil deeper and richer, but basically this type of wheat culture was found to be the best use for this land also.

The Southern Winter-Wheat Belt

When the wheat belt was pushed out of northern Illinois after 1860, it actually split into two parts. One went toward the northwest as we recounted above. The other one moved off to the southwest and became known as the southern wheat belt which permanently centered in—and was associated with—the state of Kansas. The characteristic which clearly distinguished this type of wheat culture from that to the north was that it was winter wheat. The name does not mean that it is grown during the winter, but rather that it is planted in the fall and is *established* before winter forces it to stop growing. This headstart yields an early harvest the following year, normally about June or July—when the spring wheat is just coming up, farther north. This type of crop schedule can, obviously, take advantage of winter precipitation and can also avoid the extreme, destructive heat of summer. It is the cropping sequence which has been followed in the Mediterranean region since before classical times.

The southern winter-wheat belt was centered in western Kansas but also included western Oklahoma and some of the Texas panhandle to the south, and northeastern Colorado and southwestern Nebraska to the north. This area was similar to the northern wheat belt in that it, too, was marginal for any other major cultivated crops. Rainfall was light and summers were so hot that when the wind blew, which was unfortunately frequent in the middle of summer, it could literally burn the leaves of the growing plants. But if the region never seriously challenged the Grand Canyon or Florida's Sun Coast as a national tourist attraction, it still was quite attractive to settlers because of its ability to produce wheat. In the 1880s Kansas was one of the fastest-growing states in the nation as would-be wheat farmers moved into the central part of the state.

In fact, many historical accounts of this migration contend that too many immigrants moved in and forced overexpansion of wheat farming in the period. This is said to be reflected in the dust bowls which developed in later years with the consequent exodus of discouraged farmers. There have been phases of expansion and contraction of cultivated land within this area ever since 1880, and although this indicates that conditions have undoubtedly changed periodically since that time, it does not necessarily imply that the original decision(s) in 1880 was bad in any basic sense. One factor which obviously affects the attractiveness of raising wheat is its current price. From the 1890s until the end of World War I, the price of wheat was generally high in relation to its historical level. Thus it appeared worthwhile to push wheat cultivation into areas which, before 1890 or after 1920, would not have been so attractive. Then there was the complicating factor of the weather. Rainfall within the area of the wheat belt averaged only from 10 to 20 inches a year, so that normal variations in precipitation from year to year meant the difference between good and poor crops. Sometimes precipitation tended to run in patterns, with several good or bad years in a row. In such circumstances it became difficult to tell what "normal" really was.[2] There was, for example, a series of exceptionally wet years in the 1880s which encouraged wheat farmers to extend cultivation farther out into the grasslands than they would have otherwise. When things returned to "normal," those marginal cultivated acres turned into dust, and a good part of the soil left with the wind. After it was all over it was easy to see that the farmers should not have tried planting anything (other than perhaps grass) in that first dry year. Without such solid information, however, it would actually have been foolish not to attempt to plant wheat. It is several times more valuable than the grass which could be substituted for it. Thus, it was to the interest of the farmers to try to plant wheat in marginal acreage even though they realized that it might fail for lack of moisture (although they did not know in exactly which years, of course). This might lead them to more dust bowls than a conservative policy would, which would restrict planting to only those areas where the minimum rainfall was fairly certain, but might also lead to larger average wheat crops and lower prices. Hence we have another of those trade-offs which are so ubiquitous in economic life. Clearer skies and a less eroded landscape in the southwest central states come at the cost of more expensive sandwiches and breakfast cereal.

The Livestock Industry

As one leaves the Midwest and travels westward across the Plains, the average rainfall tends to decrease. To a large extent this determines the end of corn land and the beginning of wheat. At about the 100th meridian, running roughly through the middle of the Dakotas and due south from there, the rainfall drops below 15 inches per year. As a rule of thumb this is the dividing line between grassland and cropland, because below that amount of precipitation most types of plants do not mature. This guideline has its usual share of exceptions because the wheat areas, by virtue of special strains of wheat and planting techniques, have been able to push over the line to the west. In contrast, in the latitudes

[2] A farmer really did not care what the normal rainfall *was* so much as what it *would be* during the next growing season. It is merely that in the absence of any other information, the "normal" rainfall is the best predictor of what it is likely to be in any given year.

between the two wheat zones, such as in northern Nebraska, the grassland extends east across the 100th meridian.

This may be drier country, but it would be a mistake (like the first explorers who labeled it "the Great American Desert") to consider it worthless. Large areas within this region receive from 8 to 15 inches of rainfall annually, which provides good pasture for cattle if they are dispersed and are moved around from season to season. This, of course, is just the niche for which livestock are uniquely suited, being the only type of agricultural product which provides its own motive power. The suitability of this region for cattle grazing was readily recognized. The Spanish had begun introducing cattle into the area which is now the state of New Mexico even before 1600. This was the origin of the fabled longhorn cattle, some of which escaped and perpetuated themselves as wild animals for more than two centuries until their ranges were expropriated by the commercial cattle industry in the last half of the nineteenth century.

Even before the Civil War, cattle ranches had developed along the eastern slope of the southern Rockies, with the South Platte and Arkansas River valleys having the most notable concentrations. In the 1870s and 1880s, cattle ranching spread extensively across the plains. In part this was because the ranchers had uncontested use of the Plains and in most cases simply ran their stock on the federal domain without acquiring the property or paying any fees for its use.[3] It was not until the mid-1880s that any sizeable cultivation of the area was even attempted. Even when the Plains were generally divided up among private owners, however, it was still profitable to raise cattle there. In fact, after 1880 expansion of the industry continued, especially into northern valleys, such as in Montana. That continued growth was understandable. The demand for beef continued to increase as population and per capita incomes rose, and improvements in transportation and processing reduced the net cost of delivering it to the Eastern markets.

And another important element in reducing costs which is frequently overlooked was in the actual production of range cattle themselves. (It is easy to assume that because "cowboy farming" was so colorful, no improvements in productivity occurred within it while it operated—an assumption which is not true.) One of the most dramatic advances made was in the wintering of cattle. Range cattle of that day could generally survive the winter on their own. If the snow did not become too deep, or ice coated, they could dig out the dead buffalo grass from beneath it. They did not gain much weight under such circumstances, of course, so that under the open-range system in its purest form, where the cattle were left to fend for themselves, ranchers generally tried to sell off much of their herds each fall rather than hold them over during the unproductive winter. But

---

[3] Most of the highly publicized accounts of feuds between cattleranchers and sheepherders and/or homesteaders occurred because neither party actually owned the land they were using and thus adopted informal arrangements (such as small-scale private armies) to enforce the property rights which had traditionally, but illegally, prevailed. In many ways, the conflicts on the Plains over such items as fencing is the counterpart of the squatter problem which had occurred in the more densely settled East.

the ranchers soon found that providing some shelter and extra feed in the winter was profitable. They began putting up native hay in the summer and some even began planting and irrigating hay in the river valleys.

Two other improvements in the technology of Western beef cattle have been given somewhat more publicity, although perhaps the reason for their value has been glossed over. One is the introduction of barbed wire in the 1870s. The 1880s and 1890s saw a rapid expansion in this new form of fencing material. It was much cheaper, and in some cases stronger (it could stop a good-sized bull without injuring him) than the existing alternatives, such as board or hedge barriers. The prime advantage of fencing, of course, was the labor costs it saved in rounding up and herding livestock. Even before the Plains had been converted to private ownership and ranchers had no assurance that the fences they built would remain their property, many of the cattleraisers still found them profitable to build. Even a fence which had gaps in it—and was therefore less likely to run afoul of public domain regulations—helped considerably in containing and collecting cattle. Barbed wire, by making fencing cheaper, therefore rebounded as savings in labor as well as capital costs in running a ranch.

The other improvement was the adaptation of the picturesque windmill to pump water. Before its introduction on the Plains, cattle were watered mostly from rivers and streams. And because they were reluctant to graze too far from their water, they tended to stay close to the water channels. The windmill opened up areas which were set back from the rivers, or in which the streams did not provide a dependable, year-round supply. In this sense they expanded economic resources by tapping supplies which would never have been productive otherwise.

Sheep in the West

Wheat took over where the moisture was no longer sufficient to support corn, and at the margin of wheat production cattle were brought in to use the land, and where cattle could no longer make a go of it sheep could often take over. These animals could climb into places inaccessible to cattle, live off grass which was too short or too sparse, and survive more severe winters. In short, they were the ideal way to use much of the spotty, isolated grasses in the mountainous areas of the West. Sheep. like cattle, had been introduced into the region by the Spanish and Mexican settlers who preceded the Americans. There were well-established herds in California and New Mexico before 1850. In the last half of the nineteenth century this husbandry spread throughout much of the West, but it became particularly important in the northern mountain states of Montana, Wyoming, and Idaho. Like the longhorn, the Spanish breeds were soon supplanted by English and American varieties. There was, of course, a large market for wool, particularly when tariffs were increased on imports which had traditionally supplied a good share of domestic consumption. The largest new impetus to the returns on raising sheep, however, came in the increased demand for mutton. The same processing network which was introducing Western beef to Eastern markets could also market lamb. And the sheepraisers were not slow to press their advantage, especially in periods when the price of beef was high.

The Special Economics of the Wild, Wild West   Two generations of Americans have now been raised on Saturday afternoon movies of stagecoach holdups, buffalo stampedes, and feuds between the cattleraisers and sheepherders. Such stereotyped accounts ensure that we would not be likely to neglect those colorful aspects of Western development when they appear in the course of discussing related topics, such as agriculture. They have also tended to cause such events to be thought of as much more permanent and curious than in fact they were. After we cut through some of the veneer laid on by Hollywood, we shall see that most of the exotic features of the West were actually quite predictable adaptations in the context within which they occurred.

Consider, for example, the oft-bemoaned fate of the North American bison, commonly known as the buffalo. There are numerous vivid stories of how the animals were slaughtered in large numbers in the 1860s, stripped of their hides, and the carcasses abandoned to scavaging coyotes and vultures. This destruction, it was usually pointed out, wiped out the livelihood of the Plains Indians as well as what was pronounced to be a unique national resource. Most accounts of these decimations have also noted that the animals grazed mostly on unclaimed public domain and thus (in terms of protection) were really no one's responsibility. The buffalo's dilemma was more basic than that, however. Even when their natural grazing areas were entirely taken over by private owners—who would then be able to capture all the benefits of protecting them—none found it profitable to maintain the animals (except for the 3,100 gift shops who now use them to attract tourists in western South Dakota). In a word, the buffalo's problem was that it was obsolete. The animal was fast (it could actually outrun a horse), very hardy, and could travel 1,000 miles in search of forage. In the course of thousands of years on the Plains it had demonstrated that it was magnificently adapted for survival. Unfortunately for the buffalo, that demonstration was no longer the relevant criterion.

In the latter half of the nineteenth century, the Great Plains, the natural habitat of the buffalo, became for the first time a significant economic resource in response to the demands for wheat, and particularly for choice grade beef. Here the buffalo was at a hopeless disadvantage. Its body was perfected for survival, not for livestock auctions, and the quality of the meat was not particularly good. The buffalo simply could not begin to compete with the cattle which had been deliberately developed through thousands of years to provide top-quality meat. Even buffalo robes, which were quite nice for winter sleigh rides, were not able to make the animal a long-run, paying proposition. The nineteenth-century developments in textiles had made woolen blankets reasonable, if not exact, substitutes. And because the buffalo required the same resources that cattle did, it was the one that had to go. The general destruction of the buffalo, then, was an understandable reaction to the evolving conditions governing the Great Plains. So was their unceremonious end, for that matter. As long as they existed in large herds, it was worthwhile to kill them for their hides. But at the going price of buffalo meat, as well as the cost of preparing it and shipping it to market, it was not worth anyone's effort to gather it up.

North to Dodge City   If one were to conduct a poll as to the most illustrious animal in the West, the buffalo would probably have a close competitor in the longhorn cow. This creature was the apex of rugged independence. It could endure hundreds of miles of sustained driving and yet exist indefinitely if left alone in the wilds, living off scrub vegetation which received only a few inches of rainfall a year. (Besides, those horns made a very dramatic conversation piece over the mantel, even if they did not represent the courage of acquisition which a grizzly bear did.) These attributes made the longhorn very suitable to the conditions prevailing in the Southwest in the three centuries before 1870. The creature essentially economized on the resouces which were most scarce in that environment, such as labor and transportation, and used extensive amounts of land which, of course, was then very cheap. These conditions changed dramatically as the frontier moved west, however, and the longhorn was to suffer much the same fate which the buffalo did. The cattle drives from west Texas to Kansas were based on supplies of cheap livestock and expensive transportation. The railroad put an end to both those conditions. In the late 1860s and early 1870s, rail lines were extended into the cattle collection centers of central Texas. At that point the rationale of driving cattle destined for Eastern markets overland to the Kansas terminals ceased. For a few more years drives continued in order to supply breeder stock for the farms of the northern Plains, encompassed by such current states as Montana, Wyoming, and the Dakotas. But even that traffic had disappeared by 1880. In terms of its use of land and fodder, the longhorn simply could not compete with livestock developed for beef production. Some were used to crossbreed characteristics of hardiness into the domestic stock. However, the total number existing in the United States dropped drastically after 1880, until enough remained to supply local zoos and an occasional cowboy movie.

Stagecoaches and Open Range   Part of the special appeal of the West seems to come from some of its picturesque features, such as buffalo and cattle drives. Part, however, comes from the tendency to associate with the West what, in fact, are national features. Take, for example, the stagecoach. The basics of that form of transportation were worked out in the early 1800s, primarily in the Northeastern states where it provided overland express service for passengers and mail. Before 1850, when the railroad network in the Northeastern and Great Lakes states began to reach comprehensive levels, stagecoaches served almost all communities there—of any magnitude—on a fairly regular basis. In contrast, after 1850 they lost a good portion of their market in the developed East to the railroads, which offered faster and more comfortable service. Thus, by the 1860s, when stagecoaches first began to be used in the Great Plains (other than transcontinental service before the completion of the Union Pacific–Central Pacific line), they were a declining sector in most of the economy. Even in the West they were soon pushed out of the most heavily traveled routes as the railroads were completed there. For the most part they served lightly traveled routes and small, less accessible communities which did not generate enough traffic to justify a rail line during the remainder of the century (which may account for the fact that stagecoach holdups in the movies invariably occurred in desolate, uninhabited areas).

Close behind the stagecoach as a distinctive feature of the West came the great roundup. It was, of course, a necessary part of the open-range system in which cattle were allowed to graze without confinement and thus had to be rounded up periodically for branding or for sale. It was not, however, a unique characteristic of the West which developed only in the last half of the nineteenth century. The open range has been used to provide pasture for cattle almost from the beginning of settlement in the colonies. And no wonder, because the advantage of this particular form of raising cattle depends not on some specific qualities of the West but rather on a combination of relative costs which are often likely to appear along a frontier. Turning the cattle loose to feed and fend for themselves makes sense when the cost of using the land is very low. This definition is, of course, almost synonymous with that of a frontier itself, which divides the land into two zones: that which has economic value (and is consequently settled), and that which is not yet profitable to use. Thus it is understandable that free-roaming cattle have almost always been the sign of the farthest extent of settlement on the American frontier. In the colonial period large numbers of them were set loose to forage in the uplands of the Carolinas and the backwoods of Pennsylvania and New York. When settlers first began to move into the Ohio Valley in any number in the early 1800s, they found sizeable numbers of livestock already being pastured there. And by the time the settlers began to move on to the prairies of Illinois, that area was already being kept well mowed by large numbers of cattle. Thus the use of the open range on the Great Plains in the late nineteenth century was simply the last in a long series of similar steps across the nation.

There was a similar pattern in the demise of the open range as well. It naturally disappeared when settlement began to work its way in and the price of land started to rise accordingly. Land then began to be used more intensively in such ways as planting forage crops, and fencing pasture for the cattle. In the early phase of this transition the new settlers in the range area had the responsibility of protecting their own property. In this case the first fences were erected to keep cattle *out* of a given area rather than *in* it. In terms of the local costs involved, this was a logical step in that it was cheaper to protect the relatively small property holders *inside* than it was to attempt to define and then fence the property lines of the much larger area outside.[4] As settlement proceeded and the price of land increased, however, it became cheaper to change the laws to make it the responsibility of the owners to keep their animals confined. They had to be fenced *in* rather than *out*. This point marked the end of the open range and it came almost inexorably in the face of rising land costs. Those ranchers who wished to continue to work in a format of open range had to follow the frontier westward. Those who did not were compelled to adopt more settled ways. And, ironically, this is the fate which befell many of the fabled cowboys of the old West. As the frontier moved into the areas of the most productive land in the last decades of the

---

[4] This is much the same set of conditions which explains the survival of the open range in certain parts of the Western states up to the present. It is much cheaper to issue grazing permits for a certain number of cattle on a given range than it is to divide up the land itself and require that each specific group of cattle be confined to a specified acreage within the larger area.

nineteenth century, the cowboys were caught up in a traumatic change in role. The great roundup was soon discarded in place of mending barbed-wire fences, digging wells, hauling hay, and—the ultimate insult—hoeing corn. In this sense the story of the cowboy parallels much of that of the Western economy. Its colorful features tend to be special and transitory, while its permanent forms are more bland and serviceable, like those of the rest of the economy.

Fruits, Vegetables, and Citrus Products

Suburban gardens had already developed to supply the major Northeastern cities with fresh vegetables, fruit, flowers, milk, hay, and ornamental shrubs before the Civil War. They continued to expand after 1865 if for no other reason than that the larger cities—and thus the markets they provided—were growing rapidly. One of the most notable developments in the latter half of the nineteenth century was the widening radius from which such supplies were drawn. The beginning of this trend had been evident before 1860 in the expansion of the milk sheds in response to the introduction of the railroads, and the larger distances from which fruit was being imported. The broadening tendency became quite important, however, after 1870, as farmers and distributors learned how to more fully use the speed and marketing organization which the transportation system was making available to them. The large Eastern cities, for example, extended their sources of vegetables farther south along the Atlantic coast. Cabbages, potatoes, and strawberries became regular exports of Virginia, while farther south, Georgia and South Carolina began shipping sizeable quantities of peaches, pears, cherries, and other fruit. California, which was eventually to become the largest such supplier to the nation, was somewhat less important at this time primarily because of sheer distance. But as the railroad network was completed and distributors mastered such intricacies as the refrigerator car and the marketing of perishable goods, the volume of Western produce sold fresh in Eastern markets increased rapidly. By 1900 California was known as a major supplier of cabbages, cauliflower, tomatoes, celery, and onions.

The advantage which the South Atlantic states and California held over the local farmers around the major Eastern cities was not so much one of productivity—transportation costs of that day more than offset any such margin—but rather of seasonal differences. The local seasons in both localities were out of phase with those of the Northeast. Crops could be produced earlier in the spring and later in the fall and thus greatly extend the season beyond which these food items would otherwise be locally available. The season also received "stretching" from another important development in the period—the substantial reductions in the cost of canned food products. Canning had been first adopted during the Civil War in order to feed the soldiers in the field, but in civilian markets its use was limited to those products which could be shipped over a distance only by such a method and were sufficiently expensive to absorb the high costs of the process—such as seafood. Each can was essentially a custom project, being constructed, filled, and sealed by hand. This began to change in the 1880s, however. Improvements in manufacturing allowed tin cans to be turned out automatically by machine. Canneries began to use machinery which eliminated the tedious hand labor of filling and handling the cans. And methods of mechanically sealing the cans were introduced in the 1890s. The result was that the cost of buying a wide range of fruits, vegetables, juices, soups, and relishes in the off season fell drastically, and consumers greatly increased their consumption of them. In turn, canners began contracting for the large amounts of vegetables which this market consumed. No longer bound by the constraints of local markets, however, they tended to locate their facilities where the particular crop(s) they processed grew most advantageously. That might mean corn in Indiana, peas in Minnesota, carrots in Oregon, and cherries in New York. In effect, it also meant that a good many of the locational barriers due to transportation and spoilage problems had been overcome. Consumers could now be assured of a year-round supply of a wide range of foods which had previously been available only seasonally.

The Dairy Industry

By 1860 the traditional generalized, domestic dairy industry was beginning to break down. Farmers were beginning to devote more attention to milk products for off-farm consumption and certain localities were beginning to specialize in specific types of dairy products (see Chapter 6). In the 1860s this reorganization was merely in its earliest phases, however; most of the complexity and specialization which we associate with the industry was yet to come. One of the most important changes in the sector after 1865 was the shift of a sizeable part of it to the West. As of 1860, southern Wisconsin and Michigan were largely specialized in wheat production, but this crop, as we have seen, was moving toward the West and those lands which could still produce it, albeit more cheaply. In the 1860s, then, as wheat moved out, the first local farmers' cooperatives were established in these two states to produce and market butter and cheese. Within two or three decades the North Central states—including parts of Iowa, Illinois, and Minnesota, as well as Wisconsin and Michigan—were supplying a good portion of the Northeast's butter and cheese. Fluid milk sales tended to be somewhat more restricted to local sources until after 1900 because of problems with refrigeration and processing. Thus nearby upstate New York continued to be a prime source of fresh milk for the large Eastern cities.

The westward shift of dairying was obviously encouraged by the natural endowments of the new areas, which included good soil, adequate rainfall, and also a climate which was not too hot in the summer to keep the cows from producing milk. The westward relocation was also made possible, however, by the "new chemistry" of milk. In this period the technicians of the industry were learning to take it apart and use its individual components to make a much wider array of products. So, for example, a good part of the milk produced in the upper Midwest after 1880 was never intended to be sold as milk at all. Some of it went directly into cheese production, which used the solid material from the milk while leaving the liquid, or whey, as a discard. For butter, the milk was divided a different way, between butterfat and skim milk. The former was used to make the butter and the latter ended up as a waste product. Thus both of these two major products used only part of the basic milk material, leaving the producers with the problem of finding another use for, or disposing of, the by-products.

It was in this phase of the process that the new chemistry of the milk industry made some of its most dramatic advances. For centuries, the skim milk left over from making butter had been used for animal feed, particularly for hogs. This was a rich source of feed for the animals, but it was also expensive compared with grain in that it represented both grain and fodder that had already been processed once—with the inevitable losses in conversion—by another animal. Thus, in an area where corn was comparatively cheap, milk seemed to be an expensive form of livestock feed unless there were no other uses for it. However, such uses were soon found, prompted in part by the possibility of retrieving some of those otherwise wasted by-products. One new product was milk sugar, which could be substituted for other forms of sweetening—such as sugar or corn syrup—in commercial baking. A wide range of uses grew out of another by-product developed in the 1890s—casein. In some applications it could be used as a substitute for eggs, or for glue in paper sizing, or as the base of enamel paint. In a hardened form it could be used to make such items as buttons, combs, and electrical insulators. In short, it provided an early form of the material which today we call plastic. Little did the cow realize that the milk she produced not only served as a common drink but had gone well beyond that to become a competitor of sugar, eggs, oils (in paints), adhesives, and wood.

One of the reasons that milk was becoming such a widely applicable raw material was that numerous technological advances were being made. Probably one of the more dramatic improvements was the cream separator. This was actually a simple device which separated the lighter cream from the milk by whirling it at high speeds, thus lifting it off and out by centrifugal force, but it had taken considerable effort on the part of many inventive people before it was perfected in the 1870s. It allowed the almost immediate separation of cream from milk, thus avoiding at least two major costs. One was the inventory of the milk, which was tied up while waiting for the cream to rise naturally, and the other was the capital costs of tubs and cooling tanks to hold the milk while it sat out this natural separation process. Another important innovation was the Babcock test, which allowed a simple, inexpensive measure of the cream content of a given sample of milk. This was especially important because cream was the most valuable part of the milk and almost all commercially oriented farmers were striving to increase the output of butterfat per cow. Improvements in this area came partly through the selective breeding of dairy stock. In any case, to assess the results of efforts to improve butterfat production, there had to be some comparatively cheap, easily employed measure of it available to the farmer, and the Babcock test fulfilled that demand.

The Corn Belt

Native corn has always been a ubiquitous American farm product. Even when cotton was "king" in the antebellum South, the total value of it produced was less than the value of the national corn crop. (The latter was much less obvious because a good part of it was consumed on the farm where it was raised rather than being sold elsewhere, as cotton was.) In fact, corn is one of the few crops which can be grown successfully in every one of the states of the nation (a characteristic which prompted the Future Farmers of America to adopt a cross section of an ear of corn for their insignia). Like other farming activities, however, the production of corn was to become much more specialized by area and type of farming enterprise after the Civil War. In large part, it would come to be associated with the area which formerly had comprised the prairies of the Midwest. This area would become widely known as the Corn Belt, although to be fully accurate we should refer to it as the Corn-livestock Belt. Corn, of course, is primarily an intermediate product. Most of it is fed to livestock rather than to humans, as corn-on-the-cob or cornbread. While most of the acreage in the Corn Belt is devoted to—guess what?—corn, most of that basic grain is converted into livestock products right in the neighborhood. Thus what one sees when driving through the Corn Belt is corn, but what is shipped out of the area is pork and beef.

By most absolute standards the Corn Belt is a very large area, running more than 600 miles from east to west (from eastern Nebraska to the Ohio border) and 400 miles from north to south (from southern Minnesota to central Missouri). In an economic context it is even more important because the soil is almost universally good; in fact, for a region that large, it is among the best in the world. And the fact that this large, productive area was soon devoted to producing corn and turning it into meat rather than raising dairy cattle or potatoes or wheat tells a good deal about the development which was taking place in the economy as a whole. A demand for meat on this scale suggests that incomes were reasonably high, and were growing as well. Not only were the grain products of the Corn Belt being used to feed the local livestock, but they were sufficient to finish the range cattle brought in from the Great Plains as well.

This demand for meat products also made itself felt in the quality of the product. Before 1860 most hogs and cattle were multipurpose creatures developed to serve several functions, including looking out for themselves and not troubling their owners for too much feed. In the Corn Belt, however, the emphasis was on meat production. Animals were selected and bred solely on the basis of how well they contributed to this end. The longstanding ability to forage for themselves was one of the first characteristics to be discarded. Animals which were confined in close quarters, such as barns or corrals, put on weight faster. Those which gained fastest were the ones which were sought out and perpetuated. And they tended to be just the ones which were least able to forage for themselves. Similarly, those animals with a higher meat yield were preferred to older ones which were—in the case of hogs—sometimes valued in proportion to the lard they yielded. Farming in the Corn Belt had come a long way since the times when the livestock had been allowed to roam free in the woods much of the year.

Cotton in the Postbellum South

The Civil War ended slavery and in numerous other ways had a major effect on the economy of the South. It did not, however, dislodge cotton from its dominant position in the region. And no wonder, because the demand for cotton depended not on the internal organization of the South but on the demand for cotton cloth which, in turn, was responsive to existing alternative textile materials. Simply stated, better or cheaper substitutes had not yet appeared. Thus when the war ended and Reconstruction began, the South picked itself up and went back to the cotton fields.

In fact, after the Civil War the demand for cotton continued to grow at not much less than the same long-term pace as it had before that conflict. In the fifty-year period between 1865–1915, domestic cotton production approximately tripled. Some of this increase can be explained by the increase in cotton acreage during that time. Large amounts of cotton land were put into production in central Texas; and in the more arid lands to the west, irrigation encouraged the use of new land in Arizona and California. Cotton production was also increased in the established regions by a variety of tactics. One was to push the limit of the fields farther north by using faster-maturing strains and a willingness on the part of the growers to accept a somewhat higher risk that the crop would be damaged by early frosts. Another was the tendency to plant more cotton and less of other crops, such as corn, in the typical rotation patterns. Both of these practices tended to increase the cotton supply but at the same time they indicated that cotton was becoming more, not less, important in the economic life of the South. When individual farmers substituted cotton for corn or other possible crops, it suggested that the returns on it (which the economy was communicating back to those units through prices) were rising relative to the alternatives. Cotton was not only King—to use the contemporary colloquialism—but its monarchy was becoming even more powerful in relation to the "lesser nobility" of the economy.

Southern Labor Organization in the Postbellum Period   The Civil War did not affect the basic demand for cotton but it certainly did change the institutional forms used to produce it. No longer could slavery be depended upon to automatically supply a large part of the necessary labor supply. The Negroes now had the legal right to negotiate the terms of their own work although both freed blacks and their former owners required some time to adapt to such a situation, as is understandable in such a sudden, major shift. Having been denied the option of free time (or, at best, having been granted time off only as a reward for meritorious service), the newly freed slaves had a strong inclination not to work. This was particularly true of women, children, and elderly individuals who had been kept busy under slavery but, once freed, tended to adopt labor roles much more like those of their counterparts in the white population.

But even if the freed blacks found their newly won leisure enjoyable, necessity compelled them to perform some work. Most Negroes came out of slavery with few assets other than their labor skills as a source of income. Hence, both they and their former owners had reason to work out some form of labor arrangement whereby the former earned an income and the latter were able to handle their cotton crop. One obvious arrangement was wage labor, by far the most common method of enlisting someone else's services. Cotton planters tried hiring freed blacks as laborers for several years after the Civil War, but the arrangement proved unsatisfactory for several reasons. For example, cotton has two distinct peaks of labor requirements, at the beginning and at the end of the season, planting and picking, respectively. If a planter contracted for labor on an annual basis, there was the problem of mobilizing additional labor during the busy seasons. One possible way of handling this was simply to hire temporary help. However, labor was naturally worth a higher daily rate in such periods (in formal economic terms, the marginal product was higher) and thus the longer-term rate agreed upon for season-long workers would seem low. Planters were especially vulnerable at picking time, at the end of the season, because workers could demand extra pay. This phenomenon appeared in both 1865 and 1866 when regular field hands simply refused to complete the year unless they were paid extra for the picking season.

Employees might have avoided this problem of seasonal labor requirements by instituting something like a bonus system for those who completed the entire season, or going to shorter agreements which allowed wages to be matched to the current value of labor. The latter arrangement imposed additional costs in the form of more frequent negotiations and, probably even more importantly, housing arrangements. In the years immediately following emancipation, most of the existing housing available for freed blacks was simply that used for slaves, which of course was generally bunched around the major buildings of former plantations, and it was only natural that the employer would provide housing as part of the total compensation. If the terms of labor were to be renegotiated frequently, there would be the additional cost of moving the Negro households each time they changed employers.

The Much-maligned Institution of Sharecropping What the situation seemed to dictate, therefore, was some arrangement to reduce managerial inputs on the part of the former slaveholders. The most direct means to that end would simply have been for landowners to rent out their land to the blacks. But although some of the ex-slaves had acquired some experience through supervising field operations, few yet had the backgroud to manage a complete farming operation. Thus some kind of arrangement which gave the blacks most of the day-to-day responsibilities of their own leased farms but still provided for managerial advice from landowners was desirable. This was achieved by the widespread adoption of sharecropping throughout the South just after the Civil War.

Of all the systems which have been tried in the course of the economy's history, sharecropping is one of the most publicized and degraded. It is commonly credited as a device to perpetuate the bondage of the Negroes, on the one hand, while it is criticized as a cause of soil erosion and the depreciation of Southern farms, on the other. A good many of the previous historical treatments of the system could be read as nominations for the Oscar as the most malignant arrangement in the American past. Yet if one examines the actual way in which sharecropping typically operated, the drawbacks become a little less obvious and the compensating advantages somewhat more apparent. Take, for example, the common allegation that sharecropping was a device to perpetuate the exploitation of Negroes. This argument is usually supported by the observation that sharecropping contracts typically required that one-half to two-thirds of the harvested crop be turned over to the landowner. This sounds excessively large until we remember that the landowner provided the land, various amounts of seed, fertilizer, tools, and even food (depending on the specific contract) and managerial time as well. These are all scarce resources and any economic system must recognize and enforce a recognition of their opportunity cost in some manner. If they had not been provided by the landowner, then the individual sharecropper would have been forced to get them elsewhere, paying for them out of the gross proceeds of the crop.

While the proportion of their crops which sharecroppers typically gave up— either to their landlords in the form of shares, or as purchased supplies—may seem large in isolation, it is not far out of line with other sectors. It is not unusual that payments for labor in the last level of production should equal one-third or less of the total value of the good in question. Even if we operate by the common rule of thumb that labor receives two-thirds of the total income in the American economy (which actually seems a little higher than that which has prevailed throughout most of the past), *all* that component does not have to be paid in the last stage of production; it may be contained in the inputs bought from producers. Thus, for example, the labor used in producing cotton can be that embodied in purchased tools, fertilizer, and fencing material, as well as that spent by the sharecroppers in the field. So the fact that typical sharecroppers received only a fraction of the crop they "produced" does not necessarily indicate that they were being exploited—it may simply reflect the fact that each resource, including the sharecroppers' labor, is, indeed, receiving an income which does reflect its actual contribution to output. If the labor share seems so small, it may merely be that its contribution relative to those of the others is correspondingly small.[5]

Whatever the sharecropper's share of the final cotton crop, it is not the specific system per se which allows exploitation of labor. It is the competition for labor—or the lack thereof—that exists within any given arrangement for mobilizing that resource (labor) which is crucial. Suppose that landowners are exploiting their sharecroppers in that the part of the crop they are allowed to keep is less than the amount they have contributed to its value. In such a situation the landowners will be making profits which are larger than normal on the resources they contributed to the sharecropping arrangement because the labor component has been provided at less than its opportunity cost; in effect, the excess profits on labor are subsidizing the return on other inputs. Such an imbalance would create an almost irresistible temptation for one of the two parties to attempt to rearrange things for their own advantage. The sharecroppers could gain by going to other landowners with a proposition something like the following: "Our present

[5] Stephan DeCanio, "Productivity and Income Distribution in the Post-Bellum South," *The Journal of Economic History,* vol. 34, no. 2, September 1974.

landlord is making above-normal profits on his agreement with us. We would be willing to contract with you for terms which are admittedly somewhat more favorable for ourselves but still offer you returns which are equal to, or even a little better than, that which you could make elsewhere on your capital." The landowner would stand to benefit, and if that incentive were not enough to motivate him, it would probably be sufficient to attract some other landowners into the sector. Individuals with access to capital resources could buy land on which to practice sharecropping in hopes of making higher returns from that form of investment than from others. Actually, all that is needed to move the terms of sharecropping contracts toward this equilibrium is for one of the parties to take the initiative. If, for example, all the sharecroppers were naïvely ignorant of such possibilities (or felt cowed by pressure from their landlords), the initiative of a few landlords operating strictly in their own self-interest would be sufficient to push the laborers' earnings into equality with their contribution to output. Thus it is not so much the *form* of the system which determines whether workers will receive what is coming to them, but rather the amount of competition which exists with that system.

If sharecropping was not merely a device to exploit laborers, then it must have been adopted to facilitate some particular set of conditions prevailing at that time. It can be viewed as a kind of intermediate arrangement between the landowner retaining control of the management of the land and hiring the labor, on the one hand, and renting all the land out to the laborers for their exclusive management on the other hand. In the first case the landowner provides all the management services and is also the recipient of all residual income, that is, either profits or losses as the case may be. In the latter case the laborer—made a manager by virtue of renting the land—assumes all these functions. Sharecropping is an arrangement which splits both these functions between landowner and laborer.[6] It also links their otherwise somewhat disparate interests to a common cause. The essence of sharecropping is that both landlord and tenant receive a share of total output, which means that both parties stand to gain from any modifications which increase final output.

And cotton is a crop in which such adjustments can be particularly valuable, especially in the context of the immediate post-Civil War period. Like so many of its other benign characteristics, cotton is very convenient and adaptable in its planting schedule. The plants can be put into the ground anytime from early March, in the deep South, to June, and still yield a good harvest before the first killing frost. Thus, if a group of farmers had planted corn in the spring in anticipation that the price of cotton would be low when the harvest period came, they would still have the time to plow it under and replant in cotton if it began to appear that the price of the latter would be higher by harvest time—or vice versa. One could profit from such midcourse adjustments, however, only if the manage-

---

[6] This sharing of managerial skills can be readily appreciated if one looks at the surprisingly detailed working of sharecropping contracts. They require the tenant to clean ditches or fertilize crops or commence plowing when the landlord directs. Such provisions suggest that the landowner came around fairly frequently to check up on the state of things.

ment information and the skill necessary to make such switches were readily available. For the first few years after emancipation, most freed blacks did not yet have the experience or training to make such calculations on their own. Thus, if they were going to capture the gains possible in such adaptations they would have to seek such advice from experienced individuals. In practice this meant the local landowners, who were the only ones who had both the experience and the proximity to the local situation to make such assessments. And the advantage of the sharecropping arrangement was that it harnessed the self-interest of the landlords with that of the tenants to ensure that both would cooperate. This assessment of the advantage of sharecropping would help to explain the relative demise of that institution in the South after 1870. By the time that blacks had acquired some managerial experience (and the ownership of a good share of the land they employed as well), the advantages of this form of organization were dissipated, and it became less common.

Thus, sharecropping was somewhat more beneficial for both the laborer and landowner than has commonly been assumed. Interestingly enough, it also turns out to be much less destructive of the land than has generally been propounded. Scholars who looked at the incentives embodied in the arrangement noted that it would encourage tenants to misuse and depreciate the land because their income was based on the crop they produced, not on the value of the farm capital which they left intact. While the logic of this observation is fairly clear, it overlooks the equally obvious and powerful self-interest of the individuals who owned the land and the other resources employed in sharecropping. The landowners had far more reason not to overlook this effect than the historians who believed that they were the first to detect it. After all, it was their resources which were vulnerable to misuse, and if the sharecropping contract was in effect, they would have been required to come to the farm periodically to provide managerial assistance and would therefore have natually noticed any misuse of their assets.

Landowners could have incorporated any excess depreciation into the terms they negotiated with the sharecroppers; that is, the prevailing rate at which the crop was divided would reflect not only the opportunity cost of the land and other assets employed, including that of the value of the owners' advice, but also any extra wear and tear on the capital inputs as a result of the perverse incentives in the sharecropping arrangement (much like landlords who charge higher rents to student tenants on the assumption that such a clientele will inflict more-than-average damage). While such provisions would indeed protect the landlords, it would be costly in terms of resources. Both parties would therefore be encouraged to devise a different kind of arrangement where the land and other assets would be conserved and the resulting savings could be shared between the participating parties. The simplest device would be to write safeguards on the use of the landlords' assets into the sharecropping contract, which is indeed what was usually done.[7] A typical written agreement called for a tenant to maintain the

---

[7] See Joseph D. Reid, Jr., "Sharecropping As An Understandable Market Response—The Postbellum South," *Journal of Economic History,* March 1973.

ditches and fences, paint the barn, cut a certain amount of fence rails—but nothing else from the woods without the owner's written permission—spread manure on the land, and feed and care for all the animals. In short, sharecroppers were to do all that farmowners would. And the owners and the sharecroppers agreed in the written contract on what the precise penalties would be for failing to fulfill those requirements.

Reconstruction and Racial Discrimination   Our examination of the likely operation of sharecropping suggests that it could not have been a major force in discrimination against blacks. If that judgment is correct, however, it naturally raises the question of what institutions or forces did exploit the freed blacks in the postbellum South. After all, the average incomes of blacks have remained well below those of the white population for more than a century since emancipation. Economic reasoning would suggest that such differentials in incomes should be reduced with time,[8] and our intuition tells us that a century certainly should be more than enough to accomplish such an equalization.

Our intuition may not be allowing for certain factors which would delay the equalization, however—and possibly for an extremely long period of time. In recent years the long-term experiences of immigrant ethnic groups in the United States has been carefully examined. One general conclusion of many of these studies has been that such groups maintain their ethnic identities and, to a large degree, their position of economic inferiority for several generations. The Irish, who preceded the blacks into American society and did not have the handicap of color, have just reached parity with the average of the economy. It seems likely that although education and experience—both coming with time—tend to reduce the amount by which entrant groups fall short of the average income level of a society, the creation of new technologies or skills could tend to increase that gap. This would occur, for example, if the innovations were developed within the most advanced sectors in the economy. Thus the lower-income groups would be excluded from "ground-floor" participation, and this additional gap would be added to their initial handicap. In this sense, the problem is analogous to that faced by contemporary, lesser developed economies. Not only are they at an initial disadvantage in terms of per capita incomes, but the developed nations are continuously creating new techniques which cannot be appropriated directly because they are created in the context of a different set of resource conditions as well. In effect, the lesser developed economies—and by analogy the low-income minority groups in the United States also—must themselves create new technology in

---

[8] If two assets of equal productivity are earning different incomes, employees naturally prefer to employ the lower-priced one. This tends to bid up its price, all the while shifting demand away from the higher-priced resource with the net result of reducing and eventually eliminating the difference between their prices. Forces which operate over the longer term will also tend to equalize returns to similar resources. If, for example, two laborers have different current incomes because of past differences in education, but have the same inherent capabilities, then there will be some incentive for the individual with less education to acquire more because its return would be likely to be higher than its cost. Thus, in time, investments in resources would tend to equalize their earnings (if their basic capabilities are comparable).

order to adapt those new techniques to the conditions in their economies. Thus, while the normal, ongoing activities of the economy are working to narrow existing differentials, the dynamic processes of the economy might tend to widen them. The net result for any group in an economy, then, would stem from the interaction of these forces. The important corollary, however, is that growth, notwithstanding its positive influence in raising the absolute incomes of those groups with lower-than-average incomes, might tend to worsen their relative position.

Even with these factors to explain why the catch-up process could take so long *in the absence of* discrimination, one would have to be naïve to assume that no discrimination existed against the blacks in the postbellum South. While sharecropping or the credit policies of the local general stores—another commonly alleged culprit for the period—are not likely to be major causes of discrimination, there were other channels. Probably the most important were restrictions on occupations and education. It is generally recognized that at the end of the Reconstruction, in the late 1870s, the Southern states began to enact a number of legal restrictions now commonly known as Jim Crow laws. Most of these were designed to enforce social inferiority upon blacks and were obviously irksome to them. However, the particular subset of these regulations which was probably most damaging to the economic well-being of blacks was the set which kept them out of a large share of skilled crafts in the South. This had been the primary channel through which blacks had moved up in the economic hierarchy during slavery and in the decade or so after the Civil War they were well represented among the crafts workers. With the curtailment of this avenue to skills and advancement, however, they were effectively restricted to agriculture, manual labor, and domestic service.

Barriers as blatant as legal prohibitions which prevented blacks from practicing certain trades can be readily grasped. There was, however, another form of discrimination which, although more subtle, was yet perhaps even more important and difficult to eradicate. This occurred in the financing of public education. Most of the postbellum Southern states had systems of state aid to county school districts and the formulas by which funds were apportioned among the various units invariably provided much less per pupil for those districts with high proportions of blacks than it did for those which had a high proportion of whites. Such disparities in education tend to perpetuate the gap between average black and white incomes, of course, because education is one major method of raising the economic productivity of people. Moreover, this form of discrimination was a particularly insidious one. Normally, discrimination is self-limiting in that the individual, or economic unit, which excludes certain groups of potential employees, or customers, from consideration for reasons other than productivity pays a penalty in terms of reduced earnings. If, for example, employers refuse to hire members of a certain group (even though they are equally productive), then that reduces the earnings of the excluded group relative to those of the accepted group. It also means that any employers who did not practice such discrimination can hire those workers at a lower real cost. Thus the larger the degree of discrimination, the larger the incentive for some other employers to break ranks with the general policy of discrimination in order to benefit themselves. Also, discrimination based on noneconomic grounds has a tendency to be self-limiting in that the groups which practice it pay for that action accordingly. The postbellum discrimination in Southern school funds is an exception to this rule, however. In that case the groups which practiced the discrimination made an economic gain from doing so because whatever funds they succeeded from withholding from blacks could be directly appropriated to their own purposes. Unlike the private market structure, the public allocative process encouraged, rather than discouraged, discrimination.

Despite these handicaps, American blacks have acquitted themselves reasonably well in the period since emancipation. This is not to say that they have achieved parity with the remainder of the economy, but that they have done reasonably well considering their initial position and the subsequent alternatives they faced. Their experience seems to correspond roughly to that of other major groups, or economies, who achieved major contact with other economic systems which are more productive and significantly dissimilar to their own. Almost none of the economies which are currently among the most developed achieved that position overnight. Each struggled for economic growth for long periods, often for several centuries, before reaching the high levels of productivity we associate with successful modern economies. Some, but by no means all, underdeveloped countries have shown signs of successful growth once they have achieved continuous contact with the developed sectors of the world. Almost none of them have been able to catch up with those other nations, however, except in those cases where the new nation was essentially a transplanted extension of the developed world, such as Australia or Israel. Thus the American blacks seemed to have done about as well since emancipation as any other major group with which we are familiar in modern experience. Blocked from many lines of advancement in Southern regional economy, they made the best of the prime alternative open to them—agriculture. In that sector they were able to improve their position somewhat, as suggested by the fact that by 1910 black farmers had acquired ownership of about 30 percent of the land they were cultivating. When new opportunities presented themselves, in the form of the large excess demand for labor in the North in World Wars I and II, they were quick to grasp them by migrating in large numbers. In short, the black experience since emancipation has been very similar to that of many other groups, namely, they have made the best of existing opportunities, however limited or constrained they might appear for the moment.

REGIONAL SPECIALIZATION AND
PRODUCTIVITY OF AGRICULTURE

By 1914 American agriculture had achieved much of the pattern of crop specialization which has persisted up to the present. In fact, this spatial arrangement is now so commonplace that it is easy to forget that it once was a novel development and brought gains from its implementation. For decades, students in introductory economics courses have sat through detailed—and often tedious— lectures which were designed to demonstrate that regions can improve their economic position by trading among themselves if their factor endowments differ. Such exchanges are profitable,, however, only if the additional transportation and handling costs do not wipe out the resulting gains. This, of course, was the case before 1860. Some of the regions, such as the Wheat Belts of the Plains, were not even settled yet, let alone reorganized to provide output for some external market. But after the Civil War the major improvements and extension of the nation's transportation network (which we detailed in Chapter 12) created—indeed, virtually compelled—such a sophisticated interregional specialization in agriculture.

The basic differences in local conditions which made such a division of labor profitable are not difficult to understand; indeed, they were explicitly noted by the contemporaries who put the pattern of specialization into effect. Each locality had distinct soils and fairly predictable temperatures, growing seasons, and rainfalls. Thus one could match the crop which performed best in a given environment with society's economic preferences. One would require, for example, that the rich, well-watered soil of the Corn Belt yield output which could be valued in proportion to its natural fertility. In the American context, that implied corn which, even in the mid-1800s, could yield in excess of 50 bushels an acre and be an excellent input for producing beef or pork—that increasingly important component of the American diet. Or consider the post-Civil War Dairy Belt. This is a zone in which the land is generally fertile and rainfall adequate, but the growing season and the mean temperature are less than those of the Corn Belt. This area could have produced corn (at a somewhat lower yield per acre, of course) or wheat, but the emerging demands of the rising per capita incomes of the economy dictated that the land could be used best for producing milk. The cooler climate and an even rainfall provided a long season of green pasture and produced enough forage in the form of hay and silage to supplement the winter months as well.

The advantages of this emerging pattern of specialization are subtle and thus not always readily noticed. Their effect is contained in one dramatic statistic, however. In 1870 more than 52 percent of the American population lived on farms, but only forty years later, in 1910, less than 32 percent of the nation's labor force was sufficient to feed the total population. In other words, whereas at the time of the Civil War one worker in agriculture could barely feed another off the farms, by the eve of World War I the average farmer was supporting two people in nonrural activities. Furthermore, this doubling of agriculture's capacity understates the gains because the quality of the average diet was rising as well. Food consumption included increasing amounts of such foods as meat, milk, and fresh fruits and vegetables, products which consumed a larger amount of agricultural inputs than the traditional staples they replaced. One can, for example, eat corn directly as a grain in such forms as cornbread or cereal, or one can eat it indirectly by feeding it to the hogs and then consuming it in the form of bacon or pork chops. The latter style of eating "consumes" several times as much corn as the former because it takes several pounds of corn to turn out 1 pound of pork.

Not all of this gain in agricultural productivity came from the relocation of farming, of course. There were major improvements in farm technology and in the processing and delivery of food products. But even these gains were intermingled in the developing regional specialization of agriculture. Take the rapid growth of the food-processing sector, for example.[9] Before 1860 a large portion of the total food production of the economy was consumed within a few miles of the location where it was produced. That usually meant that it required little more in the way of processing than it would have received had it been consumed on the farm. Once a good portion of the farm produce began to move to distant markets, however, the advantages of specialized (off-farm) processing became more obvious and appropriated. Some of these advantages, such as retarding spoilage or saving on weight for shipment, are readily recognizable. Other advantages—certain of which became quite important in this period—are less obvious. For example, processing is a natural point at which the householders' demands can be met concerning such amenities as prepared or convenience food. Developments in the food-processing and distribution sector during this period also increased the ability of the economy to spread the consumption of many kinds of food more evenly over the year. Whatever the combination of motivations which were propelling the food-processing sector in the fifty years after the Civil War, it clearly was one of the growth sectors of the time.

Distribution of Fresh Meat

In 1860 almost all meat which was consumed fresh was slaughtered and consumed locally. The explanation was quite simple. Without refrigeration, fresh meat spoils within a matter of days so that the time needed to deliver it to any distant location imposes a proportionally heavy discount on its quality. If one wished to import fresh meat into a given locality before 1860, the only feasible way to do it would have been to ship in the live animals and slaughter them locally. This constraint added some rather heavy increments to the cost of fresh meat, however. One could drive the cattle to market, but if they were not to lose a good part of their weight (and hence their market value), they could not be pushed too fast. In addition, they required supplementary feed which could be quite expensive when bought from wayside vendors. When the canals, steamboats, and railroads developed, they provided a faster form of carriage, but they were also expensive, especially when the livestock were not packed too closely during shipment, a practice which reduced animal losses during transit. Whatever the form of shipment, however, the basic problem with transporting livestock remained: they took up considerably more space, and therefore were more costly to ship, than the final product they represented.

This was readily recognized by packing houses and meat brokers who grap-

---

[9] Much of the remaining discussion of productivity increase in agriculture will focus on processing, rather than on-farm activities. This is not to deny that the latter gains were important because, in fact, they were. Rather, it reflects the fact that processing was newer and more novel, as were its repercussions on the rest of the economy as compared to the effect of improvements in on-farm operations. We have already discussed such improvements in the context of antebellum agriculture (Chapter 8) and as parallel developments in industry (Chapters 6 and 11).

pled each day with the problem of shipping their product as cheaply as possible. The need was to discover some method by which the meat would be delivered in good condition and without hauling all the associated, less valuable by-products along with it. Before the Civil War the packing houses at Cincinnati had worked out a method in which air could be withdrawn from containers to form a partial vacuum—much like a crude form of canning. This reduced spoilage and, when the method was reinforced by packing the containers in ice, the meat could be delivered in a very fresh state to such distant points as New York and even London. It was expensive, however, so that the total market for this sophisticated method of delivery was highly restricted.

When the growing railroad network began to pull in large quantities of beef and pork from the prairies and the Great Plains, the problem was given renewed attention. Livestock was commonly shipped by railroad from Chicago, a natural consolidation point at the vortex of the developing Corn Belt, to New York. However, the possible savings in freight costs made the participants in this trade ever-watchful for some new method which might save on those transportation charges. One device was to rely on natural refrigeration, that is, to ship fresh meat in the winter months when temperatures averaged 40 degrees or less. During this part of the year the livestock could be slaughtered at Chicago, with the resulting saving in transportation costs from Chicago to New York. The arrangement was so advantageous that the packers sought ways to extend it as much as possible, the most successful being that of cooling the meat-storage rooms and freight cars with ice. By so doing, the effective slaughter season in Chicago for fresh meat for Eastern markets was extended later into the spring and pushed back earlier into the fall. Obviously the trick was to make it into a year-round operation, using the packing houses of Chicago continuously and saving on freight costs accordingly.

The first "refrigerator" cars were introduced in the late 1860s, but they had a number of drawbacks. And no wonder; they were not the sophisticated vehicles that we know today, but were simply insulated boxes on wheels, into which the ice and the meat were loaded together. The insulation did away with the need of opening the cars and replenishing the ice on the way east, but it also discolored the meat, leading to a bad reputation for Western meat in Eastern markets, which lingered for several decades after the problem had been corrected. The solution began to emerge in the late 1870s when methods of separating the ice and the meat while yet retaining the cooling properties of the former were worked out. This was done by designing the interior of the "reefers" so that the air circulated, imparting the cooling qualities of the ice to the meat but without contacting it directly. The success of this form of transportation can be gauged by the fact that fresh Western meat (of equal quality) was underselling that produced in the East by a significant margin in 1880, and that within the next decade a good portion of Eastern livestock-fattening operations were forced out of business.

This, of course, was distressing news for Eastern cattle finishers but good news for the consumer. The lower price of fresh meat in major urban areas was more than merely a windfall gain for the beef eater, however. It represented an expansion in the economic resource base of the economy. Formerly only that land in the immediate vicinity of a consuming center was able to supply it with fresh meat. The refrigerator car changed the definition of what constituted the "vicinity." That large expanse of land in the Midwest which could turn out cheap livestock feed now began adding its weight to production. In effect, changes in technology were making Western land into an effective substitute for the more expensive Eastern acreage. There is a twist of irony in all this. While the refrigerator car was making the open spaces of the West more valuable—to the detriment of nearby Eastern land—it was also increasing the potential productivity and therefore the value of those small, select parcels of land upon which the central business districts in the major cities were located. These areas were growing rapidly (as we shall explain in more detail in Chapter 14), and one of the factors which obviously was contributing to that expansion was the availability of not-too-expensive consumables, such as meat, with which to supply the increasing working populations which were developing within the areas. Thus, while the refrigerator car was opening up the empty lands of the West and expanding the area from which the nation's beef supply was drawn, it was simultaneously contributing to an ongoing increase in the population density of the Eastern and North Central metropolitan areas. Such a seemingly simple and straightforward innovation as the ability to transport chilled beef was contributing to a growing disparity in the population distribution of the economy.

Chicago and the Rise of the Integrated Packing Plant One reason for slaughtering livestock at Chicago before sending the meat on to Eastern markets was the resultant saving in transportation costs. There was another advantage as well. There are economies in the large-scale processing of such animal products, especially in the utilization of by-products. A typical Eastern butcher, circa 1860, would extract the meat and most likely the hide from each animal he slaughtered but discard almost everything else. This was not waste or carelessness on his part, but simply a reaction to the fact that the costs of collecting and processing such waste products were greater than any returns he could expect to gain from them. This calculus worked out differently for the large packing houses. The volume of animal products they processed was sufficiently large so that it paid them to establish specialized processing operations for many of the by-products which the smaller butchers would normally discard. Thus the major Chicago packers, such as the now familiar names of Swift and Armour, began to turn out such items as lard, lard oil, tallow, soap, glue, and fertilizer. This, of course, increased the return on integrated meat-packing operations and further encouraged the shift toward this form of organization—which the refrigerator car had already encouraged.

In fact, the extra returns from these auxiliary activities were so attractive that the packers made a major effort to develop more of them. In the 1880s they began to manufacture sandpaper—a particularly attractive product from their vantage in that it used so much glue, which they were able to produce in large quantities. Another successful new line was opened up in the form of pharmaceutical products derived from raw materials of livestock. Probably in many ways the most important by-product, however, was oleomargarine. Before 1880, much of the excess fats left after butchering were simply discarded. Then the techniques were devised to convert a good portion of those fats into this new, cheap substitute for butter. The cow had come a long way. Whether dead or live, economic knowledge could use it to provide a spread for the nation's bread.

To the Consumer, from the New Wheat Belts

Most of the wheat which had been grown in the United States before 1850 was winter wheat; that is, it was planted in the fall, which gave it a head start on the following year's season, so that almost all of the harvest could be completed by the end of June. When the present, comparatively permanent wheat areas developed after the Civil War, however, this pattern was in for some major adjustments. Most obviously, the wheat lands in the Dakotas, Montana, and the Northwest were simply too cold during the winter for even winter wheat to survive. As a result, the farmers converted to spring wheat, beginning with the hard Russian, or durum, varieties, which had proven particularly resistant to drought and rust. This new stock was adapted to American conditions over the next few decades before World War I, and one of its derivatives, the Marquis cross, became a familiar standard in the industry. The durum varieties had the advantage of having a high gluten content, the sticky component which contains much of the protein of the wheat. This made it attractive nutritionally compared with other varieties of wheat, particularly in such uses as macaroni, where the stickiness of the gluten did not hinder baking as it tended to do in bread. The disadvantage of the hard spring wheat, however, was that it was difficult to grind with the existing milling techniques. The grain was so hard that the required pressure on the millstones built up heat and scorched the flour.

This problem was overcome through the introduction of "new-process" milling in the 1870s. It substituted a sequence of slower-moving rollers for the traditional set of two millstones. When combined with improved screening devices, developed at about the same time, it turned out a grade of "middling" flour which enjoyed a substantial price premium on the market. The new roller system proved to have another unanticipated advantage in that it eliminated the constant wear of the millstones. This had put troublesome grit into the flour as well as requiring the refinishing, or dressing, of the millstones every several days. This combination of improvements proved to be so strong that the new-process method was adopted generally throughout the milling industry.

One of the locations where those techniques were adoped was in the winter-wheat belt to the south, which comprised a large area consisting of much of Kansas, eastern Colorado, southwestern Nebraska, and the panhandle areas of Oklahoma and Texas. This area came into production at about the same time as the spring-wheat belt to the north and, appropriately enough, both worked out many similar problems. For example, wheat production in this region was also initiated by bringing in a foreign variety to match the local climatic and soil conditions, in this case a hard red wheat from Turkey. It proved to be the best major bread grain in the economy, and did not produce such a sticky dough. The hard husk of the grain, however, encouraged a shift to the new-process milling systems, much like the system which had been developed for the spring-wheat mills around Minneapolis.

Grain Processing in an Era of Rising Incomes   The grain-farming sector is not likely to keep pace with the growth of the total economy in the course of any sustained increase in real incomes. Food grains (that is, excluding animal feed) are an inferior good; as per capita incomes rise, the percentage of income spent on them decreases. To some extent this long-term inevitability was offset by the growth of an export market for American grain in the latter half of the nineteenth century. The influence of this offset declined later, but even if it had not, the importance of the basic function of producing food grains in the economy would have slipped anyway.

While grain production, per se, may have followed an inevitable downward path, the same is not necessarily true of the sale of grain products. In between the initial producer and the final consumer there are several intermediate steps, and each of these is subject to expansion or contraction, depending on the economic elements which impinge on each phase. Before grain can be made palatable in such forms as bread, crackers, cereals, pastries and spaghetti, it must go through a series of intermediate steps, of which milling and baking are the most obvious. Before 1850 a large portion of such intermediate activities, especially baking, were carried out in the household. This was a valuable activity (although it never made it into the national income accounts) in that it consumed resources with alternative uses, namely, labor which could be productively employed in other activities. In the latter half of the nineteenth century, however, a combination of factors caused the alternative costs of that household time to become more expensive. The proportion of women who worked outside the home began the long-term increase which has continued to this day. Average incomes rose, allowing the luxury of using someone else's labor for that formerly done in the household. And the technology of extrahousehold production of many lines of food processing improved dramatically, thereby further tilting the options toward preparing many types of food outside the household. Thus, while the basic agricultural sector was declining in this period, the intermediaries which preformed steps in preparing it for final consumption were actually a growth sector.

The most immediate example of this shift toward specialized intermediate food preparation was that of baking bread. Local bakeries had existed almost from the beginning in the larger colonial cities, but what made the activity substantially different after the Civil War was the enormous increase in the amount of output from an individual enterprise. As of the Civil War, a bakery catering to the local market (as distinguished from a few larger ones which supplied hard crackers for ships, or the military) would be hard pressed to turn out more than 100 loaves of bread a day. These were mixed, kneaded, and shaped by hand, and then baked in dome-shaped ovens which had to be cleaned and refueled between each batch. Another difficulty was in the yeast, which was usually simply a portion of old starter kept in the bakery and added to from time to time. The problem in using it in large batches of bread was that it tended to be uneven in quality and therefore had to be thoroughly mixed into the dough to avoid uneven batches. This problem was eliminated in 1870 when Charles Fleischmann invented compressed yeast. It proved to be both cheaper than the older starters and much more reliable. It also gave a major boost to the cracker industry. Until then, most cracker production had been confined to hard ships' biscuits, eaten primarily by those on sea voyages (which is to say, only those who did not have the option of anything other than those rather unpalatable staples). By 1900, Americans in almost any part of the country could buy saltines or crackers of various flavors. They came in the now-familiar interior wrapping inside the box and had a shelf life of several months. They added welcome variety to urban diets, and a new touch to the consumption patterns of more isolated rural residents, who previously could choose between only hardtack or fresh bread made by themselves.

Fleischmann's compressed yeast was only one part of the total transformation occurring in the baking industry. The market for bakery products was growing rapidly because of the expansion of urban areas and their local marketing and transportation facilities, as well as the more general reasons mentioned above. In gearing up for this predictable increase in output, the baking sector understandably achieved major production innovations, as do so many industries in the process of rapid growth. The older ovens were replaced by models that used indirect heat, which meant that the fires could be refueled without interrupting baking or reloading. Getting the dough ready for the oven was also greatly streamlined. Many of the steps of mixing, kneading, and cutting were mechanized. Moreover, once these operations had begun to reach sizeable proportions, they became a significant market for such bakery inputs as flour, sugar, and yeast in their own right and suppliers began to tailor such inputs to their advantage. Thus, for example, certain grades of flour, carefully standardized in quality and designed for mechanical preparation, began to be available. One measure of the total impact of all these changes is that the former one-worker, neighborhood bakery began to be superseded by bakeries that turned out from 10,000 to 15,000 loaves of bread a day—not counting cookies, pies, pastries, and cakes. Obviously there was a lot less aroma of hot homemade bread in the nation's neighborhoods.

Toward the Instant Breakfast   In the first half of the nineteenth century, a typical breakfast could be a large, leisurely meal. Most Americans lived in the country and required a hearty fueling for a full day of physical work. Besides, they often had a little more time in the early morning because they tended to go to bed earlier at night. Not only was there no radio, television, or stereo to pass the hours after darkness, but before kerosene and electricity, evening reading was not such a desirable pastime either. After the Civil War, however, this pattern began to change. The proportion of the population living in urban areas was increasing and better lighting in the form of kerosene, gas, and electricity was encouraging later hours at home. There was rapid growth in the readership of newspapers, books, and periodicals, and a large increase in the sale of musical instruments, such as pianos and accordians. Caught in the middle was the large country breakfast, which soon began to evolve into a faster, lighter meal. One example of that tendency was the appearance of that distinctive American food, breakfast cereal.

There was, for instance, the illustrative rise of Quaker Oats. In the early 1800s very few Americans ate oatmeal for breakfast. When oats were ground between the millstones, the result was a combination of powder and sharp, tough slivers of husks. Besides, as Samuel Johnson had remarked earlier, only the Scots ate oats; other nations, such as the English, fed them to horses. Conditions were changing, however. In about 1870, millers devised a new method of preparing oatmeal by cutting it with steel knives. Soon after, the technique of milling wheat with rollers was adapted to oats, producing the now familiar rolled oats. This made a much more palatable form of oat cereal, or porridge, and sales picked up accordingly, helped along by the arrival of immigrant groups, such as the Germans, who were familiar with the product in their homelands.

The development of rolled oats was only the first—and, by itself, rather minor—step in the transformation of the cereal industry. There was a whole series of changes in the packaging, distribution, and marketing of the product which were symptomatic of changes which were generally occurring throughout the food-processing industry. In 1870, for example, oat mills simply barreled their product and shipped it to general stores. The store proprietors would then ladle out portions as their customers requested. The barrels were not the best method of maintaining quality or cleanliness; flies or mice could get into them and often the product became stale or mildewed by the time the barrel was finished (hence the term *scraping the bottom of the barrel*). All this began to change under the catalytic influence of Henry P. Crowell, the founder of Quaker Oats Company.[10] In the 1880s he began putting rolled oats in small, 2- or 3-pound packages, just about the size a typical retail customer wanted. This assured the customer of better quality and also cut out the intermediate labor of the storekeepers.

That was just the beginning, however. The rolled oats were packaged in paper cartons, which were not only cheaper than other existing materials but also could be imprinted while still flat, before they were filled. Crowell emblazoned the front of the carton with bright, multicolored designs which certainly would have stood out on the rather bland grocer's shelves of that day. He filled the back with accounts of all the virtues of the product as well as recipes to extend its uses. The recipes on the carton were soon followed with premiums in the box as well as coupons on the back with which one could send for more recipes or premiums. To make sure that his advertising worked, Crowell undertook a major progam, many facets of which were quite novel for that day. There were, for example, advertisements placed on billboards, barns, newspapers, rural fences, giveaway

---

[10] A comprehensive account of the pioneering development of food processing and marketing in the Quaker Oats Company is given by Arthur M. Marquette, *Brands, Trademarks and Good Will: The Story of the Quaker Oats Company*, McGraw-Hill, New York, 1967.

calendars, cookbooks, grocery store walls and windows, and even the backs of church programs. In addition, there were free samples, often accompanied by parades, bands, or other free entertainment. There were also endorsements by scientists and celebrities, customer testimonials, and contests for cash prizes.

All of these were, of course, designed to get the attention of potential customers and provide a little bit of theatrics in the process. To keep them coming back, however, the product itself had to be superior to the traditional alternatives (which themselves were in the process of continual upgrading, partly through adopting those features which had proved successful for Quaker Oats). The "new" rolled oats had several advantages over the traditional components of the American breakfast, one of which was that it was faster as well as more convenient to prepare. The first rolled oats had taken about an hour to prepare—in contrast to up to two full hours for some of the more elaborate country breakfasts—but the later ones, aided by continual exhortations from the back of the carton, took progressively less time. The ultimate form of convenience in hot cereals was reached in the 1890s when Quaker Oats introduced four-minute corn mush. The only thing faster than that was cold cereal which required no preparation at all. Quaker introduced its versions of puffed wheat and puffed rice in the first decade of the twentieth century at about the same time that Kelloggs brought out corn flakes. Of course, these brands have since proved themselves by not only overpowering their initial competitors but also by surviving subsequent innovators (unlike some of the other dry cereals introduced at that time, such as Zest, Apetizo, and Brittle Bits, which have long since disappeared).

Quaker Oats' drive to capture the evolving market for convenience was evident in its other products as well. Indeed, in many ways its interests in the grain-processing industry mirrored the developments which were taking place in that sector in general. One obvious example was self-rising flour; another was prepared baby food. Other products included wheat and corn meal, cracked wheat, graham and oat flours, and pearled barley as well as the extension of the rolling techniques to wheat cereal. In addition, many of the waste products of the milling operations were converted into poultry and animal feeds now that the increasing specialization and commercialization of farming encouraged farmers to purchase a larger share of their supplies from off the farm.

The Soft-Drink Industry

When foreigners are asked to describe their image of America they usually mention large office buildings, automobiles, Singer sewing machines, possibly the Grand Canyon, cowboys and the Statue of Liberty, but almost invariably Coca-Cola or soft drinks in general. That last association is a comparatively modern one, however, because these beverages have appeared only in the last 100 years. Had the foreigners looked into what soft drinks Americans were drinking about a century ago, they would probably not have considered them significant or worth remembering at all. In the eighty years before 1870, American inventors and chemists had experimented with a variety of light refreshments. These included soda waters, some natural and some concocted. They also devised the apparatus to prepare and disperse these products. One line of development improved and expanded a line of equipment which today we would probably lump under the classification of drugstore soda fountains. The other, the one which ultimately grew to be by far the most important, was simply the adaptation of a traditional beverage container, the bottle.

The soda fountain of around 1850 was not likely to be dispensing soda drinks as we know them today; its products were mostly mineral or seltzer water. Nor was the fountain likely to be located in a drugstore yet. Many of these usually large and ornate fountains were constructed for special expositions or fairs. The drugstore soda fountain (itself now well dated) had to wait until the development of liquid carbon dioxide and auxiliary equipment, small and simple enough to be operated by the employees of a retail store. It also had to wait until the development of the drugstore as we know it today. Before 1880, the "drugstore" was mostly what we call a *pharmacy,* or an *apothecary* as it was known then, which is to say that its services were limited primarily to providing medical prescriptions. The modern drugstore could evolve only after branded medicines and other consumer products began to appear in significant numbers in the late nineteenth century.

Developments in the bottled-beverage industry were not as dramatic perhaps, but their cumulative impact on the economy was probably more important. Take the perfection of the lowly bottle cap. The late 1800s saw a wide range of attempts to develop a better bottle stopper. And no wonder; the traditional cork had a number of shortcomings. It was expensive, time-consuming to insert and remove, and was subject to damage and leakage in shipment as well. Thus, in the face of a readily recognizable growth in the market for bottled beverages, there were large rewards awaiting the successful bottle-stopper inventor and numerous candidates applied themselves to the challenge. (This environment, with the number of methods and patents it provoked, was similar to that which developed in the search for other inventions which could be generally foreseen to be profitable, such as the cast-iron stove, barbed wire, washing machines, and apple peelers.) Out of all these efforts came the familiar crown bottle cap which can be made cheaply out of sheet metal and capped on the bottle automatically by machine.

The bottle cap was one of the more important steps—but by no means the only one—toward mechanization of the bottling industry around the turn of the century. There was also the development of automatic bottle manufacturing, and filling and washing equipment, all of which obviously reduced the cost of providing this form of beverage to the market. At the same time, it encouraged the invention of a whole new series of drinks. In the 1880s Hires Root Beer—previously familiar to Americans in a concentrate form which they could make into a drink at home—began to be sold ready-made in bottles. At about the same time (1886, to be exact), Coca-Cola was introduced, the most famous and successful of them all. In the 1890s the number of contenders increased quickly, with the appearance of such famous names as Dr. Pepper, Pepsi-Cola, and Cliquoit Club. Thus, this segment of the food-processing industry was not only taking over many of the functions formerly performed in the household, but it was contributing to (or at least reflecting) a change in tastes as well.

THOSE UNHAPPY FARMERS

Anyone slighly familiar with American history knows that the thirty-year period after the Civil War was one of agrarian discontent. A large number of American farmers believed that they were not receiving a fair share of the economy's output and expressed that feeling, sometimes forcefully. Some of the farmer's ire was channeled through existing institutions in society—the press, farm periodicals, and elected representatives to the state legislature and Congress. Much of it, however, was so intense, or perhaps specific, that it led to the creation of a series of farm organizations that were initially conceived to focus that demand for redress.

In the late 1860s a farm organization called the National Grange appeared in North Central and Northeastern farm areas. The bylaws of the Grange stated that it was not to engage in political activity, but a good part of the meetings of the local chapters in their early years was spent in discussing farmers' grievances and how to mobilize group pressures to correct them. Much of the grangers' discontent soon became focused on the rate structures of railroads and grain elevators, which they believed were discriminating against them. Their pressure was instrumental in creating the first state regulation of such rates, in the 1870s, in the North Central states, especially Illinois and Wisconsin. These "granger laws," as they came to be known, set fixed, legal prices which would be charged for such services. The novel feature of the laws, however, was that rather than setting these prices themselves, the legislators established a commission which had the power to investigate and set what they deemed to be fair rates. This innovation has, of course, continued down to the present as the principal form of governmental control over sectors which are determined to be in need of "public utility" regulation.

Farther west, and in the South, the farm protest of the 1860s and 1870s was organized similarly but in a collection of local groups under the name of the Alliances. Their objectives were much the same as those of the grangers except that they advocated another set of programs as well. These consisted of government warehouses where farmers could deposit and receive loans on their produce at guaranteed prices. They also advocated a series of long-term government loans on farm real estate through the issue of more greenback currency. Both these programs have a distinctly modern tone; the crop/loan guarantee system is basically the same as one of the major programs employed by the federal government to support farm incomes in the last forty years. Such proposals did not make much headway in the nineteenth century, however. Indeed, by the end of the 1870s much of the urgency seemed to ebb from these forms of farm protests so that by 1880 both the Alliances and the Grange had reverted to the type of social organization that their bylaws had originally conceived.

Agrarian protest continued in the 1880s but its focus and the channels through which it was expressed shifted. Now it tended to become merged into broader national issues of which the principal irritant seemed to be the decline of average prices in the economy. These sentiments initially appeared in the Greenback party, which first achieved noticeable support in the 1880s. Its main concern, expressed in its name, was to increase the quantity of greenback money in circulation, thereby slowing, or even reversing, the fall in prices which was then occurring in the economy. But the Greenback party never succeeded in attracting enough national groups outside of agriculture—nor did it ever attract enough support *in* agriculture, for that matter—to enact a program. In the 1890s many advocates of greenback programs joined the newly formed Populist party which did, of course, achieve more success at the national level. It combined with the Democratic party in 1896 and made a creditable, although unsuccessful, attempt to take the presidency with its most famous spokesman, William Jennings Bryan. The year 1896 was the high-water mark for forces of "cheap" money in the economy. With the discoveries of large amounts of gold, and its addition to the money stock, prices stopped falling and the clamor for greenbacks, more silver, and other devices to increase prices subsided. Coincidentally, farm protest also seemed to dissolve in about 1896. The next twenty-five years were prosperous ones on most American farms, so much so that the period is often referred to as the "golden age of American agriculture." The causes of these good times were likely a combination of factors beyond the control (and outside the range of protests) of the farmers—such as large-scale immigration and the appropriation of most good-quality land in the West—but in any case they turned farming attention from raising a ruckus to raising corn.

The Economics of Farm Protest

The protesting farmers of the period 1865–1895 had no doubts as to where the source of their troubles lay and they could list them, quite readily, along with the appropriate remedies. The problems originated with the railroads or the grain elevators (they should be regulated), the bankers (interest rates should be controlled or the government should make loans to farmers), falling prices (the money supply should be increased through greenbacks or silver), and, in general, the monopolists who were able to exploit the "little people," such as the farmers (trusts should be broken). All these protests took place more than eighty years ago so the historical profession has had considerable opportunity to examine them in a more reflective and less polemic atmosphere. So it is surprising that—until recently at least—historical narratives have usually taken the farmers' words at face value, that is, that they were being exploited and that the specific forces they cited were, in fact, the primary causes. This sympathetic interpretation has begun to change in the last decade, however. This has been so partly because some basic economic indicators, such as regional incomes and land values, have been constructed and a few simple comparisons cast doubts on the farmers' claims. And it has been partly because of a careful reexamination of the economic logic underlying the traditional arguments.

All the irritants cited by the farmers and their subsequent sympathizers contain the common claim of exploitation. Usually, however, the argument rests on a mistaken view of how such inequities might occur. For example, consider a group which ranked right near the top of the farmers' hate list—the grain elevator operators. They bought grain from the farmers, stored it, and then resold it.[11] The farmers believed that the elevator companies had them at their mercy in that they bought the grain at harvest time—or at any other time when its price was low— and resold it when its price had risen. Hence, the farmers believed that they were being systematically cheated out of part of their product. After all, the argument went, the elevator buyers could remain in business only if they sold grain at a higher price than they paid for it.

The last observation is undeniably true. But the profit did not necessarily come out of the farmer's hide—not unless it had performed no other net economic value in itself. And that was the crux of the issue. The farmers (predictably) conceived of the grain-elevator operators as parasites; that is, their efforts added nothing to the final value of the grain but claimed part of the value of the final product nevertheless. However, one can make a good case for the elevator operators performing a positive role in preparing the grain for the final market even over and above their function of providing storage facilities. When the elevator operators acted in the role of speculators, buying at low prices and reselling at higher ones, they were also performing a social role even though they probably acted out of purely private interests. They were transferring a product from a period in which the social valuation was low to a period when it was higher; in other words, they were increasing the value of the output in the economy by shifting some of it over time from lower- to higher-value uses. Thus, they were increasing its contribution to the economy, and the profits they earned in doing so can be considered as payments for *that* function rather than as extortions from others, such as the farmers.

Ironically, one can make a good case that when the grain speculators (of which the elevator operators were the most immediate example to the farmers) succeeded in making profits for themselves, they also increased the incomes of the farmers. When they bought in periods of lower prices, they increased demand and therefore raised prices. Later, when they sold at higher prices, they increased supply and reduced prices. Thus, to the extent that they were correct in anticipating price changes by actually buying low and selling high, their actions tended to dampen fluctuations in these prices. This meant that to the extent that farmers were actually "forced" to sell their crops during periods of low prices,[12] the

---

[11] In some cases elevators simply accepted grain on commission; that is, the farmers retained ownership with the accompanying possibility of either gain or loss on their product, depending on whether the market price went up or down. In such cases the elevator operators simply acted as brokers, but in that function they were still in a position to exercise monopoly pricing power—as farmers readily noted.

[12] Even the assumption that the farmers were forced to sell their output immediately upon harvest is suspect, as the previous footnote suggested when it mentioned the possibility that farmers could retain ownership of their grain even as it started through the distribution network. It is often argued that farmers were so short of cash that they had to sell their crops immediately upon harvest in order to pay bills and meet urgent living expenses. This overlooks the possibility of borrowing, however, and if, indeed, the price of grain were to rise significantly, it would pay the farmers to pay interest on a loan to tide them over until they realized the gains from the appreciation in the price of grain. The common argument that the farmers had poor credit or were already overburdened with debts and therefore could not borrow overlooks the fact that in this case the grain itself could serve

activities of the speculators had the effect of actually increasing the farmers' incomes. Thus, speculators—those rather vague villains toward whom the farmers directed so much of their dislike—actually improved the real incomes of the farmers.

Real exploitation had to come from elsewhere. Probably the largest single source was that demon of the public and economists alike, monopolies. It is very likely that some of the grain-elevator operators, by virtue of the paucity of nearby competition, were able to charge prices for their services which yielded profits in excess of prevailing alternative investments. Generally, such extranormal returns would be dissipated by the encroachment of competitors who would attempt to appropriate some of those profits for themselves. But it is easy to conceive that the environment in which many grain elevators operated simply would not support competition. In other words, the local grain-elevator operator could easily become a natural monopoly in that only a few efficient-sized units could supply the entire requirements of the market. A combination of technological and demand conditions could rule out the likelihood of effective competition, and, as any student who has sat through an introductory course in economics can attest, *someone* can usually impose price and/or output restrictions on a monopoly to force it to operate in a way more in line with optimal social behavior than if it is left to its own devices. Thus, the farmers might well have had a real case in arguing that they were being exploited—not the vague, general complaints against middlemen, but rather the definite complaints against the disadvantages the small, local markets—in which so many of them operated—inevitably imposed.

The real possibility of local monopolies afflicting the farmers reappears dramatically in one of that group's favorite vocal targets, the railroads. Rail lines through rural areas are an almost classic example of natural monopolies in pre-motor-vehicle times. All the output from a farming locality could almost invariably be handled by a single branch line. That single railroad organization could set prices on the safe assumption that the farmers' next best means of shipping their produce to market would be a long—and more expensive—haul over rural roads to the next rail line (whose rates would probably not be much more attractive because it would have similar power over the shippers in its own neighborhood). Thus railroads, except in those areas where through main lines or large nonagricultural enterprises broke down such local monopolies, could set rates for the local farmers, smugly safe in the assumption that potential competitors would always be at a substantial disadvantage.

This, of course, was just the kind of behavior at which the granger laws were aimed. They prohibited discrimination among shippers, which they interpreted as different rates per ton/mile for different classes of goods (with some allowances

---

as collateral. Similarly, one might object that the grain-elevator operators could require the farmers to sell to them immediately upon harvest because they had a monopoly on storage and shipping facilities. But if they were making monopoly profits from that activity, then it would have paid the farmers to build their own storage facilities or, if such structures were too large in relation to the individual farmer's requirements, they could have formed cooperatives and built and operated them jointly.

for the differences in costs which were obviously not related to the mileage involved, such as storage or loading and unloading costs). The farmers and the other groups who supported this legislation believed that it would lower the prices paid by the vulnerable, isolated shippers, taking the saving out of the profits of the railroads. It did not work out quite that way. Although it undoubtedly reduced the rail rates paid by some otherwise susceptible farmers, it raised the rates of some shippers elsewhere in the economy. The system of regulation tended to be applied so that all shippers were charged rates based on the average cost of hauling goods for the entire rail system. Thus, while some rates were adjusted downward, others—which had applied to customers who had not been so susceptible to discrimination—were revised upward. This result is hardly surprising. It could have been readily predicted, given the application of a little economic reasoning to the prevailing conditions. Business firms—the railroads in this case—naturally vary their prices among markets, depending on the demand they encounter (assuming, of course, that they can effectively separate the customers to prevent resale of the product, thereby nullifying the price discrimination). Markets in which the customers have a better range of alternatives, probably reflected in a relatively elastic demand for the product (railroad transportation in this case), would be priced lower than those with fewer alternatives. Such markets would probably include manufacturers and other shippers who tended to be located in or around major urban centers. They typically had not only the alternative of several railroads but, in addition, they often had access to major water routes as well. Thus, in the absence of regulation, such shippers could generally obtain lower rates—sometimes much lower—than farmers who had access to only a single rail line. And the impact of regulation would fall not so much on the railroads as on those shippers who, before its imposition, had been able to bargain for such advantageous rates. Ultimately those higher rates would be incorporated into the costs of operations and partly passed along to the consumer in the form of higher prices. Thus, railroad regulation was not so much a victory of the farmers over the railroads as it was a case of the farmers gaining at the cost of urban enterprises. So, in fact, the farmers were hardly the helpless, underprivileged group that they claimed to be. In the struggle for power among major groups, they were clearly capable of holding their own.

Agrarian Unrest in Perspective

Our discussion has indicated that there were some conditions in the late nineteenth century which can be said to have exploited the farmer. We have also seen that farm groups were fairly perceptive in recognizing these conditions and organizing pressure against them. It is important to note, however, that the farmers' position in the economy was not unique. Other sectors also had market structures which allowed suppliers to practice price discrimination and monopoly power. And, indeed, customers in those nonagricultural markets were also known to complain and attempt to organize counterefforts. Thus, although the farmers' problems have been given a special place in historical accounts, there is no strong evidence that their position was particularly disadvantageous in any sense. In the last decade there has been a series of studies on this very question. Almost unanimously they report that farmers were receiving payments for the resources they used which were comparable to their returns in alternative uses elsewhere in the economy. In other words, farmers were doing about as well as could be expected; this, even though they were operating in an industry which was shrinking relative to the rest of the economy.

It seems appropriate, then, to adopt a new view of the agrarian protest period in the late nineteenth century. It was not so much that the conditions the farmers faced were so bad but rather that they preceived that the returns from engaging in collective pressures *would be worthwhile.* So much of the previous analysis of the farmers' protests has assumed that the farmers must have been agitated because conditions were bad. Actually, the motivation behind collective pressures should be largely independent of the prevailing conditions.[13] That is, one can be in very severe straits but unless it appears that organized activities can accomplish something, it is useless to resort to them. Similarly, one group can be doing quite well compared to others and still gain from initiating demands for aid through the political process. Almost any group will couch its quest for concessions in terms which it believes will appeal to other elements which it deems necessary to win its goals. It is just plain bad public relations to say that a change should be made simply because it benefits the group which advocates it! So, for example, it would have been foolish for the farmers to have said that railroad or grain-elevator regulations should be enacted in order to raise their incomes. Even if that was their only concern, they were much more likely to succeed by cloaking their demands in terms of advocating "fairness" (who could oppose that?) instead of the existing "discrimination." Thus, one could not unreasonably characterize the agrarian protests as being vastly overstated claims in pursuit of much smaller and more precise goals.

SUGGESTED READINGS

Bogue, Allan G.: *Money at Interest: The Farm Mortgage on the Middle Border,* Cornell, Ithaca, N.Y., 1955.

DeCanio, Stephan: "Cotton 'Overproduction' in Late Nineteenth Century Southern Agriculture," *Journal of Economic History,* vol. 33, September 1973.

Fisher, Franklin M. and Peter Temin: "Regional Specialization and the Supply of Wheat in the United States, 1867–1914," *Review of Economics and Statistics,* vol. 52, May 1970.

Fite, Gilbert.: *The Farmer's Frontier, 1865-1900,* Holt, New York, 1966.

Higgs, Robert: "Race, Tenure and Resource Allocation in Southern Agriculture, 1910," *Journal of Economic History,* vol. 33, March 1973.

Marquette, Arthur F.: *Brands, Trademarks and Good Will: The Story of the Quaker Oats*

---

[13] This statement should be qualified in two ways. First, the appearance of a difficult situation often aids groups to gain sympathy and support from other segments of the political process. Second, other things being equal, groups in distressed conditions are more likely to find the cost of engaging in protest activities to be less costly—in the vernacular, they have less to lose—and therefore they have more incentive to resort to them.

Company, McGraw-Hill, New York, 1967.

Reid, Joseph D., Jr.: "Sharecropping As An Understandable Market Response—The Post-Bellum South," *Journal of Economic History,* vol. 33, March 1973.

Shannon, Fred A.: *The Farmer's Last Frontier,* Holt, New York, 1963.

Sutch, Richard and Roger Ransom: "Debt Peonage in the Cotton South After the Civil War," *Journal of Economic History,* vol. 32, September 1972. See also the comment by William W. Brown and Morgan O. Reynolds, "Debt Peonage Reexamined," in the *Journal of Economic History,* vol. 33, December 1973.

Williamson, Harold F. (ed.): *The Growth of the American Economy,* 2d ed., Prentice-Hall, New York, 1951, Chapters 20 and 21.

Wright, Gavin: "Cotton Competition and the Post-Bellum Recovery of the American South," *Journal of Economic History,* vol. 34, September 1974.

Cities and Commerce: 1865–1914

On the eve of the Civil War about 20 percent of the American population lived in urban areas of at least 2,500 inhabitants. Fifty years later, in 1910, city residents constituted more than 45 percent of the total population. In other words, within a period of fifty years more than one-quarter of the nation's residents had been shifted from rural to urban locations. This was not the result of a net migration out of the rural areas, however, because the rural population of the nation nearly doubled. Rather, it resulted from a dramatic increase of seven times in the number of residents of urban areas. In 1860 a little more than 6 million Americans lived in cities of more than 2,500. By 1910 that figure exceeded 42 million.

Clearly, something more than simply gregariousness was prompting this drastic reorganization. One necessary condition was obviously a major increase in the productivity of agriculture which allowed such a large transfer of resources out of food production. But that in itself was not sufficient because the producers of nonfood products and services might conceivably also have located in rural areas—which is not as unlikely as it might sound initially. Before the onset of major industrialization, a good portion of nonagricultural production was carried out on farms or in small villages. And the recent pattern in the twentieth century has also been for a good portion of industry to desert central cities in search of less congested and less expensive locations. Economic activities, and the population which is drawn to them, will not necessarily locate in an urban area unless there is some advantage in doing so. The overwhelming shift of activities toward such locations in the latter half of the nineteenth century indicates that there must have been some very strong reasons for doing so.

Some of the most important forces are not too difficult to detect. Modern scholars of urban areas know that there are two major advantages to positioning economic activities close to one another. One is subsumed under the term *agglomeration,* which is to say the advantages which some activities gain when they are near other kinds of businesses. Businesses which provide services are usually quite prominent in this group. Lawyers, for example, gain from being located near the courts and the offices where the public records—such as deeds and legislation—are kept. Advertising agencies gain from being located near the media, such as newspapers, magazines, and broadcasting networks, that they need to promote their products, as well as near the headquarters of major corporations and special-interest groups which purchase such services. They also gain from having fast access to artists, draftsmen, writers, and market-research specialists who are often hired on a project-by-project basis (today such individuals are often known as free-lancers). Similarly, business headquarters often find a location in a major city advantageous because there they have access to all the specialized resources they require in managing a large enterprise, such as lawyers with expertise in finance to draw up financial instruments, such as bonds or, in corporate law, to effect mergers or contracts, and advertising and market-research firms to help the sales divisions, and personnel agencies to locate the people with the special talents which they require.

A second major advantage a firm gains from being in an urban area is the savings on transportation costs which are ultimately reflected in the costs of the resources they employ. A city forms a natural convergence of transportation lines. As such, the delivered costs of many factors of production are lower then they would be if the business were in a rural area. Probably the most important resource for most firms was labor. And in the latter half of the nineteenth century the maximum distance which laborers could commute to work on a daily basis was much shorter than it is today. One might get to work by walking, or by using the streetcar or railroad. Only the relatively rich could afford private carriages in the cities. This meant that workers were restricted to living within a few miles of their jobs (the walking option), or only along those corridors served by the public transit of that day. Thus the range of transportation alternatives restricted the labor force to be within a limited radius of the business enterprise. This, in turn, restricted the business enterprises because it meant that they could not locate far from the existing labor supplies unless they were willing to provide housing and other related urban services on their own. In other words, unless they were ready to erect a company town, they had best locate in or very close to an existing city where the necessary workers were available. The implication of all this is that certain major economic activities, which in the present day can be placed either in or outside an urban area depending on the specific circumstances, were then rather rigidly confined to urban areas. This, of course, appears to be largely the result of the restricted range of transportation services. These conditions were themselves part of the reason for the evolution of a broader range of transportation techniques, which subsequently loosened these constraints, some of which were discussed in Chapter 11 and will be considered later as well. Today, when the economy with which we are familiar has been shaped by that broader range of transportation possibilities, it is easy to forget that it has not always been this way. However, before 1914, most manufacturing, retailing, and wholesaling activities, and the housing for the workers they required, was virtually compelled to be located within the city limits. So if the cities were clearly a major growth sector of the economy in the late 1800s, the obvious explanation was that a large portion of the developing economic activity was almost forced to locate there.

CREATING PUBLIC SERVICES FOR THE NEW URBAN COMPLEXES

In 1860 only New York City had reached the population of a million persons or more, and that only if we include the adjacent areas which have since been annexed into the city, principally Brooklyn. By 1910 three cities had passed well beyond that level, with New York more than tripling its size in that fifty-year period. Perhaps even more impressive was the number of not gigantic but nevertheless quite large urban centers in the United States by that time. Five other cities (St. Louis, Boston, Cleveland, Baltimore, and Pittsburgh) exceeded 500,000 people. Eleven more had between 250,000 and 500,000 people, and thirty-one had between 100,000 and 250,000. Altogether there were fifty cities whose population exceeded 100,000 in 1910, and their aggregate inhabitants exceeded 20 million people—or more than 22 percent of the total population. A short look at the cities included in such groups indicates that urbanization was becoming a national phenomenon, not simply a special phenomenon of the Northeast. The North Central area was particularly evident in the list of major cities by 1910. The region was obviously now doing more in the way of economic activity than simply driving New England farmers out of wheat and meat production.

One important implication of this quantum jump in size was that the structure and management of cities were probably also going to have to undergo some major changes. The older means of delivering services to the populace would simply be either inadequate or too costly. There would have to be some substantial rethinking of the means by which such urban necessities as water, sewerage, streets, garbage, and lighting were handled.

City Streets

Before the Civil War, the city authorities in only a few towns had given much systematic attention to the condition of the streets within their jurisdiction. The most heavily traveled portions of towns were usually paved, after a fashion. Cobblestones or bricks were the most common material, but various other locally available materials were also tried, such as wooden planks in the Western areas.

All these materials had disadvantages. Bricks and cobblestones made for a very rough ride and tended to work loose with traffic, or in rain or freezing weather. Boards rotted and splintered within a few years. Most city streets, however, were little more than the extension of country roads, that is, they were not paved and maintenance consisted of occasional applications of gravel and grading to eliminate the worst ruts and potholes. In other words, they were in basically the same shape as they had been back in the colonial period. In dry weather they were dusty; in wet weather they became ribbons of mud.

This type of road surface soon broke down under the volume of traffic which was beginning to develop on some of the busiest streets of major cities by the mid-nineteenth century. A stronger, more durable system of paving had to be devised if the roads were to take this daily pounding and literally not bog the towns down in the mud. The first innovation was simply a smoother, more stable paving stone to replace the traditional material. These were small granite blocks, measuring from 8 to 12 inches long, about 4 inches wide and, quite important, about 8 inches deep. This material became so commonly used that an organized market in the "New York blocks" grew up along the northern Atlantic coast. A specialized trade of stonecutters developed in Maine and Massachusetts to produce the blocks. Their regular output was shipped down the coast in schooners to the major Eastern cities, and sometimes on to other towns in the interior. The blocks had several advantages over traditional materials. With their increased weight and depth they could bear much heavier loads and, if carefully installed, they made a relatively smooth road surface.

New York blocks also had a disadvantage which tended to become greater as time passed: they were very labor-intensive. It took considerable hand labor to first shape and then place them, and this element of cost increased as the cost of labor rose in the last half of the nineteenth century. Not surprisingly, public works engineers and paving contractors sought methods which reduced these labor inputs. One new technique appeared in the 1870s in the form of asphalt, which in the twentieth century has become a ubiquitous paving material. At first the basic substance was obtained from the Caribbean island of Trinidad, but within a decade or so petroleum engineers succeeded in producing a superior form from the otherwise low-value residue of oil refining. Asphalt had the obvious virtues of being not only comparatively inexpensive to lay down, but of being a relatively cheap material as well.

For some functions, it was too cheap. Whatever its other advantages, asphalt was weak in structural strength. It tended to sag and crack if the underlying roadbed shifted or did not remain almost entirely stable. Similarly, it was not strong enough for the increasing numbers of structures, such as bridges and retaining walls, which became necessary in road systems. A material which *was* tougher, and yet at the same time cheaper and more versatile than the traditional structural members such as steel and stone, was first used for roads in the 1890s. It was hydraulic cement, or what is often known today as Portland cement, and is impervious to weathering. (Earlier forms of cement had the unfortunate characteristic of being washed away in the rain and therefore had to be shielded in most uses.)[1] Within a few decades, civil engineers were routinely specifying roadways, bridges, and drainage systems out of the material on the confident assumption that if later utility crews needed to cut holes in it or run tunnels under it—which was always occurring in the streets of the major cities—it would continue to support the traffic flowing over it.

Water and Sewage Systems

Perhaps the aspect where the increase in the population density of the city most obviously overwhelmed the physical capability of the environment was in the provision of water and sewage services. Local wells simply could not provide sufficient water, nor could the ground dissipate the output of sewage, let alone deal with the further complication brought about by the fact that when they were in such close proximity it was extremely difficult to keep them separate. Philadelphia had constructed a major water-supply system as early as 1800. Most of the other large cities had been compelled to turn to external sources by the middle of the nineteenth century. This task soon developed into a much larger and more complex one than was generally conceived. It usually involved dams and reservoirs to impound a sufficient year-round water supply, plus a system of aquaducts, pumps, and pipes to bring it to the city users. There was the whole series of technical problems which usually appears with projects whose magnitude is so much greater than that of previous efforts. There was, in addition, the contemporary development of bacteriology and all the necessary extra equipment and processes which were added to water systems to prevent the spread of waterborne diseases as a result of that new science.

The basic problem with water was getting enough of it into town; the basic problem with sewage was getting enough of it outside the urban area. The modern technology of treating sewage was not yet available and the ground was simply unable to absorb the outpouring of privies and cesspools which the dense populations of the major cities created. One improvisation which usually was instituted in the larger cities in the early 1800s was the "night wagon," that seemingly eternal feature of premodern cities, which collected buckets of sewage. Such services still exist in many cities of lesser-developed nations. In the American environment, the high cost of labor alone, relative to that of the capital-intensive systems for which it serves as the substitute, have long since rendered such methods obsolete, quite aside from health and aesthetic considerations. The major solution to the sewage problem was the flush toilet, known as the "water closet" by the English, who pioneered it about 1800. It required a large increase in the per capita consumption of water, however, so that it could be made generally available only when a modern water system was introduced. Thus, the two crucial urban tasks of bringing water in and moving wastes out became entan-

---

[1] Hydraulic cement had actually been a major construction material used by the Romans. In fact, its versatility and strength account in good part for the remarkable structures the Romans were able to erect, of which so many have survived to this day. The Romans did not understand the chemistry of hydraulic cement, however, but were simply fortunate enough to have a natural supply of the material nearby.

gled. A town could not really hope to solve its sewage problem until it modernized its water system, but the institution of the former multiplied the demands placed on the latter.

Lighting Up the Town

One other rather obvious effect of the increasing density of economic activity in the larger cities was that it became more important to see what was going on, whether one was seeking a certain store, or looking out for pickpockets or absent-minded pedestrians who might wander in front of a carriage. Street lighting also made it possible to extend the working day of the central business districts, as well as that of the manufacturing areas. This extension increased the gains which could be squeezed out of the city by increasing the number of hours in which it could be profitably employed. Some advantages were fairly straightforward. Street lighting was useful in the winter months because opening and closing hours of many businesses edged into dusk, but it was also helpful in extending the many activities, such as shopping, trade and language schools, and factory shifts into the evening hours. In fact, better lighting increased the output possible from the existing resource base of the cities just as certainly as taller buildings or better transportation were in the process of doing.

As far back as the late 1600s, colonial towns had passed ordinances requiring businesses to maintain lanterns outside their establishments during certain hours. In the early 1800s several cities, most notably Baltimore, had installed gas street lights. The pressure for public lighting grew much greater after 1860, however, when the volume of economic activity in the cities began to reach modern proportions. The first major improvement was the arc light, which quickly demonstrated the large potential payoff of good public lighting by sharply increasing the evening business activity in the cities which adopted it. This was soon followed, in the 1870s, by the gas-lighting systems which were an outgrowth of ongoing improvements in petroleum refining. Gas lighting actually consisted of two major variants. One was natural gas, a by-product of both drilling and refining oil. This is the same material which serves today as a fuel for cooking and heating. The other gas system was water gas, a superior material for illumination manufactured out of a light petroleum base. Both of these materials tended to be used in place of arc lighting in the twenty years after 1870, primarily because they required far less apparatus and skilled maintenance. The final solution to the street-lighting problem occurred with the development of the incandescent light in the 1880s. But there was some delay before that invention was adapted to street use. It was initially developed for interior lighting because the existing alternatives were so much less desirable there. Over time, however, especially as the widespread installation of electric lines made it cheaper, electricity began to replace gas for outdoor lighting as well.

Getting Around Town (Better)

Only slightly less indispensable than feeding and housing the population of a city is the task of moving them around from place to place. The advantage of urban organization is that it brings people into close proximity with one another. This saves somewhat on transportation resources (relative to a more dispersed population) but, ironically, it makes local transit all the more important in that it is the ability to make fast, convenient contacts within the city which makes the arrangement of economic organization so advantageous. And the sheer increase in the number of people in the nineteenth-century American cities meant that methods of transporting much larger numbers of those people had to be found if the city was going to continue to provide its advantages in the form it was assuming.

In the first half of the nineteenth century, the only method of getting around town, other than walking, was by using horsepower. And there were only two ways of moving more than one person at a time. The horse could pull either some form of carriage (such as the omnibus, which was essentially a stretched-out stage) or a form of rail car on tracks laid down the street. Either way the speed of moving the people and the number of them moved were limited to the motive power of horses. One exception to this constraint was the railroad, which ran into almost all major cities by 1850. But it was such a dirty, noisy, and unwieldy device that it was generally restricted to separate rights-of-way. Thus, insofar as intracity passenger travel was concerned, it could play only the limited role of moving commuters along relatively restricted routes, mostly to extraurban locations. It could not shoulder much of the prime task, which was moving people relatively short distances around the town so that they both embarked and debarked close to the end points of their trip.

It is not surprising, therefore, that in the latter half of the nineteenth century considerable effort was put into devising better forms of urban transportation. (Some discussion of these improvements has already been presented in the section on electricity in Chapter 11.) One obvious approach was to find some way of using the large passenger capacities of the rail system without all the costs which steam locomotives imposed on an urban environment. The noise and danger of running the trains on street level, while still keeping them handy to the passengers, was solved by elevating the lines *above* the street level. New York City began building such a system in the 1870s. By 1890 the technique had been adopted by most major cities, including Chicago, with its now famous *El*. Transit engineers also succeeded in getting away from some of the smoke and dirt of the steam locomotives by switching to a cable system. This system supplied motive power by means of a cable which the train could hook onto, much like skiers on a rope tow powered from a central station. The cables were replaced soon after 1890 by electric power, however. It was far less cumbersome to operate. One could simply hook into the electric lines wherever it was convenient. It did not require the extensive equipment to overcome friction and keep the cables moving. Electric power was particularly advantageous in that it allowed urban transit to convert to new forms of service. Around the turn of the century it allowed the popular—though brief—extension of the interurbans to suburban areas. In this regard it predated the movement to suburbia and weekend trips to the country which we associate with the automobile today. It also caused a major shift in the form of transit within the cities, moving the train systems down from the elevateds. With overhead wires providing a clean, quiet form of power, there was a tendency for transit to move back to the street level either in the form of trolleys or (after the turn of the centry) buses. Another new form of urban transit moved down even farther from the "el" to become the subway. This proved to be the ultimate solution to the unsightly elevateds as well as a way around the cost of land which was becoming expensive in some of the larger cities.

BUILDING THE NEW METROPOLISES

Along with transforming urban transit to accommodate the huge increase in population, there was the comparable problem of providing the housing, stores, offices, factories, and public buildings where the people could live and work. And the scale and constraints of this task were such that the traditional techniques of construction in the economy simply would no longer work. Most buildings before 1850 were custom projects; that is, much of the design and construction of the building were worked out on the spot. The vast majority of all buildings were made out of wood; brick, the second most-common material, was usually restricted to urban construction. Moreover, it was exceptional for a building to be more than two stories high. All these characteristics were now inappropriate and were bound to be altered when the construction industry began grappling with the problem of the new urban complexes.

The first obvious constraint imposed on construction in the larger cities was the significantly higher cost of land. This dictated that buildings must be taller and much more densely ordered than before. For urban residences it meant a minimum of three stories near the city center, with tenements averaging as much as five or six stories in such locations as lower Manhattan. Business structures, especially those in the heart of the central business district, tended to be even higher. Existing building materials and technology did not allow them to be much higher than eight floors, however. To support the extra weight of added floors, the foundation and lower walls had to be made progressively stronger, which in 1850 meant bulkier. A building of any appreciable height soon took on the dimensions of a pyramid, with the increased width of the walls and the resulting loss of space on the lower floors more than offsetting any gains at the top. Thus, builders found that it was almost never economically worthwhile to go above eight floors in an ordinary business building.

That rule of thumb began to change in the 1880s. The effective economic height limit was another of those bottleneck factors standing in the way of a growing industry and there was considerable incentive to devise ways to circumvent it. An increase in the useful height of central business-district buildings would allow more intensive use of the advantages of agglomeration which were developing in those areas. These gains were being reflected in increasing prices of land, which in turn reinforced the pressures to find ways to use it more intensively. For at least three decades before the 1880s, builders and architects had experimented with using iron beams—and, somewhat later, steel ones, in larger buildings. Most of these efforts had been directed toward spanning larger spaces within buildings, thereby eliminating the clutter of pillars and partitions in stores and auditoriums. But in the 1880s this effort to provide more horizontal space turned into a major effort to add *vertical* space as well. The traditional limit of six to eight floors began to erode as contractors used the strength of steel to replace the excessive bulk of stone. The 1880s saw several office buildings of more than ten stories. From there on the trend was steadily upward until, on the eve of World War I in 1913, the Woolworth Building in Manhattan reached the comparatively modern height of about forty floors. Office buildings have reached much greater heights since that time, of course, with the Empire State Building, started in the 1920s, the modern World Trade Towers in New York, and the Sears, Roebuck Building in Chicago going well over 100 stories. But these buildings have prestige considerations tacked onto the usual hard-headed business calculations which underlie such decisions. Generally, the most profitable high-rise office building in the downtown area of a major city is between forty and sixty stories high. In higher units the added cost (and space) of extra elevators and utility systems offsets the gains from the space added at the top. Thus, much of the gain from increasing the heights of buildings has been achieved by the second decade of the twentieth century. Since that time there have been improvements within such buildings as well as a huge increase in the number of them. However, the basic advantages of agglomeration in the form of stacking forty acres of working people on the space where only one acre of people would otherwise be had become feasible by World War I.

New Building Materials

Wood had always been the predominant building material in the American economy, and understandably so because compared to alternative materials it was cheap and workable. Moreover, in the early 1800s it was the recipient of several more advantages which might tend to make that predominance all the more entrenched and permanent. One was the development of cheap, factory-produced, nails which reduced the cost of constructing wooden structures, especially compared to the older method of drilling holes and inserting pegs to fasten framing together. Another was the development of "balloon" construction, which was devised in the Chicago home-building sector in the 1830s. It simply recognized that when the siding of a building was added, it imparted added strength to the frame of the building. By anticipating this effect, builders could switch to the lighter two-by-four framing commonly used in home construction today rather than the heavier, self-supporting beams typical of the colonial period. Balloon framing—named after the lighter skin of the building—resulted in a considerable saving in building materials as well as some advantages in assembly.[2]

---

[2] Balloon framing was actually one of the first of a long series of steps in which builders learned to build adequately but not to overbuild. This modern characteristic often prompts the observation about homes, as well as other consumer assets, that "they don't build them like they used to." That is correct in a physical sense, but not necessarily so in terms of economics. A structure which lasts a century in modern times might be sound in a structural sense but is most likely obsolete in economic terms. The rooms are probably the wrong proportions and the utility systems hopelessly out of date. Thus, the economic return from the extra lifetime of the physical building tends to be quite low and certainly would not have been worth spending extra funds on for construction more than fifty years previously.

When it came to construction of buildings in the emerging larger cities, however, the advantages of lumber as a construction material were somewhat less marked. Ordinary varieties of wood do not have the strength of other building materials, so that when buildings began to exceed three stories in height, builders turned to other materials. Also, lumber is flammable, so owners who had good reason to be concerned about fires in the larger cities began to specify more fire-resistant materials. This private inclination was helped along considerably by city building codes which began to tighten up on fireproofing standards, especially after the great Chicago fire of 1871.

The most expensive exterior materials were the harder forms of stone, most often granite, but for particularly public locations, marble. Such materials faced the front of court houses, city offices, banks, and stores. Somewhat less expensive were the softer forms of stone, like brownstone (actually a type of reddish sandstone which darkened with exposure), which gave its name to the row houses, or town houses, which it commonly fronted in New York City and Boston. Farther to the south in such cities as Philadelphia and Baltimore, which were farther removed from the main source of brownstone in the Connecticut Valley of New England, bricks were more commonly used. Similar considerations explained their wider use in such Northwestern cities as Chicago and Detroit as well. They could be manufactured locally from any good source of clay—which seems to be one of the few natural resources that is universally available—and thus would become more attractive the farther one got from the sources of natural stone supply.

While city builders tended to use a larger proportion of such material as stone and brick on the fronts of buildings, they tended to revert to cheaper and more utilitarian lumber in the less pretentious areas behind. Most interiors, as well as the rear exteriors and sides, were constructed out of lumber. Again, the effect of the differences of availability of competing materials can be seen among cities. Compared with New York, for example, Chicago used a larger proportion of wood in construction. Many of its tenements were constructed almost entirely of lumber, even after the Great Fire demonstrated that material's susceptibility to conflagration. The Western cities also tended to use wooden roof shingles, whereas in the Eastern cities many of the larger buildings were roofed with slate. In other words, even within the context of general trends in materials, brought about by changing incomes and labor costs, the effects of differences in local conditions could still be detected.

While a shift in the types of materials used in construction was under way, a similar, perhaps even more drastic, restructuring in how they were put together was also under way. Before 1840, the construction of a building was usually an opportunity for most of the crafts workers involved to demonstrate some of their skills and creativity. Doors, window frames, moldings, railings, and cabinets were usually handcrafted right at the site of the project. In the mid-nineteenth century these functions began to move into factory production, however, because of much the same advantages in mechanization which had prompted the shift among such products as clocks, firearms, and textiles. This tendency to purchase these components ready-made, rather than craft them individually at the project, occurred first in the larger cities, understandably so, because urban markets provided a larger market and thus were often where these specialized lumber manufacturers first located. Later, as ready-made components became more standard throughout the construction sector, these enterprises tended to move toward their sources of raw material supply.

The tendency to use standardized, off-the-shelf parts carried over to other components of construction as well. This included much of the hardware, such as locks, hinges, drawer pulls, and so forth. Undoubtedly the most dramatic example of this general shift, however, was the introduction of public utilities into residential and business buildings. The first was the installation of piped-in water, which was introduced, with some variation among cities, in the middle of the nineteenth century. This created a large market for ready-made pipes, faucets, sinks, and, after considerable public debate on their healthiness, bathtubs. Soon thereafter came sewage connections and the installation of toilets and showers. There were also gas lines for lighting and natural-gas lines for heating and cooking. Then, in the 1880s, came electricity, along with light fixtures, fuse boxes, outlets, and hundreds of feet of wire. One can readily sympathize with the old-fashioned crafts workers who took pride in their work and sometimes even signed it as an expression of their creativity. By 1900 a good portion of construction work resembed assembly-line work. The compensating gain of this routinization, of course, was that offices and housing were considerably cheaper (for a given level of quality) than they would have been otherwise. It also assured that the process of urbanization, which soon after World War I would incorporate more than half of the nation's population, would not be stifled.

THE POLITICAL ECONOMY OF THE LARGE CITIES

The largest American cities of the late 1800s were not only much larger than those which had led that category near the beginning of the century but, as our discussion has repeatedly suggested, had undergone a drastic reorganization in their economic structure as well. And, as so often happens when such a dramatic reshuffling occurs in economic relations, it also caused changes in the basic institutions which regulated that economic activity. Such was the case with the municipal governments which were responsible for these emerging metropolises. At the beginning of the century, the normal functions of a city government were quite limited by modern standards. The provision of fire and police protection was a relatively small task, with much of such functions left to the voluntary, almost spontaneous, efforts of local citizens. Most cities of any size, however, did employ night guards as much to check for fires as to keep the peace. Welfare activities had a similar element of voluntary, private enterprise in them. Much of the aid to widows, orphans, the sick, disabled, and unemployed was carried out by private charity associations. Education, of course, was acknowledged as a public responsibility, but the average number of years of schooling was much less than it is today.

This pattern of the limited size and involvement of municipal governments changed radically in the last half of the nineteenth century. The larger cities were a growth sector themselves, but public management of them probably increased even faster than they did. Some of this expansion was related to the inevitable growth of the complexity of the social organization and the resultant inability of informal neighborhood actions to deal with many of the problems which arose. Public drunkeness, overdue bills, disputes between neighbors, and the other mundane problems of life which occupy so much of a typical police force's time today, began to be shifted to the hands of a professional force. This was also true for the fire-fighting services. Where once neighbors could be counted on to pitch in to fight a fire, now some areas of the city, such as the central business district or the manufacturing areas, lacked round-the-clock neighbors. Also, fires in such structures often called for specialized equipment and training. While most cities continued to employ volunteer firefighters, the larger ones began to develop full-time, trained forces as well.

The component of city services which grew the fastest, however, and which also accounted for much of the increase in the role of city governments, was that of public utilities. Formerly each household took care of its own water, waste, lighting, heating, and cooking requirements, but by the end of the nineteenth century developments in technology had converted these functions into products which were consumed collectively. And it was this commonality of the public utilities which soon forced them into the realm of municipal supervision. The special feature of such services as water or electricity is that the optimum size of output is quite large in relation to the local demand. This creates a situation which economists call a "natural monopoly," which is to say that only one firm can be efficiently maintained to provide the service. (This characteristic of public utilities is understandable when we recall that there must be a physical connection, such as water pipes or electric wires, to each customer. Competition between alternative suppliers, therefore, would require the installation of parallel physical delivery systems and, inevitably, higher unit costs of operation.) Left to itself, a private firm would undoubtedly operate as a monopolist, setting prices to maximize its own profits, which in such a case certainly would not be optimal for the consumers. A city government has two basic methods by which it can mitigate the worst of such situations. The first method by which it can do so is to allow the utility to remain under private ownership but set controls on the prices and the service it provides. And the second method is to take over ownership and management of the enterprise itself.

Both these options were quite obvious to the residents of the larger cities in the last half of the nineteenth century. They debated the relative merits of each, sometimes very intensively. Some argued, for example, that private enterprise was more efficient. Such enterprises under municipal ownership, continued the advocates of private utilities, would inevitably pad their payrolls with patronage employees. (There was probably some truth to this charge, in that such behavior was common enough in city operations of the day. It was not, however, an unmitigated cost, as we shall see below.) Proponents of public ownership countered that regulation of private monopolies was bound to fail. There was the difficulty of calculating costs, and therefore of setting prices, as well as the ever-present temptation for the monopoly to bribe the regulators. But whatever the persuasiveness of the argument presented at that time—and, it should be added, the extensive, detailed analysis which modern economists have put into the subject of public utility regulation—the choice in a specific situation seemed to be controlled by other considerations. There were large differences in public ownership of specific types of utilities. By about 1900, for example, almost 100 percent of city sewage systems were owned by their municipalities, yet the public transit systems were almost entirely privately held. Water works were about equally divided between private and public ownership, while electric companies were privately held in about 85 percent of the cases. These patterns, drawn from several thousand cities at that time, are much too marked to be simply random. Whatever the force of logic and circumstances for private vis-à-vis public ownership in general, these patterns suggest that the characteristics of particular types of services must have been important in specific decisions. Why, for example, were all of the pipes carrying sewage out of buildings owned by the cities while only half of the ones carrying water in were so managed? Surely the physical nature of the distribution system of the two services was comparable. The distinction which made the decision between private and public ownership so sharp probably originated in just how tightly private ownership could control such a system. A private waterworks could pump, store, and deliver water to its customers with the assurance that at no point would its product become (legally) mixed in with that of some other authority. There were no compelling reasons that a private firm could not provide much the same service which a public agency would. Sewer lines, on the other hand, usually joined into, or themselves served as outlets for, the city street-drainage system. Although it is conceivable that a private sewer system might charge the city for its services (or the city might charge a private sewer system for its services), it is likely that the calculation of costs would become complicated and, given the different interests involved, very heated. When there is such interrelatedness in the physical production activities, it is understandable that the function would be taken over almost exclusively by the government.

There is another fairly obvious correlation in the contrast between public and private ownership of public utilities. We noted that in 1900 almost 100 percent of public transit systems were privately owned. This may have aroused the reader's suspicion as to a possible misprint because today the vast majority of public transit systems have reverted to public ownership. In large part this has occurred because, in this particular sector, demand for the service has declined; private owners have found ownership unattractive and the municipalities, deeming the service socially necessary despite the falloff in customers, have taken over by default. What is important from our point of view here is that private ownership was dominant when the industry was relatively new, about 1900, but was taken over by the public sector when it entered its declining phase.[3] Contemporaries in the late 1800s, often the same ones who had advocated private ownership, pointed out that that form of ownership had a comparative advantage in implementing new forms of technology. There is undoubtedly some element of truth to this observation. The street-railroad systems of New York City, Chicago, and Philadelphia and more than 100 smaller towns were consolidated—into a single unit for each city, that is—and reorganized by a syndicate headed by William Whitney and T. F. Ryan. Critics of this group noted that it constituted a trust, much like the familiar ones in other sectors of the day. What they failed to distinguish, however, is that the monopoly powers inherent in such an organization lay not at the national level but in each individual city. Controlling the street railroads of Chicago and New York City jointly really gave no more control over the market than if each franchise had been owned separately. The power the syndicate had in any given city was related to the range of alternatives which existed locally. In this context, the advantages the nationwide syndicate could bring to organizing street-railroad systems was essentially that of managerial expertise. The experience and methods which had been worked out in one city could be applied to others. This deduction is supported by the recorded operations of the street-railroad syndicate. When they took over the trolleys in a city, they invariably consolidated existing lines into one network under a single management. Critics of their behavior could rightly object that this created a local monopoly which could be expected to reap monopoly profits as a result of that consolidation. One should note, however, that this response is expected in such an environment—which is one of a natural monopoly—and although it may tend to create monopoly profits it also typically reduces the cost of providing those services as well.[4]

Hence, the private syndicate, using its experience from other operations, could initially organize the street-railroad system much better than the local city government could hope to do when it was operating without the benefit of such a learning curve. And thus, in their early years, city governments had good reason to leave the management of these enterprises to private entrepreneurs, even at the cost of yielding some monopoly profits to the management. Over time,

---

[3] That switch from a growth to a declining sector occurred relatively quickly for a major sector. In 1900 street railroads and trolleys were considered good investment properties and were selling at a substantial premium over book value. By the middle of the 1920s those markups had disappeared and cities were beginning to receive some overtures from private investors to take over their investments. The primary reason for this sharp turnaround, of course, was the rapid growth of the automobile, which not only cut into the demand for alternative forms of transportation but also began a long-term reorganization of the economy, which further eroded the attractiveness of alternative methods over the longer term.

[4] Ironically, the unification of local transit lines under a single management may not increase monopoly power at all, because the market control results from a single line serving only a given neighborhood in the absence of close competitors. In other words, the monopoly is for a given route rather than for a total urban area. Consolidation may simply perpetuate those local monopolies. In any case, it probably allows those services to be produced at lower unit costs through economies in such now centralized services as maintenance, management, supervision, and utilization of equipment.

however, as learning in the management functions of street railroads tended to slow down, the loss to the city of taking over these operations on an individual basis diminished and the cities began to acquire their ownership. A similar pattern seemed to develop in public water works. As the operations of these systems became farily well established and routine, municipalities tended to buy out private owners here also.

There are at least two other considerations that were involved in this decision of whether to take a public utility into public ownership. One was the current state of city finances. The municipality would have to compensate the private owners and that usually involved issuing bonds to the amount of the purchase price. This was not necessarily bad for the residents of the city per se (abstracting from any changes in efficiency as a result of the switch in management) because the larger debt obligations which they assumed as citizens would be equally offset by the additional income to the city from charges for the use of the municipal services. Thus, increased city debt is not, in itself, a net burden. The problem was simply that the cities were, typically, undertaking large amounts of new obligations in this period. The rapid growth in roads, city buildings, and schools, not to mention the financing of the public utilities which the cities were beginning to contemplate, caused a huge increase in city debt outstanding during the latter half of the nineteenth century. Bond-rating agencies and citizens began to pull back at the thought of further indebtedness, and thus the conversion of public utilities from private to public ownership was slowed by the rapid growth of the urban government's role in the economy.

There is one last, but important, factor which became involved in the public decision as to the ownership of the utilities. Economic and political systems have different methods of reaching decisions about the level of output and the distribution of services. A privately owned enterprise, unless otherwise constrained, will provide that level and distribution of services that ensures that profits are maximized *given the number of dollars* consumers are willing to spend for the service. In contrast, a political system will tend to make such decisions on the basis of the distribution of political power, which in the American economy, conceptually at least, implies one vote per voter. Thus the two systems tend to make decisions which reflect the different distributions of interest.[5] A fairly straightforward example of this decision-making process is the question of the ownership of public transit. A private company will supply only those services it finds profitable. If constrained to provide certain services on which it loses money, it must be compensated through subsidies or extra profits on other lines of activity. If not, it will eventually use up its assets and go out of business entirely. It is usually the threat of such suspension of service which forces the public sector to assume the ownership of the utility in order to assure its continuation.

The takeover of the service by the public sector is often accompanied by an

[5] Note that the decision as to which sphere, private or public, provides a service determines which groups will tend to benefit, so that the decision about who, in fact, does provide it can be expected to be fought along such lines. We shall see examples of this process later, in the role of city governments in this period.

effort to *expand* certain elements of it, directly the opposite of the efforts under way by the private owners just before the conversion. This is to be expected. Consider the voters (and potential commuters) located next to a marginal transit route which the privately owned company would prefer to discontinue. Their aggregate demand (in dollar terms) is not sufficient to sustain the route, but the number of votes they represent (out of the relevant electorate) is certainly sufficient, and therefore a public transit authority which supersedes the private agency will respond to their pressures. As a rule of thumb, the greater the divergence between the distribution of political and economic power in regard to a given service, the more likely that public ownership will develop. That would explain, for example, the marked difference between public transit on the one hand, and electricity on the other. Public transit is an "inferior good," that is, as people's incomes rise they tend to consume less of it by shifting to more attractive alternatives, most obviously automobiles. Electric power consumption, in contrast, tends to be much more directly correlated with income. As a typical family's income rises, it tends to spend more on such items as clothes driers, air conditioners, outdoor lighting, and electric heat in the recreation room. Thus, it is likely that there would be more pressure from lower-income groups upon public authorities to take over public transit than from all groups—of varying levels of income—to take over the provision of electric power. Therefore, one more reason for the growing role of municipal governments in their local economies since the mid-1800s is that the structure of economic rewards was such that some groups found it more desirable to obtain certain of their services through that channel.

Municipal Government under the "Bosses"

During the 1860s the government of New York City was controlled by a political group, or "machine" as it is commonly known, headed by the now famous William M. Tweed. "Boss" Tweed was merely one of the best known of what was to be a fairly common form of city government over the next century. Without being accusative at this point, it seems obvious that such governments have a high degree of illegal or marginally legal operations (known now as graft or corruption). The Tweed government, for example, is known to have accepted kickbacks on public contracts in the form of unofficial payments to themselves which, of course, were reflected in a higher cost of public projects. They were also known to have padded the public payroll, that is, to employ more workers than was necessary to carry out certain city services. Furthermore, they were known to have taken bribes in return for permits on zoning variations. And, among other functions, they conducted a semiofficial welfare program, issuing aid to some of the unemployed, poor, or disrupted families through neighborhood representatives of the machine government.

These "machine governments" prompted a widespread cry for reform at the time they were operating and they have been the subject of almost continual vilification in historical treatments since their demise. The detractors of the bosses and their organizations have always vastly outnumbered those who could find many redeeming features in their operations. But that general evaluation presents a rather difficult problem in historical explanation; namely, why was this form of government so widespread and long-lived in the face of all those vocal accusations if it really did have such pervasively adverse effects on the city? There is the fairly obvious observation that these machines could acquire power and continue in it only if they received a majority vote of their respective populations. Of course, there was probably some vote "buying" going on, but that is an integral part of the explanation of these governments, to which we shall return below.

One good clue as to why this type of government could survive so widely is given in the way in which it channeled the finances it acquired. The amount of revenues which it collected outside of recognized tax revenues was often quite large. For example, an often-quoted figure is that half of the indebtedness acquired by New York City under the Tweed administration (about $65 million) went into the personal funds of the politicians. Even so, most scholars of these organizations find that very few of the officials themselves ever acquired any sizeable personal wealth from these positions. Almost all of the illegally acquired revenues were redistributed back to some (rather large) blocs of the city population. Part went into the informal ward welfare program which parceled out aid in various forms, including cash, food, fuel, and rent payments. Part also went into what was essentially a public employment program, much like later efforts such as the Civilian Conservation Corp, whose prime motivation was to put the unemployed to work. In effect, much of this illegal and unofficial activity was a redistribution of the benefits of public funds from one group to another. When the money was directed from regular tax collections, it amounted to a transfer from the regular taxpayers to those of the particular groups which the machine aided.

In effect, the machine governments were performing some of the functions, such as giving welfare and unemployment aid, which have been formally accepted into the responsibilities of higher levels of government since that time. In this context, the boss government might be viewed as a type of transitional arrangement. They performed functions which in earlier years had been carried out informally at the neighborhood level, but at a time when the neighborhoods were losing that individual responsibility in the anonymity of the growing cities. Later these functions would be formally accepted by society; when that occurred, the cities would receive much more assistance for the role of public charity which they now found thrust upon them by virtue of simple proximity. But until that recognition was obvious enough so that it would be formally and generally accepted, the cities would have to work with their own ad hoc arrangement.

If we recognize this function in the operation of the boss governments, then their previous stigma of malignancy becomes somewhat less obvious. Rather than the bosses or the machine stealing the public blind, they were acting more as intermediaries in a process in which one group in the society was—to keep the colloquial expression consistent—stealing another group blind. And if the one which was doing the "stealing" was, in fact, the one we have pictured, then the poorer elements of the city population were succeeding in taking income from the richer groups. If that is the case, many of the critics of the urban machines have been completely fooled. Rather than the established, wealthy groups exploiting everyone else, the poorer groups were typically extracting income from the rest of society. Like their contemporaries, the farmers, the urban poor were demonstrating that it is not always the lower classes which are the exploited in every society.

If the urban poor were, in fact, exploiting those with incomes higher than theirs, it was not because they were exceptionally perceptive or clever. Rather, exploitation developed because there was an opportunity for them to exert more influence through the political mechanism than through the economic sphere. In other words, we have another example of the tendency for groups to press for the use of the particular channel of decision making which benefits themselves the most, the same factor we encountered in the private/public choice in the ownership of public utilities. More specifically, what was occurring in the boss system was that the power of the lower-income groups, through the political one-man–one-vote calculus, was greater than that through their dollar expenditures. Thus they were able to use their power at the ballot box to divert more resources to their use than would have otherwise been available. Now we can see better the meaning of such terms as buying or delivering votes on the part of the machine. Of course, they "bought" votes in the sense that any political organization has to make it worthwhile for groups to support it. But at the same time the lower-income groups "sold" their votes; that was part of the implicit package of quid pro quo in which the identifiable groups swapped their disproportionate voting power for observable rewards.

The characterization of the poorer-income groups as receiving most of the net benefits is, of course, somewhat overdrawn and simplistic. Municipal machines require the support of a much broader portion of the population than merely the lower-income groups, who in the American context have never held an absolute majority in themselves. The bosses have generally commanded the support of a good portion of the middle class and the business community as well. And to do so they had to deliver the political goods, just as any other political group did which hoped to survive. Moreover, these business and middle-class groups were not likely to be impressed by a redistribution of income through taxes because they would probably be on the losing end of such a transfer.

To enlist the support of these other groups, then, the machines developed a series of other services, many of which have proven sufficiently attractive so that they have continued to be common features of government in large American cities well after most of the machines themselves have disappeared. One of the most common of these services was implicit in the frequent charges of bribery and corruption which were levied against the boss organizations. It is generally acknowledged that the machines accepted bribes to expedite zoning and building regulations, award franchises for various kinds of public services, and dismiss or reduce legal charges. These activities were illegal in the latter half of the nineteenth century even as they are today. Nevertheless, they were widely practiced— as they are yet today. This suggests that there must have been some mutual advantages to both parties in such agreements, since they were created so often and in so many different locations.

We should be able to grasp what those mutual advantages were if we look at the incentives involved in a particular case. Consider a very typical case, the issuance of the franchise to operate an electric trolley (street railroad) in the late nineteenth century. In the absence of controls on the allowable prices, such an authorization would represent a large amount of wealth. We know, for instance, that at the time of consolidation of the street-rail lines in New York City in the late 1800s, their market value was more than $150 million, while the amount of actual investment in the system totaled only about half of that. In other words, the value of the franchise, the *right* to build and construct that system, was worth about $75 million in itself. Thus, if a city government were simply to award the franchise to the highest bidder, one would expect that the price which any potential firm would be willing to pay for that license would tend to approach that amount. Thus, also, when the city issues such a permit without any severe restrictions written into it—as has usually been the case—potential owners should have been willing to pay amounts up to that amount of capitalized excess profits ($75 million in the case of the New York City street railroads) to obtain that right. In this context, it is hardly surprising that private parties would be willing to clandestinely slip the city officials a few million dollars in exchange for the franchise. From their vantage it was an immensely profitable investment, well worth the likely risks of being exposed and punished. And as for the city officials, the choice among potential franchise operators, other than the revenue they could obtain to operate their own projects, was not that important. In other words, the officials had strong reasons to be open to bribes in awarding the franchise because that source of funds enabled them to support the programs (such as the informal welfare systems) which kept them in office.

From this standpoint we can sense some of the motivations which caused business interests to support the boss administrations. They were much more convenient and cheaper to work with than the typical "law-abiding" municipalities. They were, in the usual public terms, red-tape cutters, expeditors, and friendly brokers. With them, buildings were approved faster and with the desirable variances, troubles with the housing inspector were taken care of, and complaints about the neighborhood school were dealt with. In short, insofar as the efforts of the city government were concerned, they made the city a cheaper and more convenient place in which to live and conduct business.

One fairly straightforward implication of this system of unofficial payments to the city government was that it would then have more revenue to work with than a comparable city collecting revenues only "by the book." This, in turn, meant that such an administration could provide a larger number of services out of a given tax base than that provided by a law-abiding government. Thus graft, as we have illustrated the term above, emanated to the benefit of taxpayers generally. While some may have received more benefits from the special system of distribution practiced by most of the machines, it meant that average tax assessments would be somewhat less than if the city had only legitimate revenue to fund its operations. Thus the report of the very frequent support of the middle class is understandable. They probably recognized that some shady deals were taking place—such actions have seldom slipped past enterprising, ambitious news reporters for very long—but as long as the taxes seemed reasonable and basic city services were provided smoothly, why should they complain?

When all the elements of the machine governments are put together, we can see how understandable and predictable the arrangement actually was. We saw that the poorer classes gained by trading their voting power for economic rewards. The role of the business community was simply the reverse side of the arrangement. They were essentially trading their economic power for political returns. And the other groups which supported the machine could be identified as various mixtures of the above two polar cases. Through it all, there was the obvious element of breaking the legal rules of the game, or at least overlooking them. But in this case, the costs of respecting the law were apparently not worthwhile to the majority of the citizenry. Thus, this sizeable bloc of Americans was demonstrating two characteristics which are often associated with the economy—a spirit of independence, and a capacity for productive innovation.

COMMERCE

During this period when the cities were expanding their share of the economy's product, the sector which distributed that product was itself a growth sector. In the four decades from 1860–1900, commerce's contribution to the total value of national output rose from 12 percent to 18 percent. A good part of this expansion occurred in the cities and was clearly interacting with their development. One feature which was evident in all the new merchandising forms that appeared in this period, including, ironically enough, the mail order firms, was their organization to take advantage of the new urban environment. The larger metropolitan areas offered for the first time the sheer size which allowed the specialization inherent in the new formats. Thus one more result of the development of the cities was a major reorganization of the commercial channels which served a good portion of the population.

The Middleman: Caught in the Middle

In the antebellum period there had been a rather substantial revision of the wholesale trade. The intermediate steps between the producer and the final retail customer, once filled by that jack-of-all-trades, the general merchant, were taken over by more specialized commission merchants and jobbers. Retailing also underwent some modifications, but certainly less drastic ones than those which were occurring at the wholesale level. In the larger cities, retail stores began to specialize in particular lines of merchandise, but in much of the country the generalized retail outlet continued to be dominant. Most neighborhoods were not large enough markets to support much more than a single, all-purpose retail outlet.

The effective buying power in local markets was increasing in the nineteenth century, of course, so that this localized, generalized pattern of retailing was bound to come under pressure sooner or later, especially in the larger cities where the largest local markets were. One of the first variations had actually begun to evolve before the Civil War, in the 1850s. Like so many major innovations, it developed modestly and gradually. For example, a retail dry-goods store in New York City, by the name of Macy's, began adding new types of goods to its normal line. By 1870 its range of goods included ready-made clothes, curtains and tablecloths, china, silver, dishes and kitchen utensils, books, and small household decorations and furnishings. Similar evolutions were taking place in other stores, including such now-established names as Marshall Field in Chicago, Jordan Marsh in Boston, and Gimbel's in New York City. What these stores had in common was a wide and complete selection of goods under one roof. In fact, the offerings in any one major line were so comprehensive that, by themselves, they effectively constituted an individual store, or *department* as they were called at that time—hence the name *department store.*

Although variety may have been the first noticeable characteristic of this new form of merchandising, there were others which, although less noticed, were probably as important. Another department store pioneer in New York City, A. T. Stewart, intoduced the practice of selling goods at fixed prices. His initial purpose in this tactic was simply to allow him to employ less expensive labor which could carry out the routine transactions of a sale without having the responsibility of negotiating a price. The innovation eventually became fairly universal in the economy and spread to almost all forms of retailing, well beyond the confines of the developing department stores. And that adoption is understandable. Negotiating a price for each transaction is a highly labor-intensive activity, from the standpoint of both the buyer and the seller, so that the cost of that method of setting prices was becoming increasingly expensive. Moreover, the value of the information gained through haggling over each purchase was decreasing. As the volume of transactions of a given type of product increased and the differences between market areas were reduced, prices tended to become more standardized and homogeneous anyway. Thus it was almost inevitable that, had Stewart's department store not initiated fixed-sale prices, some other store would soon have done so.

The department stores were innovators in another major aspect of retail transactions as well. They were the first type of retailers to introduce the "money back if not satisfied" guarantee. Before this time the prevailing attitude was "buy at your own risk." This was not an unreasonable way to proceed when the product varied so much from item to item—as it did, typically, in the era before mass-manufactured, or graded, products—because the buyer and seller had to arrive at some joint appraisal of each good to complete the transaction. But as the goods became more standardized, as was typical in the nineteenth century, the resources formerly used in this process of inspection and calculation could be saved. In one sense, the policy of "your money back" was a natural accompaniment of fixed prices. If the price policy proscribed bargaining, then it also prevented the salespersons and buyers from negotiating about the characteristics of the product. If the products failed to perform as anticipated, the buyers could return them. They were not taking their last chance when they took the merchandise out of the store and they did not have to inspect it accordingly. The money-back guarantee can also be seen as a labor-saving innovation. Rather than having each good undergo a careful examination upon purchase, only that minority of goods which proved to be unsatisfactory needed to undergo extensive negotiation—or renegotiation. Both the money-back guarantee and the fixed-price system, then, can be seen as natural outgrowths of the developments taking place at that time. As goods became more homogeneous, society was able to devise methods which saved on some of the resources required to deliver them to the final customers.

Bypassing the Middleman

The department stores were innovators in other ways as well. They were among the first to institute a major change in another sector of retailing practice, one that was symptomatic of the general changing structure of retailing after the Civil War. They were soon handling relatively large amounts of certain kinds of goods and, as such, were in all essential features performing the functions of the local jobber themselves. Thus they soon—rather naturally—bypassed that middleman and dealt directly with the commission merchants. But it was not long before they began to find that those brokers were also superfluous. The department stores often wished to order certain kinds of goods, or to manufacture them to certain specifications, and at such times they went directly to the manufacturer with their proposals. Thus they sometimes bypassed the middleman entirely. Not only were they supplying a large retail clientele with diversified products but they were integrating backward toward the producer in order to better serve them.

The bypass which the department stores discovered and/or forged around the wholesalers was soon followed and widened by the chain stores. The latter half of the nineteenth century saw the emergence of a series of such firms, many of which are household words today. There was, for example, the Great Atlantic and Pacific Tea Company, now commonly known simply as the A&P. It began in the 1860s doing exactly what its name implied—specializing in the sale of tea throughout the national market. It soon outran the scope of its name, however—in product, if not in location. Originally it sold tea through the mail, offering it at attractive prices by eliminating the intermediate distributors. A&P opened some of its own retail stores as well and soon found that channel was providing an increasing portion of its sales. This is surprising in one sense, because it was during this period that the mail order houses were appearing and mail service was being improved by the speed of transportation and the extension of rural delivery. But A&P was no longer merely a tea company; as long as it was operating these retail outlets, it found it advantageous to stock other items on the shelves as well. Most of those other items were either too expensive or perishable to sell by mail, so the company effectively evolved into two separate operations.

The retail stores prospered the most because A&P was finding out what had also become evident to the earliest department stores: there were special forms of economies associated with larger-sized operations, and firms which could organize to take advantage of them could make sizeable profits. The department stores had made money by matching a new package of services—a much wider variety and convenience of shopping, the assurance of product quality, and prices which were competitive with other retail outlets—with a clientele marked by more sophistication and higher incomes. The success of department stores was also partly attributable to their innovations in reaching back through the existing wholesale levels to lower the costs of the goods they handled.[6]

The chain stores also found ways to reorganize their channels of supply in order to procure goods more cheaply. By operating a relatively large number of retail outlets, the chains generated enough commerce to allow them to operate their own wholesale distribution system as well. If their retail trade was sufficiently large, they could capture all the economies inherent in wholesaling and thus enter the retail level with the advantage of paying less for acquiring their supplies. The earlier chains, such as A&P, Kroger, Grand Union, and Jewel Tea, probably did have this advantage over the independent grocers and wholesalers initially, which probably accounted for their rapid growth in the later 1800s and early 1900s, but such economies are not necessarily restricted to integrated retail/ wholesale chains—and the competition reorganized and fought back. Independent wholesalers adopted the new procedures in buying, selling, and organizing *their* operations and thus they were able to offer goods to retailers at much the same price which it cost the chain stores to supply their retail outlets.[7]

Thus the gains in retailing operations introduced by the chains are probably somewhat more than that of merely integrating back into the wholesale level. One of those other advantages can be appreciated if we note the widespread change in packaging which was occurring in consumer goods, especially food-stuffs, during this period. (Some suggestions of this change were contained in the previous chapter in the section on food processing.) As more food products were prepared and processed outside the home, they tended to be canned, bottled, wrapped, and boxed in such a way that it was difficult for consumers to check the quality of the contents before purchasing. As a result, consumers began depending on familiar brand names of products to indicate the quality of the goods inside the impenetrable label. Producers were quick to recognize—indeed to initi-ate—this channel of consumer decision making and they began to create and advertise brands as a method of expanding their sales. By the turn of the century a good many items carried by a typical grocery store were brand name goods. Looking around the shelves of such an establishment, one could expect to find

[6] This innovation is not limited to use by department stores, of course. Over time, other forms of retailing, such as discount stores, cooperatives, and chain stores, have adopted it to lower their own costs as well. And, as a result, the position of department stores in recent times has declined relative to other forms of retailing. The position they have been able to maintain is a result of those special features, such as greater variety and customer service, which are distinctively their own.

[7] The fact that the chains own their own wholesaling facilities does not mean that they can necessarily save on the middleman's charges. If they use just as many resources to perform this function as the independents do, then those opportunity costs must be recognized in the firm's total profits. If, for example, the chains were to lower the prices they charged their retail units, this would obviously make those operations appear more profitable. There would be a corresponding loss at the wholesale level, however, so that while such accounting gimmicks might make one or another division appear more profitable vis-à-vis each other, the total profit would be unaffected.

such names as Pillsbury's Best Flour, Franco-American Soups, Kellogg's Corn Flakes, and Duke's Mixture Smoking Tobacco.

As critics of the practice have so often pointed out, however, advertising costs money and eventually this must be reflected in the price which the producers must charge for the product in order to earn a normal return on all the resources they employ. From an economic viewpoint, this is not necessarily bad. If consumers value the information they receive from knowing the brand as much as any other services which the resources used could alternatively provide, then there is not a misallocation of resources. There is always an incentive for producers to seek ways which provide that information at a lower cost, however. And here, again, the chains were leaders in devising ways to reduce costs, this time in the form of house brands. The chains simply began to have goods packaged under their own recognizable label. These were prepared to the specifications of the firm (which varied somewhat among chains) by contracting with established processors—who often were also turning out the same type of goods under their own labels. The advantage of these private, or house, brands was that the chain usually spent less per item on advertising. Often it simply advertised the various goods carried under the house label in one common campaign. The main pitch of much of this advertising was simply that house goods were guaranteed to be good quality but were somewhat lower in price than the brands of the processors. This was usually correct, in that what the chains were actually doing was substituting their own names (or a closely linked version of such) for the more expensive identification of individual goods built up by more extensive advertising. In a sense, the house brands were introducing a new form of competition into markets which were in the process of changing the combination of services supplied by a typical good. In the first half of the nineteenth century if one bought flour in a store, that was all that was expected. It was up to the buyer to make sure that the product was of a certain quality, and as for any preparation beyond that point, it was unquestioned that that was also the responsibility of the buyer. But in the latter half of the nineteenth century this long-standing pattern began to change, largely in response to the complex of changes in processing, transportation, and urbanization which we have already detailed. The consumer now began to be willing to pay for quality, and to expect as a matter of course that products were of uniform good quality, and that many of the intermediate processing steps had already been completed. It was in these latter characteristics that the private brands stepped in to intensify the competition. After all, if the consumers wished to buy quality and convenience, producers could make money providing those attributes just as well as they could in providing the basic good itself.

As in the case of reorganization of wholesaling, the chain stores were leading innovators in the use of private brands. Again, as in that former case, however, the advantages of that form of merchandising were so basic and general that it was not long before other forms of retailing were adopting them. The most direct and obvious form was in the formation of supply cooperatives by the independent grocers. In this way the individual store owners could maintain their independence but still offer their customers the advantages of large-scale distribution and recognizable brand products at competitive prices. The gains inherent in chain operations extended beyond these two major contributions to higher productivity and included some—although perhaps less important, in aggregate—which the independent stores were not able to emulate. These consisted of the knowledge gained in the management and organization of one store which could be applied to improve the performance of another. The chains had an advantage over the independents in being able to transfer managers or specialists among stores in order to deal with particular local conditions. There were, for example, managers who were particularly good at getting new locations into operation, while others were better at dealing with lagging enterprises or establishing special promotions or creating advertising or establishing inventory guidelines or. . . . These specialized talents could be used more fully in a larger enterprise, like the chains, than in a collection of individually owned and managed units. Another corollary of this greater scope for specialization was that it was typically more advantageous for a chain to engage in innovative activity than it was for an independent firm. The chain store has both the specialized resources to create such innovations and a wider market area within which to recoup the benefits of such activities. No wonder, then, that chain stores were generally leaders in innovation during the latter half of the nineteenth century. And although some of that cutting edge has been eroded by the tendency for other forms of retailing enterprises to assume some of that innovative leadership, the chains established in that period have maintained a large portion of their markets since that time. Even today the names of J. C. Penny, Woolworth, Walgreen, and McCrory are common terms throughout the economy.

Integrating Forward

Pity the poor middleman in the late nineteenth century. Not only were some retailers integrating their operations backward toward the producers around him, but some of the producers were working it from the other side. This included such firms as International Harvester, Singer Sewing Machine, Swift Packing, American Tobacco, and Standard Oil. Before we conclude that this list was the beginning of a stampede which would soon eliminate the middleman altogether—which would be wrong—it is important to note that in each of the above cases there were special product characteristics which made such integration desirable. The Swift Packing Company is a good example. Initially there was no existing system of wholesalers which could have delivered meat fresh to the customers. As part of developing the product, the Swift organization was forced also to develop transportation and storage facilities near the local markets. International Harvester and Singer were not troubled by perishable products but rather by complicated machinery which required standing maintenance and repair facilities to keep the machinery functioning properly. These two firms were drawn into the establishment of factory-owned service outlets when the failure of franchise operators in this capacity began to penalize sales.

We can see that in these cases, special product characteristics dictated special distribution arrangements. This was not so with the majority of products, however. Most goods were not unique, or so difficult to adapt to general whole-sale operations, that they could not be handled by the existing firms performing that function. Moreover, there were good reasons to try to adapt new products to fit the existing system. There are economies of scale in the use of specialized, intermediate levels of commercial distribution. Thus, a product which does not use those channels pays a penalty in the form of higher per unit distribution costs. It pays to develop separate distribution facilities only if the special charac-teristics of a product impose particular problems which, in turn, impose a cost greater than a specialization-related advantage. For most products in the fifty years after the Civil War, that was not true. And that explains why commerce was a growth sector, even though entrepreneurs were able to devise methods to bypass certain elements of it. The total amount of commerce was growing more than enough to offset such losses simply because the gains implicit in those economies of scale in distribution were pulling a larger portion of the output in the economy into the commercialized sector.

This net effect can be seen in another great commercial innovation of the period, the mail order house. In their earlier years, before they went into retailing also, Montgomery Ward and Sears, Roebuck obviously worked to reduce the amount of retailing operations in the economy. But they had a counteracting effect insofar as the total volume of commerce in rural areas was concerned, one which has been celebrated in social history but which has received somewhat less attention in commercial history. As a family leafed through the latest catalog in those long winter evenings, they were, in effect, being exposed to a wide range of products which were substitutes for home production. There were ready-made clothes to replace home sewing, kitchen implements and dishes to replace hand-crafted models, and musical instruments and kerosene lamps to replace the eve-ning rehash of past harvests around the fire. Furthermore, the feature which converted many of these obvious desires into possible realities was the economies of purchasing and distribution which the catalog houses had been able to achieve. They were not only able to undersell the country store in its own territo-ry, but they also pulled the products from a good portion of former farm activity for home purposes into the American marketplace.

SUGGESTED READINGS

Groner, Alex and the Editors of American Heritage and Business Week, *American Busi-ness and Industry,* American Heritage, New York, 1972, Chapter 7.

Higgs, Robert: *The Transformation of the American Economy, 1865–1914,* Wiley, New York, 1971, Chapter 3.

Kirkland, Edward C.: *Industry Comes of Age: Business, Labor and Public Policy, 1860–1897,* Holt, New York, 1961, Chapter 12.

Williamson, Harold F.: *The Growth of the American Economy,* 2d ed., Prentice-Hall, New York, 1951, Chapter 26.

The Economics of Natural Resources: 1890 to the Present

In his report accompanying the returns of the 1890 census the Director of the U. S. Census Bureau reported that "the frontier has now disappeared." What he obviously meant was that now as one traveled westward across the United States there was no clear demarcation line where settlement ceased and vacant land began. It was not that simple, however. Although there was some settlement all the way across the country, east to west, the population was unevenly distributed. The density of people per square mile was much higher in the Northeast and North Central states than it was in the West, particularly in the Rocky Mountain states. Indeed, some of the areas that the Director of the Census Bureau reported as being settled, thereby allowing him to declare the frontier closed, would still have appeared deserted if one were to have crossed them in 1890.

Furthermore, Americans did not stop moving after 1890 merely because the frontier had been reported closed. Since then they have continued to move into previously sparsely settled areas in large numbers. The Far West, Southwest, and individual states such as Texas and Florida, have grown rapidly because of immigration. The population of other areas, such as rural New England, the upper Great Lakes, the Great Plains, and the South, have grown much less than the national average, as many of their residents have left for more attractive opportunities elsewhere. In fact, since 1920 the total acreage of developed land in the United States has been decreasing, as marginal farmland has been allowed to revert to its natural state. One by-product of this shrinkage of rural population has been the disappearance of thousands of small rural towns over the century. Another effect which is recognized by hunters with good memories is the extensive increase in the population of such wildlife as deer and turkey, as they have returned to this abandoned land. If the frontier did indeed close at one time, it seems since to have been reopened.

These changes in the use of land are only examples of a much larger pattern of changes which has gone on continually throughout American history. Some land was being abandoned before the frontier was "closed" in 1890, and some has been taken up for the first time since then. In any given year since 1607 some acreage has always been in the process of reclamation, improvement, neglect, deterioration, and being transferred from one use to another. It certainly makes one suspicious of the common conception that there is a fixed stock of it which is unchanging over time. It suggests that we should take a critical look at Will Rogers' exhortation: "Buy land, they ain't making any more of it."

What underlies all the developments in land is that it also—like labor or capital—is an economic resource. And, as an input into society's productive mechanism, it is subject to the same influence that all other resources are: land is valuable only insofar as it makes a contribution to output which society deems valuable. That effort will be affected by the demand for specific final products, the technology available to produce them, and the supply of alternative or complementary resources for production. Various combinations of these forces can make a specific parcel of land very valuable, such as footage along Fifth Avenue in New York City, which sells for $500 a square foot ($22.5 million per acre), or of no current value whatsoever, such as land under 200 feet of water off the New Jersey coast.

Thus, depending on a whole complex of economic factors a specific piece of land will or will not be productive. If it can add to output which meets some of society's wants, considerable ingenuity will be exercised to see that it gets into production. If it has no current usefulness, it will be allowed to remain idle. That distinction explains the determination of the boundary between settled and unsettled land which people commonly call the frontier. It is merely the dividing line between land that is currently productive, and therefore in use, and land that is not. For the frontier to move, westward or otherwise, means that the total complex of economic factors has changed accordingly. Thus, the expansion of the frontier is not a measure of how far society has gone in using its *given* stock of land, but rather of how changes in economic conditions have increased the effective economic supply of land. So (with apologies to Will Rogers) they may not be making any more land, but the amount currently available to the economy is changing all the time.

THE FRONTIER—REVISED

It is time to take a new look at the significance of the closing of the frontier. As our earlier discussion suggests, it should be viewed as evidence of the expanding economic capability of resources rather than as evidence of their physical limit. The soil, timber, minerals, and water of the Western United States had remained undisturbed for a long, long time before the late nineteenth century. In the several thousands of preceding years, the Indians had barely scratched the resource base, confining their activities to widely scattered small farming and hunting efforts. Nor did the European civilizations rush in to use the region immediately after discovering it. It was more than 350 years after Columbus before substantial numbers of white settlers began moving into the area, and almost 400 years after his discovery when the "closed" designation was finally placed on the frontier. It was not disinterest or inertia which kept these earlier people from using this region in the manner it was to become used in the late nineteenth century. Rather, it was simply that the capability to do so was not available then. The falling transportation costs and changing technology of the last half of the nineteenth century made these areas useable for the first time. Thus, the closing of the frontier is best seen as a reflection of an expansion of opportunities. Rather than running out of resources, we were running into ways of acquiring them.

THE CONSERVATION REACTION

The general populace was not thinking about such subtleties when the Director of the Census Bureau made his report in 1890, however. But they had seized upon one implication of the report which seemed to confirm a worry currently preoccupying them. (Actually, despite their "discovery" of this "new danger" to their society, it is one which has—and had—cropped up every few decades in American history.) Their worry was: "If we continue to use the natural resources currently available to us, isn't it inevitable that they will be exhausted one day— probably soon?" So when the report of the closing of the frontier reached them they interpreted it as evidence that such an exhaustion was closing in: "After all, if no more new territory is available, then we can only use up the resources in the area we already have."

The concern of the Americans of that decade was genuine and it explains the set of government programs which were adopted to deal with foreseen resource shortages. (We will look at the nature and consequences of those programs in more detail later.) It was, however, an evaluation which recognized only one aspect of the situation. It was obvious to observers at that time—as it has been at most times for that matter—that people will gradually deplete a stock of resources as they continue to use them. People do deplete certain types of resources, but they also almost instinctively search for less expensive substitutes and for new methods to increase output from these substitutes. In short, the tendency to use up existing resources is only one aspect of a larger interaction between people and their resources. In this context it is by no means inevitable that the effective stock of resources available to humans should shrink over time. In fact, the evidence in the Western world over the last few centuries is that it has tended to go in just the opposite direction. People's ingenuity has expanded the supply of resources faster than its consumption has reduced them.

THE MECHANICS OF NATURAL RESOURCE SCARCITY

This contest between diminishing returns and resource augmentation is so central to understanding the economic development in the past that we should be conversant with its basic elements. Figure 15-1 shows a typical, run-of-the-mill supply curve which illustrates the possible schedule of output for a typical natural resource at any given time. A specific supply curve is valid only for a given set of conditions, of course, in that it is drawn assuming the existing state of technology and prices of other resources. The usual relationship of larger output being enticed out by higher prices is evident in the upward slope of the curve. It also illustrates the economic axiom that the supply of few commodities is fixed but rather varies in response to how much of its other products society is willing to sacrifice in order to obtain the one in question. The supply curve expresses a range of options in that the higher prices necessary to call forth the additional output go to pay for the increasing quantities of the other inputs necessary to offset diminishing returns. If the resource in question is a renewable type, such as water power, where the output available in the future is not affected by how much of it we use today, then the supply curve remains fixed (always subject to technology and other resource prices remaining constant, of course). Each year we obtain the same quantity of the resource if we are willing to continue to apply the same quantity of other inputs to acquire it.

If the natural resource is a type which does not replace itself in the relevant span of people's experience, such as oil or coal or iron ore, then current consumption dissipates supplies otherwise available in the future. This condition is illustrated in Figure 15-2, where a supply curve for the current year (S_{r0}) is shown. Its intersection with the price axis—the minimum price at which output is first offered to the market—is labeled P_{r0}. Each year that this nonrenewable resource is used, however, some of it is used up forever. This will naturally come from the supplies first tapped, the cheapest sources as represented on the lowest portion of the supply curve. Thus, each year some of the lowest end of the supply curve is extinguished. This is illustrated where the section between Q_{r0} and Q_{r1} (or P_{r0} and P_{r1}) is assumed to be used up in the first year. Similarly the segment Q_{r1} to Q_{r2} (or P_{r1} to P_{r2}) is shown as being extinguished in the second year of use. This process has the effect of shifting the initial point on the supply curve to the right each year by the quantity of the resource consumed in the previous period.

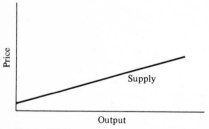

Figure 15-1

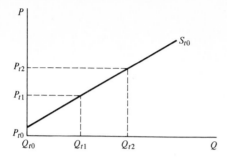

Figure 15-2

The effect on the longer-term supply of the natural resource can be illustrated if, after each year's depletion, the remaining portion of the supply curve is shifted back to the origin (Q_{t0}). This can be seen in Figure 15-3. Each supply curve is dated by its respective year, S_{t0} for the initial year, S_{t1} for the second year, and so forth. In Figure 15-3 the supply curves appear to shift upward; S_{t1} is above S_{t0} and S_{t2} is above S_{t1}. Thus, for the same quantity to be provided in the market in the second year—when S_{t1} is in effect—that was offered in the first, a higher price must be paid. This can be seen for any given quantity in Figure 15-3. The representative output Q^* shows a price of P_1 in the first year, P_2 in the second year, and P_3 in the third year.

This illustration of depletion at work will not come as much of a surprise to most observers. It merely formalizes the process they intuitively recognize must be taking place. One caution is in order, however. In a physical sense resources are never consumed. Instead, they are converted from one state in which they may be cheaply mobilized, to another state where it is necessary to apply more of other economic resources to obtain them. For example, iron molecules are not destroyed when they are mined, refined, and consumed. Some are taken from one location where they can be dug very cheaply and transported to a steel mill and converted with the aid of equally cheap coal into a commodity that is useful in a wide range of other products—at an attractive, delivered price. They are no

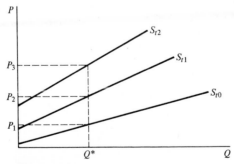

Figure 15-3

different than the iron molecules which disappear from use in the form of rust, wear, and disposal into thousands of isolated landfills across the countryside, but they require far fewer of other types of resources to retrieve. The process of natural resource depletion is merely one in which resources are converted from a state where they are cheaper to use, given current economic conditions, to another, which is more expensive, again given current economic conditions.

So our suspicions are confirmed. The process of natural resource depletion must be at work. Is it not inevitable, therefore, that sooner or later diminishing returns will dominate and permanently depress mankind's economic state? In the long run are not we condemned to poverty and mere subsistence?

We are, indeed, inexorably pressured by forces working in that direction, but there are also other influences which might be equally powerful and which are working in the opposite direction. Self-interest, the same basic force which creates diminishing returns, also leads to a number of parallel categories of behavior which tend to broaden and extend the available base of natural resources. For example, suppose we unrealistically constrain human behavior by not allowing any gains in knowledge which make resources more accessible. (We will return to recorporate this possibility later.) Even then, normal day-to-day responses of people tend to significantly stretch the available supply of natural resources. Suppose we are faced with a situation such as is illustrated in Figure 15-3. As resources are used up, their price begins to rise. This induces a variety of responses which tend to retard the depletion and therefore the tendency of the price to increase.

For example, consider steel, that ubiquitous material in the products of our society. At the first level of contact where iron ore is taken out of the ground, the higher price makes it worthwhile to dig deeper into marginal veins of ore and to modify transportation and refining processes so that a higher proportion is extracted from a given source. (This is generally true of raw materials, in that a large proportion of the physical supply remains in the ground because the cost of the complementary resources necessary to extract it are prohibitively high. When the price of oil increased dramatically during the recent "energy crisis," the proven reserves of oil within the United States doubled overnight. No one discovered any more or improved on pumping techniques, they simply recognized that at the new, higher prices it paid to put more effort into extracting oil.)

Like most intermediate goods, there is no market for steel per se. It competes with other materials as an input in a range of potential uses, such as construction, packaging, machinery, and transportation equipment. Thus, when the price of steel goes up, the use of a wide range of substitutes is encouraged. More aluminum is used in tin cans, window frames, and automobile parts. More concrete is used in buildings and bridges. And plastics are substituted in toys and appliances.

Finally, the higher price of steel motivates different behavior in the postproduction phase of steel use. Highway departments and building contractors spend more effort in painting and rust-proofing steel surfaces. A much larger effort in what is now commonly known as recycling also develops. Demolition contractors devote more care to salvaging the steel parts from old buildings and railroad tracks. Soft-drink bottlers pay more for the return of steel cans and children spend more of their Saturday mornings collecting them along the roadsides. Weekend scavengers comb the woods, swamps, and streambeds for old automobile hulks. The latter behavior was probably best illustrated in New York City where automobiles abandoned on the city streets have long been an eyesore, and a headache to the sanitation department. In early 1974, when the price of scrap steel rose to historically high levels, these ugly discards disappeared. It was suddenly profitable for private citizens to haul them to the scrap dealers.

The role of recycling in the supply component of natural resources is important and deserves special examination. As the term is commonly understood, recycling refers to reclaiming raw materials out of goods which have already been produced rather than extracting them from their natural sources. In recent years such efforts have been advocated, and sometimes legislated, in order to increase the long-term supply of natural resources. The resulting programs do increase the supply of the resource in question, but otherwise they usually do not serve the function in the total economy that their sponsors anticipate. What is frequently overlooked is that the economy can recycle materials if that tactic appears attractive. The choice is always available, at least implicitly.

The choice between extracting new materials and recovering them from discarded goods is influenced by economic considerations, which is to say, the technique which requires the least total of all the resources used in the acquisition. In the United States where labor and capital have always been expensive relative to natural resources, the methods which tend to save on the former are usually favored. And because the pattern of consumption—and therefore the sources for recycling—tend to be more scattered than the natural sources, the latter are usually preferred.

The preference for newly extracted materials is not merely a habit, or fetish, among Americans. When the conditions are appropriate, they have commonly opted to reclaim and reuse resources which would otherwise be obtained directly from natural sources. Where used materials are naturally concentrated, recycling normally appears. Thus, computer services, which turn out large quantities of paper, or packing houses, which create by-products such as hides and tallow, have almost always saved and sold such waste products. (In contrast, most American households discard their waste paper or food scraps because the cost of taking them to any form of central collection agency would exceed any possible value derived from them. American households usually participate in recycling only when someone else pays the collection costs, such as when the Boy or Girl Scouts conduct a paper drive.)

Furthermore, when the price of specific raw materials has risen in the United States, recycling efforts to retrieve them have increased. In recent years, as the price of natural gas has risen, city officials have investigated ways of obtaining it by burning the garbage in their landfills, and managers of coal mines have sought to capture the otherwise dangerous methane gas given off during coal extraction. When the price of paper goes up, grocery stores shift from burning their cardboard cartons to bundling them for recollection. And, in perhaps the ultimate form of recycling, with recent increases in the price of corn and soybeans, feedlot operators have begun to extract the remaining food material out of cattle manure and return it to the food ration.

Thus the possibility of recycling is an active option, and when the economic circumstances are appropriate, self-interest brings it into operation. If, to those concerned over the adequacy of the supply of natural resources, the amount of the recycling in the United States appears so meager, it merely reflects the economic reality of the American economy. Despite all the recent concern about the availability of our natural resources, they continue to remain among the most abundant resources in the economy. (This assertion will be demonstrated later.) Hence, recycling usually costs more in the form of other resources consumed than it saves in recovered materials. Ironically, the lack of recycling in the American economy suggests not a naïve neglect of looming scarcity of natural resources in the future, but rather an objective response to conditions which reflect their long-term availability.

Toward the Long Run (Still Constrained)

The sum of all these above reactions to an increased price of a natural resource obviously also increases its long-run supply beyond that which we would foresee at the lower price. Given the incentive and the time to adapt, a society can stretch out the supply of resources that are becoming more expensive. The long-run supply of a resource is likely to be more elastic; that is, there will be a greater increase in output in response to a given increase in price than there would be in an immediate, or short-term, schedule. In Figure 15-1, a long-term supply curve superimposed on the one depicted would be flatter and would rise less in response to a given price increase.

One way to understand why these seemingly unexpected reservoirs of resources open up is to recognize that at any given time output is organized around the prevailing price, or what is expected to be the prevailing price. This means that production techniques are employed which would appear wasteful—and would be modified—if prices were to unexpectedly increase above that level. Likewise, producers avoid constructing new factories or opening new sources which would appear profitable only at higher prices. One example of this process is the continuing "discoveries" of new sources of natural resources around the world. One might reasonably expect that all such locations should be of long-standing knowledge. After all, most of the world's land area has been explored, mapped, and generally examined. Yet the specific location of materials—let alone their development—requires a considerable input of resources to bring them to fruition. And those resources are not going to be committed to exploration until the expected returns on their use are favorable. Resources adjacent to developed areas, therefore, are most likely to be developed first. Most of the coal mined in the world, and the oil wells drilled, have, up to now, been located within the North Atlantic economies. However, when the price of one resource rises dramatically, as has that of oil, it sets off a much broader search for additional sources. Almost invariably these intensified efforts turn up "new" discoveries of the sought-after resource. Even the "total" stock of a resource is influenced by its going price.

Capital: The Classical Offset

All the above reactions to a higher price of a resource can slow, perhaps even endlessly prolong, the effect of diminishing returns. In themselves, however, they cannot reverse it. If diminishing returns are to be more than offset—still in the absence of technological progress—this must be achieved by an increase in the stock of capital. (Incidentally, this restricted model—that is without technological progress—is identical to that held by economists for over a century, before the 1950s, when they came to appreciate the importance of advances in technology in explaining growth.) Capital, like natural resources, is also a nonhuman resource which can be used in conjunction with labor. So when the amount of natural resources per capita is decreasing, an increase in the quantity of capital per person can maintain or even increase output per capita. This would also have the effect of increasing the quantity of capital used relative to each unit of natural resource used in the economy, which would tend to shift the supply curve of natural resources outward, or to the left, as, for example, a movement from S_{r1} to S_{r0} in Figure 15-3. In effect, the "other things being equal" assumed for a given supply curve has been altered by increasing the quantity—and implicitly lowering the price—of one of the resources used with it. For example, the productivity of farmland can be raised by such investments of capital as drainage systems, terracing, diking, grading, fencing, and so forth. Land and sources of raw materials can be made accessible by construction of roads, bridges, telephone systems, and steamships. And raw materials can be made more available by the construction of deeper mine shafts, the installation of more equipment to facilitate the transfer of ore, and additional screens and filters to increase the percentage of material recovered from the ore.

Capital can provide more natural resources, but can we reasonably expect that the capital itself would be provided? It comes from saving, or that portion of current output which is not consumed. And at most times in the past incomes have been well below current levels, down in what we would term the subsistence zone. At that level it is believed that all current output must be consumed merely to stay alive. Saving is a luxury that cannot be afforded at such miserable levels. Yet in fact, when careful examinations have been made of spending patterns in societies with such low per capita income, it is usually concluded that saving has been going on. It is not conducted in a form we would readily recognize, such as saving accounts or mutual funds, but it does exist in forms appropriate to their circumstances, such as land, livestock, houshold items, and gold.

If regular saving does occur in low-income societies, as the evidence so far suggests, then the concept of subsistence is due for a drastic overhaul. The absolute minimum level of income necessary for survival must be quite low, or at least much lower than commonly believed.[1] People whose income is much below that which we deem essential for survival, can— and do—set aside some of their current income for future use. One of the reasons that such behavior is puzzling to participants in modern, developed economies is that our standards of "necessary" or "minimal" have been conditioned by our own experiences. Although we may not recognize it, and certainly would not desire it, we could survive at incomes much, much lower than current levels. Residents of societies where per capita incomes are (or were) much lower than our own consider their incomes normal and can also economize to well below that level if compelled to do so.

Thus, it does not seem unreasonable to conjecture that some saving has taken place during a large part of man's economic experience. If that is the case, our appraisal of the long sweep of economic history could be subject to some major revisions. It is probably fair to say that although most historians recognize some periods of growth in the past, they view these as exceptions, or at least as offset by the disorganization, or diminishing returns, which set in from time to time. This "cyclical" view of history, perhaps best illustrated by Arnold Toynbee's writings, has mankind always coming back to the same minimal level of economic performance. If increases in society's capital stock work to offset such diminishing returns, however, then per capita incomes need not be driven back to their starting level—even in the absence of any gains in knowledge.

Consider, for example, the Dark Ages, that much aligned period of European history that fell roughly between A. D. 400 and 1000. The more historians have looked at the period, the lighter it has appeared to become. Nevertheless, the era is still generally considered one of the least progressive of the last 2,500 years of Western history. Even if we grant that no technological advances occurred in the period, it is still possible by the above logic that per capita incomes could have increased. Indeed, there is evidence that such a phenomenon was taking place if we know how to look for it. We know that there was substantial land clearance for agriculture in the period, which of course is a form of capital creation and saving. We also know that there were still sizeable amounts of such land not yet cleared, so that the supply of farm acreage—undoubtedly the most important natural resource of the time—was probably fairly elastic. If we add the commonly held assumption that population was not increasing, or at least was not increasing as fast as the other resources, then we can logically conclude that per capita income must have increased. The conclusion is particularly surprising in that this period would seem among the least likely of all in the experience of the Western world to allow growth. It emphasizes how underrated human beings' ability to counteract natural scarcities has generally been.

The Powerful Impact of Improving Technology

The human capacity to adapt offers quite a bit of resistance to diminishing returns, in and of itself. And merely an examination of that process at work produces a somewhat more optimistic forecast of human beings' long-run prospects

---

[1] After a U. N. agency estimated the minimum survival level of income for India, it was discovered that one-third of the entire population of that nation was below that level and therefore, by definition, dead.

than is generally held. As of yet, however, we have not released the constraint which we previously imposed—the prohibition on new knowledge about production relationships. Releasing that constraint, and introducing the possibility of new technology, will make the contest with diminishing returns even more one-sided, because new technology is one of the strongest forces operating against diminishing returns.

Increases in knowledge have the same effect of increasing potential output as do the appearance of new resources. If more labor, capital, or land suddenly becomes available, output can be increased by the simple expedient of increasing the inputs into the production process. If additional knowledge about the process of production becomes available, however, that allows more output to be produced from *the same amount* of inputs. Either directly or indirectly, improvements in technology have the same effect on the supply of natural resources as an increase in the capital stock. They shift the supply schedule(s) out, as illustrated by a shift from curve S_{t1} to S_{t0} in Figure 15-3, for example. By making each input go farther, better knowledge increases the effective supply of those resources to society.

The common terminology of describing improvements in technology as gains in the production process, or increases in output per unit of input, tends to convey a severe understatement of the range within which such advances occur. It makes it appear as if the improvements were confined to engineering or manufacturing, a category we would expect to be relatively unimportant in premodern times. In fact, improvements in technology can—and do— occur in *every* aspect of economic activity which contributes to human wants. They obviously take the form of improved blast furnaces, but they can also be such items as improvements in plant and animal varieties, changes in banking organization, and advances in the efficiency of transportation, craft activities, and entertainment. Furthermore, recent investigations suggest that most productivity increase is likely to be in smaller, more gradual increments rather than in dramatic breakthroughs. This suggests that the common practice of judging the technological progress of past societies by counting the number of major inventions we can attribute to them can be very misleading. The only reliable measure is some indicator of total productivity change over a period. We have only recently begun to examine past economies in that light, but the preliminary results suggest that growth is far more common than was previously believed.

In one sense we should not have been surprised, because the basic conditions which cause growth have always been at hand. When people adopt a technique which produces an increase in productivity they reap the benefit. The resources gained over and above what was required beforehand go directly to them. Thus, individuals have an incentive not only to adopt improved methods, or forms of organization, whenever they can, but also to devote efforts to developing new ones as well. It is not necessary that these efforts be carefully planned, expensive, long, or painstaking. Most of the total productivity increase in human experience has undoubtedly come from such simple events as a farm laborer's noticing that a certain angle of a hoe blade worked better, or that one hog gained weight faster—and was therefore saved for breeding stock. In fact, as the last example suggests, it is not even necessary that individuals try to create better techniques. All that is required is that they adopt them when they come along. Varieties of agricultural crops are an obvious example. Until the last century so little was known about hybridization that it could not be manipulated and encouraged. Yet for at least 6,000 years growers have been saving out the best strains, as they appeared—with a resulting substantial increase in productivity well before scientists and laboratories were turned loose on the effort. In other words, the minimal conditions necessary for improvements in technology are very, very modest. All that is required is some random mutations in natural processes, and the tendency for people to pick out the productive ones from among them.

This comprises a set of sufficient conditions for improving economic knowledge which is well within the range of behavior of premodern people, as well as that of more recent societies. Yearly growth rates may have been less in earlier years—there are a number of conceptual reasons for expecting that to have been the case—but it would appear extremely unlikely that no gains in economic knowledge, even in short periods of a decade or so, took place. We have probably been misled by the lack of records of earlier economies. It is easy to assume that if you do not have the numbers to prove it, it must not have been there.

This assumption that there was little growth in the past has led to another view, namely, that because growth has been confined to recent years, it must therefore be unusual and might well cease not too far in the future. This conception has been encouraged by another commonly held appraisal of future prospects, namely, that we cannot depend on any further improvements in knowledge. It is argued that at present we cannot foresee what advances may develop in the future and that we might have reached the point where the opportunities are becoming exhausted. This argument overlooks the fact that we have never been able to anticipate the gains in technology which have occurred in the past, either. After all, if we had really known what they were to be, they would not then have been unknown and hence subsequently had to be discovered. Of course, we have no assurance that knowledge *will* continue to improve. We can have more confidence in expecting, however, that the environment which produced such gains in the past will persist, and will, therefore, continue to encourage similar results in the future. This, after all, is no more than is generally assumed with respect to diminishing returns. Almost no one questions the likelihood that diminishing returns will continue to operate in the future with respect to natural resources, but that prediction is implicitly grounded on an assumption about the way that humans behave. It assumes that people, prompted by their own self-interest—sometimes referred to as *greed* by the less charitable—will continue to consume and use up the resources available to them. That motive, however, is the same force which instigates improvements in technology. It is no more unreasonable to assume that knowledge will continue to improve, and thereby increase the resource base, than it is to expect that people will continue to use, and thereby wear out, the resources available to them. They are both an integral part of the human response to economic scarcity.

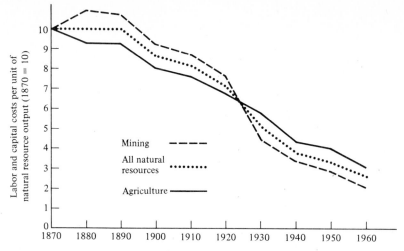

Figure 15-4 Opportunity costs of natural resources 1870–1960. *(Source: Adapted from Harold J. Barnett and Chandler Morse,* Scarcity and Growth: The Economics of Natural Resource Availability, *published for Resources for the Future, Inc., by the John Hopkins Press, Baltimore, 1963.)*

THE AMERICAN EXPERIENCE

The foregoing lengthy discussion should leave us with one crucial point about economic history: A dwindling supply of natural resources is not the omnipresent and threatening force it is commonly supposed to be. Indeed, the long-term experience of the North Atlantic economies suggests that not only can it be systematically postponed but can, over time, be pushed back still further from being a threat as well. Although capital, and especially labor, have tended to become relatively scarce as resources in the Western world, natural resources, on the other hand, have become more abundant. This experience has continued right up to the present in the United States, where we have the best measures of such tendencies. A major study by Harold J. Barnett and Chandler Morse examined the availability of natural resources relative to the economy's other major inputs, capital and labor, over the last century.[2] A summary of their primary findings are reproduced in Figure 15-4.

The figure demonstrates that natural resources have been dramatically cheapened relative to other resources during the last century. They are now only about one-third as expensive as they were in relation to labor and capital 100 years ago. Interestingly enough, almost all this has occurred in the period since the "closing" of the frontier—which emphasizes our argument that economic knowledge, not physical boundaries, form the effective limit on an economy's stock of resources. This cheapening of natural resources is even more surprising when we recall that it happened in an economy where natural resources were

---

[2] Harold J. Barnett and Chandler Morse, *Scarcity and Growth: The Economics of Natural Resource Availability,* John Hopkins, Baltimore, 1963.

already inexpensive by international standards. One might have expected that the relative scarcity of capital or labor would have directed most of society's efforts toward economizing on *their* use. Whatever the intentions involved, natural resources have become even more abundant. This development completely confounded most of the prophets. They could readily see that there was a physical dimension to natural resources which they expected would soon begin to play a limiting role in the growth process. What they failed to grasp was the economic dimension, namely, that natural resources would prove even more susceptible to innovation and augmentation than the other major factors, labor and capital.

All of this is taking a long-term view of natural resource supplies, of course. It abstracts from the continual, short-term ups and downs of prices which occur in natural resources just as in most other commodities. When we hear that the price of coal or aluminum has increased, or that gasoline purchases are limited to 10 gallons, we are tempted to extrapolate our frustration into a universal problem. It is not necessarily true, however, that the world is running out of timber when we cannot find beige paneling at the lumber store. These personal short-term frustrations reflect—indeed, enforce—the manner by which the markets for natural resources incorporate the influences operating upon them. Natural resources will always be scarce, and therefore possibly troublesome, at the margin, unless they move into the seemingly unlikely position of abundance. In the meantime, the prices of other resources continue to adapt as well, and when we step back to look at longer-term trends, natural resources continue to be relatively cheap. We can say this despite the doubts which have arisen in the mid-1970s about the availability of future supplies. Despite the concerns it generated about long-term supplies, the "energy crisis" was primarily a short-term phenomenon. The behavior of certain groups might make the price of a certain resource expensive in the short run, but, if anything, it encourages the knowledge and innovation which tend to cheapen it in the long run.

THE FIRST CONSERVATION MOVEMENT

Americans at the turn of the century did not have the advantage of hindsight about their own era, which we have today (although not about *our* own era), so they went ahead guided by their (mistaken) perceptions. They believed that they could foresee a scarcity of natural resources lurking in the future and they took a number of steps which they believed would postpone and dampen that prospect. The first step of significance came in 1891. One feature of the General Revision Act of 1891—designed to tighten up the obvious shortcomings of the various federal land regulations—allowed the President to set aside 50 million acres of timberland. This marked the beginning of the present national forests.

The efforts toward conservation received a hefty push with the election to the Presidency in 1901 of a forceful, charismatic advocate—Theodore Roosevelt. By 1907 an observer could report the establishment of the following major components of what was to become called "the first conservation movement":

1   The national forests had been further increased to 150 million acres and were being administered by the new United States Forest Service.

2   Seventy-five million acres of federal land believed to contain valuable minerals were reserved from public acquisition.

3   The federal government was explicitly committed to developing water resources in the form of reclamation (irrigation) projects and hydroelectric and flood-control dams.

From our current perspective such programs seem like small, timid efforts. We have become accustomed to much larger, more forceful intervention into the economy by the government. And, along with their seeming insignificance and—by current standards—conventionality, it is by no means obvious that these programs aided the long-run supply of resources. Our experience soon teaches us that good intentions which are not backed up by objective guidance often fail to produce the desired result.

Despite some rejoicing at the time of their creation, the national forests were to have very little effect until much later. The reason was simple. The system had been instituted by setting aside those forest lands not yet claimed by private parties in the 1890s. And that, in effect, meant the then noneconomic acreages which private parties had not found attractive enough to acquire. If one looks at a map of existing national forest land it is obvious that most of it is in the West *and* in the forested land at the highest elevations—most such land at lower elevations is in private hands. In other words, the protection the national forests provided for the lands it acquired around the turn of the century was superficial. Their basic inaccessibility kept them from being used at that time anyway. Government policy was merely formalizing what high transportation costs had already accomplished.

In the mid-twentieth century, more than fifty years after its inception, the National Forest System finally began to have an effect on the nation's supply of lumber. Unfortunately, it was negative. By this time developments in the technology of lumbering, particularly the introduction of the logging truck, had made the national forests accessible and economically attractive. Federal objectives and procedures in utilizing its forests, on the other hand, were retarding the nation's capacity to obtain wood products from these areas. With time, Congress has added other objectives besides the original goal of lumbering to the tasks of the National Forest Service. Each of these—outdoor recreation, watershed protection, and cattle grazing, for example—is a reasonable, legitimate use of the domain which should be accommodated. In implementation, however, each of these goals appears to have been mechanically applied with little recognition of its alternative cost. Suppose a particular area is designated a watershed zone. The Forest Service is likely to severely curtail recreation or lumbering activities in that area, even though small amounts of those activities would yield large returns while inflicting only small losses on the primary (watershed) function. The largest misallocation comes through the myriad constraints which have been imposed on lumbering operations, such as strong restrictions on cutting techniques, spatial patterns of harvesting, and the age and species of trees taken. The net result is that the potential supply of timber from the National Forests is substantially curtailed. Forest experts estimate that under current practices a given plot of national forest land—designated exclusively for lumber production—yields only about one-third of the timber output which private management would produce. Given the proportion of the nation's total timberland in the federal system, this results in a continuing loss equal to about one-fourth of the annual output.

This is ironic. The national forests were instituted to assure a long-run supply of timber through enlightened management. In practice they have reduced it. One cannot even argue that larger future supplies will offset current losses. Timber is a renewable resource. Unlike oil or iron ore, where existing supplies can be banked for future use, lumber not grown today cannot be made up tomorrow.

Thus, this particular attempt at conservation is a failure in terms of its own objectives—indeed, it is a net loss compared with doing nothing. And it illustrates a common misconception about the provision of future resources, namely, that in the absence of explicit intervention in the manner in which people naturally use natural resources, no conservation will take place at all. This is a mistaken view of the way a market economy—or any other economic system, for that matter—functions. In an economy which uses prices and self-interest to make its basic decisions, there are forces at work which recognize future requirements and make provisions to meet them. Suppose we adopt the possibly disdainful view that the prime motivating power behind a market economy is greed. Even that interpretation of the way things work does not necessarily lead to the conclusion that humans will quickly exhaust all the resources within their reach. Greedy entrepreneurs will recognize that they can profit by catering to consumers in the future as well as in the present, particularly if they foresee an increasing scarcity of certain resources which will raise the returns on their use later. There is, then, an implicit system of conservation in a market economy. One might object to the way it functions, or to the values it expresses, but one cannot operate with impunity under the assumption that it has no system of conservation. The opportunity cost of alternative attempts at conservation is that the market is blocked from making its contribution to that goal. In cases where that factor is overlooked, such as the experience with the national forests, society can pay a heavy cost.

Mineral Reserves

The effort to ensure future supplies of minerals through the reserve system began with equally dismal prospects. Again, the acreage which the government program acquired was in the marginal areas to which private groups had not deemed worthy of staking a claim. Unlike the case of the national forests, however, an additional factor was working which depreciated these holdings over time—technology. One obvious implication of changes in knowledge is that it sometimes opens up opportunities to profitably employ resources which were previously not economically feasible to utilize. It also removes some resources from the usable category by developing better substitutes, or allowing the resource to be obtained more cheaply elsewhere. This latter tendency was the dominant one in the experience of the federal mineral reserves. In retrospect this is hardly surprising when we remember that these reserves were marginal to begin with, and that the general experience with such resources was that in time they became more abundant (see Figure 15-4). By the mid-twentieth century almost all such reserves had proven worthless as far as the minerals they were intended to preserve were concerned. This example highlights the obvious problem of saving or preserving resources in the context of changing technology which constantly redefines what is and what is not a useful input. Society's natural resource base—and therefore the supplies deemed valuable—are altered by the very process of working with them. Attempting to save resources which will be useful in the future is, therefore, an unpredictable and doubtful task. This phenomenon was illustrated again recently when the government decided to sell off its stockpile of "strategic materials" to counteract price increases. It discovered that it had stocks of feathers (for pillows), tanning oil, and certain grades of ores which had been rendered worthless by advances in knowledge since their acquisition.

THE SECOND PHASE: CONSERVATION IN THE 1930s

For the next two decades, 1910–1930, enthusiasm for conservation efforts subsided. Public officials offered almost no support and the government programs already instituted were allowed to drift along. Then, in 1933, came the Franklin Delano Roosevelt administration and, with it, the same activist concern for natural resources which it showed for most other sectors of the economy. As usual, the New Deal efforts toward natural resource conservation involved a mixture of goals, such as developing depressed areas and aiding agriculture as well as preserving resources. Most of the government's efforts in the natural resource sector came under two categories, however: water projects and soil conservation.

The development of water resources was authorized during the "first conservation phase" in the early 1900s. Under the New Deal, extensive expenditures involving dams, river navigation, and land reclamation were undertaken. Most of these projects were in the West and the South. Included were such now-famous landmarks as Boulder and Grand Coulee Dams, but probably the best-known single project was the Tennessee Valley Authority (TVA). The New Deal administrators argued that it was necessary for the government to undertake these projects because they were needed and private groups either would not or could not provide them. In retrospect, economists have developed some analyses which tend to support that position. River projects of this kind are usually characterized by numerous external effects; that is, many of the benefits or costs they create are likely to be removed from the locality of the project and therefore not included in the calculus of private developers. For example, a privately constructed dam might create benefits downstream to other property owners in the form of reduced flooding, but a private agency would have no way of appropriating those returns and therefore would not be inclined to include them in its construction and operation decisions.

The federal government is not bound by such strict local profit maximizing and can, in principle, incorporate all relevant aspects into its decisions. As most citizens suspect, however, government actions are seldom guided exclusively by what is in the "public interest." Congressmen expect to reap votes for expenditures in their districts, and bureaucrats keep their offices and secretaries as long as they can continue to receive money to spend. Economists started to verify that this type of behavior was indeed occurring when they began advising government project planners. They had been called in when the various groups of the government decision-making structure had been unable to agree among themselves as to the relevant criteria for evaluating such projects. The economists introduced cost-benefit analysis, which is actually a generalization to add external effects to the relevant factors to which private economic units ordinarily respond. It estimates the present value of a projected investment by discounting—that is, adjusting for the opportunity cost of capital over time—the expected benefits and costs back to the initiating investment in the project. If the present value equals or exceeds the amount of the expected investment in the project, then it should be undertaken.

When the economic advisers began to review proposals for new projects, however, they found that the present value of most of them was not as large as the required investment. In fact, they found that most of the projects already carried out had similarly poor social records, some of them yielding only a small fraction of their investment back into social returns. A cynic might have expected it, coming from the government, but it was a cruel blow to the hopes of conservationists as well. They had touted water projects as an excellent technique for extending society's supply of natural resources; after all, the reasoning went, water was a renewable resource. We could continue to reuse it endlessly and avoid the necessity of dipping into nonrenewable resources. The hitch was that it takes nonrenewable resources to construct these projects and thereby gain the services of the renewable resources. And the cost-benefit reports on these water projects were saying that the social returns on using these resources in this way was less than they could yield in alternative uses.

This frustration of conservation objectives in water projects brings us to the more basic question. Obviously everyone understands that the intent of conservation is to save natural resources. What does that mean in an economic setting, however? In a world of scarcity, economic resources have alternative uses. If we use them in one function we deny them to all other functions. Thus, if we set some natural resources aside for future use, we reduce current output by the amount of that contribution. If we wish to maintain the level of total output in their absence, we must use more of other resources, capital and labor, to compensate for them. Thus, there is no such thing as a costless conservation program. If society truly wishes to set some resources aside for future use, it must be willing to make current sacrifices accordingly.

In this context the water projects initiated in the 1930s did not really constitute conservation. They consumed some of society's stock of resources in order to begin to provide a flow of output. There were no natural resources set aside for future use, however. If they had not been used on the water projects they would have been available for other uses in the economy at that time. This is equally true of other "conservation" projects, such as those involving land reclamation and river navigation. In practice they were capital investments in the economy, much like that practiced by the private sector.

A corollary of the conservation axiom is that if the program which is designed to set resources aside for future use is inefficient, that cost must be added on top of any resource sacrifice involved. Again, the experience with water projects in the 1930s illustrates the case. Generally the projects did not yield as much output, relative to the inputs they consumed, as investments elsewhere in the economy. Thus, not only were no natural resources saved—as we saw earlier—but the output available to society was penalized relative to what would have resulted from alternative investments. Thus, the attempt at conservation actually backfired. As a result of it, society had fewer resources in later years than it would have had if no such programs had been attempted. And that meant that the aggregate quantity of resources employed, including any reserved for later use, would have to be scaled down accordingly.

Soil Conservation

Perhaps one of the most memorable images of the 1930s is John Steinbeck's portrayal of the sharecroppers being forced out of the Oklahoma dust bowl. The story is given even more poignancy by the common accounts of how years of careless cultivation ruined that land and created such human misery. It is only a short step from that proposition (that soil depletion is reducing our stock of natural resources and causing poverty) to proposing the logical remedy, a soil-conservation program. And the New Deal did indeed push such programs strenuously.

This was hardly the first time that there had been soil erosion in the United States, of course. Nearly 300 years earlier, tobacco farming was wearing out the land of tidewater Virginia and some contemporary observers were warning about the deleterious long-term effects this would have. Throughout their history, Americans have generally used land so that it deteriorated faster than it did in most other economies, because it was generally cheaper than elsewhere. One example of this pattern that mystified foreign observers was the common "squatters," individuals who farmed otherwise vacant land without benefit of legal ownership. Even in cases where they had no expectation of capturing the returns to improvements in land through eventual ownership, they went ahead with some improvements, such as clearing, anyway. It would be reasonable for them to do so only if the immediate returns on the land were large in relation to the value of the improvements they would be giving up. Cheap land constantly encouraged Americans to treat it casually and wear it out relatively rapidly.

While Americans had a tendency to use up land rapidly, vis à vis other economies, they also frequently changed its function. In its natural state almost all of the land east of the Mississippi River was wooded. However, until 1850 at least, much of that land was most profitable in agriculture. That meant it had to be converted from its natural state into cropland. In the last century a good portion of that cultivated land has been reconverted into pasture land or residential areas or has simply been allowed to return to its original state. These shifts in land use have resulted because the complex of economic factors which determine them, such as technology, transportation costs, and preferences, have likewise changed. In fact, one can safely generalize that the normal state of land in the United States is transition. At any time it is likely to be in the process of being shifted into some uses and out of others. This implies that investment is being put into certain types of land by such practices as fencing, draining, and fertilizing, while it is being withdrawn from others through such expedients as not fertilizing, allowing the fences to deteriorate, and wearing out the fertility of the land.

The soil-conservation programs of the 1930s operated on the assumption that soil erosion was obviously bad and that all one needed to do, therefore, was to inform the farmers of how to stop it and they would naturally do so. In this way it is similar to modern efforts at population control in the less-developed countries which seek to provide information about family planning. The difficulty is that farmers knew what caused soil erosion in their fields well before the extension agent told them, just as even the poorest peasants know where children come from. They were allowing erosion in their fields, even though they understood its cause and its consequences. Usually the land which was being allowed to deteriorate was marginal acreage which would soon be taken out of production and was certainly not worth putting any further investment into. Thus, erosion is best seen as a method of saving on inputs—such as the additional effort required for damming or countour plowing—while that disengagement is being accomplished.

The programs the government instituted beginning in the 1930s worked to retard soil erosion. They were successful not because farmers were becoming more enlightened about soil management, but because the government was paying them to carry out specific conservation measures. And while the programs may have appeared successful in that the countryside appeared greener and more prosperous, there was no overall social gain from the program. The government was spending resources so that obsolete, noneconomic resources could continue to have the appearance of usefulness.[3] The effect was not much different than if they had continued to pay for the maintenance and restoration of icebox factories so that "those valuable resources would not be allowed to lapse into ugly and nonproductive decay." The land was simply no longer productive, given the changes which had occurred in the economy, hardly a surprising result considering the long-term history of American agriculture.

THE MODERN PHASE: BROADENING THE CONCERNS

The concern for the economy's long-term supply of natural resources has a tendency to be revived dramatically about once a generation so that it was no surprise when the issue reappeared in the late 1960s. As usual, the general con-

---

[3] Government payments for improvements to land by private farmers which would have been undertaken anyway are best considered part of the farm subsidy program. This part of the soil-conservation program tended to become increasingly important.

cern for natural resource scarcity was influenced by the specific concerns of the time. In the 1890s it had been the end of open territory that had impressed the populace. In the 1930s it was the problem of insufficient employment and national output that was pressing. In its last appearance the emphasis has been directly reversed. The concern is that acknowledged prosperity and growth will deplete the world's supply of natural resources. The watchword is *environmental quality* and a central villain is *pollution.*

Pollution

Pollution has emerged as one of the most commonly employed symbols of the recent concern over the environment. Perhaps it is because most people can cite instances of it with its associated bad effects. It is certainly much more tangible than "ecological balance" or Club of Rome predictions about population/resource ratios in the year 2040. And, unlike the latter, it makes dramatic photographs. Pictures of oil-drenched sea birds or auto-wrecking yards tell the message much more forcibly than an abstract discourse on the effect of polychlorinated vinyls on photosynthesis in the ocean.

So pollution is a villain that is readily identified—or is it so easy to spot? Most people would say that pollution is the degradation of the environment in which human beings live, and they could recite some obvious examples, such as dumping untreated sewage in a river and thereby injuring downstream water supplies, recreation, and esthetics. But sometimes the definition of pollution is equated with changes in the existing state of nature. Thus, charges of "thermal pollution" are levied against enterprises, frequently electric power plants, which raise the temperature of waterways in the process of cooling materials involved in their operations. The warmer water destroys the habitat of the traditional wildlife of that zone but, as biologists can readily elucidate, it attracts new species of birds, fish, and plants into the niches it has created. Unless one is adamantly committed to the status quo it is not immediately obvious that one state is better than another.

It would be very unfortunate if one were strongly committed to the existing state of nature because most of people's economic progress has involved altering it in some way. Thus buildings, roads, bridges, telephone lines, and irrigated fields—the visible components of people's current existence—all are manipulations of the state in which nature could otherwise be found. So are most of the basic materials, such as steel, glass, brick, fertilizer, and crushed gravel, out of which they are assembled. Keeping the "pure state" of nature is a practical impossibility. People's effective choice is among the numerous states which are the by-product of their activity within the environment. (The relation between economic activity and ecological states will be examined further.)

Thus, some interference with the otherwise existing balance of nature is inevitable, and that, in turn, implies that pollution is more widespread and difficult to eradicate than we might have assumed. Suppose we return to our example of water pollution resulting from the disposal of untreated sewage into the river. One alternative to continued dumping would be to build a treatment plant which would remove contaminants from the waste water. The amount of pollutants removed would be proportional to the size of the plant and the intensity of its operation—in short, the quantity of resources devoted to the effort. But these, in turn, must ultimately call upon other operations in the economy in the form of iron ore, chemicals, cement, and so forth. And, as is well known, these operations can be polluters in their own right. Thus, it is very difficult to eradicate pollution entirely, and some efforts to reduce local instances of it may merely shift it elsewhere. The construction of that sewage plant to reduce water pollution, for example, may lead to increased pollution from drainage of iron-ore strip mines or fallout from chemical plants.

Not only would it be very difficult to physically eliminate all pollution but the cost of doing so in terms of foregone alternatives would be extremely high. The cost of removing 80 percent or 90 percent of the pollutants from sewage water is not insignificant, but it is a cost most citizens of a modern society would be willing to pay, given its contribution to a more desirable environment. The last 10 percent or 1 percent or, to go to extremes, 0.1 percent, is more costly, however. It generally requires secondary clean-up methods that are more sophisticated and elaborate than the first-round techniques. And as more expensive processes work on smaller volumes, the cost per unit removed rises dramatically. Thus, city managers begin to get fidgety when consulting engineers describe the systems required to remove all the pollutants. They recognize that this would come out of the road or the park capital budgets and would create large recurrent costs of maintenance in the future as well. They know the telephone calls they can expect from parents if the north playground is delayed another year or the intense grilling that any proposal in increased taxes would receive from the city council.

The mayor's dilemma is a microcosm of that of society. While we would almost universally prefer to eliminate all pollution, we also have a long list of other things we want and the cost of all of them exceeds our available resources. Some wants will necessarily be postponed and it is very likely that some proposals for pollution abatement will be among them. Pollution reduction is an economic good, but it competes with other desirable goals for society's limited stock of resources. It seems very unlikely, therefore, that all pollution will be eliminated as long as scarcity continued to be a basic reality of social organization.

The Recent Political Economy of Pollution

The desire to reduce pollution competes with other reasonable wants—corn flakes, hospital beds, and chocolates for Mother's Day—for society's limited stock of resources. Until recently, however, it has labored under a handicap. Many forms of pollution, like the water projects already discussed, involve externalities. They result because pollution spills over private property boundaries, so that the polluters do not bear the full cost of the damages they create, nor, accordingly, do they have as much incentive to economize on their activity which produces pollution as they would if they did bear such costs fully. The result is that there is more pollution than private groups would choose in an arrangement where all costs are internalized or turned back to the polluter. (Note again that it is unlikely that people will be willing to pay for the elimination of *all* pollution if other wants must be left unsatisfied as a result.) In effect, pollution is subsidized by the consumers who have no way of registering their willingness to reduce the adverse effects inflicted on them.

Americans recognized and took some action to mitigate the worst of these externalities well before the recent rise of environmental concern, of course. Zoning laws, such as the prohibition of noisy foundries or reeking tanneries from locating in residential neighborhoods, are one such traditional technique for control. In recent years economists, grappling with the problem of externalities, have come increasingly to the consensus that such tactics are inadequate. What is needed for the proper management of pollution situations is some form of charges, or fines, which assesses the polluters for the social costs their activity inflicts on society. This method of control has the advantage that it makes it desirable for the polluters to find the optimal social solution, not merely the one in their own best interests, as before. If they curtail pollution, the charges levied for social damages go down accordingly. If the cost of making those changes is less than the levies they would be paying otherwise, they will gain by making the switch. On the other hand, if the charges for external damages are less than those for curtailing the pollution, they will find it to their advantage to continue to pollute. In doing so they are imposing less of a cost on society through the pollution they create than the resources they would consume—as measured by their return in alternative uses—in reducing it. Their personal interests now correspond with those of society in that they are encouraged to move toward the optimal point where the benefits from curtailing pollution equal the costs involved.

Such a program is complex to administer and probably a little esoteric for many to grasp. So when the public concern over pollution began to be translated into laws and regulations, the approach was more simplistic and less flexible. In the mid-1960s Congress set national standards for water quality and for pollutants from automobile exhausts. In 1969 it established the Environmental Protection Agency to enforce such regulations and to establish legal standards for other types of pollution, most notably air pollution. For the most part these regulations were stated in maximum physical amounts—for example, electric power plants could emit no more than so many parts of sulfur dioxide per million units of air. Most of the regulations were uniform at the national, or at least the regionwide, level. Thus, a vehicle in Montana would be required to meet the same maximum pollutant levels to which another in Pennsylvania would be subject. The standards were usually also quite stringent relative to prevailing levels of pollution. Automobile exhaust was required to be ten times cleaner in 1976 than it had been in 1970, which in turn was already several times better than that of the early 1960s. If the enforcement agencies prove able to hold to these standards, it is clear that air and water pollution will be substantially reduced in the United States. (Despite some grumbling and postponement of enforcement deadlines, it was fairly clear by the mid-1970s that such tough criteria would, in fact, be carried out.) Even in the early 1970s those effects were already evident. Two of the most notoriously polluted metropolitan areas, New York and Los Angeles, began to show significant improvements in air quality. Even that symbol of ecological cataclysm, Lake Erie, began to show clear signs of coming alive after it had been written off as permanently dead.

As of the mid-1970s it was clear that the largest and most objectionable forms of pollution were headed for substantial reductions. And, in the aggregate, it was probably a positive move in economic organization. The social valuation of the benefits exceeded the costs, especially as society had time to devise new technologies to reduce the latter.[4] Yet, as our discussion has indicated, we could have devised a better economic solution. The blanket federal regulations on pollution forestalled numerous opportunities to devise better solutions in individual localities. In some areas the cost of air pollution can be quite high. In downtown New York or Chicago the number of lungs per square mile is very high compared with that of the vast majority of the land area of the United States. So if we reduce the air pollution coming from each automobile in the nation via emission standards, for example, the resulting benefit is greater from those driven in densely populated urban areas than those used in wheatlands of the Great Plains. And because the cost of purifying automobile exhausts—such as expensive engine accessories and lower gas mileage—is independent of the benefits, urban areas will gain more from such laws than sparsely populated ones. Stringent emission standards may be close to optimal—that is, the cost of the pollution they eliminate is greater than the cost of restrictions on automobiles up to that point—in certain urban centers, but may be a net burden in other areas. The present system of uniform standards does not allow us to adjust the rules, nor, indeed, to produce the information which would allow us to tell how much the rules are costing.

Yet the rules were probably better than nothing at all and that might be the relevant alternative. The externalities which have accounted for a good part of pollution in the modern United States are defects in the private property system. Moreover, given their nature, they were unlikely to be remedied by voluntary private accords. If they were to be corrected, the enabling mechanism would have to come from the government. That consideration, in turn, shaped the type of control program which would be achieved. The benefits to be received from reducing pollution in the economy were more widely dispersed among the population than the private costs which would be incurred. It was a classic arrangement in which the concerted power of the vested interests might well be expected to prevail over the larger, but more dispersed groups benefiting from pollution reduction. If significant pollution control programs were to be enacted, it would require strong, concerted public support. That implied a relatively simple, straightforward program, and not too much delay in the refinement process or committee meetings that might allow public enthusiasm to die down. Thus, the existing structure of pollution controls reflected the reality of what could be obtained.

---

[4] The search for the catalytic converter for automobile exhausts and the "sulfur scrubber" for smokestacks are examples.

A Short History of Pollution   When Americans started to look around for it in the mid-1960s, they discovered that there was a lot more pollution than they expected to find. And because they could not remember as much in previous years, they concluded that it must be increasing quite rapidly. Actually it is difficult to assess how much the total amount of pollution has changed. It is a multidimensional irritant, occurring in air, water, and sound, with very localized properties. Engineering specialists have been unable to construct an index of pollution but they have concluded that its prime sources have changed. Some sources have become worse in recent years, but others have declined and even almost entirely disappeared. Thus, the internal combustion engine was a source of increasing pollution—until the mid-1960s, at least—as its numbers and average size grew in the twentieth century. With some qualifications, to be noted later, electric power plants, sewage systems, and garbage dumps have also been generally becoming more offensive. In contrast, soot and solid matter in the air, as distinguished from gaseous matter, have declined drastically. This, primarily, is the result of the dramatic decline in coal burning, particularly for residential heating. Along with the coal furnace went another especially offensive form of pollution. At the time of the introduction of the automobile, contemporary observers welcomed it as a method of *reducing* pollution—certainly a curious prediction in the light of current conditions. Yet the logic at that time was reasonable. The automobile would replace the horse, and that would eliminate the necessity of watching where you stepped on city streets.

Pollution Becomes a Problem   Thus, it does not appear that the recently heightened concern over pollution can be explained by a rapid increase in the amount of it. In fact, numerous efforts to reduce pollution were under way before it was generally designated as a major public problem. While some rivers have remained badly polluted until recently, others have actually been undergoing a slow, but sustained, improvement in water quality over a period of years. This was a result of the installation of sewage treatment plants and curtailment of industrial waste discharges *before* 1965. More dramatic improvements included the cleaning up of Pittsburgh and the extensive national publicity used to reduce littering of roadsides and parks.

Yet despite the absence of any clear-cut increase in pollution it became generally accepted that it was now a serious problem. And, it was a rather broadly based concern, not merely the exclusive concern of "environmental freaks." As with any other social phenomenon, there are always a limited number of vocal advocates, but only if the issue appeals to a broader portion of the populace can significant pressure be mobilized for public action. The reason for the recent upsurge in efforts to reduce pollution can be grasped in the following contrast. In 1900, Americans said that the large cities were dirty, noisy, crowded, and unpleasant to live in, but that was the way they had always been. In the 1960s Americans said that the large cities were dirty, noisy, crowded, and unpleasant to live in, and the situation was intolerable and something should be done about it. The difference was in attitudes, or, as the economists would say, on the demand side. There had indeed developed a social problem of pollution, but a good portion of the impetus was coming from the increasing intolerance of the conditions rather than a worsening of the conditions themselves. The fact which explained the difference in attitudes between 1900 and 1965 was probably the higher average income of the later date. In both years people naturally preferred to not live in a polluted environment, but it was only in the later period that they had sufficient resources with which to do something about it. This is undoubtedly what is being reflected in the change in attitude toward pollution. In 1900 it was accepted as a harsh, inevitable part of life because society could not afford to transfer resources from other current uses to eliminate it. By 1965, however, per capita incomes had risen sufficiently so that people could use some of the resources at their command to make their surroundings more pleasant.

In retrospect, this major commitment by Americans to reduce pollution in recent years is not surprising. It is quite similar to their reactions on occasions in the past when rising incomes gave them the capacity to remedy a social condition that was generally found undesirable. We have already noted such an action in the abolition of slavery. To this can be added more recent examples, such as the efforts to eliminate poverty and to provide justice to all citizens through the guarantee of legal counsel. It hardly seems surprising that, as average incomes rise, people should choose to spend some of their added purchasing power on a clearer environment as well as on refrigerators and golf clubs.

Thus, surprisingly, we come to the same conclusion about the cause of pollution that the environmentalists have often propounded; namely, that the problem is caused by economic growth. The approaches to, and the implications drawn from, each conclusion differ, however. Environmentalists usually believe that pollution is an inevitable by-product of the production process and it increases proportionately with the growth of output. But for this proposition to be true, some very important "other things being equal" factors must be held constant. These include the composition of output and the incentives to pollute. In recent years these other factors have not remained constant and, in all likelihood, changes within them have had more effect than that of increasing production. The amount of pollution is obviously strongly affected by the incentive to pollute. If air or water is treated as a common property resource, then users are encouraged to use it carelessly, thereby creating pollution. If, on the other hand, society charges for damages done to it or otherwise restricts the incentive to degrade it, less pollution will occur. For example, emission controls on automobiles reduced the amounts of pollution generated per car by more than 90 percent in the decade from 1965–1975. At the same time the number of new cars built per year only about doubled. Thus, the total amount of pollution created by automobiles fell even while the total number of them in use increased.[5]

Our above analysis would also attribute the appearance of the pollution problem to the growth of incomes, but from an increase in income per person, not necessarily from total national product. Pollution appeared as a major prob-

---

[5] Changes in the composition of output have probably also had a tendency to reduce pollution in recent years. Most well-known polluters, such as steel and paper mills, are involved with raw materials. Overall, that sector is growing much less rapidly than the service sector, which includes such relatively nonpolluting activities as education, entertainment, and medical services.

lem primarily because of an increase in the demand for more pleasant surroundings. As average incomes in the American economy have risen, a good portion of the populace has reached the position where they can afford to make the surrounding environment more desirable.

These two views on the causation of the pollution problem lead to diametrically opposed recommendations as to the policy one should advocate to reduce or eliminate it. Environmentalists would usually argue that pollution is caused by output and therefore, to reduce it, the increase in gross national product should be stopped, and possibly reversed. Our analysis, however, indicates that such a step would simply make the problem worse. Pollution will be curtailed when society has sufficient resources to do so, and the best method to reach that point is to encourage an increase in output per person. As usual, one's conception of the manner in which the world operates makes a dramatic difference in the programs one advocates.

Economics and the Ecological System

A generation ago, individuals who were concerned about the supply of natural resources called themselves *conservationists.* Today they are apt to be known as *environmentalists* or even *ecologists.* The shift in nomenclatures is not mere happenstance. It reflects a general tendency toward the broadening in the interests of such individuals. Where at one time they worried about the long-term supply of certain allegedly crucial natural resources, they now are concerned about the future of life on the entire planet. Concern for the future of copper supplies has been replaced by concern for "spaceship earth."[6]

In some forms the broader concern for the environment is merely an extension of the older conservationist worries about the supply of natural resources. Instead of focusing on specific resources within a national economy, it now ponders whether the total world supply will be sufficient for anticipated world requirements. The expressed concern is also similar to older conservationists' thinking in that it usually fails to distinguish between economic and physical stocks of resources. Take, for example, the common complaint that the American economy is using up far more than its fair share of the world's natural resources. With only 6 percent of the world's population, it takes about 40 percent of the entire world's current consumption of natural resources. Thus, it is concluded that the United States is a parasite on the rest of the world; its relatively huge consumption of natural resources reduces the future supplies of other nations. The argument begins to look shaky, however, as soon as one notices that most of the natural resources consumed by the American economy originate within its own boundaries. While the United States does import some natural resources— oil being an obvious example, as a result of recent publicity—it also exports others. It is the world's largest exporter of both coal and food products.

Americans consume more natural resources per capita because their advan-

---

[6] The term was introduced by Professor Kenneth Boulding of the University of Colorado to emphasize that the earth is essentially a closed system, dependent on its own resources for its long-term survival.

tage in technology allows them to create more of them. In this sense, they are not using any more of the world's ultimate supply than any other group, rich or poor. Rather, they are using the physical stock within their borders much better than the average of the rest of the world. The Americans' large current consumption of natural resources, therefore, is not penalizing the rest of the world at all. (This can be tested by asking if the rest of the world would have more resources in the future in the absence of America's current advantage in technology.) On the contrary, *because* the Americans have developed such advanced technology, they provide the rest of the world with the possibility of adopting it to increase the effective supply of their own resources accordingly.

POPULATION

The growth of population has received a good share of attention in the recent examination of the long-term adequacy of natural resources. That appears to be a reasonable allocation of effort because changes in the number of people certainly affect the demand for natural resources. And the adequacy of natural resources is determined by the demands placed upon them as well as by their supply. At the first level of approximation, the size of the population and the adequacy of a given stock of resources are inversely related. The larger the number of people the fewer resources there would be per person out of any given supply. This basic truism has obviously been the major driving force behind the recent campaigns to curtail population growth.

By now phrases such as family planning, zero population growth, and "stop at two," have become commonplace in modern society. How much effect they will have in changing the behavior of people from that which they would have done otherwise, however, remains to be seen. While we do not fully understand how population size is determined in an economy, we can be certain that there always have been such forces at work in economic systems. Population is clearly affected by such factors as incomes and resource supplies. We can be fairly certain, for example, that it would not continue to grow in the face of a steady deterioration in the economic environment. Thus, the most pessimistic predictions, which argue that the population will continue to increase, eventually destroying itself unless explicit measures are taken, are undoubtedly mistaken. There are natural forces which are always operating in an economy to determine the current level of population. They may not produce the results we desire, but any programs which ignore their existence will miss their objectives.

The American economy provides an interesting example of natural population dynamics at work. A pattern of change in the domestic population was well established before there was much concern about a "population problem," or indeed before there were other arrangements such as tax deductions which might have significantly affected such incentives. Around 1800, the birth rate in the United States was about fifty to fifty-five yearly per 1,000 inhabitants. The quantitative evidence on the colonial period is not as good, but the rate during that time appears to have been comparatively high also. But since 1800, the birth rate has gone through ups and downs for a decade or so, but the long-term trend has been definitely downward. In the early 1970s it was about fifteen per 1,000 year-ly, or only 30 percent of the rate prevailing two centuries before. The death rate also decreased over this period, but not nearly as rapidly as that of births, so that the net rate of increase of domestic population fell dramatically. About 1800 it was probably around 3 percent annually, but in recent years it has dropped to, or perhaps even below, zero.

The Americans' experience is by no means exceptional. The populations of most nations that have achieved relatively high per capita incomes have behaved in the same manner. In addition, national economies that have clearly begun to grow above the income levels that characterize most underdeveloped nations—Costa Rica, Taiwan, and Ceylon, for example—have begun to show the same slowdown in population growth that the now advanced nations underwent. Thus, it is with some irony that when commentators concerned about the dangers of population growth advocate worldwide measures to curtail it, they often urge the United States and the other developed nations to set a good example by slowing down their own population growth. These nations *have* been "setting a good example," and it was under way before the population advocates became con-cerned about it. Furthermore, additional reductions in population growth in the advanced nations—outside of massive depopulations—would not have much ef-fect on the "world population problem." Most of the increase in total numbers is now occurring in those nations with the lowest average incomes.

This state of affairs—low rates of population growth in the advanced econo-mies and higher rates in the less developed nations—is just the reverse of that prevailing only a century ago. At that time birth rates in the developing nations were coming down but were still relatively high. The less developed nations were barely touched yet by the worldwide transfer of technology which has since become commonplace. Their populations were generally growing slowly, having had a long time to adapt to their comparatively static economies. The reversal in the pattern of population growth is probably explained by the same basic factor, the interaction between population and improving economic welfare. We do not now have a good explanation of population change (although some interesting and promising work is developing in the field of economic demography). At-tempts have been made to explain the reduction in American growth by the reduction in the person-per-land ratio (especially nearby unsettled land). Several studies have noted that, in the nineteenth century, the closer an area was to the frontier the higher the birth rate was. This may merely be confirming a common relation which appears to exist whatever the trend in total population, namely that rural areas have higher birth rates than urban areas. What was also probably at work was a more general relation between incomes and birth rates. When a society experiences an increase in per capita incomes, it can spend it on a variety of things, including more children as well as sewing machines and potato chips. This tendency for the birth rate to rise with income is known as the "income effect" by economists.[7] At the same time rising average incomes tend to make

---

[7] The Malthusian theory of population assumes that all gains in income are spent on more children. Hence, the number of people grows as fast as total income, and per capita income can never rise above the "subsistence" level.

some costs of raising children more expensive—the "substitution effect." Generally, the cost of raising children in a society increases as the price of labor becomes more expensive relative to other resources, and an economy in which labor is scarce will devote more of its resources to increasing that factor's productivity through higher per capita expenditures on such items as education, medical care, food, and housing. And this implies that the cost of raising children in such an environment will be correspondingly higher as well.

Thus, increasing real incomes may tend to either speed up or slow down population growth, depending on whether the income or substitution effect predominates. The evidence that we have so far—which is admittedly sketchy—suggests that the advanced nations have gone through a cycle in which first the income and then the substitution effect prevailed. The income effect which was stronger in earlier years was probably overpowered by the tendency of the relative cost of labor to rise as development proceeded. Hence we observe first an increase and then a decrease in the rate of population growth.

The lesser-developed economies are currently in a situation where the income effect predominates. (Whether this will be followed by a later slowdown in population growth, we do not know. There are no necessary reasons why their experience should duplicate that of the advanced nations.) This is not surprising, as labor is cheap in most poorer economies and the cost of raising children, therefore, is correspondingly less. What may be more surprising, however, is the assertion that average incomes have been rising in most underdeveloped countries. While the measured per capita incomes of some poorer nations have undergone sizeable advances recently, there is no obvious pattern of overall growth. The basis for claiming that there has been a general increase in economic welfare relates to a component of such welfare which is not included in the standard estimates of per capita incomes—longevity. Since World War II, the death rate in almost all lesser-developed countries has fallen substantially. This has resulted primarily from the application of technology developed in the advanced nations for controlling waterborne diseases. The cost-effectiveness of doing this has proved to be surprisingly high, much higher than the same quantity of resources invested in improving the productivity of food production or education in those nations would have produced. India, for example, has been struggling with droughts and floods plus some other handicaps of her own making in the last three decades to eke out small gains in per capita income. At the same time the average life expectancy in the nation has nearly doubled, from twenty-seven to fifty-three. An increase of that magnitude in such a short time is unprecedented in world history.

Development planners have had mixed feelings about this trend because they believed that it increased the number of consumers among which hard-earned increases in output had to be divided. That is a myopic view of economic development, however, which focuses only on goods and services per person. Almost all people would prolong their lives, if possible, as indicated by expenditures for penicillin and highway dividers. Thus, even if measured per capita incomes remain the same, a reduction in the death rate, with the corresponding increase in life expectancy, represents an improvement in average well-being. Most observers of lesser-developed nations have missed an important implication of this change, and they have been somewhat puzzled by what has happened to population recently. They commonly assumed that a major motive for having children in lesser-developed economies was to provide for the parents in their old age, a form of social security in a society with few formal pension plans. Therefore, if the death rate fell, the birth rate should soon be adjusted downward because a couple could expect a higher proportion of its children to live to be adults and, therefore, a source of support. When the birth rates continued very close to their previous levels, however, the commentators dismissed it as peasant obstinancy and inertia. It would require a generation or so before they realized what was happening and adjusted accordingly.

Suppose, however, that one assumes that potential parents in lesser-developed nations view children in the same way which appears to prevail in the rest of the world? They enjoy them—on net, anyway—and if their resources allowed they would prefer to have more. Then their reaction to falling death rates is quite reasonable. Because the expected cost of raising a child is reduced they choose to raise more (that is, more to a given age, even though the rate of births remains the same). It may not be the reaction development planners would prefer, but it is a perfectly understandable adjustment to the conditions faced by the inhabitants of the less developed economies.

In summary, there appears to be a reasonable logic to the behavior of population over time. At a minimum, we can be confident that it will not run off willy-nilly on its own, oblivious to the basic economic conditions which support it. There is no evidence of "lemminglike" behavior in it which would destroy human civilization. Actually, we can reasonably make a somewhat stronger statement about the possible dangers of population dynamics. There are self-correcting forces in population growth—much more subtle and operating much earlier than Malthus' "dismal checks" of pestilence and famine. Suppose that population growth is, indeed, reducing per capita incomes by spreading the output from the existing nonhuman resources among larger numbers of customers. Then the income of an average family (assuming a given number of wage earners) would fall, and this would soon require retrenchments in spending: less expensive food or clothing, a smaller house, or fewer vacations. One way to offset these cutbacks is to have fewer children. Then less food would be necessary and a smaller house would not seem so crowded. Unless there are sudden, disastrous blows to population, such as severe crop failures or disastrous medical epidemics, it should not experience declines. Well before population pressure on resources reached crisis proportions, subtle but effective forces would have begun to reduce birth rates. In other words, population pressure is communicated back to individuals in a society in such a way that they are forced to incorporate family size along with the other basic economic decisions they must make, such as working, spending, and saving.

All of this may come as somewhat of a revelation to those who have been recently concerned that population growth will soon swallow up the earth. Because, as the reasoning goes, if population continues to grow at the present rate, it will double every twenty-five years or so. That implies a geometric increase in which there will be twice as many people twenty-five years from now, four times as many in fifty years, eight times as many in seventy-five years, and so on. Within two or three centuries there will be standing room only. Such projections assume that the present trend will continue indefinitely. It would be very surprising if it did, because no other series reporting an aggregate social condition, such as income or land development or urbanization, has ever maintained a constant trend for anything like that length of time. The law of random events almost guarantees that a trend will be disrupted before it has gone on nearly that long. Furthermore, as our discussion has indicated, a continuing geometric growth in population would create internal forces which would begin to slow it down. In the unlikely case that nothing else slowed the headlong charge toward "standing room only," the price of space itself would begin to rise dramatically. Not only would each new child entail the expense of food, measles vaccine, school clothes, and an allowance, but also a very expensive coupon entitling him to his 4 square feet on which to stand.

These internal forces of population restraint have been generally overlooked, or at least underestimated, in recent years. One reason for that is that there is very little evidence that they have been operating. From that it has been only a short step—especially for those who wanted to do so—to assume that they do not exist at all. That would be an erroneous deduction, however. The reason they have not appeared in the last three decades is that the economic base of the world has been increasing, and population has been under increasing, not diminishing, incentives. A good part of the recent concern over the growth of world population results from a mistaken view of the causation in its current dynamics. Population is growing as a result of an expanding capability of the world to support it, and not as the initiating force which is putting increasing pressure on that capability.

ECONOMIC CHOICES IN AN ECOLOGICAL SYSTEM

In recent years we have been given another push in the direction of the "no man is an island" view of things. Unless one is totally oblivious to public communication, one must realize by now that all life systems on our planet are interrelated. Materials dumped into a river affect the subgroups of life there, but they also have repercussions downstream and in the ocean, where they can operate to affect more basic parameters of life, such as temperature, rainfall, and the acquisition of energy from the sun. Humans are only one part of a larger system of living organisms, which they both depend upon and alter by their actions. Unless we recognize our influence upon the system, we could well upend our only home.

We may well appreciate the interrelation and fragility of the ecosystem, but that does not provide us with any guidelines as to how to conduct ourselves within it. Even if we know that water is an indispensable element in the basic life cycle, for example, it does not help us make the decision as to whether we should build a hydroelectric project, water the lawn, or take a bath. There are alternative objectives which might be sought and alternative ways to achieve most of them, and each option has an effect on the ecosystem. So, for example, consider a common policy suggestion of environmentalists—reducing the use of pesticides and herbicides ("weed killers"). This suggestion is made because of the well-documented tendency of such chemicals to persist and concentrate in other forms of life beyond their original purpose. If their use were reduced or eliminated, these side effects in the environment would be reduced. But their nonuse would force society to shift to alternative methods of achieving its objectives. These chemicals are now widely used in agriculture because they provide the most output of food from given resources. In their absence farmers would be required to use other techniques of production, such as planting more acreage to offset insect losses in the absence of insecticides, or using more labor for cultivation in place of herbicides. These could create their own disruptions of the ecosystem. The additional marginal acreage that is brought into production to replace losses in output from the abandonment of pesticides, for example, is probably the least fertile and accessible land. Its use will likely require the construction of new roads and towns, and possibly increase soil erosion and silting of rivers and harbors.[8] In short, the recognition of a wider horizon for the impact of people's economic activity does not provide any answers. It merely broadens the scope of the questions to be answered. As long as the alternatives are not costless, there will continue to be hard choices to be made, no matter what the scope of the perspective.

SUGGESTED READING

Barnett, Harold J., and Chandler Morse: *Scarcity and Growth: The Economics of Natural Resource Availability,* John Hopkins, Baltimore, 1963.

Heyne, Paul T.: *The Economic Way of Thinking,* Science Research, Chicago, 1973, Chapter 14.

"The Human Population," *Scientific American,* vol. 231, September 1974.

---

[8] The attempt to circumvent these losses by developing insecticides which decay more rapidly, or more insect-resistant crop varieties, is merely a variant of this process. It requires the diversion of resources and the consequent shifts which that implies for the ecosystem.

Economic Behavior amid Interruptions: 1917–1945

THE ECONOMICS OF THE WAR "OVER THERE"

In 1914, the war that the Europeans had been expecting, finally began. They had been stockpiling armaments and organizing alliances in anticipation for some time. Even so, they were not prepared for the size and the duration of the conflict that soon began to confront them. Unlike the Americans, whose estimate of the total cost of a war had been drastically revised upward by the Civil War, the Europeans had had only short or small-scale conflicts in their recent experience. Soon, however, they began to refer to the struggle as the World War, assuming that its immense scope and magnitude obviously differentiated it from all previous conflicts. In retrospect, of course, we now know it as World War I, having learned that although it was enormous by previous standards, it was merely the first major, modern war.

Sometime in the nineteenth century, probably as an unnoticed, gradual modification, the basic economics of war changed dramatically. Not only did the size of wars expand as the size of the economies that supported them grew—which, by itself, would explain a very large increase—but they tended to increase as a percentage of the economies involved as well. It is not clear now why wars have become big enterprises in recent years. Probably it was a combination of the reduction in transportation costs, an increase in the capacity of production above accepted minimal living standards for the duration of a war, and a rapid increase in the cost of military hardware. Whatever the reasons, warfare became a much larger and more demanding event in developed economies in the twentieth century.

America was not a direct combatant for the first two-thirds of World War I. There were strong feelings against breaking the long-standing precedent of "staying out of Europe's internal affairs." A conflict of this magnitude could not occur without some effects on the United States, however—even all the way across the Atlantic Ocean. By 1915, a flood of orders for American goods began to pour in from the Allies in Europe. There was a large demand for American wheat, flour, meat, and sugar to replace the European production lost when farmland was devastated or farmers were called off to war. There were standing orders for American-made ammunition to keep up with the heavy expenditure of it that this war seemed to require. And there was a brisk demand for American ships and shipping services to replace those ships not being produced in Europe's otherwise preoccupied shipyards, or else being sent to the bottom of the ocean by German submarines.

For the three years before mid-1917, the United States benefited from acting as a supplier to the warring Europeans. In several ways the situation closely paralleled the experience of the Napoleonic Wars, 125 years earlier. This additional demand for American products on the part of Europeans contributed to prosperous times in the United States. The net increase in exports exceeded $1.5 billion a year, or more than 3 percent of national income at that time. That would have had the equivalent stimulus of a tax cut of more than $40 billion in the early 1970s. This extra push came on top of an economy that was already fairly prosperous in its own right. For example, this period was marked by an extraordinary expansion in that newfangled way of getting around, the automobile. From 1913 to 1917, production nearly quadrupled, creating a broad new industry that, along with allied sectors of gasoline, tires, and road construction, exceeded $3 billion of sales in 1917.

Thus, when the Americans finally joined the fighting in 1917, the economy was operating near its maximum capacity. Unlike the later experience at the onset of World War II, there was no large reserve of idle labor and capital that could be readily pressed into the production of war supplies. In 1917 and 1918 there was no easy way out; each dollar of war production was going to come at the cost of a dollar of civilian output. From the first quarter of 1917 to the last quarter of 1918, war production increased at an annual rate of $11 billion while output of goods available to civilians fell by $13 billion.[1] (America officially entered the war in April 1917 and the Armistice was signed in November 1918). Despite the stimulus of war-related demands, in 1918 real GNP (including the

---

[1] Simon Kuznets, *National Product in Wartime*, National Bureau of Economic Research, New York, 1945. The apparent $2 billion loss in total output is probably the result of understated labor output because of military conscription.

war products) actually fell below its 1917 level. The American experience in World War I is a counterexample to those who argue that war is good for an economy. Wars usually provide an additional dose of spending, and for a society with unemployed resources that, in itself, is useful. That spending could be provided in other ways, however, some of which are much more direct and productive. A government can bolster economic activity just as well by building comfortable housing, paving muddy roads, or financing multimillion-dollar television extravaganzas. When the economy begins at full employment, it can supply the war effort only by reducing some civilian activities.

The war was obviously a powerful intrusion into the regular functioning of the economy. Within a relatively short period, 20 percent of total output was shifted from civilian to war purposes and then back again. The magnitude of this operation dazzled contemporary observers and they began to speculate as to how—and indeed whether—the transition could actually be achieved. It was a very unusual situation by American standards, so policy makers felt it necessary to advocate and implement unusual procedures. Before the beginning of the war a number of advisory commissions had been formed, but the regulatory structure received most of its power and size after America's entry into the war in April 1917. Major sectors of the economy deemed important to the war effort found themselves under the supervision of the War Industries Board, the U. S. Shipping Board, the Railroad Administration, the Fuel Administration, and the Food Administration. The last named was directed by a successful engineer by the name of Herbert Hoover, who gained considerable exposure in the position as a kind of early-day William Simon.

This instant bureaucracy was the first example of a type of federal intervention in the economy that was repeated during World War II and the price control efforts of the early 1970s. In one sense it was probably inevitable that the government would become a bigger factor in the economy. It was controlling a larger share of the resources so that it would have required considerable restraint on its part not to throw its weight around. Yet, in retrospect, it is not at all clear that the crash program of government control actually did much to speed up wartime mobilization. Even though Americans seemed to have a healthy respect for the autonomous functioning of the economy in normal times, they did not seem to appreciate how effective it could also be in extraordinary times. The same forces that seem to work so smoothly in normal times can also move quickly and persuasively to effect major changes in products and resources in extraordinary times. American planners began to appreciate some of these latent strengths of a market economy when they began to superimpose their own system of allocation on top of it. The controlling agencies had the authority to allocate raw materials and production facilities. Through a separate, but parallel, structure they also had the power to support those decisions through price controls. The planners attempted to locate existing sources of supply and then allocate them on the basis of a list of priorities—and the problems quickly began to appear. The federal allocators naturally assumed that at any given time the physical quantity of a raw material must be fixed. After all, coal is coal or cotton fiber is cotton fiber—

right? They soon discovered that there was considerable ambiguity and slippage in the concept of physical supply. Firms could affect supply substantially by varying inventories, by techniques of production, and by the effort they put into devising more economical means of production. In a normally functioning market system these actions are taken in response to prices of materials and are seldom explicitly noticed outside the firm. Central allocation in World War I overlooked such incentives, and they tended to work against the government. There was usually no incentive to economize on materials, or to report those that were available, or to seek for ways to provide more, all because such gains would go, unrewarded, into the central pool.

The priority system also ran into trouble. It was soon discovered that almost everything could be construed as contributing to the war effort and suppliers of specific goods could develop a very convincing case to that effect. When the government argued that women's fur coats, for example, were not essential to the war effort, the industry responded that they were a substitute for scarce fuel, or the prospect of buying one motivated women to work long hours in the munitions factories. Soon almost all goods were awarded priority status, and the designation had no meaning. The planners had failed to recognize that although all of one good may be more crucial than all of another one, in some sense, that is not the choice a society normally faces. Rather than choosing all steel and no glass, or vice versa, for example, an economy normally chooses some steel and some glass. The relevant choice is when to stop producing steel so that some resources remain to produce glass. Thus, the representatives of a particular good could almost always prove that *some* of their good was very important and could thereby break the all-or-nothing rating implicit in the priority system. And the planners received another lesson in the subtle advantages of the workings of the market system that they had thought it was necessary to temporarily suspend.

Just about the time that the entire bureaucracy was geared up to fight the war, however, the fighting ended. The Americans rushed to dismantle their war effort, and in doing so they demonstrated far more ingenuity and energy than they had in operating it. War contracts were canceled abruptly, the Army was quickly pulled home from France and demobilized, and federal office workers in Washington, D. C., were discharged so rapidly that their supervisors dipped into their own pockets to provide them with carfare home. Fortunately the wartime control was also benevolently dissolved in the process. Only the Food Administration was retained, and its function was shifted to war relief in Europe. Thus, Herbert Hoover spent a few more years in the limelight.

In the face of the rapid demobilization in late 1918 and early 1919, almost everyone expected a recession. It did not occur, however, probably because a combination of several factors kept total spending up. The level of food exports remained very high until Europeans could restore their agricultural systems. Exports of industrial equipment were also strong as economies around the world sought to restore their productive capacities. The domestic construction industry was also busy. The ultimate cause of the postwar prosperity in 1919 and early 1920, however, was a relatively large federal deficit. Although war-related spending had been slashed at the time of the Armistice, it took another year and a half to get federal spending down to the level of traditional revenues. In 1919 the federal budget ran a deficit of over $4 billion, equivalent to the effect that consumers would have if they were to have converted all their savings into additional spending that year.

In 1920 that recession finally caught up with the economy. Some of the forces that had worked to postpone it began to lose strength. By mid-1920, the federal budget had switched to the surplus side. Construction was being slowed by the high interest rates. And agriculture outside the United States had recovered sufficiently so that American food exports decreased—as did food prices. In fact, 1920 was a milestone for farming in the United States. It was the last year of a "golden age" of twenty-five years of American agriculture. From 1895 to 1920 demand for farm products had been buttressed first by large numbers of immigrants, until 1913, and then by exports to warring Europe. After 1920, the farm sector was forced back to the harsh basis of its long-term position in the economy. On average, the demand for food grows more slowly than the economy in general because most productivity gains are spent on nonfood items. In the 1920s the demand for American agricultural products did not increase as fast as the productivity in agriculture itself. Thus, fewer resources—specifically farmers—were required as the decade wore on. The distress that this hard-nose adjustment imposed on the farm sector would form a disquieting background to the otherwise generally prosperous 1920s.

THE ROARING TWENTIES

The decade of the 1920s is undoubtedly viewed as one of the most distinctive periods of American history. After all, it is hard to forget the Charleston, speakeasies, Stutz Bearcats, and "the great gatsby." It is very easy to visualize that time as an uninhibited, happy interlude, particularly in contrast to some of the more recent, disquieting years. Naturally, this characterization tends to carry over to descriptions of the economy in the decade. Flamboyant living styles, it is assumed, must make for a somewhat more spontaneous, kooky economy.

That would be a misleading inference to draw. Social styles and economic performance can be substantially separated. One can be a flapper on the weekend and still be a conscientious worker during the week. In addition, the stereotype of the 1920s is probably overdrawn anyway. Most of the participants of that era did not usually think of themselves as living in exceptional times. They were preoccupied with more mundane things, such as paying bills, providing for their coming retirement, or worrying about their children's problems in school. They would probably have been as surprised to find that they were living through the "roaring twenties" as residents of fifth-century Italy would have been if they had been told that they were living during the "fall of Rome," or as the inhabitants of the English Midlands in the 1780s would have been if they had been told that they were a part of the "industrial revolution."

Whatever handles have been applied to it since—appropriate or not—the economy in the decade of the 1920s behaved normally and predictably. One of its most obvious characteristics was rapid growth. In this sense it resembles recent decades much more closely than it does the years which immediately preceded it. Growth, of course, implies expanding sectors, and it is this aspect which probably accounts for the reported exuberance of the period. The widespread introduction of such new products as automobiles and radios certainly contributed to greater mobility and the development of new mores. Growth also implies shrinking sectors in an economy, and it is the obvious existence of a number of these that have bothered commentators on the twenties since then. After all, food, textiles, and coal are very basic products, and if they are in trouble, does it not suggest a fundamental problem with the entire economy? It does not. It merely indicates that, given the available supply of resources, society wishes to use more of them in other sectors. Thus the 1920s begin to appear more like recent times and, viewed in that context, they begin to look more familiar and understandable.

Expanding Sectors

Certainly the most important growth sector of the economy in the decade was that of automobiles. (See Figure 16-1.) (Somewhat more generally the sector would comprise the internal combustion engine, which would also include trucks, buses, and tractors.) In 1919, a total of 1.5 million automobiles were produced in the United States. By 1929, the average yearly output had tripled and the total stock of cars in use equaled one for each six citizens in the country. Contemporary cynics suggested that it was now conceivable for every American to be riding on the nation's roads at once. Many people who found themselves in a Sunday afternoon jam thought that that had indeed happened.

The rapid, widespread adoption of the automobile suggested that somewhat more serious considerations were involved. Its development was actually part of a broader pattern of innovation and adaptation that had been under way in the United States since the mid-nineteenth century. At that time the rising costs of central urban land, caused by the increasing size of cities, had started a search for cheaper forms of transportation. The payoff to such devices as the horsedrawn streetcar resulted because it made it feasible to extend the limits of urban housing and thus increased the effective land base of the cities. As the cities continued to grow, other innovations, such as trolleys, subways, and interurban trains, were used to "stretch out" the expensive land of city centers.

The automobile was a logical extension of this process. Although its direct costs were higher per mile than the older transport modes, the values of its unique services were even greater. The automobile offered savings in time, a resource which was growing more valuable as the value of labor increased. Driving from one's own garage directly to the office parking lot cuts out the walk to the train station, the inevitable wait at the station, the stops for the other passengers along the way, the crosstown transfer, and then the repetition of the entire trek in reverse that evening. The automobile also opened up suburban land that was otherwise inaccessible to more concentrated forms of transit. In recent years a good deal of concern has been expressed over the waste of land the automobile

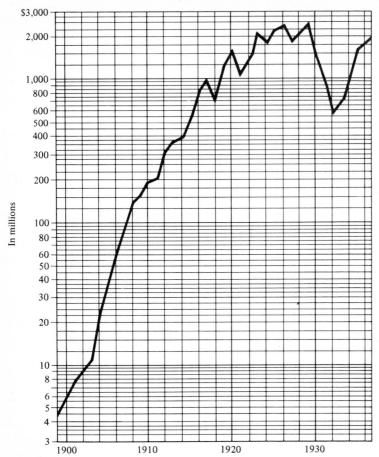

Figure 16-1 Output of passenger motor vehicles, 1899–1938. *(Source: Adapted from U. S. Bureau of the Census,* Historical Statistics of the United States, Colonial Times to 1957, *Government Printing Office, Washington, 1960, p. 420.)*

has caused by allowing suburban "sprawl." We could undoubtedly find better ways to use such land, but the criticisms miss the major points. Without the automobile most of this land would be inaccessible and the entire area would be wasted. By allowing individuals sizeable freedom in determining their own transportation patterns, it has opened large areas of land that would otherwise be denied urban use. The alternative to "sprawl" is more crowded, congested, and expensive forms of city organization.

As is typical of the early years of a growth sector, the automobile industry underwent sizeable improvements in efficiency and product design in the 1920s. Anyone watching how rapidly the car was becoming a standard feature of American life could see the huge potential gains from introducing improvements at that time. And the improvements did come, each increasing the attractiveness, and therefore the demand, for cars. The 1920s saw the widespread adoption of enclosed car bodies, which greatly increased the amount of time—such as in cold or rainy weather—during which they could be used; self-starters made driving less tiresome; four-wheel brakes and stronger tires increased safety; and the high-compression engine increased both power and fuel economy. The efficiency of manufacturing automobiles also improved. From 1919 to 1929 the output per worker increased by an average of more than 7 percent per year as assembly plants were streamlined and perfected. One obvious reason that Americans were buying more cars during this period was that they were receiving more car for each dollar they spent on them.

It is now an oft-repeated truism that the automobile substantially altered the organization of the economy. Yet while some of the changes it made are fairly obvious, others are overlooked or misconstrued. For example, it is commonly reported that the automobile greatly stimulated the demand for steel, rubber, plate glass, and petroleum because it consumed large quantities of these materials. The output of both petroleum and rubber products did increase sharply, and much of that growth can be attributed to gasoline and tires. On the other hand, the total output of plate glass and (particularly) steel did not increase much, even though the auto industry itself greatly increased its purchases of those products. One reason is that, although automobiles consumed certain inputs, they were also substitutes for other forms of transportation that used the same inputs. Cars certainly used iron and steel products for sheet metal, framing, and engine blocks, but they also severely curtailed the demand for railroad services which used the same resources for rails, boilers, and wheel trucks. While the number of automobiles sold in the 1920s almost tripled, the output of railroad rolling stock fell by 50 percent and that of streetcars, wagons, and sleighs by almost 80 percent.

The automobile also changed the landscape of America. The movement to the suburbs was already noticeable by World War I. Throughout the 1920s the automobile allowed an increasing percentage of Americans to move from multi-family units to single-family houses, each centered on its own green lawn. This changing pattern of residence was possible, of course, because the automobile allowed one to commute to work. A car also allowed—indeed encouraged—other types of driving as well. There were trips downtown for shopping or a dentist appointment, and evening forays to the library or the kid's school play or a restaurant. Another large portion of automobile driving was composed of recreation or leisure-time activities. The car made the countryside more accessible to such traditional sports as hunting or fishing, but it also encouraged the development of new interests. For example, it helped to grant Americans their wish to use a sizeable portion of their income gains on travel and entertainment. While it made going to the recently established movies easier, it single-handedly created the industry of auto touring. In the 1920s the countryside blossomed with gas stations, hotdog stands, motels—or cabin camps, as they were commonly called then—and road markers, some of the latter put up by disgruntled farmers who grew tired of directing lost tourists to the next town.

This sudden surge of traffic created what has since become a very characteristic American institution: the traffic jam. When the automobile first became popular the existing road system was obviously inadequate. Country roads had been primarily developed for wagon traffic and were generally unpaved, narrow, crooked, and routed through each small village or farmyard. Car travel on them was slow or, sometimes in wet weather, impossible, as the vehicles sank into mud up to their axles. City streets were usually paved and drained but were often constricted by streetcars or the poles of the recently installed telephone and electric systems.

As a consequence, the 1920s witnessed a major increase in expenditures for road improvements. State spending for highway construction—the largest such category—increased from $70 million in 1918 to $750 million in 1930. A good portion of rural America was connected by all-weather roads. Urban road systems were also substantially improved, with major emphasis on expediting traffic movement. This included separating opposing flows of traffic by means of bridges, road dividers, and traffic lights. It also meant much stricter controls on the operation of motor vehicles, as witnessed by driver and vehicle licenses, backed up by another new American institution—the traffic court.

Electric power was another growth sector of the twenties. The output of kilowatts more than doubled, partly because improvements in generating and distributing efficiency made them cheaper and hence more attractive. In manufacturing, the convenience and flexibility of electric power rapidly replaced traditional power sources. The large, throbbing steam engine with all its connecting belts and shafts was rapidly discarded. In its place came electric motors that could be conveniently varied in size or location as production organization dictated. Whereas 30 percent of manufacturing enterprises were powered by electricity at the beginning of the decade, that rate had jumped to more than 70 percent by the end of the decade. Such a rapid shift for an economic variable that is so large in relation to the economy suggests, by historical standards, that the gain must have been both large and obvious.

Electric power was also proving to be very useful in residential units, as reflected in the remarkable growth in electrical appliances during this period. (See Figure 16-2.) The radio was first introduced commercially in about 1922.[2] By 1930 output had reached more than 4 million sets a year, and more than 12 million households—comprising about one-third of the nation's population— owned at least one. Within that short eight-year period more than 600 commercially licensed radio stations had begun broadcasting. And large numbers of people were obviously listening to them regularly, well beyond the point where the novelty had worn off. Many of the traditional amusements that American households had used to entertain themselves in the evening were discarded; for example, the number of pianos sold fell by two-thirds in the decade. The output of electric ranges, vacuum cleaners, and refrigerators also increased dramatically

---

[2] Most of the appliances mentioned here could be operated by sources of power other than electricity. Early versions of the radio had been operated on batteries, for example. But the improvements in performance, convenience, and especially cost, brought about by electricity, were so large as to create an effectively new group of products.

in the twenties. By 1930, production of refrigerators had reached 1 million units a year, about fifty times as many as in 1921. One consequence of this was that consumption of ice cream also grew rapidly as more households obtained a simple method of storing it.

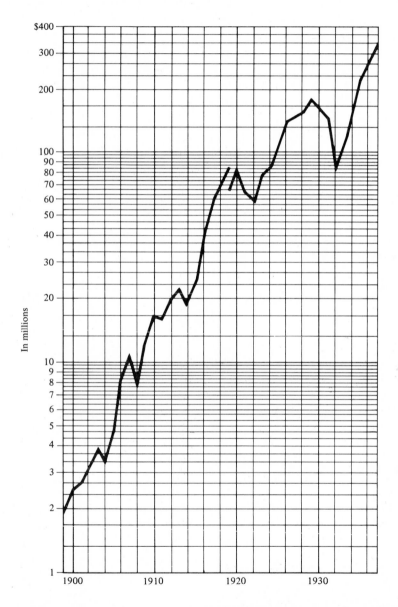

Figure 16-2 Value of household electrical appliances produced 1899–1938. *(Source: Adapted from U. S. Bureau of the Census,* Historical Statistics of the United States, Colonial Times to 1957, *Government Printing Office, Washington, D. C., 1960, p. 420.)*

Agriculture, the Traditional American Declining Sector

The end of the disorganization caused by the war in Europe brought American agriculture back to the harsh reality of its long-term position. The price of wheat fell from $2.50 a bushel in 1918 to less than a dollar in 1921. Corn followed a similar pattern—from $1.80 to $0.40. Wool prices fell by two-thirds. As a result, the price of farmland also fell substantially. In the six years after 1919 more than 30 million acres of cultivated land were abandoned. The farm population began an absolute decline for the first time in American history. (Although American *agriculture* had generally been shrinking relative to the economy prior to 1920, the total number of *farmers* had been increasing. It was simply that the nonfarm population tended to grow even faster.)

The situation was the result of a number of simultaneous forces. One force was Engel's law, which reminds us that food consumption generally grows less than per capita incomes. A second force, which reinforced the first, was a slow population growth during the decade, of 9 percent. The severe restrictions imposed in immigration just before World War I contributed to this latter slowdown, but it was also a result of the long-term reduction in birth rates that has accompanied American growth. One further factor was necessary to account for the fall in the absolute number of farmers, and that was an increase in the productivity of farming itself. If the output per input had remained constant in agriculture, then it would have required more—not less—agricultural labor to meet the growing demand for food. Yet, despite its shrinking size, American agriculture obviously achieved great gains in efficiency during the decade. And therein lies the paradox of American farming in the twentieth century: improvements in its productivity worked toward reducing its size.

In this context, American farmers were hard at work on their own demise.[3] Output per worker increased by 26 percent in agriculture over the decade. Part of this gain certainly resulted from the subtle upgrading of plants, livestock, fertilizer, implements, and pest control that obviously continued in the area. Part also resulted from more dramatic improvements, such as the introduction of the gasoline-powered tractor. It quickly replaced most of the large, unwieldy steam models. It also made major inroads into the territory of that long-standing source of motive power, the horse. In the 1920s the number of American horses was reduced by 7 million, about one-third of the initial stock. Along with them went the necessity of raising about 25 million acres of oats and hay, and also the daily chore of harnessing, feeding, and generally caring for that type of horsepower.

The forces of change were being felt in most every aspect of agriculture. Adjusting for year-to-year variations in crop conditions, wheat output increased very little in that period. Demand for it was reduced by a shift to other types of foodstuffs in response to higher incomes, and also by a reduction in the average caloric requirements per capita as the amount of manual labor in the economy

---

[3] It should be noted here that an individual farmer is better off devising or adapting improvements, whatever their aggregate effect. Generally the agricultural units pioneering the gains survive, while those who lag behind become the exodus from the sector.

declined. On the other hand, the production of certain crops, such as citrus fruits and vegetables, increased substantially, as the expanding canning industry converted them into year-round rather than seasonal foods. Canning was only one example of a general movement toward more preparation of food outside the household. The twenties saw the decline of the purchase of food products in unprocessed, bulk forms. It became increasingly common to buy canned milk and fruit as well as packaged crackers, macaroni, coffee, cheese, soup, and bacon.

The textile industry was another sector of the economy that appeared to be caught in the backlash of growth. Before the Civil War it had been a focus of growth, and the largest single component of American manufacturing. By 1920, much of the innovation and expansion had been completed so that industry managers were paying more attention to minimizing costs. Their largest single cost was labor, so they began to look for locations outside the Northeast (primarily New England) where wages were lower. (By this time one of the constraints that originally tied textiles to the Northeast—waterpower—had been eased, first by the introduction of the steam engine, and then by that of the electric motor.) The most popular area for relocation was in the Southeastern states, especially the Carolinas. One by one the lights began to go out in the mills of Lowell and Pawtucket and Holyoke.

New England cotton textile factories were beginning to feel competition from other sources as well. Synthetic fibers began to be developed in the early 1900s. The output of rayon, the most important of these, had increased by a factor of 12 in the 1920s. By 1930, it comprised 3 percent of the total market for textile fibers. Not much in an aggregate sense, but coming in a market where total output was growing very slowly, it captured a good part of the entire industry's growth.

Déjà Vu

A description of the economy in the 1920s sounds, in many ways, like a preview of more modern times. The farm sector was depressed but automobiles were booming. Manufacturing and population were moving out of New England. Immigration into Florida and California was very large. Parents worried about their children's behavior and ministers in turn worried about the parents. Real per capita income increased by about 2 percent per year in that period, very close to the record that the economy has achieved since that time.

THE GREAT CRASH

In the summer of 1929, things seemed to be going very well. For most of the preceding decade the economy had grown fairly steadily, parceling out higher incomes and new products rather generally to the population. There had been a few interruptions of the steady upward trend, in 1924 and 1927, for example, but these seemed to be insignificant anomalies. And the future was foreseen as a simple extension of the recent benevolent past. The conviction was solidifying that the economy had achieved a new, permanent path of growth and prosperity.

The designation "new era" began to be accepted as the appropriate one for the times.

Some leaders of the business community saw a small, but disquieting, exception to the general trend, however. Since early 1928 they had watched the stock market make impressive gains, gains which they believed were excessively large and threatened to produce disruptions later on when they were corrected. At the beginning of 1928, the Federal Reserve System began to operate against this "excessive speculation" by restricting the money supply to make credit more costly. Interest rates rose during the year, but the market continued its climb, seemingly oblivious to such retarding effects. In the first half of 1929, the Federal Reserve System attempted to take what it termed "direct action." This consisted of directives to member banks urging them to make only "productive loans" and to refuse all loans requested for speculation in securities. Bankers found the distinction difficult to make, even when they were willing to override their own self-interest to enforce it. Some of the board members of the Federal Reserve agreed. The problem is that purchases of equities are substitutes for investments in physical plants, or inventories, and the allocation of funds between them is affected by the returns that are expected on each. If borrowing to purchase a given asset (stock, in this case) is prohibited, the same thing can be done indirectly. For example, one can borrow to finance a new factory and then fund the purchase of securities out of current profits, rather than borrow directly on the securities.

In any case the Federal Reserve kept money tight through the first three-quarters of 1929—a cumulative period of almost two years of restraint. Stock prices—the specific sector at which this action was aimed—did not respond to this sustained pressure, however, although the rest of the economy did. Some time in the middle of 1929 the major components of output began slowing down. By the autumn of 1929 it was becoming fairly clear that both industrial production and construction were experiencing sizeable reductions. Then the stock market finally turned down. After a fairly orderly decline in September, and a partial recovery in early October, the market became chaotic in late October. On the famous "black Thursday" of October 24, nearly 13 million shares were traded and the market suffered its worse loss in a single day of its history. When the major indexes of security prices bottomed out in December, American wealth in securities had been reduced by about $25 billion. In that span of three months those losses had more than offset the entire net income the economy had earned during the period.

There has, of course, been no shortage of attempts to explain why the Great Crash occurred. Interestingly enough, many of the explanations are similar to the judgment held by most of the board members of the Federal Reserve in the year and a half immediately before the Crash: the market was marked by overspeculation, or too much buying on margin. In other words, stock prices were too high relative to some fundamental basis of their value, which they should have been reflecting, and a sizeable number of securities were bought out of emotion rather than solid judgment.[4] Our natural inclination is to sympathize with such arguments, particularly since they appear to be verified by what actually happened. Yet the specific mechanics which would make this general claim work are vague. Speculation, for example, is commonly thought of as a socially unproductive activity, attempting to make profits on changes in price without increasing society's economic welfare in any way. Carefully enunciated, however, speculation is a process in which almost everyone is necessarily engaged. It is simply having an interest in an asset whose real value can change in the future. That can consist of such commonly understood speculative positions as owning stocks or real estate, but it also includes owning fixed-income, government bonds, whose real value is affected by changes in the price level, or a teacher's certification, which is speculating on the future demand for public school instructors. Speculation, therefore, simply reflects the collective judgment of the value of a certain asset in the future. To say that there was "excessive speculation" in stocks before the Great Crash is the same as saying that *our* prediction of the prices and return on those securities would be less optimistic than that of the average participant involved. With the advantage of hindsight, one can say that the events of October 1929 proved that there was "overspeculation" just prior to that time. One can argue with equally compelling logic, however, that in the three *years* before that time there had been "insufficient speculation," in that security prices tended to keep rising above the levels at which they had previously been valued. At its best, therefore, "excess speculation" is merely another name for what happened, rather than an explanation.

The use of stock purchases on margin[5] also fails to enlighten us much as to the cause of the Great Crash. It is well known that buying on margin accentuated the decline. As prices fell, brokers were forced to sell such stock in order to sustain the minimum cash (or owner's equity) which financial regulations required. Margins can make the average price of stocks more volatile, both by adding impetus to upward movements, as well as by reinforcing downward trends, but they should not have much effect on the equilibrium level toward which stock prices move. Ultimately such prices are determined by the expected return on those equities relative to the returns anticipated on alternative investments. In severe situations, such as the Great Crash, margining might even cause prices to overshoot through forced selling. Soon, however, prices would be bid up to their competitive level as investors responded to the difference in expected returns which such a process would create. Thus, the existence of margin buying might add to the excitement, but in itself, it cannot explain most of such a dramatic shift as the Great Crash.

To explain the Crash we must look elsewhere, and, as usual, the best proce-

---

[4] Which recalls the observation of one cynic of the time that stock prices had anticipated the hereafter as well as the future.

[5] Margin purchases provide only a fraction of the cash necessary to buy a given security. The remainder is borrowed against the market value of the security itself. Such accounts are conventionally handled by the broker who arranges the purchase of the stock.

dure appears to be to go back to fundamentals.[6] The total value of outstanding stocks had increased faster than most of the major components of the economy in the late 1920s. From January 1, 1925 to October 1, 1929, for example, the total market value of securities traded on the New York Exchange rose from $27 billion to $87 billion, more than a threefold increase. Most of this growth was explained by the net issue of new shares, however. The average price per share rose only about 30 percent in the same period. Some of the new shares were issued by existing companies to raise capital for investments, such as factories, railroads, or utilities. Some reflected a shift to the corporate form of business organization as smaller proprietorships and particularly the traditional family farms declined in number relative to the size of total business activity.

Through it all, the return on corporate equity remained competitive with alternative investments. The average dividend paid out on stock remained above 4 percent of its going market value for most of the decade. Retained earnings—that part of profits reinvested in the company—made the real income somewhat higher than that. By comparison, the return on good-quality corporate bonds ranged between 4 percent and 6 percent. Both types of securities showed a parallel, downward trend in return over the decade, suggesting that stock prices were influenced by available alternatives and were not flying off on their own, oblivious to the real world.

The general tendency toward lower interest rates suggests another factor influencing the stock market's behavior. It would make any level of corporate earnings more attractive relative to the decreasing return (percentagewise) on other investments. Thus, stock prices would be bid up as investors unintentionally equalized returns in the attempt to acquire the most attractive ones for themselves.

In sum, it is not necessary to resort to such explanations as excess speculation, margin buying, or any other special circumstances to explain the behavior of the stock market before October 1929. It was reasonable and understandable in the context of the evolving structure and resource returns of the economy at that time. In fact, the stock market collectively "understood" conditions in the economy better than most of those who were worried about its wayward behavior. That, as we shall see, became a contributing factor to the entire problem.

The rise in stock prices up to October 1929 can be explained by fundamentals, and, interestingly enough, so can the Crash itself. The prime explanation for

---

[6] Undoubtedly, some of the participants in the stock market in the late 1920s approached it in the spirit of a weekend gamble. They bet at the New York Exchange rather than at the window of the local race track because the brokerage office was closer. That, of course, is hardly unique to American security markets in the late 1920s. For almost any group of assets in any age on which we can obtain evidence, some of the participants acted as if they were involved in a lottery. Yet it takes only a fraction of the players in a particular market, responding to more basic objectives, to compel the entire market to adhere to the same guidelines. If, for example, 80 percent of the buyers of securities acquire their holdings at random, the remaining 20 percent can determine the prices among particular stocks by their selective purchases. Similarly, if pure speculators are particularly attracted to the stock market, then the remaining investors would be attracted to the lower prices in alternative assets, such as bonds, real estate, agricultural commodities, and antiques.

the going price of most stocks was the profits expected to accrue to them in the future. Current earnings, liquid assets, or the scrap value of existing facilities are usually only a fraction of the current valuation of a corporation.[7] If profits had reached the level that was expected of them as of 1929, stock prices would have remained at their existing level. As of the fall of 1929, however, those expectations had to be revised downward drastically. By then it was increasingly obvious that real income had begun to fall sharply. With it went the profit expectations that supported stock prices as of early October 1929. So stock prices were written down by a sizeable amount in light of this new information about their prospects. Given the performance of the economy over the next decade, the Crash can be seen as a reasonable adjustment. Indeed, the stock market anticipated the long, dreary years of the Depression much better than most pundits of the time.

This, in turn, raises the question of what caused such a major downturn in the economy to begin with. Part of the explanation undoubtedly lies in the falloff of certain types of investments, such as automobiles and construction. Such dips, at least in moderate form, had occurred every three years or so in the preceding decade. Yet there almost certainly must have been additional contributing forces to turn the "dip" into such a steep retreat. The obvious primary candidate is the prior two-year reign of tight money imposed by the Federal Reserve during its preoccupation with the stock market. That was a major drag on the economy which would otherwise have been undergoing an increase both in output and in the financial assets which commonly accompany economic activity in a sophisticated economy. In short, an unusually severe monetary policy accentuated the downturn in the economy. So, ironically, and in a roundabout way, the Federal Reserve did get its way with the stock market. Its tight-policy stance had not succeeded in reducing prices directly. However, it had succeeded in slowing down the entire economy and, indirectly, it knocked out the rationale for those prevailing stock prices.

THE GREAT DECLINE

The decline of real income from 1929 into 1930—about 11 percent—was severe enough in itself. But real output, even after adjustments for the sharp drop in prices that was occurring, continued to fall. (See Figure 16-3.) National income was 9 percent lower in 1931 than in 1930, a whopping 18 percent lower in 1932 than 1931, and—as if to make the slide appear endless—3 percent lower in 1933 than in 1932. All told, real national income fell by 36 percent in the four-year period and the per capita loss was even larger in that the population continued to grow during the period.

Historians have looked back over the American past for something equally catastrophic. Some have suggested that the lengthy depression of the 1870s or the very sharp decline in 1839 could have been similar in magnitude. But neither of

---

[7] If the possibility of future profits is somehow destroyed, these are the only salvable assets. The usual option of selling the concern is conditional on prospective buyers' foreseeing future profits from it for themselves.

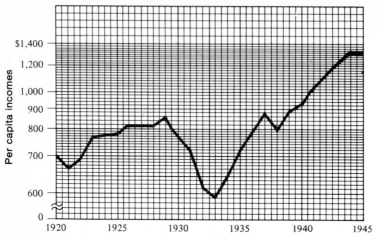

Figure 16-3   Real per capita output, 1920–1945. *(Source: Adapted from U. S. Bureau of the Census,* Historical Statistics of the United States, Colonial Times to 1957, *Government Printing Office, Washington, 1960, p. 139.)*

these two experiences, nor any others, came near the sizeable, sustained losses in real output of the 1930s. The Great Depression was a unique experience for the American economy. Nothing like it had happened before, and, hopefully, given the preventive advantage of hindsight, nothing like it will happen again.

Such great events in history naturally provoke great interest and—given the recent methodological diversity in the practice of history—a great variety of answers. Many explanations have been offered for the Great Depression. However, most of them falter over a rather basic guideline. The experience of the 1930s was an extraordinary economic event. Explanations which build on the operations of forces that are normally present in the economy are very suspect. For example, an obvious and commonly invoked candidate to explain the Great Depression is the crash of the stock market which occurred very near the beginning of the experience. There are several problems with that hypothesis, however. American security, or commodity, markets had been operating on a regular basis for at least a century before 1929. They had experienced numerous, sizeable, sharp declines before. (Citizens of the nineteenth century referred to them as "panics.") The stock market had probably become more important by 1929, but then other forms of assets—trade credit, for example—that were also subject to such fluctuations probably had become less important.

The stock market also appears to be an unlikely explanation for the Great Depression if we look at the probable magnitude of its effects. The fall in security values would have affected the economy through three major channels. First, the decrease in aggregate wealth would have reduced perceived permanent income and, therefore, consumption expenditures. The effect relative to total expenditures of that time, however, would probably have been 1 or 2 percent.[8]

---

[8] There are at least two ways to verify this basic result. First, one knows that the loss of stock value was equal to about one-quarter of prevailing national income. The (now lost) income emanating

Second, another influence would have been the reduction in the incentive to invest, because of the increase in the cost of raising capital by means of new stock. Lower stock prices—at given earnings per share—would raise the effective percentage, or interest, cost of raising funds through new issues of stock. For example, if a share of stock currently representing earnings of $1 a year were selling for $20, the effective rate of return would be 5 percent. Both the company and the stockholders would want to earn at least $1 a year per share on any new investments they financed by selling new shares. Otherwise the return per share would be reduced when the number of shares was increased. If the price per share was to fall to $10—at the same dollar-per-share earnings—then the effective return on the stock would rise to 10 percent. It would then be correspondingly more difficult to devise new investments which would justify the issuance of additional shares.

In any case, the fall in the average level of stock prices only makes that particular form of raising capital more expensive. But there were other ways of obtaining funds for investment, such as through bonds, bank loans, equipment leases, commercial paper, and selling franchises. Most of these methods became less expensive means of raising capital, beginning in the fall of 1929. So acquiring investment funding through stock issues was not much of a roadblock. Actually, the problem in the 1930s was generally just the reverse. There was so little incentive for investment due to depressed economy that available funds went begging.

Third, and finally, the Great Crash is commonly believed to have provoked such feelings of despair that both investment and consumption spending were cut back substantially. The reasoning given for this argument is usually only intuitive. The fall in stock prices is asserted to have been such a traumatic event that large numbers of people must have run for cover, or, more specifically, clamped a fearfully tight grip on their checkbooks. It is difficult to make a reasonable measurement of such a nebulous force, however. At least no one has succeeded yet. But the little insight which economic theory provides on the question suggests that it is not likely to be important. Spending decisions are made for specific items in the context of their price, utility, and possible alternatives, not in the aggregate, amorphous context of whether spending is generally desirable or not. One is more likely to decide to purchase (or delay purchasing) a washing machine on the basis of its price relative to its saving in labor, soap, and household tranquility than on whether the economy appears to be moving up or down. It might be possible to detect such shock effects on an increased savings rate, then. The record suggests just the opposite, however. The savings rate fell. While the shock effect still might have been operating, it would have been more than offset by the influence of falling incomes. With real per capita income dropping by an

---

from this amount of wealth at the prevailing return of 5 percent would equal about 1.25 percent of current income. A second approach is to relate the total capital stock of the economy at a given time to its yearly output. A not unreasonable capital/output ratio for the United States at this time was three to one. Thus, the stock market crash wrote down the total capital stock of the United States by about one-twelfth. If we estimate capital's contribution to national income as about 20 percent at this time, we conclude that income would have been lowered by about 1.66 percent by the stock market crash.

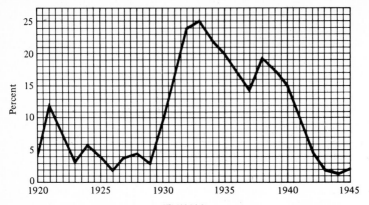

Figure 16-4 Percentage of labor force unemployed, 1920–1945. *(Source: Adapted from U. S. Bureau of the Census, Historical Statistics of the United States, Colonial Times to 1957, Government Printing Office, Washington, 1960, p. 73.)*

average of 12 percent in the four years after 1929, consumers were drawing down their savings rates to keep current consumption levels from falling as dramatically. Saving for a perceived future catastrophe was a luxury Americans could not afford at that time. It took all they had just to cope with the painfully real one they had on their hands already. (See Figure 16-4.)

So the stock market Crash appears to fall well short of explaining the Depression of the 1930s. Some other familiar explanations also fail for much the same reasons—they describe what are actually quite common phenomena that are not likely, therefore, to cause uncommon events. (That is, those that actually existed. Some never occurred outside the unverified speculations of commentators.) For example, one set of explanations emphasized the development of "structural imbalances" in the economy during the twenties, which caused the problems of the thirties. A common variant was to point to the depressed conditions of the farm, railroad, and textile sectors and argue that they constituted a long-term drag on the economy. That is merely selective perception, however, because a growing economy inevitably has declining sectors as well as expanding ones. Although agriculture might not be contributing as much to spending as it had previously, the automobile or electric appliance industries provided an expanding and offsetting, share.

Another common approach is to argue that changes in the distribution of purchasing power among the subgroups in the economy during the 1920s was responsible for much of the distress of the 1930s. For example, because wages did not rise as fast as labor productivity, profits came to absorb a large share of income. The evidence usually offered to support this is incomplete and misleading. By one measure, output per worker-hour in manufacturing was reported to be increasing faster than wages. This might be a correct observation—the representativeness of the estimate is not clear—and still not prove the asserted conclusion. Wages tend to reflect the alternative, marginal uses of labor, not necessarily their average product in a given employment. Gains in labor productivity can be channeled into higher profits—until competition dissipates them—but also into lower product prices to consumers, or to the increase in the use of other factors of production. In fact, the increase of wages and salaries in aggregate was very close to that of the economy as a whole during the 1920s. While profits and entrepreneurial income did increase during the decade, they did so at the cost of lower dividends and unincorporated business income, not that of labor.

Another "structuralist" argument for the Great Depression is that incomes became more unequally distributed during the 1920s. This is seen to have increased savings in that the rich are believed to save a higher portion of their income than do the poor.[9] The portion of income received by the top 5 percent of the population did increase from about 24 percent at the beginning of the expansion in 1922 to 26 percent in 1929. Even if the poor had spent every penny they received while the rich had saved all theirs it would still account for only 2 percent of total income, not nearly enough to account for the nearly 50 percent shortfall in output below its potential by 1933. The argument also suffers from another serious shortcoming—one that it shares with many of the other structuralist explanations—namely, timing. The Depression developed quite suddenly relative to the causes that are advanced to explain it. The change in income distribution, for example, occurred rather gradually. It seems unlikely that its full effect would have appeared suddenly, and for the first time, in the third quarter of 1929.

If we are to find the demon (or demons) which explains the exceptional severity of the Great Depression, therefore, we should probably look among unusual or nonrecurring forces that were at work at this time. One obvious candidate is discretionary economic policies by which we mean programs undertaken by the explicit decisions of policymakers rather than the autonomous results of the economy left to its own lights. The two primary discretionary policies were fiscal—the use of federal taxes and spending to affect the aggregate economy— and monetary, the control of money and credit by the Federal Reserve for the same purpose. We can readily dismiss the first possibility. Even though Herbert Hoover was more sophisticated about economic affairs than he is commonly given credit for, there was no fiscal policy of any consequence from 1929 to 1933. The federal budget did tend to develop a deficit during the period, but only because revenues were falling off as rapidly as the economy. Most contemporaries believed the deficit was due to irresponsible behavior on the part of the government, which would then demoralize the business sector and cause it to postpone anticipated investments (presumably what was left of them, by this time). So in 1932 a tax *increase* was enacted. Through hindsight we now know that such a step was counterproductive, much like a steambath taken to reduce a fever. The appropriate policy would have been a tax *cut* to pump more spending into the economy, creating a deficit as an inevitable by-product. But such a policy was considered perilous, if not downright heresy. The necessity of a bal-

---

[9] This relationship usually appears if one looks at cross-section data, that is, the percentage of income saved out of various levels of income in a given year. This may be only a deceptive, short-term effect, however, in that people who receive unusually high incomes tend to save more while those who suffer unusually low incomes draw down their savings. There is much less evidence that the rich save a higher proportion of their incomes on a permanent basis.

anced budget was so generally accepted that that well-known radical, Franklin Delano Roosevelt, endorsed it in his presidential campaign of 1932. Fiscal policy, even of inadvertent origin, does not explain the Great Depression.

For several decades after the 1930s, monetary policy was also believed to have played a neutral, or insignificant, role in the economic troubles of the 1930s. For example, it was generally accepted that monetary policy had been kept "easy" in the formative years of 1930 to 1933. The evidence offered for this theory commonly included the observations that interest rates were low and loans readily available to qualified borrowers. It therefore followed, because the economy degenerated so badly anyway, that monetary policy must be a weak instrument.

The conclusion was hasty and mistaken. Interest rates were low in a nominal sense, but very high in real terms. Quoted rates of 1 or 2 percent work out to be closer to an actual level of 10 percent when we recognize that prices fell by an average of 8 percent a year from 1929 to 1933. Borrowers might get what appeared to be a low rate on a bank loan, but they would be forced to pay it back in dollars whose value had risen considerably in the meantime. The only way that credit could have been provided cheaply during those traumatic years would have been to have instituted a negative interest rate! Lenders would have had to accept somewhat fewer dollars from borrowers in return for the gain in value of each of the dollars.

Similarly, funds were readily available—at real rates approaching 10 percent, of course—to borrowers who qualified for the prime rate, but the premium for risky borrowers became substantial in these years. (This extreme penalty for risk was caused by the degeneration of the financial system, as we shall see.) The interest rate of B-grade corporate bonds, for example, exceeded 8 percent for almost all of 1932 and 1933. Thus, such a borrower would be paying an effective real rate of more than 16 percent a year. And to make matters worse, it was much more difficult to avoid such penalties by qualifying for the prime rate. In an economy where everything seemed to be coming apart, hardly any businesses, even the most established, seemed completely riskless anymore.

Thus, in real terms, money was expensive from 1929 to 1933. No wonder that bankers reported they had funds available for loans. There were very few opportunities in the troubled economy of that time to use capital whose effective cost ranged from 10 percent to 18 percent annually. Yet the true state of the money eluded many contemporaries of the time, as it has fooled many historians since then. They were so accustomed to small—or even no—changes in the general price level that they continued to think of nominal and real interest rates as being the same thing. Most important, the distinction eluded the Federal Reserve, which held the power and the responsibility for providing the proper amount of money, and as the economy went through the drastic retrenchment of the early 1930s the Federal Reserve continued to believe it was doing all that was within its power to make money and credit readily available. Just how mistaken that judgment was can be seen in our examination of the scenario of the Great Decline.

The Dismal Chronology of the Great Decline

In the first year of the downturn, from autumn 1929 to autumn 1930, real income fell by 12 percent per capita. Yet while its average pace was slowing considerably, the basic structure and functioning of the economy appeared to remain the same. In October 1930, however, a seemingly local banking crisis in the Midwest spread unsettling ripples all across the country before it died out in January 1930. The initial cause was simply a crop failure in the Corn Belt. This proved to be the final blow to a number of banks that had already been weakened by the decade-long problems of their agricultural clients. Of far more significance was that when some panicky depositors in other parts of the country went to withdraw funds from their local banks, they found that some of them had also become vulnerable. When the dust settled, banks with deposits of about $600 million had closed their doors.

In relation to the total economy, $600 million was a small amount, about 3 percent of the money supply in 1930. Yet its repercussions ran far beyond what the direct measure would indicate. The bank panic set off a scramble for liquidity on the part of both the banks and the general public. Banks began to prepare themselves in case their depositors also descended en masse to convert their passbooks into cash. They began rearranging their portfolios, shifting a larger portion of their assets into cash or into securities readily converted into cash, such as government notes. Depositors, who were coming to distrust their bankers as much as the bankers were growing leery of them, also tried to shift out of bank deposits into larger holdings of cash. As a result of this heightened desire for liquidity, the price of assets which were easily converted to cash rose, while those that were illiquid declined. Just before October 1930, for example, interest rates were decreasing on most assets as a result of deflation and the decline in the economy. After the onset of the bank panic, the rates on relatively liquid assets, such as government securities, continued to decrease. However, the rates on assets that were less marketable, such as B-grade corporate bonds, reversed their course and rose. This made the position of the banking system even more difficult and vulnerable. Banks that held such relatively risky securities suffered capital losses as their prices fell.[10] When it came time to raise additional cash to meet the demands of their depositors, or to open their books to the next bank examiner, some discovered that they had become insolvent as well as illiquid.

Conditions deteriorated further in March 1931, when a second banking panic developed, more severe than the first. In the six months from February to August of that year, bank deposits had fallen by $2.7 billion, or 7 percent of their initial amount. The quest for liquidity intensified, with banks attempting to increase their holdings of cash. Everyone tried to dispose of illiquid assets such as mortgages, equipment leases, and lower-grade bonds.

---

[10] Market interest rates and prices on long-term bonds with fixed income payments move in opposite directions. A bond that originally sold for $1,000 and paid a yearly return of 5 percent ($50) would sell for only $500 when prevailing interest rates were 10 percent, because $50 in yearly earnings can be obtained from $500 investment in other assets.

By this time the trend—which was to continue to its bitter end in 1933—was becoming well established. In their understandable quest to protect their assets against the emerging risks of institutional custody, Americans were collectively dismantling their financial sector. Modern banking systems depend on the nearly universal pattern that most assets entrusted to them will not be recalled in the immediate future. They can therefore be committed to longer-term assets, such as mortgages or bonds, with minimum risk. Such leverage allows a financial system to provide a quantity of money and financial assets out of a given monetary base (such as gold) which is several times larger than it could provide if no such system existed. It is a great economizing device while it works. If the general public begins to distrust its safety and stability, however, it can unravel very quickly. And on those rare occasions when it does disintegrate, it can take a good portion of the economy with it. As a sizeable fraction of the banking system failed, or held "holidays," from 1929 to 1933, the money supply of the economy fell by one-third. That reduction and the financial disorganization which accompanied it goes a long way toward explaining the unusual severity of the Great Depression.

Where Were the Fire Fighters?

The breakdown of the monetary system seems even more unfortunate because it could have been prevented. In 1913, Congress had established the Federal Reserve System, a central bank with some characteristically American twists. It was intended for just such eventualities as the Great Decline, with its accompanying banking panics. Yet somehow it never really got into action during those four traumatic years. Part of the reason undoubtedly was that it underestimated the severity of the decline. Even in early 1931, when real income had already fallen more than 15 percent and the banking system was under assault, some board members were observing that panics had the laudable effect of weeding out weak banks.

The same miscalculation was evident in the assessment which the governing board of the Federal Reserve made of its monetary policy. It believed that it was pursuing a very liberal course. After all, the reasoning went, it had reduced the discount rate from 6 percent to 1.5 percent and interest rates in general had fallen to very low levels. By historical standards, such indicators would suggest an easy-money policy, but relative to the extraordinary conditions then prevailing it was instead quite stringent. As we noted, when changes in the price level are included, the real rate of interest had actually *risen*. From a level of about 5 percent in mid-1929 it had doubled to 10 percent by mid-1931.

Furthermore, the Federal Reserve Board could not even take undisputed credit for the fall in interest rates which had occurred. It believed that the ongoing decline reflected the easy-money policy it thought it was following. A decrease in interest rates, it reasoned, came from an increase in the supply of funds. It forgot to check the other side of the market, where demand had fallen drastically as most of the investment opportunities in the economy vanished. The only easy-money policy in operation in early 1931 was a highly selective and perverse one. As the total level of economic and financial activity in the economy fell precipitously, it *was* relatively easy to obtain funding for new projects. Otherwise, as measured by the more comprehensive indicators, money was exceptionally tight. Real interest rates were at their highest levels in American history and the stock of money was fading at a rate which, over the period 1929–1933, averaged 10 percent yearly.

The experience during the Great Decline could have been much less severe and traumatic if the Federal Reserve had adopted a more positive monetary policy. What was called for was a large injection of liquidity into the banking system. If, for example, the Federal Reserve had begun to buy large quantities of bonds, or had actively encouraged member banks to borrow at its rediscount window, the pressure on the banking system would have been correspondingly reduced. Individual banks could have used the liquid assets that would have come flowing into their tills to meet the clammerings of their depositors. It would not have been necessary, therefore, to tear down the entire structure of bank assets in order to obtain the fractional portion of liquidity which such a dismantling yielded. And it would also not have had the side effect of severely reducing the money supply, that crucial medium of exchange in a specialized economy.

Of course, it did not happen that way. The appropriate first aid was not administered and the patient suffered severe, lasting damage. Even worse, while the Federal Reserve failed to do its part, it prohibited the banking system from using the natural defenses it normally used when facing a crisis without external assistance. Throughout the nineteenth century, it was common, accepted practice to "suspend payments" when a bank found itself unable to meet its depositors' demands for cash. This simply meant that a bank would refuse to provide specie (gold coin) in exchange for its own bank notes or checks. The step was taken only infrequently, and then for only short periods, just long enough for a bank to borrow, or to convert assets into cash. Suspension of payments did impose costs on the public; for its duration the normal conduct of business was interrupted. Yet it was generally accepted that the cost was necessary. The alternative was a general dismantling of the financial system which—as the 1930s demonstrated— could be far more severe. With the creation of the Federal Reserve System in 1913, it was noted that suspensions and their costs should no longer be necessary. After all, the new system could be counted to provide the necessary liquidity when the crunch came—and so the Federal Reserve prohibited its member banks from suspending payments. Thereafter, it would be assumed that if a bank failed to meet the legitimate requests of its depositors for cash it was insolvent, and it would be closed permanently and liquidated.

Things might not have been too bad if the Federal Reserve fulfilled its part of the deal. The implied threats of bankruptcy might have made the banks behave a little too conservatively in terms of the efficiency with which they provided financial resources, but the system would be somewhat more resistant to periodic disruptions. It was something like encouraging the passengers to learn how to swim by pointing out that the ship no longer carried lifeboats, but quickly adding that the new captain was absolutely certain he could prevent any possibility of disaster. In fact, of course, the captain proved that he could not recognize a sinking ship even when his own went down under him. The passengers had no hope except to swim for it on their own and, because they had not anticipated that it would be necessary, many of them (read *individual banks*) discovered that they could not make shore and perished in the process. Moral: Do not throw away the lifeboats until you are certain that the captain can cope with any emergency. And a corollary: A central bank which fails to provide the generally expected emergency support for an economy is worse than no central bank at all.

Almost as soon as the second banking crisis began to subside in mid-1931, the economy was buffeted by shock waves from abroad. (See Figure 16-5.) In September 1931, Britain abandoned the gold standard (that is, the direct link between the quantity of domestically held gold and currency). It was widely assumed that the resulting pressure would force the United States to follow suit. As a consequence, holders of dollars began to cash them in for gold, on the assumption that dollars would soon be devalued. But the Federal Reserve moved to support the dollar by raising the rediscount rate and generally tightening monetary conditions, and these steps once again made the dollar more attractive than gold and soon stopped the outflow of the latter. At the same time, however, they made conditions in the domestic economy worse. In effect, the banking system was put through its third major panic in a span of just over a year. In the five months after September 1931, bank deposits fell by 15 percent and the money supply by 12 percent. These work out to phenomenal annual rates of decrease of 36 percent and 29 percent, respectively. Not surprisingly, in 1932 real income was 18 percent below that of 1931.

In the spring of 1932 the Federal Reserve began to entertain the idea that the economy just might be in trouble and could possibly use some help. This inclination was encouraged by pressure from Congress, which was listening to its constituents, especially with elections coming up in the fall.[11] As a result, the FRS at this time undertook its only strong, concerted action to strengthen the economy during the four-year slide. From April to June of 1932 it purchased $1 billion of bonds, pumping an equivalent amount of liquid assets into the banking system. The effect was soon noticeable in that the decline in the money supply fell off to a fraction of its recent rate and industrial production actually began to increase in the late summer. It was a bit too bold an experiment for the Federal Reserve, however, so by the end of the summer they had lapsed back to the usual hands-off monetary (non)policy. The economy was left to follow its own course down to the ultimate end.

In late 1932, the by now well-battered banking system entered yet another crisis. The good news was that it was to be the last one; the bad news that it was

---

[11] There has been considerable debate as to how much insulation a central bank should be afforded from democratically elected governments. The argument for sizeable independence rests on allowing the central bank to provide the "best" monetary policy, unpressured by short-term political partisanship. This particular situation supports the opposite case, however—namely, that strong political influence can be a virtue when it is more responsive to conditions in the economy than is the central bank.

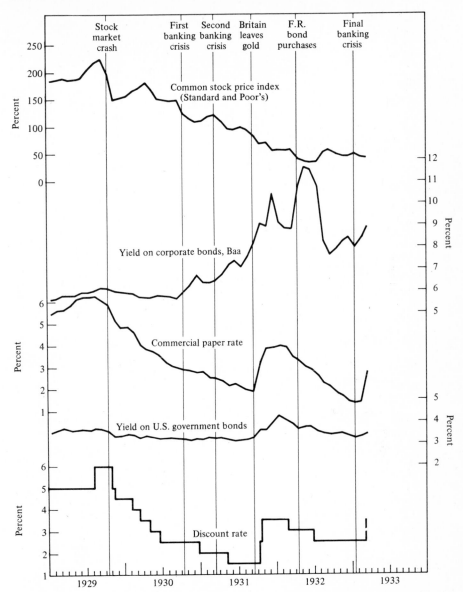

Figure 16-5 Common stock prices, interest yields, and discount rates of Federal Reserve Bank of New York, monthly, 1929 to March 1933. (*Source: Milton Friedman and Anna Jacobsen Schwartz,* The Great Contraction, 1929–1933, *Princeton University Press, Princeton, 1965, p. 8.)*

the worst of them all. (See Figure 16-6.) It was hardly a surprise that another crisis should occur in the financial system about this time. Many of the nation's banks were in shaky condition. Their profits had been reduced and frequently entirely eliminated by falling bond prices, defaulted loans and mortgages, and the necessity of keeping a good portion of their assets in low-return, liquid assets. Furthermore, the populace—with good reason—generally considered the banks risky institutions in which to entrust their assets. So when a few weak banks closed their doors in the fall of 1932, the depositors in the other banks began to descend upon them, anxious to retrieve their assets before the same fate befell them. It was, of course, a self-fulfilling prophecy. When large numbers of people believe that a bank will fail, they act so that it does, in fact, fail. In the absence of external assistance, a modern financial system cannot instantly convert to cash a sizeable portion of its assets that it has committed to long-term obligations.

That external assistance, meaning in this case the Federal Reserve, was not forthcoming. Even worse, the Federal Reserve's preoccupation with the nation's gold stock led it into a policy that intensified the banking panic even further. Franklin Delano Roosevelt had been elected President in November of 1932 and it was generally expected that he would devalue the dollar when he took office—as, indeed, he did. Dollar holders naturally began to switch those assets

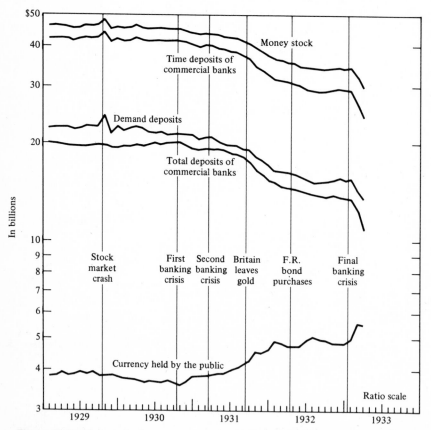

Figure 16-6 Money stock, currency, and commerical bank deposits, monthly, 1929 to March 1933.*(Source: Milton Friedman and Anna Jacobsen Schwartz, The Great Contraction, 1929–1933, Princeton University Press, Princeton, 1965, p. 6.)*

to gold. The Federal Reserve reacted to this in the same way it had to England's departure from the gold standard in 1931. It began applying pressure to the financial markets by raising interest rates and by tightening credit conditions so that it would be more attractive to hold onto dollars. Normally this would have been the correct response, and by 1933 it had become a well-established, almost instinctive reaction of central bankers to such an event. Until this time all major currencies had operated under the gold standard, which meant that the quantity of domestic currency was rigidly linked to the nation's holding of gold. Central banks religiously protected their gold stock because its loss depleted their money supply and depressed the level of domestic economic activity. In the America of early 1933, however, the gold stock was not the key constraint on the financial sector. There was enough gold in the economy to support a much larger volume of money and financial assets. The big roadblock at the moment was the lack of any method of providing the assured liquidity necessary to allow the banking industry to operate normally. And the Federal Reserve's efforts to alleviate the constraint which was least binding at the moment—gold—made the restriction from the most pressing constraint—the liquidity of the banking system—all the more severe.

And during the process the financial system went through one last, massive shake-out. Governors of states whose banks were especially besieged began declaring bank holidays. These were statewide bank closings intended to provide a respite during which weak banks could be consolidated and the remainder could brace themselves for the next onslaught. Throughout February the holidays became more frequent and widespread, and by the first of March half of all states had used them. The state of New York's declaration of a banking holiday on March 4 further disrupted those banks which remained open elsewhere in the economy. It also paralyzed New York City, which served as the wholesale and clearing center for American financial transactions. When Roosevelt took office on March 6, one of his first actions was to declare a national three-day banking holiday to stop the economy's entire banking system from being pulled down by the fast-developing collapse.

In one sense the executive branch was taking over, by default, a function which the Federal Reserve had failed to perform. The bank holidays were a form of payment suspensions whose effect was much like that practiced by individual banks during the panics before 1913. The statewide or nationwide holidays were a blunter tool in that they closed down *all* banks in a jurisdiction rather than only those that were experiencing liquidity deficiencies. Yet the technique worked, in the same basic manner, by relieving the pressure on the banks so that they could have a chance to reorganize their holdings to meet the demands of their depositors. More than all the accusations which critics might hurl at them, the resort to bank holidays is most incriminating to the behavior of the Federal Reserve during this period. Government authorities were, in effect, dictating, as necessary, a technique that the Federal Reserve had banned because, under their administration, it should be no longer necessary.

The bank holidays stopped the worst of the destructiveness, but a lot of damage had already been done. In the first two months of 1933 the money supply fell by 12 percent. Had such a rate continued for the full year, more than three-quarters of the initial money stock would have been destroyed by the year's end! It did not last that long because after the banking holiday stopped the momentum of the panic, it was discovered that the conditions which could propel another one had finally been depleted. A good part of the financial sector as it has commonly appeared in modern times had been dismantled over the preceding four traumatic years. The aggregate balance kept in checking accounts had been sharply reduced as consumers attempted to protect themselves against further possible panics. Financial institutions had similarly reduced their holdings of mortgages, long-term loans, and less liquid categories of bonds in order to be ready for the next onslaught of panicked depositors. From 1929 to 1933 the amount of currency in circulation relative to total bank deposits rose substantially; where it had comprised less than 10 percent of the total money stock in 1929, it had reached 20 percent by early 1933. Such adjustments finally stopped bank runs, but they came at the cost of sizeable losses in efficiency and organization in the economy. As of 1933 it took more resources to provide the same amount of financial services, and, in the process of reaching that point, bank stockholders and depositors had suffered large losses in wealth.

Another by-product of the retrenchment probably had a much more important effect on the aggregate economy, however. In making the shift to a more "panic-proof" banking system, the economy's money supply was slashed by a full third. It is possible for an economy to absorb such a major reduction without undue difficulty if it is given sufficient notice. We saw, for example, that in the thirty-year period from 1865–1895 the money supply fell, relative to the level of output, by a comparable amount. That adjustment, however, proceeded through the reasonably smooth, gradual process of reducing prices by about 2 percent a year. Individuals had time to adapt themselves to the ongoing deflation and to build it into their commitments in prices, wages, and interest rates. From 1929 to 1933 there was no such opportunity. The fall in prices came suddenly and irregularly. The year-to-year decreases in the four years after 1929 were 2 percent, 7 percent, 17 percent, and 12 percent, respectively. Businesses and individuals caught by such unanticipated reductions in the prices of goods with which they were involved were subject to disorganization and losses.

Actually the unanticipated fall in prices was only part of the severe wrenching that the economy was being put through. As the total volume of money and related financial assets contracted, there were correspondingly fewer dollars serving as the economy's purchasing power. If the average level of prices had fallen immediately at the same rate as the supply of monetary assets, it would have remained sufficient to purchase the same real volume of goods and services. Prices did not fall that rapidly, however, because it takes much longer than the duration of the Great Decline for such a major adjustment.

The first, immediate effect of the reduction in the money supply was that there was much less spending money available. Managers of individual enterprises saw this as a reduction in the demand for their particular products, and they were soon forced to adjust in the only ways open to them—reducing output and and discharging resources. This, of course, then led to secondary multiplier effects. The wages and dividends lost when the first-round of repercussions was felt implied that much less spending in the second and subsequent rounds, so that further resources would be idled. All this unemployment and retrenchment resulted because the contraction initially came as a surprise to most parties. If the prices of all goods and resources were to fall immediately, at the same rate that the money supply was contracting, the same total amount of output could continue to be sold. Prices in money terms would be lower, but all real variables, such as income and consumption, would be unaffected.

Prices cannot adjust that rapidly, however, for at least two reasons. First, most contracts and financial obligations are specified in dollar values. Such values cannot be scaled down in proportion to the reduction in total money supply without violating their basic function. If, for example, the outstanding balance of a mortgage were to be written down, the creditor would be subject to arbitrary losses. Since a developed economy normally has a sophisticated array of such financial contracts whose maturities stretch decades into the future, instantaneous adjustments cannot be made without creating immense havoc in the economy. If that were allowed, economic units would not make the long-term commitments so productive in organizing resources. But with that profile of financial assets trailing off well into the future, it takes a long time before all assets can catch up to any current change.

Second, it is difficult to keep prices and output decisions in line with up-to-the-minute conditions simply because it is not easy to tell what the latter actually are. If the demand for steel falls off this month, does that reflect a permanent reduction in the demand for it, requiring production cutbacks and perhaps price reductions, or is it merely a random occurrence, such as when a good number of purchasing agents go on vacation at the same time?

It takes some time to adjust to a single, overall price decrease. When they come irregularly, as well as in rapid succession, as they did from 1929 to 1933, however, it makes management of economic units much more difficult. And in many ways that overwhelming character of economic decline probably best summarizes the experience of the great contraction. Individuals were faced with a rapid falloff in aggregate demand, an almost complete immobilization of the money and credit system, and the uncertainty as to when—indeed, whether—the economy would ever bottom out. It finally did, of course, but by then the damage had reached historically huge proportions.

THE LONG CLIMB BACK UP

When the economy finally bottomed out in March 1933, Americans could take consolation in one thing anyway: there was now a lot of potential to increase output. Furthermore, the usual historical rules seemed to be working for them. The American economy has tended to recover from specific depressions at about

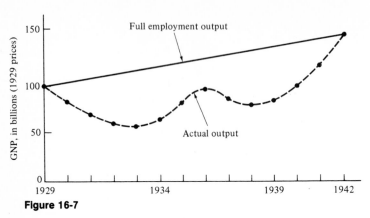

Figure 16-7

the same pace that it entered them. If this were to be the case this time, there would be a dramatic period of growth. The economy had taken slightly less than four years to reach its depressed state in 1933 and so, by the usual dynamics, it should return to full employment sometime in 1937. That would imply four consecutive years in which real incomes would increase by better than 10 percent. It was a pleasing prospect, especially in the context of conditions at that time.

It was not to be, however. In 1937 the economy was still operating at only 80 percent of its total capacity and, to add insult to injury, it began another minidepression on top of its already depressed state. It was not until 1942, in obvious response to war-related spending for World War II, that the economy finally reached full employment. (See Figure 16-7.) That was nine years after 1933, not the four that might have been expected. Some set of forces appeared to have been operating to retard normal recovery. That is surprising, especially because accounts of the 1930s usually emphasize how much aid the economy was given to increase its output. The federal government undertook innumerable programs to put spending and economic stimulation into the economy. Unfortunately, intentions and results are not necessarily the same thing, as we shall see as we examine the decade in more detail.

The federal government did increase its total spending after 1933. It began a large number of programs to aid specific sectors of the economy and it consistently reported deficits in the official budget. Yet the net effect of all this activity on the aggregate level of the economy was not positive. This surprising result was demonstrated by E. Cary Brown in a study that has by now become a minor classic. Brown's work has been scrutinized and extended since its original publication, but its basic finding has emerged in even stronger form.[12] The structure of

[12] The original work is E. Cary Brown, "Fiscal Policy in the Thirties: A Reappraisal," *American Economic Review*, December 1956. Reprinted with omissions in Robert W. Fogel and Stanley L. Engerman (eds.), *The Reinterpretation of American Economic History*, Harper & Row, New York, 1971. The most important extension of Brown's work is reported by Larry C. Pepper, "Full-Employment Surplus Analysis and Structural Change: The 1930's," *Explorations in Economic History*, Winter 1973.

federal taxes and expenditures was such that they would tend to develop a surplus and retard the expansion of the economy as it moved toward full employment. The reported budget deficit was actually only a by-product of the massive contraction in the economy, and was created by the correspondingly large falloff in revenues (what economists call the built-in stabilizer effect). As the economy rose above that deflated level, however, taxes grew faster than expenditures, thus creating a surplus and pulling back on total economic activity well before full employment was reached. For the ten years from 1930 to 1939 the average surplus at the full employment level exceeded 1 percent of GNP. Only in one year, 1937, did the budget contribute a deficit to the recovery. Furthermore, state and local governments ran consistent surpluses after 1933, thereby reinforcing the retarding tendency.

MONETARY POLICY, 1933–1941

Nor did the Federal Reserve provide the economy with much assistance during the recovery phase of the Depression. It continued its "above the battle" stance of neutrality, not making much more effort against the distress around it than it had during the decline. In one sense it was not quite as important after 1933. The effective range of the Federal Reserve's responsibility had been narrowed as the federal government had stepped into those areas where the central bank had recently failed to prevent severe disorganization. We have already noted the resort to bank holidays. To that should be added the creation of a series of federal funding agencies, such as the Reconstruction Finance Corporation (RFC), which provided government-backed loans to banks, state and local governments, railroads, and other businesses; and the Home Owners' Loan Corporation, which guaranteed mortgages of urban housing. These intermediaries either issued their own long-term securities or backed those issued by private financial companies. In either case they guaranteed the value and thereby ensured the liquidity of a range of long-term financial assets that had proven particularly vulnerable in the monetary distress from 1930 to 1933.

The federal government's most dramatic expansion into the monetary sector was probably the devaluation of gold in 1933. By raising the price of gold in terms of dollars—thereby cheapening it relative to other currencies—Roosevelt hoped to increase American exports, particularly farm products. The move undoubtedly had some effect in that direction, although devaluations elsewhere, and the generally depressed state of the nation's most important international trade, made it difficult to sell much of anything anywhere in those days. A less anticipated effect of devaluation was to substantially increase the stock of gold on which the nation's money supply was based. The act of raising the dollar price of gold in and of itself increased the monetary base of the United States from $4 billion to nearly $7 billion, directly. After 1933 the advantages of holding wealth in dollars—partly because of the devaluation, but also certainly because of turmoil in much of the rest of the world—swelled the nation's gold stock to nearly $23 billion by 1942. Historically, such a huge influx would have been directly transformed into a larger domestic money supply. And in the depressed conditions of the 1930s it would certainly have given aggregate demand a major push, thereby reducing unemployment. That effect had been considerably weakened, however, because at the time of devaluation gold had been taken out of circulation as money in the United States. Thus, as the "golden avalanche" of gold poured into the country during the middle and late 1930s, it was effectively insulated from any significant effect on the economy and merely piled up in Fort Knox.

The increase in the gold supply was prevented from increasing the domestic money supply, and the Federal Reserve made no attempt to increase it through the banking system. From 1934 to 1937 the Federal Reserve failed to increase its holdings of government bonds, a step which would have improved the lending potential of the banks. Almost all the increase in bank reserves in this four-year period took the form of financial assets created by the new federal agencies. In fact, most of the explicit actions the Federal Reserve took had a retarding effect on the recovery of the economy. In 1936 and 1937, for example, it increased reserve requirements. It was concerned about an old bugaboo—inflation. This at a time when unemployment had just dropped below 15 percent for the first time in more than six years! The relapse the economy underwent in 1937 and 1938 must be at least partly attributed to that action.

THE NEW DEAL

One other force, in addition to monetary and fiscal policy, was going to intrude into the day-to-day functioning of the economy during its recovery period. In March 1933, the month in which the economy reached its lowest level, Franklin Delano Roosevelt was inaugurated President. That was not entirely coincidence. FDR's election was obviously an expression of discontent with the current state of the economy and a strong mandate for something to be done. From the vantage point of more recent years, Roosevelt and his program would seem to be moderate, merely advocating a role for government which has by now become commonplace. In 1932 and 1933, however, he was considered somewhat of a radical, albeit a necessary one perhaps, considering the prevailing distressed conditions. He ran on a platform not only of economic recovery, but also of economic reform. In the early 1930s it was easy to believe that economic troubles of the prevailing magnitude could be explained only by some basic defect in the economy. The prescription, therefore, was a structural reform appropriate to the particular defect that the observer believed he detected. And thus, when FDR turned his attention to the economy, he was attempting not only to revive it but also to remodel it.

Roosevelt's "first hundred days" have since been singled out as one of the most active periods of the federal executive in American history. Within a few months—an extremely rapid pace by the usual standards of a large bureaucracy—programs had been initiated to attempt to alleviate the distress of most major sectors of the economy. Efforts were designed to bail out banking, agriculture, industry, and homeowners, among others. So many such programs were created within such a short time that people simply began to refer to them by their initials. There were, for example, the AAA, NIRA, NRA, FERA, CWA, PWA, CCC, WPA, RFC, and so forth. And soon thereafter people understandably began to refer to the total collection of New Deal programs as "alphabet soup."

The Roosevelt administration preferred to think of its programs as *salve* rather than *soup*. It was trying to reduce the current distress of various sectors in the hope that it would aid recovery, or at least make things easier until recovery occurred. Although at first most of the programs were considered temporary, many of them developed more permanent features when the problems of specific sectors failed to disappear. And there were distressingly large numbers of such persistent problems. The underlying cause of most of these troubled sectors lay in the generally depressed state of the aggregate economy itself, and until that situation was remedied the efforts in the specific areas would be little more than displacing problems from one sector to another.

For example, take agriculture, which was everyone's first candidate for the distressed list because of its well-publicized problems ever since 1920. In an attempt to aid it, the New Deal introduced the Agricultural Adjustment Act (AAA). This was the forerunner of most subsequent American farm programs in that it tried to raise the farmers' incomes by increasing the prices they received for their produce. This was done by guaranteeing the price of their products above the price they would normally receive on the free market. The program could be accomplished either by having the government act as a buyer of last resort, picking up all unsold produce on the market at the guaranteed price, or by paying farmers *not* to plant crops—a kind of "soil bank." Both methods were used in the 1930s. And both were helpful in working toward the goal of the AAA program, namely, raising the income of the farm sector. Unfortunately, that was not its only effect. Higher food prices, which benefited farmers, hurt consumers. In effect, the nonfarm populace was being forced to subsidize the farm sector through a reduction in its own real income. In addition, taxpayers had to pick up the federal subsidy which made the program possible. If the government had financed the program by running a deficit, thus tending to increase the nation's total output at the same time, the real cost of its intervention would have been less. But, as we have seen, the federal government worked to balance its budget and, as a consequence, each program funded out of Treasury funds took an equivalent amount of expenditure away from other sectors.

Then there was the National Recovery Act (NRA), or the "Blue Eagle" as it came to be known—after the emblem which firms placed on their door to indicate compliance. This program was intended to eliminate the instability and uncertainty believed to be hindering the recovery of most sectors of the economy by convening a board representing business, labor, and consumers for each specific sector. Their task was to work out a plan of prices, output, and employment on which all parties could depend with some assurance and, therefore, make commitments for the future. Such boards were duly organized, conducted their deliberations, and announced their plans. But things did not quite work out as expected. In the first place, the power of the various groups represented on the boards tended to reflect their vested interests in the proceedings. Almost always the business representatives dominated and shaped the board's deliberations. Labor representatives usually succeeded in obtaining some concessions for their constituency, but consumer interests were mostly ignored. The typical plan resulting from these deliberations shared the following features: higher prices and reduced aggregate output for the producers, and higher wages at frequently reduced working hours for the employees. In retrospect, these results are hardly surprising. The boards of the NRA allowed the participating industries to do exactly what the antitrust laws had been shaped to prevent over the past forty years: explicitly collaborate to make monopoly profits. The pattern of the industry-by-industry agreements suggests that is precisely what occurred. Producers raised prices and reduced output, as monopolists would be expected to behave vis-à-vis a more competitive industry. Labor representatives also appeared to be following the same tactics in their positions, perhaps also appropriating some of the monopoly gains of the producers in order to provide the necessary appearance of unanimity for the industry accord. Even so, the actual effect of the NRA was fairly obvious to anyone who examined it carefully. In 1935 the Supreme Court declared it unconstitutional and a subterfuge to bypass the antitrust laws.

Its passing was not widely mourned because by that time it had become clear that, whatever its effects on the competitiveness within industries, it was not aiding the recovery of the economy. In fact, if its actual operation is considered dispassionately, it was likely to be judged a net retardant. Its primary effect was to make a number of industries less competitive. It is by now a well-established axiom in economics that monopolies—compared with competitive markets—reduce total output by misallocating society's stock of resources. That is the long-term effect, after all adjustments are completed. The short-term effect is to reduce both output and employment of resources in the monopolized industry. This displacement is eventually offset by increases elsewhere, but the immediate effect is to reduce national income.

Today the practice of raising prices in the face of widespread unemployment would seem rather curious. One of the factors which made the practice tolerated, even supported, at the time of the NRA was the widespread belief in the necessity of "reflation" to restore the economy to full employment. Since prices had fallen so much in the decline, it was assumed they must return to their original levels if the levels of output were to do likewise. That view not only confuses cause and effect but also, if used as a guide for policy, is counterproductive. In one sense the cause of the Great Depression was—as we saw—that prices had not fallen *enough* during the downturn. If the average level of all resources and product prices had fallen at the same rate as the money supply, aggregate demand and aggregate supply could continue to be equalized at the full employment level of output.

Furthermore, it is not necessary for prices to rise for the economy to return to production at its capacity level. If aggregate demand increases until all the possible output can be "bought back" at existing prices, full employment will be achieved. Raising prices under the NRA, therefore, tended to counteract recovery. With higher prices and no increase in aggregate demand, fewer products could be bought.

Finally, in 1936, there was the establishment of the Social Security Administration. It, perhaps more than any other single program of the New Deal, illustrates the problem of achieving the joint goals of recovery and social restructuring. Social Security was set up to provide a variety of insurance services—retirement, disability, and support of dependents—which were believed to be important and were not being provided otherwise. Whatever the merits of Social Security as a device to promote social objectives—obviously a large question in itself, and one that can be, and has been, argued at length—it had a retarding effect on the recovery of the economy at the time of its creation. Like most insurance or annuity plans, it operates by first taking in premiums, or contributions, in the period when eligibility is established, and then paying out benefits later as the circumstances warrant. Thus, it is hardly surprising that in its early years the Social Security fund ran a surplus. It began to receive contributions in the late 1930s, but hardly anyone could yet qualify for benefits. Whatever its social desirability, the middle of the Depression was not an auspicious time to initiate the program.

This discussion of specific programs introduced during the New Deal could be continued at considerable length. We could add minimum wages, banking regulations, Tennessee Valley Authority (TVA), labor union legislation, and public works. Yet all that additional detail is not likely to change the basic appraisal of the New Deal that has emerged so far. Despite all the activity and new initatives accompanying it, Roosevelt's administration did not aid the recovery of the economy after 1933. In fact, a complete appraisal would probably report that it was a net hindrance. Without it, the economy would have done a little better.

This finding is surprising; or at least it contradicts most of the standard histories of the period. It also runs counter to a widely held opinion at that time, namely that "things are so bad that anything you do would help." Flailing around at random, however, does not always help. It makes considerable difference whether you are clearing brush or performing brain surgery. The appraisal that "anything will help" probably came from the view that part of the problem in getting out of the Depression was psychological. Things had continued to grow worse for so long that people were numbed and unwilling to spend or invest any longer. In fact, fear was not the effective barrier to recovery, however much people were troubled. They were spending every cent available to them. In 1933, net saving in the economy dropped to zero. Because the GNP had fallen so drastically, the income earned in the process of creating it was also severely reduced, and until spending could somehow be increased, the Depression would remain, fear or no fear.[13]

---

[13] This view of the nature of the Depression is well expressed in Roosevelt's famous slogan: "The only thing we have to fear is fear itself." Actually, what the nation should have feared was *believing* that fear was the only thing to fear. The Depression could be overcome only by real spending, no matter how much confidence people had that things would become better.

The basic problem was that for the economy to have made a rapid recovery to full employment in the 1930s would have required a big push from something outside its normal day-to-day functioning. The private sector was able to make some recovery independent of—or perhaps in spite of—the lack of a favorable environment, but only the federal government could have feasibly provided the necessary massive effort. It has been frequently suggested that Roosevelt was beginning to catch on to this imperative in the late 1930s. His meeting with Lord Keynes, the father of modern macroeconomics, is noted, as are the federal budget deficits of those years. Yet these appearances are superficial; the underlying record of the period contradicts them. The federal budget was consistently restrictive, as our discussion has demonstrated. In retrospect, it is clear that much of the waste of the 1930s could have been avoided by the simple expedient of large budget deficits. But that, of course, was not practiced until the exigency of World War II forced them upon us. By then the lesson was very obvious, if a little late.

By this measure, most of the programs of the New Deal were wasted motion insofar as recovery was concerned. While Roosevelt may have been considered a radical by some, he was not radical enough in the one crucial dimension. This is a harsh judgment and we should temper it with the recognition that we can be so dogmatic only in hindsight. If we were now living in the late 1930s, the necessity of running a large budget deficit would be much less obvious than it is today. At that time, Keynes notwithstanding, the economics profession was just beginning to work out the relations between aggregate output and public policy. And even if public leaders in the late 1930s had clairvoyantly grasped the essentials of what has since become generally accepted knowledge, they would have had a difficult task in convincing the public to accept it. Roosevelt should no more be blamed for not using deficit spending against the Depression than Nero should be for allowing Rome to burn because he would not use chemical fire extinguishers. The knowledge necessary to overcome a depression as severe as that of the 1930s was simply not yet generally available.

THE LESSONS OF THE THIRTIES: MONETARY AND FISCAL POLICY SINCE 1941

Perhaps the most important long-term result of the Depression was that the knowledge of how to overcome a contraction of that magnitude has since become generally available. The experience of the 1930s made economists go back to their drawing boards. Until 1929 they had commonly assumed that modern economies were self-righting. Subjected to such severe shocks as major changes in business conditions, or the money supply, it was believed that any modern economy soon returns to its full employment level of output without external aid. That view is still probably true within the normal range of fluctuations. The problem was that the experience of the 1930s was well outside the normal range—undoubtedly because, in that case, the exogenous forces tended to make it even worse. Economists had not yet built the possibility of perverse behavior by the central bank into their models.

In any case, a good part of the resources of the economics profession has since been channeled into improving what is now known as macroeconomics. Economists have worked out more carefully the relations between aggregate consumption, saving, investment, output, employment, and so forth. Like any other active body of knowledge, some behavior still remains puzzling and unexplained. Yet development of macroeconomics has proceeded well beyond the level of the problem that instigated it as a distinctive field. We now almost certainly understand macroeconomic relations well enough so that we could prevent an economic collapse of the magnitude of the Great Depression. This is not to say that we can prevent all economic fluctuations, nor that the powers which control levers of public policy will necessarily respond appropriately. We do know, however, the appropriate monetary and fiscal policies in such circumstances, and the order of magnitude in which each should be supplied.

We also know, now that we understand how to look for such things, that monetary and fiscal policies did work—albeit applied perversely—in the 1930s. They were applied for reasons other than those which would motivate such actions today, and sometimes they were unknowingly applied so as to be counterproductive to the objectives sought, but they did work. Large-scale changes on the money supply—the techniques of monetary policy—were employed once. From 1928 to 1933 the money supply was substantially and steadily reduced, and the result was correspondingly large decreases in both output and prices. The policy was exactly the opposite to that which we would have recommended in hindsight, but it did demonstrate that the mechanism of monetary policy is sufficiently potent to accomplish what we might ask of it. Fiscal policy also was given an inadvertent demonstration. The Depression ended when the economy was converted to a wartime footing and the federal government decided—for reasons independent of this question—to finance the war primarily through borrowing rather than through increased taxes. In short, we can attribute a good part of the behavior of the economy during those unfortunate years to bad monetary and fiscal policies. Rather than suggesting that the economy malfunctioned in some basic way, the record indicates that it was public policy that went awry. The experience of that period underlines the importance of understanding and applying the tools of economic policy.

Events since 1945 suggest that Americans have absorbed that lesson quite well. The federal government committed itself by the Employment Act of 1946 to seek to maintain full employment. It simultaneously established the Council of Economic Advisors to aid the President in formulating economic policy. In 1964, for the first time, taxes were cut to explicitly stimulate the economy. Since that step all major components of the political spectrum of the nation have come to embrace the principle of government responsibility for aggregate economic output. Of course there is still disagreement about the specific goals to be achieved, or, more precisely, the relative importance of each, but all parties agree that the government *should* be the self-initiating shock absorber for the economy.

In one way the lesson has been learned too well. Since 1964 there has been a noticeable tendency for the public to expect more of countercyclical policy than it can reasonably deliver. After the apparant success of the tax cut in stimulating the economy in 1964,[14] public officials, frequently with the encouragement of their economic advisors, sought to "fine tune" the economy. The plan was to squeeze the last fractional amount of unemployment out of the economy while at the same time avoiding possible side effects, such as more inflation or larger balance-of-payments deficits. A new group of tools was introduced in an attempt to provide greater flexibility and to reduce the lag in getting at the problems of the economy compared to the "heavy weapons" of fiscal and monetary policy. Thus, such now familiar devices as wage-price guidelines, "jaw-boning," and workforce-retraining programs, among others, appeared. Generally, the results of these programs has proved to be disappointing. Exhortations to the public or to specific sectors of the economy to spend—or not to spend—or to practice price "restraint," were largely ignored or circumvented. The programs designed to attack the problems of specific sectors did not move through the federal decision hierarchy any faster than matters of fiscal policy could. The "last small amount" of unemployment proved to be highly resistant to these new weapons.

Fiscal policy was not used much after its successful introduction in 1964. A tax surcharge (effectively, an increase in taxes) was imposed in 1968, but because it had been well anticipated and was announced as temporary it did not seem to have much effect. Generally, fiscal policy proved to be such a slow and unwieldly device to enact within the federal government that interest in it waned. In contrast, monetary policy seemed to gain in favor as the 1960s passed. Partly in response to some of the findings about the role of money in the 1930s that we have reported, it became commonly accepted that "money matters." In the late 1960s the Federal Reserve shifted to a more expansionary policy of a faster growth in the money supply. Unemployment was reduced somewhat, but prices seemed to increase even faster. In 1969 the Federal Reserve reversed itself, preventing the money supply from increasing at all for more than a full year. The result was a sharp rise in unemployment, but only a slight falloff in inflation. Once more the Federal Reserve shifted back to an easy-money policy.

By this time the result was fairly predictable. Employment responded a little, but most of the effect of the monetary policy appeared to be going into higher prices. "Fine tuning" was simply not working. It was to be given one more try, however. In mid-1971, in response to historically high inflation and the immediate problem of a run on the American dollar in foreign exchange markets, a comprehensive system of price controls was instituted. As most economists would

---

[14] While the upsurge in the economy during the 1964 experience clearly coincided with the effects which would have been expected to come from the tax cut, there were other factors at work at the same time. For example, it has been noted that the money supply also increased rapidly during the same period. So, until a more careful appraisal is made of the economy during this time, a more definitive judgment will have to wait.

have predicted, it proved extremely complex and difficult to manage. When it did succeed in holding prices below their equilibrium levels, it merely converted pressure for price increases into other forms of costs, such as shortages. When it expired in 1974, few mourned its passing.

Hence, in the mid-1970s, monetary and fiscal policy was back to where it started in 1964. Despite all the effort, "fine tuning" remains an unattained goal, not a functioning technique. Therefore, the problem of fluctuations in the aggregate level of economic activity is subject to the same basic constraint we have detected throughout the past—economic knowledge. Until we know more about such forces as lags, credit mechanisms, spending determinants, and so on, we will therefore be forced to bear the costs of these major fluctuations in economic activity.

SUGGESTED READINGS

Brown, E. Cary: "Fiscal Policy in the Thirties: A Reappraisal," *American Economic Review,* vol. 46, December 1956.

Chandler, Lester V.: *America's Greatest Depression, 1929–1941,* Harper & Row, New York, 1970.

Friedman, Milton and Anna Jacobson Schwartz: *The Great Contraction, 1929–1933,* Princeton, Princeton, N. J., 1965.

Gordon, Robert A.: *Economic Instability and Growth: The American Record,* Harper & Row, New York, 1974.

Mitchell, Broadus: *Depression Decade: From New Era Through New Deal, 1932–1940,* Harper & Row, New York, 1969.

North, Douglass C.: *Growth and Welfare in the American Past,* 2d ed., Prentice-Hall, Englewood Cliffs, N. J., 1973, Chapter 13.

Soule, George H.: *Prosperity Decade,* Holt, New York, 1947.

Stein, Herbert: *The Fiscal Revolution in America,* The University of Chicago Press, Chicago, 1969.

Scarcity Continued: Timeless Problems in a Modern Setting

Most people instinctively believe that they can deduce something useful about the present and the future if they can understand the past. In most cases this view is an untested assumption—in certain cases it almost amounts to an article of faith—but it is based on the seemingly plausible premise that the forces which propel history are reasonably continuous over time so that if one discerns them in the context of past events, it is easier to decipher what is developing in the present. This view of history as productive prologue is summed up in Santayana's dictum that "those who forget the past are compelled to relearn it." That evaluation of the use of history is not unanimous, of course. Some people are naturally skeptics, and others have been disillusioned by a barrage of conflicting claims by advocates who have used history to support their positions about current events. The doubters would probably agree with Carlyle's assessment that "history does not repeat itself, only historians repeat each other." Or this evaluation might be summed up in Henry Ford's succinct comment that "history is bunk."

Oddly enough, both views probably have some truth to them. The problem is to discern which guideline applies in a given case. Like any other discipline, or field of knowledge, there is a range of unresolved questions in history. Historians can no more completely explain all past events than physicists can explain what happens to matter which disappears into "black holes" or medical researchers can avoid catching the common cold. Hence, one should take a careful, searching look at the logic which underlies any assertion that history "proves" something in a given circumstance. Whether or not the past tells us anything useful about the present depends on how skillfully and completely the narrator has matched the specific circumstances in the contemporary case with a set of parallel conditions in the historical case, or cases. All individuals who cite historical precedents to support their case are implicitly practicing such a procedure. The crucial measure of their efforts, however, is how completely and accurately they have constructed that analog.

There are two basic ways to go about this process of using history to illuminate the present. One is the labor-intensive method of constructing detailed, exact parallels; that is, to carefully comb history to find situations which were closely comparable to the current situation which one wishes to examine. This usually runs up against the problem that two situations are seldom exactly alike and therefore the investigator is forced to estimate the importance of the differing elements. At this point the historian is, in effect, shifting to the use of the other basic method of historical inquiry, which is theory. Theory is simply specified rules, or relationships, which are believed to hold over a given range of situations. It is not, of course, or should not be, constructed in a vacuum. Rather, it is a generalization of facts or relationships observed in other situations. In other words, it is a substitution of facts in other cases for the ones which are missing in the specific case in question. This suggests that the usefulness of a theory depends on how carefully and comprehensively it has been tailored to the facts in those other situations. And our ability to explain historical occurrences depends on how well the theory we use is constructed.

For example, throughout this text we have used a few basic tenets of economics, sometimes implicitly, to help explain the common economic dilemmas which each group or individual has faced at each time in the past. These guidelines indicate that in each situation the parties involved would have interpreted and responded to those problems in certain predictable ways. This is not to say that we can completely predict the result of those responses, however, but rather that in the economic sphere we expect certain basic efforts to continually appear.

Two of those basic responses have appeared quite frequently in the course of this text. Both are fairly direct results of the underlying economic fact of scarcity. When people wish to consume more in the way of output than the resource base of the economy allows, they must choose that which they will actually consume and that which they must necessarily forgo. This is the basic nature of costs—that the forgone alternatives are relinquished in the course of choosing a given expenditure, or course of action. Such decisions must inevitably be made, somewhere and somehow, in any society where scarcity prevails—which includes every one about which we have minimal information so far. Individuals, or groups of individuals, are not apt to look at the question so stoically, however. They see costs as a direct problem to themselves, and often realize that goods, or privileges, which others have could be shifted to themselves. Thus the pressures of scarcity caused the farmers to direct their ire against the manufacturers or the railroads, and caused the American colonists to contend with their mother country over the right to tax and control local governments. Scarcity, in short, makes each generation believe that it is up against a set of problems unique to itself. Certain *specific* problems might be confined to a given group, or era, but problems in general are universal.

The second implication of scarcity is that not only does it force individuals to confine their consumption within the currently feasible limits, but it also encourages them to attempt to expand those limits. In other words, innovation is also a common response to normal economic conditions. An important by-product of this reaction and the one which is so important in economic history is the consequent changes it induces into the economy. We may not be able to predict in what form successful innovations will appear, but we can safely predict that they, just like economic situations which contemporaries define as problems, will constantly reappear. Thus, while our basic conception of economic history does not help us predict in advance what problems or innovations will occur, it does indicate that some of both will almost certainly be present.

One test of these generalizations, or theory, lies readily at hand. Current or recent developments in the economy can serve as a kind of minitest of the proposition that economic behavior remains basically the same, resulting in similar manifestations. Consider the two explicit predictions which our experience of prior economic history suggests should be present: problems and innovative responses. Does such behavior continue into the present, or alternatively, does its absence suggest that that particular model, or theory, has limited usefulness?

MODERN PROBLEMS

It does not take an expert in historical patterns to confirm that the participants in the modern American economy believe that they, too, are—or have been—facing a number of pressing economic problems. Over the last three decades there has been considerable concern over unemployment and inflation, food prices, natural resource supplies, poverty, balance of payments deficits, pollution and environmental quality, and a series of problems of larger metropolitan areas lumped under the common rubric of urban decay. The list is far from complete, but what they all share is the characteristic that if scarcity were to disappear, most of the problems themselves would also vanish. For example, the concern about unemployment would be unnecessary if all people had command of all the resources they desired. There would be no pressure to find a job because there would be no sacrifice from not having one. If some people felt that certain activities which are now commonly considered work were actually creative and pleasurable, then without any constraints on the resources available to them, they could simply enjoy those activities for themselves. In the absence of requirements to work, any activity which people engage in would become recreation. Similar considerations apply to the contemporary concern over inflation. If we had all the goods and services we desired, prices would cease to have any meaning in that they would not perform any rationing function. If, out of force of habit, they were kept on goods after scarcity ceased, the most that inflation probably would do would be to amuse people as they observed those little numbers becoming larger.

Thus, in the absence of scarcity—that is, the population desiring more goods than it is collectively capable of producing—many of the problems which individuals, and governments, spend so much time struggling with would simply disappear. Indeed, many of the conflicts which are not entirely economic would be considerably muted as well. Consider the problem of racial discrimination, which results in costs to individuals' sense of self-esteem as well as to their range of economic choices. If there were no scarcity, however, discrimination would not have such a severe bite. Without the economic pressure to compel people to compete for jobs, or housing, or education, there would be that much less opportunity for discrimination to operate. In fact, while it might continue, minorities would have the resources to sidestep entirely the activities where it existed, if they so wished. Or take the case of that other perpetual worry of nations, their foreign relations. A considerable portion of the aggressive drive would probably drop out of nations' policies if the economic gains they "won" were useless and, moreover, if they could use some of their own overabundance of goods to buy out the aggressiveness of their neighbors.

While these examples help to clarify just why it is that social problems exist, they also strongly suggest why they are so intractable and likely to persist into the foreseeable future. And a close look at some of the problems which were considered to be the most severe in recent years suggests that problems are just as likely to be found in an economy with high incomes as in one with much lower incomes.

Poverty in a Wealthy Society

If one wishes a clear example of higher incomes fostering a problem, consider the ironic case of poverty in the American economy. In recent years the United States has had one of the highest per capita incomes in the world, even considering recent declines in the value of the dollar vis-à-vis other major currencies which have tended to make direct comparisons less favorable. Yet beginning in the early 1960s a sizeable portion of the electorate became concerned about the poor in their midst. What is striking about the emergence of this "problem" is that Americans were setting standards of poverty which were considerably above the average income of most of the rest of the world, and even further above what citizens of those economies would consider poverty. The official American standard of poverty in the mid-1970s was calculated at about $4,500 a year for a family of four in an urban area. This was not particularly generous in terms of prevailing living standards. It provided a small apartment, nutritious but not particularly appetizing food, and some amounts for utilities, clothes, and bus fares. With such an income it would be very difficult to own an automobile, buy medical insurance, pay average doctor and dentist bills, purchase life or disability insurance, make contributions to a pension plan for retirement income, or buy anything in the way of entertainment or vacations other than perhaps a few paperbacks and a television set.

Poverty is relative. People generally perceive it in relation to what they see as normal, or standard, levels. That, in turn, is obviously influenced by the levels of income and consumption which they, and those they see around them, enjoy. It is true that two-thirds of the world's population lives on incomes of $500 a year or less—a fraction of the official definition of poverty in the United States. Americans do not see those individuals very often, however, and even if they are told that such conditions exist, they find it hard to think of that rather amorphous group as their neighbors. There is another, more direct, example of this tendency to define poverty relative to prevailing local conditions. It is sometimes reported that although the United States is richer on the average than Europe, there is less poverty in Europe. This is correct if we use each area's own definition of poverty. The Europeans generally set their standard of poverty lower in terms of *real* income than Americans do, however, so that such a comparison is misleading. By any common standard—either the Europeans' or the Americans'—a larger portion of Europe is poor.

Thus, it is not the absolute level of income which defines poverty so much as a noticeable shortfall from the prevailing standard of living in a given society. Poverty is relative, and, therefore, even when an economy has reached average income levels which approximate superluxury by today's standards, some individuals, or groups, will fall below that level and be considered poor, nevertheless.[1] Thus the traditional folklore had it right: the poor will always be with us, not necessarily below some absolute level of income, but below the average level— and therefore poor.

If relative poverty is a permanent feature of economic systems, the toleration, or acceptance, of that condition is not. Ironically, it is the wealthier societies that dislike it the most, for obvious reasons. Undoubtedly people in societies at all levels of income would prefer to aid the less fortunate, or the poor, in their midst. But their capacity to do so is obviously constrained by the resources at their disposal which can be freed for that purpose. Richer societies do not have "extra" or leftover resources, but they do have more resources per capita. This implies that the marginal satisfaction some individuals receive from spending the last dollar on such basic items as food and housing is declining in relation to alternative expenditures. One of those other possible expenditures brings with it the satisfaction one gets from removing poverty or hardship from the community.[2] Thus society's economic capability to reduce poverty is related to its average level of income. But there is an important feedback effect at this point. A

---

[1] During the Great Depression in the 1930s, President Roosevelt made the now famous remark that one-third of the nation was poorly housed, poorly fed, and poorly clothed. One wag, noting that an unequal distribution of income would probably always prevail, remarked that one day one-third of the nation would probably live in shabby mansions, drink cheap champagne, and wear secondhand fur coats.

[2] An economist would include these effects under the category of income elasticity. In certain income ranges, specifically in the moderate and upper-income brackets, the income elasticity of food is less than one, while that of other products, such as the reduction of poverty of income in this case, is greater than one. This is to say that the percentage of each additional dollar of income spent on food will be less than that of the average rate out of current income. Thus, as income rises, the average percentage spent on food will fall. Just the opposite occurs in the case of superior goods (income elasticity greater than one), such as expenditures on poverty, as incomes increase.

society's perception of a "problem" is influenced by its economic capability to deal with it. To use a somewhat extreme example, many people would prefer to do without the nuisance of rain or snow if that were possible. If a community of such people were wealthy enough to erect a plastic dome and install a controlled sprinkler system to make up for the lack of natural rainfall, they might consider rain and snow to be problems, and intolerable ones at that! However, because the cost of such a project appears to be extremely expensive relative to other services which might be procured from those resources, it is considered a visionary gimmick rather than a pressing social need. Rather than pressuring the city council to start feasibility studies, the citizens simply put on their raincoats, carry umbrellas, and appropriate funds for snow removal.

Poverty is viewed analogously. In the nineteenth century, communities did undertake relief efforts for the obviously indigent, but they made no pretense of eliminating poverty in general. To them it was a normal part of life. Although it was disagreeable, it would be prohibitively expensive to eliminate. Thus, as long as people see that a disagreeable aspect of life is not feasible to eliminate, it remains simply "a fact of life." Once community incomes rise to the level where it becomes possible to mitigate the situation, however, it becomes a "problem." Paradoxically, economic problems are created just as much by rising as by falling incomes.

This transformation can be readily seen in the case of poverty by a brief examination of the expenditures in the economy to aid low-income groups. In 1930 there was almost no effort at the federal level to reduce poverty. Any programs that existed were carried out by local governments or volunteer private groups. It is unlikely that they totaled as much as 2 percent of national product. By 1970 that fraction had risen dramatically, with the federal government alone contributing more than 3 percent to the effort. If we add the efforts of state and local governments as well, this value rises to 5 percent of national income as a direct expenditure to reduce poverty. There is also a wide range of indirect arrangements, such as the progressive federal income tax, urban renewal programs, and aid to compensatory education projects, which are intended to shift even more resources to lower-income groups. By any rough measure, therefore, expenditures to aid the lower-income portion of the population have grown much faster than real per capita incomes in the economy. Expenditures to aid the poor are a superior good (that is, their income elasticity is greater than one) in the modern economy. This confirms the irony of the poverty "problem." It is likely to occur only in a relatively wealthy society, because only such a level of resource availability will encourage people to consider it solvable and therefore onerous if it persists.

Food and Fuel Prices

According to standard historical accounts, a good part of the population in the Middle Ages spent a considerable portion of its time worrying about where its next meal was going to come from. In the nineteenth century a gift of a winter's supply of firewood or coal to a poor widow was considered the ultimate in the way of charity, and for good reason; the cost of heating an average urban family's dwelling in the mid-nineteenth century could amount to 25 percent of their income in the winter months. Such once-common associations have now been generally forgotten, however. The average modern American family spends less than 20 percent of its disposable income on food. Although hunger is still a real feature in the daily lives of some of the poor, a much larger number of Americans worry that they are eating too much, as witnessed by the large expenditures for diet products and weight-reducing programs (as one observer remarked, that sector which lives off the fat of the land). Similarly, the cost of fuels in their modern form (gasoline, heating oil, and electricity) has taken a progressively smaller portion of the average household budget in the twentieth century. Behind this common trend in typical consumption patterns lies similar forces of technological advances which have cheapened the products, as well as increased the general incomes, thus tending to make the costs less significant.

Those reductions in cost were much more than mere short-term dips; they were substantial and sustained. For example, in the thirty years from 1940 to 1970 the real cost of electricity per kilowatt-hour fell by more than 75 percent. And today, the real cost of electricity is only a small fraction—less than 5 percent—of the prevailing rate around the turn of the century, soon after that service became generally available. This is certainly among the highest rates of technological improvements which have occurred in such a short period of time, even for the twentieth century. Although the gains are not quite so dramatic in the case of other sources of energy, such as petroleum and coal, they are nevertheless substantial. The real price of gasoline fell by more than 70 percent in the four decades from 1930 to 1970.

These substantial, long-term decreases in the cost of power set off the predictable response of consumers of an increase in their consumption of fuel products. The consumption of electricity, for example, increased eight times per capita between 1940 and 1973. Some of this went to power the wide array of appliances known in American society—stoves, refrigerators, air conditioners, washers and driers, and so on. But a large part of the increase must be accounted for by other uses of electric power which were developed in response to its low price. One of these was the substantial increase in residential heating. As the cost of electric power decreased, it became comparatively cheaper than the existing alternatives, such as heating oil, coal, and wood. There was also a dramatic increase in the amount of outdoor lighting, especially for streets. Such lighting contributes to safety, both against motor vehicle accidents and against street crime, and also extends the effective operating hours of business and commercial districts. Another major use of electricity has been as a source of power in industry. The most obvious example has been the growth of aluminum production in the twentieth century, but there has also been a major expansion in such uses as steel furnaces, electroplating, electrolysis of materials, as well as the proliferation of automated machinery.

During the period of the "energy crisis," which was initiated in 1973 by the dramatic increase in the price of petroleum, it became quite common for Americans to berate themselves for their careless use of energy supplies. It was common to hear that the society was wasteful—or "fuelish," as one of the slogans put it. But this was a rather selective judgment prompted by the preoccupation of the times. There was no evidence that people were wasteful in any absolute sense of the term. No one was seen pouring gasoline into the street catch basins, nor was anyone noted arcing electricity off into the air. Rather, if Americans were wasteful in using energy supplies, it must have been in a relative sense. Their consumption must be too large compared with other resources, such as labor and capital. What this comes down to is the argument that Americans were not correctly recognizing the true scarcity of energy supplies. But as we saw, there was no such scarcity until 1973. Up to that time the cost of energy supplies had been decreasing so that it was only reasonable for Americans to use them relatively lavishly. In fact, given that their cost was decreasing compared with the other main categories of resources (labor and capital), this practice constituted a net gain for the economy. In other words, the cost of using more natural resources was less than the cost of the capital and labor which they replaced.

This was the logic of the substitution which was evident in so many of the "wasteful" examples which were suddenly discovered when the "energy crisis" appeared. Thus, for example, there was the finding that industrial plants were typically using 10 to 30 percent more electricity, steam, and oil than was necessary. That fact became evident when companies sent their operating engineers out into the plants to look for ways to conserve energy. The cost of this extra effort is a good deal of labor time, both in routine and managerial activities, and that, of course, is expensive in the American environment. The extra effort may be worthwhile given the sharp increase in the cost of energy, but it certainly would not have been so before that increase. Similarly, American-made automobiles are frequently pictured as gas-guzzling monsters. They are often unfavorably compared with European models, which get better gas mileage from lighter cars, but without sacrificing comfort and handling qualities. Such gains are achieved by a considerable investment in engineering, however, so that, in effect, the Europeans were using labor to substitute for the larger consumption of gasoline and other materials which the American designs consumed more intensively. That this was a calculated, or rational, strategy, rather than mere nonchalance on the part of the Americans, can be seen in the response of the domestic manufacturers to the dramatic increase in the price of gasoline in 1973 and 1974. Within one year they had added accessories such as manifold pressure gauges, radial tires, stiffer shock absorbers, and higher gear ratios to their existing models. And in those models, scheduled for production several years later and, therefore, still in the design stage, they began a major weight- and fuel-saving effort. In other words, they could respond to such costs if and when it actually became profitable to do so.

Competing with the Rest of the World for Food   One of the numerous paradoxes of American economic history is that even though the economy has been one of the leaders in terms of prevailing levels of technology, a good share of its comparative advantage has always been in agriculture. This is not what conventional wisdom would suggest; advanced economies are generally expected to be industrialized and to export industrialized products, while lesser-developed nations are supposed to be agricultural or raw-material producers and exporters. The American experience is interesting, however, in that although it obviously began with an abundance of natural resources, when its population was small in relation to the initial physical stock of resources, developments in technology *increased* the effective natural resource base.[3]

Throughout almost all its history, America has exported agricultural products, including tobacco in the colonial period, cotton and wheat in the nineteenth century, and corn and soybeans in the modern period. Tobacco and cotton were important in relation to the total economy in earlier years, but in the twentieth century agricultural exports (indeed, the foreign sector in general) were not so large or obvious in relation to the domestic economy. This isolation—or at least the general assumption of isolation—ended abruptly in the early 1970s, however. At that time a series of devaluations of the dollar relative to foreign currencies occurred. By increasing the number of dollars which were equivalent to a given amount of foreign currency, American exports appeared cheaper (in terms of their own domestic currency) to potential foreign buyers. The net effect within the American economy was an increase in the demand for wheat (in terms of dollars) with a consequent rise in its price. This increase was quite marked because of the relatively inelastic supply in the short-run coupled with the apparently nearly complete failure of the industry to anticipate such a major shift.

Whatever the exact reason, Americans discovered that they were part of the world after all. If there was a crop failure in the Ukraine or the Indian subcontinent, it appeared most directly in the price of bread in the local supermarket. And Americans found themselves, in effect, competing against the starving peasants of other lands. And they were not always gracious in doing so, either. Most of the energy they expended in response to this development was dissipated in displeasure with the higher grocery prices rather than sympathy with the plight of that much larger part of the world that was coping with the same problem—but with far fewer resources.

The reason for this self-interested myopia is understandable, however, if we go back to the basic economic forces which must have been at work. Food prices have become relatively low in the United States, compared with those of most other nations. They are not a free good, however, so that each dollar spent on food is a dollar's worth of purchasing power withdrawn from other commodities.

---

[3] There are frequent references in the popular literature of the nation about the abundance of natural resources within the economy. This is misleading, however. Whatever the physical abundance of resources, it is their economic feasibility which counts. We can speak today of good farmland, or huge supplies of coal or timber, only after the technology to use them has been developed. In 1500 the present farmland, coal, and timber were no more useful to Europeans than the Sahara Desert or Antarctica. No nation has an advantage over any other in terms of physical endowments. That issue is decided by the evolution of knowledge which makes some regions more economically productive than others. America's "amber waves of grain" are not a cause of economic growth, but a symbol of its success.

Thus, consumer spending (and tolerance) should not be expected to show any special consideration because of a favorable historical record. When the price of food rises dramatically, as it did in the early 1970s, this bites into consumers' real incomes just as much as if it were to hit another major component of consumer spending which had not experienced such a long period of beneficial contraction. In other words, as long as scarcity persists, it does not make any difference how well economic events have progressed up to the moment. All goods which remain scarce compete with each other, and when any one becomes more expensive than the others, it sets off an inevitable sequence of competition and reshuffling.

This adjustment and reorganization proceeded in the various markets for food products in the United States much as it did in the case of energy supplies, and at about the same time. The long-term trend up to that time, stretching back for at least a century and a half, was for food to become cheaper. Although the amount of food consumed per capita did not increase much—in fact, if anything, it probably decreased as Americans worked at less physically strenuous occupations—the quality did. The populace used its increasing purchasing power to upgrade, and to increase the variety of, its diet. Thus, although it was not consuming more food per capita in a physical sense, it required more resources to provide each unit of output being turned out. The dimensions of the product were being altered to match the shifting conditions in the economy. One of those alterations, of course, was that labor tended to become more scarce. Thus, any features which could be built into food products that would save on subsequent labor were likely candidates for adoption. And over time there was such a trend in the preparation of American food products. A given item was increasingly likely to be processed, packaged, and, in general, closer to being ready for immediate use. This increased the cost of food products, but it saved on resources which were even more expensive in the American setting.

The experience of the 1970s demonstrated that this was a reasoned response, not simply an accidental trend. When the price of food went up sharply, American consumers shifted back toward food products with less of that labor-saving component in them. There was more home baking, cooking, and canning. This was reflected in the larger sales of home freezers, garden seeds, glass jars, flour, and tomato plants. It was also seen in a backhanded way in the sales of beef. Cattleraisers had happily noted in recent years that the per capita sales of that item had gone up a few pounds each year in the last few decades. Rather optimistically, they projected that this trend would continue into the indefinite future. That trend was based on rising real incomes and a decrease in the relative cost of food, however, so that when both these trends were interrupted in 1973 and 1974, beef sales per capita actually decreased. The cattleraisers learned the hard way that difficult economic choices still had to be made, and that established economic patterns could be completely overthrown if conditions dictated.

The Central Cities: Postwar Problems

When food and energy suddenly appeared as matters of general public concern in the 1970s, they were relative upstarts compared with another long-standing dilemma of the post-World War II period. By that time Americans had been watching, worrying over, and devising programs to aid the declining centers of their larger cities for more than three decades. And the duration of the concern was clearly related to the magnitude and imperviousness of the problem. A sizeable fraction of the population lived in these areas, and their difficulties and complaints reverberated throughout the political system and the public media of the economy. Thus, the major elements of the "urban problem" were fairly well recognized—an exodus of middle-income residents, factories, and retail establishments out of the central city to the suburbs. This was accompanied by deterioration of the housing, public transportation systems, and general environment in the central areas. The municipal governments were caught in the middle of these forces, facing a relative decline in their fiscal base as economic resources leave their domain, on the one hand, and feeling increased demands for their services from those who remain, on the other hand. It was a difficult period in which to be a mayor of a large American city.

The urban problem might be especially difficult to cope with, but the main element comprising its source is not too difficult to detect. In essence, it was the outgrowth of an earlier economic success, one which we detailed earlier (in Chapters 11, 12, and 14). In the latter half of the nineteenth century large cities were a growth sector of the American economy. They combined two advantages—of agglomeration and of access to transportation networks—in one locality. These advantages were sufficient to more than offset the higher costs of conducting economic activities in these areas, and therefore they pulled a sizeable portion of them away from the less densely populated areas of the economy. But the possibility of saving on costs always opens up the opportunity to create alternatives which bypass such arrangements. The cost in this particular case was that of urban land, whose price had been bid up by the concentration of activity which had developed upon it. The resulting innovation was, of course, the internal combustion engine in the form of automobiles, trucks, and buses, which allowed a much greater decentralization of economic activities. Most of this impact was felt on one of the two advantages which had previously drawn economic activity into the city—the proximity to transportation networks. Now transportation channels became much less of a constraint because, to exaggerate only slightly, one could connect into the existing road system over a wide area without much penalty in costs. As a result, the city started on a long-term pattern of spatial redistribution, which is still going on some seventy-five years later.

The most immediate effect was on housing patterns in urban areas. By the eve of World War I, a shift toward single-family housing in the suburbs was evident. At first this was primarily an upper-income exodus because the earliest automobiles were relatively expensive. But as the price of cars came down—as exemplified by the Model T—and incomes rose, a progressively larger section of the population elected to drive to and from work each day. [4] As many observers

---

[4] Americans, especially when caught in one, often believe that traffic jams are a relatively recent phenomenon, resulting primarily from the increase of automobiles since World War II. Actual-

have since remarked, this increased the expense of commuting to work. The advantages of using lower-priced land for housing more than offset this penalty, however. Part of the savings of using cheaper suburban land came from the less expensive forms of structures which could be used for single-family housing. It was not necessary to build the massive foundations, or thick walls, or the extra hallways and lobbies necessary in multistory housing. One understandable corollary of this cheaper land was that the residents also chose to consume more of it simply in the form of added space. Thus, there was a strong tendency to spread out rather than to go up in devising housing plans. The now standard pattern of single-family homes being placed in the midst of their own one-quarter to one-half acre lots quickly appeared.

Housing was not the only urban activity to migrate to the suburbs in response to the lower cost of land. It was soon followed by the relocation of such services as stores, gas stations, restaurants, doctors' and lawyers' offices, libraries, and schools. Obviously, such economic activities were attracted by the advantage of being near the customers they served, but they also reflected the cheap, prevailing cost of land. Probably the most dramatic example was the evolution of the shopping center. The stores contained in it were one, or at most two stories high, often in marked contrast to the downtown branches of the same company where six to ten stories was common for department stores. The contrast was even more dramatic in the case of parking. It is not unusual for 80 percent of the land area of a shopping center to be devoted to parking space. Such an allocation would be prohibitively expensive in a downtown location where land sells in the six-figure-bracket—or higher—and private parking lots charge several dollars a day. Thus, the suburban stores are employing a cheap local resource to provide certain attributes of service, such as convenience, which retail enterprises in the center of a major city cannot afford.

But the exodus from the central cities did not stop with housing and its associated service sector. Any activity which could gain more from being located on cheaper land than it would lose by giving up central city contacts would be encouraged to move to the periphery also. Manufacturing was undoubtedly the largest sector in this category. Before the development of the internal combustion engine, factories were commonly confined to the central areas of cities—except for those such as textile mills, which were restricted to a certain power source—where they had access to transportation networks and the labor, materials, and shipping facilities which went with them. But these advantages also came at the cost of constraining the organization and operations of the firm because of the high cost of land. A quick glance at most older manufacturing facilities in the United States indicates that many of them are multistory structures in which the flow of materials and sequential processes worked its way up or, more commonly, down from floor to floor. This created added expense in the form of elevators

---

ly, some of the worst traffic jams occurred in the 1920s when sales of automobiles rose rapidly to nearly 5 million units—about half the present rate, but the cumulative road system was still undeveloped because construction for motor vehicles was just getting under way.

and conveyers, as well as sometimes placing severe restrictions on the layout of equipment patterns. There were also added expenses in ready access to inventories and loading facilities.

When the automobile and the truck allowed a number of manufacturing enterprises to move out of the central city, these constraints fell away and operations were reorganized to reduce costs. The typical suburban factory now has a low profile, spreading out across the landscape to expedite the flow of work processes. It also mitigates one of those other bottlenecks of multistory buildings—storage, and access to raw materials and inventory. These areas can be placed on open floors where they are directly accessible by modern materials handling equipment, such as lift trucks, and moved directly either into the factory or out to truck loading. Moreover, the suburban location allows for the necessary parking lots for the large numbers of automobiles which the employees use to get to work.

And as the housing and the stores and the factories moved outward toward the suburbs, the road system was gradually expanded and modified to service them. This included local residential streets, traffic control systems, and business service roads, as well as the more obvious network of limited access expressways. In recent years there has been considerable public debate as to whether the construction of this extensive network of roads was desirable. After all, some of the critics noted, this large expenditure on highways virtually dictated that something like the present spatial pattern of suburban location would result. (That existing pattern, of course, as much as the roads themselves, was what the critics were unhappy about.) Public officials and highway designers replied that it simply was not so. The relocation of economic activity was proceeding so rapidly and with so much self-momentum that they were only reacting to events, building roads which should have been built a decade earlier. There is undoubtedly some truth in both positions, although they are not necessarily inconsistent with each other. Without any investment in, and modernization of, the highway system, the twentieth century trend toward suburbanization certainly would have been stifled. It is the comparatively cheap, flexible, and convenient transportation those roads allow which provides much of the raison d'être for this pattern of economic location. But while the absence of such a road system would curtail that arrangement, it was not in itself the initiating reason for it. The demand for roads to build and service suburbia was derived from more basic considerations—namely, the availability of lower-cost land and the possibility of substituting it in a variety of ways for other, scarcer resources. Suburban land is a substitute for more expensive urban land and, indirectly, for building materials, elevators, waiting for the subway, and the noise of the quarreling couple in the apartment next door. Of course, the critics are right in saying that such features of suburbia as developments which sprawl haphazardly across the landscape and the elimination of open farmland and natural areas are undesirable. What they fail to recognize and what causes a substantial majority of the population to act as if they did not believe it to be so, is that the alternative costs are greater. One can forgo suburbanization only at the cost of greater urban crowding, larger demands on public

transit and services, higher manufacturing costs, and confinement to the fire
escape or the city park on hot summer evenings. Most Americans behave as if
they find those latter costs to be the greater ones.

Meanwhile, Back in the "Decaying" Urban Centers   As the economic functions which were tied to transportation services pulled out of the central city, they
left behind them the inevitable collection of difficult adjustments and problems.
And the difficulties were exacerbated in this case because the lifespan of so many
of the assets involved were unusually lengthy. Consider, for example, the case of
central city housing. Structures which were built in the first two or three decades
of the twentieth century are still in large part structurally sound and capable of
providing good housing services in exchange for only moderate investments in
maintenance and refurbishing. But although the supply remains—or could remain, if it were worthwhile for it to do so—the demand has melted away. It left
town in moving vans and in the backs of station wagons when a large part of the
middle- and higher-income working class moved out to the suburbs. Landlords
were left with housing which still had decades of good use in it, but not the
customers for which it was designed.

In such difficult circumstances, you do the best you can, and so the rental
housing market sought out what other tenants might be available. One of the
most noticeable groups, certainly the one which has attracted the most public
attention in recent years, has been the lower-income racial minorities. Included
are the Puerto Ricans who have settled mostly in the larger cities of the Northeast, the Mexican-Americans in California, and the native blacks who moved in
large numbers out of the South into all major cities of the North. It has frequently
been suggested that this concentration of population in the older housing of the
central cities results from discrimination. Undoubtedly some such pressure has
played a part in reinforcing that pattern, but even in its absence there were
strong, almost compelling reasons, why those groups should move into that particular type of housing. For one thing, housing there offered the advantage of
transportation. This is important to lower-income groups because they typically
own fewer automobiles per capita than groups further up the income scale. In a
sense they are in the same position the middle and upper classes were in some
fifty years ago, no longer because of the constraint of the lack of transportation
technology, however, but because they lack the income to purchase that now
available attribute.

There is also the rather obvious fact that much of the older central-city
housing is now poor quality and is deteriorating.[5] Again, it is not surprising that
the lower-income groups should choose that particular type of housing. Although
they would obviously prefer something better, they must balance their expenditures on housing against other desires, such as food, clothing, and medical care.

---

[5] It is understandable that owners of such housing should allow it to depreciate so quickly.
After all, its economic return has been reduced by the loss of the clientele for which it was originally
designed. Rapid depreciation is simply withholding maintenance expenses in order to obtain as much
cash flow back out of the structure as is now possible.

When the price is adjusted for other factors, such as location,[6] lower-quality older housing costs less than modern units. This price differential, based on quality, is accentuated even further by the typical increase in resident occupancy which occurs when lower-income groups take over a neighborhood. The higher density of population per unit implies a lower cost per resident as well as a further reduction in quality.

Thus, we have a plausible explanation for what has often been called "slum" housing in the larger cities in the middle of the twentieth century. It is not necessary to resort to such hypotheses as discrimination, or exploitation of tenants, to explain its existence. It is simply a way of extracting some economic value out of a stock of housing which has been made obsolete by changes in technology and incomes. Certainly it does not provide housing services which are either high quality or attractive, but the relevant alternative is simply either those services or none at all. Viewed in this context, its existence is, ironically, a gain for the poor. In its absence they would be forced to compete more directly for newer and more expensive housing, and against groups with higher incomes.

Another indication that slum housing was not a particularly profitable sector was that very little of it was constructed anew when the older units were demolished. Instead, the land on which it had been located in central areas was typically converted to office buildings, parking lots, expressways, or, when it was used for new housing, for luxury or high-income buildings. Sometimes it is reported that slum properties are very profitable, that they repay their owners higher profits than most alternative investments. If one looks carefully at the account books of such businesses, however, the phenomenon is mostly illusionary. Slum properties usually have a high rate of cash flow, partly because they tend to skimp on maintenance and modernizing. The high return is mostly disinvestment in a form of earning asset which had only a limited expected lifetime remaining. Furthermore, the rate of return on investment may appear high if the existing owners are not the ones who first owned the buildings at the completion of their construction. The present owners would have paid a price which reflected the contemporary evaluation of future profits at the time they were resold. And since their expected future profits were probably already being marked down, it would take less profit for the current owners to recoup their investment than it would for the initial owners to get back the full opportunity cost of the capital they had put into the project. Thus, although slum housing might seem currently profitable, it appears much less so if viewed in the context of the total resources invested in it over its entire lifespan.

The Continuing Decline of Mass Transit   When a new good or service is introduced, one of the most noticeable effects is usually its impact on substitute products. The widespread adoption of the internal combustion engine as the primary means of transportation in the twentieth century was no exception; in

---

[6] The land on which the central-city housing is located is typically higher priced, and therefore the rents must reflect this opportunity cost even if the prevailing price for the housing services does not cover all long-term costs of that part of the rent. If the cost of the land is not being compensated, an owner can simply demolish the existing housing and sell the land.

fact, it was one of the more dramatic examples of how devastating such an innovation can sometimes be on the competition. Between 1880 and 1915 very large investments were made in public transit in all major American cities, as well as in many medium-sized communities and even in some small ones. These took the form of subways, elevated rail lines, street railroads, and interurbans. Very importantly for the scenario which developed afterward, they required large investments in specialized, long-lasting facilities. The second best uses of subway tunnels, elevated train tracks, and electric street cars, are quite poor and unremunerative. Thus, as the demand for such services decreased during the twentieth century, there was little else which could be done with them but to adjust the frequency of service to the number of passengers and keep the systems running. With only a few exceptions, such as those of San Francisco and Washington, D. C., most of the mass transit systems operating in the United States are quite old. Some of the rolling stock has been replaced but many of the roadbeds and right-of-ways were constructed in the neighborhood of seventy years ago. They are kept in operation because, coupled with some political considerations, the marginal costs of running the systems are relatively low. It would certainly not pay to construct such a system anew at the present time. Even using the best technology currently available, only a small fraction of the total resources necessary to erect and operate it would be recovered. This rather basic reality explains why, despite the frequent exhortations that new mass transit systems should be constructed to reduce traffic congestion, or save on energy, or improve the aesthetics of the cities, very few have been built recently. The amount of cash which taxpayers would have to shell out to construct such new systems has forestalled most such efforts. Those few programs which have been initiated have been heavily subsidized by funds from outside the project revenues of the system itself. And, characteristically enough, most federal aid to mass transit in recent years has gone to help finance the increasing deficits of older systems rather than initiating many new ones.

The problems of mass transit are understandable enough if we look carefully at what its primary competitor, the automobile, has going for it. In recent years it has become commonplace to characterize the car as a luxury, a form of transportation which is personally convenient but which will have to be curtailed in the new austerity which has arrived. What this appraisal overlooks is that the automobile has been so widely adopted exactly because it uses fewer total resources than alternative forms of transportation. This judgment flies in the face of most common-sense impressions but it can be understood if we examine the full range of costs involved. For example, some observers have pointed out that over a given route a fully loaded railroad car can carry far more passengers at a lower cost per capita than a parallel procession of automobiles. True enough, but that is an artificial and unrepresentative comparison. It requires a high density of passenger traffic over a very restricted route. And there is probably only one city in the United States which approaches such volumes of concentrated traffic that mass transit is actually cheaper per commuter than that of automobiles. That, of course, is New York City, which contains fully one-half of the total economy's volume of mass transit ridership (exclusive of buses). The reason for this striking comparison is quite simple. Mass transit systems require large capital investments in track, roadbed, bridges, and tunnels—more so than comparable highway systems—so that is takes a large volume of passengers to spread out the costs sufficiently to push the cost per user down to the level of the automobile. In other words, in the vast majority of locations where most Americans live, cars are actually a cheaper form of passenger travel, considering only direct costs.

Furthermore, the spatial distribution of population has tended to change in the course of the twentieth century so as to make the advantage of the automobile even greater. In discussions of the comparative costs of mass transit and motor vehicles, it is common to establish a kind of rough model of daily transportation in which people live in the suburbs and commute each day into the city, where most of the jobs are located. This might have been an adequate approximation of the state of things at the beginning of the twentieth century in the United States—if we construe the suburbs to be quite close, indeed, part of the city proper itself—but it has long ceased to represent conditions as they are. The 1970 census reported that the majority of people do not drive into the larger cities to go to work. Rather, they tend to drive *around* them from one suburb to another. Even more surprising, a good number drive *out* of the central cities to work in the suburbs. Even in the New York City metropolitan area, for example, which is the most centralized and mass transit–intensive center in the nation, the majority of the work force uses their personal automobiles each day to commute around, but not into, the city center.

Another indication of the ongoing process of decentralization is the population density, measured in the number of residents per square mile, of the central-city areas, which has been dropping steadily for more than three decades. For such areas as Manhattan Island, it is now less than half the level it was in 1920. This comes as a surprise to many citizens, because they have heard that urbanization is continuing and they have also been exposed to numerous reports of crime, congestion, and pollution, which are said to have resulted from increasing crowding of American cities. Certainly the total urban population has grown in recent years, but this has occurred within a total urban area which has increased even faster. The net result has been that the average population density has decreased as the existing population has been spread more thinly over the total area. This redistribution has been most marked in the central cities where the number of housing units has contracted dramatically. Interestingly enough, a good part of the land freed by this exodus of residents has been used to adapt the downtown areas to the age of the automobile. A fair amount of land gained from the demolition of older housing has gone into the construction of parking lots and garages and motor hotels as well as new highway extensions to handle traffic into and out of the downtown area. Thus, even the central business district, the area of the city which would have seemed most impervious to the automobile, has succumbed to its all-pervasive influence. The automobile has not only bested mass transit in the competition to carry people into and out of the central city, but it has also caused a longer-term relocation of activities which have made its advantage even greater as time has passed.

And the automobile still had another advantage over existing forms of transportation which we have yet to detail. The car was not only a cheaper way to get to and from work each day, but one could either stop directly at the grocery store or the dentist's office on the way home or make the journey with no stops at all. There was no waiting for the bus or train, nor the necessity of a transfer and a walk to cover the last five blocks home. In other words, the automobile provided a number of advantages because of its flexibility for personal use, some of which translated directly into savings of resources and some of which disappeared, unmeasured, in the form of greater consumer welfare. The savings from the internal combustion engine could be gauged directly in access to lower-cost land which previously had been unavailable, or in the savings in labor time for such occupations as repair personnel, salespeople, or delivery people. It could also be seen—if not measured directly—in such new consumer options as switching from its regular weekday function of commuting to evening shopping trips and week-end trips to the lake upstate.

It was the sum of all such advantages which made the automobile a net saver of total resources consumed in transportation as well as simply a more pleasant way to travel. When one suggests that mass transit consumes less energy than automobiles and should, therefore, be encouraged in order to mitigate the "energy crisis," one is immediately skeptical. Of course, it requires more energy units to transport passengers in their individual automobiles than it does to consolidate them and carry them in a single train. The problem is simply that they all do not want to go where or when the single train is going,[7] and as a consequence the trains are—or would be—used well below their optimum capability with resulting increases in average costs per passenger. Furthermore, if society decided that it was really essential to cease using internal combustion engines as the prime source of transportation in the economy, it would be compelled to either build many more rail systems or relocate a good portion of the population into denser concentrations. Both tactics would require considerable additional investment, of course, and with each the expenditure of large amounts of energy in the process. Even if that extra consumption did not push the total usage of energy over the amount consumed by automobiles, if left to themselves, it would consume large amounts of resources in nonenergy forms. And those inputs could be otherwise turned to the production of further energy or alternative systems, such as recycling, which could reduce the demands for it. In other words, the consumers are not making so wasteful a choice insofar as energy is concerned when they opt to use automobiles. In terms of energy—or resources in general, which are a substitute for more of it—they have chosen the least-expensive medium.

Financing the Governments of the Larger Cities   Each year the mayors of America's major cities make their customary trips to Washington, D. C., and their respective state capitals to request additional aid for their jurisdictions. And each year the crux of the plea is pretty much the same: the larger cities are caught in a vicious cycle. The middle class, which contributes much of the tax revenue to

---

[7] It seems significant to note here that the increase in the use of public transit and the railroad during the "energy crisis" was temporary and soon resumed its long-term downward trend despite the continued higher price of gasoline after 1973.

the cities, is moving out and the poorer groups, which are large consumers of public services, are moving in: there is a decrease in the "tax suppliers" and an increase in the "tax eaters." Furthermore, according to the city officials, prospects of stopping the deterioration are not so good either. If they cut back on services or raise taxes to cover the gap, they only increase the rate of exodus from the central areas and make things even worse. By their own evaluation, they are caught in a vicious downward spiral. The future looks dim; in the words of one cynical resident of Detroit, "Will the last one to leave town please turn off the lights."

It would probably come as a dramatic surprise to someone who has heard such reports and taken them at their face value to undertake a tour of America's major cities for the first time. One striking fact is that in almost every large urban center, and most smaller ones as well, a huge amount of new construction is going on. This is particularly noticeable in the central business districts where, almost without exception, the number of large office buildings has grown dramatically since World War II. It is obvious in New York City where the forty- and fifty-story buildings are marching north toward Central Park and west toward the Hudson River. It is true of Chicago where the John Hancock, the Sears, and the Standard Oil of Indiana buildings have raised the level of the skyline into a new league compared with that of two decades ago. And it is even true of Los Angeles, where for a long time residents joked about the possibility of a central business district for all those seemingly self-contained suburbs. But perhaps most dramatic of all, this growth is true of a number of major cities which are just one cut below the largest but seem to be expanding more rapidly—Houston, Atlanta, Denver, Boston, Dallas, and San Francisco. Anyone who has been in a number of large American cities knows that they still have considerable vitality left in them; or, in the words of Mark Twain upon reading his own obituary in the newspaper, "The reports of [my] death have been greatly exaggerated."

In fact, what has been occurring in the larger American cities is not their death, as has been so often reported, but a change in their personalities. While the function of the cities as transportation centers has been largely stripped from them, their other major service, that of agglomeration, has continued to grow all through the transition period. Thus, the total volume of business activity in most central business districts has not decreased much—in some cases it has actually expanded—in the middle third of the twentieth century. While the factories, warehouses, and railroad stations have disappeared, the space has not remained idle. They have been replaced by the headquarters of corporations, banks, consulting firms, communications firms, publishing houses, and advertising agencies. This, of course, is what all those new office buildings have been constructed for. They are providing the productive proximity within which all those services can interact and reinforce each other. In other words, agglomeration is alive and well and growing in America's larger cities.

Thus, although one of the two major economic functions which larger cities performed at the beginning of the twentieth century had been taken from them (transportation), the other one had kept on growing (agglomeration). In fact, it turned out to be somewhat of a growth sector, a rather fortuitous trend insofar as the cities were concerned. (We shall return to examine the reasons behind this pattern more carefully.) Not only that, but, in terms of the cities' revenue base, which the local officials spent much time worrying about, the newer office buildings were generally net tax suppliers. They required some city water and sewage (which were usually self-financed through user fees), fire and police protection and street services, but they did not directly consume some of the more expensive components of city expenditures, such as schools and social welfare services.[8] Thus they made a major net contribution to the financial base of the city. Just how important this source actually has been is indicated if we examine one such typical structure. A modern fifty-story office building contains about 2 million square feet of floor space and at a construction cost of $50 per square foot has a total value of about $100 million. At typical tax rates this would yield the municipal treasury about $3 million, or the equivalent of that provided by about 3,000 single-family homes. For a large city this can add up to quite a hefty sum. The real estate on Manhattan in the mid-1970s had a market value of about $150 billion, of which probably half was office—as distinguished from housing—property. (This enormous sum is not surprising if we consider that most of the land, even without any of the buildings on it, sells for more than $1 million an acre.) This would yield the city of New York more than $2 billion in property taxes which, by itself, accounted for about a third of the city's locally derived revenues and about 20 percent of its total expenditures. No wonder City Hall shudders every time the president of a major corporation suggests that the company just might consider moving out of town.

The cities are able to tap this beneficial source of revenue because of one underlying condition—agglomeration. There are huge amounts of net economic output created by this concentration of business activity, and because it can occur only in certain established centers, it is immobile. Thus, cities can tax the rent—that is, the economic return above the next best use of the land—without any fear that it too will get up and move to the suburbs. This factor also explains why so many corporations continue to keep their headquarters in the larger cities despite their occasional mumblings about the costs and inconvenience of such. While they can move their operations to the suburbs, they cannot simultaneously move the benefits of agglomeration along with them. That, in the final analysis, is why so many of them stay, simply because the gains of agglomeration are sufficient to more than offset the costs and hassles of big city operations.

It also puts the periodic complaints of the city officials in a somewhat new light. Rather than being the victims of the changing economic conditions, the larger cities seemed to be doing quite well in taking advantage of evolving oppor-

---

[8] A similar consideration often appears in the form of an argument that commuters who come into the city to work during the day do not contribute their fair share to the revenue of the town—namely, because they do not pay any property taxes, which are the primary source of local revenues. This appraisal overlooks the fact that they do not consume as many services as full-time residents and that the buildings in which they work probably contribute more than their "fair share" of city financing.

tunities. (This reinforces the observation we have made several times that those, like the farmers, who complain of being exploited are quite capable of defending themselves and dishing it out to others.) This is quickly evident if one takes a short look at some representative municipal budgets over the last two decades or so. They have grown rapidly, often faster than that of the economy overall, which hardly suggests that they are under the severe pressure that they sometimes claim. But one can get a good clue concerning their querulous behavior if the changing sources of their financial support are noted. The larger cities have tended to obtain an increasing share of their revenue as grants from other levels of government, particularly state and federal. Thus, they are operating in an arena in which bargaining—and cries of need—affect the amount of support which they can expect to obtain. Rather than reflecting actual distress, therefore, some of the cries of distress coming from the cities can be interpreted as simply smart politics. The central cities may be a declining sector in relation to the rest of the total economy, but they have shown that they can improvise and compete with the rest of the economy on quite even terms.

CONTINUING BOTTLENECKS AND INNOVATIVE RESPONSES

The continuing increases in the amount of economic activity which was positioning itself in the larger cities to take advantage of agglomeration underlines one of the stronger—and most intriguing—trends in economic activity in recent years. It suggests that resources for innovation and decision making—the basic functions which much of this activity seems to be contributing to—are becoming scarcer. This is suggested by the higher costs the economic units seem willing to bear in order to keep these resources (primarily a collection of trained and talented people) together to increase their productivity. Actually, this trend of increasing scarcity of decision making has probably been developing over the last couple of centuries. It has seldom been appreciated, however, as we can see by a short digression.

The Predictions of the Great Economists

In the early nineteenth century an otherwise little-known English parson by the name of Thomas Malthus made a permanent name for himself by advancing a model of the probable long-run course of human affairs. It envisioned a rather dismal future in which the human population would invariably expand to dissipate any gains made in increasing capital or natural resources. Thus, human beings were condemned forever to a miserable existence because, ultimately, natural resources would be scarce, and not capable of being augmented as rapidly as the number of consumers of them. Malthus has been dusted off again in recent years and elevated as a man of great foresight. That, of course, has been in response to the renewed concern over the adequacy of natural resource supplies. It was a little premature, however, as we shall see, because a good deal of evidence has come in on the question since the parson made his bold projection.

In the mid-nineteenth century another prophet, who was to gain permanent fame thereafter, made a different prediction. This, of course, was Karl Marx, and he foresaw that in the long run the scarce economic factor would be capital. Like Malthus, he expected that there would always be extra people around, but that would result from the ready tendency of capital to "automate" them out of jobs rather than as Malthus felt, that they would simply increase in numbers too rapidly. Marx is also resurrected from time to time, but not so much because of his prediction about the long-run shortage of capital but because he provides one of the few full-fledged alternatives to the existing system when people become weary of it.

The continued popularity of these two famous forecasters suggests that the assumptions they made about human beings' long-term prospects are not merely out of date, unrepresentative opinions. They are still quite commonly held, as can be verified by looking at the predictions which are currently being made about what is ahead for the economy. One recurrent worry is automation, with the threat that machines will replace so many jobs that a large portion of the potential work force will be permanently unemployed. Another variant of this same prediction is that the future will be characterized by increasing leisure and people will have to learn how to use their unaccustomed free time. The total amount of work available will be so small that we shall be forced to share the "privilege" of productive employment, putting in only a few hours a week on a job. In short, we shall be working hard at not working. What all these predictions have in common is the implicit assumption that labor will eventually become the abundant resource, with one of the nonhuman resources, either capital or natural resources, being the effective constraint on output. It is surprising how little people's intuitive reactions have changed over time.

These views are unfortunate in one way because the accumulated evidence strongly suggests that they are wrong. The resource which has become scarcer over time—at least in the most developed economies of the world—is labor. All the great prophets, and a good share of the intuitive wisdom of the common folk as well, are contradicted by the observable trends. In one sense, however, this common misconception is understandable. Labor is commonly pictured as a pick-and-shovel type of activity, that is, as a routine activity which can be readily replaced by some form of machinery. Some forms of labor *are,* in fact, of this type, and such functions have tended to be automated out of existence. But muscle power is not the main contribution of labor to the economic process. The special contribution which people—as distinguished from land or capital—can bring to the production process is discretion. Labor can adjust, improvise, make decisions, and, in general, add the useful function of flexibility and adaptability to economic activity. And this attribute of judgment has proved to be the scarcest resource. It has proven easier to substitute one raw material for another (and to devise new ones), and to create new forms of capital which performed tasks more efficiently than previous models, than it has to replace the decision-making capability embodied in people. In the long run, human resourcefulness has proved to be the scarcest factor.

This is why labor has become even more expensive and has increased the share of the national product (currently by more than three-quarters, if incomes to unincorporated businesses are counted at least partially as returns to labor). Part of this increased share of labor, of course, reflects the return on the growing amount of human capital in the form of education and on-the-job training. But that, in turn, indicates the growing scarcity of labor in that the expansion of human capital vis-à-vis labor corresponds to the increasing scarcity of the latter relative to the former. And this increasing scarcity of labor is what is being reflected and counteracted in the increasing concentration, in the larger cities, of people in occupations with large innovative elements in them. As usual, an economy tends to organize to ensure that its scarce resources are employed so as to yield correspondingly high returns. In the central business districts, considerable amounts of land (in terms of its economic valuation) and capital (in the form of all those expensive high-rise office buildings) are being used to raise the product of the scarcest factor of all—ingenuity.

Innovation: The Continuing Assault on Scarce Resources

Our historical experience suggests that not only does the severe scarcity of a given resource encourage the use of methods which stretch its use, but it also heightens the search for new methods to substitute for it and to bypass it as well. There is a great deal of current sentiment to the effect that labor is a particularly difficult resource to economize on.[9] Particularly in the service industries, goes the usual argument, it is very difficult to increase the productivity of labor. But while these views continued to be propounded in the abstract, economic forces were subtly at work discrediting the assumption. One of these developments has now grown to be a commonplace word in the modern vocabulary, even though its impact on the aggregate supply of labor has not been generally appreciated.

In 1947 three scientists, John Bardeen, Walter Brattain, and William Schockley, working in the Bell Telephone Laboratories, devised the first transistor. It was a simple, solid state device for regulating current which could do almost everything the vacuum tube was then doing but was much smaller, used less power, did not require any warm-up period, and was much less subject to wear and damage. It was soon clear that it was going to substantially reduce the cost of most electronic equipment. What was not immediately obvious but has become increasingly so since then is that this was just the beginning. Like most basic inventions, there was to be a long period of learning and refinement as the original breakthrough worked its way down the learning curve. The original "chip" was reduced in size, increased in speed and reliability, and substantially reduced in cost. This was soon followed by the integrated circuit, or chip, in which a series of transistors were strung together to perform a sequence of steps as one step. In the 1960s and 1970s the number of functions on a single chip was

---

[9] We have previously encountered this argument back in Chapter 6 where we found that it was based on an incomplete specification of the problem and that, in addition, there was some evidence that it was not actually true. It is interesting to note that the argument that it is difficult to replace labor runs directly counter to the argument that in the long run labor will be a redundant factor and a large portion of the labor force will be involuntarily unemployed.

steadily increased, while the cost per chip was similarly decreased. The aggregate result was a spectacular reduction in the cost of a single calculation, or function, performed by transistors. The most immediately obvious result was the development of an entirely new, large growth industry in the form of computers. That was a direct response to the enormous reduction in the cost of processing and storing data which had, in turn, encouraged and created an entirely new dimension of uses for that service. But the use of the transistor soon went well beyond the rather passive function of processing data, to which the earliest generations of computers had been confined. Later models were capable of being integrated into industrial processing and assembly lines, adjusting the controls in response to information fed back from the system, as well as directing complex preprogrammed sequences of operations.

Some of the more interesting applications of the transistor, however, developed outside the larger main frame computer operations. They proved to be useful over a wide range of relatively small operations where mechanical and/or electric mechanisms had previously regulated some function—and, of course, in a wide range of functions where they had not before, the transistor made the cost low enough to be feasibly accomplished automatically. So, for example, the transistor began to replace the mechanical workings of watches and clocks, appliances, and automobiles. The "brain" of the transistors could be combined with various kinds of sensing devices (such as temperature or pressure) to take over such previously manually controlled operations as the heating and lighting in buildings, or the humidity in greenhouses or cold storage plants. The ultimate range of such applications will probably be much wider than it is now even conceived, simply because the costs of building such devices are still coming down and the passage of time will inevitably suggest new applications.

When the effects of the transistor as embodied in the computer first began to be anticipated, it was widely believed that they would displace large numbers of clerical workers who were considered to be performing "routine jobs." In retrospect, no such mass exodus developed. It was not that computers did not replace a wide range of routine computation, filing, inventory, and billing functions, because they did. But at the same time they substantially lowered the cost of information and encouraged the expansion of other types of office functions which had been prohibitively expensive before. One of the places where certain of these new functions were particularly noticeable was upstairs in the executive suites. The scope of information and the speed with which it became available to management was significantly increased. This meant that many of the elements of the usually complex decisions which must be made at the top were specified more precisely and the possible options became clearer. This is not to imply that decision making became any easier, but it does suggest that the improved inputs going into such choices should improve the quality of the results.[10] A similar

___

[10] Individuals who work with computers have an acronym, GIGO, which stands for Garbage In, Garbage Out, meaning that the usefulness of the results depends on the quality of the programing which processed them, not on the mechanical computations themselves.

process was evident in scientific and research activities. The great gains in mechanical computation and processing greatly extended the range and amount of questions with which innovative scholars could cope. In other words, the transistor was extending the work of some of the most scarce and productive resources in the economy—the innovative and decision-making component of the labor force. By reducing the inputs required to assemble some of the elements of that process, it freed them for other, nonmechanical efforts.

Thus, human ingenuity had found at least one way to save on one of its scarcest resources, ingenuity itself. And the human response to scarcity continues in modern America much as it has throughout its past. Obviously we do not know exactly what will result from such behavior in the future, but we can be quite certain the age-old process, with its constant appearance of problems and innovative responses, will continue to compel considerable energy and attention.

Index